the life of thomas paine

the life of

Moncure Daniel Conway

First published 1892
Reissued, edited by
Hypatia Bradlaugh Bonner, 1909

thomas paine

ARNO PRESS / A NEW YORK TIMES COMPANY / NEW YORK, 1977

PUBLISHER'S NOTE

The Rev. Moncure D. Conway began his *Life of Thomas Paine* in 1888; for the next three years he gathered together the material that would create the first scholarly, fully documented life of the revolutionary thinker and activist. When the *Life* was published in 1892 it revealed, through a mass of letters and original documents, many not available before, an entirely new image of the man Tom Paine. Conway's research created the background of the era of revolt in which Paine lived; but it was Paine's own words, quoted in abundance, that gave this biographical study its authenticity. Paine's sincerity, his total dedication to the cause of political and personal freedom, and, most surprising, his generosity and benevolence, were all inescapable proof that the great theoretician of rebellion was quite simply one of the most maligned men in American history. The "educated ignorance concerning Paine," which first prompted Conway to write his book, could no longer be safe before the simple facts of the man's life and work. To make the record even more secure from distortion, Conway would continue his labor on Paine until he had gathered together the most complete collection of his writing that had ever been assembled. The four volumes of *The Writings of Thomas Paine* were published between 1894 and 1897. They were to remain for more than half a century the most trustworthy guide to the mind and spirit of Paine, a great anthology where he himself spelled out his lifelong struggles against political repression. These volumes were an anthology in a more limited sense, for they showed in page after page of brilliant writing that Thomas Paine was a literary as well as a political genius, master of a style perfectly attuned to the time, the place, and the occasion. For generations of readers, Conway's two works on Paine would be the best introduction to the man and his world.

Moncure Daniel Conway was born on March 17, 1832, near Falmouth, Stafford County, Virginia. His family was of the plantation aristocracy, slave-owning and rigorously Methodist. The young son was educated at Dickinson College, in Carlisle, Pennsylvania, and then at the Harvard Divinity School. Although he had traveled through the countryside as a Methodist circuit rider before he was twenty, his intellectual development was gradually turning him away from the inherited beliefs of his family. His reading of Emerson, which prompted his decision to enter Harvard, and his acquaintance with the intellectual circles in Cambridge and Concord, led him to the more liberal religious attitudes of the Unitarians. When he was prepared for his first pulpit, it was at the Unitarian Church in Washington.

Conway's first pastorate was abruptly terminated in 1856 as a result of his outspoken anti-slavery views. The same fate awaited his next assignment, at the First Congregational Church of Cincinnati. Now more than just his pulpit oratory contributed to the hostility of his sedate and conservative congregation. He had already begun the extensive periodical writings in which he would, for the rest of his life, give expression to his unorthodox views on religious, social, and poltical issues. The boldness and the clarity with which he wrote and spoke left no doubts in his audience: the Rev. M. Conway was too radical for Sunday praying in Cincinnati.

In 1862 Conway moved to Concord, Massachusetts, to take up editorship of the newspaper *The Commonwealth*, which he used as a platform for his attacks on slavery and secession. The following year he moved to England, where he was to remain for the next two decades, and began a series of lectures to popularize the Northern cause in an essentially pro-South country. Conway's hatred of the injustice of slavery and his concern for its victims was a crusade that would outlast Emancipation and the end of hostilities. Clarence Darrow, himself a crusader in many causes, wrote in 1901 of a meeting with the aging Conway:

> He told me with what enthusiasm he entered that cause, how it had been his life, and that when Lincoln issued his proclamation, he thought all had been accomplished, and he felt that he had been one of the warriors in a great battle that had ended in favor of human liberty. He came back to America a few years ago, went South again, went over the scenes of his early youth and life—an old man still young in his enthusiasm for justice, truth and liberty; but he said, as he looked the field over now, he felt that

the abolitionists had been befooled and cheated and defrauded, that this great victory which he believed they had won was not a victory at all, that the enemies of human liberty had really turned victory into defeat, that the colored man today was a slave as much as he was when Moncure D. Conway entered the great fight for human liberty fifty years ago. He said, as he looked over the South and looked over the conditions of the Negro in the South, he believed that they had less—less to eat, less to wear, less comfortable homes to live in, less to satisfy their material wants than they had as slaves—and that some way or other the powers of injustice and wrong which are ever battling in this world against justice, liberty and truth, that these had succeeded and had undone all the glorious work of Garrison, of Phillips, and Conway and Beecher, and that host of men who worked so valiantly for the black man's cause.

From 1863 to 1884 Conway held the pulpit of South Place Chapel, Finsbury, London. He became in many ways the epitome of the kind of liberal thinker who made South Place almost synonymous with religious and political unorthodoxy. The congregation at South Place was not revolutionaries, nor was it given to socially unacceptable behavior to advance its cause. They were, rather, an intelligent and sophisticated group, typically Victorian in the earnestness with which they sought some new moral order to replace the ruins of traditional religious and social habits. If their genteel liberalism seems to us inadequate in terms of the problems of Victorian society, they deserve credit at least for bringing the issues into the open and permitting sober, proper citizens to discuss them. This was no minor achievement in an era when, as Dickens had complained, the Veneerings and the Podsnaps had varnished all things disagreeable out of sight. Merely to speak out against social injustice or ecclesiastic tyranny, and to maintain one's standing in the community, was a useful function. The urbane, gregarious, personally captivating, and eloquent Rev. Moncure Conway seemed most fitted by experience and temperament to act as spokesman for such well-intentioned, even-tempered reformers.

During his entire tenure at South Place, and for four years after his return to England in 1893, Conway kept up his acquaintance with literary, political, and artistic circles. Unorthodoxy did not make him suspect, and his round of socializing was extraordinary. As the *Autobiography*, published in two volumes in 1904, makes abundantly clear, he was an inveterate collector of important people; among those he mentions are Thackeray, Dickens, Newman, Renan, Carlyle, Disraeli, Burne-Jones, William Morris, G. H. Lewes, George Eliot, Gladstone, Herbert Spencer, Browning—in short, the entire Victorian pantheon. And as the account of his career shows, his calling to the cloth did not interfere with more worldly pursuits: he lectured throughout England and America on a wide variety of topics, particularly on the revolutionary impact of scientific thinking on religious belief. In the Franco-Prussian War he served as a front-line correspondent for the *New York World*, and he found time to write fiction and to travel extensively through Europe and the Orient.

His geniality made him welcome wherever he traveled; the calm rationality of his discourse made even his most controversial views acceptable to an audience often too comfortable to question its values too closely. There is, perhaps, something paradoxical about Conway undertaking a major work on Tom Paine; one man preached revolutionary ideas and was praised for it, rewarded over a lifetime with society's favors; he never became an outcast. The other called a new nation to arms, and when the battle was won found himself ridiculed and calumniated. Conway's memory has faded, and that is an unmerited slight of history. But he has not suffered the fate from which he rescued Tom Paine. Conway was drawn to Paine by a similarity in their beliefs that was greater than the differences in their temperaments; for both, the disguises of social injustice were transparent; for both, the written and spoken word were the first weapons; and for both, the religion of humanity was the only rational faith for man. These principles, held through a long lifetime, are such as one is grateful to find in Tom Paine's first worthy biographer.

New York, 1969

The illustration reproduced on the title page is taken from the plaster bust of Tom Paine by the American artist John Wesley Jarvis (1780-1840). Jarvis was a close friend of Paine and remained loyal to him in the last years of his life when he was ostracized and hounded into poverty. (For five months in 1806 and 1807 Paine lived in Jarvis' house in New York City.) Jarvis was a self-trained artist who made intensive study of anatomy and phrenology and modeled carefully from life. The plaster bust of Paine, actually based on a death mask taken by Jarvis in 1809, is a remarkably vivid and realistic character study. The bust was not given its final form until 1817. The illustration is reproduced by courtesy of the New-York Historical Society.

Reproduced opposite is the portrait of Paine, also by Jarvis, executed around 1805. The work is an oil on canvas, measuring 25¾ by 20½ inches, and is in the collection of the National Gallery of Art, Washington, D.C.

THE
LIFE OF THOMAS PAINE

WITH A HISTORY OF HIS LITERARY, POLITICAL, AND RELIGIOUS CAREER IN AMERICA, FRANCE, AND ENGLAND

BY

MONCURE DANIEL CONWAY

AUTHOR OF "OMITTED CHAPTERS OF HISTORY DISCLOSED IN THE LIFE AND PAPERS OF
EDMUND RANDOLPH," "GEORGE WASHINGTON AND MOUNT VERNON,"
"WASHINGTON'S 'RULES OF CIVILITY,'" ETC.

TO WHICH IS ADDED A SKETCH OF PAINE
BY WILLIAM COBBETT
(HITHERTO UNPUBLISHED)

EDITED BY HYPATIA BRADLAUGH BONNER

(ISSUED FOR THE RATIONALIST PRESS ASSOCIATION, LIMITED, BY KIND PERMISSION OF
THE AUTHOR'S EXECUTORS AND MESSRS. G. P. PUTNAM'S SONS)

LONDON
WATTS & CO.
17 JOHNSON'S COURT, FLEET STREET, E.C.
1909

INSCRIBED

TO

GEORGE HOADLY

EDITOR'S PREFACE

UNTIL Dr. Moncure D. Conway undertook the great labor of investigating original documents, and comparing and weighing contemporary evidence, and in 1892 published the result in two thick volumes, no one had been in a position to form a really just estimate of the personality of Thomas Paine. The earliest biographies of Paine were avowedly and malignantly hostile, and it was not until ten years after his death that friendly biographies began to appear, all of which—with one exception, Rickman's—were written by strangers who possessed very little first-hand information. After the lapse of another sixty or seventy years it seemed a well-nigh hopeless task to sift out the true from the false, and piece together the scattered fragments of authentic information into an intelligible and convincing narrative, but Dr. Conway proved equal to the achievement, and gave the world a story which carries conviction by its transparent candour and absolute sincerity. Instead of the "filthy little atheist" of Mr. Roosevelt's imagination, in his pages we have revealed to us a clear-sighted, wise, brave, and benevolent man, the associate of the statesmen of his day, the "heart and brain" of the American Revolution, the believer in a possible "Religion of Humanity," the undaunted pleader for the life of Louis XVI. Instead of one whose character "was a compound of all that is most base, disgusting and wicked, without the relief of any one quality that was great or good" (Harford), we see a man whose great and overwhelming desire was to do something for the common good, who was ever moving quietly and steadily on his way, looking neither to the right nor to the left, neither seduced by bribery nor deterred by threat.

Dr. Conway's pages have not always been pleasant reading to the orthodox holding fast to the idea of Paine's baseness, or to the heterodox who have accepted the orthodox portrait of Paine. Sir Leslie Stephen, for example, who had on more than one occasion repeated the pious calumnies approved "in the service of religion," read Dr. Conway's book in a spirit of the bitterest hostility ; yet, having read it, he scrupulously reconsidered his position and honorably made amends.   Would that other repeaters of calumny might have the candor to follow this excellent example!

Dr. Conway's death, in November, 1907, was a great loss to all who had come under his influence, but it is pleasant to think that he lived long enough to witness the beginnings of that better feeling towards Paine's memory which his book has unquestionably been bringing about. There can be little doubt that few things would have given him greater satisfaction than to have helped to commemorate the centenary of Paine's death by preparing his book for publication in a form which would render it accessible to the great public whose means will not permit them to purchase the original edition.   I have felt the preparation of this edition a somewhat heavy responsibility, for it is certain that Dr. Conway himself was in a position to supplement and further elucidate his work. He continued to investigate and collect fresh information concerning Paine ; some of this new matter he was able to use in the collection of Paine's writings which he published in four volumes in 1894–6, and where I have found it possible I have referred to this fresh matter in a note. Where Dr. Conway's quotations from Paine bore no indication of their exact source, and where I feared they might be obscure to those unacquainted with Paine's writings, I have added a note giving the reference in Dr. Conway's edition.   Those who do not possess these volumes can with the help of the reference easily identify the passage in some of the cheaper editions which are now obtainable of most of Paine's works.   In one or two cases I have corrected the quotations given in the biography by the revised reading which Dr. Conway adopted in his edition of the "Writings."

HYPATIA BRADLAUGH BONNER.

May 14, 1909.

AUTHOR'S PREFACE

AT Hornsey, England, I saw a small round mahogany table, bearing at its centre the following words: "This Plate is inscribed by Thos. Clio Rickman in Remembrance of his dear friend Thomas Paine, who on this table in the year 1792 wrote several of his invaluable Works."

The works written by Paine in Rickman's house were the second part of "The Rights of Man" and "A Letter to the Addressers." Of these two books vast numbers were circulated, and though the government prosecuted them, they probably contributed largely to make political progress in England evolutionary instead of revolutionary. On this table he set forth constitutional reforms that might be peacefully obtained, and which have been substantially obtained. And here he warned the "Addressers," petitioning the throne for suppression of his works: "It is dangerous in any government to say to a nation, *Thou shalt not read.* This is now done in Spain, and was formerly done under the old government of France; but it served to procure the downfall of the latter, and is subverting that of the former; and it will have the same tendency in all countries; because Thought, by some means or other, is got abroad in the world, and cannot be restrained, though reading may."

At this table the Quaker chieftain, whom Danton rallied for hoping to make revolutions with rosewater, unsheathed his pen and animated his Round Table of Reformers for a conflict free from the bloodshed he had witnessed in América, and saw threatening France. This little table was the field chosen for the battle of free speech; its abundant ink-spots were the shed blood of hearts transfused with humanity. I do not wonder that Rickman was wont to show the table to his visitors, or that its present owner, Edward Truelove[1]—a bookseller who has suffered imprisonment for selling proscribed books—should regard it with reverence.

The table is what was once called a candle-stand, and there stood on it, in my vision, Paine's clear, honest candle, lit from his "inner light," now covered by a bushel of prejudice. I myself had once supposed his light an infernal torch; now I sat at the ink-spotted candle-stand to write the first page of this history, for which I can invoke nothing higher than the justice that inspired what Thomas Paine here wrote.

[1] At the death of Mr. Truelove, which occurred on April 21st, 1899, the table was acquired by the late Dr. Clair J. Grece, of Redhill.—H. B. B.

The educated ignorance concerning Paine is astounding. I once heard an English prelate speak of "the vulgar atheism of Paine." Paine founded the first theistic society in Christendom; his will closes with the words, "I die in perfect composure, and resignation to the will of my Creator, God." But what can be expected of an English prelate when an historian like Jared Sparks, an old Unitarian minister, could suggest that a letter written by Franklin, to persuade some one not to publish a certain attack on religion, was "probably" addressed to Paine. (Franklin's "Writings," vol. x., p. 281.) Paine never wrote a page that Franklin could have so regarded, nor anything in the way of religious controversy until three years after Franklin's death. "The remarks in the above letter," says Sparks, "are strictly applicable to the deistical writings which Paine afterwards published." On the contrary, they are strictly inapplicable. They imply that the writer had denied a "particular providence," which Paine never denied, and it is asked, "If men are so wicked with religion, what would they be without it?" Paine's "deism" differed from Franklin's only in being more fervently religious. No one who had really read Paine could imagine the above question addressed to the author to whom the Bishop of Llandaff wrote: "There is a philosophical sublimity in some of your ideas when speaking of the Creator of the Universe." The reader may observe at work, in this example, the tiny builder, prejudice, which has produced the large formation of Paine mythology. Sparks, having got his notion of Paine's religion at second hand, becomes unwittingly a weighty authority for those who have a case to make out. The American Tract Society published a tract entitled "Don't Unchain the Tiger," in which it is said: "When an infidel production was submitted— probably by Paine—to Benjamin Franklin, in manuscript, he returned it to the author, with a letter from which the following is extracted: 'I would advise you not to attempt unchaining the Tiger, but to burn this piece before it is seen by any other person.'" Thus our Homer of American history nods, and a tract floats through the world misrepresenting both Paine and Franklin, whose rebuke is turned from some anti-religious essay against his own convictions. Having enjoyed the personal friendship of Mr. Sparks, while at college, and known his charity to all opinions, I feel certain that he was an unconscious victim of the Paine mythology to which he added. His own creed was, in essence, little different from Paine's. But how many good, and even liberal, people will find by the facts disclosed in this volume that they have been accepting the Paine mythology and contributing to it? It is a notable fact that the most effective distortions of Paine's character and work have proceeded from unorthodox writers—some of whom seem not above throwing a traditionally hated head to the orthodox mob. A recent instance is the account given of Paine in Leslie Stephen's "History of English Thought in the Eighteenth Century." On its appearance I recognized the old effigy of Paine elaborately con- structed by Oldys and Cheetham, and while writing a paper on the subject

(*Fortnightly Review*, March, 1879) discovered that those libels were the only "biographies" of Paine in the London Library, which (as I knew) was used by Mr. Stephen. The result was a serious miscarriage of historical and literary justice. In his second edition Mr. Stephen adds that the portrait presented "is drawn by an enemy," but on this Mr. Robertson pertinently asks why it was allowed to stand? ("Thomas Paine : an Investigation," by John M. Robertson, London, 1888). Mr. Stephen, eminent as an agnostic and editor of a biographical dictionary, is assumed to be competent, and his disparagements of a fellow-heretic necessitated by verified facts. His scholarly style has given new lease to vulgar slanders. Some who had discovered their untruth, as uttered by Paine's personal enemies, have taken them back on Mr. Stephen's authority. Even brave O. B. Frothingham, in his high estimate of Paine, introduces one or two of Mr. Stephen's depreciations (Frothingham's "Recollection and Impressions," 1891).[1]

There has been a sad absence of magnanimity among eminent historians and scholars in dealing with Paine. The vignette in Oldys—Paine with his "Rights of Man" preaching to apes;—the Tract Society's picture of Paine's death-bed—hair on end, grasping a bottle,—might have excited their inquiry. Goethe, seeing Spinoza's face demonized on a tract, was moved to studies of that philosopher which ended in recognition of his greatness. The chivalry of Goethe is indeed almost as rare as his genius, but one might have expected in students of history an historic instinct keen enough to suspect in the real Paine some proportion to his monumental mythology, and the pyramidal cairn of curses covering his grave. What other

---

[1] In 1892 Mr. Stephen wrote (*National Reformer*, Sept. 11th): "The account I gave of Paine . . . was, I have no doubt, erroneous. My only excuse, if it be an excuse, was the old one, 'pure ignorance.'" He went on to say that he intended to take the first opportunity of going into the question again with Mr. Conway's additional information. "It will be a great pleasure to me if I find, as I expect to find, that he [Paine] was greatly maligned and to make some redress for my previous misguided remarks. I will venture to say for myself, that I would not consciously be unjust to any man, even to a priest, and should be especially sorry to do anything short of justice to a man of Paine's real importance." In August of the following year Mr. Stephen honorably made good his promise of "redress" by an article on "Thomas Paine" in the *Fortnightly Review*. "For some three generations," he says, "the name of Paine has been regarded by the respectable classes as synonymous with vulgar brutality. Mr. Moncure Conway has recently published a biography intended to destroy this orthodox legend. He has carefully collected all available information, and probably knows all that can now be known upon the subject. He states in his preface that a book of mine published some years ago accepted certain scandals about Paine ; and as I misled at least one of my readers, I think it a duty to confess my error frankly. My description of Paine's last years was taken from a statement by a witness whom Mr. Conway has proved to be utterly unworthy of credit. . . . I am the more sorry to have been unintentionally an accomplice, because in any case the charges were but slightly relevant. Paine's brandy is less to the purpose than Pitt's port, and much less to the purpose than Coleridge's opium. Patriots may love Pitt, and poets may love Coleridge in spite of weaknesses which really affected their careers. But Paine's lapse into drink, such as it was, did not take place till his work was substantially done ; and his writings were the product of brains certainly not sodden by brandy, but clear, vigorous, and in some ways curiously free from passion." Mr. Stephen, afterwards Sir Leslie Stephen, K.C.B., died Feb. 22d, 1904.—H.B.B.

last-century writer on political and religious issues survives in the hatred and devotion of a time engaged with new problems? What power is confessed in that writer who was set in the place of a decadent Satan, hostility to him being a sort of sixth point of Calvinism, and fortieth article of the Church? Large indeed must have been the influence of a man still perennially denounced by sectarians after heretical progress has left him comparatively orthodox, and retained as the figure-head of "Freethought" after his theism has been abandoned by its leaders. "Religion," said Paine, "has two principal enemies, Fanaticism and Infidelity." It was his strange destiny to be made a battle-field between these enemies. In the smoke of the conflict the man has been hidden. In the catalogue of the British Museum Library I counted 327 entries of books by or concerning Thomas Paine, who in most of them is a man-shaped or devil-shaped shuttlecock tossed between fanatical and "infidel" rackets.

Here surely were phenomena enough to attract the historic sense of a scientific age, yet they are counterpart of an historic suppression of the most famous author of his time. The meagre references to Paine by other than controversial writers are perfunctory; by most historians he is either wronged or ignored. Before me are two histories of "American Slavery" by eminent members of Congress; neither mentions that Paine was the first political writer who advocated and devised a scheme of emancipation. Here is the latest "Life of Washington" (1889), by another member of Congress, who manages to exclude even the name of the man who, as we shall see, chiefly converted Washington to the cause of independence. And here is a history of the "American Revolution" (1891), by John Fiske, who, while recognizing the effect of "Common Sense," reveals his ignorance of that pamphlet, and of all Paine's works, by describing it as full of scurrilous abuse of the English people,—whom Paine regarded as fellow sufferers with the Americans under royal despotism.

It may be said for these contemporaries that the task of sifting out the facts about Paine was formidable. The intimidated historians of the last generation, passing by this famous figure, left an historic vacuum, which has been filled with mingled fact and fable to an extent hardly manageable by any not prepared to give some years to the task. Our historians might, however, have read Paine's works, which are rather historical documents than literary productions. None of them seem to have done this, and the omission appears in many a flaw in their works. The reader of some documents in this volume, left until now to slumber in accessible archives, will get some idea of the cost to historic truth of this long timidity and negligence. But some of the results are more deplorable and irreparable, and one of these must here be disclosed.

In 1802 an English friend of Paine, Redman Yorke, visited him in Paris. In a letter written at the time Yorke states that Paine had for some time been preparing memoirs of his own life, and his correspondence, and showed him two volumes of the same. In a letter of Jan. 25, 1805, to Jefferson, Paine speaks of his wish to publish his works, which will make, with his manuscripts, five octavo volumes of four hundred pages each. Besides which he means to publish "a miscellaneous volume of correspondence, essays, and some pieces of poetry." He had also, he says, prepared historical prefaces, stating the circumstances under which each work was written. All of which confirms Yorke's statement, and shows that Paine had prepared at least two volumes of autobiographic matter and correspondence. Paine never carried out the design mentioned to Jefferson, and his manuscripts passed by bequest to Madame Bonneville. This lady, after Paine's death, published a fragment of Paine's third part of "The Age of Reason," but it was afterwards found that she had erased passages that might offend the orthodox. Madame Bonneville returned to her husband in Paris, and the French "Biographical Dictionary" states that in 1829 she, as the depositary of Paine's papers, began "editing" his life. This, which could only have been the autobiography, was never published. She had become a Roman Catholic. On returning (1833) to America, where her son, General Bonneville, also a Catholic, was in military service, she had personal as well as religious reasons for suppressing the memoirs. She might naturally have feared the revival of an old scandal concerning her relations with Paine. The same motives may have prevented her son from publishing Paine's memoirs and manuscripts. Madame Bonneville died at the house of the General, in St. Louis. I have a note from his widow, Mrs. Sue Bonneville, in which she says : "The papers you speak of regarding Thomas Paine are all destroyed—at least all which the General had in his possession. On his leaving St. Louis for an indefinite time all his effects—a handsome library and valuable papers included—were stored away, and during his absence the storehouse burned down, and all that the General stored away were burned."

There can be little doubt that among these papers burned in St. Louis were the two volumes of Paine's autobiography and correspondence seen by Redman Yorke in 1802. Even a slight acquaintance with Paine's career would enable one to recognize this as a catastrophe. No man was more intimately acquainted with the inside history of the revolutionary movement, or so competent to record it. Franklin had deposited with him his notes and papers concerning the American Revolution. He was the only Girondist who survived the French Revolution who was able to tell their secret history. His personal acquaintance included nearly every great or famous man of his time, in England, America, France. From this witness must have come testimonies, facts, anecdotes, not to be derived from other sources, concerning Franklin, Goldsmith, Ferguson, Rittenhouse, Rush, Fulton, Washington, Jefferson, Monroe, the Adamses, Lees, Morrises, Condorcet, Vergennes, Sieyès, Lafayette, Danton, Genêt, Brissot, Robespierre, Marat, Burke,

Erskine, and a hundred others.   All this, and probably invaluable letters from these
men, have been lost through the timidity of a woman before the theological
" boycott " on the memory of a theist, and the indifference of this country to
its most important materials of History.

When I undertook the biography of Edmund Randolph I found that the
great mass of his correspondence had been similarly destroyed by fire in New
Orleans, and probably a like fate will befall the Madison papers, Monroe papers,
and others, our national neglect of which will appear criminal to posterity.   After
searching through six States to gather documents concerning Randolph which
should all have been in Washington City, the writer petitioned the Library
Committee of Congress to initiate some action towards the preservation of our
historical manuscripts.   The Committee promptly and unanimously approved the
proposal, a definite scheme was reported by the Librarian of Congress, and—there
the matter rests.   As the plan does not include any device for advancing partisan
interests, it stands a fair chance of remaining in our national *oubliette* of intellectual
desiderata.

In writing the " Life of Paine " I have not been saved much labor by
predecessors in the same field.   They have all been rather controversial pam-
phleteers than biographers, and I have been unable to accept any of their statements
without verification.   They have been useful, however, in pointing out regions of
inquiry, and several of them—Rickman, Sherwin, Linton—contain valuable citations
from contemporary papers.   The truest delineation of Paine is the biographical
sketch by his friend Rickman.   The " Life " by Vale, and sketches by Richard
Carlile, Blanchard, and others, belong to the controversial *collectanea* in which
Paine's posthumous career is traceable.   The hostile accounts of Paine, chiefly
found in tracts and encyclopædias, are mere repetitions of those written by George
Chalmers and James Cheetham.

The first of these was published in 1791 under the title : " The Life of Thomas
Pain, Author of ' The Rights of Men,' with a Defence of his Writings.   By
Francis Oldys, A.M., of the University of Pennsylvania.   London.   Printed for
John Stockdale, Pickadilly."   This writer, who begins his vivisection of Paine by
accusing him of adding " e " to his name, assumed in his own case an imposing
pseudonym.   George Chalmers never had any connection with the University of
Philadelphia, nor any such degree.   Sherwin (1819) states that Chalmers admitted
having received £500 from Lord Hawksbury, in whose bureau he was a clerk, for
writing the book ; but though I can find no denial of this I cannot verify it.   In his
later editions the author claims that his book had checked the influence of Paine,
then in England, and his " Rights of Man," which gave the government such alarm
that subsidies were paid several journals to counteract their effect.   (See the letter
of Freching, cited from the Vansitart Papers, British Museum, by W. H. Smith, in

the *Century*, August, 1891.) It is noticeable that Oldys, in his first edition, entitles his work a "Defence" of Paine's writings—a trick which no doubt carried this elaborate libel into the hands of many "Paineites." The third edition has, "With a Review of his Writings." In a later edition we find the vignette of Paine surrounded by apes. Cobbett's biographer, Edward Smith, describes the book as "one of the most horrible collections of abuse which even that venal day produced." The work was indeed so overweighted with venom that it was sinking into oblivion when Cobbett reproduced its libels in America, for which he did penance through many years. My reader will perceive, in the earlier chapters of this work, that Chalmers tracked Paine in England with enterprise, but there were few facts that he did not manage to twist into his strand of slander.

In 1809, not long after Paine's death, James Cheetham's "Life of Thomas Paine" appeared in New York. Cheetham had been a hatter in Manchester, England, and would probably have continued in that respectable occupation had it not been for Paine. When Paine visited England and there published "The Rights of Man" Cheetham became one of his idolaters, took to political writing, and presently emigrated to America. He became editor of *The American Citizen*, in New York. The cause of Cheetham's enmity to Paine was the discovery by the latter that he was betraying the Jeffersonian party while his paper was enjoying its official patronage. His exposure of the editor was remorseless; the editor replied with personal vituperation; and Paine was about instituting a suit for libel when he died. Of Cheetham's ingenuity in falsehood one or two specimens may be given. During Paine's trial in London, for writing "The Rights of Man," a hostile witness gave testimony which the judge pronounced "impertinent"; Cheetham prints it "important." He says that Madame de Bonneville accompanied Paine on his return from France in 1802; she did not arrive until a year later. He says that when Paine was near his end Monroe wrote asking him to acknowledge a debt for money loaned in Paris, and that Paine made no reply. But before me is Monroe's statement, while President, that for his advances to Paine "no claim was ever presented on my part, nor is any indemnity now desired." Cheetham's book is one of the most malicious ever written, and nothing in it can be trusted.

Having proposed to myself to write a critical and impartial history of the man and his career, I found the vast Paine literature, however interesting as a shadow measuring him who cast it, containing conventionalized effigies of the man as evolved by friend and foe in their long struggle. But that war has ended among educated people. In the laborious work of searching out the real Paine I have found a general appreciation of its importance, and it will be seen in the following pages that generous assistance has been rendered by English clergymen, by official persons in Europe and America, by persons of all beliefs and no beliefs. In no instance have I been impeded by any prejudice, religious or political. The curators of archives, private collectors, owners of important documents bearing on the subject, have welcomed my effort to bring the truth to light. The mass of material thus accumulated is great, and its compression has been a difficult task. But the interest that led me to the subject has increased at every step; the story has abounded in thrilling episodes and dramatic surprises; and I have proceeded with a growing conviction that the simple facts, dispassionately told, would prove of importance far wider than Paine's personality, and find welcome with all students of history. I have brought to my task a love for it, the studies of some years, and results of personal researches made in Europe and America: qualifications which I count less than another which I venture to claim—the sense of responsibility, acquired by a public teacher of long service, for his words, which, be they truths or errors, take on life, and work their good or evil to all generations.

CONTENTS

CHAPTER   PAGE

Editor's Preface   .   .   .   .   .   .   *v*

Author's Preface   .   .   .   .   .   .   *vii*

I.   Early Influences   1

II.   Early Struggles   6

III.   Domestic Trouble   13

IV.   The New World   16

V.   Liberty and Equality   20

VI.   "Common Sense"   25

VII.   Under the Banner of Independence   .   . . 32

VIII.   Soldier and Secretary   37

IX.   French Aid, and the Paine-Deane Controversy   . . 48

X.   A Story by Gouverneur Morris   .   .   . 56

XI.   Cause, Country, Self 59

XII.   A Journey to France   68

XIII.   The Muzzled Ox Treading Out the Grain .   . . 72

XIV.   Great Washington and Poor Paine 80

XV.   Pontifical and Political Inventions 86

XVI.   Returning to the Old Home   .   .   . 93

XVII.   A British Lion with an American Heart   .   . . 98

XVIII.   Paine's Letters to Jefferson in Paris 103

XIX.   The Key of the Bastille   109

XX.   "The Rights of Man"   113

XXI.   Founding the European Republic 124

XXII.   The Right of Evolution   134

XXIII.   The Deputy for Calais in the Convention .   . . 142

XXIV.   Outlawed in England   150

XXV.   "Kill the King, but not the Man" 156

XXVI.   An Outlawed English Ambassador 162

XXVII.   Revolution *vs.* Constitution 168

XXVIII.   A Garden in the Faubourg St. Denis   .   . . 180

XXIX.   A Conspiracy   187

CONTENTS

CHAPTER		PAGE
XXX.	A Testimony under the Guillotine	195
XXXI.	A Minister and his Prisoner	200
XXXII.	Sick and in Prison	207
XXXIII.	A Restoration	217
XXXIV.	The Silence of Washington	222
XXXV.	"The Age of Reason"	228
XXXVI.	Friendships	246
XXXVII.	Theophilanthropy	253
XXXVIII.	The Republican Abdiel	264
XXXIX.	The Last Year in Europe	273
XL.	The American Inquisition	279
XLI.	New Rochelle and the Bonnevilles	287
XLII.	A New York Prometheus	299
XLIII.	Personal Traits	310
XLIV.	Death and Resurrection	317
Appendix A.	The Cobbett Papers	328
Appendix B.	The Hall Manuscripts	339
Appendix C.	Portraits of Paine	344
Appendix D.	Brief List of Paine's Works	348
Index	:	349

THE LIFE OF THOMAS PAINE

CHAPTER I

EARLY INFLUENCES

THE history here undertaken is that of an English mechanic, of Quaker training, caught in political cyclones of the last century, and set at the centre of its revolutions, in the old world and the new.

In the church register of Euston Parish, near Thetford, England, occurs this entry: "1734. Joseph Pain and Frances Cocke were married June 20th." These were the parents of Thomas Paine. The present rector of Euston Church, Lord Charles Fitz Roy, tells me that the name is there plainly "Pain," but in the Thetford town-records of that time it is officially entered "Joseph Paine."

Paine and Cocke are distinguished names in the history of Norfolk County. In the sixteenth century Newhall Manor, on the road between Thetford and Norwich, belonged to a Paine family. In 1553 Thomas Paine, Gent., was, by license from Queen Mary, trustee for the Lady Elizabeth, daughter of Henry VIII., by Queen Anne Bullen. In St. Thomas Church, Norwich, stands the monument of Sir Joseph Paine, Knt., the most famous mayor and benefactor of that city in the seventeenth century. In St. John the Baptist Church is the memorial of Justice Francis Cocke (d. 1628). Whether our later Joseph and Thomas were related to these earlier Paines has not been ascertained, but Mr. E. Chester Waters, of London, an antiquarian especially learned in family histories, expressed to me his belief that the Norfolk County Paines are of one stock. There is equal probability that John Cocke, Deputy Recorder of Thetford in 1629, pretty certainly ancestor of Thomas Paine's mother, was related to Richard Cock, of Norwich, author of "English Law, or a Summary Survey of the Household of God upon Earth" (London, 1651). The author of "The Rights of Man" may therefore be a confutation of his own dictum: "An hereditary governor is as inconsistent as an hereditary author." One Thomas Payne, of the Norfolk County family, was awarded £20 by the Council of State (1650) "for his sufferings by printing a book for the cause of Parliament." Among the sequestrators of royalist church livings was Charles George Cock, "student of Christian Law, of the Society of the Inner Temple, now [1651] resident of Norwich." In Blomefield's "History of Norfolk County" other notes may be found suggesting that whatever may have been our author's genealogy he was spiritually descended from these old radicals.

At Thetford I explored a manuscript —"Freeman's Register Book" (1610–1756)—and found that Joseph Paine (our author's father) was made a freeman of Thetford April 18, 1737, and Henry Cock May 16, 1740. The freemen of this borough were then usually members of trade guilds. Their privileges amounted to little more than the right of pasturage on the commons. The appointment did not imply high position, but popularity and influence. Frances Cocke had no doubt resided in Euston Parish, where she was married. She was a member of the Church of England and daughter of an attorney of Thetford. Her husband was a Quaker, and is said to have been disowned by the Society of Friends for being married by a priest. A search made for me by official members of that Society in Norfolk County failed to discover either the membership or disownment of any one of the name. Joseph's father, a farmer, was probably a Quaker. Had the son (b. 1708) been a Quaker by conversion he would hardly have defied the rules of the Society at twenty-six.

Joseph was eleven years younger than his wife. According to Oldys he was "a reputable citizen and though poor an honest man," but his wife was "a woman of sour temper and an eccentric character." Thomas Paine's writings contain several affectionate allusions to his father, but none to his mother. "They say best men are moulded out of faults," and the moulding begins before birth.

Thomas Paine was born January 29, 1736-7, at Thetford. The house was in Bridge Street, (now White Hart), and has recently made way for a pretty garden and fountain. I was inclined to adopt a more picturesque tradition that the birthplace was in old Heathenman Street, as more appropriate for a *païen* (no doubt the origin of Paine's name), who also bore the name of the doubting disciple. An appeal for allowances might be based on such a conjunction of auspices, but a manuscript of Paine's friend Rickman, just found by Dr. Clair J. Grece, identifies the house beyond question.

Thomas Paine is said by most of his biographers never to have been baptized. This rests solely on a statement by Oldys:

"It arose probably from the tenets of the father, and from the eccentricity of the mother, that our author was never baptized, though he was privately named; and never received, like true Christians, into the bosom of any church, though he was indeed confirmed by the bishop

of Norwich: This last circumstance was owing to the orthodox zeal of Mistress Cocke, his aunt, a woman of such goodness, that though she lived on a small annuity, she imparted much of this little income to his mother. . . .

"As he was not baptized, the baptism of Thomas Pain is not entered on the parish books of Thetford. It is a remarkable fact, that the leaves of the two registers of the parishes of St. Cuthbert's and St. Peter's, in Thetford, containing the marriages, births, and burials, from the end of 1733, to the beginning of 1737, have been completely cut out. Thus, a felony has been committed against the public, and an injury done to individuals, by a hand very malicious and wholly unknown. Whether our author, when he resided in Thetford in 1787, looked into these registers for his own birth; what he saw, or what he did, we will not conjecture. They contain the baptism of his sister Elizabeth, on the 28th of August, 1738."

This is Oldysian. Of course, if there was any mischief Paine did it, albeit against his own interests. But a recent examination shows that there has been no mutilation of the registers. St. Peter's and St. Cuthbert's had at the time one minister. In 1736, just before Paine's birth, the minister (John Price) died, and his successor (Thomas Vaughan) appears to have entered on his duties in March, 1737. A little before and during this interregnum the registers were neglected. In St. Cuthbert's register is the entry: "Elizabeth, Daughter of Joseph Payne and Frances his wife of this parish, was born Aug't the 29th, 1738, baptized September ye 20, 1738." This (which Oldys has got inaccurately, *suo more*) renders it probable that Thomas Paine was also baptized. Indeed, he would hardly have been confirmed otherwise.

The old historian of Norfolk County, Francis Blomefield, introduces us to Thetford (Sitomagus, Tedford, Theford, "People of the Ford") with a strain of poetry:

"No situation but may envy thee,
    Holding such intimacy with the sea,
    Many do that, but my delighted muse
    Says, Neptune's fairest daughter is the Little Ouse."

After reading Blomefield's history of the ancient town, and that of Martin, and after strolling through the quaint streets, I thought some poet should add to this praise for picturesqueness some tribute on Thetford's historic vistas. There is indeed " a beauty buried every-where," as Browning says.

Evelyn, visiting his friend Lord Arlington at Euston in September, 1677, writes :

"I went to Thetford, the Burrough Towne, where stand the ruines of a religious house ; there is a round mountaine artificially raised, either for some castle or monument, which makes a pretty landscape. As we went and return'd, a tumbler shew'd his extraordinary addresse in the Warren. I also saw the Decoy, much pleas'd with the stratagem."

Evelyn leaves his own figure, his princely friends, and the tumbler in the foreground of "a pretty landscape" visible to the antiquarian all around Thetford, whose roads, fully followed, would lead past the great scenes of English history. In general appearance the town (population under five thou-sand) conveys the pleasant impression of a fairly composite picture of its eras and generations. There is a continuity between the old Grammar School, occupying the site of the ancient cath-edral, and the new Guildhall, with its Mechanics' Institute. The old churches summon their flocks from eccentric streets suggestive of literal sheep-paths. Of the ignorance with which our democratic age sweeps away as cobwebs fine threads woven by the past around the present, Thetford showed few signs, but it is sad to find " Guildhall " effacing " Heathen-man " Street, which pointed across a thousand years to the march of the " heathen men " (Danes) of Anglo-Saxon chronicles.

"A. 870. This year the [heathen] army rode across Mercia into East Anglia, and took up their winter quarters in Thetford ; and the same winter King Edmund fought against them, and the Danes got the victory, and slew the king, and subdued all the land, and destroyed all the minsters which they came to. The names of their chiefs who slew the king were Hingwar and Habba."

If old Heathenman Street be followed historically, it would lead to Bury St.

Edmunds, where, on the spot of his coronation, the young king " was placed in a goodly shrine, richly adorned with jewels and precious stones," and a royal saint added to the calendar. The blood of St. Edmund reconsecrated Thetford.

"A. 1094. Then at Candlemas the king [William Rufus] went to Hastings, and whilst he waited there for a fair wind he caused the monastery on the field of battle to be consecrated ; and he took the staff from Herbert Losange, bishop of Thetford."

The letters of this Bishop Herbert, discovered at Brussels, give him an honorable place in the list of Thetford authors ; wherein also occur the names of Richard of Thetford, author of a treatise on preaching, Jeffrey de Roch-erio, who began a history of the monarchy, and John Brame, writer and translator of various treatises. The works of these Thetford authors are preserved at Cambridge.

Thetford was, in a way, connected with the first newspaper enterprise. Its member of Parliament, Sir Joseph Wil-liamson, edited the *London Gazette*, established by the Crown to support its own policy. The Crown claimed the sole right to issue any journal, and its license was necessary for every book. In 1674 Sir Joseph, being Secretary of State (he bought the office for £5,000), had control of the *Gazette* and of litera-ture. In that year, when Milton died, his treatise on " Christian Doctrine " was brought to Williamson for license. He said he could " countenance nothing of Milton's writings," and the treatise was locked up by this first English editor, to be discovered a hundred and forty-nine years later.

On his way to the Grammar School (founded by bequest of Sir Richard Ful-merston, 1566) Paine might daily read an inscription set in the Fulmerston alms-house wall : " Follow peace and holines with all men without the which no man shall see the Lord." But many memorials would remind him of how Williamson, a poor rector's son, had sold his talent to a political lord and reached power to buy

and sell Cabinet offices, while suppressing Milton. Thomas Paine, with more
talent than Williamson to dispose of,
was born in a time semi-barbaric at its
best, and savage at its worst. Having
got in the Quaker meeting an old head
on his young shoulders, he must bear
about a burden against most things
around him. The old churches were
satanic steeple-houses, and if he strolled
over to that in which his parents were
married, at Euston, its new splendors
were accused by surrounding squalor.

Mr. F. H. Millington of Thetford, who
has told Williamson's story,[1] has made
for me a search into Paine's time there.

"In Paine's boyhood [says Mr. Millington in
a letter I have from him] the town (about 2,000
inhabitants) possessed a corporation with mayor,
aldermen, sword-bearers, macemen, recorder.
The corporation was a corrupt body, under the
dominance of the Duke of Grafton, a prominent
member of the Whig government. Both members of Parliament (Hon. C. Fitzroy and Lord
Augustus Fitzroy) were nominees of Grafton.
The people had no interest and no power, and I
do not think politics were of any account in
Paine's childhood. From Paine's 'Rights of
Man' (Part ii., p. 108) it is clear that his native
town was the model in his mind when he wrote
on charters and corporations. The Lent Assizes
for the Eastern Circuit were held here, and Paine
would be familiar with the procedure and pomp
of a court of justice. He would also be familiar
with the sight of men and women hung for
trivial offences. Thetford was on the main road
to London, and was a posting centre. Paine
would be familiar with the faces and equipages
of some of the great Whig nobles in Norfolk.
Walpole might pass through on his way to
Houghton. The river Ouse was navigable to
Lynn, and Paine would probably go on a barge
to that flourishing seaport. Bury St. Edmunds
was a provincial capital for the nobility and
gentry of the district. It was twelve miles from
Thetford, and in closest connection with it.
The religious life of Thetford would be quiet.
The churches were poor, having been robbed at
the reformation. The Quakers were the only
non-conformists in the town. There is a tradition
that Wesley visited the town; if he did Paine
would no doubt be among his hearers. On the
whole, I think it easy to trace in Paine's works
the influence of his boyhood here. He would
see the corrupting influence of the aristocracy,

the pomp of law, the evils of the unreformed
corporations; the ruins of great ecclesiastical
establishments, much more perfect than now,
would bring to his mind what a power the
church had been. Being of a mechanical turn of
mind no doubt he had often played about the
paper-mill which was, and is, worked by water-
power."

When Paine was a lad the grand
gentlemen who purloined parks and
mansions from the Treasury were sending children to the gallows for small
thefts instigated by hunger. In his
thirteenth year he might have seen
under the shadow of Ely Minster, ten
miles away, the execution of Amy
Hutchinson, aged seventeen, for poison-
ing her husband. "Her face and hands
were smeared with tar, and having a
garment daubed with pitch, after a short
prayer the executioner strangled her, and
twenty minutes after the fire was kindled
and burnt half an hour." (*Notes and
Queries*, September 27, 1873.) Against
the prevailing savagery a human protest
was rarely heard outside the Quaker
meeting. Whether disowned or not,
Paine's father remained a Quaker, and
is so registered at burial; and his eminent son has repeatedly mentioned his
own training in the principles of that
Society. Remembering the extent to
which Paine's Quakerism had influenced
his political theories, and instances of
their bearing on great events, I found
something impressive in the little meeting-house in Cage Lane, Thetford.
This was his more important birthplace.
Its small windows and one door open
on the tombless graveyard at the back,
—perhaps that they might not be
smashed by the mob, or admit the
ribaldry of the street. The interior is
hardly large enough to seat fifty people.
Plymouth Brethren have for some years
occupied the place, but I was told that
the congregation, reduced to four or
five, would soon cease to gather there.
Adjoining the meeting-house, and in
contact with it, stands the ancient gaol,
from which may have been derived the
name "Cage Lane." In its front are two
iron-grated arches, at one of which was

---

[1] "Sir Joseph Williamson, Knt., A.D. 1630–
1701. A Page in the History of Thetford." A
very valuable contribution to local history.

the pillory, at the other the stocks,—the latter remembered by some now living.

On "first day," when his schoolmates went in fine clothes to grand churches, to see gay people, and hear fine music, little Thomas, dressed in drab, crept affrighted past the stocks to his childhood's pillory in the dismal meeting-house. For him no beauty or mirth, no music but the oaths of the pilloried, or shrieks of those awaiting the gallows. There could be no silent meeting in Cage Lane. Testimonies of the "Spirit" against inhumanity, delivered beside instruments of legal torture, bred pity in the child, who had a poetic temperament. The earliest glimpses we have of his childhood are in lines written on a fly caught in a spider's web, and an epitaph for a crow which he buried in the garden :

> "Here lies the body of John Crow, .
> Who once was high, but now is low ;
> Ye brother Crows take warning all,
> For as you rise, so must you fall."

This was when he was eight years of age. It seems doubtful whether the child was weeping or smiling, but the humor, if it be such, is grim, and did not last long. He had even then already, as we shall see, gained in the Quaker meeting a feeling that "God was too good" to redeem man by his son's death, as his Aunt Cocke instructed him, and a heart so precocious was a sad birthright in the Thetford of that day. We look in vain for anything that can be described as true boyhood in Paine. Oldys was informed, no doubt rightly, that "he was deemed a sharp boy, of unsettled application ; but he left no performances which denote juvenile vigour or uncommon attainments." There are, indeed, various indications that, in one way and another, Thetford and Quakerism together managed to make the early years of their famous son miserable. Had there been no Quakerism there had been no Thomas Paine ; his consciousness of this finds full recognition in his works ; yet he says :

"Though I reverence their philanthropy, I cannot help smiling at the conceit, that if the taste of a Quaker had been consulted at the creation, what a silent and drab-coloured creation it would have been ! Not a flower would have blossomed its gaieties, nor a bird been permitted to sing."

There is a pathos under his smile at this conceit. Paine wrote it in later life, amid the flowers and birds of his garden, which he loved, but whose gaieties he could never imitate. He with difficulty freed himself from his early addiction to an unfashionable garb ; he rarely entered a theatre, and could never enjoy cards.

By the light of the foregoing facts we may appreciate the few casual reminiscences of his school-days found in Paine's writings :

"My parents were not able to give me a shilling, beyond what they gave me in education; and to do this they distressed themselves.

"My father being of the Quaker profession, it was my good fortune to have an exceeding good moral education, and a tolerable stock of useful learning. Though I went to the grammar school (the same school, Thetford in Norfolk, that the present counsellor Mingay went to, and under the same master), I did not learn Latin, not only because I had no inclination to learn languages, but because of the objection the Quakers have against the books in which the language is taught. But this did not prevent me from being acquainted with the subjects of all the Latin books used in the school. The natural bent of my mind was to science. I had some turn, and I believe some talent, for poetry; but this I rather repressed than encouraged, as leading too much into the field of imagination.

"I happened, when a schoolboy, to pick up a pleasing natural history of Virginia, and my inclination from that day of seeing the western side of the Atlantic never left me."

Paine does not mention his proficiency in mathematics, for which he was always distinguished. To my own mind his "turn" for poetry possesses much significance in the light of his career. In excluding poets from his "Republic" Plato may have had more reasons than he has assigned. The poetic temperament and power, repressed in the purely literary direction, are apt to break out in glowing visions of ideal society and fiery denunciations of the unlovely world. Paine was not under the master of Thetford School (Colman), who taught Latin, but under the usher, Rev. William

Knowler, who admitted the Quaker lad to some intimacy, and related to him his adventures while serving on a man-of-war. Paine's father had a small farm, but he also carried on a stay-making business in Thetford, and his son was removed from school, at the age of thirteen, to be taught the art and mystery of making stays. To that he stuck for nearly five years. But his father became poorer, his mother probably more discontented, and the boy began to dream over the adventures of Master Knowler on a man-of-war.

CHAPTER II

EARLY STRUGGLES

In the middle of the eighteenth century England and France were contending for empire in India and in America. For some service the ship *Terrible*, Captain Death, was fitted out, and Thomas Paine made an effort to sail on her. It seems, however, that he was overtaken by his father on board, and carried home again. "From this adventure I was happily prevented by the affectionate and moral remonstrances of a good father, who from the habits of his life, being of the Quaker profession, looked on me as lost." This privateer lost in an engagement one hundred and seventy-five of its two hundred men. Thomas was then in his seventeenth year. The effect of the paternal remonstrances, unsupported by any congenial outlook at Thetford, soon wore off, and, on the formal declaration of war against France (1756), he was again seized with the longing for heroic adventure, and went to sea on the *King of Prussia*, privateer, Captain Mendez. Of that he soon got enough, but he did not return home.

Of Paine's adventures with the privateer there is no record. Of yet more momentous events of his life for some years there is known nothing beyond the barest outline. In his twentieth year he found work in London (with Mr. Morris, stay-maker, Hanover Street, Long Acre) and there remained near two years. These were fruitful years. "As soon as I was able I purchased a pair of globes, and attended the philosophical lectures of Martin and Ferguson, and became afterwards acquainted with Dr. Bevis, of the society called the Royal Society, then living in the Temple, and an excellent astronomer."

In 1758 Paine found employment at Dover with a stay-maker named Grace. In April, 1759, he repaired to Sandwich, Kent, where he established himself as a master stay-maker. There is a tradition at Sandwich that he collected a congregation in his room in the market-place, and preached to them "as an independent, or a Methodist." Here, at twenty-two, he married Mary Lambert. She was an orphan and a waiting-woman to Mrs. Richard Solly, wife of a woollen-draper in Sandwich. The Rev. Horace Gilder, Rector of St. Peter's, Sandwich, has kindly referred to the register, and finds the entry : " Thomas Pain, of the parish of St. Peter's, in the town of Sandwich, in Kent, bachelor, and Mary Lambert, of the same parish, spinster, were married in this church, by licence, this 27th day of Sept., 1759, by me William Bunce, Rector." Signed, " Thomas Pain, Mary Lambert. In the presence of Thomas Taylor, Maria Solly, John Joslin."

The young couple began housekeeping on Dolphin Key, but Paine's business did not thrive, and he went to Margate. There, in 1760, his wife died. Paine then concluded to abandon the stay-making business. His wife's father had once been an exciseman. Paine resolved to prepare himself for that office, and corresponded with his father on the subject. The project found favour, and Paine, after passing some months of study in London, returned to Thetford in July, 1761. Here, while acting as a supernumerary officer of excise, he continued his studies, and enjoyed the friendship of Mr. Cocksedge, the Recorder of Thetford. On December 1, 1762, he was appointed to gauge brewers' casks at Grantham. On August 8, 1764, he was set to watch smugglers at Alford.

Thus Thomas Paine, in his twenty-fifth year, was engaged in executing Excise Acts, the application of which to America prepared the way for independence. Under pressure of two great hungers—for bread, for science—the young exciseman took little interest in politics. "I had no disposition for what is called politics. It presented to my mind no other idea than is contained in the word jockeyship." The excise, though a Whig measure, was odious to the people, and smuggling was regarded as not only venial but clever. Within two years after an excise of £1 per gallon was laid on spirits (1746), twelve thousand persons were convicted for offences against the Act, which then became a dead letter. Paine's post at Alford was a dangerous one. The exciseman who pounced on a party of smugglers got a special reward, but he risked his life. The salary was only fifty pounds, the promotions few, and the excise service had fallen into usages of negligence and corruption to which Paine was the first to call public attention. "After tax, charity, and sitting expenses are deducted, there remains very little more than forty-six pounds; and the expenses of horse-keeping in many places cannot be brought under fourteen pounds a year, besides the purchase at first, and the hazard of life, which reduces it to thirty-two pounds per annum, or one shilling and ninepence farthing per day."[1]

[1] "Case of the officers of excise." *The*

It is hardly wonderful that Paine with his globes and scientific books should on one occasion have fallen in with the common practice of excisemen called "stamping,"—that is, setting down surveys of work on his books, at home, without always actually travelling to the traders' premises and examining specimens. These detective rounds were generally offensive to the warehouse people so visited, and the scrutiny had become somewhat formal. For this case of "stamping," frankly confessed, Paine was discharged from office, August 27, 1765.[2]

Writings of Paine (Conway), vol. iv, p. 500. Every Outride Officer had to keep his own horse.—H. B. B.

[2] I am indebted to Mr. G. J. Holyoake for documents that shed full light on an incident which Oldys has carefully left in the half-light congenial to his insinuations. The minute of the Board of Excise, dated August 27, 1765, is as follows:

"Thomas Paine, officer of Alford (Lincolnshire), Grantham collection, having on July 11th stamped the whole ride, as appears by the specimens not being signed in any part thereof, though proper entry was shown in journal, and the victualler's stocks drawn down in his books as if the same had been surveyed that day, as by William Swallow, Supervisor's letter of 3rd instant, and the collector's report thereon, also by the said Paine's own confession of the 13th instant, ordered to be discharged; that Robert Peat, dropped malt assistant in Lynn collection, succeed him."

The following is Paine's petition for restoration:

"LONDON, July 3, 1766. Honorable Sirs, —In humble obedience to your honors' letter of discharge bearing date August 29, 1765, I delivered up my commission and since that time have given you no trouble. I confess the justice of your honors' displeasure and humbly beg to add my thanks for the candour and lenity with which you at that unfortunate time indulged me. And though the nature of the report and my own confession cut off all expectations of enjoying your honors' favour then, yet I humbly hope it has not finally excluded me therefrom, upon which hope I humbly presume to entreat your honors to restore me. The time I enjoyed my former commission was short and unfortunate—an officer only a single year. No complaint of the least dishonesty or intemperance ever appeared against me; and, if I am so happy as to succeed in this, my humble petition, I will endeavour that my future conduct shall as much engage your honors' approbation as my former has merited

After Paine's dismission he supported himself as a journeyman with Mr. Gudgeon, a stay-maker of Diss, Norfolk, where he is said to have frequently quarrelled with his fellow-workmen. To be cast back on the odious work, to be discharged and penniless at twenty-eight, could hardly soothe the poor man's temper, and I suppose he did not remain long at Diss. He is traceable in 1766 in Lincolnshire, by his casual mention of the date in connection with an incident related in his fragment on "Forgetfulness." He was on a visit at the house of a widow lady in a village of the Lincolnshire fens, and as they were walking in the garden, in the summer evening, they beheld at some distance a white figure moving. He quitted Mrs. E. and pursued the figure, and when he at length reached out his hand, "the idea struck me," he says, "will my hand pass through the air, or shall I feel anything?" It proved to be a love-distracted maiden who, on hearing of the marriage of one she supposed her lover, meant to drown herself in a neighboring pond.

That Thomas Paine should sue for an office worth, beyond its expenses, thirty-two pounds, argues not merely penury, but an amazing unconsciousness, in his twenty-ninth year, of his powers. In London, for some months there stood between him and starvation only a salary of twenty-five pounds, given him by a Mr. Noble for teaching English in his academy in Goodman's Fields. This was the year 1766, for though Paine was restored to the excise on July 11th of this year no place was found for him. In January, 1767, he was employed by

your displeasure. I am, your honors' most dutiful humble servant, THOMAS PAINE."
Board's minute : "July 4, 1766. Ordered that he be restored on a proper vacancy."
Mr. B. F. Dun, for thirty-three years an officer of excise, discovered the facts connected with Paine's discharge, and also saw Paine's letter and entry books. In a letter before me he says : "I consider Mr. Paine's restoration as creditable to him as to the then Board of Excise."

Mr. Gardiner in his school at Kensington. Rickman and others have assigned to this time Paine's attendance of lectures of Martin and Ferguson, which I have however connected with his twentieth year. He certainly could not have afforded globes during this pauperized year 1766. In reply to Rickman's allusion to the lowly situations he had been in at this time, Paine remarked : "Here I derived considerable information ; indeed I have seldom passed five minutes of my life, however circumstanced, in which I did not acquire some knowledge."

According to Oldys he remained in the school at Kensington but three months. "His desire of preaching now returned on him," says the same author, "but applying to his old master for a certificate of his qualifications to the bishop of London, Mr. Noble told him that, since he was only an English scholar, he could not recommend him as a proper candidate for ordination in the church." It would thus appear that Paine had not parted from his employer in Goodman's Fields in any unpleasant way. Of his relation with his pupils only one trace remains—a letter in which he introduces one of them to General Knox, September 17, 1783 : "Old friend, I just take the opportunity of sending my respects to you by Mr. Darby, a gentleman who was formerly a pupil of mine in England."

Oldys says that Paine, "without regular orders," preached in Moorfields and elsewhere in England, "as he was urged by his necessities, or directed by his spirit." Although Paine's friendly biographers have omitted this preaching episode, it is too creditable to Paine's standing with the teacher with whom he had served a year for Oldys to have invented it. It is droll to think that the Church of England should ever have had an offer of Thomas Paine's services. The Quakerism in which he had been nurtured had never been formally adopted by him, and it offered no opportunities for the impulse to preach which seems to mark a phase in the life of every active English brain.

On May 15, 1767, Paine was appointed excise officer at Grampound, Cornwall, but "prayed leave to wait another vacancy." On February 19, 1768, he was appointed officer at Lewes, Sussex, whither, after a brief visit to Thetford, he repaired.

Not very unlike the old Norfolk borough in which Paine was born was Lewes, and with even literally an Ouse flowing through it. Here also marched the "Heathen Men," who have left only the legend of a wounded son of Harold nursed into health by a Christian maiden. The ruined castle commands a grander landscape than the height of Thetford, and much the same historic views. Seven centuries before Paine opened his office in Lewes came Harold's son, possibly to take charge of the excise as established by Edward the Confessor, just deceased.

'Paine" was an historic name in Lewes also. In 1688 two French refugees, William and Aaron Paine, came to the ancient town, and found there as much religious persecution as in France. It was directed chiefly against the Quakers. But when Thomas Paine went to dwell there the Quakers and the "powers that be" had reached a *modus vivendi*, and the new exciseman fixed his abode with a venerable Friend, Samuel Ollive, a tobacconist. The house then adjoined a Quaker meeting-house, now a Unitarian chapel. It is a quaint house, always known and described as "the house with the monkey on it." The projecting roof is supported by a female nondescript rather more human than anthropoid. I was politely shown through the house by its occupant, Mr. Champion, and observed in the cellar traces of Samuel Ollive's — afterwards Paine's — tobacco mill. The best room upstairs long bore on its wall "Tom Paine's study." The plaster has now flaked off but the proprietor, Mr. Alfred Hammond, told me that he remembers it there in 1840. Not far from the house is the old mansion of the Shelleys,—still called "The Shelleys,"—ancestors of a poet born with the "Rights of Man," and a child of Paine's revolution. And—such are the moral zones and poles in every English town—here in the graveyard of Jireh Chapel is the tomb of William Huntington S. S. [Sinner Saved] bearing this epitaph :

" Here lies the Coalheaver, beloved of God, but abhorred of men : the omniscient Judge, at the grand assize, shall ratify and confirm that to the confusion of many thousands ; for England and its metropolis shall know that there hath been a prophet among them. W. H : S. S."

While Paine was at Lewes this Hunt *alias* Huntington was a pious tramp in that part of England, well known to the police. Yet in his rubbish there is one realistic story of tramp-life which incidentally portrays an exciseman of the time, Huntington (born 1744), one of the eleven children of a day-laborer earning from seven to nine shillings a week in Kent, was sent by some friends to an infant school.

"And here I remember to have heard my mistress reprove me for something wrong, telling me that God Almighty took notice of children's sins. It stuck to my conscience a great while ; and who this God Almighty could be I could not conjecture ; and how he could know my sins without asking my mother I could not conceive. At that time there was a person named Godfrey, an exciseman in the town, a man of a stern and hard-favoured countenance, whom I took notice of for having a stick covered with figures, and an ink-bottle hanging at the button-hole of his coat. I imagined that man to be employed by God Almighty to take notice, and keep an account of children's sins ; and once I got into the market-house, and watched him very narrowly, and found that he was always in a hurry by his walking so fast ; and I thought he had need to hurry, as he must have a deal to do to find out all the sins of children. I watched him out of one shop into another, all about the town, and from that time eyed him as a most formidable being, and the greatest enemy I had in all the world."

To the shopkeepers this exciseman was really an adversary and an accuser, and one can well believe that his very physiognomy would be affected by such work, and the chronic consciousness of being unwelcome. We may picture Paine among the producers of Lewes—with but four or five thousand people,

then a notorious seat of smugglers—
with his stick and ink-bottle ; his face
prematurely aged, and gathering the
lines and the keen look which mask for
casual eyes the fundamental candor and
kindliness of his face.

Paine's surveys extended to Brighton ;
the brilliant city of our time being then
a small fishing-town known as Brighthelmston. It was scarce ten miles
distant, and had no magistrates, offenders
being taken to Lewes. There was a good
deal of religious excitement in the
neighborhood about the time Paine
went there to reside, owing to the preaching of Rev. George Whitefield, chaplain
of Lady Huntingdon, at a chapel built
by her ladyship at Brighthelmston. Lady
Huntingdon already had a quasi-
miraculous fame which in Catholic times
would have caused her to be honored
as St. Selina. In those days a pious
countess was more miraculous than the
dream that foretold about Lady
Huntingdon's coming. Surrounded by
crowds, she had to send for her chaplain,
Whitefield, who preached in a field till
a chapel was built. At the time when
Lady Huntingdon was exhorting the poor
villagers of Brighton, two relatives of
hers, Governor Shirley of Massachusetts
and his aide-de-camp Colonel George
Washington, were preparing the way for
the great events in which Paine was to
bear a part. When Paine went on his
survey he might have observed the
Washington motto, possibly a trace of
the pious countess, which long remained
on a house in Brighton : *Exitus acta
probat*. There was an ancient Washington
who fought at the battle of Lewes ; but
probably if our exciseman ever thought
of any Washington at all it was of the
anomalous Colonel in Virginia founding
a colonial association to disuse excisable
articles imported from England. But if
such transatlantic phenomena, or the
preaching of Whitefield in the neighborhood, concerned Paine at all, no trace
of their impression is now discoverable.
And if there were any protest in him at
that time, when the English Government

had reached its nadir of corruption, it
cannot be heard. He appears to have
been conventionally patriotic, and was
regarded as the Lewes laureate. He
wrote an election song for the Whig
candidate at New Shoreham, for which
the said candidate (Rumbold by name)
paid him three guineas ; and he wrote a
song on the death of General Wolfe,
which, when published some years later,
was set to music, and enjoyed popularity
in the Anacreontic and other societies.
While Britannia mourns for her Wolfe,
the sire of the gods sends his messengers
to console "the disconsolate dame,"
assuring her that her hero is not dead
but summoned to lead "the armies
above" against the proud giants marching
against Heaven.

The ballad recalls Paine the *païen*,
but the Thetford Quaker is not apparent.
And, indeed, there are various indications
about this time that some reaction had
set in after the preaching phase. "Such
was his enterprise on the water," says
Oldys, "and his intrepidity on the ice
that he became known by the appellation
of *Commodore*." William Carver (MS.)
says he was at this time "tall and slim,
about five feet eight inches."

At Lewes, where the traditions concerning Paine are strong, I met Miss
Rickman, a descendant of Thomas
"Clio" Rickman—"Clio," under which
his musical contributions to the Revolution were published, having become
part of his name. Rickman was a youth
in the Lewes of Paine's time, and
afterwards his devoted friend. His
enthusiasm was represented in children
successively named Paine, Washington,
Franklin, Rousseau, Petrarch, Volney.
Rickman gives an account of Paine at
Lewes :

"In this place he lived several years in habits
of intimacy with a very respectable, sensible,
and convivial set of acquaintance, who were
entertained with his witty sallies and informed
by his more serious conversations. In politics
he was at this time a Whig, and notorious for
that quality which has been defined perseverance
in a good cause and obstinacy in a bad one. He
was tenacious of his opinions, which were bold,

acute, and independent, and which he maintained with ardour, elegance, and argument. At this period, at Lewes, the White Hart evening club was the resort of a social and intelligent circle who, out of fun, seeing that disputes often ran very warm and high, frequently had what they called the 'Headstrong Book.' This was no other than an old Greek Homer which was sent the morning after a debate vehemently maintained, to the most obstinate haranguer in the Club : this book had the following title, as implying that Mr. Paine the best deserved and the most frequently obtained it : 'The Headstrong Book, or Original Book of Obstinacy.' Written by ***** ****, of Lewes, in Sussex, and Revised and Corrected by THOMAS PAINE.

"'Immortal PAINE, while mighty reasoners jar,
We crown thee General of the Headstrong War ;
Thy logic vanquish'd error, and thy mind
No bounds but those of right and truth confined.
Thy soul of fire must sure ascend the sky,
Immortal PAINE, thy fame can never die ;
For men like thee their names must ever save
From the black edicts of the tyrant grave.'

"My friend Mr. Lee, of Lewes, in communicating this to me in September, 1810, said : 'This was manufactured nearly forty years ago, as applicable to Mr. Paine, and I believe you will allow, however indifferent the manner, that I did not very erroneously anticipate his future celebrity.' "

It was probably to amuse the club at the White Hart, an ancient tavern, that Paine wrote his humorous poems.

On March 26, 1771, Paine married Elizabeth, daughter of Samuel Ollive, with whom he had lodged. This respected citizen had died in July, 1769, leaving in Lewes a widow and one daughter in poor circumstances. Paine then took up his abode elsewhere, but in the following year he joined the Ollives in opening a shop, and the tobacco-mill went on as before. His motive was probably compassion, but it brought him into nearer acquaintance with the widow and her daughter. Elizabeth is said to have been pretty, and, being of Quaker parentage, she was no doubt fairly educated. She was ten years younger than Paine, and he was her hero. They were married in St. Michael's Church, Lewes, on the 26th of March, 1771, by Robert Austen, curate, the witnesses being Henry Verrall and Thomas Ollive, the lady's brother.

Oldys is constrained to give Paine's ability recognition. "He had risen by superior energy, more than by greater honesty, to be a chief among the excisemen." They needed a spokesman at that time, being united in an appeal to Parliament to raise their salaries, and a sum of money, raised to prosecute the matter, was confided to Paine. In 1772 he prepared the document, which was printed, but not published until 1793.[1] Concerning the plea for the excisemen it need only be said that it is as clear and complete as any lawyer could make it. There was, of course, no room for originality in the simple task of showing that the ill-paid service must be badly done, but the style is remarkable for simplicity and force.

Paine put much time and pains into this composition, and passed the whole winter of 1772-3 trying to influence members of Parliament and others in favor of his cause. "A rebellion of the excisemen," says Oldys, "who seldom have the populace on their side, was not much feared by their superiors." Paine's pamphlet and two further leaflets of his were printed. The best result of his pamphlet was to secure him an acquaintance with Oliver Goldsmith, to whom he addressed the following letter :

"HONORED SIR,—Herewith I present you with the Case of the Officers of Excise. A compliment of this kind from an entire stranger may appear somewhat singular, but the following

---

[1] The document was revived as a pamphlet, though its subject was no longer of interest, at a time when Paine's political writings were under prosecution, and to afford a vehicle for an "introduction," which gives a graphic account of Paine's services in the United States. On a copy of this London edition (1793) before me, one of a number of Paine's early pamphlets bearing marks of his contemporary English editor, is written with pencil : "With a preface (Qy. J. Barlow)." From this, and some characteristics of the composition, I have no doubt that the vigorous introduction was Barlow's. The production is entitled, "The case of the Officers of Excise ; with remarks on the qualifications of Officers ; and of the numerous evils arising to the Revenue, from the insufficiency of the present salary. Humbly addressed to the Hon. and Right Hon. Members of both Houses of Parliament."

reasons and information will, I presume, sufficiently apologize, I act myself in the humble station of an officer of excise, though somewhat differently circumstanced to what many of them are, and have been the principal promoter of a plan for applying to Parliament this session for an increase of salary. A petition for this purpose has been circulated through every part of the kingdom, and signed by all the officers therein. A subscription of three shillings per officer is raised, amounting to upwards of £500, for supporting the expenses. The excise officers, in all cities and corporate towns, have obtained letters of recommendation from the electors to the members in their behalf, many or most of whom have promised their support. The enclosed case we have presented to most of the members, and shall to all, before the petition appear in the House. The memorial before you met with so much approbation while in manuscript, that I was advised to print 4000 copies ; 3000 of which were subscribed for the officers in general, and the remaining 1000 reserved for presents. Since the delivering them I have received so many letters of thanks and approbation for the performance, that were I not rather singularly modest, I should insensibly become a little vain. The literary fame of Dr. Goldsmith has induced me to present one to him, such as it is. It is my first and only attempt, and even now I should not have undertaken it, had I not been particularly applied to by some of my superiors in office. I have some few questions to trouble Dr. Goldsmith with, and should esteem his company for an hour or two, to partake of a bottle of wine, or any thing else, and apologize for this trouble, as a singular favour conferred on

"His unknown
"Humble servant and admirer,
"THOMAS PAINE.

Excise Coffee House,
"Broad Street, Dec. 21, 1772.

"P.S. Shall take the liberty of waiting on you in a day or two."[1]

To one who reads Paine's argument, it appears wonderful that a man of such ability should, at the age of thirty-five, have had his horizon filled with such a cause as that of the underpaid excisemen. Unable to get the matter before Parlia-

ment, he went back to his tobacco-mill in Lewes, and it seemed to him like the crack of doom when, 8 April, 1774, he was dismissed from the excise. The cause of Paine's second dismission from the excise being ascribed by his first biographer (Oldys) to his dealing in smuggled tobacco, without contradiction by Paine, his admirers have been misled into a kind of apology for him on account of the prevalence of the custom. But I have before me the minutes of the Board concerning Paine, and there is no hint whatever of any such accusation.[2] The order of discharge from Lewes is as follows :

"Friday 8th April 1774. Thomas Pain, Officer of Lewes 4th O. Ride Sussex Collection having quitted his Business, without obtaining the Board's Leave for so doing, and being gone off on Account of the Debts which he hath contracted, as by Letter of the 6th instant from Edward Clifford, Supervisor, and the said Pain having been once before Discharged, Ordered that he be again discharged."

In Paine's absence in London, writing his pleas for the excisemen, laboring with members of Parliament, his tobacco-mill had been still, his groceries unsold, and his wife and her mother had been supported from the bank of flattering hope. No sooner was it known that the hope of an increased salary for the exciseman had failed than he found himself in danger of arrest for debt. It was on this account that he left Lewes for a time, but it was only that he might take steps to make over all of his possessions to his creditors. This was done. The following placard appeared :

"To be sold by auction, on Thursday the 14th of April, and following day, all the household furniture, stock in trade and other effects of Thomas Pain, grocer and tobacconist, near the West Gate, in Lewes : Also a horse tobacco and snuff mill, with all the utensils for cutting tobacco and grinding off snuff ; and two unopened crates of cream-coloured stone ware."

---

[1] Goldsmith responded to Paine's desire for his acquaintance. I think Paine may be identified as the friend to whom Goldsmith, shortly before his death, gave the epitaph first printed in Paine's *Pennsylvania Magazine*, January, 1775, beginning,

"Here Whitefoord reclines, and deny it who can,
Though he merrily lived he is now a *grave* man."

In giving it Goldsmith said, "It will be of no use to me where I am going."

[2] I am indebted for these records to the Secretary of Inland Revenue, England, and to my friend Charles Macrae, who obtained them for me.

This sale was announced by one Whitfield, grocer, and if there were other creditors they were no doubt paid by the results, for Paine had no difficulty in returning to Lewes. He once more had to petition the Board, which shortly before had commended his assiduity. Its commissioner, George Lewis Scott, labored in his behalf. In vain. Whether it was because it was a rule that a second discharge should be final, or that his failure to move Parliament had made him a scapegoat for the disappointed excisemen, his petition was rejected. At thirty-seven Paine found himself penniless.

CHAPTER III

DOMESTIC TROUBLE

THE break-up of Paine's business at Lewes brought to a head a more serious trouble. On June 4th of the same miserable year, 1774, Paine and his wife formally separated.

The causes of their trouble are enveloped in mystery. It has been stated by both friendly and hostile biographers that there was from the first no cohabitation, and that concerning the responsibility for this neither of them was ever induced to utter a word. Even his friend Rickman was warned off the subject by Paine, who, in reply to a question as to the reason of the separation, said : "It is nobody's business but my own; I had cause for it, but I will name it to no one."

William Huntington, in his "Kingdom of Heaven," mentions a usage of some Quakers in his time, "that when a young couple are espoused, they are to be kept apart for a season to mourn"; this being their interpretation of Zech. xii., 12–14. As Huntington was mainly acquainted with this Sussex region, it is not inconceivable that Elizabeth Ollive held some such notion, and that this led to dissension ending in separation. Nor is it inconceivable that Paine himself, finding his excise office no support, and his shop a failure, resolved that no offspring should suffer his penury or increase it. It is all mere guesswork.

Mr. Alfred Hammond, of Lewes, who owns the property, showed me the documents connected with it. After the death of Samuel Ollive in 1769, Esther, his widow, enjoyed the messuage until her own death, in 1800, when a division among the heirs became necessary. Among the documents is one which recites some particulars of the separation between Paine and his wife.

" Soon after the Testator's death, his daughter Elizabeth married Thos. Pain from whom she afterwards lived separate under articles dated 4th June 1774, and made between the said Thos. Pain of the first part, the said Elizabeth of the 2nd part, and the Rev. James Castley, Clerk, of the 3d part, by which Articles, after reciting (inter alia) that Dissentions had arisen between the said Thos. Pain and Elizabeth his wife, and that they had agreed to live separate. And also reciting the Will of the said Saml. Ollive and that the said Elizabeth should have and take her share of the said Monies of the said House when the same should become due and payable and that he would give any Discharge that should then be required to and for the use of the said Elizabeth: The said Thos. Pain did covenant to permit the said Elizabeth to live separate from him and to carry on such Trade and Business as she should think fit, notwithstanding her coverture and as if she were a Feme Sole. And that he would not at any time thereafter claim or demand the said monies which she should be entitled to at the time of the sale of the said House in Lewes aforesaid, or any of the Monies Rings Plate Cloathes Linen Woollen Household Goods or Stock in Trade which the said Elizabeth should or might at any time thereafter buy or purchase or which should be devised or given to her or she should otherwise acquire and that she should and might enjoy and absolutely dispose of the same as if she were a Feme Sole and unmarried. And also that it should and might be lawful for the said Elizabeth to have receive and take to her own separate use and benefit her said share of the Monies for which the said Messuage or Tenement in Lewes should be sold when the same should become due and payable."

Another paper is a Release to Francis Mitchener, October 14, 1800, in which it is recited:

"That the said Elizabeth Pain had ever since lived separate from him the said Thos. Pain, and never had any issue, and the said Thomas Pain had many years quitted this Kingdom and resided (if living) in parts beyond the seas, but had not since been heard of by the said Elizabeth Pain, nor was it known for certain whether he was living or dead."

This release is signed by Robert Blackman and wife, and eight others, among these being the three children of Samuel Ollive, who under his will were to "share alike"—Samuel, Thomas, and Elizabeth (Mrs. Paine). The large seals attached to the signatures were fortunately well preserved, for each represents the head of Thomas Paine. By the assistance of Mr. Hammond I am able to present this little likeness of Paine that must have been made when he was about thirty-five, or nearly twenty years earlier than any other portrait of him. The reader must form his own conjecture as to the origin of this seal, its preservation by the wife, and use on this document. At this time, and probably since her separation, Elizabeth Paine would appear to have resided with her brother Thomas, a watchmaker in Cranbrook, Kent. That she and the family did not know Paine's whereabouts in 1800, or whether he were dead or alive, argues that they had not followed his career or the course of public events with much interest. One would be glad to believe that Elizabeth cherished kindly remembrance of the man who, considering his forlorn condition, had certainly shown generosity in the justice with which he renounced all of his rights in the property she had brought him, and whose hand she might naturally have suspected behind the monies anonymously sent her. We will therefore hope that it was from some other member of the family that Oldys obtained,—unless, like his "A.M. of the University of Philadelphia," it was invented,—the letter said to have been written by Paine's mother to his wife.[1] The letter may have been manipulated, but it is not improbable that rumors, "exaggerated by enmity or misstated by malice," as Oldys confesses, elicited some such outburst from Thetford.[2] The excisemen, angry at the failure to get their case before Parliament, and having fixed on Paine as their scapegoat, all other iniquities were naturally laid on him. Eighteen years

[1] "THETFORD, NORFOLK, July 27, 1774. Dear Daughter,—I must beg leave to trouble you with my inquiries concerning my unhappy son and your husband: various are the reports, which I find come originally from the Excise-office. Such as his vile treatment to you, his secreting upwards of 30l. intrusted with him to manage the petition for advance of salary; and that since his discharge, he have petitioned to be restored, which was rejected with scorn. Since which I am told he have left England. To all which I beg you'll be kind enough to answer me by due course of post.—You'll not be a little surprized at my so strongly desiring to know what's become of him after I repeat to you his undutiful behavior to the tenderest of parents; he never asked of us anything, but what was granted, that were in our poor abilities to do; nay, even distressed ourselves, whose works are given over by old age, to let him have 20l. on bond, and every other tender mark a parent could possibly shew a child; his ingratitude, or rather want of duty, has been such, that he have not wrote to me upwards of two years.—If the above account be true, I am heartily sorry, that a woman whose character and amiableness deserves the greatest respect, love, and esteem, as I have always on enquiry been informed your's did, should be tied for life to the worst of husbands. I am, dear daughter, your affectionate mother,
                                    "F. PAIN.
"P.S. For God's sake, let me have your answer, as I am almost distracted."

[2] When Paine had the money he did forward twenty pounds to his parents, and made provision for his mother when she was a widow. As to writing to her, in those unhappy years, he probably thought it better to keep his burdens to himself. He may also have been aware of his mother's severity without knowing her interest in him.

later, when the scapegoat who had gone into the American wilderness returned with the renown of having helped to make it a nation, he addressed a letter to Lewes, which was about to hold a meeting to respond to a royal proclamation for suppressing seditious writings. His tone is not that of a man who supposed that Lewes had aught against him on the score of his wife.

" It is now upwards of eighteen years since I was a resident inhabitant of the town of Lewes. My situation among you as an officer of the revenue, for more than six years, enabled me to see into the numerous and various distresses which the weight of taxes even at that time of day occasioned ; and feeling, as I then did, and as it is natural for me to do, for the hard condition of others, it is with pleasure I can declare, and every person then under my survey, and now living, can witness the exceeding candor, and even tenderness, with which that part of the duty that fell to my share was executed. The name of Thomas Paine is not to be found in the records of the Lewes justices, in any one act of contention with, or severity of any kind whatever towards, the persons whom he surveyed, either in the town or in the country ; of this Mr. Fuller and Mr. Shelley, who will probably attend the meeting, can, if they please, give full testimony. It is, however, not in their power to contradict it. Having thus indulged myself in recollecting a place where I formerly had, and even now have, many friends, rich and poor, and most probably some enemies, I proceed to the import of my letter. Since my departure from Lewes, fortune or providence has thrown me into a line of action which my first setting out in life could not possibly have suggested to me. . . . Many of you will recollect, that whilst I resided among you, there was not a man more firm and open in supporting the principles of liberty than myself, and I still pursue, and ever will, the same path."

Finally, it should be added that Rickman, a truthful man, who admits Paine's faults, says : " This I can assert, that Mr. Paine always spoke tenderly and respectfully of his wife ; and sent her several times pecuniary aid, without her knowing even whence it came."

While Paine was in London, trying to get before Parliament a measure for the relief of excisemen, he not only enjoyed the friendship of Goldsmith, but that of Franklin. In the Doctor's electrical experiments he took a deep interest ; for Paine was devoted to science, and the extent of his studies is attested by his description of a new electrical machine and other scientific papers, signed " Atlanticus," in the *Pennsylvania Magazine*. The sale of his effects in Lewes paid his debts, but left him almost penniless. He came to London, and how he lived is unknown—that is, physically, for we do find some intimation of his mental condition. In a letter written many years after to John King, a political renegade, Paine says :

" When I first knew you in Ailiffe-street, an obscure part of the City, a child, without fortune or friends, I noticed you ; because I thought I saw in you, young as you was, a bluntness of temper, a boldness of opinion, and an originality of thought, that portended some future good. I was pleased to discuss, with you, under our friend *Oliver's* lime-tree, those political notions, which I have since given the world in my ' Rights of Man.' You used to complain of abuses, as well as me, and write your opinions on them in free terms—What then means this sudden attachment to *Kings ?* "

This " Oliver " was probably the famous Alderman Oliver who was imprisoned in the Tower during the great struggle of the City with the Government, on account of Wilkes. Paine tells us that in early life he cared little for politics, which seemed to him a species of " jockeyship " ; and how apt the term is is shown by the betting-book kept at Brooks' Club, in which are recorded the bets of the noblemen and politicians of the time on the outcome of every motion and course of every public man or minister. But the contemptuous word proves that Paine was deeply interested in the issues which the people had joined with the king and his servile ministers. He could never have failed to read with excitement the letters of Junius, whose "brilliant pen," he afterwards wrote, " enraptured without convincing ; and though in the plenitude of its rage it might be said to give elegance to bitterness, yet the policy survived the blast." We may feel sure that he had heard with joy that adroit verdict of the jury at the King's Bench on Woodfall, Junius' printer, which secured liberty of the Press until, twenty-two years later, it was reversed by revolutionary panic, in the same court, for Paine himself. Notwithstanding the private immorality of Wilkes, in which his associates were aristocratic, the most honorable political elements in England, and the Independents and Presbyterians, were resolute in defending the rights of his constituents against the authority arrogated by the Commons to exclude him. Burke then stood by Wilkes, as John Bright stood by Bradlaugh at a later day. And while Paine was laboring to carry his excise bill through Parliament he had good opportunity to discover how completely that body's real opinions were overruled by royal dictation. It was at that time that George III., indifferent to his brother's profligacies, would not forgive his marriage with a commoner's sister, and forced on Parliament a Marriage Act which made all marriages in the royal family illegitimate without his consent. The indignant resignation of Fox modified the measure slightly, limiting the King's interference at the twenty-sixth year of the marrying parties, and then giving the veto to Parliament. For this the King turned his wrath on Fox. This was but one of the many instances of those years—

all told in Trevelyan's admirable work [1] —which added to Paine's studies of the Wilkes conflicts a lasting lesson in the conservation of despotic forces. The barbaric eras of prerogative had returned under the forms of ministerial government. The Ministry, controlled by the Court, ruled by corruption of commoners.

It was a *régime* almost incredible to us now, when England is of all nations most free from corruption and Court influence in politics ; and it was little realized in English colonies before the Revolution. But Franklin was in London to witness it, and Paine was there to grow familiar with the facts. To both of them the systematic inhumanity and injustice were brought home personally. The discharged and insulted postmaster could sympathize with the dismissed and starving exciseman. Franklin recognized Paine's ability, and believed he would be useful and successful in America. So on this migration Paine decided, and possibly the determination brought his domestic discords to a crisis.

[1] " The Early History of Charles James Fox," 1880.

CHAPTER IV

THE NEW WORLD

PAINE left England in October and arrived in America November 30, 1774. He bore a letter of introduction from Dr. Franklin to Richard Bache, his son-in-law, dated September 30, 1774 :

" The bearer Mr. Thomas Paine is very well recommended to me as an ingenious worthy young man. He goes to Pennsylvania with a view of settling there. I request you to give him your best advice and countenance, as he is quite a stranger there. If you can put him in a way of obtaining employment as a clerk, or assistant tutor in a school, or assistant surveyor, of all of which I think him very capable, so that

he may procure a subsistence at least, till he can make acquaintance and obtain a knowledge of the country, you will do well, and much oblige your affectionate father."

On March 4, 1775, Paine writes Franklin from Philadelphia :

" Your countenancing me has obtained for me many friends and much reputation, for which please accept my sincere thanks. I have been applied to by several gentlemen to instruct their sons on very advantageous terms to myself, and a printer and bookseller here, a man of reputation and property, Robert Aitkin, has lately attempted a magazine, but having little or no turn that way himself, he has applied to me for assistance. He had not above six hundred subscribers when I first assisted him. We have now upwards of fifteen hundred, and daily increasing. I have not entered into terms with him. This is only the second number. The first I was not concerned in."

It has been often stated that Paine was befriended by Dr. Rush, but there is no indication of this. Their acquaintance was casual.

"About the year 1773 [says Dr. Rush[1]—the date is an error for 1774] I met him accidentally in Mr. Aitkin's bookstore, and was introduced to him by Mr. Aitkin. We conversed a few minutes, when I left him. Soon afterwards I read a short essay with which I was much pleased, in one of Bradford's papers, against the slavery of the Africans in our country, and which I was informed was written by Mr. Paine. This excited my desire to be better acquainted with him. We met soon after in Mr. Aitkin's bookstore, where I did homage to his principles and pen upon the subject of the enslaved Africans. He told me the essay to which I alluded was the first thing he had ever published in his life. After this Mr. Aitkin employed him as the editor of his Magazine, with a salary of fifty pounds currency a year. This work was well supported by him. His song upon the death of Gen. Wolfe, and his reflections upon the death of Lord Clive, gave it a sudden currency which few works of that kind have since had in our country."

As the anti-slavery essay was printed March 8, 1775, it appears that Paine had been in America more than three months before Rush noticed him.

The first number of the *Pennsylvania Magazine*, or *American Museum*, appeared at the end of January, 1775. Though "not concerned" in it pecuniarily, not yet being editor, his contributions increased the subscription list, and he was at once engaged. For eighteen months Paine edited this magazine, and probably there never was an equal amount of good literary work done on a salary of fifty pounds a year. It was a handsome magazine, with neat vignette—book, plough, anchor, and olive-twined shield,—the motto, *Juvat in sylvis habitare*. The future author

[1] In a letter written July 17, 1809, to James Cheetham in answer to a request for information. See Cheetham's *Life of Paine.*—H.B.B.

of the "Rights of Man" and "Age of Reason" admonishes correspondents that religion and politics are forbidden topics! The first number contains a portrait of Goldsmith and the picture of a new electrical machine. A prefatory note remarks that "the present perplexities of affairs" have "encompassed with difficulties the first number of the magazine, which, like the early snow-drop, comes forth in a barren season, and contents itself with modestly foretelling that choicer flowers are preparing to appear." The opening essay shows a fine literary touch, and occasionally a strangely modern vein of thought. "Our fancies would be highly diverted could we look back and behold a circle of original Indians haranguing on the sublime perfections of the age; yet 'tis not impossible but future times may exceed us almost as much as we have exceeded them."

Here is a forerunner of Macaulay's New Zealander sketching the ruins of St. Paul's. It is followed by a prediction that the coming American magazine will surpass the English, "because we are not exceeded in abilities, have a more extensive field for inquiry, and whatever may be our political state, our happiness will always depend upon ourselves." A feature of the magazine was the description, with plates, of recent English inventions not known in the new world — threshing-machine, spinning-machine, etc.,—such papers being by Paine. These attracted the members of the Philosophical Society, founded by Franklin, and Paine was welcomed into their circle by Rittenhouse, Clymer, Rush, Muhlenberg, and other representatives of the scientific and literary metropolis. Many a piece composed for the Headstrong Club at Lewes first saw the light in this magazine,—such as the humorous poems, "The Monk and the Jew," "The Farmer and Short's Dog, Porter"; also the famous ballad "On the Death of General Wolfe," printed March, 1775, with music. Lewes had not, indeed, lost sight of him, as is shown by a communication in April from Dr. Matthew Wilson, dated from that town, relating to a new kind of fever raging in England.

The reader who has studied Paine's avowed and well-known works finds no difficulty in tracking him beneath the various signatures by which he avoided an appearance of writing most of the articles in the *Pennsylvania Magazine*, though he really did. He is now "Atlanticus," now "Vox Populi," or "Æsop," and oftener affixes no signature. The Thetford Quaker is still here in "Reflections on the Death of Lord Clive" (reprinted as a pamphlet in England), "A New Anecdote of Alexander the Great," and "Cursory Reflections on the Single Combat or Modern Duel." The duel was hardly yet challenged in America when Paine wrote (May, 1775).

"From the peculiar prevalence of this custom in countries where the religious system is established which, of all others, most expressly prohibits the gratification of revenge, with every species of outrage and violence, we too plainly see how little mankind are in reality influenced by the precepts of the religion by which they profess to be guided, and in defence of which they will occasionally risk even their lives."

But with this voice from Thetford meeting-house mingles the testimony of "common sense." In July, 1775, he writes :

"I am thus far a Quaker, that I would gladly agree with all the world to lay aside the use of arms, and settle matters by negotiations ; but, unless the whole world wills, the matter ends, and I take up my musket, and thank heaven he has put it in my power. . . . We live not in a world of angels. The reign of Satan is not ended, neither can we expect to be defended by miracles."

Titles he sees through (May, 1775):

"The Honorable plunderer of his country, or the Right Honorable murderer of mankind, create such a contrast of ideas as exhibit a monster rather than a man. . . . The lustre of the Star, and the title of My Lord, overawe the superstitious vulgar, and forbid them to enquire into the character of the possessor : Nay more, they are, as it were, bewitched to admire in the great the vices they would honestly condemn in themselves. . . . The reasonable freeman sees through the magic of a title, and examines the man before he approves him. To him the honors of the worthless seem to write their masters' vices in capitals, and their Stars shine to no other end than to read them by. . . . Modesty forbids men separately, or collectively, to assume titles. But as all honors, even that of kings, originated from the public, the public may justly be called the true fountain of honor. And it is with much pleasure I have heard the title 'Honorable' applied to a body of men, who nobly disregarding private ease and interest for public welfare, have justly merited the address of *The Honorable Continental Congress.*"

He publishes (May, 1775), and I think wrote, a poetical protest against cruelty to animals, to whose rights Christendom was then not awakened. His pen is unmistakable in "Reflections on Unhappy Marriages" (June, 1775) : "As extasy abates coolness succeeds, which often makes way for indifference, and that for neglect. Sure of each other by the nuptial bond, they no longer take any pains to be mutually agreeable. Careless if they displease, and yet angry if reproached ; with so little relish for each other's company that anybody else's is more welcome, and more entertaining." It is a more pointed statement of the problem already suggested, in the April magazine, by his well-known fable "Cupid and Hymen," whose controversies are now settled in the Divorce Court.

In his August (1775) number is found the earliest American plea for woman. It is entitled "An Occasional Letter on the Female Sex," and unsigned, but certainly by Paine. His trick of introducing a supposititious address from another person, as in the following extract, appears in many examples.

"Affronted in one country by polygamy, which gives them their rivals for inseparable companions ; inslaved in another by indissoluble ties, which often join the gentle to the rude, and sensibility to brutality : Even in countries where they may be esteemed most happy, constrained in their desires in the disposal of their goods, robbed of freedom of will by the laws, the slaves of opinion, which rules them with absolute sway, and construes the slightest appearances into guilt, surrounded on all sides by judges who are at once their tyrants and seducers, and who after having prepared their faults, punish every lapse with dishonor—nay usurp the right of degrading them on suspicion !—who does not feel for the tender sex ? Yet such I am sorry to say is the lot of woman over the whole earth. Man with regard to them, in all climates and in all ages, has been either an insensible husband or an oppressor ; but they have sometimes experienced the cold and deliberate oppression of pride, and sometimes the violent and terrible tyranny of jealousy. When they are not beloved they are nothing ; and when they are they are tormented. They have almost equal cause to be afraid of indifference and love. Over three quarters of the globe Nature has placed them between contempt and misery."

" Even among people where beauty receives the highest homage we find men who would deprive the sex of every kind of reputation. ' The most virtuous woman,' says a celebrated Greek, ' is she who is least talked of.' That morose man, while he imposes duties on women, would deprive them of the sweets of public esteem, and in exacting virtues from them would make it a crime to aspire to honor. If a woman were to defend the cause of her sex she might address him in the following manner :

" ' How great is your injustice ! If we have an equal right with you to virtue, why should we not have an equal right to praise? The public esteem ought to wait upon merit. Our duties are different from yours, but they are not less difficult to fulfil, or of less consequence to society : They are the foundations of your felicity, and the sweetness of life. We are wives and mothers. 'Tis we who form the union and the cordiality of families ; 'tis we who soften that savage rudeness which considers everything as due to force, and which would involve man with man in eternal war. We cultivate in you that humanity which makes you feel for the misfortunes of others, and our tears forewarn you of your own danger. Nay, you cannot be ignorant that we have need of courage not less than you : More feeble in ourselves, we have perhaps more trials to encounter. Nature assails us with sorrow, law and custom press us with constraint, and sensibility and virtue alarm us by their continual conflict. Sometimes also the name of citizen demands from us the tribute of fortitude. When you offer your blood to the state, think that it is ours. In giving it our sons and our husbands we give it more than ourselves. You can only die on the field of battle, but we have the misfortune to survive those whom we love the most. Alas ! while your ambitious vanity is unceasingly laboring to cover the earth with statues, with monuments, and with inscriptions to eternize, if possible, your names, and give

yourselves an existence when this body is no more, why must we be condemned to live and to die unknown ? Would that the grave and eternal forgetfulness should be our lot. Be not our tyrants in all : Permit our names to be sometime pronounced beyond the narrow circle in which we live : Permit friendship, or at least love, to inscribe its emblems on the tomb where our ashes repose ; and deny us not the public esteem which, after the esteem of one's self, is the sweetest reward of well-doing.' "

Thus the *Pennsylvania Magazine*, in the time that Paine edited it, was a seed-bag from which this sower scattered the seeds of great reforms ripening with the progress of civilization. Through the more popular press he sowed also. Events selected his seeds of American independence, of republican equality, freedom from royal, ecclesiastical, and hereditary privilege, for a swifter and more imposing harvest : but the whole circle of human ideas and principles was recognized by this lone wayfaring man. The first to urge extension of the principles of independence to the enslaved negro ; the first to arraign monarchy, and to point out the danger of its survival in presidency ; the first to propose articles of a more thorough nationality to the new-born States ; the first to advocate international arbitration ; the first to expose the absurdity and criminality of duelling ; the first to suggest more rational ideas of marriage and divorce ; the first to advocate national and international copyright ; the first to plead for the animals ; the first to demand justice for woman : what brilliants would our modern reformers have contributed to a coronet for that man's brow, had he not presently worshipped the God of his fathers after the way that theologians called heresy ! " Be not righteous overmuch," saith cynical Solomon ; " neither make thyself overwise : why shouldest thou destroy thyself ? "

CHAPTER V

LIBERTY AND EQUALITY

WITH regard to Paine's earliest publication there has been needless confusion. In his third *Crisis* he says to Lord Howe : " I have likewise an aversion to monarchy, as being too debasing to the dignity of man ; but I never troubled others with my notions till very lately, nor ever published a syllable in England in my life." It has been alleged that this is inconsistent with his having written in 1772 " The Case of the Officers of Excise." But this, though printed (by William Lee of Lewes) was not published until 1793. It was a document submitted to Parliament, but never sold. The song on Wolfe, and other poetical pieces, though known to the Headstrong Club in Lewes, were first printed in Philadelphia.[1]

In America Wolfe again rises before Paine's imagination. In the *Pennsylvania Journal*, January 4th, appears a brief " Dialogue between General Wolfe and General Gage in a Wood near Boston." Wolfe, from the Elysian Fields, approaches Gage with rebuke for the errand on which he has come to America, and reminds him that he is a citizen as well as a soldier. " If you have any regard for the glory of the British name, and if you prefer the society of Grecian, Roman, and British heroes in the world of spirits to the company of Jeffries, Kirk, and other royal executioners, I conjure you immediately to resign your commission."

Although this " Dialogue " was the first writing of Paine published, it was not the first written for publication. The cause that first moved his heart and pen was that of the negro slave. Dr. Rush's date of his meeting with Paine, 1773, —a year before his arrival,—is one of a number of errors in his letter, among

---

[1] Mr. W. H. Burr maintains that Paine wrote in the English *Crisis* (1775) under the name of " Casca." As Casca's articles bear intrinsic evidence of being written in London—such as his treating as facts General Gage's fictions about Lexington—the theory supposes Paine to have visited England in that year. But besides the facts that Rush had an interview with Paine near the middle of March, and Franklin in October, the accounts of Aitkin, preserved in Philadelphia, show payments to Paine in May, July, and August, 1775. As Mr. Burr's further theory, that Paine wrote the letters of Junius, rests largely on the identification with " Casca," it might be left to fall with disproof of the latter. It is but fair, however, to the labors of a courageous writer, and to the many worthy people who have adopted his views, to point out the impossibilities of their case. An able summary of the facts discoverable concerning the personality of Junius, in Macaulay's " Warren Hastings," says : " As to the position, pursuits, and connexions of Junius, the following are the most important facts which can be considered as clearly proved : first, that he was acquainted with the technical forms of the Secretary of State's office ; secondly, that he was intimately acquainted with the business of the War Office ; thirdly, that he, during the year 1770, attended debates in the House of Lords, and took notes of speeches, particularly of the speeches of Lord Chatham ; fourthly, that he bitterly resented the appointment of Mr. Chamier to the place of Deputy Secretary of War ; fifthly, that he was bound by some strong tie to the first Lord Holland."

Now during the period of Junius' letters (Jan. 21, 1769, to Jan. 21, 1772) Paine was occupied with his laborious duties as exciseman at Lewes, and with the tobacco-mill from which he vainly tried to extort a living for himself and wife, and her mother. Before that period there was no time at which Paine could have commanded the leisure or opportunities necessary to master the political and official details known to Junius, even had he been interested in them. He declares that he had no interest in politics, which he regarded as a species of " jockeyship." How any one can read a page of Junius and then one of Paine, and suppose them from the same pen appears to me inconceivable. Junius is wrapped up in the affairs of Lord This and Duke That, and a hundred details. I can as easily imagine Paine agitated with the movements of a battle of chessmen. But apart from this, the reader need only refer to the facts of his life before coming to America to acquit him of untruth in saying that he had published nothing in England, and that the cause of America made him an author.

these being his report that Paine told him the antislavery essay was the first thing he had ever published. Paine no doubt told him it was the first thing he ever wrote and offered for publication; but it was not published until March 8th. Misled by Rush's words, Paine's editors and our historians of the antislavery movement have failed to discover this early manifesto of abolitionism. It is a most remarkable article. Every argument and appeal, moral, religious, military, economic, familiar in our subsequent antislavery struggle, is here found stated with eloquence and clearness. Having pointed out the horrors of the slave trade and of slavery, he combats the argument that the practice was permitted to the Jews. Were such a plea allowed it would justify adoption of other Jewish practices utterly unlawful "under clearer light." The Jews indeed had no permission to enslave those who never injured them, but all such arguments are unsuitable "since the time of reformation came under Gospel light. All distinctions of nations, and privileges of one above others, are ceased. Christians are taught to account all men their neighbours, and love their neighbours as themselves; and do to all men as they would be done by; to do good to all men; and man-stealing is ranked with enormous crimes." Bradford might naturally hesitate some weeks before printing these pointed reproofs. "How just, how suitable to our crime is the punishment with which Providence threatens us? We have enslaved multitudes, and shed much innocent blood, and now are threatened with the same." In the conclusion, a practical scheme is proposed for liberating all except the infirm who need protection, and settling them on frontier lands, where they would be friendly protectors instead of internal foes ready to help any invader who may offer them freedom.

This wonderful article is signed "Justice and Humanity." Thomas Paine's venture in this direction was naturally welcomed by Dr. Rush, who some years before had written a little pamphlet against the slave trade, and deploring slavery, though he had not proposed or devised any plan for immediate emancipation. Paine's paper is as thorough as Garrison himself could have made it. And, indeed, it is remarkable that Garrison, at a time when he shared the common prejudices against Paine, printed at the head of his *Liberator* a motto closely resembling Paine's. The motto of Paine was: "The world is my country, my religion is to do good"; that of the *Liberator*: "Our country is the world, our countrymen are all mankind." Garrison did characteristic justice to Paine when he had outgrown early prejudices against him.[1] On April 12th, thirty-five days after Paine's plea for emancipation, the first American Antislavery Society was formed, in Philadelphia.

Although the dialogue between Wolfe and Gage (January 4th) shows that Paine shared the feeling of America, the earlier numbers of his *Pennsylvania Magazine* prove his strong hope for reconciliation. That hope died in the first collision; after Lexington he knew well that separation was inevitable. A single sentence in the magazine intimates the change. The April number, which appeared soon after the "Lexington massacre," contains a summary of Chatham's speech, in which he said the crown would lose its lustre if "robbed of so principal a jewel as America." Paine adds this footnote: "The principal jewel of the crown actually dropt out at the coronation." There was probably no earlier printed suggestion of independence by any American.[2]

[1] It will be seen by the "Life of William Lloyd Garrison," i., p. 219, and iii., p. 145, that Mr. Garrison did not know of Paine's motto ("Rights of Man," ii., chap. v.). His review of Paine's works appeared November 21, 1845. The *Liberator* first appeared January 1, 1831.

[2] The *London Chronicle*, of October 25, 1774, printed Major Cartwright's "American Independence the Interest and Glory of Great Britain," and it was reprinted in the *Pennsylvania Journal*. Although it has little relation to the form in which the question presently suggested

There are three stages in the evolution of the Declaration of Independence. The colonies reached first the resolution of resistance, secondly of separation, and thirdly of republicanism.

In the matter of resistance the distribution of honors has been rather literary than historical. In considering the beginnings of the Revolution our minds fly at once to the Tea-party in Boston harbor, then to Lexington, where seven Massachusetts men fell dead, and seven years of war followed. But two years before the tea was thrown overboard, and four years before the Lexington massacre, North Carolinians had encountered British troops, had left two hundred patriots fallen, and seen their leaders hanged for treason. Those earliest martyrs are almost forgotten because, in the first place, North Carolina produced no historians, poets, magazines, to rehearse their story from generation to generation. In the second place, the rebellion which Governor Tryon crushed at Alamance, though against the same oppressions, occurred in 1771, before the colonies had made common cause.

Governmental anachronisms have a tendency to take refuge in colonies. Had Great Britain conceded to Americans the constitutional rights of Englishmen there could have been no revolution. Before the time of George III. British governors had repeatedly revived in America prerogatives extinct in England, but the colonists had generally been successful in their appeals to the home Government. Even in 1774 the old statesmen in America had not realized that a king had come who meant to begin in America his mad scheme of governing as well as reigning. When, in September, 1774, the first Continental Congress assembled, its members generally expected to settle the troubles with the "mother country" by petitions to Parliament. There is poetic irony in the fact that the first armed resistance to royal authority in America was by the North Carolina "Regulators." On the frontiers, before official courts were established, some kind of law and order had to be maintained, and they were protected by a volunteer police called "Regulators." In the forests of Virginia, two hundred years ago, Peter Lynch was appointed judge by his neighbors because of his wisdom and justice, and his decisions were enforced by "Regulators." Judge Lynch's honorable name is now degraded into a precedent for the cowardly ruffians who hunt down unarmed negroes, Italians, and Chinamen, and murder them without trial, or after their acquittal. But such was not the case with our frontier courts and "Regulators," which were civilized organizations, though unauthorized. For several years before the Revolution lawful and civilized government in some of the colonies depended on unauthorized administrations. The authorized powers were the "lynchers," as they would now be called, with traditional misrepresentation of Peter Lynch. The North Carolina Regulators of 1771 were defending the English constitution against a king and a governor acting as lawlessly as our vile lynchers and "White Caps." It was remarked, by Paine among others that after the royal authority was abolished, though for a long time new governments were not established, "order and harmony was preserved as inviolate as in any country in Europe."[1]

In the dialogue between Wolfe and Gage, Paine writes as an Englishman; he lays no hand on the constitution, nor considers the sovereign involved in ministerial iniquities. Apart from his Quaker sentiments he felt dismay at a conflict which interrupted his lucrative school, and the literary opportunities afforded by his magazine. "For my

itself, the article is interesting as an indication that separation was then more talked of in England than in America. Twelve years before the Revolution a pamphlet in favor of separation was written by Josiah Tucker of Bristol, England. Then as now colonists were more loyal than the English at home.

[1] "The Rights of Man," part ii., chapter i.

own part," he wrote to Franklin, "I thought it very hard to have the country set on fire about my ears almost the moment I got into it." And indeed there was a general disgust among the patriots during the year 1775, while as yet no great aim or idea illumined the smoke of battle. They were vehemently protesting that they had no wish for separation from England, just as in the beginning of our civil war leading Unionists declared that they would not interfere with slavery. In March, 1775, Franklin maintained the assurance he had given Lord Chatham in the previous year, that he had never heard in America an expression in favour of independence, "from any person drunk or sober." Paine says that on his arrival he found an obstinate attachment to Britain : "it was at that time a kind of treason to speak against it." "Independence was a doctrine scarce and rare even towards the conclusion of the year 1775." In May, George Washington, on his way to Congress, met the Rev. Jonathan Boucher, in the middle of the Potomac ; while their boats paused, the clergyman warned his friend that the path on which he was entering might lead to separation from England. "If you ever hear of my joining in any such measures," said Washington, "you have my leave to set me down for everything wicked." [1] Although Paine, as we shall see, had no reverence for the crown, and already foresaw American independence, he abhorred the method of war. In the first number of his magazine he writes : "The speeches of the different governors pathetically lament the present distracted state of affairs. Yet they breathe a spirit of mildness as well as tenderness, and give encouragement to hope that some happy method of accommodation may yet arise.

But on April 19th came the "massacre at Lexington," as it was commonly called.

How great a matter is kindled by a small fire ! A man whose name remains unknown, forgetful of Captain Parker's order to his minute-men not to fire until fired on, drew his trigger on the English force advancing to Concord ; the gun missed fire, but the little flash was answered by a volley ; seven men lay dead. In the blood of those patriots at Lexington the Declaration of Independence was really written. From town-meetings throughout the country burning resolutions were hurled on General Gage in Boston, who had warned Major Pitcairn, commander of the expedition, not to assume the offensive. From one county, Mecklenburg, North Carolina, were sent to Congress twenty resolutions passed by its committee, May 31st, declaring "all laws and commissions confirmed by or derived from the authority of the King and Parliament are annulled and vacated," and that, "whatever person shall hereafter receive a commission from the crown, or attempt to exercise any such commission heretofore received, shall be deemed an enemy to his country." [2]

Many years after the independence of America had been achieved, William Cobbett, on his return to England after

---

[1] *Notes and Queries* (Eng.), series 3 and 5. See also in *Lippincott's Magazine*, May, 1889, my paper embodying the correspondence of Washington and Boucher.

[2] These resolutions further organized a provisional government to be in force until "the legislative body of Great Britain resign its unjust and arbitrary pretensions with respect to America." In 1819 a number of witnesses stated that so early as May 20th Mecklenburg passed an absolute Declaration of Independence, and it is possible that, on receipt of the tidings from Lexington, some popular meeting at Charlottetown gave vent to its indignation in expressions, or even resolutions, which were tempered by the County Committee eleven days later. The resolutions embodying the supposititious "Declaration," written out (1800) from memory by the alleged secretary of the meeting (Dr. Joseph McKnitt Alexander), are believed by Dr. Welling to be "an honest effort to reproduce, according to the best of his recollection, the facts and declarations contained in the genuine manuscripts of May 31, after that manifesto had been forgotten." — (*North American Review*, April, 1874). But the testimony is very strong in favor of two sets of resolutions.

a long sojourn in the United States, wrote as follows :

" As my Lord Grenville introduced the name of Burke, suffer me, my Lord, to introduce that of a man who put this Burke to shame, who drove him off the public stage to seek shelter in the pension list, and who is now named fifty million times where the name of the pensioned Burke is mentioned once. The cause of the American colonies was the cause of the English Constitution, which says that no man shall be taxed without his own consent. . . . A little thing sometimes produces a great effect ; an insult offered to a man of great talent and unconquerable perseverance has in many instances produced, in the long run, most tremendous effects ; and it appears to me very clear that some beastly insults, offered to Mr. Paine while he was in the Excise in England, was the real cause of the Revolution in America ; for, though the nature of the cause of America was such as I have before described it ; though the principles were firm in the minds of the people of that country ; still, it was Mr. Paine, and Mr. Paine alone, who brought those principles into action."

In this passage Cobbett was more epigrammatic than exact. Paine, though not fairly treated, as we have seen, in his final dismissal from the excise, was not insulted. But there is more truth in what Cobbett suggests as to Paine's part than he fully realized. Paine's unique service in the work of independence may now be more clearly defined. It was that he raised the Revolution into an evolution. After the " Lexington massacre " separation was talked of by many, but had it then occurred America might have been another kingdom. The members of Congress were of the rich conservative " gentry," and royalists. Had he not been a patriot, Peyton Randolph, our first President, would probably have borne a title like his father, and Washington would certainly have been knighted. Paine was in the position of the abolitionists when the secession war began. They also held peace principles, and would have scorned a war for the old slave-holding union as Paine would have scorned a separation from England preserving its political institutions. The war having begun, and separation become probable, Paine hastened to connect it with

humanity and with republicanism. As the abolitionists resolved that the secession war should sweep slavery out of the country, Paine made a brave effort that the Revolution should clear away both slavery and monarchy. It was to be in every respect a new departure for humanity. So he anticipated the Declaration of Independence by more than eight months with one of his own, which was discovered by Moreau in the file of the *Pennsylvania Journal*, October 18th.[1]

" A SERIOUS THOUGHT.

" When I reflect on the horrid cruelties exercised by Britain in the East Indies—How thousands perished by artificial famine—How religion and every manly principle of honor and honesty were sacrificed to luxury and pride —When I read of the wretched natives being blown away, for no other crime than because, sickened with the miserable scene, they refused to fight—When I reflect on these and a thousand instances of similar barbarity, I firmly believe that the Almighty, in compassion to mankind, will curtail the power of Britain.

" And when I reflect on the use she hath made of the discovery of this new world— that the little paltry dignity of earthly kings hath been set up in preference to the great cause of the King of kings—That instead of Christian examples to the Indians, she hath basely tampered with their passions, imposed on their ignorance, and made them the tools of treachery and murder—And when to these and many other melancholy reflections I add this sad remark, that ever since the discovery of America she hath employed herself in the most horrid of all traffics, that of human flesh, unknown to the most savage nations, hath yearly (without provocation and in cold blood) ravaged the hapless shores of Africa, robbing it of its unoffending inhabitants to cultivate her stolen dominions in the West—When I reflect on these, I hesitate not for a moment to believe that the Almighty will finally separate America from Britain. Call it Independency or what you will, if it is the cause of God and humanity it will go on.

" And when the Almighty shall have blest us, and made us a people *dependent only upon him*, then may our first gratitude be shown by an act of continental legislation, which shall put a stop to the importance of Negroes for sale, soften the hard fate of those already here, and in time procure their freedom.

" HUMANUS."

[1] Mr. Moreau mentions it as Paine's in his MS. notes in a copy of Cheetham's book, now owned by the Pennsylvania Historical Society. No one familiar with Paine's style at the time can doubt its authorship.

CHAPTER VI

"COMMON SENSE"

In furrows ploughed deep by lawless despotism, watered with blood of patriots, the Thetford Quaker sowed his seed— true English seed. Even while he did so he was suspected of being a British spy, and might have been roughly handled in Philadelphia had it not been for Franklin. Possibly this suspicion may have arisen from his having, in the antislavery letter, asked the Americans " to consider with what consistency or decency they complain so loudly of attempts to enslave them, while they hold so many thousands in slavery." Perfectly indifferent to this, Paine devoted the autumn of 1775 to his pamphlet " Common Sense," which with the new year " burst from the press with an effect which has rarely been produced by types and paper in any age or country." So says Dr. Benjamin Rush, and his assertion, often quoted, has as often been confirmed.

Of the paramount influence of Paine's " Common Sense " there can indeed be no question.[1] It reached Washington soon after tidings that Norfolk, Virginia, had been burned (Jan. 1st) by Lord Dunmore, as Falmouth (now Portland), Maine, had been, Oct. 17, 1775, by ships under Admiral Graves. The General wrote to Joseph Reed, from Cambridge, Jan. 31st: "A few more of such flaming arguments as were exhibited at Falmouth and Norfolk, added to the sound doctrine and unanswerable reasoning contained in the pamphlet 'Common Sense,' will not leave numbers at a loss to decide upon the propriety of the separation."[2]

Henry Wisner, a New York delegate in Congress, sent the pamphlet to John Mc-Kesson, Secretary of the Provincial Congress sitting in New York City, with the following note : " Sir, I have only to ask the favour of you to read this pamphlet, consulting Mr. Scott and such of the Committee of Safety as you think proper, particularly Orange and Ulster, and let me know their and your opinion of the general spirit of it. I would have wrote a letter on the subject, but the bearer is waiting." In pursuance of this General Scott suggested a private meeting, and McKesson read the pamphlet aloud. New York, the last State to agree to separation, was alarmed by the pamphlet, and these leaders at first thought of answering it, but found themselves without the necessary arguments. Henry Wisner, however, required arguments rather than orders, and despite the instructions of his State gave New York the honor of having one name among those who, on July 4th, voted for independence.[3] Joel Barlow, a student in Yale College at the beginning of the Revolution, has borne testimony to the great effect of Paine's pamphlet, as may be seen in his biography by Mr. Todd. An original copy of Paine's excise pamphlet (1792) in my possession contains a note in pencil, apparently contemporary, suggesting that the introduction was written by Barlow. In this introduction —probably by Barlow, certainly by a competent observer of events in America —it is said :

[1] " This day was published, and is now selling by Robert Bell, in Third Street, [Phil.] price two shillings, 'Common Sense,' addressed to the inhabitants of North America."—*Pennsylvania Journal*, Jan. 10, 1776.

[2] " The Writings of George Washington." Collected and edited by Worthington Chauncey Ford, vol. iii., p. 396.

[3] *Mag. Am. Hist.*, July, 1880, p. 62, and Dec., 1888, p. 479. The Declaration passed on July 4th was not signed until Aug. 2d, the postponement being for the purpose of removing the restrictions placed by New York and Maryland on their delegates. Wisner, the only New York delegate who had voted for the Declaration, did not return until after the recess. In Trumbull's picture at the Capitol Thomas Stone, a signer for Maryland, is left out, and Robert Livingston of New York is included, though he did not sign it.

"On this celebrated publication ['Common Sense'], which has received the testimony of praise from the wise and learned of different nations, we need only remark (for the merit of every work should be judged by its effect) that it gave spirit and resolution to the Americans, who were then wavering and undetermined, to assert their rights, and inspired a decisive energy into their counsels : we may therefore venture to say, without fear of contradiction, that the great American cause owed as much to the pen of Paine as to the sword of Washington."[1]

Edmund Randolph, our first Attorney-General, who had been on Washington's staff in the beginning of the war, and conducted much of his correspondence, ascribed independence primarily to George III., but next to "Thomas Paine, an Englishman by birth, and possessing an imagination which happily combined political topics, poured forth in a style hitherto unknown on this side of the Atlantic, from the ease with which it insinuated itself into the hearts of the people who were unlearned, or of the learned."[2] This is from a devout churchman, writing after Paine's death. Paine's malignant biographer, Cheetham (1809), is constrained to say of "Common Sense": "Speaking a language which the colonists had felt but not thought, its popularity, terrible in its consequences to the parent country, was unexampled in the history of the press."[3]

Let it not be supposed that Washington, Franklin, Jefferson, Randolph, and the rest, were carried away by a meteor. Deep answers only unto deep. Paine's ideas went far because they came far. He was the authentic commoner, representing English freedom in the new world. There was no dreg in the poverty of his people that he had not tasted, no humiliation in their dependence, no outlook of their hopelessness, he had not known, and with the addition of intellectual hungers which made his old-world despair conscious. The squalor and abjectness of Thetford, its corporation held in the hollow of Grafton's hand, its commoners nominated by him, the innumerable villages equally helpless, the unspeakable corruption of the Government, the repeated and always baffled efforts of the outraged people for some redress,—these had been brought home to Paine in many ways, had finally driven him to America, where he arrived on the hour for which none had been so exactly and thoroughly trained. He had thrown off the old world, and that America had virtually done the same constituted its attraction for him. In the opening essay in his magazine, written within a month of his arrival in the country (Nov. 30, 1774), Paine speaks of America as a "nation," and his pregnant sentences prove how mature the principles of independence had become in his mind long before the outbreak of hostilities.

"America has now outgrown the state of infancy. Her strength and commerce make large advances to manhood ; and science in all its branches has not only blossomed, but even ripened upon the soil. The cottages as it were of yesterday have grown to villages, and the villages to cities ; and while proud antiquity like a skeleton in rags, parades the streets of other nations, their genius, as if sickened and disgusted with the phantom, comes hither for recovery. . . . America yet inherits a large portion of her first-imported virtue. Degeneracy is here almost a useless word. Those who are conversant with Europe would be tempted to believe that even the air of the Atlantic disagrees with the constitution of foreign vices ; if they survive the voyage they either expire on their arrival, or linger away in an incurable consumption. There is a happy something in the climate of America which disarms them of all their power both of infection and attraction."

In presently raising the standard of republican independence, Paine speaks of separation from England as a foregone conclusion. "I have always considered the independency of this continent as an event which sooner or later must arrive." Great Britain having forced a

---

[1] And yet—such was the power of theological intimidation—even heretical Barlow could find no place for Paine in his *Columbiad* (1807).

[2] Randolph "History" (MS.), a possession of the Virginia Historical Society, has been confided to my editorial care for publication.

See also the historians, Ramsay (Rev., i., p. 336, London, 1793), Gordon (Rev., ii., p. 78, New York, 1794), Bryant and Gay (U.S., iii., p. 471, New York, 1879).

collision, the very least that America can demand is separation.

"The object contended for ought always to bear some just proportion to the expence. The removal of North, or the whole detestable junto, is a matter unworthy the millions we have expended. A temporary stoppage of trade was an inconvenience which would have sufficiently ballanced the repeal of all the acts complained of, had such repeals been obtained; but if the whole Continent must take up arms, if every man must be a soldier, 'tis scarcely worth our while to fight against a contemptible ministry only. Dearly, dearly do we pay for the repeal of the acts, if that is all we fight for; for, in a just estimation, 'tis as great a folly to pay a Bunker-hill price for law as for land. . . . It would be policy in the king, at this time, to repeal the acts for the sake of reinstating himself in the government of the provinces, in order that he may accomplish by craft and subtlety, in the long run, what he cannot do by force and violence in the short one. Reconciliation and ruin are nearly related."

Starting with the lowest demand, separation, Paine shows the justice and necessity of it lying fundamentally in the nature of monarchy as represented by Great Britain, and the potential republicanism of colonies composed of people from all countries. The keynote of this is struck in the introduction. The author withholds his name "because the object of attention is the Doctrine itself, not the Man"; and he affirms, "the cause of America is in a great measure the cause of all mankind."

No other pamphlet published during the Revolution is comparable with "Common Sense" for interest to the reader of to-day, or for value as an historical document. Therein as in a mirror is beheld the almost incredible England, against which the colonies contended. And therein is reflected the moral, even religious, enthusiasm which raised the struggle above the paltriness of a rebellion against taxation to a great human movement,—a war for an idea. The art with which every sentence is feathered for its aim is consummate.

The work was for a time generally attributed to Franklin. It is said the Doctor was reproached by a loyal lady for using in it such an epithet as "the royal brute of Britain." He assured her that he had not written the pamphlet, and would never so dishonor the brute creation.

In his letter to Cheetham (1809) already referred to, Dr. Rush claims to have suggested the work to Paine, who read the sheets to him and also to Dr. Franklin. This letter, however, gives so many indications of an enfeebled memory, that it cannot be accepted against Paine's own assertion, made in the year following the publication of "Common Sense," when Dr. Rush and Dr. Franklin might have denied it.

"In October, 1775, Dr. Franklin proposed giving me such materials as were in his hands towards completing a history of the present transactions, and seemed desirous of having the first volume out the next spring. I had then formed the outlines of 'Common Sense,' and finished nearly the first part; and as I supposed the doctor's design in getting out a history was to open the new year with a new system, I expected to surprise him with a production on that subject much earlier than he thought of; and without informing him of what I was doing, got it ready for the press as fast as I conveniently could, and sent him the first pamphlet that was printed off."

On the other hand, Paine's memory was at fault when he wrote (December 3, 1802): "In my publications, I follow the rule I began with in 'Common Sense,' that is, to consult nobody, nor to let anybody see what I write till it appears publicly." This was certainly his rule, but in the case of "Common Sense" he himself mentions (*Penn. Jour.*, April 10, 1776) having shown parts of the MS. to a "very few." Dr. Rush is correct in his statement that Paine had difficulty in finding "a printer who had boldness enough to publish it," and that he (Rush) mentioned the pamphlet to the Scotch bookseller, Robert Bell. For Bell says, in a contemporary leaflet: "When the work was at a stand for want of a courageous Typographer, I was then recommended by a gentleman nearly in the following words: 'There is Bell, he is a Republican printer, give it to him, and I will answer for his courage to print it.'" Dr. Rush probably required some knowledge of the contents of the pamphlet before he made this recommendation.

That Dr. Rush is mistaken in saying the manuscript was submitted to Franklin, and a sentence modified by him, is proved by the fact that on February 19th, more than a month after the pamphlet appeared, Franklin introduced Paine to Gen. Charles Lee with a letter containing the words, "He is the reputed and, I think, the real author of 'Common Sense.'" Franklin could not have thus hesitated had there been in the work anything of his own, or anything he had seen. Beyond such disclosures to Dr. Rush, and one or two others, as were necessary to secure publication, Paine kept the secret of his authorship as long as he could. His recent arrival in the country might have impaired the force of his pamphlet.

The authorship of "Common Sense" was guessed by the "Tory" President of the University of Philadelphia, the Rev. William Smith, D.D., who knew pretty well the previous intellectual resources of that city. Writing under the name of "Cato" he spoke of "the foul pages of interested writers, and strangers intermeddling in our affairs." [1] To which "The Forester" (Paine) answers: "A freeman, Cato, is a stranger nowhere, —a slave, everywhere." [2]

The publication of "Common Sense" had been followed by a number of applauding pamphlets, some of them crude or extravagant, from Bell's press. "Cato" was anxious to affiliate these "additional doses" on the author of "Common Sense," who replies:

"Perhaps there never was a pamphlet, since the use of letters were known, about which so little pains were taken, and of which so great a number went off in so short a time. I am certain that I am within compass when I say one hundred and twenty thousand. The book was turned upon the world like an orphan to shift for itself; no plan was formed to support it, neither hath the author ever published a syllable on the subject from that time till after the appearance of Cato's fourth letter."

This letter of "The Forester" is dated April 8th (printed on the 10th). "Common Sense," published January 10th, had, therefore, in less than three months, gained this sale. In the end probably half a million copies were sold. In reply to "Cato's" sneer about "interested writers," Paine did not announce the fact that he had donated the copyright to the States for the cause of independence. It was sold at two shillings, and the author thus gave away a fortune in that pamphlet alone. It never brought him a penny; he must even have paid for copies himself, as the publisher figured up a debt against him, on account of "Common Sense," for £29 12s. 1d. [3] Notwithstanding this

---

[1] In his edition of the "Writings of Thomas Paine" Dr. Conway notes that the letters written by "Cato" appeared in the *Pennsylvania Gazette*; Paine replied in the *Pennsylvania Journal*. He wrote in all four letters, which appeared in the issues for April 3, 10, 24, and May 8, 1776.—H.B.B.

[2] "The writer of 'Common Sense' and 'The Forester' is the same person. His name

is Paine, a gentleman about two years ago from England,—a man who, General Lee says, has genius in his eyes."—John Adams to his wife.

[3] See Almon's *Remembrancer*, 1780. On p. 136 Dr. Conway quotes a statement made by Paine in 1779 that he stood "£39 11s. 0d. out of pocket in Bradford's books" on account of his "Common Sense" pamphlet. In January of that year in a letter to the Hon. Henry Laurens Paine writes: "The first edition [of "Common Sense"] was printed by Bell on the recommendation of Dr. Rush. I gave him the pamphlet on the following conditions: That if any loss should arise I would pay it—and in order to make him industrious in circulating it, I gave him one-half of the profits if it should produce any. I gave a written order to Col. Joseph Dean and Captain Thos. Prior, both of this city, to receive the other half, and lay it out for mittens for the troops that were going to Quebec. I did this to do honor to the cause. Bell kept the whole and abused me into the bargain. The price he set upon them was two shillings. I then enlarged the pamphlet with an appendix, and an address to the Quakers, which made it one-third bigger than before, printed 6,000 at my own expense, 3,000 by B. Towne and 3,000 by Cist and Steyner, and delivered them ready stitched and fit for sale to Mr. Bradford at the Coffee House; and though the work was thus increased, and consequently should have borne a higher price, yet, in order that it might

experience and the popularity he had acquired, Paine also gave to the States the copyright of his *Crisis* (thirteen numbers), was taunted by Tories as a "garreteer," ate his crust contentedly, peace finding him a penniless patriot, who might easily have had fifty thousand pounds in his pocket.

The controversy between "Cato" and "The Forester" was the most important that preceded the Declaration of Independence. The president of the University represented "Toryism" in distress. The "massacre at Lexington" disabled him from justifying the Government, which, however, he was not prepared to denounce. He was compelled to assume the tone of an American, while at the same time addressing his appeal "To the People of Pennsylvania," trying to detach its non-resident Quakers and its mercantile interest from sympathy with the general cause. Having a bad case, in view of Lexington, he naturally resorted to abuse of the plaintiff's attorney. He soon found that when it came to Quaker sentiment and dialect, his unknown antagonist was at home.

"Remember, thou hast thrown me the glove, Cato, and either thee or I must tire. I fear not the field of fair debate, but thou hast stepped aside and made it personal. Thou hast tauntingly called me by name ; and if I cease to hunt thee from every lane and lurking hole of mischief, and bring thee not a trembling culprit before the public bar, then brand me with

produce the general service I wished, I confined Mr. Bradford to sell them at only one shilling each, or tenpence by the dozen, and to enable him to do this with sufficient advantage to himself I let him have the pamphlets at 8½d. Pennsylvania Currency. The sum of 8½d. each was reserved to pay the expenses of printing, paper, advertising etc., and such as might be given away. The state of the account at present is that I am £39 11s. out of pocket, being the difference between what I have paid for printing etc., and what I have received from Bradford. He has a sufficiency in his hands, to balance with and clear me, which is all I aimed at, but by his unaccountable dilatoriness and unwillingness to settle accounts, I fear I shall be obliged to sustain a real loss exclusive of my trouble."—H.B.B.

reproach by naming me in the list of your confederates."

"The Forester" declares his respect for the honest and undisguised opponents of independence. "To be nobly wrong is more manly than to be meanly right." But "Cato" wears the mask of a friend, and shall be proved a foe.

The so-called "Tories" of the American Revolution have never had justice done them. In another work I have told the story of John Randolph, King's Attorney in Virginia, and there were many other martyrs of loyalty in those days.[1] Four months after the affair at Lexington, Thomas Jefferson wrote to John Randolph, in London : "Looking with fondness towards a reconciliation with Great Britain, I cannot help hoping you may be able to contribute towards expediting the good work." This was written on August 25, 1775 ; and if this was the feeling of Jefferson only ten months before the Declaration, how many, of more moderate temper, surrounded "Cato" and "The Forester" in loyal and peace-loving Philadelphia? But "Cato" was believed ungenuine. The Rev. Dr. William Smith, who wrote under that name, a native of Aberdeen with an Oxonian D.D., had been a glowing Whig patriot until June, 1775. But his wife was a daughter of the loyalist, William Moore. This lady of fashion was distinguished by her contempt for the independents, and her husband, now near fifty, was led into a false position.[2]

[1] "Omitted Chapters of History, Disclosed in the Life and Papers of Edmund Randolph," p. 20.
[2] R. H. Lee, in a letter to his brother (July 5, 1778) says : "We had a magnificent celebration of the anniversary of independence. The Whigs of the city dressed up a woman of the town with the monstrous head-dress of the Tory ladies, and escorted her through the town with a great concourse of people. Her head was elegantly and expensively dressed, I suppose about three feet high and proportionate width, with a profusion of curls, etc. The figure was droll, and occasioned much mirth. It has lessened some heads already, and will probably

He held the highest literary position in Philadelphia, and perhaps felt some jealousy of Paine's fame. He picked out all the mistakes he could find in "Common Sense," and tried in every way to belittle his antagonist. Himself a Scotchman, his wife an Englishwoman, he sneered at Paine for being a foreigner; having modified his principles to those of the loyalist's daughter, he denounced Paine as an "interested writer." He was out of his element in the controversy he began with personalities. He spoke of the trouble as a lovers' quarrel. Paine answers:

"It was not in the power of France or Spain, or all the other powers in Europe, to have given such a wound, or raised us to such mortal hatred as Britain hath done. We see the same kind of undescribed anger at her conduct, as we would at the sight of an animal devouring its young."

The strongest point of "Cato" was based on the proposed embassy for negotiation, and he demanded reverence for "Ambassadors coming to negotiate a peace." To this "The Forester" replied:

"Cato discovers a gross ignorance of the British Constitution in supposing that these men *can* be empowered to act as Ambassadors. To prevent his future errors, I will set him right. The present war differs from every other, in this instance, viz., that it is not carried on under the prerogative of the crown, as other wars have always been, but under the authority of the

whole legislative power united; and as the barriers which stand in the way of a negotiation are not proclamations, but acts of Parliament, it evidently follows that were even the King of England here in person, he could not ratify the terms or conditions of a reconciliation; because, in the single character of King, he could not stipulate for the repeal of any acts of Parliament, neither can the Parliament stipulate for him. There is no body of men more jealous of their privileges than the Commons: Because they sell them."

Paine wrote three letters in reply to "Cato," the last of which contained a memorable warning to the people on the eve of the Declaration of Independence: "*Forget not the hapless African.*" That was forgotten, but the summing up made Dr. William Smith an object of detestation. He never ventured into political controversy again, and when he returned from exile to Philadelphia, a penitent patriot, he found his old antagonist, Thomas Paine, honored by a degree from the University of Pennsylvania into which the college had been absorbed.

On May 8th a fourth letter, signed "The Forester," appeared in the same paper (*Pennsylvania Journal*), which I at first suspected of not being from Paine's pen.[1] This was because of a sentence beginning: "The clergy of the English Church, of which I profess myself a member," etc. There is no need to question the truth of this, for, as we have seen, Paine had been confirmed, and no doubt previously baptized; nor is there reason to disbelieve the statement of Oldys that he wished to enter holy orders. There was a good deal of rationalism in the American church at that time, and that Paine, with his religious fervor and tendency to inquire, should have maintained his

---

bring the rest within the bounds of reason, for they are monstrous indeed. The Tory wife of Dr. Smith has christened this figure Continella, or the Duchess of Independence, and prayed for a pin from her head by way of relic. The Tory women are very much mortified, notwithstanding this."—"Omitted Chapters of History," p. 40. "Cato's" brilliant wife had to retire before "Continella" in the following year. ·The charter of the College of Philadelphia was taken away, and its president retired to an obscure living at Chestertown, Maryland. He had, however, some of the dexterity of the Vicar of Bray; when the cause he had reviled was nearly won he founded a "Washington" college in Maryland. He was chosen by that diocese for a bishop (1783), but the General Convention refused to recommend him for consecration. In 1789 he managed to regain his place as college president in Philadelphia.

[1] A theft of Paine's usual signature led to his first public identification of himself (Feb. 13, 1779). "As my signature, 'Common Sense,' has been counterfeited, either by Mr. [Silas] Deane, or some of his adherents in Mr. Bradford's paper of Feb. 3, I shall subscribe this with my name, Thomas Paine." He, however, in Almon's *Remembrancer* (vol. viii.) is indexed by name in connection with a letter of the previous year signed "Common Sense."

place in that scholarly church is natural. His quakerism was a philosophy, but he could by no means have found any home in its rigid and dogmatic societies in Philadelphia. The casual sentence above quoted was probably inserted for candor, as the letter containing it opens with a censure on the attitude of the Quakers towards the proposal for independence. The occasion was an election of four burgesses to represent Philadelphia in the State Assembly, a body in which Quakers (loyalists) preponderated. Had the independents been elected they must have taken the oath of allegiance to the crown, with which the State was at war. Indeed Paine declares that the "Tories" succeeded in the election because so many patriots were absent for defence of their country. Under these circumstances Paine urges the necessity of a popular convention. The House of Assembly is disqualified from "sitting in its own case."

The extracts given from this letter are of historic interest as reflecting the conflict of opinions in Pennsylvania amid which the Declaration was passed two months later.

"Whoever will take the trouble of attending to the progress and changeability of times and things, and the conduct of mankind thereon, will find that *extraordinary circumstances* do sometimes arise before us, of a species, either so purely natural or so perfectly original, that none but the man of nature can understand them. When precedents fail to assist us, we must return to the first principles of things for information, and *think*, as if we were the *first men* that *thought*. And this is the true reason, that in the present state of affairs, the wise are become foolish, and the foolish wise. I am led to this reflection by not being able to account for the conduct of the Quakers on any other ; for although they do not seem to perceive it themselves, yet it is amazing to hear with what unanswerable ignorance many of that body, wise in other matters, will discourse on the present one. Did they hold places or commissions under the king, were they governors of provinces, or had they any interest apparently distinct from us, the mystery would cease ; but as they have not, their folly is best attributed to that superabundance of *worldly knowledge* which in original matters is too cunning to be wise.

Back to the first plain path of nature, friends, and begin anew, for in this business your first footsteps were wrong. You have now travelled to the summit of inconsistency, and that, with such accelerated rapidity as to acquire autumnal ripeness by the first of May. Now your *rotting time comes on*." [1]

"The Forester" reminds the Quakers of their predecessors who, in 1704, defended the rights of the people against the proprietor. He warns them that the people, though unable to vote, represent a patriotic power tenfold the strength of Toryism, by which they will not submit to be ruled.

"He that is wise will reflect, that the safest asylum, especially in times of general convulsion, when no settled form of government prevails, is *the love of the people*. All property is safe under their protection. Even in countries where the lowest and most licentious of them have risen into outrage, they have never departed from the path of *natural* honor. Volunteers unto death in defence of the person or fortune of those who had served or defended them, division of property never entered the mind of the populace. It is incompatible with that spirit which impels them into action. An avaricious mob was never heard of ; nay, even a miser, pausing in the midst of them, and catching their spirit, would from that instant cease to be covetous."

The Quakers of Pennsylvania and New Jersey had held a congress in Philadelphia and issued (January 20th) "The Ancient Testimony and Principles of the People called Quakers renewed, with respect to the King and Government ; and touching the Commotions now prevailing in these and other Parts of America ; addressed to the People in General." Under this lamb-like tract, and its bleat of texts, was quite discoverable the "Tory" wolf; but it was widely circulated and became a danger. The Quakers of Rhode Island actually made efforts to smuggle provisions into Boston during the siege. Paine presently reviewed this testimony in a pamphlet, one extract from which will show that he could preach a better Quaker sermon than any of them :

[1] In "The Forester's Letters," vol. i, p. 155, of Dr. Conway's edition of "The Writings of Thomas Paine," this sentence is rendered : "Now your *resting time* comes on."—H.B.B.

" O ye partial ministers of your own acknowledged principles ! If the bearing arms be sinful, the first going to war must be more so, by all the difference between wilful attack and unavoidable defence. Wherefore, if ye really preach from conscience, and mean not to make a political hobby-horse of your religion, convince the world thereof by proclaiming your doctrine to our enemies, for they likewise bear arms. Give us proof of your sincerity by publishing it at St. James's, to the commanders in chief at Boston, to the admirals and captains who are piratically ravaging our coasts, and to all the murdering miscreants who are acting in authority under HIM whom ye profess to serve. Had ye the honest soul of Barclay ye would preach repentance to your king ; ye would tell the Royal Wretch his sins, and warn him of eternal ruin ; ye would not spend your partial invectives against the injured and insulted only, but, like faithful ministers, cry aloud and spare none." [1]

[1] Paine was not then aware of the extent of the intrigues of leading Quakers with the enemy. The State archives of England and France contain remarkable evidences on this subject. Paul Wentworth, in a report to the English Government (1776 or 1777), mentions the loyalty of Pemberton and the Quakers. Wentworth says that since the publication of " Common Sense" it had become hard to discover the real opinions of leading men. " Mr. Payne," he says, "should not be forgot. He is an Englishman, was schoolmaster in Philadelphia ; must be driven to work ; naturally indolent ; led by His passions." These " passions," chiefly for liberty and humanity, seem to have so driven the indolent man to work that, according to Wentworth, his pamphlet " worked up [the people] to such a high temper as fitted them for the impression of the Declaration, etc." The Quakers, however, held out long, though more covertly. M. Gérard de Rayneval, in a letter from Philadelphia, Sept. 18, 1778, reports to his Government : " During the occupation of Philadelphia by the English, proofs were obtained of the services rendered them by the Quakers ; some of these were caught acting as spies, etc." La Luzerne writes (May 4, 1781): " All the Quakers in Philadelphia who have taken up arms, or voluntarily paid war taxes, have been excommunicated ; these, increasing in number, declare themselves loyal." See for further information on this matter, " New Materials for the History of the American Revolution," etc. By John Durand. New York, 1889.

CHAPTER VII

UNDER THE BANNER OF INDEPENDENCE

As in North Carolina had occurred the first armed resistance to British oppressions (1771), and its Mecklenburg County been the first to organize a government independent of the Crown, so was that colony the first to instruct its delegates in Congress to vote for national independence. She was followed in succession by South Carolina,[2] Virginia,[3] Massachusetts, Rhode Island, Connecticut, New Hampshire, Georgia, New Jersey, Delaware, and Pennsylvania. Maryland passed patriotic resolutions, but not sufficiently decisive for its delegates to act. New York alone forbade its delegates to vote for independence.

Meanwhile, on June 7th, Richard Henry Lee, on behalf of the Virginians,

[2] Colonel Gadsden, having left the Continental Congress to take command in South Carolina, appeared in the provincial Congress at Charleston February 10, 1776. " Col. Gadsden (having brought the first copy of Paine's pamphlet ' Common Sense,' etc.) boldly declared himself . . . for the absolute Independence of America. This last sentiment came like an explosion of thunder on the members" (Rev. John Drayton's *Memoirs, etc.*, p. 172). The sentiment was abhorred, and a member "called the author of ' Common Sense' —— "; but on March 21st the pamphlet was reinforced by tidings of an Act of Parliament (Dec. 21, 1775) for seizure of American ships, and on March 23d South Carolina instructed its delegates at Philadelphia to agree to whatever that Congress should " judge necessary, etc."

[3] A thousand copies of " Common Sense " were at once ordered from Virginia, and many more followed. On April 1st Washington writes to Joseph Reed : " By private letters which I have lately received from Virginia, I find ' Common Sense' is working a wonderful change there in the minds of many men." On June 29th union with England was " totally dissolved " by Virginia.

had submitted resolutions of independence; but as six States hesitated, Congress adjourned the decision until July 1st, appointing, however (June 11th), a committee to consider the proper form of the probable Declaration— Jefferson, John Adams, Franklin, Roger Sherman, and Robert R. Livingston. But this interval, from June 7th to July 1st, was perilous for independence. News came of the approach of Lord Howe bearing from England the " olive branch." The powerful colonies New York and Pennsylvania were especially anxious to await the proposals for peace. At this juncture Paine issued one of his most effective pamphlets, " A Dialogue between the Ghost of General Montgomery, Just Arrived fron the Elysian Fields, and an American Delegate, in a Wood near Philadelphia." Montgomery, the first heroic figure fallen in the war, reproaches the hesitating delegate for willingness to accept pardon from a royal criminal for defending " the rights of humanity." He points out that France only awaits their declaration of independence to come to their aid, and that America " teems with patriots, heroes, and legislators who are impatient to burst forth into light and importance."

The most effective part of the pamphlet, however, was a reply to the commercial apprehensions of New York and Pennsylvania. " Your dependance upon the Crown is no advantage, but rather an injury, to the people of Britain, as it increases the power and influence of the King. The people are benefited only by your trade, and this they may have after you are independant of the Crown." There is a shrewd prescience of what actually happened shown in this opportune work. Of course the gallant ghost remarks that " monarchy and aristocracy have in all ages been the vehicles of slavery." The allusion to the arming of negroes and Indians against America, and other passages, resemble clauses in one of the paragraphs eliminated from the original Declaration of Independence.

At this time Paine saw much of Jefferson, and there can be little doubt that the antislavery clause struck out of the Declaration was written by Paine, or by some one who had Paine's antislavery essay before him. In the following passages it will be observed that the antitheses are nearly the same—" infidel and Christian," " heathen and Christian."

PARAGRAPH STRUCK OUT OF THE DECLARATION.

" He has waged cruel war against human nature itself, violating its most sacred rights of life and liberty in the persons of a distant people who never offended him, captivating and carrying them into slavery in another hemisphere, or to incur miserable death in their transportation thither. This piratical warfare, the opprobrium of INFIDEL powers, is the warfare of the CHRISTIAN king of Great Britain. Determined to keep open a market where MEN should be bought and sold, he has prostituted his negative for suppressing every legislative attempt to prohibit or restrain this execrable commerce. And that this assemblage of horrors might want no fact of distinguished dye, he is now exciting those very people to rise in arms among us, and to purchase that liberty of which he has deprived them by murdering the people on whom he has obtruded them, thus paying off former crimes committed against the LIBERTIES of one people with crimes which he urges them to commit against the LIVES of another."

THOMAS PAINE.

" —these inoffensive people are brought into slavery, by stealing them, tempting kings to sell subjects, which they can have no right to do, and hiring one tribe to war against another, in order to catch prisoners. By such wicked and inhuman ways the English, etc. . . . an hight of outrage that seems left by *Heathen* nations to be practised by pretended *Christians*."

" —that barbarous and hellish power which has stirred up the Indians and Negroes to destroy us ; the cruelty hath a double guilt—it is dealing brutally by us and treacherously by them."

Thus did Paine try to lay at the corner the stone which the builders rejected, and which afterwards ground their descendants to powder. Jefferson withdrew the clause on the objection of Georgia and South Carolina, which wanted slaves, and of Northerners interested in supplying them. That, however, was not known till all the parties were dead. Paine had no reason to suppose that the Declaration of human freedom and equality, passed July 4th, could fail eventually to include the African slaves. The Declaration embodied every principle he had been asserting, and indeed Cobbett is correct in saying that whoever may have written the Declaration Paine was its author. The world being his country, and America having founded its independence on such universal interests, Paine could not hesitate to become a soldier for mankind.[1] His Quaker principles, always humanized, were not such as would applaud a resistance in which he was not prepared to participate. While the signers of the Declaration of Independence were affixing their

[1] Professor John Fiske (whose "American Revolution" suffers from ignorance of Paine's papers) appreciates the effect of Paine's "Common Sense" but not its cause. He praises the pamphlet highly, but proves that he has only glanced at it by his exception: "The pamphlet is full of scurrilous abuse of the English people; and resorts to such stupid arguments as the denial of the English origin of the Americans" (i., p. 174). Starting with the principle that the cause of America is "the cause of all mankind," Paine abuses no people, but only their oppressors. As to Paine's argument, it might have appeared less "stupid" to Professor Fiske had he realized that in Paine's mind negroes were the equals of whites. However, Paine does not particularly mention negroes; his argument was meant to carry its point, and it might have been imprudent for him, in that connection, to have classed the slaves with the Germans, who formed a majority in Pennsylvania, and with the Dutch of New York. In replying to the "Mother-Country" argument it appears to me far from stupid to point out that Europe is our parent country, and that if English descent made men Englishmen, the descendants of William the Conqueror and half the peers of England were Frenchmen, and, if the logic held, should be governed by France.

names—a procedure which reached from August 2d into November—Paine resigned his *Pennsylvania Magazine*, and marched with his musket to the front. He enlisted in a Pennsylvania division of the Flying Camp of ten thousand men, who were to be sent wherever needed. He was under General Roberdeau, and assigned at first to service at Amboy, afterwards at Bergen. The Flying Camp was enlisted for a brief period and when that had expired Paine travelled to Fort Lee, on the Hudson, and renewed his enlistment. Fort Lee was under the command of General Nathaniel Greene, who, on or about September 19th, appointed Paine a Volunteer aide-de-camp. General Greene in a gossipy letter to his wife (November 2d) says: "Common Sense (Thomas Paine) and Colonel Snarl, or Cornwell, are perpetually wrangling about mathematical problems." On November 20th came the surprise of Fort Lee; the boiling kettles and baking ovens of a dinner to be devoured by the British were abandoned, with three hundred tents, for a retreat made the more miserable by hunger and cold. By November 22d the whole army had retreated to Newark, where Paine began writing his famous first *Crisis*.[2]

He could only write at night; during the day there was constant work for every soldier of the little force surrounding Washington. "I am wearied almost to death with the retrograde motion of

[2] See Almon's *Remembrancer*, 1777, p. 28, for Paine's graphic journal of this retreat, quoted from the *Pennsylvania Journal*. In reply to those who censured the retreat as pusillanimous, he states that "our army was at one time less than a thousand effective men and never more than 4,000," the pursuers being "8,000 exclusive of their artillery and light horse"; he declares that posterity will call the retreat "glorious—and the names of Washington and Fabius will run parallel to eternity." In the *Pennsylvania Packet* (March 20, 1779) Paine says: "I had begun the first number of the *Crisis* while on the retreat, at Newark, with a design of publishing it in the Jersies, as it was General Washington's intention to have made a stand at Newark, could he have been timely reenforced; instead of which nearly half the army left him at that place, or soon after, their time being out."

things," wrote Washington to his brother (November 9th), "and I solemnly protest that a pecuniary reward of twenty thousand pounds a year would not induce me to undergo what I do ; and, after all, perhaps to lose my character, as it is impossible, under such a variety of distressing circumstances, to conduct matters agreeably to public expectation." On November 27th he writes from Newark to General Lee : "It has been more owing to the badness of the weather that the enemy's progress has been checked than to any resistance we could make." Even while he wrote, the enemy drew near, and the next day (November 28th) entered one end of Newark as Washington left the other. At Brunswick, he was joined by General Williamson's militia, and on the Delaware by the Philadelphia militia, and could muster five thousand against Howe's whole army. " I tremble for Philadelphia," writes Washington to Lund Washington (December 10th). "Nothing in my opinion, but General Lee's speedy arrival, who has been long expected, though still at a distance (with about three thousand men), can save it." On December 13th, Lee was a prisoner, and on the 17th Washington writes to the same relative :

" Your imagination can scarce extend to a situation more distressing than mine. Our only dependence now is upon the speedy enlistment of a new army. If this fails, I think the game will be pretty well up, as from disaffection and want of spirit and fortitude, the inhabitants, in-instead of resistance, are offering submission and taking protection from Gen. Howe in Jersey."

The day before, he had written to the President of Congress that the situation was critical, and the distresses of his soldiers "extremely great, many of 'em being entirely naked and most so thinly clad as to be unfit for service." On December 18th he writes to his brother :

" You can form no idea of the perplexity of my situation. No man, I believe, ever had a greater choice of difficulties, and less means to extricate himself from them. However, under a full persuasion of the justice of our cause, I cannot entertain an Idea that it will finally sink, tho' it may remain for some time under a cloud."

Under that cloud, by Washington's side, was silently at work the force that lifted it. Marching by day, listening to the consultations of Washington and his generals, Paine wrote by the camp fires ; the winter storms, the Delaware's waves, were mingled with his ink ; the half-naked soldiers in their troubled sleep dreaming of their distant homes, the skulking deserter creeping off in the dusk, the pallid face of the heavy-hearted commander, made the awful shadows beneath which was written that leaflet which went to the Philadelphia printer along with Washington's last foreboding letters to his relatives in Virginia. It was printed on December 19th,[1] and many copies reached the camp above Trenton Falls on the eve of that almost desperate attack on which Washington had resolved. On the 23d December he wrote to Colonel Joseph Reed :

" Christmas-day, at night, one hour before day, is the time fixed upon for our attempt on Trenton. For Heaven's sake keep this to yourself, as the discovery of it may prove fatal to us ; our numbers, sorry I am to say, being less than I had any conception of ; but necessity, dire necessity will, nay must, justify *any* attempt."

America has known some utterances of the lips equivalent to decisive victories in the field,—as some of Patrick Henry's, and the address of President Lincoln at Gettysburg. But of utterances by the pen none have achieved such vast results as Paine's *Common Sense* and his first *Crisis*. Before the battle of Trenton. the half-clad, disheartened soldiers of Washington were called together in groups to listen to that thrilling exhortation. The opening words alone were a victory.

" These are the times that try men's souls. The summer soldier and the sunshine patriot will, in this crisis, shrink from the service of his country ; but he that stands it now, deserves the love and thanks of man and woman. Tyranny, like hell, is not easily conquered ; yet we have this consolation with us, that the harder the conflict the more glorious the triumph : what we

[1] The pamphlet was dated December 23rd, but it had appeared on the 19th in the *Pennsylvania Journal.*

obtain too cheap we esteem too lightly ; 'tis dearness only that gives everything its value. Heaven knows how to put a proper price upon its goods ; and it would be strange indeed if so celestial an article as Freedom should not be highly rated."

Not a chord of faith, or love, or hope was left untouched. The very faults of the composition, which the dilettanti have picked out, were effective to men who had seen Paine on the march, and knew these things were written in sleepless intervals of unwearied labors. He speaks of what Joan of Arc did in " the fourteenth century," and exclaims : " Would that heaven might inspire some Jersey maid to spirit up her countrymen, and save her fair fellow sufferers from ravage and ravishment ! " Joan was born in 1410, but Paine had no cyclopædia in his knapsack. The literary musket reaches its mark. The pamphlet was never surpassed for true eloquence—that is, for the power that carries its point. With skilful illustration of lofty principles by significant details, all summed with simplicity and sympathy, three of the most miserable weeks ever endured by men were raised into epical dignity. The wives, daughters, mothers, sisters, seemed stretching out appealing hands against the mythically monstrous Hessians. The great commander, previously pointed to as "a mind that can even flourish upon care," presently saw his dispirited soldiers beaming with hope, and bounding to the onset,—their watchword : *These are the times that try men's souls!* Trenton was won, the Hessians captured, and a New Year broke for America on the morrow of that Christmas Day, 1776.[1]

[1] Paine's enemy, Cheetham, durst not, in the face of Washington's expression of his "lively sense of the importance of your [Paine's] works," challenge well known facts, and must needs partly confess them : " The number was read in the camp, to every corporal's guard, and in the army and out of it had more than the intended effect. The convention of New York, reduced by dispersion, occasioned by alarm, to nine members, was rallied and reanimated. Militiamen who, already tired of the war, were straggling from the army, returned. Hope succeeded to despair, cheerfulness to gloom, and firmness to irresolution. To the confidence which it inspired may be attributed much of the brilliant little affair which in the same month followed at Trenton." Even Oldys is somewhat impressed by Paine's courage : " The Congress fled. All were dismayed. Not so our author."

Paine's Trenton musket had hardly cooled, or the pen of his first *Crisis* dried, before he began to write another. It appeared about four weeks after the battle and is addressed to Lord Howe. The Thetford mechanic has some pride in confronting this English lord who had offered the Americans mercy. " Your lordship, I find, has now commenced author, and published a Proclamation ; I have published a Crisis." The rumors of his being a hireling scribe, or gaining wealth by his publications, made it necessary for Paine to speak of himself at the conclusion :

"What I write is pure nature, and my pen and my soul have ever gone together. My writings I have always given away, receiving only the expense of printing and paper, and sometimes not even that. I never counted either fame or interest, and my manner of life, to those who know it, will justify what I say. My study is to be useful, and if your lordship loves mankind as well as I do, you would, seeing you cannot conquer us, cast about and lend your hand towards accomplishing a peace. Our independence, with God's blessing, we will maintain against all the world ; but as we wish to avoid evil ourselves, we wish not to inflict it on others. I am never over-inquisitive into the secrets of the cabinet, but I have some notion that, if you neglect the present opportunity, it will not be in our power to make a separate peace with you afterwards ; for whatever treaties or alliances we form we shall most faithfully abide by ; wherefore you may be deceived if you think you can make it with us at any time."

Thus the humble author of the *Crisis* offers the noble author of the Proclamation "mercy," on condition of laying down his arms, and going home ; but it must be at once !

If Howe, as is most likely, considered this mere impudence, he presently had reason to take it more seriously. For there were increasing indications that Paine was in the confidence of those who controlled affairs. On January 21st he was appointed by the Council of

Safety in Philadelphia secretary to the commission sent by Congress to treat with the Indians at Easton, Pennsylvania. The commissioners, with a thousand dollars' worth of presents, met the Indian chiefs in the German Reformed Church (built 1776), and, as they reported to Congress, "after shaking hands, drinking rum, while the organ played, we proceeded to business." [1] The report was, no doubt, written by Paine, who for his services was paid £300 by the Pennsylvania Assembly (one of its advances for Congress, afterwards refunded). In a public letter, written in 1807, Paine relates an anecdote concerning this meeting with the Indians.

"The chief of the tribes, who went by the name of King *Last-night*, because his tribe had sold their lands, had seen some English men-of-war in some of the waters of Canada, and was impressed with the power of those great canoes; but he saw that the English made no progress against us by land. This was enough for an Indian to form an opinion by. He could speak some English, and in conversation with me, alluding to the great canoes, he gave me his idea of the power of a king of England, by the following metaphor. 'The king of England,' said he, 'is like a fish. When he is in the water he can wag his tail; when he comes on land he lays down on his side.' Now if the English Government had but half the sense this Indian had, they would not have sent Duckworth to Constantinople, and Douglas to Norfolk, to lay down on their side."

On April 17th, when Congress transformed the "Committee of Secret Correspondence" into the "Committee of Foreign Affairs," Paine was elected its secretary. [2] His friend, Dr. Franklin, had reached France in December, 1776, where Arthur Lee and Silas Deane were already at work. Lord Howe might, indeed, have done worse than take Paine's advice concerning the "opportunity," which did not return. General Howe did, indeed, presently occupy a fine abode in Philadelphia, but only kept it warm, to be afterwards the executive mansion of President Washington.

[1] Condit's "History of Easton," pp. 60, 118.

[2] His salary "nominally $70 per month was really about $15." See chap. 14.—H.B.B.

CHAPTER VIII

SOLDIER AND SECRETARY

AFTER their disaster at Trenton, the English forces suspended hostilities for a long time. Paine, maintaining his place on General Greene's staff, complied with the wish of all the generals by wielding his pen during the truce of arms. He sat himself down in Philadelphia, "Second Street, opposite the Quaker meeting,"—as he writes the address. The Quakers regarded him as Antichrist pursuing them into close quarters. Untaught by castigation, the leaders of the Society, and chiefly one John Pemberton, disguised allies of the Howes, had put forth, November 20, 1776, a second and more dangerous "testimony." In it they counsel Friends to refuse obedience to whatever "instructions or ordinances" may be published, not warranted by "that happy constitution under which they and others long enjoyed tranquillity and peace." In his second *Crisis* (January 13, 1777) Paine refers to this document, and a memorial, from "a meeting of a reputable number of the inhabitants of the city of Philadelphia," called attention of the Board of Safety to its treasonable character. The Board, however, not having acted, Paine devoted his next three months to a treatment of that and all other moral and political problems which had been developed by the course of the Revolution, and must be practically dealt with. In reading this third *Crisis*, one feels in every sentence its writer's increased sense of responsibility. Events had given him the seat of a lawgiver. His first pamphlet had dictated the Declaration of Independence, his second had largely won its first victory, his third demonstrated the impossibility of subjugation, and offered England peace on the only possible terms. The American heart had responded without a dissonant note; he held it in his hand; he knew that what he was writing in that room "opposite the Quaker meeting" were Acts of Congress. So it proved. The third *Crisis* was dated April 19, 1777, the second anniversary of the first collision (Lexington). It was as effective in dealing with the internal enemies of the country as the first had been in checking its avowed foes. It was written in a city still largely, if not preponderantly, "Tory," and he deals with them in all their varieties, not arraigning the Friends as a Society. Having carefully shown that independence, from being a natural right, had become a political and moral necessity, and the war one "on which a world is staked," he says that "Tories" endeavoring to insure their property with the enemy should be made to fear still more losing it on the other side. Paine proposes an "oath or affirmation" renouncing allegiance to the King, pledging support to the United States. At the same time let a tax of ten, fifteen, or twenty per cent. be levied on all property. Each who takes the oath may exempt his property by holding himself ready to do what service he can for the cause; they who refuse the oath will be paying a tax on their insurance with the enemy.

"It would not only be good policy but strict justice to raise fifty or one hundred thousand pounds, or more, if it is necessary, out of the estates and property of the King of England's votaries, resident in Philadelphia, to be distributed as a reward to those inhabitants of the city and State who should turn out and repulse the enemy should they attempt to march this way."

These words were written at a moment when a vigorous opposition, in and out of Congress, was offered to Washington's Proclamation (Morristown, January 25, 1777) demanding that an oath of allegiance to the United States should be required of all who had taken such an oath to the King, non-jurors to remove within the enemy's lines, or be treated as enemies. Paine's proposal was partly followed on June 13th, when Pennsylvania exacted an oath of allegiance to the State from all over eighteen years of age.

Paine was really the Secretary of Foreign Affairs. His election had not been without opposition, and, according to John Adams, there was a suggestion that some of his earlier writings had been unfavorable to this country.[1] What the reference was I cannot understand unless it was to his antislavery essay, in which he asked Americans with what consistency they could protest against being enslaved while they were enslaving others. That essay, I have long believed, caused a secret, silent, hostility to the author by which he suffered much without suspecting it. But he was an indefatigable secretary. An example of the care with which foreign representatives were kept informed appears in a letter to William Bingham, agent of Congress at Martinique.

"PHILADELPHIA, July 16, 1777.—SIR,— A very sudden opportunity offers of sending you the News-papers, from which you will collect the situation of our Affairs. The Enemy finding their attempt of marching thro' the Jersies to this City impracticable, have retreated to Staten Island seemingly discontented and dispirited and quite at a loss what step next to pursue. Our Army is now well recruited and formidable. Our Militia in the several States ready at a day's notice to turn out and support the Army when occasion requires; and tho' we cannot, in the course of a Campaign, expect everything to go just as we wish it; yet the general face of our Affairs assures us of final success.

"In the Papers of June 18th & 25 and July 2d you will find Genl. Washington and Arnold's Letters of the Enemy's movement in, and retreat from the Jersies. We are under some apprehensions for Ticonderoga, as we find the Enemy are

---

[1] America.—H.B.B.

unexpectedly come into that Quarter. The Congress have several times had it in contemplation to remove the Garrison from that Place—as by Experience we find that Men shut up in Forts are not of so much use as in the field, especially in the highlands where every hill is a natural fortification.

"I am Sir
"Your Obt. Humble Servt.
"THOMAS PAINE.

"Secretry. to the Committee for Foreign Affairs." [1]

After the occupation of Philadelphia by the British (September 26, 1777), Paine had many adventures, as we shall presently see. He seems to have been with Washington at Valley Forge when the Pennsylvania Assembly and President (Thomas Wharton, Jr.) confided to him the delicate and arduous task assigned by the following from Timothy Matlack, Secretary of the Assembly:

"LANCASTER, Oct. 10, 1777. SIR,—The Hon'ble house of As'y have proposed and Council have adopted a plan of obtaining more regular and constant intelligence of the proceeding of Gen. Washington's army than has hitherto been had. Everyone agrees that you are the proper person for this purpose, and I am directed by his Exc'y, the pr't, to write to you hereon (the Prs't being engaged in writing to the Gen'l, and the Express in waiting).

"The Assembly have agreed to make you a reasonable compensation for your services in this business, if you think proper to engage in it, which I hope you will; as it is a duty of importance that there are few, however well disposed, who are capable of doing in a manner that will answer all the intentions of it—perhaps a correspondence of this kind may be the fairest opportunity of giving to Council some important hints that may occur to you on interesting subjects.

"Proper expresses will be engaged in this business. If the expresses which pass from headquarters to Congress can be made use of so much the better;—of this you must be judge.

"I expect Mr. Rittenhouse will send you a copy of the testimony of the late Y. M. by this opp'y, if time will admit it to be copied—'t is a poor thing.—Yours, &c., T. M." [2]

What with this service, and his correspondence with foreign agents, Paine had his hands pretty full. But at the same time he wrote important letters to leading members of Congress, then in session at York, Pennsylvania.

The subjoined letter sheds fresh light on a somewhat obscure point in our revolutionary history,—the obscurity being due to the evasions of American historians on an episode of which we have little reason to be proud. An article of Burgoyne's capitulation (October 17th) was as follows:

"A free passage to be granted to the army under General Burgoyne to great Britain, upon condition of not serving again in North America during the present contest: and the port of Boston to be assigned for entry of transports to receive the troops whenever General Howe shall so order."

A letter was written by Paine to Hon. Richard Henry Lee, dated at "Headquarters, fourteen miles from Philadelphia," October 30th, 1777.

"I wrote you last Tuesday 21st Inst., including a Copy of the King's speech, since which nothing material has happened at Camp. Genl. McDougal was sent last Wednesday night 22d to attack a Party of the Enemy who lay over the Schuylkill at Grey's Ferry where they have a Bridge. Gens. Greene & Sullivan went down to make a diversion below German Town at the same Time. I was with this last Party, but as the Enemy withdrew their Detachment We had only our Labor for our Pains.

"No Particulars of the Northern Affair have yet come to head Qrs., the want of which has caused much Speculation. A copy, said to be the Articles of Capitulation was recd. 3 or 4 days ago, but they rather appear to be some proposals made by Burgoyne, than the Capitulation itself. By those Articles it appears to me that Burgoyne has capitulated upon Terms, which we have a right to doubt the full performance of, Vizt., 'That the Offrs. and Men shall be Transported to England and not serve in or against North America during the present War'—or words to this effect.

"I remark, that this Capitulation, if true, has the air of a National treaty; it is binding, not only on Burgoyne as a *General*, but on England as a *Nation;* because the Troops are to be subject to the conditions of the Treaty after they return to England and are out of his Command. It regards England and America as Separate Sovereign States, and puts them on an equal footing by staking the faith and honor of the former for the performance of a Contract entered into with the latter.

"What in the Capitulation is stiled the '*Present War*' England affects to call a '*Rebellion*' and while she holds this Idea and

---

[1] MS., for which I am indebted to Mr. Simon Gratz, Philadelphia.

[2] Pa. Arch., 1779, p. 659. Paine at once set to work: pp. 693, 694.

denies any knowledge of America as a Separate Sovereign Power, she will not conceive herself bound by any Capitulation or Treaty entered into by her Generals which is to bind her as a *Nation*, and more especially in those Cases where both Pride and present Advantage tempt her to Violation. She will deny Burgoyne's Right and Authority for making such a Treaty, and will, very possibly, show her insult by first censuring him for entering into it, and then immediately sending the Troops back.

"I think we ought to be exceedingly cautious how we trust her with the power of abusing our Credulity. We have no authority for believing she will perform that part of the Contract which subjects her not to send the Troops to America during the War. The insolent Answer given to the Commissrs. by Ld. Stormont, '*that the King's Ambassadors recd. no Letters from Rebels but when they came to crave Mercy*,' sufficiently instructs us not to entrust them with the power of insulting Treaties of Capitulation.

"Query, Whether it wd. not be proper to detain the Troops at Boston & direct the Commissioners at Paris to present the Treaty of Capitulation to the English Court thro' the hands of Ld. Stormont, to know whether it be the intention of that Court to abide strictly by the Conditions and Obligations thereof, and if no assurance be obtained to keep the Troops until they can be exchanged here.

"Tho' we have no immediate knowledge of any alliance formed by our Commissioners with France or Spain, yet we have no assurance there is not, and our immediate release of those prisoners, by sending them to England, may operate to the injury of such Allied Powers, and be perhaps directly contrary to some contract subsisting between us and them prior to the Capitulation. I think we ought to know this first.—Query, ought we not (knowing the infidelity they have already acted) to suspect they will evade the Treaty by putting back into New York under pretence of distress.—I would not trust them an inch farther than I could see them in the present state of things.

"The Army was to have marched yesterday about 2 or 3 Miles but the weather has been so exceedingly bad for three days past as to prevent any kind of movement, the waters are so much out and the rivulets so high there is no passing from one part of ye Camp to another.

"I wish the Northern Army was down here. I am apt to think that nothing materially offensive will take place on our part at present. Some Means must be taken to fill up the Army this winter. I look upon the recruiting service at an end and that some other plan must be adopted. Suppose the Service be by draft—and that those who are not drawn should contribute a Dollar or two Dollars a Man to him on whom the lot falls,—something of this kind would proportion the Burthen, and those who are drawn would have something either to encourage them to go, or to provide a substitute with—After closing

this Letter I shall go again to Fort Mifflin ; all was safe there on the 27th, but from some preparations of the Enemy they expect another attack somewhere.

"The enclosed return of provision and Stores is taken from an account signed by Burgoyne and sent to Ld. George Germain. I have not time to Copy the whole. Burgoyne closes his Letter as follows, '.By a written account found in the Commissary's House at Ticonderoga Six thousand odd hundred Persons were fed from the Magazine the day before the evacuation.'

"I am Dear Sir, Yr. Affectionate Hble. Servt.

"T. PAINE.

"Respectful Compts. to Friends.

"If the Congress has the Capitulation and Particulars of ye Surrender, they do an exceeding wrong thing by not publishing ym. because they subject the whole Affair to Suspicion."[1]

Had this proposal of Paine, with regard to Burgoyne's capitulation, been followed at once, a blot on the history of our Revolution might have been prevented. The time required to march the prisoners to Boston and prepare the transports would have given England opportunity to ratify the articles of capitulation. Washington, with characteristic inability to see injustice in anything advantageous to America, desired Congress to delay in every possible way the return of the prisoners to England, "since the most virtuous adhesion to the articles would not prevent their replacing in garrison an equal number of soldiers who might be sent against us." The troops were therefore delayed on one pretext and another until Burgoyne declared that "the publick faith is broke." Congress seized on this remark to resolve that the embarkation should be suspended until an "explicit ratification of the Convention of Saratoga shall be properly ratified by the Court of Great Britain." This resolution, passed January 8, 1778, was not communicated to Burgoyne until February 4th. If any

---

[1] I am indebted for this letter to Dr. John S. H. Fogg of Boston. It bears the superscription : "Honble. Richd. Henry Lee Esq. (in Congress) York Town. Forwarded by yr. humble Servt. T. Matlack, Nov. 1, 1777." Endorsed in handwriting of Lee : "Oct : 1777. Mr. Paine, Author of 'Common Sense.'"

one should have suffered because of a remark made in a moment of irritation it should have been Burgoyne himself; but he was presently allowed to proceed to England, while his troops were retained,—a confession that Burgoyne's casual complaint was a mere pretext for further delay. It may be added that the English Government behaved to its surrendered soldiers worse than Congress. The question of ratifying the Saratoga Convention was involved in a partisan conflict in Parliament, the suffering prisoners in America were forgotten, and they were not released until the peace,— five years after they had marched " with the honours of war," under a pledge of departure conceded by Gen. Gates in reply to a declaration that unless conceded they would "to a man proceed to any act of desperation sooner than submit."

Concerning this ugly business there is a significant silence in Paine's public writings. He would not have failed to discuss the matter in his *Crisis* had he felt that anything honorable to the American name or cause could be made out of it.[1]

In his letter to Hon. R. H. Lee (October 30, 1777) Paine mentions that he is about leaving the headquarters near Philadelphia for Fort Mifflin. Mr. Asa Bird Gardener, of New York, who has closely studied Paine's military career, writes me some account of it.

"Major-Gen. Greene was charged with the defence of the Delaware, and part of Brig.-Gen. Varnum's brigade was placed in garrison at Fort Mercer, Red Bank, and at Fort Mifflin, Mud Island. A bloody and unsuccessful assault was made by Count Donop and 1,200 Hessians on Fort Mercer, defended by the 1st and 2d Reg'ts. R. I. Continental Inf'y. The entire British fleet was then brought up opposite Fort Mifflin, and the most furious cannonade, and most desperate but finally unsuccessful defence of the place was made. The entire works were demolished, and most of the garrison killed and wounded. Major-Gen. Greene being anxious for the garrison and desirous of knowing its ability to resist sent Mr. Paine to ascertain. He accordingly went to Fort Mercer, and from thence, on Nov. 9 (1777) went with Col. Christopher Greene, commanding Fort Mercer, in an open boat to Fort Mifflin, during the cannonade, and were there when the enemy opened with two-gun batteries and a mortar battery. This *very* gallant act shows what a fearless man Mr. Paine was, and entitles him to the same credit for service in the Revolution as any Continental could claim."

The succession of mistakes, surprises, panics, which occasioned the defeats before Philadelphia and ended in the occupation of that city by the British general, seriously affected the reputation of Washington. Though Paine believed that Washington's generalship had been at fault (as Washington himself probably did [2]), he could utter nothing that might injure the great cause. He mistrusted the singleness of purpose of Washington's opponents, and knew that the commander-in-chief was as devoted as himself to the American cause, and would never surrender it whatever should befall. While, therefore, the intrigues were going on at Yorktown, Pennsylvania, whither Congress had retreated, and Washington with his ill-fed and ill-clad army were suffering at Valley Forge, Paine was writing his fifth *Crisis*, which had the most happy effect. It was dated at Lancaster, March 21, 1778. Before that time (February 19th) General Gates had made his peace with Washington, and the intrigue was breaking up, but gloom and dissatisfaction remained. The contrast between the luxurious " Tories " surrounding Howe in Philadelphia, and Washington's wretched five thousand at Valley Forge, was demoralizing the country. The first part of this *Crisis*, addressed " to General Sir William Howe," pointed wrangling patriots to the common enemy ; the second, addressed " to the

---

[1] Professor Fiske ("Am. Revolution," i., p. 341) has a ferocious attack on Congress for breaking faith in this matter, but no doubt he has by this time read, in Ford's "Writings of Washington" (vol. vi.), the letters which bring his attack on the great commander's own haloed head.

[2] See his letter to the President of Congress. Ford's "Writings of Washington," vol. vi., p. 82.

inhabitants of America," sounded a note of courage, and gave good reason for it. Never was aid more artistic than that Paine's pen now gave Washington. The allusions to him are incidental, there is no accent of advocacy. While mentioning "the unabated fortitude of a Washington," he lays a laurel on the brow of Gates, on that of Herkimer, and even on the defeated. While belittling all that Howe had gained, telling him that in reaching Philadelphia, he "mistook a trap for a conquest," he reunites Washington and Gates, in the public mind, by showing the manœuvres of the one near Philadelphia part of the other's victory at Saratoga. It is easy for modern eulogists of Washington to see this, but when Paine said it,—apparently aiming only to humiliate Howe,—the sentence was a sunbeam parting a black cloud. Coming from a member of Greene's staff, from an author whose daring at Fort Mifflin had made him doubly a hero ; from the military correspondent of the Pennsylvania Council, and the Secretary of the Congressional Committee of Foreign Affairs,—Paine's optimistic view of the situation had immense effect. He hints his official knowledge that Britain's "reduced strength and exhausted coffers in a three years' war with America hath given a powerful superiority to France and Spain," and advises Americans to leave wrangling to the enemy. "We never had so small an army to fight against, nor so fair an opportunity of final success as *now*."

The fifth *Crisis* was written mainly at Lancaster, Pa., at the house of William Henry, Jr., where he several times found shelter while dividing his time between Washington's headquarters and York.[1] Every number of the *Crisis* was thus written with full information from both the military and political leaders. This *Crisis* was finished and printed at York,

and there Paine begins No. VI. The "stone house on the banks of the Cadorus," at York, is still pointed out by a trustworthy tradition as that to which he bore the chest of congressional papers with which he had fled to Trenton, when Howe entered Philadelphia.[2] It is a pleasant abode in a picturesque country, and no doubt Paine would have been glad to remain there in repose. But whoever slept on his watch during the Revolution Paine did not. The fifth *Crisis* printed, he goes to forward the crisis he will publish next. In April he is again at Lancaster, and on the 11th writes thence to his friend Henry Laurens, President of Congress.[3]

"LANCASTER, April 11, 1778. Sir,—I take the liberty of mentioning an affair to you which I think deserves the attention of Congress. The persons who came from Philadelphia some time ago with, or in company with, a flag from the Enemy, and were taken up and committed to Lancaster Jail for attempting to put off counterfeit Contl. money, were yesterday brought to Tryal and are likely to escape by means of an artful and partial Construction of an Act of this State for punishing such offences. The Act makes it felony to counterfeit the money *emitted* by Congress, or to circulate such counterfeits knowing them to be so. The offenders' Council explained the word 'emitted' to have only a retrospect meaning by supplying the Idea of '*which have been*' 'emitted by Congress.' Therefore say they the Act cannot be applied to any money emitted after the date of the Act. I believe the words 'emitted by Congress' means only, and should be understood, to distinguish Continental Money from other Money, and not one Time from another Time. It has, as I conceive,. no reference to any Particular Time, but only to the particular authority which distinguishes Money so emitted from Money emitted by the State. It is meant only as a discription of the Money, and not of the Time of striking it, but includes the Idea of all Time as inseparable from the Continuance of the authority of Congress. But be this as it

---

[1] This I learn by a note from Mr. Henry's descendant, John W. Jordan. At this time Paine laid before Henry his scheme for steam-navigation.

[2] The house is marked "B. by J. B. Cookis in the year 1761." It is probable that Congress deemed it prudent to keep important documents a little way from the edifice in the centre of the town where it met, a building which no longer stands.

[3] I am indebted to Mr. Simon Gratz, of Philadelphia, for this and several other letters of Paine to Laurens.

may; the offence is Continental and the consequences of the same extent. I can have no Idea of any particular State pardoning an offence against all, or even their letting an offender slip *legally* who is accountable to all and every State alike for his crime. The place where he commits it is the least circumstance of it. It is a mere accident and has nothing or very little to do with the crime itself. I write this hoping the Information will point out the necessity of the Congress supporting their emissions by claiming every offender in this line where the present deficiency of the Law or the Partial Interpretation of it operates to the Injustice and Injury of the whole Continent.

"I beg leave to trouble you with another hint. Congress I learn has something to propose thro' the Commissrs. on the Cartel respecting the admission and stability of the Continental Currency. As Forgery is a Sin against all men alike, and reprobated by all civil nations, Query, would it not be right to require of General Howe the Persons of Smithers and others in Philadelphia suspected of this crime; and if He, or any other Commander, continues to conceal or protect them in such practices, that, in such case, the Congress will consider the crime as the Act of the Commander-in-Chief. Howe affects not to know the Congress—he ought to be made to know them; and the apprehension of Personal Consequences may have some effect on his Conduct. I am, Dear Sir,
"Your obt. and humble Servt.,
"T. PAINE.

"Since writing the foregoing the Prisoners have had their Tryal, the one is acquitted and the other convicted only of a Fraud; for as the law now stands, or rather as it is explained, the counterfeiting—or circulating counterfeits—is only a fraud. I do not believe it was the intention of the Act to make it so, and I think it misapplied Lenity in the Court to suffer such an Explanation, because it has a tendency to invite and encourage a Species of Treason, the most prejudicial to us of any or all the other kinds. I am aware how very difficult it is to make a law so very perfect at first as not to be subject to false or perplexed conclusions. There never was but one Act (said a Member of the House of Commons) which a man might not creep out of, *i.e.* the Act which obliges a man to be buried in woollen. T.P."

The active author and secretary had remained in Philadelphia two days after Howe had crossed the Schuylkill, namely, until September 21st. The events of that time, and of the winter, are related in a letter to Franklin, in Paris, which is of too much historical importance for any part of it to be omitted. It is dated Yorktown, May 16, 1778.

"Your favor of Oct. 7th did not come to me till March. I was at Camp when Capt. Folger arrived with the Blank Packet. The private Letters were, I believe, all safe. Mr. Laurens forwarded yours to York Town where I afterwards recd. it.

"The last winter has been rather barren of military events, but for your amusement I send you a little history how I have passed away part of the time.

"The 11th of Sepr. last I was preparing Dispatches for you when the report of cannon at Brandywine interrupted my proceeding. The events of that day you have doubtless been informed of, which, excepting the Enemy keeping the ground, may be deemed a drawn battle. Genl. Washington collected his Army at Chester, and the Enemy's not moving towards him next day must be attributed to the disability they sustained and the burthen of their wounded. On the 16th of the same month, the two Armies were drawn up in order of battle near the White horse on the Lancaster road, when a most violent and incessant storm of rain prevented an action. Our Army sustained a heavy loss in their Ammunition, the Cartouch Boxes, especially as they were not of the most seasoned leather, being no proof agst. the almost incredible fury of the weather, which obliged Genl. Washn. to draw his Army up into the country till those injuries could be repaired, and a new supply of ammunition procured. The Enemy in the mean time kept on the West Side of Schuylkill. On Fryday the 19th about one in the morning the first alarm of their crossing was given, and the confusion, as you may suppose, was very great. It was a beautiful still moonlight morning and the streets as full of men women and children as on a market day. On the eveng. before I was fully persuaded that unless something was done the City would be lost; and under that anxiety I went to Col. Bayard, speaker of the house of Assembly, and represented, as I very particularly knew it, the situation we were in, and the probability of saving the City if proper efforts were made for that purpose. I reasoned thus—Genl. Washn. was about 30 Miles up the Schuylkill with an Army properly collected waiting for Ammunition, besides which, a reinforcement of 1500 men were marching from the North River to join him; and if only an appearance of defence be made in the City by throwing up works at the heads of streets, it will make the Enemy very suspicious how they throw themselves between the City and Genl. Washington, and between two Rivers, which must have been the case; for notwithstanding the knowledge which military gentlemen are supposed to have. I observe they move exceedingly cautiously on new ground, are exceedingly suspicious of Villages and Towns, and more perplexed at seemingly little things which they cannot clearly understand than at great ones which they are fully acquainted with. And I think it very probable that Genl. Howe would have mistaken our necessity for a deep laid scheme and not have ventured himself in the middle of it. But admitting that he had, he must either have brought his whole Army down, or a part of it. If the whole, Gen. W. would have followed him, perhaps the same day, in two or three days at most, and our assistance in the City would have been material. If only a part of it, we should have been a match for them, and Gen. W. superior to those which remained above. The chief thing was, whether the cityzens would turn out to defend the City. My proposal to Cols. Bayard and Bradford was to call them together the next morning, make them fully acquainted with the situation and the means and prospect of preserving themselves, and that the City had better voluntarily assess itself 50,000 for its defence than suffer an Enemy to come into it. Cols. Bayard and Bradford were in my opinion, and as Genl. Mifflin was then in town, I next went to him, acquainted him with our design, and mentioned likewise that if two or three thousand men could be mustered up whether we might depend on him to command them, for without some one to lead, nothing could be done. He declined that part, not being very well, but promised what assistance he could.— A few hours after this the alarm happened. I went directly to Genl. Mifflin but he had sett off, and nothing was done. I cannot help being of opinion that the City might have been saved, but perhaps it is better otherwise.

"I staid in the City till Sunday [Sep. 21st], having sent my Chest and everything belonging to the foreign Committee to Trenton in a Shallop. The Enemy did not cross the river till the Wednesday following. Hearing on the Sunday that Genl. Washn. had moved to Swederford I set off for that place but learning on the road that it was a mistake and that he was six or seven miles above the place, I crossed over to Southfield and the next Morning to Trenton, to see after my Chest. On the Wednesday Morning I intended returning to Philadelphia, but was informed at Bristol of the Enemy's crossing the Schuylkill. At this place I met Col. Kirkbride of Pennsburg Manor, who invited me home with him. On Fryday the 26th a Party of the Enemy about 1500 took possession of the City, and the same day an account arrived that Col. Brown had taken 300 of the Enemy at the old french lines at Ticonderoga and destroyed all their Water Craft, being about 200 boats of different kinds.

"On the 29th Sept. I sett off for Camp without well knowing where to find it, every day occasioning some movement. I kept pretty high up the country, and being unwilling to ask questions, not knowing what company I might be in, I was three days before I fell in with it. The Army had moved about three miles lower down that morning. The next day they made a movement about the same distance, to the 21 Mile Stone on the Skippach Road—Head Quarters

at John Wince's. On the 3d Octr. in the morning they began to fortify the Camp, as a deception ; and about 9 at Night marched for German Town. The Number of Continental Troops was between 8 and 9000, besides Militia, the rest remaining as Guards for the security of Camp. Genl. Greene, whose Quarters I was at, desired me to remain there till Morning. I set off for German Town about 5 next morning. The Skirmishing with the Pickets began soon after. I met no person for several miles riding, which I concluded to be a good sign ; after this I met a man on horseback who told me he was going to hasten on a supply of ammunition, that the Enemy were broken and retreating fast, which was true. I saw several country people with arms in their hands running cross a field towards German Town, within about five or six miles, at which I met several of the wounded on waggons, horseback, and on foot. I passed Genl. Nash on a litter made of poles, but did not know him. I felt unwilling to ask questions lest the information should not be agreeable, and kept on. About two miles after this I passed a promiscuous crowd of wounded and otherwise who were halted at a house to refresh. Col : Biddle D.Q.N.G. was among them, who called after me, that if I went farther on that road I should be taken, for that the firing which I heard ahead was the Enemy's. I never could, and cannot now learn, and I believe no man can inform truly the cause of that day's miscarriage.

"The retreat was as extraordinary. Nobody hurried themselves. Every one marched his own pace. The Enemy kept a civil distance behind, sending every now and then a Shot after us, and receiving the same from us. That part of the Army which I was with collected and formed on the Hill on the side of the road near White Marsh Church ; the Enemy came within three quarters of a mile and halted. The orders on Retreat were to assemble that night on the back of Perkiominy Creek, about 7 miles above Camp, which had orders to move. The Army had marched the preceding night 14 miles and having full 20 to march back were exceedingly fatigued. They appeared to me to be only sensible of a disappointment, not a defeat, and to be more displeased at their retreating from German Town, than anxious to get to their rendezvous. I was so lucky that night to get to a little house about 4 miles wide of Perkiominy, towards which place in the morning I heard a considerable firing, which distressed me exceedingly, knowing that our army was much harassed and not collected. However, I soon relieved myself by going to see. They were discharging their pieces, wch. tho' necessary, prevented several Parties going till next day. I breakfasted next morning at Genl. W. Quarters, who was at the same loss with every other to account for the accidents of the day. I remember his expressing his Surprise, by saying, that at the time he supposed every thing secure, and was about giving orders for the Army to proceed down to

Philadelphia ; that he most unexpectedly saw a Part (I think of the Artillery) hastily retreating. This partial Retreat was, I believe, misunderstood, and soon followed by others. The fog was frequently very thick, the Troops young and unused to breaking and rallying, and our men rendered suspicious to each other, many of them being in Red. A new Army once disordered is difficult to manage, the attempt dangerous. To this may be added a prudence in not putting matters to too hazardous a tryal the first time. Men must be taught *regular* fighting by practice and degrees, and tho' the expedition failed, it had this good effect—that they seemed to feel themselves more important *after* it than *before*, as it was the first general attack they had ever made.

" I have not related the affair at Mr. Chew's house German Town, as I was not there, but have seen it since. It certainly afforded the Enemy time to rally—yet the matter was difficult. To have pressed on the left 500 Men in ye rear, might by a change of circumstances been ruinous. To attack them was loss of time, as the house is a strong stone building, proof against any 12 pounder. Genl. Washington sent a flag, thinking it would procure their surrender and expedite his march to Philadelphia ; it was refused, and circumstances changed almost directly after.

" I staid in Camp two days after the Germantown action, and lest any ill impression should get among the Garrisons at Mud Island and Red Bank, and the Vessels and Gallies stationed there, I crossed over to the Jersies at Trenton and went down to those places. I laid the first night on board the Champion Continental Galley, who was stationed off the mouth of Schuylkill. The Enemy threw up a two Gun Battery on the point of the river's mouth opposite the Pest House. The next morning was a thick fog, and as soon as it cleared away, and we became visible to each other, they opened on the Galley, who returned the fire. The Commodore made a signal to bring the Galley under the Jersey shore, as she was not a match for the Battery, nor the Battery a sufficient object for the Galley. One Shot went thro' the fore sail, wch. was all. At noon I went with Col. [Christopher] Greene, who commanded at Red Bank, over to fort Mifflin (Mud Island). The Enemy opened that day 2 two-gun Batteries, and a Mortar Battery, on the fort. They threw about 30 Shells into it that afternoon, without doing any damage ; the ground being damp and spongy, not above five or six burst ; not a man was killed or wounded. I came away in the evening, laid on board the Galley, and the next day came to Col. Kirkbride's [Bordentown N.J.] ; staid a few days, and came again to Camp. An Expedition was on foot the evening I got there in which I went as Aid de Camp to Genl. Greene, having a Volunteer Commission for that purpose. The Occasion was—a Party of the Enemy, about 1500, lay over the Schuyl-

kill at Grey's ferry. Genl. McDougall with his Division was sent to attack them ; and Sullivan & Greene with their Divisions were to favor the enterprise by a feint on the City, down the Germantown road. They set off at about nine at night, and halted at day break, between German Town and the City, the advanced Party at the three Miles Run. As I knew the ground I went with two light horse to discover the Enemy's Picket, but the dress of the light horse being white made them, I thought, too visible, as it was then twilight ; on which I left them with my horse, and went on foot, till I distinctly saw the Picket at Mr. Dickerson's place,—which is the nearest I have been to Philadelphia since Sepr., except once at Coopers ferry, as I went to the forts. Genl. Sullivan was at Dr. Redman's house, and McDougall's beginning the attack was to be the Signal for moving down to the City. But the Enemy either on the approach of McDougall, or on information of it, called in their Party, and the Expedition was frustrated.

" A Cannonade, by far the most furious I ever heard, began down the river, soon after daylight, the first Gun of which we supposed to be the Signal ; but was soon undeceived, there being no small Arms. After waiting two hours beyond the time, we marched back, the cannon was then less frequent ; but on the road between German town and White marsh we were stuned with a report as loud as a peal from a hundred Cannon at once ; and turning round I saw a thick smoke rising like a pillar, and spreading from the top like a tree. This was the blowing up of the Augusta. I did not hear the explosion of the Berlin.

" After this I returned to Col. Kirkbride's where I staid about a fortnight, and set off again to Camp. The day after I got there Genls. Greene, Wayne, and Cadwallader, with a Party of light horse, were ordered on a reconnoitering Party towards the forts. We were out four days and nights without meeting with any thing material. An East Indiaman, whom the Enemy had cut down so as to draw but little water, came up, without guns, while we were on foot on Carpenter's Island, going to Province Island. Her Guns were brought up in the evening in a flat, she got in the rear of the Fort, where few or no guns could bear upon her, and the next morning, played on it incessantly. The night following the fort was evacuated. The obstruction the enemy met with from those forts, and the *Chevaux de frise* was extraordinary, and had it not been that the Western Channel, deepened by the current, being somewhat obstructed by the *Chevaux de frise* in the main river, which enabled them to bring up the light Indiaman Battery, it is a doubt whether they would have succeeded at last. By that assistance they reduced the fort, and got sufficient command of the river to move some of the late sunk *Chevaux de frise*. Soon after this the fort on Red Bank, (which had bravely repulsed the Enemy a little time before) was avacuated, the Gallies ordered up to Bristol, and the Capts. of such other armed Vessels as *thought* they could not pass on the Eastward side of Wind mill Island, very precipitately set them on fire. As I judged from this event that the Enemy would winter in Philadelphia, I began to think of preparing for York Town, which however I was willing to delay, hoping that the ice would afford opportunity for new Manœuvres. But the season passed very barrenly away. I staid at Col. Kirkbride's till the latter end of Janay. Commodore Haslewood, who commanded the remains of the fleet at Trenton, acquainted me with a scheme of his for burning the Enemy's Shipping, which was by sending a charged boat across the river from Cooper's ferry, by means of a Rocket fixt in its stern. Considering the width of the river, the tide, and the variety of accidents that might change its direction, I thought the project trifling and insufficient ; and proposed to him, that if he would get a boat properly choyed, and take a Batteau in tow, sufficient to bring three or four persons off, that I would make one with him and two other persons who might be relied on to go down on that business. One of the Company, Capn. Blewer of Philadelphia, seconded the proposal, but the Commodore, and, what I was more surprized at, Col. Bradford, declined it. The burning of part of the Delaware fleet, the precipitate retreat of the rest, the little service rendered by them and the great expense they were at, make the only national blot in the proceedings of the last Campaign. I felt a strong anxiety for them to recover their credit, wch., among others, was one motive for my proposal. After this I came to camp, and from thence to York Town, and published the Crisis No. 5, To Genl. Howe. I have began No. 6, which I intend to address to Ld. North.

"I was not at Camp when Genl. Howe marched out on the 20th of Decr. towards White marsh. It was a most contemptible affair, the threatenings and seeming fury he sate out with, and haste and Terror the Army retreated with, make it laughable. I have seen several persons from Philadelphia who assure me that their coming back was a mere uproar, and plainly indicated their apprehensions of a pursuit. Genl. Howe, in his Letter to Ld. Go. Germain, dated Dec. 13th, represented Genl. Washington's camp as a strongly fortified place. There was not, Sir, a work thrown up in it till Genl. Howe marched out, and then only here and there a breast work. It was a temporary Station. Besides which, our men begin to think Works in the field of little use.

" Genl. Washington keeps his Station at the Valley forge. I was there when the Army first began to build huts ; they appeared to me like a family of Beavers ; every one busy ; some carrying Logs, others Mud, and the rest fastening them together. The whole was raised in a few days, and is a curious collection of buildings in the true rustic order.

" As to Politics, I think we are now safely

landed. The apprehension which Britain must be under from her neighbors must effectually prevent her sending reinforcements, could she procure them. She dare not, I think, in the *present* situation of affairs trust her troops so far from home.

" No Commissrs. are yet arrived. I think fighting is nearly over, for Britain, mad, wicked, and foolish, has done her utmost. The only part for her now to act is frugality, and the only way for her to get out of debt is to lessen her Government expenses. Two Millions a year is a sufficient allowance, and as much as she ought to expend exclusive of the interest of her Debt. The Affairs of England are approaching either to ruin or redemption. If the latter, she may bless the resistance of America.

" For my own part, I thought it very hard to have the Country set on fire about my Ears almost the moment I got into it ; and among other pleasures I feel in having uniformly done my duty, I feel that of not having discredited your friendship and patronage.

" I live in hopes of seeing and advising with you respecting the History of the American Revolution, as soon as a turn of Affairs make it safe for me to take a passage to Europe. Please to accept my thanks for the Pamphlets, which Mr. Temple Franklin informs me he has sent. They are not yet come to hand. Mr. & Mrs. Bache are at Mainheim, near Lancaster ; I heard they were well a few days ago. I laid two nights at Mr. Duffield's, in the winter. Miss Nancy Clifton was there, who said the Enemy had destroyed or sold a great quantity of your furniture. Mr. Duffield has since been taken by them and carried into the City, but is now at his own house. I just now hear they have burnt Col. Kirkbride's, Mr. Borden's, and some other houses at Borden Town. Governor Johnstone (House of Commons) has wrote to Mr. Robt. Morriss informing him of Commissioners coming from England. The letter is printed in the Newspapers without signature, and is dated Febry. 5th, by which you will know it.[1]

" Please, Sir, to accept this, rough and incorrect as it is, as I have [not] time to copy it fair, which was my design when I began it ; besides which, paper is most exceedingly scarce.

" I am, Dear Sir, your Obliged and Affectionate humble Servt.,

"T. PAINE.
" The Honble. BENJ. FRANKLIN, Esqr.

Paine's prophecy at the close of his fifth *Crisis* (March, 1778), that England, reduced by her war with America, was in peril from France, was speedily con-

[1] The arrival of the Commissioners caused Paine to address his *Crisis VI.* to them instead of to Lord North, as he tells Franklin is his intention. The above letter was no doubt written in the old stone house at York.

firmed. The treaty between France and America (February 6th) was followed by a war-cloud in Europe, which made the Americans sanguine that their own struggle was approaching an end. It was generally expected that Philadelphia would be evacuated. On this subject Paine wrote the following letter to Washington :

"York Town, June 5, 1778.—Sir,—As a general opinion prevails that the Enemy will quit Philadelphia, I take the Liberty of transmitting you my reasons why it is probable they will not. In your difficult and distinguished Situation every hint may be useful.

"I put the immediate cause of their evacuation, to be a declaration of War in Europe made by them or against them : in which case, their Army would be wanted for other Service, and likewise because their present situation would be too unsafe, being subject to be blocked up by France and attacked by you and her jointly.

"Britain will avoid a War with France if she can ; which according to my arrangement of Politics she may easily do—She must see the necessity of acknowledging, sometime or other, the Independance of America ; if she is wise enough to make that acknowledgment *now*, she of consequence admits the Right of France to the quiet enjoyment of her Treaty, and therefore no War can take place upon the Ground of having concluded a Treaty with revolted British Subjects.

"This being admitted, their apprehension of being doubly attacked, or of being wanted elsewhere, cease of consequence ; and they will then endeavor to hold all they can, that they may have something to restore, in lieu of something else which they will demand ; as I know of no Instance where conquered Places were surrendered up prior to, but only in consequence of a Treaty of Peace.

"You will observe, Sir, that my reasoning is founded on the supposition of their being reasonable Beings, which if they are not, then they are not within the compass of my System. I am, Sir, with every wish for your happiness, Your Affectionate and Obt. humble Servant,
"THOS. PAINE.

"His Excellency GENL. WASHINGTON, Valley Forge."

Shortly after this letter to Washington tidings came that a French fleet, under Count d'Estaing, had appeared on the coast, and was about to blockade the Delaware. The British apparently in panic, really by order from England, left Philadelphia, June 18th. This seeming flight was a great encouragement. Congress was soon comfortably seated in Philadelphia, where Paine had the pleasure of addressing his next *Crisis* to the British Peace Commissioners.

In Philadelphia Congress was still surrounded by a hostile population ; Paine had still to plead that there should be no peace without republican independence. Even so late as November 24, 1778, the French Minister (Gérard) writes to his Government : "Scarcely one quarter of the ordinary inhabitants of Philadelphia now here favour the cause (of independence). Commercial and family ties, together with an aversion to popular government, seem to account for this. The same feeling exists in New York and Boston, which is not the case in the rural districts." While Franklin was offered in Paris the bribe of a peerage, and the like for several revolutionary leaders, similar efforts were made in America to subdue the "rebellion" by craft. For that purpose had come the Earl of Carlisle, Sir George Johnstone, and William Eden. Paine omits the name of Johnstone, America's friend. Referring to the invitation of the Peace Commissioners, that America should join them against France, he says : "Unless you were capable of such conduct yourselves, you would never have supposed such a character in us." He reminds the commissioners, who had threatened that America must be laid waste so as to be useless to France, that increased wants of America must make her a more valuable purchaser in France. Paine includes Sir H. Clinton with the commissioners, and suspects the truth that he had brought orders, received from England, overruling an intention of the peace envoys to burn Philadelphia if their terms were rejected. He says he has written a *Crisis* for the English people because there was a convenient conveyance ; "for the Commissioners — *poor Commissioners !* — having proclaimed that '*yet forty days and Nineveh shall be overthrown,*' have waited out the date, and, discontented with their God, are returning to their gourd. And all the harm I wish them is that it may not wither about their ears, and that they may not make their exit in the belly of a whale."

CHAPTER IX

FRENCH AID, AND THE PAINE–DEANE CONTROVERSY

In Bell's addenda to "Common Sense," which contained Paine's Address to the Quakers (also letters by others), appeared a little poem which I believe his, and the expression of his creed.

"THE AMERICAN PATRIOT'S PRAYER.

" Parent of all, omnipotent
    In heaven, and earth below,
Through all creation's bounds unspent,
    Whose streams of goodness flow,

" Teach me to know from whence I rose,
    And unto what designed ;
No private aims let me propose,
    Since link'd with human kind.

" But chief to hear my country's voice,
    May all my thoughts incline ;
'T is reason's law, 't is virtue's choice,
    'T is nature's call and thine.

" Me from fair freedom's sacred cause
    Let nothing e'er divide ;
Grandeur, nor gold, nor vain applause,
    Nor friendship false misguide.

" Let me not faction's partial hate
    Pursue to this Land's woe ;
Nor grasp the thunder of the state
    To wound a private foe.

" If, for the right to wish the wrong
    My country shall combine,
Single to serve th' erroneous throng,
    Spight of themselves, be mine."

Every sacrifice contemplated in this self-dedication had to be made. Paine had held back nothing from the cause. He gave America the copyrights of his eighteen pamphlets. While they were selling by thousands, at two or three shillings each, he had to apologize to a friend for not sending his boots, on the ground that he must borrow the money to pay for them ! He had given up the magazine so suited to his literary and scientific tastes, had dismissed his lucra-

tive school in Philadelphia, taken a musket on his Quaker shoulders, shared the privations of the retreat to the Delaware, braved bullets at Trenton and bombs at Fort Mifflin. But now he was to give up more. He was

" Single to serve th' erroneous throng,
    Spight of themselves,"

and thereby lose applause and friendship. An ex-Congressman, sent to procure aid in France, having, as Paine believed, attempted a fraud on the scanty funds of this country, he published his reasons for so believing. In doing so he alarmed the French Ambassador in America, and incurred the hostility of a large party in Congress ; the result being his resignation of the secretaryship of its Foreign Affairs Committee.

It has been traditionally asserted that, in this controversy, Paine violated his oath of office. Such is not the fact. His official oath, which was prepared for Paine himself—the first secretary of a new committee,—was framed so as to leave him large freedom as a public writer.

" That the said secretary, ʳprevious to his entering on his office, take an oath, to be administered by the president, well and faithfully to execute the trust reposed in him, according to his best skill and judgment ; and to disclose no matter, the knowledge of which shall be acquired in consequence of his office, *that he shall be directed to keep secret.*"

Not only was there no such direction of secrecy in this case, but Congress did not know the facts revealed by Paine. Compelled by a complaint of the French Minister to disown Paine's publication,

Congress refused to vote that it was "an abuse of office," or to discharge him. The facts should be judged on their merits, and without prejudice. I have searched and sifted many manuscripts in European and American archives to get at the truth of this strange chapter in our revolutionary history, concerning which there is even yet an unsettled controversy.[1] The reader who desires to explore the subject will find an ample literature concerning it, but with confusing omissions, partly due to a neglect of Paine's papers.

The suggestion of French aid to America was first made in May, 1775, by Durbourg, and a scheme was submitted by Beaumarchais to the King. This was first brought to light in November, 1878, in the *Magazine of American History*, where it is said: "It is without date, but must have been written after the arrival of the American Commissioners in Paris." This is an error. A letter of December 7, 1775, from Beaumarchais proves that the undated one had been answered. Moreover, on June 10, 1776, a month before Deane had reached Paris, and six months before Franklin's arrival, the million for America had been paid to Beaumarchais and receipted. It was Deane's ruin that he appeared as if taking credit for, and bringing within the scope of his negotiations, money paid before his arrival. It was the ruin of Beaumarchais that he deceived Deane about that million.

In 1763 France had suffered by her struggle with England humiliations and territorial losses far heavier than those suffered by her last war with Germany. With the revolt of the English colonies in America the hour of French revenge struck. Louis XVI. did not care much about it, but his minister Vergennes did. Inspired by him, Beaumarchais, adventurer and playwright, consulted Arthur Lee, secret agent of Congress in London, and it was arranged that Beaumarchais should write a series of letters to the King, to be previously revised by Vergennes. The letters are such as might be expected from the pen that wrote "The Marriage of Figaro." He paints before the King the scene of France driven out of America and India; he describes America as advancing to engage the conqueror of France with a force which a little help would make sufficient to render England helpless beside her European foes—France and Spain. Learning through Vergennes that the King was mindful of his treaty with England, Beaumarchais made a proposal that the aid should be rendered as if by a commercial house, without knowledge of the Government. This, the most important document of the case, suppressed until 1878, was unknown to any of the writers who have discussed this question, except Durand and Stillé the latter alone having recognized its bearing on the question of Beaumarchais' good faith. Beaumarchais tells the King that his "succor" is not to end the war in America, but "to continue and feed it to the great damage of the English"; that "to sacrifice a million to put England to the expense of a hundred millions, is exactly the same as if you advance a million to gain ninety-nine." Half of the million (livres) is to be sent to America in gold, and half in powder. So far from this aid being gratuitous, the powder is to be taken from French magazines at "four to six sols per pound," and sent to America "on the basis of twenty sols per pound." "The constant view of the affair in which the mass of Congress ought to be kept is the certainty that your Majesty is not willing to enter in any way into the affair, but that

---

[1] "Beaumarchais et son Temps," par M. De Lomenie, Paris, 1856. "Histoire de la Participation de la France à l'Établissement des Etats Unis d'Amérique," par M. Doniol, Paris. "Beaumarchais and 'The Lost Million,'" by Charles J. Stillé (privately printed in Philadelphia). "New Materials for the History of the American Revolution," by John Durand, New York, 1889. *Magazine of American History*, vol. ii., p. 663. "Life and Times of Benjamin Franklin," by James Parton, New York, 1864. "Papers in Relation to the Case of Silas Deane," Philadelphia, printed for the Seventy-six Society, 1855.

a company is very generously about to turn over a certain sum to the prudent management of a faithful agent to give successive aid to the Americans by the shortest and the surest means of return in tobacco."

How much of this scheme actually reached the King, and was approved by him, is doubtful. He still hesitated, and another appeal was made (February 29, 1776) embodying one from Arthur Lee, who says: "We offer to France, in return for her secret assistance, a secret treaty of commerce, by which she will secure for a certain number of years after peace is declared all the advantages with which we have enriched England for the past century, with, additionally, a guarantee of her possessions according to our forces." Nothing is said by Arthur Lee about other payments. The Queen had now become interested in the gallant Americans, and the King was brought over to the scheme in April. On May 2, 1776, Vergennes submits to the King the order for a million livres which he is to sign ; also a letter, to be written by the hand of the Minister's son aged fifteen, to Beaumarchais, who, he says, will employ M. Montandoin (the name was really Montieu) to transmit to the Americans "such funds as your Majesty chooses to appropriate for their benefit." There are various indications that the pecuniary advantages, in the way of "sols" and tobacco, were not set before the King, and that he yielded to considerations of State policy.

After receiving the million (June 10th) Beaumarchais wrote to Arthur Lee in London (June 12, 1776): "The difficulties I have found in my negotiations with the Minister have *determined me to form a company* which will enable the munitions and powder to be transmitted sooner to *your friend* on condition of his returning tobacco to Cape Francis."

To Arthur Lee, whom he had met at the table of Lord Mayor John Wilkes, Beaumarchais had emphasized the "generous" side of his scheme. Tobacco was indeed to be sent, chiefly to give a commercial color to the transaction for the King's concealment, but there appeared no reason to do more with Lee, who had no power of contract, than impress him with the magnanimity and friendship of the French Government. This Lee was to report to the Secret Committee of Congress, which would thus be prepared to agree to any arrangement of Beaumarchais' agent, without any suspicion that it might be called on to pay twenty sols a pound for powder that had cost from four to six. Lee did report it, sending a special messenger (Story) to announce to Congress the glad tidings of French aid and much too gushingly its quasi-gratuitous character.

A month later Silas Deane, belated since March 5th by wind and wave, reached Paris, and about July 17, 1776, by advice of Vergennes, had his first interview with Beaumarchais. Had Beaumarchais known that an agent, empowered by Congress to purchase munitions, was on his way to France, he would have had nothing to do with Lee ; now he could only repudiate him, and persuade Deane to disregard him. Arthur Lee informed Deane that Beaumarchais had told him that he had received two hundred thousand pounds sterling of the French administration for the use of Congress, but Deane believed Beaumarchais, who "constantly and positively denied having said any such thing." It had been better for Deane if he had believed Lee.[1] It turned out in the end that Beaumarchais had received

[1] M. Doniol and Mr. Durand are entirely mistaken in supposing that Lee was "substantially a traitor." That he wrote to Lord Shelburne that "if England wanted to prevent closer ties between France and the United States she must not delay," proves indeed the reverse. He wanted recognition of the independence of his country, and peace, and was as willing to get it from England as from France. He was no doubt well aware that French subsidies were meant, as Beaumarchais reminded the King, to continue the war in America, not to end it. Arthur Lee had his faults, but lack of patriotism was not among them.

the sum Lee named, and the French Government—more anxious for treaty concessions from America than for Beaumarchais' pocket—assured the American Commissioners that the million was a royal gift.

This claim to generosity, however, or rather the source of it, was a secret of the negotiation. In October, 1777, the commissioners wrote to Congress a letter which, being intercepted, reached that body only in duplicate, March, 1778, saying they had received assurances "that no repayment will ever be required from us for what has already been given us either in money or military stores." One of these commissioners was Silas Deane himself (the others Franklin and Lee). But meanwhile Beaumarchais had claimed of Congress, by an agent (De Francy) sent to America, payment of his bill, which included the million which his Government declared had been a gift. This complication caused Congress to recall Deane for explanations.

Deane arrived in America in July, 1778. There were suspicious circumstances around him. He had left his papers in Paris ; he had borrowed money of Beaumarchais for personal expenses, and the despatch he had signed in October, saying the million was a gift, had been intercepted, other papers in the same package having duly arrived. Thus appearances were against Deane. The following statement, in Paine's handwriting, was no doubt prepared for submission to Congress, and probably was read during one of its secret discussions of the matter. It is headed " Explanatory Circumstances."

" 1st. The lost dispatches are dated Oct. 6th and Oct. 7th. They were sent by a private hand—that is, they were not sent by the post. Capt. Folger had the charge of them. They were all under one cover containing five separate Packets ; three of the Packets were on commercial matters only—one of these was to Mr. R[obert] Morris, Chairman of the Commercial Committee, one to Mr. Hancock (private concerns), another to Barnaby Deane, S. Deane's brother. Of the other two Packets, one of them was to the Secret Committee, then stiled the Committee for foreign Affairs, the other was to Richard H. Lee—these two last Packets had nothing in them but blank white French Paper.

" 2d. In Sept'r preceding the date of the dispatches Mr. B[eaumarchais] sent Mr. Francis [De Francy] to Congress to press payment to the amount mentioned in the official Letter of Oct. 6. Mr. F[rancy] brought a letter signed only by S. Deane—the Capt. of the vessel (Landais) brought another letter from Deane ; both of these letters were to enforce Mr. B[eaumarchais'] demand. Mr. F[rancy] arrived with his letters and demand. The official despatches (if I may so say) arrived blank. Congress therefore had no authoritative information to act by. About this time Mr. D[eane] was recalled and arrived in America in Count D'Estaing's fleet. He gave out that he had left his accounts in France.

" With the Treaty of Alliance come over the Duplicates of the lost Despatches. They come into my office not having been seen by Congress ; and as they contain an injunction not to be conceded by [to ?] Congress, I kept them secret in the office because at that time the foreign Committee were dispersed and new members not appointed.

" On the 5th of Dec. 1778, Mr. D[eane] published an inflamatory piece against Congress. As I saw it had an exceeding ill effect out of doors I made some remarks upon it—with a view of preventing people running mad. This piece was replied to by a piece under the Signature of Plain Truth—in which it was stated, that Mr. D[eane] though a stranger in France and to the Language, and without money, had by himself procured 30,000 stand of Arms, 30,000 suits of Cloathing, and more than 200 pieces of Brass Cannon. I replied that these supplies were in a train of Execution before he was sent to France. That Mr. Deane's private letters and his official despatches jointly with the other two Commissioners contradicted each other.

" At this time I found Deane had made a large party in Congress—and that a motion had been made but not decided upon for dismissing me from the foreign office, with a kind of censure."

Deane was heard by Congress twice (August 9 and 21, 1778) but made a bad impression, and a third hearing was refused. In wrath he appealed in the Press " to the free and virtuous Citizens of America " (December 5, 1778), against the injustice of Congress. This Paine answered in the *Pennsylvania Packet* of December 15, 1778. His motives are told in the following letter addressed to the Hon. Henry Laurens :

"PHILADELPHIA, Dec. 15, 1778.—DEAR SIR.—In this morning's paper is a piece addressed to Mr. Deane, in which your name is mentioned. My intention in relating the circumstances with wch. it is connected is to prevent the Enemy drawing any unjust conclusions from an accidental division in the House on matters no ways political. You will please to observe that I have been exceedingly careful to preserve the honor of Congress in the minds of the people who have been so exceedingly fretted by Mr. Deane's address—and this will appear the more necessary when I inform you that a proposal has been made for calling a Town Meeting to demand justice for Mr. Deane. I have been applied to smoothly and roughly not to publish this piece. Mr. Deane has likewise been with the Printer. I am, &c."

To Paine, who had given his all to the American cause, nothing could appear more natural than that France and her King should do the same with pure disinterestedness. Here were Lafayette and other Frenchmen at Washington's side. However, the one thing he was certain of was that Deane had no claim to be credited with the French subsidies. Had Henry Laurens been President of Congress it would have been easy to act on that body through him; but he had resigned, and the new president, John Jay, was a prominent member of the Deane party. So Paine resolved to defeat what he considered a fraud on the country at whatever cost. In the course of the controversy he wrote (January 2, 1779):

"If Mr. Deane or any other gentleman will procure an order from Congress to inspect an account in my office, or any of Mr. Deane's friends in Congress will take the trouble of coming themselves, I will give him or them my attendance, and shew them in handwriting which Mr. Deane is well acquainted with, that the supplies he so pompously plumes himself upon were promised and engaged, and that as a present, before he ever arrived in France; and the part that fell to Mr. Deane was only to see it done, and how he has performed that service the public are acquainted with."

Although Paine here gave the purport of the commissioners' letter, showing plainly that Deane had nothing to do with obtaining the supplies, he is not so certain that they were gratuitous, and adds, in the same letter (January 2d): "The supplies here alluded to are those which were sent from France in the Amphitrite, Seine, and Mercury, about two years ago. They had at first the appearance of a present, but whether so or on credit the service was a great and a friendly one." To transfer the debt to the French Government would secure such a long credit that the American cause would not suffer. Perhaps no official notice might have been taken of this, but in another letter (January 5th) Paine wrote : " Those who are now her [America's] allies, prefaced that alliance by an early and generous friendship ; yet that we might not attribute too much to human or auxiliary aid, so unfortunate were these supplies that only one ship out of three arrived ; the Mercury and Seine fell into the hands of the enemy."

It was this last paragraph that constituted Paine's indiscretion. Unless we can suppose him for once capable of a rôle so Machiavellian as the forcing of France's hand, by revealing the connection between the King and the subsidies of Beaumarchais, we can only praise him for a too-impulsive and self-forgetting patriotism. It was of course necessary for the French Minister (Gérard) to complain, and for Congress to soothe him by voting the fiction that his most Christian Majesty "did not preface his alliance with any supplies whatever sent to America." But in order to do this, Paine had somehow to be dealt with. A serio-comical performance took place in Congress. The members knew perfectly well that Paine had documents to prove every word he had printed : but as they did not yet know these documents officially, and were required by their ally's minister to deny Paine's statement, they were in great fear that Paine, if summoned, might reveal them. As the articles were only signed " Common Sense," it was necessary that the Secretary should acknowledge himself their author, and Congress, in dread of discovering its own secrets, contrived that he should be allowed to utter at the bar only one word.

Congress received M. Gérard's complaint on January 5th, and on the 6th, to which action thereon had been adjourned, the following memorial from Paine.

"HONORABLE SIRS.—Understanding that exceptions have been taken at some parts of my conduct, which exceptions as I am unacquainted with I cannot reply to : I therefore humbly beg leave to submit every part of my conduct public and private, so far as relate to public measures, to the judgment of this Honble. House, to be by them approved or censured as they shall judge proper—at the same time reserving to myself that conscious satisfaction of having ever intended well and to the best of my abilities executed these intentions.

"The Honble. Congress in April, 1777, were pleased, not only unsolicited on my part, but wholly unknown to me, to appoint me unanimously Secretary to the Committee for foreign affairs, which mode of appointment I conceive to be the most honorable that can take place. The salary they were pleased to affix to it was 70 dollars per month. It has remained at the same rate ever since, and is not at this time equal to the most moderate expences I can live at ; yet I have never complained, and always conceiving it my duty to bear a share of the inconveniences of the country, have ever cheerfully submitted to them. This being my situation, I am at this time conscious of no error, unless the cheapness of my services, and the generosity with which I have endeavored to do good in other respects, can be imputed to me as a crime, by such individuals as may have acted otherwise.

"As my appointment was honorable, therefore whenever it shall appear to Congress that I have not fulfilled their expectations, I shall, tho' with concern at any misapprehension that might lead to such an opinion, surrender up the books and papers intrusted to my care.

"Were my appointment an office of profit it might become me to resign it, but as it is otherwise I conceive that such a step in me might imply a dissatisfaction on account of the smallness of the pay. Therefore I think it my duty to wait the orders of this Honble. House, at the same time begging leave to assure them that whatever may be their determination respecting me, my disposition to serve in so honorable a cause, and in any character in which I can best do it, will suffer no alteration. I am, with profound respect, your Honors' dutiful and obt. hble. Servant,

"THOMAS PAINE."

On the same day Paine was summoned before Congress (sitting always with closed doors), and asked by its president (Jay) if he wrote the articles.

He replied "Yes," and was instantly ordered to withdraw. On the following day Paine, having discovered that Deane's party were resolved that he should have no opportunity to reveal any fact in Congress, submitted a second memorial.

"HONORABLE SIRS.—From the manner in which I was called before the House yesterday, I have reason to suspect an unfavorable disposition in them towards some parts in my late publications. What the parts are against which they object, or what those objections are, are wholly unknown to me. If any gentleman has presented any Memorial to this House which contains any charge against me, or any-ways alludes in a censurable manner to my character or interest, so as to become the ground of any such charge, I request, as a servant under your authority, an attested copy of that charge, and in my present character as a freeman of this country, I demand it. I attended at the bar of this House yesterday as their servant, tho' the warrant did not express my official station, which I conceive it ought to have done, otherwise it could not have been compulsive unless backed by a magistrate. My hopes were that I should be made acquainted with the charge, and admitted to my defence, which I am all times ready to make either in writing or personally.

"I cannot in duty to my character as a freeman submit to be censured unheard. I have evidence which I presume will justify me. And I entreat this House to consider how great their reproach will be should it be told that they passed a sentence upon me without hearing me, and that a copy of the charge against me was refused to me ; and likewise how much that reproach will be aggravated should I afterwards prove the censure of this House to be a libel, grounded upon a mistake which they refused fully to inquire into.

"I make my application to the heart of every gentleman in this House, that, before he decides on a point that may affect my reputation, he will duly consider his own. Did I court popular praise I should not send this letter. My wish is that by thus stating my situation to the House, they may not commit an act they cannot justify.

"I have obtained fame, honor, and credit in this country. I am proud of these honors. And as they cannot be taken from me by any unjust censure grounded on a concealed charge, therefore it will become my duty afterwards to do justice to myself. I have no favor to ask more than to be candidly and honorably dealt by ; and such being my right I ought to have no doubt but this House will proceed accordingly. Should Congress be disposed to hear me, I have to request that they will give me sufficient time to prepare."

It was, of course, a foregone conclusion that the story of what had occurred in France must not be told. M. Gérard had identified himself with the interests of Beaumarchais, as well as with those of his Government, and was using the privileges of the alliance to cover that speculator's demand. Paine, therefore, pleaded in vain. Indeed, the foregoing memorial seems to have been suppressed, as it is not referred to in the journal of the House for that day (January 7th). On the day following his resignation was presented in the following letter :

"Honorable Sirs.—Finding by the Journals of this House, of yesterday, that I am not to be heard, and having in my letter of the same day, prior to that resolution, declared that I could not 'in duty to my character as a freeman submit to be censured unheard,' therefore, consistent with that declaration, and to maintain that Right, I think it my duty to resign the office of Secretary to the Committee for foreign Affairs, and I do hereby resign the same. The Papers and documents in my charge I shall faithfully deliver up to the Committee, either on honor or oath, as they or this House shall direct.

" Considering myself now no longer a servant of Congress, I conceive it convenient that I should declare what have been the motives of my conduct. On the appearance of Mr. Deane's Address to the Public of the 5 of Dec, in which he said 'The ears of the Representatives were shut against him,' the honor and justice of this House were impeached and its reputation sunk to the lowest ebb in the opinion of the People. The expressions of suspicion and degradation which have been uttered in my hearing and are too indecent to be related in this letter, first induced me to set the Public right ; but so grounded were they, almost without exception, in their ill opinion of this House, that instead of succeeding as I wished in my first address, I fell under the same reproach and was frequently told that I was defending Congress in their bad designs. This obliged me to go farther into the matters, and I have now reason to believe that my endeavours have been and will be effectual.

"My wish and my intentions in all my late publications were to preserve the public from error and imposition, to support as far as laid in my power the just authority of the Representatives of the People, and to cordiallize and cement the Union that has so happily taken place between this country and France.

"I have betrayed no Trust because I have constantly employed that Trust to the public good. I have revealed no secrets because I have told nothing that was, or I conceive ought to be a secret. I have convicted Mr. Deane of error, and in so doing I hope I have done my duty.

" It is to the interest of the Alliance that the People should know that before America had any agent in Europe the 'public-spirited gentlemen' in that quarter of the world were her warm friends. And I hope this Honorable House will receive it from me as a farther testimony of my affection to that Alliance, and of my attention to the duty of my office, that I mention, that the duplicates of the Dispatches of Oct. 6 and 7, 1777, from the *Commissioners,* the originals of which are in the Enemy's possession, seem to require on *that account* a reconsideration.

"His Excellency, the Minister of France, is well acquainted with the liberality of my sentiments, and I have had the pleasure of receiving repeated testimonies of his esteem for me. I am concerned that he should in any instance misconceive me. I beg likewise to have it understood that my appeal to this Honorable House for a hearing yesterday was as a *matter of Right* in the character of a Freeman, which Right I ought to yield up to no Power whatever. I return my utmost thanks to the Honorable Members of this House who endeavored to support me in that Right, so sacred to themselves and to their constituents ; and I have the pleasure of saying and reflecting that as I came into office an honest man, I go out of it with the same character."

This letter also was suppressed, and the same fate was secured by Mr. Jay for several other letters written by Paine to Congress. On March 30, 1779, he quotes a letter of the commissioners of November 30, 1777, saying that the supplies from France were "the effects of private benevolence." On April 21st he reminds Congress that "they began their hard treatment of me while I was defending their injured and insulted honor, and which I cannot account for on any other ground than supposing that a private unwarrantable connection was formed between Mr. Deane and certain Members of this Honorable House." On April 23d he again addresses the " Honorable Sirs ":

"On inquiring yesterday of Mr. Thomson, your Secretary, I find that no answer is given to any of my letters. I am unable to account for the seeming inattention of Congress in collecting information at this particular time, from whatever quarter it may come ; and this wonder is the more increased when I recollect that a private offer was made to me, about three months ago, amounting in money to £700 a year ; yet however polite the proposal might be, or however friendly it might be designed, I thought it my duty to decline it; as it was accompanied with a condition which I conceived had a tendency to prevent the information I have since given, and shall yet give to the Country on Public Affairs.

"I have repeatedly wrote to Congress respecting Mr. Deane's dark incendiary conduct, and offered every information in my power. The opportunities I have had of knowing the state of foreign affairs is greater than that of many gentlemen of this House, and I want no other knowledge to declare that I look on Mr. Deane to be, what Mr. Carmichael calls him, a rascal."

The offer of money came from M. Gérard. This clever diplomatist perceived in all Paine's letters his genuine love of France, and esteem for the King who had so generously allied himself with the Americans in their struggle for independence. Since M. Gérard's arrival Paine had been on friendly terms with him. I have explored the State Archives of France for M. Gérard's versions of these affairs, and find them more diplomatic than exact. Immediately on the appearance of Paine's first attack on Deane, the Minister appears to have visited Paine. He reports to Vergennes, January 10th, that he had been at much pains to convince Paine of his error in saying that the supplies furnished by Beaumarchais had been "promised as a gift"; but he had not retracted; and he (Gérard), then thought it necessary to refer what he wrote to Congress. "Congress, however, did not wait for this to show me its indignation." The journals of Congress do not, however, reveal any reference to the matter previous to M. Gérard's memorial of January 5th. In his next letter M. Gérard asserts that Congress had dismissed Paine, whereas Paine resigned, and a motion for his dismission was lost. This letter is dated January 17th.

"When I had denounced to Congress the assertions of M. Payne, I did not conceal from myself the bad effects that might result to a head puffed up by the success of his political writings, and the importance he affected. I foresaw the loss of his office, and feared that, separated from the support which had restrained him, he would seek only to avenge himself with his characteristic impetuosity and impudence. All

means of restraining him would be impossible, considering the enthusiasm here for the license of the press, and in the absence of any laws to repress audacity even against foreign powers. The only remedy, my lord, I could imagine to prevent these inconveniences, and even to profit by the circumstances, was to have Payne offered a salary in the King's name, in place of that he had lost. He called to thank me, and I stipulated that he should publish nothing on political affairs, nor about Congress, without advising with me, and should employ his pen mainly in impressing on the people favorable sentiments towards France and the Alliance, of the kind fittest to foster hatred and defiance towards England. He appeared to accept the task with pleasure. I promised him a thousand dollars per annum, to begin from the time of his dismission by Congress. He has already begun his functions in declaring in the Gazette that the affair of the military effects has no reference to the Court and is not a political matter. You know too well the prodigious effects produced by the writings of this famous personage among the people of the States to cause me any fear of your disapproval of my resolution."

M. Gérard adds that he has also employed Dr. Cooper, an intimate friend of Dr. Franklin. On May 29th he informs Vergennes that the Paine arrangement did not work.

"A piece in a Gazette of the third by M. Payne, under his usual title of Common Sense proves his loss of it. In it he declares that he is the only honest man thus far employed in American affairs, and demands that the nation shall give him the title and authority of Censorgeneral, especially to purify and reform Congress. This bit of folly shows what he is capable of. He gives me marks of friendship, but that does not contribute to the success of my exhortations."

In another despatch of the same date M. Gérard writes:

"I have had the honor to acquaint you with the project I had formed to engage Sir Payne [le Sr. Payne] to insert in the public papers paragraphs relative to the Alliance, calculated to encourage the high idea formed by the people of the king, and its confidence in his friendship: but this writer having tarnished his reputation and being sold to the opposition, I have found another."

He goes on to say that he has purchased two eminent gentlemen, who write under the names "Honest Politician" and "Americanus."

M. Gérard, in his statements concerning his relations with Paine, depended on the unfamiliarity of Vergennes with the Philadelphia journals. In these Paine had promptly made known the overtures made to him.

"Had I been disposed to make money I undoubtedly had many opportunities for it. The single pamphlet 'Common Sense' would at that time of day have produced a tolerable fortune, had I only taken the same profits from the publication which all writers have ever done ; because the sale was the most rapid and extensive of anything that was ever published in this country, or perhaps in any other. Instead of which I reduced the price so low, that instead of getting, I stand £39, 11, 0 out of pocket on Mr. Bradford's books, exclusive of my time and trouble ; and I have acted the same disinterested part by every publication I have made.

"At the time the dispute arose respecting Mr. Deane's affairs, I had a conference with Mr. Gérard at his own request, and some matters on that subject were freely talked over, which it is here necessary to mention. This was on the 2d of January. On the evening of the same day or the next, Mr. Gérard through the medium of another gentleman made me a very genteel and profitable offer. My answer to the offer was precisely in these words : ' Any service I can render to either of the countries in alliance, or to both, I ever had done and shall readily do, and Mr. Gérard's *esteem* will be the only compensation I shall desire.' "

Paine never received a cent of M. Gérard's money, but he became convinced that the French Government might be compromised by his allusion to its early generosity to America, and on January 26th wrote that the letter to which he had alluded had not mentioned " the King of France by any name or title nor yet the nation of France." This was all that the French Minister could get out of Paine, and it was willingly given. The more complaisant " Honest Politician " and " Americanus " however, duly fulfilled the tasks for which they had been employed by the French Ambassador. This will be seen by reference to their letters in the *Pennsylvania Gazette* of June 23d. In June and July Paine entered on a controversy with "Americanus " on the terms upon which America should insist, in any treaty of peace. He intimates his suspicion that " Americanus " is a hireling.

It should be mentioned that the English archives prove that in Paris Deane and Gérard had long been intimate and often closeted with Vergennes. (See the reports of Wentworth and others in Stevens' *Fac-Similes*.) Deane and Gérard came over together, on one of d'Estaing's ships. According to the English information Gérard was pecuniarily interested in the supplies sent to America, and if so had private reasons for resisting Paine's theory of their gratuitous character.

CHAPTER X

A STORY BY GOUVERNEUR MORRIS

THE Paine–Deane incident had a number of curious sequels, some of which are related in a characteristic letter of Gouverneur Morris to John Randolph, which has not, I believe, hitherto been printed. Gouverneur Morris had much to do with the whole affair ; he was a member of Congress during the controversy, and he was the Minister in France who, fifteen years later, brought to light the receipt for the King's million livres charged by Beaumarchais against this country.

WASHINGTON, Jany. 20, 1812.

" It would give me pleasure to communicate the information you ask, but I can only speak from memory respecting matters, some of which were transacted long ago and did not command my special attention. But it is probable that the material facts can be established by documents in the Secretary of State's office.

" It will, I believe, appear from the correspondence between Mr. Arthur Lee and the

Secret and Commercial Committee, that early in our dispute with Great Britain the French Court made through him a tender of military supplies, and employed as their agent for that purpose M. Beaumarchais, who, having little property and but slender standing in society might (if needful) be disavowed, imprisoned, and punished for presuming to use the King's name on such an occasion. In the course of our Revolutionary War, large supplies were sent by M. Beaumarchais under the name of Roderique Hortalez and Co., a supposed mercantile name. But the operations were impeded by complaints of the British Ambassador, Lord Stormont, which obliged the French Court to make frequent denials, protestations, seizure of goods and detention of ships. Every step of this kind bound them more strongly to prevent a disclosure of facts.

"After the Congress returned to Philadelphia, M. de Francy, agent of M. Beaumarchais, applied to Congress for payment. This application was supported on the ground of justice by many who were not in the secret, for the Congress had then so much good sense as not to trust itself with its own secrets. There happened unluckily at that time a feud between Mr. Lee and Mr. Deane. The latter favored (in appearance at least) M. Beaumarchais' claim. Paine, who was clerk to the Secret and Commercial Committee, took part in the dispute, wrote pieces for the Gazettes, and at length, to overwhelm Deane and those who defended him with confusion, published a declaration of the facts confidentially communicated to the Committee by Mr. Lee, and signed this declaration as American Secretary for Foreign Affairs.[1] The French Minister M. Gérard, immediately made a formal complaint of that publication, and an equally formal denial of what it contained. The Congress was therefore obliged to believe, or at least to act as if they believed, that Paine had told a scandalous falsehood. He was in consequence dismissed, which indeed he deserved for his impudence if for nothing else.[2]

"Beaumarchais and his agent had already received from the Committee tobacco and perhaps other articles of produce on account of his demand ; what and how much will of course be found from investigating the files of the Treasury. But he wanted and finally obtained a larger and more effectual payment. Bills were drawn in his favor on Dr. Franklin, our Minister in France, at long sight, for about one hundred thousand pounds sterling. This was done in the persuasion that the Doctor would, when they were presented, communicate the fact to Comte de Vergennes, from whom he would afterwards be obliged to solicit the means of payment. It was hoped that the French Court would then interfere

and either lay hold of the bills or compel M. Beaumarchais to refund the money, so that no real deduction would on that account be afterwards made from the loans or subsidies to us. The death of all who were privy to it has spread an impenetrable veil over what passed on this occasion between M. Beaumarchais and his employer, but the bills were regularly paid, and we were thereby deprived in a critical moment of the resources which so large a sum would have supplied. When this happened, M. de la Luzerne, then Minister of France at Philadelphia, expressed himself with so much freedom and so much indignation respecting M. Beaumarchais and his claim, that there was reason to believe nothing more would have been heard of it. In that persuasion, perhaps, Dr. Franklin, when he came to settle our national accounts with M. de Vergennes, was less solicitous about a considerable item than he otherwise might have been. He acknowledged as a free gift to the United States the receipt on a certain day of one million livres, for which no evidence was produced. He asked indeed for a voucher to establish the payment, but the Count replied that it was immaterial whether we had received the money or not, seeing that we were not called on for repayment. With this reassuring the old gentleman seems to have been satisfied, and the account was settled accordingly. Perhaps the facts may have been communicated to him under the seal of secrecy, and if so he showed firmness in that he had shared in the plunder with Deane and Beaumarchais.

"Things remained in that state till after the late king of France was dethroned. The Minister of the United States at Paris[3] was then directed to enquire what had become of the million livres. The correspondence will of course be found in the office of the Secretary of State. It seems that he had the good fortune to obtain copies of M. Beaumarchais' receipt for a million, bearing date on the day when the gift was said to have been made, so that no reasonable doubt could exist as to the identity of the sum.[4]

"So much, my dear Sir, for what memory can command. You will, I think, find papers containing a more accurate statement in the New York 'Evening Post,' about the time when Mr. Rodney's opinion was made public. At least I recollect having seen in that gazette some facts with which I had not been previously acquainted or which I had forgotten. A gentleman from Connecticut, who was on the Committee of Claims last year, can I believe give you the papers. I remember also to have been told by a respectable young gentleman, son of the late Mr. Richard Henry Lee, that important evidence on this

---

[1] Error. Paine signed "Common Sense," and in one instance "Thomas Paine."

[2] Paine resigned. Several motions for his dismissal were lost.

[3] Gouverneur Morris himself.

[4] This was the receipt dated June 10, 1776, on which the King had marked "Bon," and was obtained by Morris in 1794.

subject, secured from his uncle Arthur, was in his possession, and I believe it may be obtained from Mr. Carroll of Annapolis, or his son-in-law Mr. Harper of Baltimore.[1]

"The Hon'le Mr. JOHN RANDOLPH, of Roanoke."

Beaumarchais, barely escaping the guillotine, died in poverty in Holland. He bequeathed his claim to his daughter who (1835) was paid 800,000 francs, but the million which he had received from the King and then charged on the United States, was never paid. Silas Deane suffered a worse fate. His claims for commissions and services in France remained unpaid, and after his return to France he occupied himself with writing to his brother Simeon and others the intercepted letters printed by Rivington in 1782. In these letters he urges submission to England. Franklin took the charitable view that his head had been turned by his misfortunes. He went over to England, where he became the friend of Benedict Arnold, and died in poverty in 1789. In recent years his heirs were paid $35,000 by Congress. But his character and his performances in France, during the Revolution, remain an enigma.

The determination with which Paine, to his cost, withstood Deane, may seem at first glance quixotic. His attack was animated by a belief that the supplies sent from France were a covert gift, and, at any rate, that the demand for instant payment to agents was fraudulent. Evidence having been supplied, by the publication of Beaumarchais' notes to Arthur Lee, under pseudonym of "Mary Johnston," that returns in tobacco were expected, this, if not a mercantile mask, was still a matter of credit, and very different from payments demanded by Beaumarchais and Deane from the scanty treasury of the struggling colonies.[2] But

[1] The documents referred to are no doubt among the Lee Papers preserved at the University of Virginia, which I have examined.

[2] In one of Deane's intercepted letters (May 20, 1781) there is an indication that he had found more truth in what Paine had said about the gratuitous supplies than Beaumarchais had led

there was something more behind the vehemence of Paine's letters. This he intimated, but his revelation seems to have received no attention at the time. He says (January 5th) : "In speaking of Mr. Deane's contracts with foreign officers, I concealed, out of pity to him, a circumstance that must have sufficiently shown the necessity of recalling him, and either his want of judgment or the danger of trusting him with discretionary power. It is no less than that of his throwing out a proposal, in one of his foreign letters, for contracting with a German prince to command the American army." This personage, who was "to supersede General Washington," he afterwards declares to be Prince Ferdinand. It is known that Count de Broglie had engaged Kalb and Deane to propose him as generalissimo of America, but the evidence of this other proposal has disappeared with other papers missing

him to believe. "The first plan of the French Government evidently was to assist us just so far as might be absolutely necessary to prevent an accommodation, and to give this assistance with so much secresy as to avoid any rupture with Great Britain. On this plan succors were first permitted to be sent out to us by private individuals, and only on condition of future payment, but afterward we were thought to be such cheap and effectual instruments of mischief to the British nation that more direct and gratuitous aids were furnished us." But now M. Doniol has brought to light the *Réflexions* and *Considérations* of the French Minister, Count de Vergennes, which led to his employment of Beaumarchais, which contain such propositions as these : " It is essential that France shall at present direct its care towards this end : she must nourish the courage and perseverance of the insurgents by flattering their hope of effectual assistance when circumstances permit." " It will be expedient to give the insurgents secret aid in munitions and money ; utility suggests this small sacrifice." " Should France and Spain give succors, they should seek compensation only in the political object they have at heart, reserving to themselves subsequent decision, after the events and according to the situations." " It would be neither for the king's dignity or interest to bargain with the insurgents." It is certain that Beaumarchais was required to impress these sentiments on Arthur Lee, who continued to take them seriously, and made Paine take them so, after Beaumarchais was taking only his own interests seriously.

from Deane's diplomatic correspondence. I find, however, that ex-provost Stillé, who has studied the proceedings of Beaumarchais thoroughly, has derived from another source an impression that he (Beaumarchais) made an earlier proposition of the same kind concerning Prince Ferdinand. It would be unsafe to affirm that Deane did more than report the proposals made to him, but his silence concerning this particular charge of his antagonist, while denying every other categorically, is suspicious. At that early period Washington had not loomed up in the eye of the world. The French and Germans appear to have thought of the Americans and their commander as we might think of rebellious red men and their painted chief. There is nothing in Deane's letters from Europe to suggest that he did not share their delusion, or that he appreciated the necessity of independence. Paine, who conducted the foreign correspondence, knew that the secrets of the American office in Paris were open to Lord Stormont, who stopped large supplies prepared for America, and suspected Deane of treachery. It now appears that one of Deane's assistants, George Lupton, was an English "informer." (Stevens' *Fac-Similes*, vii., No. 696.) Deane had midnight meetings in the Place Vendôme with an English "Unknown" (now known as the informer Paul Wentworth) to whom he suggested that the troubles might be ended by England's forming a "federal union" with America. All of which shows Deane perilously unfit for his mission, but one is glad to find him appearing no worse in Wentworth's confidental portraiture (January 4, 1778) of the American officials :

"Dr. Franklin is taciturn, deliberate, and cautious ; Mr. Deane is vain, desultory, and subtle ; Mr. Arthur Lee, suspicious and indolent ; Alderman Lee, peevish and ignorant ; Mr. Izzard, costive and dogmatical—all of these insidious, and Edwards vibrating between hope and fear, interest and attachment."

CHAPTER XI

CAUSE, COUNTRY, SELF

WHATEVER might be thought of Paine's course in the Deane-Beaumarchais affair, there could be no doubt that the country was saved from a questionable payment unjustly pressed at a time when it must have crippled the Revolution, for which the French subsidies were given. Congress was relieved, and he who relieved it was the sufferer. From the most important congressional secretaryship he was reduced to a clerkship in Owen Biddle's law office.

Paine's patriotic interest in public affairs did not abate. In the summer of 1779 he wrote able articles in favor of maintaining our right to the Newfoundland fisheries in any treaty of peace that might be made with England. Congress was secretly considering what instructions should be sent to its representatives in Europe, in case negotiations should arise, and the subject was discussed by "Americanus" in a letter to the *Pennsylvania Gazette*, June 23d. This writer argued that the fisheries should not be mentioned in such negotiations ; England would stickle at the claim, and our ally, France, should not be called on to guarantee a right which should be left to the determination of natural laws. This position Paine combated ; he maintained that independence was not a change of ministry, but a real thing ; it should mean prosperity as well as political liberty. Our ally would be aggrieved by a concession to Great Britain of any means of making our alliance useful. "There are but two natural sources of wealth—the Earth and the Ocean,—and to lose the right to either is, in our situation, to put up the other for sale." The fisheries are needed, "*first*, as an Employment. *Secondly*, as producing national Supply and Commerce, and a means of national wealth. *Thirdly*, as a Nursery for Seamen." Should Great Britain be in such straits as to ask for peace, that would be the right opportunity to settle the matter. "To leave the Fisheries wholly out, on any pretence whatever, is to sow the seeds of another war." (*Pennsylvania Gazette*, June 30th, July 14th, 21st.)

The prospects of peace seemed now sufficiently fair for Paine to give the attention which nobody else did to his own dismal situation. His scruples about making money out of the national cause were eccentric. The manuscript diary of Rickman, just found by Dr. Clair Grece, contains this note :

"Franklin, on returning to America from France, where he had been conducting great commercial and other concerns of great import and benefit to the States of America, on having his accounts looked over by the Committee appointed to do so, there was a deficit of £100,000. He was asked how this happened. 'I was taught,' said he very gravely, 'when a boy to read the scriptures and to attend to them, and it is there said : muzzle not the ox that treadeth out his master's grain.' No further inquiry was ever made or mention of the deficient £100,000, which, it is presumed, he devoted to some good and great purpose to serve the people, —his own aim through life."

Rickman, who named a son after Franklin, puts a more charitable construction on the irregularities of the Doctor's accounts than Gouverneur Morris (p. 57). The anecdote may not be exact, but it was generally rumored, in congressional circles, that Franklin had by no means been muzzled. Nor does it appear to have been considered a serious matter. The standard of political ethics being thus lowered, it is easy to understand that Paine gave more offence by his Diogenes-lantern than if he had quietly taken his share of the grain he trod out. The security of independence

and the pressure of poverty rendered it unnecessary to adhere to his quixotic Quaker repugnance to the sale of his inspirations, and he now desired to collect these into marketable shape. His plans are stated in a letter to Henry Laurens.

"PHILADELPHIA, Sepr. 14, 1779.—DEAR SIR,—It was my intention to have communicated to you the substance of this letter last Sunday had I not been prevented by a return of my fever ; perhaps finding myself unwell, and feeling, as well as apprehending, inconveniences, have produced in me some thoughts for myself as well as for others. I need not repeat to you the part I have acted or the principle I have acted upon ; and perhaps America would feel the less obligation to me, did she know, that it was neither the place nor the people but the Cause itself that irresistibly engaged me in its support ; for I should have acted the same part in any other Country could the same circumstances have arisen there which have happened here. I have often been obliged to form this distinction to myself by way of smoothing over some disagreeable ingratitudes, which, you well know, have been shewn to me from a certain quarter.

"I find myself so curiously circumstanced that I have both too many friends and too few, the generality of them thinking that from the public part I have so long acted I cannot have less than a mine to draw from. What they have had from me they have got for nothing, and they consequently suppose I must be able to afford it. I know but one kind of life I am fit for, and that is a thinking one, and, of course, a writing one— but I have confined myself so much of late, taken so little exercise, and lived so very sparingly, that unless I alter my way of life it will alter me. I think I have a right to ride a horse of my own, but I cannot now even afford to hire one, which is a situation I never was in before, and I begin to know that a sedentary life cannot be supported without jolting exercise. Having said thus much, which, in truth, is but loss of time to tell to you who so well know how I am situated, I take the liberty of communicating to you my design of doing some degree of justice to myself, but even this is accompanied with some present difficulties, but it is the easiest, and, I believe, the most useful and reputable of any I can think of. I intend this winter to collect all my Publications, beginning with Common Sense and ending with the fisheries, and publishing them in two volumes Octavo, with notes. I have no doubt of a large subscription. The principal difficulty will be to get Paper and I can think of no way more practicable than to desire Arthur Lee to send over a quantity from France in the Confederacy if she goes there, and settling for it with his brother. After that work is compleated, I intend prosecuting a history of the Revolution by means of a subscription—but this undertaking will be attended with such an amazing expense, and will take such a length of Time, that unless the States individually give some assistance therein, scarcely any man could afford to go through it. Some kind of an history might be easily executed made up of daily events and triffling matters which would lose their Importance in a few years. But a proper history cannot even be began unless the secrets of the other side of the water can be obtained, for the first part is so interwoven with the Politics of England, that, that which will be the last to get at must be the first to begin with—and this single instance is sufficient to show that no history can take place of some time. My design, if I undertake it, is to comprise it in three quarto volumes and to publish one each year from the time of beginning, and to make an abridgment afterwards in an easy agreeable language for a school book. All the histories of ancient wars that are used for this purpose, promotes no Moral Reflection, but like the beggars opera renders the villain pleasing in the hero. Another thing that will prolong the completion of an history is the want of Plates which only can be done in Europe, for that part of a history which is intended to convey discription of places or persons will ever be imperfect without them. I have now, Sir, acquainted you with my design, and unwilling, as you know I am, to make use of a friend while I can possibly avoid it, I am really obliged to say that I should now be glad to consult with two or three on some matters that regard my situation till such time as I can bring the first of those subscriptions to bear, or set them on foot, which cannot well be until I can get the paper ; for should I [be] disappointed of that, with the subscriptions in my hand, I might be reflected upon, and the reason, tho' a true one, would be subject to other explanations.

"Here lies the difficulty I alluded to in the beginning of this letter, and I would rather wish to borrow something of a friend or two in the interim that run the risk I have mentioned, because should I be disappointed by the Paper being taken or not arriving in time, the reason being understood by them beforehand will not injure me, but in the other case it would, and in the mean Time I can be preparing for publication. I have hitherto kept all my private matters a secret, but as I know your friendship and you a great deal of my situation, I can with more ease communicate them to you than to another.

"P. S. If you are not engaged to-morrow evening I should be glad to spend part of it with you—if you are, I shall wait your opportunity." [1]

It was a cruel circumstance of Paine's poverty that he was compelled to call attention not only to that but to his services, and to appraise the value of his

own pen. He had to deal with hard men, on whom reserve was wasted. On September 28th he reminded the Executive Council of Pennsylvania of his needs and his uncompensated services, which, he declared, he could not afford to continue without support. The Council realized the importance of Paine's pen to its patriotic measures, but was afraid of offending the French Minister. Its president, Joseph Reed, on the following day (September 29th) wrote to that Minister intimating that they would like to employ Paine if he (the Minister) had no objection. On October 11th Gérard replies with a somewhat equivocal letter, in which he declares that Paine had agreed to terms he had offered through M. de Mirales, but had not fulfilled them. " I willingly," he says, "leave M. Payne to enjoy whatever advantages he promises himself by his denial of his acceptance of the offers of M. de Mirales and myself. I would even add, Sir, that if you feel able to direct his pen in a way useful to the public welfare—which will perhaps not be difficult to your zeal, talents, and superior lights,—I will be the first to applaud the success of an attempt in which I have failed." [2] On the same date Paine, not having received any reply to his previous letter, again wrote to the Council.

"HONBLE. SIRS.—Some few days ago I presented a letter to this Honble. Board stating the inconveniences which I lay under from an attention to public interest in preference to my own, to which I have recd. no reply. It is to me a matter of great concern to find in the government of this State, that which appears to be a disposition in them to neglect their friends and to throw discouragements in the way of genius and Letters.

"At the particular request of the Gentleman who presides at this board, I took up the defence of the Constitution, at a time when he declared to me that unless he could be assisted he must give it up and quit the state ; as matters then pressed too heavy upon him, and the opposition was gaining ground ; yet this Board has since suffered me to combat with all the inconveniences incurred by that service, without any attention to my interest or my situation.

---

[1] I am indebted to Mr. Simon Gratz of Philadelphia for a copy of this letter.

[2] " Life and Correspondence of Joseph Reed." By his grandson. 1847.

For the sake of not dishonoring a cause, good in itself, I have hitherto been silent on these matters, but I cannot help expressing to this board the concern I feel on this occasion, and the ill effect which such discouraging examples will have on those who might otherwise be disposed to act as I have done.

"Having said this much, which is but a little part of which I am sensible, I have a request to make which if complied with will enable me to overcome the difficulties alluded to and to withdraw from a service in which I have experienced nothing but misfortune and neglect. I have an opportunity of importing a quantity of printing paper from France, and intend collecting my several pieces, beginning with Common Sense, into two Volumes, and publishing them by Subscription, with notes; but as I cannot think of beginning the Subscription until the paper arrive, and as the undertaking, exclusive of the paper, will be attended with more expense than I, who have saved money both in the Service of the Continent and the State, can bear, I should be glad to be assisted with the loan of fifteen hundred pounds for which I will give bond payable within a year. If this should not be complied with, I request that the services I have rendered may be taken into consideration and such compensation made me therefor as they shall appear to deserve.

"I am, Honble. Sirs, your obt. and humble servt.,

"THOMAS PAINE."

The constitution which Paine, in the above letter, speaks of defending was that of 1776, which he had assisted Dr. Franklin, James Cannon, and others, in framing for Pennsylvania. It was a fairly republican constitution, and by its enfranchisement of the people generally reduced the power enjoyed by the rich and reactionary under the colonial government. In Stillé's biography of John Dickinson the continued conflicts concerning this constitution are described. In 1805, when a constitutional convention was proposed in Pennsylvania, Paine pointed out the superiority of its constitution of 1776, which "was conformable to the Declaration of Independence and the Declaration of Rights, which the present constitution [framed in 1790] is not."[1] The constitution of

1776, and Paine's exposure of the services rendered to the enemy by Quakers, cleared the Pennsylvania Assembly of the members of that society who had been supreme. This process had gone on. The oath of allegiance to the State, proposed by Paine in 1777, and adopted, had been followed in 1778 (April 1st) by one imposing renunciation of all allegiance to George III., his heirs and successors, to be taken by all trustees, provosts, professors, and masters. This was particularly aimed at the nest of "Tories" in the University of Philadelphia, whose head was the famous Dr. William Smith. This provost, and all members of the University except three trustees, took the oath, but the influence of those who had been opposed to independence remained the same. In 1779 the Assembly got rid of the provost (Smith), and this was done by the act of November which took away the charter of the University.[2] It was while this agitation was going on, and the Philadelphia "Tories" saw the heads of their chieftains falling beneath Paine's pen, that his own official head had been thrown to them by his own act. The sullen spite of the "Tories" did not fail to manifest itself. In conjunction with Deane's defeated friends, they managed to give Paine many a personal humiliation. This was, indeed, easy enough, since Paine, though willing to fight for his cause, was a non-resistant in his own behalf. It may have been about this time that an incident occurred which was remembered with gusto by the aged John Joseph Henry after the "Age of

---

[1] Paine forgot the curious inconsistency in this constitution of 1776, between the opening Declaration of Rights in securing religious freedom and equality to all who "acknowledge

the being of a God," and the oath provided for all legislators, requiring belief in future rewards and punishments, and in the divine inspiration of the Old and New Testaments. This deistical oath, however, was probably considered a victory of latitudinarianism, for the members of the convention had taken a rigid trinitarian oath on admission to their seats.

[2] See "A Memoir of the Rev. William Smith, D.D.," by Charles J. Stillé, Philadelphia, 1869. Provost Stillé, in this useful historical pamphlet, states all that can be said in favor of Dr. Smith, but does not refer to his controversy with Paine.

Reason" had added horns and cloven feet to his early hero. Mr. Mease, Clothier-General, gave a dinner party, and a company of his guests, on their way home, excited by wine, met Paine. One of them remarking, "There comes 'Common Sense,'" Matthew Slough said, "Damn him, I shall common-sense him," and thereupon tripped Paine into the gutter.[1]

But patriotic America was with Paine, and missed his pen; for no *Crisis* had appeared for nearly a year. Consequently on November 2, 1779, the Pennsylvania Assembly elected him its Clerk. On the same day there was introduced into that Assembly an act for the abolition of slavery in the State, which then contained six thousand negro slaves. The body of this very moderate measure was prepared by George Bryan, but the much admired preamble has been attributed by tradition to the pen of Paine.[2] That this tradition is correct is now easily proved by a comparison of its sentiments and phraseology with the antislavery writings of Paine presented in previous pages of this work. The author, who alone seems to have been thinking of the negroes and their rights during that revolutionary epoch, thus had some reward in writing the first proclamation of emancipation in America. The act passed March 1, 1780. The Preamble is as follows:

"I. When we contemplate our abhorrence of that condition, to which the arms and tyranny of Great Britain were exerted to reduce us, when we look back on the variety of dangers to which we have been exposed, and how miraculously our wants in many instances have been supplied,

and our deliverances wrought, when even hope and human fortitude have become unequal to the conflict, we are unavoidably led to a serious and grateful sense of the manifold blessings, which we have undeservedly received from the hand of that Being, from whom every good and perfect gift cometh. Impressed with these ideas, we conceive that it is our duty, and we rejoice that it is in our power, to extend a portion of that freedom to others, which hath been extended to us, and release from that state of thraldom, to which we ourselves were tyrannically doomed, and from which we have now every prospect of being delivered. It is not for us to enquire why, in the creation of mankind, the inhabitants of the several parts of the earth were distinguished by a difference in feature or complexion. It is sufficient to know that all are the work of the Almighty Hand. We find in the distribution of the human species, that the most fertile as well as the most barren parts of the earth are inhabited by men of complexions different from ours, and from each other; from whence we may reasonably as well as religiously infer, that He, who placed them in their various situations, hath extended equally his care and protection to all, and that it becometh not us to counteract his mercies. We esteem it a peculiar blessing granted to us, that we are enabled this day to add one more step to universal civilization, by removing, as much as possible, the sorrows of those, who have lived in undeserved bondage, and from which, by the assumed authority of the Kings of Great Britain, no effectual, legal relief could be obtained. Weaned, by a long course of experience, from those narrow prejudices and partialities we had imbibed, we find our hearts enlarged with kindness and benevolence towards men of all conditions and nations; and we conceive ourselves at this particular period particularly called upon by the blessings which we have received, to manifest the sincerity of our profession, and to give a substantial proof of our gratitude.

"II. And whereas the condition of those persons, who have heretofore been denominated Negro and Mulatto slaves, has been attended with circumstances, which not only deprived them of the common blessings that they were by nature entitled to, but has cast them into the deepest afflictions, by an unnatural separation and sale of husband and wife from each other and from their children, an injury, the greatness of which can only be conceived by supposing that we were in the same unhappy case. In justice, therefore, to persons so unhappily circumstanced, and who, having no prospect before them whereon they may rest their sorrows and their hopes, have no reasonable inducement to render their service to society, which they otherwise might, and also in grateful commemoration of our own happy deliverance from that state of unconditional submission to which we were doomed by the tyranny of Britain.

"III. *Be it enacted,* &c."

---

[1] This incident is related in the interest of religion in Mr. Henry's "Account of Arnold's Campaign against Quebec." The book repeats the old charge of drunkenness against Paine, but the untrustworthiness of the writer's memory is shown in his saying that his father grieved when Paine's true character appeared, evidently meaning his "infidelity." His father died in 1786, when no suspicion either of Paine's habits or orthodoxy had been heard.

[2] "Life and Correspondence of Joseph Reed," ii., p. 177; *North American Review*, vol. lvii, No. cxx.

The New Year, 1780, found Washington amid much distress at Morristown. Besides the published letters which attest this I have found an extract from one which seems to have escaped the attention of Washington's editors.[1] It was written at Morristown, January 5th.

"It gives me extreme Pain that I should still be holding up to Congress our wants on the score of Provision, when I am convinced that they are doing all that they can for our relief. Duty and necessity, however, constrain me to it. The inclosed copies of Letters from Mr. Flint, the Assistant Commissary, and from Gen. Irvine, who commands at present our advanced troops, contain a just Representation of our situation. To add to our Difficulties I very much fear that the late violent snowstorm has so blocked up the Roads, that it will be some days before the scanty supplies in this quarter can be brought to camp. The troops, both officers and men, have borne their Distress, with a patience scarcely to be conceived. Many of the latter have been four or five days without meat entirely and short of Bread, and none but very scanty Supplies— Some for their preservation have been compelled to maraud and rob from the Inhabitants, and I have it not in my power to punish or reprove the practice. If our condition should not undergo a very speedy and considerable change for the better, it will be difficult to point out all the consequences that may ensue. About forty of the Cattle mentioned by Mr. Flint got in last night."

The times that tried men's souls had come again. The enemy, having discovered the sufferings of the soldiers at Morristown, circulated leaflets inviting them to share the pleasures of New York. Nor were they entirely unsuccessful. On May 28th was penned the gloomiest letter Washington ever wrote. It was addressed to Reed, President of Pennsylvania, and the Clerk (Paine) read it to the Assembly. "I assure you," said the Commander's letter, "every idea you can form of our distresses will fall short of the reality. There is such a combination of circumstances to exhaust the patience of the soldiery that it begins at length to be worn out, and we see in every line of the army the most serious features of

mutiny and sedition." There was throughout the long letter a tone of desperation which moved the Assembly profoundly. At the close there was a despairing silence, amid which a member arose and said, "We may as well give up first as last." The treasury was nearly empty, but enough remained to pay Paine his salary, and he headed a subscription of relief with $500.[2] The money was enclosed to Mr. M'Clenaghan, with a vigorous letter which that gentleman read to a meeting held in a coffeehouse the same evening. Robert Morris and M'Clenaghan subscribed £200 each, hard money. The subscription, dated June 8th, spread like wildfire, and resulted in the raising of £300,000, which established a bank that supplied the army through the campaign, and was incorporated by Congress on December 21st.

Paine, by his timely suggestion of a subscription, and his "mite," as he called it, proved that he could meet a crisis as well as write one. He had written a cheery *Crisis* in March, had helped to make good its hopefulness in May, and was straightway busy on another. This was probably begun on the morning when M'Clenaghan came to him with a description of the happy effect and result produced by his letter and subscription on the gentlemen met at the coffee-house. This *Crisis* (June 9, 1780) declares that the reported fate of Charleston, like the misfortunes of 1776, had revived the same spirit ; that such piecemeal work was not conquering the continent; that France was at their side ; that an association had been formed for supplies, and hard-money bounties. In a postscript he adds : "Charleston is gone, and I believe for the want of a sufficient supply of provisions. The man that does not now feel for the honor of the best and noblest cause that ever a country engaged in, and exert himself accordingly, is no

---

[1] It is in the Ward Collection at Lafayette College, Easton, Pa., copied by a (probably) contemporary hand.

[2] The salary was drawn on June 7th, and amounted to £1,699. For particulars concerning Paine's connection with the Assembly I am indebted to Dr. William H. Egle, State Librarian of Pennsylvania.

longer worthy of a peaceable residence among a people determined to be free."

Meanwhile, on "Sunday Morning, June 4th," Paine wrote to President Reed a private letter :

"SIR,—I trouble you with a few thoughts on the present state of affairs. Every difficulty we are now in arises from an empty treasury and an exhausted credit. These removed and the prospect were brighter. While the war was carried on by emissions at the pleasure of Congress, any body of men might conduct public business, and the poor were of equal use in government with the rich. But when the means must be drawn from the country the case becomes altered, and unless the wealthier part throw in their aid, public measures must go heavily on.

"The people of America understand *rights* better than *politics*. They have a clear idea of their object, but are greatly deficient in comprehending the means. In the first place, they do not distinguish between sinking the debt and raising the current expenses. They want to have the war carried on, the Lord knows how.

"It is always dangerous to spread an alarm of danger unless the prospect of success be held out with it, and that not only as probable, but naturally essential. These things premised, I beg leave to mention, that suppose you were to send for some of the richer inhabitants of the City, and state to them the situation of the army and the treasury, not as arising so much from defect in the departments of government as from a neglect in the country generally, in not contributing the necessary support in time. If they have any spirit, any foresight of their own interest or danger, they will promote a subscription either of money or articles, and appoint a committee from among themselves to solicit the same in the several Counties ; and one State setting the example, the rest, I presume, will follow. Suppose it was likewise proposed to them to deposit their plate to be coined for the pay of the Army, crediting the government for the value, by weight.

"If measures of this kind could be promoted by the richer of the Whigs, it would justify your calling upon the other part to furnish their proportion without ceremony, and these two measures carried, would make a draft or call for personal service the more palatable and easy.

"I began to write this yesterday. This morning, it appears clear to me that Charleston is in the hands of the enemy, and the garrison prisoners of war. Something must be done, and that something, to give it popularity, must begin with men of property. Every care ought now to be taken to keep goods from rising. The rising of goods will have a most ruinous ill effect in every light in which it can be viewed.

"The army must be reunited, and that by the most expeditious possible means. Drafts should

first be countenanced by subscriptions, and if men would but reason rightly, they would see that there are some thousands in this State who had better subscribe thirty, forty, or fifty guineas apiece than run the risk of having to settle with the enemy. Property is always the object of a conqueror, wherever he can find it. A rich man, says King James, makes a bonny traitor ; and it cannot be supposed that Britain will not reimburse herself by the wealth of others, could she once get the power of doing it. We must at least recruit eight or ten thousand men in this State, who had better raise a man apiece, though it should cost them a thousand pounds apiece, than not have a sufficient force, were it only for safety sake. Eight or ten thousand men, added to what we have now got, with the force that may arrive, would enable us to make a stroke at New York, to recover the loss of Charleston— but the measure must be expeditious.

"I suggest another thought. Suppose every man, working a plantation, who has not taken the oath of allegiance, in Philadelphia County, Bucks, Chester, Lancaster, Northampton, and Berks, were, by the new power vested in the Council, called immediately upon for taxes in kind at a certain value. Horses and wagons to be appraised. This would not only give immediate relief, but popularity to the new power. I would remark of taxes in kind, that they are hard-money taxes, and could they be established on the non-jurors, would relieve us in the articles of supplies.

"But whatever is necessary or proper to be done, must be done immediately. We must rise vigorously upon the evil, or it will rise upon us. A show of spirit will grow into real spirit, but the Country must not be suffered to ponder over their loss for a day. The circumstance of the present hour will justify any means from which good may arise. We want rousing.

"On the loss of Charleston I would remark —the expectation of a foreign force arriving will embarrass them whether to go or to stay ; and in either case, what will they do with their prisoners? If they return, they will be but as they were as to dominion ; if they continue, they will leave New York an attackable post. They can make no new movements for a considerable time. They may pursue their object to the Southward in detachments, but then in every main point they will naturally be at a stand ; and we ought immediately to lay hold of the vacancy.

"I am, Sir,
"Your obedient humble servant,
"THOMAS PAINE."

If Paine had lost any popularity in consequence of his indirect censure by Congress, a year before, it had been more than regained by his action in heading the subscription, and the inspiriting effect of his pamphlets of March and June, 1780. The University of the State of Pennsylvania, as it was now styled, celebrated the Fourth of July by conferring on him the degree of Master of Arts.[1] Among the trustees who voted to confer on him this honor were some who had two years before refused to take the American oath of allegiance.

In the autumn appeared Paine's *Crisis Extraordinary*. It would appear by a payment made to him personally, that in order to make his works cheap he had been compelled to take his publications into his own hands.[2] The sum of $360 paid for ten dozen copies of this pamphlet was really at the rate of five cents per copy. It is a forcible reminder of the depreciation of the Continental currency. At one period Paine says he paid $300 for a pair of woollen stockings.

Although the financial emergency had been tided over by patriotic sacrifices, it had disclosed a chaos. Congress, so far from being able to contend with Virginia on a point of sovereignty, was without power to levy taxes. "One State," writes Washington (May 31st), "will comply with a requisition of Congress;

---

[1] Mr. Burk, Secretary of the University of Pennsylvania, sends me some interesting particulars. The proposal to confer the degree on Paine was unanimously agreed to by the trustees present, who were the Hon. Joseph Reed, President of the Province; Mr. Moore, Vice-President; Mr. Sproat (Presbyterian minister), Mr. White (the Bishop), Mr. Helmuth, Mr. Weiborg (minister of the German Calvinist Church), Mr. Farmer (Roman Catholic Rector of St. Mary's), Dr. Bond, Dr. Hutchkinson, Mr. Muhlenberg (Lutheran minister). There were seven other recipients of the honor on that day, all eminent ministers of religion; and M.D. was conferred on David Ramsay, a prisoner with the enemy.

[2] "In Council. Philadelphia, October 10th, 1780. SIR,—Pay to Thomas Paine Esquire, or his order, the amount of three hundred and sixty dollars Continental money in State money, at sixty to one, amount of his account for 10 dozen of the Crisis Extraordinary. WM. MOORE, Vice President.—To DAVID RITTENHOUSE Esquire, Treasurer."

"SIR,—Please to pay the within to Mr. Willm. Harris, and you will oblige yr. obt. Hble. Sert., *Thos. Paine.*—DAVID RITTENHOUSE ESQ."

"Rcd. in full, H. WM. HARRIS." [Harris printed the pamphlet.]

---

another neglects to do it; a third executes it by halves; and all differ either in the manner, the matter, or so much in point of time, that we are always working up hill, and ever shall be; and, while such a system as the present one or rather want of one prevails, we shall ever be unable to apply our strength or resources to any advantage." In the letter of May 28th, to the President of Pennsylvania, which led to the subscription headed by Paine, Washington pointed out that the resources of New York and Jersey were exhausted, that Virginia could spare nothing from the threatened South, and Pennsylvania was their chief dependence. "The crisis, in every point of view, is extraordinary." This sentence of Washington probably gave Paine his title, *Crisis Extraordinary*. It is in every sense a masterly production. By a careful estimate he shows that the war and the several governments cost two millions sterling annually. The population being 3,000,000, the amount would average 13*s.* 4*d.* per head. In England the taxation was £2 per head. With independence a peace establishment in America would cost 5*s.* per head; with the loss of it Americans would have to pay the £2 per head like other English subjects. Of the needed annual two millions, Pennsylvania's quota would be an eighth, or £250,000; that is, a shilling per month to her 375,000 inhabitants,— which subjugation would increase to three-and-threepence per month. He points out that the Pennsylvanians were then paying only £64,280 per annum, instead of their real quota of £250,000, leaving a deficiency of £185,720, and consequently a distressed army. After showing that with peace and free trade all losses and ravages would be speedily redressed, Paine proposes that half of Pennsylvania's quota, and £60,000 over, shall be raised by a tax of 7*s.* per head. With this sixty thousand (interest on six millions) a million can be annually borrowed. He recommends a war-tax on landed property, houses, imports, prize goods, and liquors. "It would be an addition to the pleasures of society to know that, when the health of the army goes round, a few drops from every glass become theirs."

On December 30, 1780, Dunlap advertised Paine's pamphlet "Public Good." Under a charter given the Virginia Company in 1609 the State of Virginia claimed that its southern boundary extended to the Pacific; and that its northern boundary, starting four hundred miles above, on the Atlantic coast, stretched due northwest. To this Paine replies that the charter was given to a London company extinct for one hundred and fifty years, during which the State had never acted under that charter. Only the heirs of that company's members could claim anything under its extinct charter. Further the State unwarrantably assumed that the northwestern line was to extend from the northern point of its Atlantic base; whereas there was more reason to suppose that it was to extend from the southern point, and meet a due west line from the northern point, thus forming a triangular territory of forty-five thousand square miles. Moreover, the charter of 1609 said the lines should stretch "from sea to sea." Paine shows by apt quotations that the western sea was supposed to be a short distance from the Atlantic, and that the northwestern boundary claimed by Virginia would never reach the said sea, "but would form a spiral line of infinite windings round the globe, and after passing over the northern parts of America and the frozen ocean, and then into the northern parts of Asia, would, when eternity should end, and not before, terminate in the north pole." Such a territory is nondescript, and a charter that describes nothing gives nothing. It may be remarked here that though the Attorney-General of Virginia, Edmund Randolph, had to vindicate his State's claim, he used a similar argument in defeating Lord Fairfax's claim to lands in Virginia which had not been discovered when his grant was issued.[1]

[1] "Omitted Chapters of History Disclosed in

All this, however, was mere fencing preliminary to the real issue. The western lands, on the extinction of the Virginia companies, had reverted to the Crown, and the point in which the State was really interested was its succession to the sovereignty of the Crown over all that territory. It was an early cropping up of the question of State sovereignty. By royal proclamation of 1763 the province of Virginia was defined so as not to extend beyond heads of rivers emptying in the Atlantic. Paine contended that to the sovereignty of the Crown over all territories beyond limits of the thirteen provinces the United States had succeeded. This early assertion of the federal doctrine, enforced with great historical and legal learning, alienated from Paine some of his best Southern friends. The controversy did not end until some years later. After the peace, a proposal in the Virginia Legislature to present Paine with something for his services, was lost on account of this pamphlet.[2]

the Life and Papers of Edmund Randolph," pp. 47, 60.

[2] Of course this issue of State *v.* National sovereignty was adjourned to the future battlefield, where indeed it was not settled. Congress accepted Virginia's concession of the territory in question (March 1, 1784), without conceding that it was a donation; it accepted some of Virginia's conditions, but refused others, which the State surrendered. A motion that this acceptance did not imply endorsement of Virginia's claim was lost, but the contrary was not affirmed. The issue was therefore settled only in Paine's pamphlet, which remains a document of paramount historical interest.

There was, of course, a rumor that Paine's pamphlet was a piece of paid advocacy. I remarked among the Lee MSS., at the University of Virginia, an unsigned scrap of paper saying he had been promised twelve thousand acres of western land. Such a promise could only have been made by the old Indiana, or Vandalia, Company, which was trying to revive its defeated claim for lands conveyed by the Indians in compensation for property they had destroyed. Their agent, Samuel Wharton, may have employed Paine's pen for some kind of work. But there is no faintest trace of advocacy in Paine's "Public Good." He simply maintains that the territories belong to the United States, and should be sold to pay the public

The students of history will soon be enriched by a "Life of Patrick Henry," by his grandson, William Wirt Henry, and a "Life of George Mason," by his descendant, Miss Rowland. In these works by competent hands important contributions will be made (as I have reason to know) to right knowledge of the subject dealt with by Paine in his "Public Good." It can here only be touched on ; but in passing I may say that Virginia had good ground for resist-

ing even the semblance of an assertion of sovereignty by a Congress representing only a military treaty between the colonies ; and that Paine's doctrine confesses itself too idealistic and premature by the plea, with which his pamphlet closes, for the summoning of a "continental convention, for the purpose of forming a continental constitution, defining and describing the powers and authority of Congress."

CHAPTER XII

A JOURNEY TO FRANCE

THE suggestion of Franklin to Paine, in October, 1775, that he should write a history of the events that led up to the conflict, had never been forgotten by either. From Franklin he had gathered important facts and materials concerning the time antedating his arrival in America, and he had been a careful chronicler of the progress of the Revolution. He was now eager to begin this work. At the close of the first year of his office as Clerk of the Assembly, which left him with means of support for a time, he wrote to the Speaker (November 3, 1780) setting forth his intention of collecting materials for a history of the Revolution, and saying that he could not fulfil the duties of Clerk if re-elected.[1] This and another

letter (September 14, 1780), addressed to the Hon. John Bayard, Speaker of the late Assembly, were read, and ordered to lie on the table. Paine's office would appear to have ended early in November ; the next three months were devoted to preparations for his history.

But events determined that Paine should make more history than he was able to chronicle. Soon after his *Crisis Extraordinary* (dated October 6, 1780) had appeared, Congress issued its estimate of eight million dollars (a million less than Paine's) as the amount to be raised. It was plain that the money could not be got in the country, and France must be called on for help. Paine drew up a letter to Vergennes, informing him that a paper dollar was

---

debt,—a principle as fatal to the claim of a Company as to that of a State.

[1] Dr. Egle informs me that the following payments to Paine appear in the Treasurer's account: 1779, November 27, £450. 1780, February 14. For public service at a treaty held at Easton in 1777, £300. February 14. Pay as clerk ; £582. 10. 0. March 18. On account as clerk, £187. 10. 0. March 27, "for his services" (probably those mentioned on p. 39), £2,355. 7. 6. June 7, "for 60 days' attendance and extra expenses," £1,699. 1. 6. (This was all paper money, and of much less value than

it seems. The last payment was drawn on the occasion of his subscription of the $500, apparently hard money, in response to Washington's appeal.) In March, 1780, a Fee Act was passed regulating the payment of officers of the State in accordance with the price of wheat ; but this was ineffectual to preserve the State paper from depreciation. In June, 1780, a list of lawyers and State officers willing to take paper money of the March issue as gold and silver was published, and in it appears "Thomas Paine, clerk to the General Assembly."

worth only a cent, that it seemed almost impossible to continue the war, and asking that France should supply America with a million sterling per annum, as subsidy or loan. This letter was shown to M. Marbois, Secretary of the French Legation, who spoke discouragingly. But the Hon. Ralph Izard showed the letter to some members of Congress, whose consultation led to the appointment of Col. John Laurens to visit France. It was thought that Laurens, one of Washington's aids, would be able to explain the military situation. He was reluctant, but agreed to go if Paine would accompany him.

It so happened that Paine had for some months had a dream of crossing the Atlantic, with what purpose is shown in the following confidential letter (September 9, 1780), probably to Gen. Nathaniel Greene :

"SIR,—Last spring I mentioned to you a wish I had to take a passage for Europe, and endeavour to go privately to England. You pointed out several difficulties in the way, respecting my own safety, which occasioned me to defer the matter at that time, in order not only to weigh it more seriously, but to submit to the government of subsequent circumstances. I have frequently and carefully thought of it since, and were I now to give an opinion on it as a measure to which I was not a party, it would be this :—that as the press in that country is free and open, could a person possessed of a knowledge of America, and capable of fixing it in the minds of the people of England, go suddenly from this country to that, and keep himself concealed, he might, were he to manage his knowledge rightly, produce a more general disposition for peace than by any method I can suppose. I see my way so clearly before me in this opinion, that I must be more mistaken than I ever yet was on any political measure, if it fail of its end. I take it for granted that the whole country, ministry, minority, and all, are tired of the war ; but the difficulty is how to get rid of it, or how they are to come down from the high ground they have taken, and accommodate their feelings to a treaty for peace. Such a change must be the effect either of necessity or choice. I think it will take, at least, three or four more campaigns to produce the former, and they are too wrong in their opinions of America to act from the latter. I imagine that next spring will begin with a new Parliament, which is so material a crisis in the politics of that country, that it ought to be attended to by this ; for, should it start wrong, we may look forward to six or

seven years more of war. The influence of the press rightly managed is important ; but we can derive no service in this line, because there is no person in England who knows enough of America to treat the subject properly. It was in a great measure owing to my bringing a knowledge of England with me to America, that I was enabled to enter deeper into politics, and with more success, than other people ; and whoever takes the matter up in England must in like manner be possessed of a knowledge of America. I do not suppose that the acknowledgment of Independence is at this time a more unpopular doctrine in England than the declaration of it was in America immediately before the publication of the pamphlet 'Common Sense,' and the ground appears as open for the one now as it did for the other then.

" The manner in which I would bring such a publication out would be under the cover of an Englishman who had made the tour of America *incog.* This will afford me all the foundation I wish for and enable me to place matters before them in a light in which they have never yet viewed them. I observe that Mr. Rose in his speech on Governor Pownall's bill, printed in Bradford's last paper, says that 'to form an opinion on the propriety of yielding independence to America requires an accurate knowledge of the state of that country, the temper of the people, the resources of their Government,' &c. Now there is no other method to give this information a national currency but this,—the channel of the press, which I have ever considered the tongue of the world, and which governs the sentiments of mankind more than anything else that ever did or can exist.

" The simple point I mean to aim at is, to make the acknowledgment of Independence a popular subject, and that not by exposing and attacking their errors, but by stating its advantages and apologising for their errors, by way of accommodating the measure to their pride. The present parties in that country will never bring one another to reason. They are heated with all the passion of opposition, and to rout the ministry, or to support them, makes their capital point. Were the same channel open to the ministry in this country which is open to us in that, they would stick at no expense to improve the opportunity. Men who are used to government know the weight and worth of the press, when in hands which can use it to advantage. Perhaps with me a little degree of literary pride is connected with principle ; for, as I had a considerable share in promoting the declaration of Independence in this country, I likewise wish to be a means of promoting the acknowledgment of it in that ; and were I not persuaded that the measure I have proposed would be productive of much essential service, I would not hazard my own safety, as I have everything to apprehend should I fall into their hands ;

but, could I escape in safety, till I could get out a publication in England, my apprehensions would be over, because the manner in which I mean to treat the subject would procure me protection.

"Having said thus much on the matter, I take the liberty of hinting to you a mode by which the expense may be defrayed without any new charge. Drop a delegate in Congress at the next election, and apply the pay to defray what I have proposed ; and the point then will be, whether you can possibly put any man into Congress who could render as much service in that station as in the one I have pointed out. When you have perused this, I should be glad of some conversation upon it, and will wait on you for that purpose at any hour you may appoint. I have changed my lodgings, and am now in Front Street opposite the Coffee House, next door to Aitkin's bookstore.

"I am, Sir, your ob't humble servant,
                    "THOMAS PAINE."

The invitation of Colonel Laurens was eagerly accepted by Paine, who hoped that after their business was transacted in France he might fulfil his plan of a literary descent on England. They sailed from Boston early in February, 1781, and arrived at L'Orient in March.

Young Laurens came near ruining the scheme by an imprudent advocacy, of which Vergennes complained, while ascribing it to his inexperience. According to Lamartine, the King "loaded Paine with favors." The gift of six millions was "confided into the hands of Franklin and Paine." The author now revealed to Laurens, and no doubt to Franklin, his plan for going to England, but was dissuaded from it. From Brest, May 28th, he writes to Franklin in Paris :

"I have just a moment to spare to bid you farewell. We go on board in an hour or two, with a fair wind and everything ready. I understand that you have expressed a desire to withdraw from business, and I beg leave to assure you that every wish of mine, so far as it can be attended with any service, will be employed to make your resignation, should it be accepted, attended with every possible mark of honor which your long services and high character in life justly merit."[1]

---

[1] He confides to Franklin a letter to be forwarded to Bury St. Edmunds, the region of his birth. Perhaps he had already been corresponding with some one there about his projected visit. Ten years later the *Bury Post* vigorously supported Paine and his "Rights of Man."

They sailed from Brest on the French frigate *Resolve* June 1st, reaching Boston August 25th, with 2,500,000 livres in silver, and in convoy a ship laden with clothing and military stores.

The glad tidings had long before reached Washington, then at New Windsor. On May 14, 1781, the General writes to Philip Schuyler :

"I have been exceedingly distressed by the repeated accounts I have received of the sufferings of the troops on the frontier, and the terrible consequences which must ensue unless they were speedily supplied. What gave a particular poignancy to the sting I felt on the occasion was my inability to afford relief."

On May 26th his diary notes a letter from Laurens reporting the relief coming from France. The information was confided by Washington only to his diary, lest it should forestall efforts of self-help. Of course Washington knew that the starting of convoys from France could not escape English vigilance, and that their arrival was uncertain ; so he passed near three months in preparations, reconnoitrings, discussions. By menacing the British in New York he made them draw away some of the forces of Cornwallis from Virginia, where he meant to strike ; but his delay in marching south brought on him complaints from Governor Jefferson, Richard Henry Lee, and others, who did not know the secret of that delay. Washington meant to carry to Virginia an army well clad, with hard money in their pockets, and this he did. The arrival of the French supplies at Boston, August 25th, was quickly heralded, and while sixteen ox-teams were carrying them to Philadelphia, Washington was there getting, on their credit, all the money and supplies he wanted for the campaign that resulted in the surrender of Cornwallis.

For this great service Paine never received any payment or acknowledgment. The plan of obtaining aid from France was conceived by him, and mainly executed by him. It was at a great risk that he went on this expedition ; had he been captured he could have hoped for little mercy from the British. Laurens, who had nearly upset the business, got the glory and the pay ; Paine, who had given up his clerkship of the Assembly, run the greater danger, and done the real work, got nothing. But it was a rôle he was used to. The young Colonel hastened to resume his place in Washington's family, but seems to have given little attention to Paine's needs, while asking attention to his own. So it would appear by the following friendly letter of Paine, addressed to "Col. Laurens, Head Quarters, Virginia :

"PHILADELPHIA, Oct. 4, 1781.—DEAR SIR, —I received your favor (by the post,) dated Sep. 9th, Head of Elk, respecting a mislaid letter. A gentleman who saw you at that place about the same time told me he had likewise a letter from you to me which he had lost, and that you mentioned something to him respecting baggage. This left me in a difficulty to judge whether after writing to me by post, you had not found the letter you wrote about, and took that opportunity to inform me about it. However, I have wrote to Gen. Heath in case the trunk should be there, and inclosed in it a letter to Blodget in case it should not. I have yet heard nothing from either. I have preferred forwarding the trunk, in case it can be done in a reasonable time, to the opening it, and if it cannot, then to open it agreeably to your directions, tho' I have no idea of its being there.

"I went for your boots, the next day after you left town, but they were not done, and I directed the man to bring them to me as soon as finished, but have since seen nothing of him, neither do wish him to bring them just now, as I must be obliged to borrow the money to pay for them ; but I imagine somebody else has taken them off his hands. I expect Col. Morgan in town on Saturday, who has some money of mine in his hands, and then I shall renew my application to the bootmaker.

"I wish you had thought of me a little before you went away, and at least endeavored to put matters in a train that I might not have to re-experience what has already past. The gentleman who conveys this to you, Mr. Burke, is an assistant judge of South Carolina, and one to whose friendship I am much indebted. He lodged some time in the house with me.

"I enclose you the paper of this morning, by which you will see that Gillam had not sailed (or at least I conclude so) on the 4th of July, as Major Jackson was deputy toast master, or Burgos-master, or something, at an entertainment on that day. As soon as I can learn anything concerning Gillam I will inform you of it.

"I am with every wish for your happiness and success, &c.

"Please to present my Compts. and best wishes to the General. I have wrote to the Marquis and put all my politics into his letter. A paper with Rivington's account of the action is enclosed in the Marquis' letter." [1]

It will be seen by the following letter to Franklin's nephew that Paine was now on good terms with the Congressmen who had opposed him in the Deane matter. The letter (in the Historical Society of Pennsylvania) is addressed to " Mr. Jonathan Williams, Merchant, Nantz," per " Brig Betsey."

"PHILADELPHIA, Nov. 26, 1781,—DEAR SIR, —Since my arrival I have received a letter from you dated Passy May 18, and directed to me at Brest. I intended writing to you by Mr. Baseley who is consul at L'Orient but neglected it till it was too late.—Mem: I desired Baseley to mention to you that Mr. Butler of S : Carolina is surprised at Capt Rob——n's drawing on him for money ; this Mr. Butler mentioned to me, and as a friend I communicate it to you.—I sent you Col. Laurens's draft on Madam Babut (I think that is her name) at Nantz for 12 L' d'ors for the expence of the Journey but have never learned if you received it.

"Your former friend Silas Deane has run his last length. In france he is reprobating America, and in America (by letters) he is reprobating france, and advising her to abandon her alliance relinquish her independence, and once more become subject to Britain. A number of letters, signed Silas Deane, have been published in the New York papers to this effect : they are believed, by those who formerly were his friends, to be genuine ; Mr. Robt. Morris assured me that he had been totally deceived in Deane, but that he now looked upon him to be a bad man, and his reputation totally ruined. Gouverneur Morris hopped round upon one leg, swore they had all been duped, himself among the rest, complimented me on my quick sight,—and by Gods says he nothing carries a man through the world like honesty :—and my old friend Duer 'Sometimes a sloven and sometimes a Beau,' says, Deane is a damned artful rascal. However Duer has fairly cleared himself. He received a letter from him a considerable time before the appearance of these in the New York papers—which was so contrary to what he expected to receive, and of such a traitorous cast, that he communicated it to Mr. Luzerne the Minister.

"Lord Cornwallis with 7247 officers and men are nabbed nicely in the Cheasepeake, which I presume you have heard already, otherwise I

---

[1] The original is in Mr. W. F. Havermeyer's collection.

should send you the particulars. I think the enemy can hardly hold out another campaign. General Greene has performed wonders to the southward, and our affairs in all quarters have a good appearance. The french Ministry have hit on the right scheme, that of bringing their force and ours to act in conjunction against the enemy.

"The Marquis de la fayette is on the point of setting out for france, but as I am now safely on this side the water again, I believe I shall postpone my second journey to france a little longer. —Lest Doctr. Franklin should not have heard of Deane I wish you would write to him, and if anything new transpires in the meantime and the Marquis do not set off too soon, I shall write by him.

"Remember me to Mr. & Mrs. Johnstone, Dr. Pierce, Mr. Watson & Ceasey and Mr.

Wilt. Make my best wishes to Mrs. Williams, Mrs. Alexander, and all the good girls at St. Germain.

"I am your friend &c.
"THOMAS PAINE.

"P. S. Mind, I 'll write no more till I hear from you. The French fleet is sailed from the Cheasepeake, and the British fleet from New York—and since writing the above, a vessel is come up the Delaware, which informs that he was chased by two french frigates to the southward of Cheasepeake, which on their coming up acquainted him that the french fleet was a head in chase of a fleet which they supposed to be the British.

"N. B. The french fleet sailed the 4th of this month, and the british much about the same time—both to the southward."

CHAPTER XIII

THE MUZZLED OX TREADING OUT THE GRAIN

WHILE Washington and Lafayette were in Virginia, preparing for their grapple with Cornwallis, Philadelphia was in apprehension of an attack by Sir Henry Clinton, for which it was not prepared. It appeared necessary to raise for defence a body of men, but the money was wanting. Paine (September 20th) proposed to Robert Morris the plan of "empowering the tenant to pay into the Treasury one quarter's rent, to be applied as above [*i. e.*, the safety of Philadelphia], and in case it should not be necessary to use the money when collected, the sums so paid to be considered a part of the customary taxes." This drastic measure would probably have been adopted had not the cloud cleared away. The winter was presently made glorious summer by the sun of Yorktown.

Washington was received with enthusiasm by Congress on November 28th. In the general feasting and joy Paine participated, but with an aching heart. He was an unrivalled literary lion; he had to appear on festive occasions; and he was without means. Having given

his all,—copyrights, secretaryship, clerkship,—to secure the independence of a nation, he found himself in a state of dependence. He fairly pointed the moral of Solomon's fable: By his wisdom he had saved the besieged land, yet none remembered that poor man, so far as his needs were concerned. If in his confidential letter to Washington, given below, Paine seems egotistical, it should be borne in mind that his estimate of his services falls short of their appreciation by the national leaders. It should not have been left to Paine to call attention to his sacrifices for his country's cause, and the want in which it had left him. He knew also that plain speaking was necessary with Washington.

"SECOND STREET, OPPOSITE THE QUAKER MEETING-HOUSE, Nov. 30, 1781.

"SIR,—As soon as I can suppose you to be a little at leisure from business and visits, I shall, with much pleasure, wait on you, to pay you my respects and congratulate you on the success you have most deservedly been blest with.

"I hope nothing in the perusal of this letter will add a care to the many that employ your mind; but as there is a satisfaction in speaking where one can be conceived and understood, I divulge to you the secret of my own situation; because I would wish to tell it to somebody, and as I do not want to make it public, I may not have a fairer opportunity.

"It is seven years, *this day*, since I arrived in America, and tho' I consider them as the most honorary time of my life, they have nevertheless been the most inconvenient and even distressing. From an anxiety to support, as far as laid in my power, the reputation of the Cause of America, as well as the Cause itself, I declined the customary profits which authors are entitled to, and I have always continued to do so; yet I never thought (if I thought at all on the matter,) but that as .I dealt generously and honorably by America, she would deal the same by me. But I have experienced the contrary—and it gives me much concern, not only on account of the inconvenience it has occasioned to me, but because it unpleasantly lessens my opinion of the character of a country which once appeared so fair, and it hurts my mind to see her so cold and inattentive to matters which affect her reputation.

"Almost every body knows, not only in this country but in Europe, that I have been of service to her, and as far as the interest of the heart could carry a man I have shared with her in the worst of her fortunes, yet so confined has been my private circumstances that for one summer I was obliged to hire myself as a common clerk to Owen Biddle of this city for my support: but this and many others of the like nature I have always endeavored to conceal, because to expose them would only serve to entail on her the reproach of being ungrateful, and might start an ill opinion of her honor and generosity in other countries, especially as there are pens enough abroad to spread and aggravate it.

"Unfortunately for me, I knew the situation of Silas Deane when no other person knew it, and with an honesty, for which I ought to have been thanked, endeavored to prevent his fraud taking place. He has himself proved my opinion right, and the warmest of his advocates now very candidly acknowledge their deception.

"While it was every body's fate to suffer I chearfully suffered with them, but tho' the object of the country is now nearly established and her circumstances rising into prosperity, I feel myself left in a very unpleasant situation. Yet I am totally at a loss what to attribute it to; for wherever I go I find respect, and every body I meet treats me with friendship; all join in censuring the neglect and throwing blame on each other, so that their civility disarms me as much as their conduct distresses me. But in this situation I cannot go on, and as I have no inclination to differ with the Country or to tell the story of her neglect, it is my design to get to Europe, either to France or Holland. I have literary fame, and I am sure I cannot experience worse fortune than I have here. Besides a

person who understood the affairs of America, and was capable and disposed to do her a kindness, might render her considerable service in Europe, where her situation is but imperfectly understood and much misrepresented by the publications which have appeared on that side the water, and tho' she has not behaved to me with any proportionate return of friendship, my wish for her prosperity is no ways abated, and I shall be very happy to see her character as fair as her cause.

"Yet after all there is something peculiarly hard that the country which ought to have been to me a home has scarcely afforded me an asylum.

"In thus speaking to your Excellency, I know I disclose myself to one who can sympathize with me, for I have often cast a thought at your difficult situation to smooth over the unpleasantness of my own.

"I have began some remarks on the Abbe Raynal's 'History of the Revolution.' In several places he is mistaken, and in others injudicious and sometimes cynical. I believe I shall publish it in America, but my principal view is to republish it in Europe both in French and English.

"Please, Sir, to make my respectful compts. to your Lady, and accept to yourself the best wishes of,

"Your obedt. humble servant,
"THOMAS PAINE.[1]

"His Excellency General WASHINGTON."

Paine's determination to make no money by his early pamphlets arose partly from his religious and Quaker sentiments. He could not have entered into any war that did not appear to him sacred, and in such a cause his "testimony" could not be that of a "hireling." His "Common Sense," his first *Crisis*, were inspirations, and during all the time of danger his pen was consecrated to the cause. He had, however, strict and definite ideas of copyright, and was the first to call attention of the country to its necessity, and even to international justice in literary property. In the chaotic condition of such matters his own sacrifices for the national benefit had been to some extent defeated by the rapacity of his first publisher, Bell, who pocketed much of what Paine had intended for the nation. After he had left Bell for Bradford, the former not

---

[1] I am indebted to Mr. Simon Gratz of Philadelphia for a copy of this letter.

only published another edition of "Common Sense," but with "large additions," as if from Paine's pen. When the perils of the cause seemed past Paine still desired to continue his literary record clear of any possible charge of payment, but he believed that the country would appreciate this sensitiveness, and, while everybody was claiming something for services, would take care that he did not starve. In this he was mistaken. In that very winter, after he had ventured across the Atlantic and helped to obtain the six million livres, he suffered want. Washington appears to have been the first to consider his case. In the diary of Robert Morris, Superintendent of Finance, there is an entry of January 26, 1782, in which he mentions that Washington had twice expressed to him a desire that some provision should be made for Paine.[1] Morris sent for Paine and, in the course of a long conversation, expressed a wish that the author's pen should continue its services to the country; adding that though he had no position to offer him something might turn up. In February Morris mentions further interviews with Paine, in which his assistant, Gouverneur Morris, united; they expressed their high appreciation of his services to the country, and their desire to have the aid of his pen in promoting measures necessary to draw out the resources of the country for the completion of its purpose. They strongly disclaimed any private or partial ends, or a wish to bind his pen to any particular plans. They proposed that he should be paid eight hundred dollars per annum from some national fund. Paine having consented, Robert Morris wrote to Robert R. Livingston on the subject, and the result was a meeting of these two with Washington, at which the following was framed:

"PHILADELPHIA, Feb. 10, 1782.—The subscribers, taking into consideration the important

---

[1] Sparks' "Diplomatic Correspondence," xii., p. 95.

situation of affairs at the present moment, and the propriety and even necessity of informing the people and rousing them into action; considering also the abilities of Mr. Thomas Paine as a writer, and that he has been of considerable utility to the common cause by several of his publications: They are agreed that it will be much for the interest of the United States that Mr. Paine be engaged in their service for the purpose above mentioned. They are therefore agreed that Mr. Paine be offered a salary of $800 per annum, and that the same be paid him by the Secretary of Foreign Affairs. The salary to commence from this day, and to be paid by the Secretary of Foreign Affairs out of monies to be allowed by the Superintendent of Finance for secret services. The subscribers being of opinion that a salary publicly and avowedly given for the above purpose would injure the effect of Mr. Paine's publications, and subject him to injurious personal reflections.

"ROBT. MORRIS.
"ROBT. LIVINGSTON.
"GO. WASHINGTON."

Before this joint note was written, Paine's pen had been resumed. March 5th is the date of an extended pamphlet, that must long have been in hand. It is introduced by some comments on the King's speech, which concludes with a quotation of Smollett's fearful description of the massacres and rapine which followed the defeat of the Stuarts at Culloden in 1746. This, a memory from Paine's boyhood at Thetford, was an effective comment on the King's expression of his desire "to restore the public tranquillity," though poor George III., who was born in the same year as Paine, would hardly have countenanced such vengeance. He then deals—no doubt after consultation with Robert Morris, Superintendent of Finance— with the whole subject of finance and taxation, in the course of which he sounds a brave note for a more perfect union of the States, which must be the foundation-stone of their independence. As Paine was the first to raise the flag of republican independence he was the first to raise that of a Union which, above the States, should inherit the supremacy wrested from the Crown. These passages bear witness by their nicety to the writer's consciousness that he was touching a sensitive subject. The States were jealous of their " sovereignty," and he could only delicately intimate the necessity of surrendering it. But he manages to say that " each state (with a small *s*) is to the United States what each individual is to the state he lives in. And it is on this grand point, this movement upon one centre, that our existence as a nation, our happiness as a people, and our safety as individuals, depend." He also strikes the federal keynote by saying : " The United States will become heir to an extensive quantity of vacant land "—the doctrine of national inheritance which cost him dear.

Before the Declaration, Paine minted the phrases " Free and Independent States of America," and " The Glorious Union." In his second *Crisis*, dated January 13, 1777, he says to Lord Howe : "'*The* UNITED STATES *of* AMERICA' will sound as pompously in the world or in history as 'the kingdom of Great Britain.'"

The friendliness of Robert Morris to the author is creditable to him. In the Deane controversy, Paine had censured him and other members of Congress for utilizing that agent of the United States to transact their commercial business in Europe. Morris frankly stated the facts, and, though his letter showed irritation, he realized that Paine was no respecter of persons where the American cause was concerned.[1] In 1782 the Revolution required nicest steering. With the port in sight, the people were prone to forget that it is on the coast that dangerous rocks are to be found. Since the surrender of Cornwallis they were over-confident, and therein likely to play into the hands of the enemy, which had lost confidence in its power to conquer the States by arms. England was now making efforts to detach America and France from each other by large inducements. In France Paine was shown by Franklin and Vergennes the overtures that had been made, and told the secret history of the offers of mediation from Russia and Austria. With these delicate

[1] Almon's *Remembrancer* 1778–9, p. 382.

matters he resolved to deal, but before using the documents in his possession consulted Washington and Morris. This, I suppose, was the matter alluded to in a note of March 17, 1782, to Washington, then in Philadelphia :

" You will do me a great deal of pleasure if you can make it convenient to yourself to spend a part of an evening at my apartments, and eat a few oysters or a crust of bread and cheese ; for besides the favour you will do me, I want much to consult with you on a matter of public business, tho' of a secret nature, which I have already mentioned to Mr. Morris, whom I likewise intend to ask, as soon as yourself shall please to mention the evening when."

A similar note was written to Robert Morris four days before. No doubt after due consultation the next *Crisis*, dated May 22, 1782, appeared. It dealt with the duties of the alliance :

" General Conway," he says, " who made the motion in the British parliament for discontinuing *offensive* war in America, is a gentleman of an amiable character. We have no personal quarrel with him. But he feels not as we feel ; he is not in our situation, and that alone without any other explanation is enough. The British parliament suppose they have many friends in America, and that, when all chance of conquest is over, they will be able to draw her from her alliance with France. Now if I have any conception of the human heart, they will fail in this more than in anything that they have yet tried. This part of the business is not a question of policy only, but of honor and honesty."

Paine's next production was a public letter to Sir Guy Carleton, commanding in New York, concerning a matter which gave Washington much anxiety. On April 12th Captain Huddy had been hanged by a band of "refugees," who had sallied from New York into New Jersey (April 12th). The crime was traced to one Captain Lippencott, and, after full consultation with his officers, Washington demanded the murderer. Satisfaction not being given, Washington and his generals determined on retaliation, and Colonel Hazen, who had prisoners under guard at Lancaster, was directed to have an officer of Captain Huddy's rank chosen by lot to suffer death. Hazen included the officers who had capitulated with Cornwallis, though they were expressly relieved from liability to reprisals (Article 14). The lot fell upon one of these, young Captain Asgill (May 27th). It sufficiently proves the formidable character of the excitement Huddy's death had caused in the army that Washington did not at once send Asgill back. The fact that he was one of the capitulation officers was not known outside the military circle. Of this circumstance Paine seems ignorant when he wrote his letter to Sir Guy Carleton, in which he expresses profound sympathy with Captain Huddy, and warns Carleton that by giving sanctuary to the murderer he becomes the real executioner of the innocent youth. Washington was resolved to hang this innocent man, and, distressing as the confession is, no general appears to have warned him of the wrong he was about to commit.[1] But Paine, with well-weighed words, gently withstood the commander, prudently ignoring the legal point, if aware of it.

[1] Historians have evaded this ugly business. I am indebted to the family of General Lincoln, then Secretary of War, for the following letter addressed to him by Washington, June 5, 1782: "Col. Hazen's sending me an officer under the capitulation of Yorktown for the purpose of retaliation has distressed me exceedingly. Be so good as to give me your opinion of the propriety of doing this upon Captain Asgill, if we should be driven to it for want of an unconditional prisoner. Presuming that this matter has been a subject of much conversation, pray with your own let me know the opinions of the most sensible of those with whom you have conversed. Congress by their resolve has unanimously approved of my determination to retaliate. The army have advised it, and the country look for it. But how far is it justifiable upon an officer under the faith of a capitulation, if none other can be had is the question? Hazen's sending Captain Asgill on for this purpose makes the matter more distressing, as the whole business will have the appearance of a farce, if some person is not sacrificed to the mains of poor Huddy; which will be the case if an unconditional prisoner cannot be found, and Asgill escapes. I write you in exceeding great haste; but beg your sentiments may be transmitted as soon as possible (by express), as I may be forced to a decision in the course of a few days.—I am most sincerely and affectionately, D'r Sir, yr. obed't,

"G. WASHINGTON."

"For my own part, I am fully persuaded that a suspension of his fate, still holding it *in terrorem*, will operate on a greater quantity of their passions and vices, and restrain them more, than his execution would do. However, the change of measures which seems now to be taking place, gives somewhat of a new cast to former designs; and if the case, without the execution, can be so managed as to answer all the purposes of the last, it will look much better hereafter, when the sensations that now provoke, and the circumstances which would justify his exit shall be forgotten."

This was written on September 7th, and on the 30th Washington, writing to a member of Congress, for the first time intimates a desire that Asgill shall be released by that body.

In October came from Vergennes a letter, inspired by Marie Antoinette, to whom Lady Asgill had appealed, in which he reminds Washington that the Captain is a prisoner whom the King's arms contributed to surrender into his hands. That he had a right, therefore, to intercede for his life. This letter (of July 29, 1782) was laid before Congress, which at once set Asgill at liberty. Washington was relieved, and wrote the Captain a handsome congratulation.

Although Paine could never find the interval of leisure necessary to write consecutively his "History of the Revolution," it is to a large extent distributed through his writings. From these and his letters a true history of that seven years can be gathered, apart from the details of battles; and even as regards these his contributions are of high importance, notably as regards the retreat across the Delaware, the affairs at Trenton and Princeton, and the skirmishes near Philadelphia following the British occupation of that city. The latter are vividly described in his letter to Franklin (p. 43), and the former in his review of the Abbé Raynal.

In his letter to Washington, of November 30, 1781, Paine mentioned that he had begun "some remarks" on the Abbé's work "On the Revolution of the English Colonies in North America." It was published early in September, 1782. The chief interest of the pamphlet, apart from the passages concerning the military events of 1770, lies in its reflections of events in the nine months during which the paper lingered on his table. In those months he wrote four numbers of the *Crisis*, one of urgent importance on the financial situation. The review of the Abbé's history was evidently written at intervals. As a literary production it is artistic. With the courtliness of one engaged in "an affair of honor," he shakes the Abbé's hand, sympathizes with his misfortune in having his manuscript stolen, and thus denied opportunity to revise the errors for which he must be called to account. His main reason for challenging the historian is an allegation that the Revolution originated in the question "whether the mother country had, or had not, a right to lay, directly or indirectly, a slight tax upon the colonies." The quantity of the tax had nothing to do with it. The tax on tea was a British experiment to test its declaratory Act affirming the right of Parliament "to bind America in all cases whatever," and that claim was resisted in the first stage of its execution. Secondly, the Abbé suffers for having described the affair at Trenton as accidental. Paine's answer is an admirable piece of history. Thirdly, the Abbé suggests that the Americans would probably have accommodated their differences with England when commissioners visited them in April, 1778, but for their alliance with France. Paine affirms that Congress had rejected the English proposals (afterwards brought by the commissioners) on April 22d, eleven days before news arrived of the French alliance.[1] The Abbé is metaphysically

punished for assuming that a French monarchy in aiding defenders of liberty could have no such motive as "the happiness of mankind." Not having access to the archives of France, Paine was able to endow Vergennes with the enthusiasm of Lafayette, and to see in the alliance a new dawning era of international affection. All such alliances are republican The Abbé is leniently dealt with for his clear plagiarisms from Paine, and then left for a lecture to England. That country is advised to form friendship with France and Spain ; to expand its mind beyond its island, and improve its manners. This is the refrain of a previous passage.

"If we take a review of what part Britain has acted we shall find everything which should make a nation blush. The most vulgar abuse, accompanied by that species of haughtiness which distinguishes the hero of a mob from the character of a gentleman ; it was equally as much from her manners as her injustice that she lost the colonies. By the latter she provoked their principle, by the former she wore out their temper ; and it ought to be held out as an example to the world, to show how necessary it is to conduct the business of government with civility."

The close of this essay, written with peace in the air, contains some friendly advice to England. She is especially warned to abandon Canada, which, after loss of the thirteen colonies, will be a constant charge. Canada can never be populous, and of all that is done for it "Britain will sustain the expense, and America reap the advantage."

In a letter dated "Bordentown, September 7, 1782," Paine says to Washington :

"I have the honour of presenting you with fifty copies of my Letter to the Abbé Raynal, for the use of the army, and to repeat to you my acknowledgments for your friendship.

"I fully believe we have seen our worst days

---

[1] Here Paine is more acute than exact. On June 3, 1778, the English Commissioners sent Congress the resolutions for negotiation adopted by Parliament, February 17th. Congress answered that on April 22d it had published its sentiments on these acts. But these sentiments had admitted a willingness to negotiate if Great Britain should "as a preliminary thereto, either withdraw their fleets and armies, or else, in positive and express terms, acknowledge the independence of the said States." But in referring the commissioners (June 6th) to its

manifesto of April 22d, the Congress essentially modified the conditions : it would treat only as an independent nation, and with "sacred regard" to its treaties. On June 17th Congress returned the English Commissioners their proposal (sent on the 9th) unconsidered, because of its insults to their ally.

over. The spirit of the war, on the part of the enemy, is certainly on the decline full as much as we think. I draw this opinion not only from the present promising appearance of things, and the difficulties we know the British Cabinet is in ; but I add to it the peculiar effect which certain periods of time have, more or less, on all men. The British have accustomed themselves to think of *seven years* in a manner different to other portions of time. They acquire this partly by habit, by reason, by religion, and by superstition. They serve seven years' apprenticeship—they elect their parliament for seven years—they punish by seven years' transportation, or the duplicate or triplicate of that term—they let their leases in the same manner, and they read that Jacob served seven years for one wife, and after that seven years for another ; and the same term likewise extinguishes all obligations (in certain cases) of debt, or matrimony : and thus this particular period of time, by a variety of concurrences, has obtained an influence on their mind. They have now had seven years of war, and are no farther on the Continent than when they began. The superstitious and populous part will therefore conclude that *it is not to be*, and the rational part of them will think they have tried an unsuccessful and expensive experiment long enough, and that it is in vain to try it any longer, and by these two joining in the same eventual opinion the obstinate part among them will be beaten out, unless, consistent with their former sagacity, they get over the matter at once by passing a new declaratory Act *to bind Time in all cases whatsoever*, or declare him a rebel."

The rest of this letter is the cautious and respectful warning against the proposed execution of Captain Asgill, quoted elsewhere. Washington's answer is cheerful, and its complimentary close exceptionally cordial.

HEAD-QUARTERS, VERPLANK'S POINT, September 18, 1782.—SIR,—I have the pleasure to acknowledge your favor, informing me of your proposal to present me with fifty copies of your last publication for the amusement of the army. For this intention you have my sincere thanks, not only on my own account, but for the pleasure, which I doubt not the gentlemen of the army will receive from the perusal of your pamphlets. Your observations on the *period of seven years*, as it applies itself to and affects British minds, are ingenious, and I wish it may not fail of its effects in the present instance. The measures and the policy of the enemy are at present in great perplexity and embarrassment—but I have my fears, whether their necessities (which are the only operating motives with them, are yet arrived to that point, which must drive them unavoidably into what they will esteem disagreeable and dishonorable terms of peace,—such,

for instance, as an absolute, unequivocal admission of American independence, upon the terms on which she can accept it. For this reason, added to the obstinacy of the King, and the probable consonant principles of some of the principal ministers, I have not so full a confidence in the success of the present negociation for peace as some gentlemen entertain. Should events prove my jealousies to be ill founded, I shall make myself happy under the mistake, consoling myself with the idea of having erred on the safest side, and enjoying with as much satisfaction as any of my countrymen the pleasing issue of our severe contest.

"The case of Captain Asgill has indeed been spun out to a great length—but, with you, I hope that its termination will not be unfavourable to this country.

"I am, sir, with great esteem and regard,
"Your most obedient servant,
"G. WASHINGTON."

A copy of the answer to the Abbé Raynal was sent by Paine to Lord Shelburne, and with it in manuscript his newest *Crisis*, dated October 29, 1782. This was suggested by his lordship's speech of July 10th, in which he was reported to have said : "The independence of America would be the ruin of England." "Was America then," asks Paine, "the giant of empire, and England only her dwarf in waiting?[1] Is the case so strangely altered, that those who once thought we could not live without them are now brought to declare that they cannot exist without us ? "

Paine's prediction that it would be a seven years' war was nearly true. There was indeed a dismal eighth year, the army not being able to disband until the enemy had entirely left the country,—a year when peace seemed to "break out" like another war. The army, no longer uplifted by ardors of conflict with a foreign foe, became conscious of its hunger, its nakedness, and the prospect of returning in rags to pauperized homes. They saw all the civil officers of the country paid, while those who had defended them were unpaid ; and the

[1] Paine was here repeating a simile used by Mr. Wedderburne about the year 1776. "*Relinquish America !*" says he. '*What is it but to desire a giant to shrink spontaneously into a dwarf?*" See *Crisis*, vol. i, p. 363, "Writings of Thomas Paine." (Conway.)—H. B. B.

only explanations that could be offered —the inability of Congress, and incoherence of the States—formed a new peril. The only hope of meeting an emergency fast becoming acute, was the unanimous adoption by the States of the proposal of Congress for a five-per-cent. duty on imported articles, the money to be applied to the payment of interest on loans to be made in Holland. Several of the States had been dilatory in their consent, but Rhode Island absolutely refused, and Paine undertook to reason with that State. In the *Providence Gazette*, December 21st, appeared the following note, dated " Philadelphia, November 27, 1782 " :

" SIR,—Inclosed I send you a Philadelphia paper of this day's date, and desire you to insert the piece signed ' A Friend to Rhode Island and the Union.' I am concerned that Rhode Island should make it necessary to address a piece to her, on a subject which the rest of the States are agreed in.—Yours &c. Thomas Paine."

The insertion of Paine's letter led to a fierce controversy, the immediate subject of which is hardly of sufficient importance to detain us long.[1] Yet this controversy, which presently carried Paine to Providence, where he wrote and published six letters, raised into general discussion the essential principles of Union. Rhode Island's jealousy of its " sovereignty "—in the inverse ratio of its size,—made it the last to enter a Union which gave it equal legislative power with the greatest States ; it need not be wondered then that at this earlier period, when sovereignty and self-interest combined, our pioneer of nationality had to undergo some martyrdom. " What," he asked, " would the sovereignty of any individual state be, if left to itself to contend with a foreign power ? It is on our united sovereignty that our greatness and safety, and the

[1] It may be traced through the *Providence Gazette* of December 21, 28 (1782), January 4, 11, 18, 25, February 1 (1783) ; also in the *Newport Mercury*. Paine writes under the signature of " A Friend to Rhode Island and the Union." I am indebted to Professor Jamieson of Brown University for assistance in this investigation.

security of our foreign commerce, rest. This united sovereignty then must be something more than a name, and requires to be as completely organized for the line it is to act in as that of any individual state, and, if anything, more so, because more depends on it." He received abuse, and such ridicule as this (February 1st) :

" In the Name of Common Sense, Amen, I, Thomas Paine, having according to appointment, proceeded with all convenient speed to answer the objections to the five per cent, by endeavouring to cover the design and blind the subject, before I left Philadelphia, and having proceeded to a *convenient* place of action in the State of Rhode Island, and there republished my first letter," etc.

In the same paper with this appeared a letter of self-defence from Paine, who speaks of the personal civility extended to him in Rhode Island, but of proposals to stop his publications. He quotes a letter of friendship from Colonel Laurens, who gave him his war-horse, and an equally cordial one from General Nathaniel Greene, Rhode Island's darling hero, declaring that he should be rewarded for his public services.

This visit to Rhode Island was the last work which Paine did in pursuance of his engagement, which ended with the resignation of Morris in January. Probably Paine received under it one year's salary, $800—certainly no more. I think that during the time he kept his usual signature, " Common Sense," sacred to his individual " testimonies."

On his return to Philadelphia Paine wrote a memorial to Chancellor Livingston, Secretary for Foreign Affairs, Robert Morris, Minister of Finance, and his assistant Gouverneur Morris, urging the necessity of adding " a Continental Legislature to Congress, to be elected by the several States." Robert Morris invited the Chancellor and a number of eminent men to meet Paine at dinner, where his plea for a stronger union was discussed and approved. This was probably the earliest of a series of consultations preliminary to the constitutional Convention.

The newspaper combat in Rhode Island, which excited general attention, and the continued postponement of all prospect of paying the soldiers, had a formidable effect on the army. The anti-republican elements of the country, after efforts to seduce Washington, attempted to act without him. In confronting the incendiary efforts of certain officers at Newburg to turn the army of liberty into mutineers against it, Washington is seen winning his noblest victory after the revolution had ended. He not only subdued the reactionary intrigues, but the supineness of the country, which had left its soldiers in a condition that played into the intriguers' hands.

On April 18th Washington formerly announced the cessation of hostilities. On April 19th—eighth anniversary of the collision at Lexington—Paine printed the little pamphlet entitled "Thoughts on Peace and the Probable Advantages Thereof," included in his works as the last *Crisis*. It opens with the words : "The times that tried men's souls are over—and the greatest and completest revolution the world ever knew, gloriously and happily accomplished." He again, as in his first pamphlet, pleads for a supreme nationality, absorbing all cherished sovereignties. This is Paine's " farewell address."

" It was the cause of America that made me an author. The force with which it struck my mind, and the dangerous condition the country ap eared to me in, by courting an imp ssible and an unnatural reconciliation with those who were determined to reduce her. instead of striking out into the only line that could cement and save her, a Declaration of Independence, made it impossible for me, feeling as I did, to be silent : and if, in the course of more than seven years, I have rendered her any service, I have likewise added something to the reputation of literature, by freely and disinterestedly employing it in the great cause of mankind. . . . But as the scenes of war are closed, and every man preparing for home and happier times, I therefore take my leave of the subject. I have most sincerely followed it from beginning to end, and through all its turns and windings : and whatever country I may hereafter be in, I shall always feel an honest pride at the part I have taken and acted, and a gratitude to nature and providence for putting it in my power to be of some use to mankind."

CHAPTER XIV

GREAT WASHINGTON AND POOR PAINE

THE world held no other man so great and so happy as Washington, in September, 1783,—the month of final peace. Congress, then sitting at Princeton, had invited him to consult with them on the arrangements necessary for a time of peace, and prepared a mansion for him at Rocky Hill. For a time the General gave himself up to hilarity, as ambassadors of congratulation gathered from every part of the world. A glimpse of the festivities is given by David Howell of Rhode Island in a letter to Governor Greene.

" The President, with all the present members, chaplains, and great officers of Congress, had the honor of dining at the General's table last Friday. The tables were spread under a marquise or tent taken from the British. The repast was elegant, but the General's company crowned the whole. As I had he good fortune to be seated facing the General, I had the pleasure of hearing all his conversation. The President of Congress was seated on his right, and the Minister of France on his left. I observed with much pleasure that the General's front was uncommonly open and pleasant ; the contracted, pensive phiz betokening deep thought and much care, which I noticed at Prospect Hill in 1775, is done away, and a pleasant smile and sparkling vivacity of wit and humour succeeds. On the President observing that in the present situation of our affairs he believed that Mr. [Robert] Morris had his hands full, the General replied at the same instant, ' he wished he had his pockets full too.' On Mr. Peters observing that the man who made these cups (for we drank wine out of silver cups) was turned a Quaker preacher, the General replied that 'he wished he had turned a Quaker preacher before he made the cups.' You must also hear the French Minister's remark on the General's humor—'You tink de penitence wou'd have been good for de cups.' Congress has ordered an Egyptian statue of General Washington, to be erected at the place where they may establish their permanent residence. No honors short of those which the Deity vindicates to himself can be too great for Gen. Washington."

At this time Paine sat in his little home in Bordentown, living on his crust. He had put most of his savings in this house (on two-tenths of an acre) so as to be near his friend Col. Joseph Kirkbride. The Colonel was also of Quaker origin, and a hearty sympathizer with Paine's principles. They had together helped to frame the democratic constitution of Pennsylvania (1776), had fought side by side, and both had scientific tastes. Since the burning of his house, Bellevue (Bucks), Colonel Kirkbride had moved to Bordentown, N.J., and lived at Hill Top, now part of a female college. A part of Paine's house also stands. At Bordentown also resided Mr. Hall, who had much mechanical skill, and whom he had found eager to help him in constructing models of his inventions. To such things he now meant to devote himself, but before settling down permanently he longed to see his aged parents and revisit his English friends. For this, however, he had not means. Robert Morris advised Paine to call the attention of Congress to various unremunerated services. His secretaryship of the Foreign Affairs Committee, terminated by an admitted injustice to him, had been burdensome and virtually unpaid; its nominal $70 per month was really about $15. His perilous journey to France, with young Laurens, after the millions that wrought wonders, had not brought him even a paper dollar. Paine, therefore, on June 7th, wrote to Elias Boudinot, President of Congress, stating that though for his services he had "neither sought, received, nor stipulated any honors, advantages, or emoluments," he thought Congress should

inquire into them. The letter had some effect, but meanwhile Paine passed three months of poverty and gloom, and had no part in the festivities at Princeton.

One day a ray from that festive splendour shone in his humble abode. The great Commander had not forgotten his unwearied fellow-soldier, and wrote him a letter worthy to be engraved on the tombs of both.

"ROCKY HILL, Sept. 10, 1783.

" DEAR SIR,

"I have learned since I have been at this place, that you are at Bordentown. Whether for the sake of retirement or economy, I know not. Be it for either, for both, or whatever it may, if you will come to this place, and partake with me, I shall be exceedingly happy to see you.

"Your presence may remind Congress of your past services to this country; and if it is in my power to impress them, command my best services with freedom, as they will be rendered cheerfully by one who entertains a lively sense of the importance of your works, and who, with much pleasure, subscribes himself,

"Your sincere friend,

" G. WASHINGTON."

The following was Paine's reply :—

"BORDEN TOWN, Sept. 21st.—SIR,—I am made exceedingly happy by the receipt of your friendly letter of the 10th instant, which is this moment come to hand; and the young gentleman that brought it, a son of Col. Geo. Morgan, waits while I write this. It had been sent to Philadelphia, and on my not being there, was returned, agreeable to directions on the outside, to Col. Morgan at Princetown, who forwarded it to this place.

"I most sincerely thank you for your good wishes and friendship to me, and the kind invitation you have honoured me with, which I shall with much pleasure accept.

"On the resignation of Mr. Livingston in the winter and likewise of Mr. R. Morris, at [the same] time it was judged proper to discontinue the matter which took place when you were in Philadelphia.[1] It was at the same time a pleasure to me to find both these gentlemen (to whom I was before that time but little known) so warmly disposed to assist in rendering my situation permanent, and Mr. Livingston's letter to me, in answer to one of mine to him, which I enclose, will serve to show that his friendship to me is in concurrence with yours.

"By the advice of Mr. Morris I presented a letter to Congress expressing a request that they would be pleased to direct me to lay before

[1] See page 74.

them an account of what my services, such as they were, and situation, had been during the course of the war. This letter was referred to a committee, and their report is now before Congress, and contains, as I am informed, a recommendation that I be appointed historiographer to the continent.[1] I have desired some members that the further consideration of it be postponed, until I can state to the committee some matters which I wish them to be acquainted with, both with regard to myself and the appointment. And as it was my intention, so I am now encouraged by your friendship to take your confidential advice upon it before I present it. For though I was never at a loss in writing on public matters, I feel exceedingly so in what respects myself.

"I am hurt by the neglect of the collective ostensible body of America, in a way which it is probable they do not perceive my feelings. It has an effect in putting either my reputation or their generosity at stake ; for it cannot fail of suggesting that either I (notwithstanding the appearance of service) have been undeserving their regard or that they are remiss towards me. Their silence is to me something like condemnation, and their neglect must be justified by my loss of reputation, or my reputation supported at their injury ; either of which is alike painful to me. But as I have ever been dumb on everything which might touch national honor so I mean ever to continue so.

"Wishing you, Sir, the happy enjoyment of peace and every public and private felicity I remain &c.

"THOMAS PAINE.

"Col. Kirkbride at whose house I am, desires me to present you his respectful compliments."

Paine had a happy visit at Washington's headquarters, where he met old revolutionary comrades, among them Humphreys, Lincoln, and Cobb. He saw Washington set the river on fire on Guy Fawkes Day with a roll of cartridge-paper. When American art is more mature we may have a picture of war making way for science, illustrated by the night-scene of Washington and Paine on a scow, using their cartridge-paper to fire the gas released from the river-bed by soldiers with poles![2]

There was a small party in Congress which looked with sullen jealously on Washington's friendliness with Paine.

[1] This had been Washington's suggestion.
[2] See Paine's essay on "The Cause of the Yellow Fever." These experiments on the River at Rocky Hill were followed by others in Philadelphia, with Rittenhouse.

The States, since the conclusion of the war, were already withdrawing into their several shells of "sovereignty," while Paine was arguing with everybody that there could be no sovereignty but that of the United States,—and even that was merely the supremacy of Law. The arguments in favor of the tax imposed by Congress, which he had used in Rhode Island, were repeated in his last *Crisis* (April 19th), and it must have been under Washington's roof at Rocky Hill that he wrote his letter "To the People of America" (dated December 9th), in which a high national doctrine was advocated. This was elicited by Lord Sheffield's pamphlet, "Observations on the Commerce of the United States," which had been followed by a prohibition of commerce with the West Indies in American bottoms. Lord Sheffield had said : "It will be a long time before the American States can be brought to act as a nation ; neither are they to be feared as such by us." Paine calls the attention of Rhode Island to this, and says : "America is now sovereign and independent, and ought to conduct her affairs in a regular style of character." She has a perfect right of commercial retaliation.

"But it is only by acting in union that the usurpations of foreign nations on the freedom of trade can be counteracted, and security extended to the commerce of America. And when we view a flag, which to the eye is beautiful, and to contemplate its rise and origin inspires a sensation of sublime delight, our national honor must unite with our interest to prevent injury to the one, or insult to the other."

Noble as these sentiments now appear, they then excited alarm in certain Congressmen, and it required all Washington's influence to secure any favourable action in Paine's case. In 1784, however, New York presented Paine with "two hundred and seventy-seven acres, more or less, which became forfeited to and vested in the People of this State by the conviction of Frederick Devoe."[3]

[3] The indenture, made June 16, 1784, is in the Register's Office of Westchester County, Vol. T.

With such cheerful prospects, national and personal, Paine rose into song, as appears by the following letter (" New York, April 28th ") to Washington :

DEAR SIR,—As I hope to have in a few days the honor and happiness of seeing you well at Philadelphia, I shall not trouble you with a long letter.

" It was my intention to have followed you on to Philadelphia, but when I recollected the friendship you had shewn to me, and the pains you had taken to promote my interests, and knew likewise the untoward disposition of two or three Members of Congress, I felt an exceeding unwillingness that your friendship to me should be put to further tryals, or that you should experience the mortification of having your wishes disappointed, especially by one to whom delegation is his daily bread.

" While I was pondering on these matters, Mr. Duane and some other friends of yours and mine, who were persuaded that nothing would take place in Congress (as a single man when only nine states were present could stop the whole), proposed a new line which is to leave it to the States individually ; and a unanimous resolution has passed the senate of this State, which is generally expressive of their opinion and friendship. What they have proposed is worth at least a thousand guineas, and other States will act as they see proper. If I do but get enough to carry me decently thro' the world and independently thro' the History of the Revolution, I neither wish nor care for more ; and that the States may very easily do if they are disposed to it. The State of Pennsylvania might have done it alone.

" I present you with a new song for the Cincinnati ; and beg to offer you a remark on that subject.[1] The intention of the name appears to me either to be lost or not understood. For it is material to the future freedom of the country that the example of the late army retiring to private life, on the principles of Cincinnatus, should he commemorated, that in future ages it may be imitated. Whether every

part of the institution is perfectly consistent with a republic is another question, but the precedent ought not to be lost.

" I have not yet heard of any objection in the Assembly of this State, to the resolution of the Senate, and I am in hopes there will be none made. Should the method succeed, I shall stand perfectly clear of Congress, which will be an agreeable circumstance to me ; because whatever I may then say on the necessity of strengthening the union, and enlarging its powers, will come from me with a much better grace than if Congress had made the acknowledgment themselves.

" If you have a convenient opportunity I should be much obliged to you to mention this subject to Mr. President Dickinson. I have two reasons for it, the one is my own interest and circumstances, the other is on account of the State, for what with their parties and contentions, they have acted to me with a churlish selfishness, which I wish to conceal unless they force it from me.

" As I see by the papers you are settling a tract of land, I enclose you a letter I received from England on the subject of settlements. I think lands might be disposed of in that country to advantage. I am, dear Sir, &c."

The estate at New Rochelle had a handsome house on it (once a patrimonial mansion of the Jays), and Paine received distinguished welcome when he went to take possession. This he reciprocated, but he did not remain long at New Rochelle.[2] Bordentown had become his home ; he had found there a congenial circle of friends,— proved such during his poverty. He was not, indeed, entirely relieved of poverty by the New York *honorarium*, but he had expectation that the other

---

of Grantees, p. 163. The confiscated estate of the loyalist Devoe is the well-known one at New Rochelle on which Paine's monument stands. I am indebted for investigations at White Plains, and documents relating to the estate, to my friend George Hoadly, and Mr. B. Davis Washburn.

[1] Paine wrote four patriotic American Songs : " Hail, Great Republic of the World " (tune " Rule Britannia ") ; " To Columbia, who Gladly Reclined at her Ease " ; " Ye Sons of Columbia, who Bravely have Fought,"—both of the latter being for the tune of " Anacreon in Heaven " ; and " Liberty Tree " (tune " Gods of the Greeks "), beginning, " In a chariot of light, from the regions of Day," etc.

[2] " An old lady, now a boarding-house keeper in Cedar Street, remembers when a girl visiting Mr. Paine when he took possession of his house and farm at New Rochelle, and gave a village fête on the occasion ; she then only knew him as ' Common Sense,' and supposed that was his name. On that day he had something to say to everybody, and young as she was she received a portion of his attention ; while he sat in the shade, and assisted in the labor of the feast, by cutting or breaking sugar to be used in some agreeable liquids by his guests. Mr. Paine was then, if not handsome, a fine agreeable looking man."—*Vale*, 1841. The original house was accidentally destroyed by fire, while Paine was in the French Convention. The present house was, however, occupied by him after his return to America.

States would follow the example. In a letter to Jefferson also Paine explained his reason for desiring that the States, rather than Congress, should remunerate him. That Washington appreciated this motive appears by letters to Richard Henry Lee and James Madison.

"MOUNT VERNON, June 12th.—Unsollicited by, and unknown to Mr. Paine, I take the liberty of hinting the services and the distressed (for so I think it may be called) situation of that Gentleman.

"That his Common Sense, and many of his Crisis, were well timed and had a happy effect upon the public mind, none, I believe, who will recur to the epocha's at which they were published will deny.—That his services hitherto have passed of [f] unnoticed is obvious to all ;— and that he is chagreened and necessitous I will undertake to aver.—Does not common justice then point to some compensation ?

"He is not in circumstances to refuse the bounty of the public. New York, not the least distressed nor most able State in the Union, has set the example. He prefers the benevolence of the States individually to an allowance from Congress, for reasons which are conclusive in his own mind, and such as I think may be approved by others. His views are moderate, a decent independency is, I believe, the height of his ambition, and if you view his services in the American cause in the same important light that I do, I am sure you will have pleasure in obtaining it for him.—I am with esteem and regard, Dr. sir, yr. most obdt. servt.,
              "GEORGE WASHINGTON."[1]

"MOUNT VERNON, June 12th.—DEAR SIR,— Can nothing be done in our Assembly for poor Paine? Must the merits and services of *Common Sense* continue to glide down the stream of time, unrewarded by this country?

"His writings certainly have had a powerful effect on the public mind,—ought they not then to meet an adequate return? He is poor! he is chagreened! and almost if not altogether in despair of relief.

"New York, it is true, not the least distressed nor best able State in the Union, has done something for him. This kind of provision he prefers to an allowance from Congress, he has reasons for it, which to him are conclusive, and such, I think, as would have weight with others. His views are moderate—a decent independency is, I believe, all he aims at. Should he not obtain this? If you think so I am sure you will not only move the matter but give it your support. For me it only remains to feel for his situation and to assure you of the sincere esteem and

regard with which I have the honour to be, D Sir,
          "Yr. Most Obedt. Humble Servt.,
                    "G. WASHINGTON.[2]
"JAMES MADISON, Esq."

A similar letter was written to Patrick Henry and perhaps to others. A bill introduced into the Virginia Legislature (June 28th) to give Paine a tract of land, being lost on the third reading, Madison (June 30th) offered a "bill for selling the public land in the county of Northampton, called the Secretary's land, and applying part of the money arising therefrom to the purchase of a tract to be vested in Thomas Payne and his heirs." The result is described by Madison (July 2d) to Washington :

"The easy reception it found, induced the friends of the measure to add the other moiety to the proposition, which would have raised the market value of the donation to about four thousand pounds, or upwards, though it would not probably have commanded a rent of more than one hundred pounds per annum. In this form the bill passed through two readings. The third reading proved that the tide had suddenly changed, for the bill was thrown out by a large majority. An attempt was next made to sell the land in question, and apply two thousand pounds of the money to the purchase of a farm for Mr. Paine. This was lost by a single voice. Whether a greater disposition to reward patriotic and distinguished exertions of genius will be found on any succeeding occasion, is not for me to predetermine. Should it finally appear that the merits of the man, whose writings have so much contributed to enforce and foster the spirit of independence in the people of America, are unable to inspire them with a just beneficence, the world, it is to be feared, will give us as little credit for our policy as for gratitude in this particular."

R. H. Lee—unfortunately not present, because of illness—writes Washington (July 22d) :

"I have been told that it miscarried from its being observed that he had shown enmity to this State by having written a pamphlet injurious to our claim of Western Territory. It has ever appeared to me that this pamphlet was the consequence of Mr. Paine's being himself imposed upon, and that it was rather the fault of the place than the man."[3]

---

[1] I found this letter (to Lee) among the Franklin MSS. in the Philosophical Society, Philadelphia.

[2] I am indebted for this letter to Mr. Frederick McGuire, of Washington.

[3] "Arthur Lee was most responsible for the failure of the measure, for he was active in culti-

So the news came that Virginia had snubbed Paine, at the moment of voting a statue to Washington. But his powerful friend did not relax his efforts, and he consulted honest John Dickinson, President of Pennsylvania. Under date of November 27th, the following was written by Paine to General Irwin, Vice-President of Pennsylvania:

"The President has made me acquainted with a Conversation which General Washington had with him at their last interview respecting myself, and he is desirous that I should communicate to you his wishes, which are, that as he stands engaged on the General's request to recommend to the Assembly, so far as lies in his power, their taking into consideration the part I have acted during the war, that you would join your assistance with him in the measure.— Having thus, Sir, opened the matter to you in general terms, I will take an opportunity at some time convenient to yourself to state it to you more fully, as there are many parts in it that are not publicly known.—I shall have the pleasure of seeing you at the President's to-day to dine and in the mean time I am etc."

On December 6th the Council sent this message to the General Assembly of Pennsylvania:

"GENTLEMEN: The President having reported in Council a conversation between General Washington and himself respecting Mr. Thomas Paine, we have thereby been induced to take the services and situation of that gentleman at this time into our particular consideration.

"Arriving in America just before the war broke out, he commenced his residence here, and became a citizen of this Commonwealth by taking the oath of allegiance at a very early period. So important were his services during the late contest, that those persons whose own merits in the course of it have been the most distinguished concur with a highly honourable unanimity in entertaining sentiments of esteem for him, and interesting themselves in his deserts. It is unnecessary for us to enlarge on this subject. If the General Assembly shall be pleased to appoint a Committee, they will receive information that we doubt not will in every respect prove satisfactory.

vating a prejudice against Paine. This was somewhat ungracious, as Paine had befriended Lee in his controversy with Deane."—Ford's "Writings of Washington," x., p. 395. Had there been any belief at this time that Paine had been paid for writing the pamphlet objected to, "Public Good," it would no doubt have been mentioned.

"We confide that you will, then, feel the attention of Pennsylvania is drawn towards Mr. Paine by motives equally grateful to the human heart, and reputable to the Republic; and that you will join with us in the opinion that a suitable acknowledgment of his eminent services, and a proper provision for the continuance of them in an independent manner, should be made on the part of this State."

Pennsylvania promptly voted to Paine £500,—a snug little fortune in those days.

Paine thus had a happy New Year. Only two States had acted, but they had made him independent. Meanwhile Congress also was willing to remunerate him, but he had put difficulties in the way. He desired, as we have seen, to be independent of that body, and wished it only to pay its debts to him; but one of these—his underpaid secretaryship—would involve overhauling the Paine-Deane case again. Perhaps that was what Paine desired; had the matter been passed on again the implied censures of Paine on the journal of Congress would have been reversed. When therefore a gratuity was spoken of Paine interfered, and wrote to Congress, now sitting in New York, asking leave to submit his accounts. This letter was referred to a committee (Gerry, Pettit, King).

"Mr. Gerry," says Paine, "came to me and said that the Committee had consulted on the subject, and they intended to bring in a handsome report, but that they thought it best not to take any notice of your letter, or make any reference to Deane's affair, or your salary. They will indemnify you without it. The case is, there are some motions on the journals of Congress for censuring you, with respect to Deane's affair, which cannot now be recalled, because they have been printed. Therefore [we] will bring in a report that will supersede them without mentioning the purport of your letter."

On the committee's report Congress resolved (August 26th):

"That the early, unsolicited, and continued labors of Mr. Thomas Paine, in explaining and enforcing the principles of the late revolution by ingenious and timely publications upon the nature of liberty, and civil government, have been well received by the citizens of these States, and merit the approbation of Congress;

and that in consideration of these services, and the benefits produced thereby, Mr. Paine is entitled to a liberal gratification from the United States."

This of course was not what Paine wished, and he again (September 27th) urged settlement of his accounts. But, on October 3d, Congress ordered the Treasurer to pay Paine $3,000, " for the considerations mentioned in the resolution of the 26th of August last." " It was," Paine maintained to the last, " an indemnity to me for some injustice done me, for Congress had acted dishonorably by me." The Committee had proposed $6,000, but the author's enemies had managed to reduce it. The sum paid was too small to cover Paine's journey to France with Laurens, which was never repaid.

The services of Thomas Paine to the American cause cannot, at this distance of time, be estimated by any records of them, nor by his printed works. They are best measured in the value set on them by the great leaders most cognizant of them, — by Washington, Franklin, Jefferson, Adams, Madison, Robert Morris, Chancellor Livingston, R. H. Lee, Colonel Laurens, General Greene, Dickinson. Had there been anything dishonourable or mercenary in Paine's career, these are the men who would have known it ; but their letters are searched in vain for even the faintest hint of anything disparaging to his patriotic self-devotion during those eight weary years. Their letters, however, already quoted in these pages, and others omitted, show plainly that they believed that all the States owed Paine large " returns (as Madison wrote to Washington) of gratitude for voluntary services," and that these services were not merely literary. Such was the verdict of the men most competent to pass judgment on the author, the soldier, the secretary. It can never be reversed.

To the radical of to-day, however, Paine will seem to have fared pretty well for a free lance ; and he could now beat all his lances into bridge iron, without sparing any for the wolf that had haunted his door.

CHAPTER XV

PONTIFICAL AND POLITICAL INVENTIONS

PAINE was the literary lion in New York—where Congress sat in 1785— and was especially intimate with the Nicholsons, whose house was the social *salon* of leading republicans.[1] One may easily read between the lines of the following note to Franklin that the writer is having "a good time" in New York, where it was written September 23d :

"MY DEAR SIR,—It gives me exceeding great pleasure to have the opportunity of congratulating you on your return home, and to a land of Peace ; and to express to you my heartfelt wishes that the remainder of your days may be to you a time of happy ease and rest.

[1] " Commodore Nicholson was an active republican politician in the city of New York, and his house was a headquarters for the men of his way of thinking. The young ladies' letters are full of allusions to the New York society of that day, and to calls from Aaron Burr, the Livingstons, the Clintons, and many others. . . . An other man still more famous in some respects was a frequent visitor at their house. It is now almost forgotten that Thomas Paine, down to the time of his departure for Europe in 1787, was a fashionable member of society, admired and courted as the greatest literary genius of his

day. . . . Here is a little autograph, found among the papers of Mrs. Gallatin [*née* Nicholson] ; its address is to : ' Miss Hannah N., at the Lord knows where.—You Mistress Hannah if you don't come home, I'll come and fetch you. T. PAINE.' "—Adams' " Life of Gallatin."

Should Fate prolong my life to the extent of yours, it would give me the greatest felicity to have the evening scene some resemblance of what you now enjoy.

"In making you this address I have an additional pleasure in reflecting, that, so far as I have hitherto gone, I am not conscious of any circumstance in my conduct that should give you one repentant thought for being my patron and introducer to America.

"It would give me great pleasure to make a journey to Philadelphia on purpose to see you, but an interesting affair I have with Congress makes my absence at this time improper.

"If you have time to let me know how your health is, I shall be much obliged to you.

"I am, dear Sir, with the sincerest affection and respect,

"Your obedient, humble servant,
"THOMAS PAINE.

"The Hon'ble BENJAMIN FRANKLIN, Esquire.

"My address is Messrs. Lawrence and Morris, Merchants."

To this came the following reply, dated Philadelphia, September 24th :

"DEAR SIR,—I have just received your friendly congratulations on my return to America, for which, as well as your kind wishes for my welfare, I beg you to accept my most thankful acknowledgments. Ben is also very sensible of your politeness, and desires his respects may be presented.

"I was sorry on my arrival to find you had left this city. Your present arduous undertaking, I easily conceive, demands retirement, and tho' we shall reap the fruits of it, I cannot help regretting the want of your abilities here where in the present moment they might, I think, be successfully employed. Parties still run very high —Common Sense would unite them. It is to be hoped therefore it has not abandoned us forever."[1]

---

[1] The remainder of the letter (MS. Philosoph. Soc., Philadelphia) seems to be in the writing of William Temple Franklin, to whom probably Paine had enclosed a note : "Mr. Williams whom you inquire after accompanied us to America, and is now here. We left Mrs. Wms. and her sisters well at St. Ger's, but they proposed shortly returning to England to live with their uncle, Mr. J. Alexander, who has entirely settled his affairs with Mr. Walpole and the Bank. Mr. Wm. Alex'r I suppose you know is in Virginia fulfilling his tobacco contract with the Farmer Gen'l. The Marquis la Fayette we saw a few days before we left Passy—he was well and on the point of setting off on an excursion into Germany, and a visit to the Emperor K. of Prussia.—I purpose shortly being at New York, where I will with pleasure give you any further information you may wish, and shall be very

The "arduous undertaking" to which Franklin refers was of course the iron bridge. But it will be seen by our next letter that Paine had another invention to lay before Franklin, to whom he hastened after receiving his $3,000 from Congress :

"Dec. 31, 1785.—DEAR SIR,—I send you the Candles I have been making ;—In a little time after they are lighted the smoke and flame separate, the one issuing from one end of the Candle, and the other from the other end. I suppose this to be because a quantity of air enters into the Candle between the Tallow and the flame, and in its passage downwards takes the smoke with it ; for if you allow a quantity of air up the Candle, the current will be changed, and the smoke reascends, and in passing this the flame makes a small flash and a little noise.

"But to express the Idea I mean, of the smoke descending more clearly it is this,—that the air enters the Candle in the very place where the melted tallow is getting into the state of flame, and takes it down before the change is completed—for there appears to me to be two kinds of smoke, humid matter which never can be flame, and enflameable matter which would be flame if some accident did not prevent the change being completed—and this I suppose to be the case with the descending smoke of the Candle.

"As you can compare the Candle with the Lamp, you will have an opportunity of ascertaining the cause—why it will do in the one and not in the other. When the edge of the enflamed part of the wick is close with the edge of the Tin of the Lamp no counter current of air can enter—but as this contact does not take place in the Candle a counter current enters and prevents the effect [?] in the candles which illuminates the Lamp. For the passing of the air thro' the Lamp does not, I imagine, burn the smoke, but burns up all the oil into flame, or by its rapidity prevents any part of the oil flying off in the state of half-flame which is smoke.

"I do not, my Dear Sir, offer these reasons to you but to myself, for I have often observed that by lending words for my thoughts I understand my thoughts the better. Thoughts are a kind of mental smoke, which require words to illuminate them.

"I am affectionately
your Obt. & Hble. servant,
"THOMAS PAINE.

"I hope to be well enough tomorrow to wait on you."

---

happy to cultivate the acquaintance and friendship of Mr. Paine, for whose character I have a sincere regard and of whose services I, as an American, have a grateful sense."

Paine had now to lay aside his iron arch and bridge a financial flood. A party had arisen in Philadelphia, determined to destroy the "Bank of North America." Paine had confidence in this bank, and no one knew its history better, for it had grown out of the subscription he headed (May, 1780) with $500 for the relief of Washington's suffering army. It had been incorporated by Congress, and ultimately by Pennsylvania, April 1, 1782. Investments and deposits by and in the Bank had become very large, and to repeal its charter was to violate a contract. The attack was in the interest of paper money, of which there was a large issue. The repeal had to be submitted to popular suffrage, and even Cheetham admits that Paine's pamphlet "probably averted the act of despotism." The pamphlet was entitled, "Dissertations on Government, the Affairs of the Bank, and Paper Money" (54 pages 8vo). It was written and printed, Paine says in his preface (dated February 18, 1786), "during the short recess of the Assembly." This was between December 22d and February 26th.

The first fourteen pages of the work are devoted to a consideration of general principles. Englishmen who receive their constitutional instruction from Walter Bagehot and Albert Dicey will find in this introduction by Paine the foundation of their Republic. In discussing "sovereignty" he points out that the term, when applied to a people, has a different meaning from the arbitrariness it signifies in a monarchy. "Despotism may be more effectually acted by many over a few, than by one over all." "A republic is a sovereignty of justice, in contradistinction to a sovereignty of will." The distinct powers of the legislature are stated—those of legislation and those of agency. "All laws are acts, but all acts are not laws." Laws are for every individual; they may be altered. Acts of agency or negotiation are deeds and contracts.

"The greatness of one party cannot give it a superiority or advantage over the other. The state or its representative, the assembly, has no more power over an act of this kind, after it has passed, than if the state was a private person. It is the glory of a republic to have it so, because it secures the individual from becoming the prey of power, and prevents might from overcoming right. If any difference or dispute arise between the state and the individuals with whom the agreement is made respecting the contract, or the meaning or extent of any of the matters contained in the act, which may affect the property or interest of either, such difference or dispute must be judged of and decided upon by the laws of the land, in a court of justice and trial by jury; that is, by the laws of the land already in being at the time such act and contract was made."

"That this is justice," adds Paine, "that it is the true principle of republican government, no man will be so hardy as to deny." So, indeed, it seemed in those days. In the next year those principles were embodied in the Constitution; and in 1792, when a State pleaded its sovereign right to repudiate a contract ("Chisholm *vs.* Georgia"), the Supreme Court affirmed every contention of Paine's pamphlet, using his ideas and sometimes his very phrases.

Our first Attorney-General (Edmund Randolph, of Virginia) eloquently maintained that the inferiority of one party, or dignity of the other, could not affect the balances of justice. Individuals could not be left the victims of States. So it was decided. Justice Wilson remarked that the term sovereignty is unknown to the Constitution: "The term 'sovereign' has for its correlative, 'subject.'" A State contracting as a merchant cannot, when asked to fulfil its contract, take refuge in its "sovereignty." "The rights of individuals," said Justice Cushing, "and the justice due to them are as dear and precious as those of States. Indeed the latter are founded on the former; and the great end and object of them must be to secure and support the rights of individuals, or else vain is government."[1] But the decline of republicanism set in; the shameful Eleventh Amend-

[1] See "Omitted Chapters of History Disclosed in the Life and Papers of Edmund Randolph," Chap. XVIII., for a full history of this subject.

ment was adopted; Chisholm was defrauded of his victory by a retrospective action of this amendment; and America stands to-day as the only nation professing civilization, which shields repudiation under "State sovereignty."

In the strength of these principles Paine was able to overwhelm the whole brood of heresies,—State privilege, legal tender, repudiation, retrospective laws.

His arguments are too modern to need repetition here; in fineness and force they are like the ribs of his bridge: as to-day commerce travels on Paine's iron span, so on his argumentative arch it passes over freshets endangering honest money.

For a like reason it is unnecessary to give here all the details of his bridge sent by Paine to his correspondents. Of this invention more is said in further chapters, but the subjoined letters are appropriate at this point. The first two were written at Bordentown, where Paine settled himself in the spring.

To Franklin, undated.—"I send you the two essays I mentioned. As the standing or not standing of such an arch is not governed by opinions, therefore opinions one way or the other will not alter the fact. The opinions of its standing will not make it stand, the opinions of its falling will not make it fall; but I shall be exceedingly obliged to you to bestow a few thoughts on the subject and to communicate to me any difficulties or doubtfulness that may occur to you, because it will be of use to me to know them. As you have not the model to look at I enclose a sketch of a rib, except that the blocks which separate the bars are not represented."

To Franklin, June 6th.—"The gentleman, Mr. Hall, who presents you with this letter, has the care of two models for a bridge, one of wood, the other of cast iron, which I have the pleasure of submitting to you, as well for the purpose of showing my respect to you, as my patron in this country, as for the sake of having your opinion and judgment thereon.—The European method of bridge architecture, by piers and arches, is not adapted to many of the rivers in America on account of the ice in the winter. The construction of those I have the honor of presenting to you is designed to obviate the difficulty by leaving the whole passage of the river clear of the incumbrance of piers. . . . My first design in the wooden model was for a bridge over the Harlem River, for my good friend General Morris of Morrisania . . . but I cannot help thinking that

it might be carried across the Schuylkill. . . . Mr. Hall, who has been with me at Borden Town, and has done the chief share of the working part, for we have done the whole ourselves, will inform you of any circumstance relating to it which does not depend on the mathematical construction. Mr. Hall will undertake to see the models brought safe from the stage boat to you; they are too large to be admitted into the house, but will stand very well in the garden. Should there be a vessel going round to New York within about a week after my arrival in Philadelphia I shall take that convenience for sending them there, at which place I hope to be in about a fortnight."

Address and date not given; written in Philadelphia, probably in June—"Honorable Sir,—I have sent to His Excellency, the President [Franklin] two models for a Bridge, the one of wood the other of cast-iron bars, to be erected over rivers, without piers. As I shall in a few days go to New York, and take them with me, I do myself the honor of presenting an invitation to Council to take a view of them before they are removed. If it is convenient to Council to see and examine their construction to-day, at the usual time of their adjournment, I will attend at the President's at half after twelve o'clock, or any other day or hour Council may please to appoint." [1]

To the Hon. Thomas Fitzsimmons; addressed "To be left at the Bank, Philadelphia." Written at Bordentown, November 19th.—"I write you a few loose thoughts as they occur to me. Next to the gaining a majority is that of keeping it. This, at least (in my opinion), will not be best accomplished by doing or attempting a great deal of business, but by doing no more than is absolutely necessary to be done, acting moderately and giving no offence. It is with the whole as it is with the members individually, and we always see at every new election that it is more difficult to turn out an old member against whom no direct complaint can be made than it is to put in a new one though a better man. I am sure it will be best not to touch any part of the plan of finance this year. If it falls short, as most probably it will, it would be (I speak for myself) best to reduce the interest that the whole body of those who are stiled public creditors may share it equally as far as it will go. If any thing can be saved from the Civil List expences it ought not to be finally mortgaged to make up the deficiency; it may be applied to bring the creditors to a balance for the present year. There is more to be said respecting this debt than has yet been said. The matter has never been taken up but by those who are interested in the matter. The public has been

---

[1] This and the two letters preceding are among the Franklin MSS. in the Philosophical Society, Philadelphia.

deficient and the claimants exorbitant—neglect on one side and greediness on the other. That which is truly Justice may be always advocated. But I could no more think of paying six per cent Interest in real money, in perpetuity, for a debt a great part of which is quondam than I could think of not paying at all. Six per cent on any part of the debt, even to the original holders is ten or twelve per cent, and to the speculators twenty or thirty or more. It is better that the matter rest until it is fuller investigated and better understood, for in its present state it will be hazardous to touch upon.

"I have not heard a word of news from Philadelphia since I came to this place. I wrote a line to Mr. Francis and desired him to give me a little account of matters but he does not, perhaps, think it very necessary now.

"I see by the papers that the subject of the Bank is likely to be renewed. I should like to know when it will come on, as I have some thought of coming down at that time, if I can.

"I see by the papers that the Agricultural Society have presented a petition to the house respecting building a Bridge over the Schuylkill —on a model prepared for that purpose. In this I think they are too hasty. I have already constructed a model of a Bridge of Cast Iron, consisting of one arch. I am now making another of wrought Iron of one arch, but on a different Plan. I expect to finish it in about three weeks and shall send it first to Philadelphia. I have no opinion of any Bridge over the Schuylkill that is to be erected on piers— the sinking of piers will sink more money than they have any Idea of and will not stand when done. But there is another point they have not taken into their consideration; which is, that the sinking three piers in the middle of the river, large and powerful enough to resist the ice, will cause such an alteration in the bed and channel of the river that there is no saying what course it may take, or whether it will not force a new channel somewhere else." [1]

To George Clymer, Esquire, "to be left at the Bank, Philadelphia." Written at Bordentown, November 19th.—"I observe by the minutes that the Agricultural Society have presented a petition to the house for an act of incorporation for the purpose of erecting a bridge over the Schuylkill on a model in their possession. I hope this business will not be gone into too hastily. A Bridge on piers will never answer for that river, they may sink money but they never will sink piers that will stand. But admitting that the piers do stand— they will cause such an alteration in the Bed and channel of the river, as will most probable alter its course either to divide the channel, and require two bridges of cause it to force a new channel in

some other part. It is a matter of more hazard than they are aware of the altering by obstructions the bed and channel of a River ; the water must go somewhere—the force of the freshets and the Ice is very great now but will be much greater then.

"I am finishing as fast as I can my new model of an Iron Bridge of one arch which if it answers, and I have no doubt but it will, the whole difficulty of erecting Bridges over that river, or others of like circumstances, will be removed, and the expense not greater, (and I believe not so great) as the sum mentioned by Mr. Morris in the house, and I am sure will stand four times as long or as much longer as Iron is more durable than wood. I mention these circumstances to you that you may be informed of them—and not let the matter proceed so far as to put the Agricultural Society in a difficult situation at last.

"The giving a Society the exclusive right to build a bridge, unless the plan is prepared before hand, will prevent a bridge being built ; because those who might afterwards produce models preferable to their own, will not present them to any such body of men, and they can have no right to take other peoples labours or inventions to compleat their own undertakings by.

"I have not heard any news since I came to this place. I wish you would give me a line and let me know how matters are going on.—The Stage Boat comes to Borden Town every Wednesday and Sunday from the Crooked Billet Wharf." [2]

At the close of the war Paine was eager to visit England. He speaks of it in his letter of June 7, 1783, to Elias Boudinot, already referred to—but he had not the means. The measures for his remuneration had delayed him two and a half years, and it now became imperative that he should put in a fair way of success his invention of the bridge. The models made a good impression on Franklin and the Council, and a committee was appointed to investigate it. Early in the year following the Pennsylvania Assembly appointed another committee. But meanwhile Paine's correspondence with his parents determined him to visit them at once, and look after the interests of his invention upon his return.[3] He no doubt

[1] I am indebted for this letter to Mr. Simon Gratz of Philadelphia.

[2] For this letter I am indebted to Mr. Charles Roberts, of Philadelphia.

[3] It is known that he received an affectionate letter from his father, now in his 78th year, but it has not been found, and was probably burned with the Bonneville papers in St. Louis.

also thought, and it may have been suggested by Franklin, that the success of his bridge would be assured in America and England if it should receive approval of the engineers in France. In March, 1787, he is in Philadelphia, consulting committees, and on the 31st writes to Franklin of his prospects and plans :

"I mentioned in one of my essays my design of going this spring to Europe.—I intend landing in france and from thence England,—and that I should take the model with me. The time I had fixed with myself was May, but understanding (since I saw you yesterday) that no french packet sails that month, I must either take the April packet or wait till June. As I can get ready by the April packet I intend not omitting the opportunity. My Father and Mother are yet living, whom I am very anxious to see, and have informed them of my coming over the ensuing summer.

"I propose going from hence by the stage on Wednesday for New York, and shall be glad to be favoured with the care of any letters of yours to France or England. My stay in Paris, when with Col. Laurens, was so short that I do not feel myself introduced there, for I was in no house but at Passy, and the Hotel Col. Laurens was at. As I have taken a part in the Revolution and politics of this country, and am not an unknown character in the political world, I conceive it would be proper on my going to Paris, that I should pay my respects to Count Vergennes, to whom I am personally unknown ; and I shall be very glad of a letter from you to him affording me that opportunity, or rendering my waiting on him easy to me ; for it so often happens that men live to forfeit the reputation at one time they gained at another, that it is prudent not to presume too much on one's self. The Marquis La Fayette I am the most known to of any gentleman in France. Should he be absent from Paris there are none I am much acquainted with. I am on exceeding good terms with Mr. Jefferson which will necessarily be the first place I go to. As I had the honor of your introduction to America it will add to my happiness to have the same friendship continued to me on the present occasion.

"Respecting the model, I shall be obliged to you for a letter to some of the Commissioners in that department. I shall be glad to hear their opinion of it. If they will undertake the experiment of two Ribs, it will decide the matter and promote the work here,—but this need not be mentioned. The Assembly have appointed another Committee, consisting of Mr. Morris, Mr. Clymer, Mr. Fitzsimons, Mr. Wheeler, Mr. Robinson, to confer with me on the undertaking. The matter therefore will remain suspended till my return next winter. It is worth waiting this event, because if a single arch to that extent will answer, all difficulties in that river, or others of the same condition, are overcome at once.

"I will do myself the pleasure of waiting on you to-morrow."

During the time when Paine was perfecting his bridge, and consulting the scientific committees, the country was absorbed with preparations for forming a national Constitution and Union. When the States were nominating and electing delegates to the Convention of 1787, no one seems to have suggested Paine for a seat in it, nor does he appear to have aspired to one. The reasons are not far to seek. Paine was altogether too inventive for the kind of work contemplated by the colonial politicians. He had shown in all his writings, especially in his " Dissertations on Government," that he would build a constitution as he built his bridge : it must be mathematical, founded and shaped in impregnable principles, means adopted and adapted strictly for an ideal national purpose. His iron span did not consider whether there might be large interests invested in piers, or superstitions in favor of oak ; as little did his antislavery essays consider the investments in slavery, or his " Public Good " the jealous sovereignty of States. A recent writer says that Paine's " Common Sense " was " just what the moment demanded," and that it " may be briefly described as a plea for independence and a continental government." [1] In setting the nation at once to a discussion of the principles of such government, he led it to assume the principle of independence ; over the old English piers on their quicksands, which some would rebuild, he threw his republican arch, on which the people passed from shore to shore. He and Franklin did the like in framing the Pennsylvania constitution of 1776, by which the chasm of "Toryism" was spanned. Every pamphlet of Paine was of the nature of an invention, by which

[1] " The Development of Constitutional Liberty in the English Colonies of America," by Eben Greenough Scott, 1890.

principles of liberty and equality were framed in constructions adapted to emergencies of a republic. But when the emergencies were past, the old contrivances regained their familiar attractions, and these were enhanced by independence. Privilege, so odious in Lords, was not so bad when inherited by democracy ; individual sovereignty, unsuited to King George, might be a fine thing for President George ; and if England had a House of Peers, why should we not make one out of a peerage of States ? "Our experience in republicanism," wrote Paine, "is yet so slender, that it is much to be doubted whether all our public laws and acts are consistent with, or can be justified on, the principles of a republican government."[1] But the more he talked in this way, or reminded the nation of the "Declaration of Independence" and the "Bill of Rights," the more did he close the doors of the Constitutional Convention against himself.

In those days there used to meet in Franklin's library a "Society for Political Inquiries." It had forty-two members, among them Washington, James Wilson, Robert Morris, Gouverneur Morris, Clymer, Rush, Bingham, Bradford, Hare, Rawle, and Paine. A memorandum of Rawle says : "Paine never opened his mouth, but he furnished one of the few essays which the members of the Society were expected to produce. It was a well written dissertation on the expediency of incorporating towns."[2] That

in such company, and at such a time, Paine should be silent, or discuss corporations, suggests political solitude. Franklin, indeed, agreed with him, but was too old to struggle against the reaction in favor of the bicameral and other English institutions.

M. Chanut ("Nouv. Biog. Générale") says that Paine's bridge was not erected on the Schuylkill because of "the imperfect state of iron manufacture in America." Something of the same kind might be said of the state of political architecture. And so it was, that while the Convention was assembling in Independence Hall, he who first raised the standard of Independence, and before the Declaration proposed a Charter of the "United Colonies of America," was far out at sea on his way to rejoin his comrades in the old world, whose hearts and burdens he had represented in the new.

---

[1] "Dissertations on Government." Vol. II, "The Writings of Thomas Paine." (Conway.) H.B.B.

[2] "Memoir of Penn. Hist. Soc., 1840." The gist of Paine's paper (read Apr. 20, 1787) is no doubt contained in "The Rights of Man," Part II. Ch. 5.

The printed Rules of the Society (founded February 9, 1787) are in the Philosophical Society, Philadelphia. The preamble, plainly Paine's, says : "Important as these inquiries are to all, to the inhabitants of these republics they are objects of peculiar magnitude and necessity. Accustomed to look up to those nations, from whom we have derived our origin, for our laws, our opinions, and our manners, we have retained with undistinguishing reverence their errors, with their improvements ; have blended with our public institutions the policy of dissimilar countries ; and have grafted on our infant commonwealth the manners of ancient and corrupted monarchies. In having effected a separate government, we have as yet effected but a partial independence. The revolution can only be said to be compleat, when we shall have freed ourselves, no less from the influence of foreign prejudices than from the fetters of foreign power."

CHAPTER XVI

RETURNING TO THE OLD HOME

EVEN now one can hardly repress regret that Paine did not remain in his beloved Bordentown. There he was the honored man; his striking figure, decorated with the noblest associations, was regarded with pride; when he rode the lanes on his horse Button, the folk had a pleasant word with him; the best homes prized his intimacy, and the young ladies would sometimes greet the old gentleman with a kiss. From all th.s he was drawn by the tender letter of a father he was never to see again. He sailed in April for a year's absence; he remained away fifteen,—if such years may be reckoned by calendar.

The French packet from New York had a swift voyage, and early in the summer Paine was receiving honors in Paris. Franklin had given him letters of introduction, but he hardly needed them.[1] He was already a hero of the progressives, who had relished his artistic dissection of the Abbé Raynal's disparagement of the American Revolution. Among those who greeted him was Auberteuil, whose history of the American Revolution Paine had corrected, an early copy having been sent him (1783) by Franklin for that purpose. But Paine's main object in France was to secure a verdict from the Academy of Sciences, the supreme authority, on his bridge, a model of which he carried with him. The Academy received him with the honors due to an M.A. of the University of Pennsylvania, a member of the Philosophical Society, and a friend of Franklin. It appointed M. Leroy, M. Bossou, and M. Borda a committee to report on his bridge. On August 18th

he writes to Jefferson, then Minister in Paris :

"I am much obliged to you for the book you are so kind to send me. The second part of your letter, concerning taking my picture, I must feel as an honor done to me, not as a favour asked of me—but in this, as in other matters, I am at the disposal of your friendship.

"The committee have among themselves finally agreed on their report; I saw this morning it will be read in the Academy on Wednesday. The report goes pretty fully to support the principles of the construction, with their reasons for that opinion."

On August 15th, a cheery letter had gone to George Clymer in Philadelphia, in which he says :

"This comes by Mr. Derby, of Massachusetts, who leaves Paris to-day to take shipping at L' [Orient] for Boston. The enclosed for Dr. Franklin is from his friend Mr. Le Roy, of the Academy of Sciences, respecting the bridge, and the causes that have delayed the completing report. An arch of 4 or 5 hundred feet is such an unprecedented thing, and will so much attract notice in the northern part of Europe, that the Academy is cautious in what manner to express their final opinion. It is, I find, their custom to give reasons for their opinion, and this embarrasses them more than the opinion itself. That the model is strong, and that a bridge constructed on the same principles will also be strong, they appear to be well agreed in, but to what particular causes to assign the strength they are not agreed in. The Committee was directed by the Academy to examine all the models and plans for iron bridges that had been proposed in France, and they unanimously gave the preference to our own, as being the simplest, strongest, and lightest. They have likewise agreed on some material points."[2]

Dr. Robinet says that on this visit (1787) Paine, who had long known the "soul of the people," came into relation with eminent men of all groups, philoso-

[1] "This letter goes by Mr. Paine, one of our principal writers at the Revolution, being the author of 'Common Sense,' a pamphlet that had prodigious effects."—*Franklin to M. de Veillard.*

[2] For this letter I am indebted to Mr. Curtis Guild, of Boston. The letter goes on to describe, with drawings, the famous bridge at Schaffhausen, built by Grubenmann, an uneducated carpenter, the model being shown Paine by the King's architect, Perronet. The Academy's committee presently made its report, which was even more favorable than Paine had anticipated.

phical and political,—Condorcet, Achille Duchâtelet, Cardinal De Brienne, and, he believes, also Danton, who, like the English republican, was a freemason.[1] This intercourse, adds the same author, enabled him to print in England his remarkable prophecy concerning the change going on in the French mind. Dr. Robinet quotes from a pamphlet presently noticed, partly written in Paris during this summer. Although it was Paine's grievous destiny soon to be once more a revolutionary figure, it is certain that he had returned to Europe as an apostle of peace and good-will. While the engineers were considering his daring scheme of an iron arch of five hundred feet, he was devising with the Cardinal Minister, De Brienne, a bridge of friendship across the Channel. He drew up a paper in this sense, on which the Minister wrote and signed his approval. The bridge-model approved by the Academy he sent to Sir Joseph Banks, President of the Royal Society; the proposal for friendship between France and England, approved by the Cardinal Minister, he carried by his own hand to Edmund Burke.

On his arrival in London Paine gave to the printer a manuscript on which he had been engaged, and straightway went to Thetford.[2] His father had died the year before.[3] His mother, now in her ninety-first year, he found in the comfort his remittances had supplied. The house,

---

[1] "Danton Emigré," p. 7. Paine wrote a brief archæological treatise on freemasonry, but I have not met with the statement that he was a freemason except in Dr. Robinet's volume, —certainly high authority.

[2] The exact time of his arrival in England is doubtful. Oldys says: "He arrived at the White Bear, Picadilly, on the 3d of September, 1787, just thirteen years after his departure for Philadelphia." Writing in 1803 Paine also says it was in September. But his "Rubicon" pamphlet is dated "York Street, St. James's Square, 20th August, 1787." Possibly the manuscript was dated in Paris and forwarded to the London printer with the address at which he wished to find proof on his arrival.

[3] St. Cuthbert's Register: "Burials, 1786. Joseph Payne (a Quaker) aged 78 years. November 14th."

with its large garden, stands in Guildhall (then Heathenman) Street. I was politely shown through it by its present occupant, Mr. Brett. Mr. Stephen Oldman, Sr., who went to school in the house, told me that it was identified by "old Jack Whistler," a barber, as the place where he went to shave Paine, in 1787. At this time Paine settled on his mother an allowance of nine shillings per week, which in the Thetford of that period was ample for her comfort. During this autumn with his mother he rarely left her side. As she lived to be ninety-four it may be that he sat beside her in the Quaker meeting-house, to which she had become attached in her latter years.

Eloquent and pathetic must have been the silence around the gray man when, after so many tempests, he sat once more in the little meeting-house where his childhood was nurtured. From this, his spiritual cradle, he had borne away a beautiful theory, in ignorance of the contrasted actuality. Theoretically the Society of Friends is a theocracy; the Spirit alone rules and directs, effacing all distinctions of rank or sex. As a matter of fact, one old Quaker, or the clerk of a meeting, often over-rules the "inner lights" of hundreds. Of the practical working of Quaker government Paine had no experience; he had nothing to check his ideal formed in boyhood. His whole political system is explicable only by his theocratic Quakerism. His first essay, the plea for negro emancipation, was brought from Thetford meeting-house. His "Common Sense," a new-world scripture, is a "testimony" against the proud who raised their paltry dignities above the divine presence in the lowliest. "But where, say some, is the King of America? I'll tell you, friend, he reigns above." Paine's love of his adopted country was not mere patriotism; he beheld in it the land of promise for all mankind, seen from afar while on his Thetford Pisgah. Therefore he made so much of the various races in America.

"The mere independence of America, were it to have been followed by a system of government modelled after the corrupt system of the English government, would not have interested me with the unabated ardour that it did. It was to bring forward and establish the representative system of government that was the leading principle with me."

So he spake to Congress, and to its president he said that he would have done the same for any country as for America. The religious basis of his political system has a droll illustration in an anecdote of his early life told by himself. While bowling with friends at Lewes, Mr. Verril remarked that Frederick of Prussia "was the best fellow in the world for a king; he had so much of the devil in him." It struck Paine that "if it were necessary for a king to have so much of the devil in him, kings might very beneficially be dispensed with." From this time he seems to have developed a theory of human rights based on theocracy; and so genuinely that in America, while the Bible was still to him the word of God, he solemnly proposed, in the beginning of the Revolution, that a crown should be publicly laid on that book, to signify to the world that "in America the Law is King."

While in America the States were discussing the Constitution proposed by the Convention, Paine sat in the silent meeting at Thetford dreaming of the Parliament of Man, and federation of the world. In America the dawn of the new nation was a splendor, but it paled the ideals that had shone through the night of struggle. The principles of the Declaration, which would have freed every slave, —representation proportionate to population, so essential to equality, the sovereignty of justice instead of majorities or of States,—had become "glittering generalities." The first to affirm the principles of the Declaration, Paine awaited the unsummoned Convention that would not compromise any of them away. For politicians these lofty ideas might be extinguished by the rising of a national sun; but in Paine there remained the

deep Quaker well where the stars shone on through the garish day.[1]

Seated in the Quaker meeting-house beside his mother, and beside his father's fresh grave, Paine revises the past while revising the proofs of his pamphlet. The glamor of war, even of the American Revolution, fades; the shudder with which he saw in childhood soldiers reeking from the massacres of Culloden and Inverness returns; he begins his new career in the old world with a "testimony" against war.[2]

"When we consider, for the feelings of Nature cannot be dismissed, the calamities of war and the miseries it inflicts upon the human species, the thousands and tens of thousands of every age and sex who are rendered wretched by the event, surely there is something in the heart of man that calls upon him to think! Surely there is some tender chord, tuned by the hand of the Creator, that still struggles to emit in the hearing of the soul a note of sorrowing sympathy. Let it then be heard, and let man learn to feel that the true greatness of a nation is founded on principles of humanity. . . . War involves in its progress such a train of unforeseen and unsupposed circumstances, such a combination of foreign matters, that no human wisdom can calculate the end. It has but one thing certain, and that is to increase taxes. . . . I defend the cause of the poor, of the manufacturer, of the tradesman, of the farmer, and of all those on whom the real burthen of taxes fall—but above all, I defend the cause of humanity."

So little did Paine contemplate or desire revolution in England or France. His exhortation to young Pitt is to avoid war with Holland, to be friendly with France, to shun alliances involving aid in war, and to build up the wealth and liberties of England by uniting the people with the throne. He has discovered that this healthy change is going on in France. The French people are allying "the Majesty of the Sovereign with the Majesty of the Nation." "Of all alliances this is infinitely the strongest and the

---

[1] "In wells where truth in secret lay
He saw the midnight stars by day."—
                              W. D. Howells.
[2] "Prospects on the Rubicon; or, An Investigation into the causes and Consequences of the Politics to be Agitated at the Meeting of Parliament." London, 1787. Pp. 68.

safest to be trusted to, because the interest so formed and operating against external enemies can never be divided." Freedom doubles the value of the subject to the government. When the desire of freedom becomes universal among the people, then, "and not before, is the important moment for the most effectual consolidation of national strength and greatness." The government must not be frightened by disturbances incidental to beneficent changes. "The creation we enjoy arose out of a chaos." [1]

Paine had seen a good deal of Jefferson in Paris, and no doubt their conversation often related to struggles in the Constitutional Convention at Philadelphia. Jefferson wished the Constitution to include a Declaration of Rights, and wrote Paine some comments on the argument of James Wilson (afterward of the Supreme Court), maintaining that such a Declaration was unnecessary in a government without any powers not definitely granted, and that such a Declaration might be construed to imply some degree of power over the matters it defined. Wilson's speeches, powerfully analyzing the principles of liberty and federation, were delivered on October 6th and November 24th, and it will appear by the subjoined paper that they were more in accord with Paine's

than with Jefferson's principles. The manuscript, which is among Jefferson's papers, bears no date, but was no doubt written at Thetford early in the year 1788.

"After I got home, being alone and wanting amusement, I sat down to explain to myself (for there is such a thing) my ideas of national and civil rights, and the distinction between them. I send them to you to see how nearly we agree.

"Suppose twenty persons, strangers to each other, to meet in a country not before inhabited. Each would be a Sovereign in his own natural right. His will would be his law, but his power, in many cases, inadequate to his right ; and the consequence would be that each might be exposed, not only to each other, but to the other nineteen. It would then occur to them that their condition would be much improved, if a way could be devised to exchange that quantity of danger into so much protection ; so that each individual should possess the strength of the whole number. As all their rights in the first case are natural rights, and the exercise of those rights supported only by their own natural individual power, they would begin by distinguishing between those rights they could individually exercise, fully and perfectly, and those they could not. Of the first kind are the rights of thinking, speaking, forming and giving opinions, and perhaps are those which can be fully exercised by the individual without the aid of exterior assistance ; or in other words, rights of personal competency. Of the second kind are those of personal protection, of acquiring and possessing property, in the exercise of which the individual natural power is less than the natural right.

"Having drawn this line they agree to retain individually the first class of Rights, or those of personal competency ; and to detach from their personal possession the second class, or those of defective power, and to accept in lieu thereof a right to the whole power produced by a condensation of all the parts. These I conceive to be civil rights, or rights of compact, and are distinguishable from natural rights because in the one we act wholly in our own person, in the other we agree not to do so, but act under the guarantee of society.

"It therefore follows that the more of those imperfect natural rights or rights of imperfect power we give up, and thus exchange, the more security we possess ; and as the word liberty is often mistakenly put for security, Mr. Wilson has confused his argument by confounding the terms. But it does not follow that the more natural rights of *every kind* we assign the more security we possess, because if we resign those of the first class we may suffer much by the exchange ; for where the right and the power are equal with each other in the individual, naturally, they ought to rest there.

---

[1] The pamphlet was reprinted in London in 1793 under the title : " Prospects on the War, and Paper Currency. The second edition, corrected." Advertisement (June 20th) : " This pamphlet was written by Mr. Paine in the year 1787, on one of Mr. Pitt's armaments, namely, that against Holland. His object was to prevent the people of England from being seduced into a war, by stating clearly to them the consequences which would inevitably befall the credit of this country should such a calamity take place. The minister has at length, however, succeeded in his great project, after three expensive armaments within the space of seven years ; and the event has proved how well founded were the predictions of Mr. Paine. The person who has authority to bring forward this pamphlet in its present shape, thinks his doing so a duty which he owes both to Mr. P—— and the people of England, in order that the latter may judge what credit is due to (what a great judge calls) THE WILD THEORIES OF MR. PAINE."

"Mr. Wilson must have some allusion to this distinction, or his position would be subject to the inference you draw from it.

"I consider the individual sovereignty of the States retained under the act of confederation to be of the second class of right. It becomes dangerous because it is defective in the power necessary to support it. It answers the pride and purpose of a few men in each State, but the State collectively is injured by it."

The paper just quoted may be of importance to those students of Yale College who shall compete for the Ten Eyck prize of 1892, on the interesting subject, "Thomas Paine: Deism and Democracy in the Days of the American Revolution." There was no nearer approach to democracy, in Paine's theory, than that of this paper sent to Jefferson. The Constitutional Convention represented to him the contracting People, all the individuals being parties to a Compact whereby every majority pledges itself to protect the minority in matters not essential to the security of all. In representative government thus limited by compact he recognized the guaranty of individual freedom and influence by which the mass could be steadily enlightened. Royall Tyler considered some of his views on these subjects "whimsical paradoxes"; but they are not so "unaccountable" as he supposed. Tyler's portraiture of Paine in London, though somewhat adapted to prejudices anent "The Age of Reason," is graphic, and Paine's anti-democratic paradox wittily described.

"I met this interesting personage at the lodgings of the son of a late patriotic American governour [Trumbull]. . . . He was dressed in a snuff-coloured coat, olive velvet vest, drab breeches, coarse hose. His shoe buckles of the size of a half dollar. A bob-tailed wig covered that head which worked such mickle woe to courts and kings. If I should attempt to describe it, it would be in the same stile and principle with which the veteran soldier bepraiseth an old standard : the more tattered, the more glorious. It is probable that this was the same identical wig under the shadow of whose curls he wrote Common Sense, in America, many years before. He was a spare man, rather under size ; subject to the extreme of low, and highly exhilarating spirits ; often sat reserved in company ; seldom mingled in common chit chat : But when a man of sense and elocution was present, and the company numerous, he delighted in advancing the most unaccountable, and often the most whimsical paradoxes ; which he defended in his own plausible manner. If encouraged by success, or the applause of the company, his countenance was animated with an expression of feature which, on ordinary occasions, one would look for in vain, in a man so much celebrated for acuteness of thought ; but if interrupted by extraneous observation, by the inattention of his auditory, or in an irritable moment, even by the accidental fall of the poker, he would retire into himself, and no persuasion could induce him to proceed upon the most favourite topic. . . . I heard Thomas Paine once assert in the presence of Mr. Wolcott, better known, in this country, by the facetious name of Peter Pindar, that the minority, in all deliberative bodies, ought, in all cases, to govern the majority. Peter smiled. You must grant me, said *Un*common Sense, that the proportion of men of sense, to the ignorant among mankind, is at least as twenty, thirty, or even forty-nine, to an hundred. The majority of mankind are consequently most prone to errour ; and if we atchieve the right, the minority ought in all cases to govern. Peter continued to smile archly." [1]

In the end this theory was put to a vote of the company present, and all arose with Paine except Peter Pindar, who thereupon said, "I am the wise minority who ought, in all cases, to govern your ignorant majority."

[1] "The Algerine Captive," 1797. (Paine's shoe-buckles in the National Museum, Washington, are of the fashionable kind.)

CHAPTER XVII

A BRITISH LION WITH AN AMERICAN HEART

THE influence of Paine's Quaker training has been traced in his constructive politics, but its repressive side had more perhaps to do with his career. "I had some turn," he said, "and I believe some talent, for poetry; but this I rather repressed than encouraged." It is your half-repressed poets that kindle revolutions. History might be different had Paine not been taught fear of music and poetry. He must have epical commonwealths. The American Republic having temporarily filled his ideal horizon in the political direction, the disguised Muse turned his eye upon the possibilities of nature. Morally utilitarian, he yet rarely writes about physics without betraying the poetic passion for nature of a suppressed Wordsworth. Nature is his Aphrodite and his Madonna.

"Bred up in antediluvian notions, she has not yet acquired the European taste of receiving visitors in her dressing-room; she locks and bolts up her private recesses with extraordinary care, as if not only resolved to preserve her hoards but conceal her age, and hide the remains of a face that was young and lovely in the days of Adam." [1]

Defining for Jefferson the distinction between attraction and cohesion, he says:

"I recollect a scene at one of the theatres which very well explains the difference. A condemned lady wishes to see her child and the child its mother: that is Attraction. They were admitted to meet, but when ordered to part threw their arms around each other and fastened their persons together: this is Cohesion." [2]

All the atoms or molecules are little mothers and daughters and lovers clasping each other; it is an interlocking of figures; "and if our eyes were good enough we should see how it was done."

[1] "Useful and Entertaining Hints," The Writings of Thomas Paine (Conway), Vol. I. p. 22.—H.B.B.
[2] "Scientific Memoranda," The Writings of Thomas Paine (Conway), Vol. IV. p. 437.—H.B.B.

He has a transcendental perception of unity in things dissimilar. On his walks to Challiot he passes trees and fountains, and writes a little essay, with figures, explaining to his friend that the tree is also a fountain, and that by measuring diameters of trunks and tubes, or branches, the quantity of timber thrown up by sap-fountains might be known. Some of his casual speculations he calls "conceits." They are the exuberance of a scientific imagination inspired by philanthropy and naturalistic religion. The "inner light" of man corresponds to an "inner spirit" of nature. The human mind dimmed by ignorance, perverted by passion, turns the very gifts of nature to thorns, amid which her divine beauty sleeps until awakened by the kiss of science.

It would be difficult to find anything in the literature of mechanical invention more naïvely picturesque than this Quaker, passed through furnaces of two revolutions, trying to humanize gunpowder. Here is a substance with maximum of power and minimum of bulk and weight:

"When I consider the wisdom of nature I must think that she endowed matter with this extraordinary property for other purposes than that of destruction. Poisons are capable of other uses than that of killing. If the power which an ounce of gunpowder contains could be detailed out as steam or water can be it would be a most commodious natural power." [3]

Having failed to convert revolutions to Quakerism, Paine tries to soften the heart of gunpowder itself, and insists that its explosiveness may be restrained and detailed like strokes on a boy's top to obtain continual motion. The sleeping top, the chastened repose of perfect motion, like the quiet of the spinning worlds, is the Quaker inventor's ideal, and he begs the President of the United States to try the effect of the smallest

[3] Id., p. 438.—H.B.B.

pistol made—the size of a quill—on a wheel with peripheral cups to receive the discharges.[1]

"The biographers of Paine," wrote his friend, Joel Barlow, "should not forget his mathematical acquirements and his mechanical genius." But it would require a staff of specialists, and a large volume, to deal with Paine's scientific studies and contrivances— with his planing machine, his new crane, his smokeless candle, his wheel of concentric rim, his scheme for using gunpowder as a motor, above all his iron bridge. As for the bridge, Paine feels that it is a sort of American revolution carried into mechanics ; his eagle cannot help spreading a little in the wondering eyes of the Old World. " Great scenes inspire great ideas," he writes to Sir George Staunton.

"The natural mightiness of America expands the mind, and it partakes of the greatness it contemplates. Even the war, with all its evils, had some advantages. It energized invention and lessened the catalogue of impossibilities. At the conclusion of it every man returned to his home to repair the ravages it had occasioned, and to think of war no more. As one amongst thousands who had borne a share in that memorable revolution, I returned with them to the re-enjoyment of quiet life, and, that I might not be idle, undertook to construct a single arch for this river [Schuylkill]. Our beloved General had engaged in rendering another river, the Potowmac, navigable. The quantity of iron I had allowed in my plan for this arch was five hundred and twenty tons, to be distributed into thirteen ribs, in commemoration of the Thirteen United States."

It is amusing after this to find Paine, in his patent, declaring his special license from "His Most Excellent Majesty King George the Third."[2] Had poor George

been in his right senses, or ever heard of the invention, he might have suspected some connection between this insurrection of the iron age and the American "rebellion." However, Paine is successful in keeping America out of his specification, albeit a poetic touch appears.

"The idea and construction of this arch is taken from the figure of a spider's circular web, of which it resembles a section, and from a conviction that when nature empowered this insect to make a web she also instructed her in the strongest mechanical method of constructing it. Another idea, taken from nature in the construction of this arch, is that of increasing the strength of matter by dividing and combining it, and thereby causing it to act over a larger space than it would occupy in a solid state, as is seen in the quills of birds, bones of animals, reeds, canes, &c. The curved bars of the arch are composed of pieces of any length joined together to the whole extent of the arch, and take curvature by bending."

Paine and his bridge came to England at a fortunate moment. Blackfriars Bridge had just given way, and two over the Tyne, one built by Smeaton, had collapsed by reason of quicksands under their piers. And similarly Pitt's policy was collapsing through the treacherous quicksands on which it was based. Paper money and a "sinking fund" at home, and foreign alliances that disregarded the really controlling interests of nations, Paine saw as piers set in the Channel.[3] He at once took his place in England as a sort of institution. While the engineers beheld with admiration his iron arch clearing the treacherous riverbeds, statesmen saw with delight his prospective bridges spanning the political

[1] I am reluctantly compelled to give only the main ideas of several theses of this kind by Paine, found among Jefferson's papers. The portion of the "Jefferson Papers" at Washington written by Paine would fill a good volume.

[2] "No. 1667. Specification of Thomas Paine. Constructing Arches, Vaulted Roofs, and Ceilings." The specification, dated August 28, 1788, declares his invention to be "on principles new and different to anything hitherto practised." The patents for England, Scotland, and Ireland were granted in September. An iron arch of

one hundred feet was designed by Pritchard and erected by Darby at Coalbrook Dale, Shropshire, in 1779, but it did not anticipate the invention of Paine, as may be seen by the article on "Iron Bridges" in the Encyclopædia Britannica, which also well remarks that Paine's "daring in engineering does full justice to the fervor of his political career."

[3] It is droll to find even Paine's iron bridge resting somewhat on a "paper" pier. "Perhaps," he writes Jefferson, "the excess of paper currency, and the wish to find objects for realizing it, is one of the motives for promoting the plan of the Bridge."

"Rubicon." Nothing could be more felicitous than the title of his inaugural pamphlet, "Prospects on the Rubicon." It remembered an expression in Parliament at the beginning of the war on America.

"'The Rubicon is passed' was once given as a reason for prosecuting the most expensive war that England ever knew. Sore with the event, and groaning beneath a galling yoke of taxes, she has again been led ministerially on to the shore of the same delusive and fatal river."

The bridge-builder stretches his shining arches to France, Holland, Germany,— free commerce and friendship with all peoples, but no leagues with the sinking piers called thrones.

At Rotherham, in Yorkshire, where Messrs. Walker fitted up a workshop for Paine, he was visited by famous engineers and political personages. There and in London he was "lionized," as Franklin had been in Paris. We find him now passing a week with Edmund Burke, now at the country-seat of the Duke of Portland, or enjoying the hospitalities of Lord Fitzwilliam at Wentworth House. He is entertained and consulted on public affairs by Fox, Lord Lansdowne, Sir George Staunton, Sir Joseph Banks; and many an effort is made to enlist his pen. Lord Lansdowne, it appears, had a notion of Paine's powers of political engineering so sublime that he thought he might bridge the Atlantic, and reconnect England and America! All of this may be gathered from the Jefferson papers, as we shall presently see; but it should be remarked here that Paine's head was not turned by his association with the gentry and aristocracy. The impression he made on these eminent gentlemen was largely due to his freedom from airs. They found him in his workshop, hammer in hand, proud only of free America and of his beautiful arch.

Professor Peter Lesley of Philadelphia tells me that when visiting in early life the works at Rotherham, Paine's workshop and the very tools he used were pointed out. They were preserved with care. He conversed with an aged and intelligent workman who had worked under Paine as a lad. Professor Lesley, who had shared some of the prejudice against Paine, was impressed by the earnest words of this old man. Mr. Paine, he said, was the most honest man, and the best man he ever knew. After he had been there a little time everybody looked up to him, the Walkers and their workmen. He knew the people for miles round, and went into their homes; his benevolence, his friendliness, his knowledge, made him beloved by all, rich and poor. His memory had always lasted there.

In truth Paine, who had represented the heart of England, in America, was now representing the heart of America to England. America was working by his hand, looking through his eyes, and silently publishing to the people from whom he sprung what the new nation could make out of a starving English staymaker. He was a living Declaration of Independence. The Americans in London—the artists West and Trumbull, the Alexanders (Franklin's connections), and others—were fond of him as a friend and proud of him as a countryman.

The subjoined letter to Benjamin West (afterwards P.R.A.) shows Paine's pleasant relations with that artist and with Trumbull. It is dated March 8, 1789.

"I have informed James of the matter which you and I talked of on Saturday, and he is much rejoiced at an opportunity of shewing his gratitude to you for the permission you indulged him with in attending Mr. Trumbull at your rooms. As I have known his parents upwards of twenty years, and the manners and habits he has been educated in, and the disposition he is of, I can with confidence to myself undertake to vouch for the faithful discharge of any trust you may repose in him; and as he is a youth of quick discernment and a great deal of silent observation he cannot be easily imposed upon, or turned aside from his attention, by any contrivance of workmen. I will put him in a way of keeping a diary of every day's work he sees done, and of any observations he may make, proper for you to be informed of, which he can send once or twice a week to you at Windsor; and any directions you may have to give him in your absence can be conveyed through Mr. Trumbull, or what other method you please, so that James is certified they come from you.

"James has made a tender of his service to Mr. Trumbull, if it should be of any use, when his picture is to be exhibited; but that will probably not be till nearly the time the impressions will be struck off. James need not entirely omit his drawing while he is attending the plates. Some employment will, in general, fix a person to a place better than having only to stand still and look on. I suppose they strike off about three impressions in an hour, and as James is master of a watch he will find their average of works,—and also how fast they can work when they have a mind to make haste,—and he can easily number each impression, which will be a double check on any being carried off. I intend visiting him pretty often, while he is on duty, which will be an additional satisfaction to yourself for the trust you commit to him." [1]

This chapter may well close with a letter from Paine in London (January 6, 1789) to his young friend "Kitty Nicholson,"—known at the Bordentown school, and in New York,—on the occasion of her marriage with Colonel Few.[2] Let those who would know the real Thomas Paine read this letter!

"I sincerely thank you for your very friendly and welcome letter. I was in the country when it arrived and did not receive it soon enough to answer it by the return of the vessel.

"I very affectionately congratulate Mr. and Mrs. Few on their happy marriage, and every branch of the families allied by that connection; and I request my fair correspondent to present me to her partner, and to say, for me, that he has obtained one of the highest Prizes on the wheel. Besides the pleasure which your letter gives me to hear you are all happy and well, it relieves me from a sensation not easy to be dismissed; and if you will excuse a few dull thoughts for obtruding themselves into a congratulatory letter I will tell you what it is. When I see my female friends drop off by matrimony I am sensible of something that affects me like a loss in spite of all the appearances of joy: I cannot help mixing the sincere compliment of regret with that of congratulation. It appears as if I had outlived or lost a friend. It seems to me as if the original was no more, and that which she is changed to forsakes the circle and forgets the scenes of former society. Felicities are cares superior to those she formerly cared for,

create to her a new landscape of Life that excludes the little friendships of the past. It is not every lady's mind that is sufficiently capacious to prevent those greater objects crowding out the less, or that can spare a thought to former friendships after she has given her hand and heart to the man who loves her. But the sentiment your letter contains has prevented these dull Ideas from mixing with the congratulation I present you, and is so congenial with the enlarged opinion I have always formed of you, that at the time I read your letter with pleasure I read it with pride, because it convinces me that I have some judgment in that most difficult science—a Lady's mind. Most sincerely do I wish you all the good that Heaven can bless you with, and as you have in your own family an example of domestic happiness you are already in the knowledge of obtaining it. That no condition we can enjoy is an exemption from care —that some shade will mingle itself with the brightest sunshine of Life—that even our affections may become the instruments of our sorrows —that the sweet felicities of home depend on good temper as well as on good sense, and that there is always something to forgive even in the nearest and dearest of our friends,—are truths which, tho' too obvious to be told, ought never to be forgotten; and I know you will not esteem my friendship the less for impressing them upon you.

"Though I appear a sort of wanderer, the married state has not a sincerer friend than I am. It is the harbour of human life, and is, with respect to the things of this world, what the next world is to this. It is home; and that one word conveys more than any other word can express. For a few years we may glide along the tide of youthful single life and be wonderfully delighted; but it is a tide that flows but once, and what is still worse, it ebbs faster than it flows, and leaves many a hapless voyager aground. I am one, you see, that have experienced the fate I am describing.[3] I have lost my tide; it passed by

---

[1] I have not been able to find anything more of Paine's *protégé* James, whose parents were known to him before his departure for America. I am indebted to Mr. W. E. Benjamin for the letter.

[2] To a representative of this family I am indebted for the letter. Concerning the Nicholsons, see page 86.

[3] Paine's marriage and separation from his wife had been kept a secret in America, where the "Tories" would have used it to break the influence of his patriotic writings. It may be stated here, in addition to what is said on p. 13, that, in the absence of any divorce law in England, a separation under the Common Law was generally held as pronouncing the marriage a nullity *ab initio*. According to Chalmers Paine was dissatisfied with articles of separation drawn up by an attorney, Josias Smith, May 24, 1774, and insisted on new ones, to which the clergyman was a party. The "common lawyers" regarded the marriage as completely annulled, and Paine thus free to marry again. However, he evidently never thought of doing so, and that his relations with ladies were as chaste as affectionate appears in this letter to Mrs. Few, and in his correspondence generally.

while every thought of my heart was on the wing for the salvation of my dear America, and I have now, as contentedly as I can, made myself a little bower of willows on the shore that has the solitary resemblance of a home. Should I always continue the tenant of this home, I hope my female acquaintance will ever remember that it contains not the churlish enemy of their sex, not the inaccessible cold hearted mortal, nor the capricious tempered oddity, but one of the best and most affectionate of their friends.

"I did not forget the Dunstable hat, but it was not on wear here when I arrived. That I am a negligent correspondent I freely confess, and I always reproach myself for it. You mention only one letter, but I wrote twice ; once by Dr. Derby, and another time by the Chevalier St. Triss—by whom I also wrote to Gen. Morris, Col. Kirkbride, and several friends in Philadelphia, but have received no answers. I had one letter from Gen. Morris last winter, which is all I have received from New York till the arrival of yours.

"I thank you for the details of news you give. Kiss Molly Field for me and wish her joy,—and all the good girls of Bordentown. How is my favorite Sally Morris, my boy Joe, and my horse Button? pray let me know. Polly and Nancy Rogers,—are they married? or do they intend to build bowers as I have done? If they do, I wish they would twist their green willows somewhere near to mine.

"I am very much engaged here about my Bridge—There is one building of my Construction at Messrs. Walker's Iron Works in Yorkshire, and I have direction of it. I am lately come from thence and shall return again in two or three weeks.

"As to news on this side the water, the king is mad, and there is great bustle about appointing a Regent. As it happens, I am in pretty close intimacy with the heads of the opposition—the Duke of Portland, Mr. Fox and Mr. Burke. I have sent your letter to Mrs. Burke as a specimen of the accomplishments of the American Ladies. I sent it to Miss Alexander, a lady you have heard me speak of, and I asked her to give me a few of her thoughts how to answer it. She told me to write as I felt, and I have followed her advice.

"I very kindly thank you for your friendly invitation to Georgia and if I am ever within a thousand miles of you, I will come and see you ; though it be but for a day.

"You touch me on a very tender part when you say my friends on your side the water 'cannot be reconciled to the idea of my resigning my adopted America, even for my native England.' They are right. Though I am in as elegant style of acquaintance here as any American that ever came over, my heart and myself are 3000 miles apart ; and I had rather see my horse Button in his own stable, or eating the grass of Bordentown or Morrisania, than see all the pomp and show of Europe.

"A thousand years hence (for I must indulge in a few thoughts), perhaps in less, America may be what England now is ! The innocence of her character that won the hearts of all nations in her favor may sound like a romance, and her inimitable virtue as if it had never been. The ruins of that liberty which thousands bled for, or suffered to obtain, may just furnish materials for a village tale or extort a sigh from rustic sensibility, while the fashionable of that day, enveloped in dissipation, shall deride the principle and deny the fact.

"When we contemplate the fall of Empires and the extinction of nations of the ancient world, we see but little to excite our regret than the mouldering ruins of pompous palaces, magnificent monuments, lofty pyramids, and walls and towers of the most costly workmanship. But when the Empire of America shall fall, the subject for contemplative sorrow will be infinitely greater than crumbling brass or marble can inspire. It will not then be said, here stood a temple of vast antiquity,—here rose a Babel of invisible height, or there a palace of sumptuous extravagance ; but here, ah painful thought ! the noblest work of human wisdom, the grandest scene of human glory, the fair cause of freedom rose and fell !

"Read this and then ask if I forget America— But I'll not be dull if I can help it, so I leave off, and close my letter to-morrow, which is the day the mail is made up for America.

"January 7th. I have heard this morning with extreme concern of the death of our worthy friend Capt. Read. Mrs. Read lives in a house of mine at Bordentown, and you will much oblige me by telling her how much I am affected by her loss ; and to mention to her, with that delicacy which such an offer and her situation require, and which no one knows better how to convey than yourself, that the two years' rent which is due I request her to accept of, and to consider herself at home till she hears further from me.

"This is the severest winter I ever knew in England ; the frost has continued upwards of five weeks, and is still likely to continue. All the vessels from America have been kept off by contrary winds. The 'Polly' and the 'Pigeon' from Philadelphia and the 'Eagle' from Charleston are just got in.

"If you should leave New York before I arrive (which I hope will not be the case) and should pass through Philadelphia, I wish you would do me the favour to present my compliments to Mrs. Powell, the lady whom I wanted an opportunity to introduce you to when you were in Philadelphia, but was prevented by your being at a house where I did not visit.

"There is a Quaker favorite of mine at New York, formerly Miss Watson of Philadelphia ; she is now married to Dr. Lawrence, and is an acquaintance of Mrs. Oswald : be so kind as to make her a visit for me. You will like her conversation. She has a little of the Quaker primness—but of the pleasing kind—about her.

"I am always distressed at closing a letter, because it seems like taking leave of my friends after a parting conversation.—Captain Nicholson, Mrs. Nicholson, Hannah, Fanny, James, and the little ones, and you my dear Kitty, and your partner for life—God bless you all! and send me safe back to my much loved America!
"THOMAS PAINE—æt. 52.
"or if you better like it
"'Common Sense.'

"This comes by the packet which sails from Falmouth, 300 miles from London; but by the first vessel from London to New York I will send you some magazines. In the meantime be so kind as to write to me by the first opportunity. Remember me to the family at Morrisania, and all my friends at New York and Bordentown. Desire Gen. Morris to take another guinea of Mr. Constable, who has some money of mine in his hands, and give it to my boy Joe. Tell Sally to take care of 'Button.' Then direct for me at Mr. Peter Whiteside's London. When you are at Charleston remember me to my dear old friend Mrs. Lawrence, Col. and Mrs. L. Morris, and Col. Washington; and at Georgia, to Col. Walton. Adieu."

CHAPTER XVIII

PAINE'S LETTERS TO JEFFERSON IN PARIS

A NOTE of Paine to Jefferson, dated February 19, 1788, shows him in that city [1] consulting with Lafayette about his bridge, and preparing a memorial for the government. The visit was no doubt meant to secure a patent, and also arrange for the erection of the bridge. This appears to be his last meeting with Jefferson in Europe. He must have returned soon to England, where a letter of June 15th reports to Jefferson large progress in his patent, and other arrangements. Paine's letters were by no means confined to his personal affairs. In one of his letters Jefferson says: "I have great confidence in your communications, and since Mr. Adams' departure I am in need of authentic information from that country." Jefferson subscribes his letters—"I am with great and sincere attachment, dear Sir, your affectionate friend and servant," —and Paine responded with wonted fidelity. For more than a year the United States government was supplied by Paine, mainly through Jefferson, with information concerning affairs in England. It will be seen by some of the subjoined extracts that Paine was recognized by English statesmen as a sort of American Minister, and that the in-

[1] Paris.—H.B.B.

formation he transmits is rarely, if ever, erroneous. All this would appear more clearly could space be here given to the entire letters. The omissions are chiefly of items of news now without interest, or of technical details concerning the bridge. It is only just to remind the reader, before introducing the quotations, that these letters were confidential, and to a very intimate friend, being thus not liable to any charge of egotism from the public, for whose eye they were not intended.

"LONDON, BROAD STREET BUILDINGS, No. 13. Sept. 9, 1788.—That I am a bad correspondent is so general a complaint against me, that I must expect the same accusation from you —But hear me first—When there is no matter to write upon, a letter is not worth the trouble of receiving and reading and while any thing which is to be the subject of a letter, is in suspence, it is difficult to write and perhaps best to let it alone—'least said is soonest mended,' and nothing said requires no mending.

"The model has the good fortune of preserving in England the reputation which it received from the Academy of Sciences. It is a favorite hobby horse with all who have seen it; and every one who has talked with me on the subject advised me to endeavor to obtain a Patent, as it is only by that means that I can secure to myself the direction and management. For this purpose I went, in company with Mr. Whiteside to the office which is an appendage to Lord Sydney's—told them who I was, and made an affidavit that the construction was my own Invention. This was the only step I took in the business. Last Wednesday I received a Patent for England, the next day a Patent for Scotland, and I am to have one for Ireland.

"As I had already the opinion of the scientific Judges both in France and England on the Model, it was also necessary that I should have that of the practical Iron men who must finally be the executors of the work. There are several capital Iron Works in this country, the principal of which are those in Shropshire, Yorkshire, and Scotland. It was my intention to have communicated with Mr. Wilkinson, who is one of the proprietors of the Shropshire Iron Works, and concerned in those in France, but his departure for Sweden before I had possession of the patents prevented me. The Iron Works in Yorkshire belonging to the Walkers near to Sheffield are the most eminent in England in point of establishment and property. The proprietors are reputed to be worth two hundred thousand pounds and consequently capable of giving energy to any great undertaking. A friend of theirs who had seen the model wrote to them on the subject, and two of them came to London last Fryday to see it and talk with me on the business. Their opinion is very decided that it can be executed either in wrought or cast Iron, and I am to go down to their Works next week to erect an experiment arch. This is the point I am now got to, and until now I had nothing to inform you of. If I succeed in erecting the arch all reasoning and opinion will be at an end, and, as this will soon be known, I shall not return to France till that time ; and until then I wish every thing to remain respecting my Bridge over the Seine, in the state I left matters in when I came from France. With respect to the Patents in England it is my intention to dispose of them as soon as I have established the certainty of the construction.

"Besides the ill success of Black friars Bridge, two Bridges built successively on the same spot, the last by Mr. Smeaton, at Hexham, over the Tyne in Northumberland, have fallen down, occasioned by quicksands under the bed of the river. If therefore arches can be extended in the proportion the model promises, the construction in certain situations, without regard to cheapness or dearness, will be valuable in all countries. . . . As to English news or Politics, there is little more than what the public papers contain. The assembling the States General, and the reappointment of Mr. Neckar, made considerable impression here. They overawe a great deal of the English habitual rashness, and check that triumph of presumption which they indulged themselves in with respect to what they called the deranged and almost ruinous condition of the finances of France. They acknowledge unreservedly that the natural resources of France are greater than those of England, but they plume themselves on the superiority of the means necessary to bring national resources

forth. But the two circumstances above mentioned serve very well to lower this exaltation.

"Some time ago I spent a week at Mr. Burke's, and the Duke of Portland's in Buckinghamshire. You will recollect that the Duke was the member during the time of the coalition—he is now in the opposition, and I find the opposition as much warped in some respects as to Continental Politics as the Ministry.—What the extent of the Treaty with Russia is, Mr. B[urke] says that he and all the opposition are totally unacquainted with ; and they speak of it not as a very wise measure, but rather tending to involve England in unnecessary continental disputes. The preference of the opposition is to a connection with Prussia if it could have been obtained. Sir George Staunton tells me that the interference with respect to Holland last year met with considerable opposition from part of the Cabinet. Mr. Pitt was against it at first, but it was a favourite measure with the King, and that the opposition at that crisis contrived to have it known to him that they were disposed to support his measures. This together with the notification of the 16th of September gave Mr. Pitt cause and pretence for changing his ground.

"The Marquis of Landsdown is unconnected either with the Ministry or the opposition. His politics is distinct from both. His plan is a sort of armed neutrality which has many advocates. In conversation with me he reprobated the conduct of the Ministry towards France last year as operating to '*cut the throat of confidence*' (this was his expression) between France and England at a time when there was a fair opportunity of improving it.

"The enmity of this country against Russia is as bitter as it ever was against America, and is carried to every pitch of abuse and vulgarity. What I hear in conversations exceeds what may be seen in the news-papers. They are sour and mortified at every success she acquires, and voraciously believe and rejoice in the most improbable accounts and rumors to the contrary. You may mention this to Mr. Simelin on any terms you please for you cannot exceed the fact.

"There are those who amuse themselves here in the hopes of managing Spain. The notification which the Marquis del Campo made last year to the British Cabinet, is perhaps the only secret kept in this country. Mr. B[urke] tells me that the opposition knows nothing of it. They all very freely admit that if the Combined fleets had had thirty or forty thousand land forces, when they came up the channel last war, there was nothing in England to oppose their landing, and that such a measure would have been fatal to their resources, by at least a temporary destruction of national credit. This is the point on which this country is most impressible. Wars carried on at a distance, they care but little about, and seem always disposed to enter into them. It is bringing the matter home to them that makes them fear and feel, for their weakest part is at home. This I take to be the reason of the attention they are paying to Spain ; for while France and Spain make a common cause and *start* together, they may easily overawe this country.

" I intended sending this letter by Mr. Parker, but he goes by the way of Holland, and as I do not chuse to send it by the English Post, I shall desire Mr. Bartholemy to forward it to you.

" Remember me with much affection to the Marquis de la Fayette. This letter will serve for two letters. Whether I am in London or the country any letter to me at Mr. Whiteside's, Merchant, No. 13 Broad Street Buildings, will come safe. My compliments to Mr. Short."

" LONDON, September 15.—I have not heard of Mr. [Lewis] Littlepage since I left Paris,—if you have, I shall be glad to know it. As he dined sometimes at Mr. Neckar's, he undertook to describe the Bridge to him. Mr. Neckar very readily conceived it. If you have an opportunity of seeing Mr. Neckar, and see it convenient to renew the subject, you might mention that I am going forward with an experiment arch.—Mr. Le Couteulx desired me to examine the construction of the Albion Steam Mills erected by Bolton and Watt. I have not yet written to him because I had nothing certain to write about. I have talked with Mr. Rumsey, who is here, upon this matter, and who appears to me to be master of that subject, and who has procured a model of the Mill, which is worked originally from the steam. . . . When you see Mr. Le Roy please to present my compliments. I hope to realize the opinion of the Academy on the Model, in which case I shall give the Academy the proper information. We have no certain accounts here of the arrangement of the new Ministry. The papers mention Count St. Preist for Foreign Affairs. When you see him please to present my compliments. . . . Please to present my compliments to M. and Madame de Corney."

" LONDON, December 16.—That the King is insane is now old news. He yet continues in the same state, and the Parliament are on the business of appointing a Regent. The Dukes of York and Gloucester have both made speeches in the house of Peers. An embarrassing question, whether the Prince of Wales has a right in himself by succession during the incapacity of his father, or whether the right must derive to him thro' Parliament, has been agitated in both Houses. [Illegible] and the speeches of York and Gloucester of avoiding the question. This day is fixt for bringing the matter on in the house of Commons. A change of Ministry is expected, and I believe determined on. The Duke of Portland and his friends will in all probability come in. I shall be exceedingly glad to hear from you, and to know if you have received my letters, and also when you intend

setting off for America, or whether you intend to visit England before you go. In case of change of Ministry here there are certain matters I shall be glad to see you upon. Remember me to the Marquis de la Fayette. We hear good things from France, and I sincerely wish them all well and happy. Remember me to Mr. Short and Mr. Mazzei." [1]

" LONDON, Jan. 15, 1789.—My last letter requested to know if you had any thoughts of coming to England before you sailed to America. There will certainly be a change of ministry, and probably some change of measures, and it might not be inconvenient if you could know before your sailing, for the information of the new Congress, what measures the new Ministry here intended to pursue or adopt with respect to commercial arrangements with America. I am in some intimacy with Mr. Burke, and after the new ministry are formed he has proposed to introduce me to them. The Duke of Portland, at whose seat in the country I was a few days last summer, will be at the head of the Treasury, and Mr. Fox Secretary for Foreign Affairs. The King continues, I believe, as mad as ever. It appears that he has amassed several millions of money, great part of which is in foreign funds. He had made a Will, while he had his senses, and devised it among his children, but a second Will has been produced, made since he was mad, dated the 25th of Oct., in which he gives his property to the Queen. This will probably produce much dispute, and it is attended with many suspicious circumstances. It came out in the examination of the physicians, that one of them, Dr. Warrens, on being asked the particular time of his observing the King's insanity, said the twenty-second of October, and some influence has been exerted to induce him to retract that declaration, or to say that the insanity was not so much as to prevent him making a Will, which he has refused to do."

" LONDON, February 16.—Your favor of the 23d December continued to the —— of Janry. came safe to hand,—for which I thank you. I begin this without knowing of any opportunity of conveyance, and shall follow the method of your letter by writing on till an opportunity offers.

" I thank you for the many and judicious observations about my bridge. I am exactly in your Ideas as you will perceive by the following account.—I went to the Iron Works the latter

---

[1] Mazzei was a scientific Italian who settled in Virginia with a Tuscan colony before the Revolution, in which he took up arms and was captured by the British. His colony had been under the patronage of Jefferson, to whose fortunes he was alway devoted, though the publication of Jefferson's famous letter to him, reflecting on Washington's administration, caused his patron much trouble.

end of Octr. My intention at the time of writing to you was to construct an experiment arch of 250 feet, but in the first place, the season was too far advanced to work out of doors and an arch of that extent could not be worked within doors, and *nextly*, there was a prospect of a real Bridge being wanted on the spot of 90 feet extent. The person who appeared disposed to erect a Bridge is Mr. Foljambe nephew to the late Sir George Saville, and member in the last Parliament for Yorkshire. He lives about three miles from the works, and the River Don runs in front of his house, over which there is an old ill constructed Bridge which he wants to remove. These circumstances determined me to begin an arch of 90 feet with an elevation of 5 feet. This extent I could manage within doors by working half the arch at a time. . . . A great part of our time, as you will naturally suppose, was taken up in preparations, but after we began to work we went on rapidly, and that without any mistake, or anything to alter or amend. The foreman of the works is a Relation to the Proprietors, an excellent mechanic, and who fell into all my Ideas with great ease and penetration. I staid at the works till one half the Rib, 45 feet, was compleated and framed horizontally together and came up to London at the meeting of Parliament on the 4th of December. The foreman, whom, as I told him, I should appoint 'President of the Board of Works,' in my absence,' wrote me word that he has got the other half together with much less trouble than the first. He is now preparing for erecting and I for returning.

"February 26.—A few days ago I received a letter from Mr. Foljambe in which he says: 'I saw the Rib of your Bridge. In point of elegance and beauty, it far exceeded my expectations and is certainly beyond any thing I ever saw.'—My model and myself had many visitors while I was at the works. A few days after I got there, Lord Fitz-William, heir to the Marquis of Rockingham, came with Mr. Burke. The former gave the workmen five guineas and invited me to Wentworth House, a few miles distant from the works, where I went, and staid a few days.

"This Bridge I expect will bring forth something greater, but in the meantime I feel like a Bird from its nest and wishing most anxiously to return. Therefore, as soon as I can bring any thing to bear, I shall dispose of the contract and bid adieu. I can very truly say that my mind is not at home.

"I am very much rejoiced at the account you give me of the state of affairs in France. I feel exceedingly interested in the happiness of that nation. They are now got or getting into the right way, and the present reign will be more Immortalized in France than any that ever preceded it. They have all died away, forgotten in the common mass of things, but this will be to France like an Anno Mundi, or an Anno Domini. The happiness of doing good and the

Pride of doing great things unite themselves in this business. But as there are two kinds of Pride—the little and the great, the privileged orders will in some degree be governed by this Division. Those of little pride (I mean little-minded pride) will be schismatical, and those of the great pride will be orthodox, with respect to the States General. Interest will likewise have some share, and could this operate freely it would arrange itself on the orthodox side. To enrich a Nation is to enrich the individuals which compose it. To enrich the farmer is to enrich the farm—and consequently the Landlord ;—for whatever the farmer is, the farm will be. The richer the subject, the richer the revenue, because the consumption from which Taxes are raised is in proportion to the abilities of people to consume ; therefore the most effectual method to raise both the revenue and the rental of a country is to raise the condition of the people,—or that order known in France by the Tiers Etat. But I ought to ask pardon for entering into reasonings in a letter to you, and only do it because I like the subject.

"I observe in all the companies I go into the impression which the present circumstances of France has upon this Country. *An internal Alliance* in France [between Throne and People] is an alliance which England never dreamed of, and which she most dreads. Whether she will be better or worse tempered afterwards I cannot judge of, but I believe she will be more cautious in giving offence. She is likewise impressed with an Idea that a negotiation is on foot between the King [Louis XVI.] and the Emperor for adding Austrian Flanders to France. This appears to me such a probable thing, and may be rendered so conducive to the interest and good of all the parties concerned, that I am inclined to give it credit and wish it success. I hope then to see the Scheld opened, for it is a sin to refuse the bounties of nature. On these matters I shall be glad of your opinion. I think the States General of Holland could not be in earnest when they applied to France for the payment of the quota to the Emperor. All things considered to request it was meanness, and to expect it absurdity. I am more inclined to think they made it an opportunity to find how they stood with France. Absalom (I think it was) set fire to his brother's field of corn to bring on a conversation.

"March 12.—With respect to Political matters here, the truth is, the people are fools. They have no discernment into principles and consequences. Had Mr. Pitt proposed a National Convention, at the time of the King's insanity, he had done right ; but instead of this he has absorbed the right of the Nation into a right of Parliament,—one house of which (the Peers) is hereditary in its own right, and over which the people have no controul (not so much as they have over their King) ; and the other elective by only a small part of the Nation. Therefore he has lessened instead of increased the rights of the people ; but as they have not sense enough to see it, they have been huzzaing him. There can be no fixed principles of government, or anything like a constitution in a country where the Government can alter itself, or one part of it supply the other.

"Whether a man that has been so compleatly mad as not to be managed but by force and the mad shirt can ever be confided in afterwards as a reasonable man, is a matter I have very little opinion of. Such a circumstance, in my estimation, if mentioned, ought to be a perpetual disqualification.

"The Emperor I am told has entered a caveat against the Elector of Hanover (not the electoral vote) for King of the Romans. John Bull, however, is not so mad as he was, and a message has been manufactured for him to Parliament in which there is nothing particular. The Treaty with Prussia is not yet before Parliament but is to be.

"Had the Regency gone on and the new administration been formed I should have been able to communicate some matters of business to you, both with respect to America and France ; as an interview for that purpose was agreed upon and to take place as soon as the persons who were to fill the offices should succeed. I am the more confidential with those persons, as they are distinguished by the name of the Blue & Buff,— a dress taken up during the American War, and is the undress uniform of General Washington with Lapels which they still wear.[1] But, at any rate, I do not think it is worth while for Congress to appoint any Minister to this Court. The greater distance Congress observes on this point the better. It will be all money thrown away to go to any expence about it—at least during the present reign. I know the nation well, and the line of acquaintance I am in enables me to judge better than any other American can judge —especially at a distance. If Congress should have any business to state to the Government here, it can be easily done thro' their Minister at Paris—but the seldomer the better.

"I believe I am not so much in the good graces of the Marquis of Landsdowne as I used to be—I do not answer his purpose. He was always talking of a sort of reconnection of England and America, and my coldness and reserve on this subject checked communication."

"LONDON, April 10.—The King continues in his amended state, but Dr. Willis, his son, and attendants, are yet about his person. He has not been to Parliament nor made any public appearance, but he has fixed the 23d April for a public thanksgiving, and he is to go in great Parade to offer up his Devotions at St. Paul's on

---

[1] On this Blue and Buff Society, Canning wrote some satirical verses. He also described "French philanthropy" as "Condorcet filtered through the dregs of Paine."

that day. Those about him have endeavored to dissuade him from this ostentatious pilgrimage, most probably from an apprehension of some effect it may have upon him, but he persists. . . . The acts for regulating the trade with America are to be continued as last year. A paper from the Privy Council respecting the American fly is before Parliament. I had some conversation with Sir Joseph Banks upon this subject, as he was the person whom the Privy Council referred to. I told him that the Hessian fly attacked only the green plant, and did not exist in the dry grain. He said that with respect to the Hessian fly, they had no apprehension, but it was the weevil they alluded to. I told him the weevil had always more or less been in the wheat countries of America, and that if the prohibition was on that account it was as necessary fifty or sixty years ago, as now ; that I believe it was only a political manœuvre of the Ministry to please the landed interest, as a balance for prohibiting the exportation of wool to please the manufacturing interest. He did not reply, and as we are on very sociable terms I went farther by saying—The English ought not to complain of the non-payment of Debts from America while they prohibit the means of payment.

"I suggest to you a thought on this subject. The debts due before the war, ought to be distinguished from the debts contracted since, and all and every mode of payment and remittance under which they *have been discharged at the time they were contracted* ought to accompany those Debts, so long as any of them shall continue unpaid ; because the circumstances of payment became united with the debt, and cannot be separated by subsequent acts of one side only. If this was taken up in America, and insisted on as a right co-eval with and inseparable from those Debts, it would force some of the restrictions here to give way.

"You speak very truly of this country when you say 'that they are slumbering under a half reformation of Politics and religion, and cannot be excited by any thing they hear or see to question the remains of prejudice.' Their ignorance on some matters, is unfathomable, for instance the Bank of England discounts Bills at 5 p cent, but a proposal is talked of for discounting at $4\frac{1}{2}$; and the reason given is the vast quantity of money, and that money of the good houses discounts at $4\frac{1}{2}$; from this they deduce the great ability and credit of the nation. Whereas the contrary is the case. This money is all in paper, and the quantity is greater than the object to circulate it upon, and therefore shows that the market is glutted, and consequently the ability for farther paper excretions is lessened.—If a war should ever break out, between the countries again, this is the spot where it ought to be prosecuted, they neither feel nor care for any thing at a distance, but are frightened and spiritless at every thing which happens at home. The Combined fleet coming up the Channel, Paul Jones, and the Mob of 1738, are the dreadful eras of this country. But for national puffing none equals them. The addresses which have been presented are stuffed with nonsense of this kind. One of them published in the *London Gazette* and presented by a Sir William Appleby begins thus,—' Britain, the Queen of Isles, the pride of Nations, the Arbitress of Europe, perhaps of the world.' . . . On the receipt of your last, I went to Sir Joseph Banks to inform him of your having heard from Ledyard, from Grand Cairo, but found he had a letter from him of the same date. Sir Joseph is one of the society for promoting that undertaking. He has an high opinion of Ledyard, and thinks him the only man fitted for such an exploration. As you may probably hear of Ledyard by accounts that may not reach here, Sir Joseph will be obliged to you to communicate to him any matters respecting him that may come to you (Sir Joseph Banks, Bart., Soho Square). . . .

"While writing this I am informed that the Minister has had a conference with some of the American creditors, and proposed to them to assume the debts and give them ten shillings on the pound—the conjecture is that he means, when the new Congress is established, to demand the payment. If you are writing to General Washington, it may not be amiss to mention this—and if I hear farther on the matter I will inform you.[1] But, as being a money matter it cannot come forward but thro' Parliament, there will be notice given of the business. This would be a proper time to show that the British Acts since the Peace militate against the payment by narrowing the means by which those debts might have been paid when they were contracted, and which ought to be considered as constituant parts of the contract."

"June 17.—I received your last to the 21st May. I am just now informed of Messrs. Parker and Cutting setting off to-morrow morning for Paris by whom this will be delivered to you. Nothing new is showing here. The trial of Hastings, and the Examination of evidence before the house of Commons into the Slave Trade still continue.

" I wrote Sir Joseph Banks an account of my Experiment Arch. In his answer he informs me of its being read before the Royal Society who expressed 'great satisfaction at the Communication.' ' I expect' says Sir Joseph ' many improvements from your Countrymen who think with vigor, and are in a great measure free from those shackles of Theory which are imposed on the minds of our people before they are capable of exerting their mental faculties to advantage.' In the close of his letter he says : ' We have lost poor Ledyard. He had agreed with certain Moors to conduct him to Sennar. The time for their departure was arrived when he found him-

self ill, and took a large dose of Emetic Tartar, burst a blood-vessel in the operation, which carried him off in three days. We sincerely lament his loss, as the papers we have received from him are full of those emanations of spirit, which taught you to construct a Bridge without any reference to the means used by your predecessors in that art.' I have wrote to the Walkers and proposed to them to manufacture me a compleat Bridge and erect it in London, and afterwards put it up to sale. I do this by way of bringing forward a Bridge over the Thames—which appears to me the most advantageous of all objects. For, if only a fifth of the persons, at a half penny each, pass over a new Bridge as now pass over the old ones the tolls will pay 25 per Cent besides what will arise from carriage and horses. Mrs. Williams tells me that her letters from America mention Dr. Franklin as being exceedingly ill. I have been to see the Cotton Mills,—the Potteries— the Steel furnaces—Tin plate manufacture— White lead manufacture. All those things might be easily carried on in America. I saw a few days ago part of a hand bill of what was called a geometrical wheelbarrow,—but cannot find where it is to be seen. The Idea is one of those that needed only to be thought of,—for it is very easy to conceive that if a wheelbarrow, as it is called, be driven round a piece of land, —a sheet of paper may be placed in it—so as to receive by the tracings of a Pencil, regulated by a little Mechanism—the figure and content of the land—and that neither Theodolite nor chain are necessary."

"ROTHERHAM, YORKSHIRE, July 13.—The Walkers are to find all the materials, and fit and frame them ready for erecting, put them on board a vessel & send them to London. I am to undertake all expense from that time & to compleat the erecting. We intend first to exhibit it and afterwards put it up to sale, or dispose of it by private contract, and after paying the expences of each party the remainder to be equally divided—one half theirs, the other mine. My principal object in this plan is to open the way for a Bridge over the Thames. . . . I shall now have occasion to draw upon some funds I have in America. I have one thousand Dollars stock in the Bank at Philadelphia, and two years interest due upon it last April, £180 in the hands of General Morris ; £40 with Mr. Constable of New York ; a house at Bordentown, and a farm at New Rochelle. The stock and interest in the Bank, which Mr. Willing manages for me, is the easiest negotiated, and full sufficient for what I shall want. On this fund I have drawn fifteen guineas payable to Mr. Trumbull, tho' I shall not want the money longer than till the Exhibition and sale of the Bridge. I had rather draw than ask to borrow of any body here. If you go to America this year I shall be very glad if you can manage this matter for me, by giving me credit for two

---

[1] This and other parts of Paine's correspondence were forwarded to Washington.

hundred pounds, on London, and receiving that amount of Mr. Willing. I am not acquainted with the method of negotiating money matters, but if you can accommodate me in this, and will direct me how the transfer is to be made, I shall be much obliged to you. Please direct to me under cover to Mr. Trumbull. I have some thoughts of coming over to France for two or three weeks, as I shall have little to do here until the Bridge is ready for erecting.

September 15.—When I left Paris I was to return with the Model, but I could now bring over a compleat Bridge. Tho' I have a slender opinion of myself for executive business, I think, upon the whole that I have managed this matter tolerable well. With no money to spare for such an undertaking I am the sole Patentee here, and connected with one of the first and best established houses in the Nation. But absent from America I feel a craving desire to return and I can scarcely forbear weeping at the thoughts of your going and my staying behind.

"Accept my dear Sir, my most hearty thanks for your many services and friendship. Remember me with an overflowing affection to my dear America—the people and the place. Be so kind to shake hands with them for me, and tell our beloved General Washington, and my old friend Dr. Franklin how much I long to see them. I wish you would spend a day with General Morris of Morrisania, and present my best wishes to all the family.—But I find myself wandering into a melancholy subject that will be tiresome to read,—so wishing you a prosperous passage, and a happy meeting with all your friends and mine, I remain yours affectionately, etc.

"I shall be very glad to hear from you when you arrive. If you direct for me to the care of Mr. Benjamin Vaughn it will find me.—Please present my friendship to Captain Nicholson and family of New York, and to Mr. and Mrs. Few.

"September 18.—I this moment receive yours of ye 13 int. which being Post Night,

affords me the welcome opportunity of acknowledging it. I wrote you on the 15th by post—but I was so full of the thoughts of America and my American friends that I forgot France.

"The people of this Country speak very differently on the affairs of France. The mass of them, so far as I can collect, say that France is a much freer Country than England. The Peers, the Bishops, &c. say the National Assembly has gone too far. There are yet in this country, very considerable remains of the feudal System which people did not see till the revolution in france placed it before their eyes. While the multitude here could be terrified with the cry and apprehension of Arbitrary power, wooden shoes, popery, and such like stuff, they thought themselves by comparison an extraordinary free people; but this bugbear now loses its force, and they appear to me to be turning their eyes towards the Aristocrats of their own Nation. This is a new mode of conquering, and I think it will have its effect.

"I am looking out for a place to erect my Bridge, within some of the Squares would be very convenient. I had thought of Soho Square, where Sir Joseph Banks lives, but he is now in Lincolnshire. I expect it will be ready for erecting and in London by the latter end of October. Whether I shall then sell it in England or bring it over to Paris, and re-erect it there, I have not determined in my mind. In order to bring any kind of a contract forward for the Seine, it is necessary it should be seen, and, as œconomy will now be a principle in the Government, it will have a better chance than before.

"If you should pass thro' Bordentown in Jersey, which is not out of your way from Philadelphia to New York, I shall be glad you would enquire out my particular friend Col. Kirkbride. You will be very much pleased with him. His house is my home when in that part of the Country—and it was there that I made the Model of my Bridge."

CHAPTER XIX

THE KEY OF THE BASTILLE

In June, 1777, the Emperor Joseph II. visited his sister, the Queen of France, and passed a day at Nantes. The Count de Menou, commandant of the place, pointed out in the harbor, among the flags raised in his honor, one bearing thirteen stars. The Emperor turned away his eyes, saying: "I cannot look on that; my own profession is to be royalist."

Weber, foster-brother of Marie Antionette, who reports the Emperor's remark, recognized the fate of France in those thirteen stars. That republic, he says, was formed by the subjects of a King, aided by another King. These French armies, mingling their flags with those of America, learned a new language. Those warriors, the flower of their age, went out Frenchmen and returned Americans. They returned to a court, but decorated with republican emblems and showing the scars of Liberty. Lafayette, it is said, had in his study a large *carton*, splendidly framed, in two columns : on one was inscribed the American Declaration of Independence; the other was blank, awaiting the like Declaration of France.[1]

The year 1789 found France afflicted with a sort of famine, its finances in disorder ; while the people, their eyes directed to the new world by the French comrades of Washington, beheld that great chieftain inaugurated as president of a prosperous republic. The first pamphlet of Thomas Paine, expurgated in translation of anti-monarchism, had been widely circulated, and John Adams (1779) found himself welcomed in France as the supposed author of "Common Sense." The lion's skin dropped from Paine's disgusted enemy, and when, ten years later, the lion himself became known in Paris, he was hailed with enthusiasm. This was in the autumn of 1789, when Paine witnessed the scenes that ushered in the "crowned republic," from which he hoped so much. Jefferson had sailed in September, and Paine was recognized by Lafayette and other leaders as the representative of the United States. To him Lafayette gave for presentation to Washington the Key of the destroyed Bastille, ever since visible at Mount Vernon,—symbol of the fact that, in Paine's words, "the principles of America opened the Bastille."

But now an American enemy of Paine's principles more inveterate than Adams found himself similarly eclipsed in Paris by the famous author. Early in 1789 Gouverneur Morris came upon the stage of events in Europe. He was entrusted

[1] "Mémoires concernant Marie-Antoinette," pp. 34–79.

by the President with a financial mission which, being secret, swelled him to importance in the imagination of courtiers. At Jefferson's request Gouverneur Morris posed to Houdon for the bust of Washington ; and when, to Morris' joy, Jefferson departed, he posed politically as Washington to the eyes of Europe. He was scandalized that Jefferson should retain recollections of the Declaration of Independence strong enough to desire for France "a downright republican form of government"; and how it happened that under Jefferson's secretaryship of state this man, whom even Hamilton pronounced "an exotic" in a republic, was presently appointed Minister to France, is a mystery remaining to be solved.

Morris had a "high old time" in Europe. Intimacy with Washington secured him influence with Lafayette, and the fine ladies of Paris, seeking official favours for relatives and lovers, welcomed him to the boudoirs, baths, and bedrooms to which his diary now introduces the public.

It was but natural that such a man, just as he had been relieved of the overlaying Jefferson, should try to brush Paine aside. On January 26, 1790, he enters in his diary :

"To-day, at half-past three, I go to M. de Lafayette's. He tells me that he wishes to have a meeting of Mr. Short, Mr. Paine, and myself, to consider their judiciary, because his place imposes on him the necessity of being right. I tell him that Paine can do him no good, for that, although he has an excellent pen to write, he has but an indifferent head to think."

Eight years before, Gouverneur Morris had joined Robert Morris in appealing to the author to enlighten the nation on the subject of finance and the direction of the war. He had also confessed to Paine that he had been duped by Silas Deane, who, by the way, was now justifying all that Paine had said of him by hawking his secret letter-books in London. Now, in Paris, Morris discovers that Paine has but an indifferent head to think.[1]

Gouverneur Morris was a fascinating man. His diary and letters, always entertaining, reveal the secret of his success in twisting the Constitution and Jefferson and Washington around his fingers in several important junctures. To Paine also he was irresistible. His cordial manners disarm suspicion, and we presently find the author pouring into the ear of his secret detractor what state secrets he learns in London.

On March 17, 1790, Paine left Paris to see after his Bridge in Yorkshire, now near completion. On the day before, he writes to a friend in Philadelphia how prosperously everything is going on in France, where Lafayette is acting the part of a Washington ; how the political reformation is sure to influence England ; and how he longs for America.

"I wish most anxiously to see my much loved America. It is the country from whence all reformation must originally spring. I despair of seeing an abolition of the infernal traffic in negroes. We must push that matter further on your side of the water. I wish that a few well-instructed could be sent among their brethren in bondage ; for until they are able to take their own part nothing will be done."[2]

On his arrival in London he has the happiness of meeting his old friend General Morris of Morrisania, and his wife. Gouverneur is presently over there, to see his brother ; and in the intervals of dancing attendance at the opera on titled ladies—among them Lady Dunmore, whose husband desolated the Virginia coast,—he gets Paine's confidences.[3] Poor Paine was an easy victim of any show of personal kindness, especially when it seemed like the magnanimity of a political opponent.

The historic sense may recognize a picturesque incident in the selection by Lafayette of Thomas Paine to convey the Key of the Bastille to Washington. In the series of intellectual and moral movements which culminated in the French Revolution, the Bastille was especially the prison of Paine's forerunners, the writers, and the place where their books were burned. "The gates of the Bastille," says Rocquain, "were opened wide for abbés, savants, brilliant intellects, professors of the University and doctors of the Sorbonne, all accused of writing or reciting verses against the King, casting reflections on the Government, or publishing books in favor of Deism; and contrary to good morals. Diderot was one of the first arrested, and it was during his detention that he conceived the plan of his ' Encyclopedia.' "[4]

The coming Key was announced to Washington with the following letters :

"LONDON, May 1, 1790.—Sir,—Our very good friend the Marquis de la Fayette has entrusted to my care the Key of the Bastille, and a drawing, handsomely framed, representing the demolition of that detestable prison, as a present to your Excellency, of which his letter will more particularly inform. I feel myself happy in being the person thro' whom the Marquis has conveyed this early trophy of the Spoils of despotism, and the first ripe fruits of American principles transplanted into Europe, to his great master and patron. When he mentioned to me the present he intended you, my heart leaped with joy. It is something so truly in character that no remarks can illustrate it, and is more happily expressive of his remembrance of his American friends than any letters can convey. That the principles of America opened the Bastille is not to be doubted, and therefore the Key comes to the right place.

---

[1] " Diary and Letters of Gouverneur Morris." Edited by Anne Cary Morris, i., p. 286.

[2] One cannot help wondering how, in this matter, Paine got along with his friend Jefferson, who, at the very time of his enthusiasm for the French Revolution, had a slave in his house at Challiot. Paine was not of the philanthropic type portrayed in the " Biglow Papers " :

"I du believe in Freedom's cause
    Ez fur away ez Payris is ;
I love to see her stick her claws
    In them infarnal Phayrisees.
It 's well enough agin a king
    To dror resolves and triggers,
But libbaty 's a kind o' thing
    That don't agree with niggers. '

[3] " Diary," etc., i., pp. 339, 341.

[4] "L'Esprit revolutionnaire avant la Revolution." A good service has been done by Miss Hunting in translating and condensing the admirable historical treatise of M. Félix Rocquain on " The Revolutionary Spirit Preceding the Revolution," for which Professor Huxley wrote a preface.

"I beg leave to suggest to your Excellency the propriety of congratulating the King and Queen of France (for they have been our friends,) and the National Assembly, on the happy example they are giving to Europe. You will see by the King's speech, which I enclose, that he prides himself on being at the head of the Revolution ; and I am certain that such a congratulation will be well received and have a good effect.

"I should rejoice to be the direct bearer of the Marquis's present to your Excellency, but I doubt I shall not be able to see my much loved America till next Spring. I shall therefore send it by some *American* vessel to New York. I have permitted no drawing to be taken here, tho' it has been often requested, as I think there is a propriety that it should first be presented. B[ut] Mr. West wishes Mr. Trumbull to make a painting of the presentation of the Key to you.

"I returned from France to London about five weeks ago, and I am engaged to return to Paris when the Constitution shall be proclaimed, and to carry the American flag in the procession. I have not the least doubt of the final and compleat success of the French Revolution. Little Ebbings and Flowings, for and against, the natural companions of revolutions, sometimes appear ; but the full current of it, is, in my opinion, as fixed as the Gulph Stream.

"I have manufactured a Bridge (a single arch) of one hundred and ten feet span, and five feet high from the cord of the arch. It is now on board a vessel coming from Yorkshire to London, where it is to be erected. I see nothing yet to disappoint my hopes of its being advantageous to me. It is this only which keeps me [in] Europe, and happy shall I be when I shall have it in my power to return to America. I have not heard of Mr. Jefferson since he sailed, except of his arrival. As I have always indulged the belief of having many friends in America, or rather no enemies, I have [*mutilated*] to mention but my affectionate [*mutilated*] and am Sir with the greatest respect, &c.

"If any of my friends are disposed to favor me with a letter it will come to hand by addressing it to the care of Benjamin Vaughn Esq., Jeffries Square, London."

"LONDON, May 31, 1790.—SIR,—By Mr. James Morris, who sailed in the May Packet, I transmitted you a letter from the Marquis de la Fayette, at the same time informing you that the Marquis had entrusted to my charge the Key of the Bastille, and a drawing of that prison, as a present to your Excellency. Mr. J. Rutledge, jun'r, had intended coming in the ship ' Marquis de la Fayette,' and I had chosen that opportunity for the purpose of transmitting the present ; but, the ship not sailing at the time appointed, Mr. Rutledge takes his passage on the Packet, and I have committed to his care that trophie of Liberty which I know it will give you pleasure to receive. The french Revolution is not only compleat but triumphant, and the envious despotism of this nation is compelled to own the magnanimity with which it has been conducted.

"The political hemisphere is again clouded by a dispute between England and Spain, the circumstances of which you will hear before this letter can arrive. A Messenger was sent from hence the 6th inst. to Madrid with very peremptory demands, and to wait there only forty-eight hours. His return has been expected for two or three days past. I was this morning at the Marquis del Campo's but nothing is yet arrived. Mr. Rutledge sets off at four o'clock this afternoon, but should any news arrive before the making up the mail on Wednesday June 2, I will forward it to you under cover.

"The views of this Court as well as of the Nation, so far as they extend to South America, are not for the purpose of freedom, but conquest. They already talk of sending some of the young branches to reign over them, and to pay off their national debt with the produce of their Mines. The Bondage of those countries will, as far as I can perceive, be prolonged by what this Court has in contemplation.

"My Bridge is arrived and I have engaged a place to erect it in. A little time will determine its fate, but I yet see no cause to doubt of its success, tho' it is very probable that a War, should it break out, will as in all new things prevent its progress so far as regards profits.

"In the partition in the Box, which contains the Key of the Bastille, I have put up half a dozen Razors, manufactured from Cast-steel made at the Works where the Bridge was constructed, which I request you to accept as a little token from a very grateful heart.

"I received about a week ago a letter from Mr. G. Clymer. It is dated the 4th February, but has been travelling ever since. I request you to acknowledge it for me and that I will answer it when my Bridge is erected. With much affection to all my friends, and many wishes to see them again, I am, etc."

Washington received the Key at New York, along with this last letter, and on August 10, 1790, acknowledges Päine's "agreeable letters."

"It must, I dare say, give you great pleasure to learn by repeated opportunities, that our new government answers its purposes as well as could have been reasonably expected, that we are gradually overcoming the difficulties which presented in its first organization, and that our prospects in general are growing more favorable."

Paine is said by several biographers to have gone to Paris in the May of this year. No doubt he was missed from London, but it was probably because he had gone to Thetford, where his mother died about the middle of May. Gouverneur Morris reports interviews with him August 8th and 15th, in London. The beautiful iron bridge, 110 feet long, had been erected in June at Leasing-Green (now Paddington-Green) at the joint expense of Paine and Peter Whiteside, an American merchant in London. It was attracting a fair number of visitors, at a shilling each, also favorable press notices, and all promised well.

So Paine was free to run over to Paris, where Carlyle mentions him, this year, as among the English "missionaries." [1] It was a brief visit, however, for October finds him again in London, drawn probably by intimations of disaster to the interests of his Bridge. Whiteside had failed, and his assignees, finding on his books £620 debited to Paine's Bridge, came upon the inventor for the money ; no doubt unfairly, for it seems to have

[1] "Her Paine ; rebellious Staymaker ; unkempt ; who feels that he, a single needleman, did, by his 'Common Sense' pamphlet, free America ;—that he can and will free all this World ; perhaps even the other."—French Revolution.

been Whiteside's investment, but Paine, the American merchants Cleggett and Murdoch becoming his bail, scraped together the money and paid it. Probably he lost through Whiteside's bankruptcy other moneys, among them the sum he had deposited to supply his mother with her weekly nine shillings. Paine was too much accustomed to straitened means to allow this affair to trouble him much. The Bridge exhibition went on smoothly enough. Country gentlemen, deputations from riverside towns, visited it, and suggested negotiations for utilizing the invention. The snug copyright fortune which the author had sacrificed to the American cause seemed about to be recovered by the inventor.

But again the Cause arose before him ; he must part from all—patent interests, literary leisure, fine society—and take the hand of Liberty, undowered, but as yet unstained. He must beat his bridge-iron into a Key that shall unlock the British Bastille, whose walls he sees steadily closing around the people.

CHAPTER XX

'*THE RIGHTS OF MAN*'

EDMUND BURKE'S " Reflexions on the Revolution in France" appeared about November 1, 1790. Paine was staying at the Angel inn, Islington, and there immediately began his reply. With his sentiment for anniversaries, he may have begun his work on November 4th, in honor of the English Revolution, whose centenary celebration he had witnessed three years before. In a hundred years all that had been turned into a more secure lease of monarchy. Burke's pamphlet founded on that Revolution a claim that the throne represented a perpetual popular franchise. Paine

might have heard under his window the boys, with their

" Please to remember
The fifth of November,"

and seen their effigy of Guy Fawkes, which in two years his own effigy was to replace. But no misgivings of that kind haunted him. For his eyes the omens hung over the dark Past ; on the horizon a new day was breaking in morning stars and stripes. With the inspiration of perfect faith, born of the sacrifices that had ended so triumphantly in America,

Paine wrote the book which, coming from such deep, the deeps answered.

Although Paine had been revising his religion, much of the orthodox temper survived in him; notably, he still required some sort of Satan to bring out his full energy. In America it had been George III., duly hoofed and horned, at whom his inkstand was hurled; now it is Burke, who appeared with all the seductive brilliancy of a fallen Lucifer. No man had been more idealized by Paine than Burke. Not only because of his magnificent defence of American patriots, but because of his far-reaching exposures of despotism, then creeping, snake-like, from one skin to another. At the very time that Paine was writing "Common Sense," Burke was pointing out that "the power of the crown, almost dead and rotten as prerogative, has grown up anew, with much more strength and far less odium, under the name of influence." He had given liberalism the sentence : "The forms of a free and the ends of an arbitrary government are things not altogether incompatible." He had been the intimate friend of Priestley and other liberals, and when Paine arrived in 1787 had taken him to his heart and home. Paine maintained his faith in Burke after Priestley and Price had remarked a change. In the winter of 1789, when the enthusiastic author was sending out jubilant missives to Washington and others, announcing the glorious transformation of France, he sent one to Burke, who might even then have been preparing the attack on France, delivered early in the Parliament of 1790. When, soon after his return from Paris, Paine mingled with the mourners for their lost leader, he was informed that Burke had for some time been a "masked pensioner," to the extent of £1,500 per annum. This rumor Paine mentioned, and it was not denied, whether because true, or because Burke was looking forward to his subsequent pension of £2,500, is doubtful. Burke's book preceded the events in France which caused

reaction in the minds of Wordsworth and other thinkers in England and America. The French were then engaged in adapting their government to the free principles of which Burke himself had long been the eloquent advocate. It was not without justice that Erskine charged him with having challenged a Revolution in England, by claiming that its hereditary monarchy was bound on the people by a compact of the previous century, and that, good or bad, they had no power to alter it. The power of Burke's pamphlet lay largely in his deftness with the methods of those he assailed. He had courted their company, familiarized himself with their ideas, received their confidences. This had been especially the case with Paine. So there seemed to be a *soupçon* of treachery in his subtleties and his disclosures.

But after all he did not know Paine. He had not imagined the completeness with which the struggle in America had trained this man in every art of controversy. Grappling with Philadelphia Tories, Quakers, reactionists, with aristocrats on the one hand and anarchists on the other, Paine had been familiarized beyond all men with every deep and by-way of the subject on which Burke had ventured. Where Burke had dabbled Paine had dived. Never did man reputed wise go beyond his depth in such a bowl as when Burke appealed to a revolution of 1688 as authoritative. If one revolution could be authoritative, why not another? How did the seventeenth century secure a monopoly in revolution? If a revolution in one century could transfer the throne from one family to another, why might not the same power in another transfer it to an elective monarch, or a president, or leave it vacant?

To demolish Burke was the least part of Paine's task. Burke was, indeed, already answered by the government established in America, presided over by a man to whom the world paid homage. To Washington, Paine's work was dedicated. His real design was to write a

Constitution for the English nation. And to-day the student of political history may find in Burke's pamphlet the fossilized, and in Paine's (potentially) the living, Constitution of Great Britain.

For adequacy to a purpose Paine's "Common Sense" and his "Rights of Man" have never been surpassed. Washington pronounced the former unanswerable, and Burke passed the like verdict on the latter when he said that the refutation it deserved was "that of criminal justice." There was not the slightest confusion of ideas and aim in this book. In laying down first principles of human government, Paine imports no preference of his own for one form or another. The people have the right to establish any government they choose, be it democracy or monarchy,—if not hereditary. He explains with nicety of consecutive statement that a real Constitution must be of the people, and for the people. That is, for the people who make it; they have no right, by any hereditary principle, to bind another people, unborn. His principle of the rights of man was founded in the religious axiom of his age that all men derived existence from a divine maker. To say men are born equal means that they are created equal. Precedent contradicts precedent, authority is against authority, in all our appeals to antiquity, until we reach the time when man came from the hands of his maker. "What was he then? Man. Man was his high and only title, and a higher cannot be given him." "God said Let us make man in our own image." No distinction between men is pointed out. All histories, all traditions, of the creation agree as to the unity of man. Generation being the mode by which creation is carried forward, every child derives its existence from God. "The world is as new to him as it was to the first man that existed, and his natural right to it is of the same kind." On these natural rights Paine founds man's civil rights. To secure his natural rights the individual deposits some of them—*e.g.* the right to judge in his own cause—in the common stock of society.

Paine next proceeds to distinguish governments which have arisen out of this social compact from those which have not. Governments are classified as founded on—(1) superstition; (2) power; (3) the common interests of society, and the common rights of man: that is, on priestcraft, on conquest, on reason. A national constitution is the act of the people antecedent to government; a government cannot therefore determine or alter the organic law it temporarily represents. Pitt's bill to reform Parliament involves the absurdity of trusting an admittedly vitiated body to reform itself. The judges are to sit in their own case. "The right of reform is in the nation in its original character, and the constitutional method would be by a general convention elected for the purpose." The organization of the aggregate of rights which individuals concede to society, for the security of all rights, makes the Republic. So far as the rights have been surrendered to extraneous authority, as of priestcraft, hereditary power, or conquest,—it is Despotism.

To set forth these general principles was Paine's first design. His next aim was to put on record the true and exact history of events in France up to the year 1791. This history, partly that of an eye-witness, partly obtained from the best men in France—Lafayette, Danton, Brissot, and others,—and by mingling with the masses, constitutes the most fresh and important existing contribution to our knowledge of the movement in its early stages. The majority of histories of the French Revolution, Carlyle's especially, are vitiated by reason of their inadequate attention to Paine's narrative. There had been then few serious outbreaks of the mob, but of these Burke had made the most. Paine contends that the outrages can no more be charged against the French than the London riots of 1780 against the English nation; then retorts that mobs are the inevitable consequence of mis-government.

"It is by distortedly exalting some men, that others are distortedly debased. A vast mass of mankind are degradedly thrown into the back-ground of the human picture, to bring forward, with greater glare, the puppet show of state and aristocracy. In the commencement of a revolu-tion, those men are rather followers of the camp than of the standard of liberty, and have yet to be instructed how to use it."

Part I. of "The Rights of Man" was printed by Johnson in time for the opening of Parliament (February), but this publisher became frightened, and only a few copies bearing his name found their way into private hands,—one of these being in the British Museum. J. S. Jordan, 166 Fleet Street, consented to publish it, and Paine, entrusting it to a committee of his friends—William Godwin, Thomas Holcroft, and Thomas Brand Hollis—took his departure for Paris.[1] From that city he sent a brief preface which appeared with Jordan's first edition, March 13, 1791. Oldys (Chalmers) asserts that the work was altered by Jordan. This assertion, in its sweeping form, is disproved not only by Holcroft's note to Godwin, but by a comparison of the "Johnson" and "Jordan" volumes in the British Museum.[2]

[1] "I have got it—If this do not cure my cough it is a damned perverse mule of a cough—The pamphlet—From the row—But mum—We don't sell it—Oh, no—Ears and Eggs—Verbatim, ex-cept the addition of a short preface, which, as you have not seen, I send you my copy—Not a single castration (Laud be unto God and J. S. Jordan!) can I discover—Hey for the New Jerusalem! The Millennium! And peace and eternal beatitude be unto the soul of Thomas Paine!"—C. Kegan Paul's "William Godwin." In supposing that Paine may have gone to Paris before his book appeared (March 13th), I have followed Rickman, who says the work was written "partly at the Angel, at Islington, partly in Harding Street, Fetter Lane, and finished at Versailles." He adds that "many hundred thousand more copies were rapidly sold." But I have no certain trace of Paine in Paris in 1791 earlier than April 8th.

[2] This comparison was made for me by a careful writer, Mr. J. M. Wheeler, of London, who finds, with a few corrections in spelling,

The preface to which Holcroft alludes is of biographical interest both as regards Paine and Burke. As it does not appear in the American edition it is here inserted :

"From the part Mr. Burke took in the American Revolution, it was natural that I should consider him a friend to mankind ; and as our acquaintance commenced on that ground, it would have been more agreeable to me to have had cause to continue in that opinion, than to change it.

"At the time Mr. Burke made his violent speech last winter in the English Parliament against the French Revolution and the National Assembly, I was in Paris, and had written him, but a short time before, to inform him how prosperously matters were going on. Soon after this I saw his advertisement of the Pamphlet he intended to publish. As the attack was to be made in a language but little studied, and less understood, in France, and as everything suffers by translation, I promised some of the friends of the Revolution in that country, that whenever Mr. Burke's Pamphlet came forth, I would answer it. This appeared to me the more necessary to be done, when I saw the flagrant misrepresentations which Mr. Burke's Pamphlet contains ; and that while it is an outrageous abuse of the French Revolution, and the principles of Liberty, it is an imposition on the rest of the world.

"I am the more astonished and disappointed at this conduct in Mr. Burke, as (from the circum-stance I am going to mention) I had formed other expectations.

"I had seen enough of the miseries of war, to wish it might never more have existence in the world, and that some other mode might be found out to settle the differences that should occasion-ally arise in the neighborhood of nations. This certainly might be done if Courts were disposed to set honestly about it, or if countries were enlightened enough not to be made the dupes of Courts. The people of America had been bred up in the same prejudices against France, which at that time characterized the people of England ; but experience and an acquaintance with the French Nation have most effectually shown to the Americans the falsehood of those prejudices ; and I do not believe that a more cordial and confidential intercourse exists between any two countries than between America and France.

"When I came to France in the spring of 1787, the Archbishop of Thoulouse was then Minister, and at that time highly esteemed. I

but one case of softening : "P. 60, in Johnson Paine wrote 'Everything in the English govern-ment appears to me the reverse of what it ought to be' which in Jordan is modified to 'Many things,' etc."

became much acquainted with the private Secretary of that Minister, a man of an enlarged benevolent heart ; and found that his sentiments and my own perfectly agreed with respect to the madness of war, and the wretched impolicy of two nations, like England and France, continually worrying each other, to no other end than that of a mutual increase of burdens and taxes. That I might be assured I had not misunderstood him, nor he me, I put the substance of our opinions into writing, and sent it to him ; subjoining a request that if I should see among the people of England any disposition to cultivate a better understanding between the two nations than had hitherto prevailed, how far I might be authorized to say that the same disposition prevailed on the part of France? He answered me by letter in the most unreserved manner, and that not for himself only, but for the Minister, with whose knowledge the letter was declared to be written.

" I put this letter into the hands of Mr. Burke almost three years ago, and left it with him, where it still remains, hoping, and at the same time naturally expecting, from the opinion I had conceived of him, that he would find some opportunity of making a good use of it, for the purpose of removing those errors and prejudices which two neighboring nations, from the want of knowing each other, had entertained, to the injury of both.

" When the French Revolution broke out, it certainly afforded to Mr. Burke an opportunity of doing some good, had he been disposed to it ; instead of which, no sooner did he see the old prejudices wearing away, than he immediately began sowing the seeds of a new inveteracy, as if he were afraid that England and France would cease to be enemies. That there are men in all countries who get their living by war, and by keeping up the quarrels of Nations, is as shocking as it is true : but when those who are concerned in the government of a country, make it their study to sow discord, and cultivate prejudices between Nations, it becomes the more unpardonable.

" With respect to a paragraph in this work alluding to Mr. Burke's having a pension, the report has been some time in circulation, at least two months ; and as a person is often the last to hear what concerns him the most to know, I have mentioned it, that Mr. Burke may have an opportunity of contradicting the rumor, if he thinks proper."

" The Rights of Man " produced a great impression from the first. It powerfully reinforced the " Constitutional Society," formed seven years before, which Paine had joined. The book was adopted as their new *Magna Charta*. Their enthusiasm was poured forth on March 23d in resolutions which Daniel Williams,

secretary, is directed to transmit "to all our corresponding Constitutional Societies in England, Scotland, and France." In Ireland the work was widely welcomed. I find a note that "at a numerous meeting of the Whigs of the Capital [Dublin] on Tuesday the 5th of April, Hugh Crothers in the chair," a committee was appointed to consider the most effectual mode of disseminating Mr. Paine's pamphlet on " The Rights of Man."

In order to be uniform with Burke's pamphlet the earlier editions of " The Rights of Man," were in the three-shilling style. The proceeds enriched the Society for Constitutional Information, though Paine had been drained of funds by the failure of Whiteside. Gouverneur Morris, as appears by the subjoined extracts from his diary, is disgusted with Paine's " wretched apartments " in Paris, in which, however, the reader may see something finer than the diarist's luxury, which the author might have rivalled with the means devoted to his Cause. This was perhaps what Morris and Paine's friend Hodges agreed in deeming a sort of lunacy.

" April 8. Return home, and read the answer of Paine to Burke's Book ; there are good things in the answer as well as in the book. Paine calls on me. He says that he found great difficulty in prevailing on any bookseller to publish his book ; that it is extremely popular in England, and, of course, the *writer*, which he considers as one of the many uncommon revolutions of this age. He turns the conversation on times of yore, and as he mentions me among those who were his enemies, I frankly acknowledge that I urged his dismissal from the office he held of secretary to the Committee of Foreign Affairs."

" April 16. This morning I visit Paine and Mr. Hodges. The former is abroad, the latter is in the wretched apartments they occupy. He speaks of Paine as being a little mad, which is not improbable."

" April 25. This morning Paine calls and tells me that the Marquis de Lafayette has accepted the position of head of the National Guards."

" May 1. Dine with Montmorin. Bouinville is here. He is just returned from England. He tells me that Paine's book works mightily in England."

Up to this point Paine had, indeed,

carried England with him,—for England was at heart with Fox and the Opposition. When Burke made his first attack on the French Revolution (February 9, 1790), he was repeatedly called to order; and Fox—with tears, for their long friendship was breaking forever—overwhelmed Burke with his rebuke. Even Pitt did not say a word for him. His pamphlet nine months later was ascribed to inspiration of the King, from whom he expected favors; and although the madmen under whom the French Revolution fell presently came to the support of his case, Burke personally never recovered his place in the esteem of England. That the popular instinct was true, and that Burke was playing a deeper game than appeared was afterwards revealed in the archives of England and France.[1]

There was every reason why Paine's reply should carry liberal statesmen with him. His pamphlet was statesmanlike. The French Constitution at that time was the inchoate instrument beginning with the " Declaration of Rights," adopted on Lafayette's proposal (August 26, 1789), and containing provisions contrary to Paine's views. It recognized the reigning house, and made its executive power hereditary. Yet so free was Paine from pedantry, so anxious for any peaceful advance, that it was at the expected inauguration of this Constitution he had consented to bear the American flag, and in his reply to Burke he respects the right of a people to establish even hereditary executive, the right of constitutional reform being retained. " The French constitution distinguishes between the king and the sovereign; it considers the station of the king as

official, and places sovereignty in the nation." In the same practical way he deals with other survivals in the French Constitution—such as clericalism, and the property qualification for suffrage— by dwelling on their mitigations, while reaffirming his own principles on these points.

A very important part of Paine's answer was that which related to the United States. Burke, the most famous defender of American revolutionists, was anxious to separate their movement from that in France. Paine, with ample knowledge, proved how largely the uprising in France was due to the training of Lafayette and other French officers in America, and to the influence of Franklin, who was " not the diplomatist of a court, but of man." He also drew attention to the effect of the American State Constitutions, which were a grammar of liberty.[2] He points out that under this transatlantic influence French liberalism had deviated from the line of its forerunners,—from Montesquieu, " obliged to divide himself between principle and prudence "; Voltaire, "both the flatterer and satirist of despotism "; Rousseau, leaving " the mind in love with an object without describing the means of possessing it "; Turgot, whose maxims are directed to " reform the ad-

---

[1] " Thirty thousand copies of Burke's book were circulated in all the courts and among the European aristocracy as so many lighted brands to set Europe in flames. During this time the author, by his secret correspondence, excited Queen Marie-Antoinette, the court, the foreigners, to conspire against the Revolution. 'No compromises with rebels!' he wrote; 'appeal to sovereign neighbors; above all trust to the support of foreign armies.'"—"Histoire de France," par Henri Martin, i., p. 151.

[2] Dr. Franklin had these constitutions translated, and presented them in a finely bound volume to the King. According to Paine, who must have heard it from Franklin, Vergennes resisted their publication, but was obliged to give way to public demand. Paine could not allude to the effect of his own work, " Common Sense," which may have been the more effective because its argument against monarchy was omitted from the translation. But his enemies did not fail to credit his pen with the catastrophes in France. John Adams declares that the Constitution of Pennsylvania was ascribed wrongly to Franklin; it was written by Paine and three others; Turgot, Condorcet, and the Duke de la Rochefoucauld were enamored of it, and two of them " owed their final and fatal catastrophe to this blind love " (Letter to S. Perley, June 19, 1809). Whence Cheetham, dwelling on the enormity of the "single representative assembly," queries: " May not Paine's constitution of Pennsylvania have been the cause of the tyranny of Robespierre?"

ministration of government rather than the government itself." To these high praise is awarded, but they all had to be filtered through America.

And it goes without saying that it was not the reactionary America with which John Adams and Gouverneur Morris had familiarized Burke. "The Rights of Man" was the first exposition of the republicanism of Jefferson, Madison, and Edmund Randolph that ever appeared. And as this republicanism was just then in deadly struggle with reaction, the first storm raised by Paine's book occurred in America. It was known in America that Paine was about to beard the British lion in his den, and to expectant ears the roar was heard before its utterance.

"Paine's answer to Burke (writes Madison to Jefferson, May 1st) has not yet been received here [New York]. The moment it can be got, Freneau tells me, it will be published in Child's paper [*Daily Advertiser*]. It is said that the pamphlet has been suppressed, and that the author withdrew to France before or immediately after its appearance. This may account for his not sending copies to his friends in this country."

Mr. Beckley, however, had by this time received a copy and loaned it to Jefferson, with a request that he would send it to J. B. Smith, whose brother, S. H. Smith, printed it with the following Preface :

"The following Extracts from a note accompanying a copy of this pamphlet for republication is so respectable a testing of its value, that the Printer hopes the distinguished writer will excuse its present appearance. It proceeds from a character equally eminent in the councils of America, and conversant in the affairs of France, from a long and recent residence at the Court of Versailles in the Diplomatic department ; and at the same time that it does justice to the writings of Mr. Paine, it reflects honor on the source from which it flows by directing the mind to a contemplation of that Republican firmness and Democratic simplicity which endear their possessor to every friend of the Rights of Man.

"After some prefatory remarks the Secretary of State observes :

"'I am extremely pleased to find it will be reprinted, and that something is at length to be publickly said against the political heresies which have sprung up among us.

"'I have no doubt our citizens will rally a *second* time round the *standard* of Common Sense.'"

As the pamphlet had been dedicated to the President,[1] this encomium of the Secretary of State ("Jefferson" was not mentioned by the sagacious publisher) gave it the air of a manifesto by the administration. Had all been contrived, Paine's arrow could not have been more perfectly feathered to reach the heart of the anti-republican faction. The Secretary's allusion to "political heresies" was so plainly meant for the Vice-President that a million hands tossed the gauntlet to him, and supposed it was his own hand that took it up. These letters, to *The Columbian Centinel* (Boston), were indeed published in England as by "John Adams," and in the trial of Paine were quoted by the Attorney-General as proceeding from "the second in the executive government" of America. Had it been generally known, however, that they were by the Vice-President's son, John Quincy Adams, the effect might not have been very different on the father. Edmund Randolph, in view of John Adams' past services, felt some regret at the attacks on him, and wrote to Madison : "I should rejoice that the controversy has been excited, were it not that under the character of [Publicola] he, who was sufficiently depressed before, is now irredeemable in the public opinion without being the real author." The youth, however, was only in his twenty-fourth year, and pretty certainly under his father's inspiration.

It is improbable, however, that John

[1] "Sir, I present you a small treatise in defence of those principles of freedom which your exemplary virtue hath so eminently contributed to establish. That the rights of men may become as universal as your benevolence can wish, and that you may enjoy the happiness of seeing the new world regenerate the old, is the prayer of, Sir, your much obliged, and obedient humble servant, THOMAS PAINE."

Adams could have written such scholarly and self-restrained criticisms on any work by Paine, mere mention of whom always made him foam at the mouth. Publicola's arguments could not get a fair hearing amid surviving animosities against England and enthusiasm for a republican movement in France, as yet not a revolution, which promised the prevalence of American ideas in Europe. The actual England of that era, whose evils were powerfully portrayed by Paine, defeated in advance any theoretical estimate of the advantages of its unwritten Constitution. America had, too, an inventor's pride in its written Constitution, as yet untried by experience. Publicola assailed, successfully as I think, Paine's principle that a vitiated legislature could never be trusted to reform itself. It was answered that there is no reason why the people may not delegate to a legislature, renewed by suffrage, the power of altering even the organic law. Publicola contends that the people could not act in their original character in changing a constitution, in opposition to an existing legislature, without danger of anarchy and war; that if the people were in harmony with their legislature it could be trusted to carry out their amendments; that a legislature without such constitutional powers would nevertheless exercise them by forced constructions; and that the difficulty and delay of gathering the people in convention might conceivably endanger the commonwealth, were the power of fundamental alteration not delegated to the legislature,—a concurrent right being reserved by the people.

This philosophical statement, interesting in the light of French revolutions and English evolutions, recoiled on Publicola from the walls of Paine's real fortress. This was built of the fact that in England the majority was not represented even in the Commons, and that the people had no representation at all in two branches of their government. Moreover, Paine's plea had been simply for such reconstitution of government as would enable the people to reform it without revolution or

convulsion. Publicola was compelled to admit that the English people had no resort but the right of revolution, so that it appeared mere Monarchism to argue against Paine's plea for a self-amending constitution in England.

Publicola's retort on the Secretary's phrase, "political heresies" (infelicitous from a freethinker),—"Does he consider this pamphlet of Mr. Paine's as the canonical book of political scripture,"—hurt Jefferson so much that he supposed himself harmed. He was indeed much annoyed by the whole affair, and straightway wrote to political leaders letters—some private, others to be quoted,—in which he sought to smooth things by declaring that his note was not meant for publication. To Washington he writes (May 8th) the Beckley-Smith story, beginning:

"I am afraid the indiscretion of a printer has committed me with my friend Mr. Adams, for whom, as one of the most honest and disinterested men alive, I have a cordial esteem, increased by long habits of concurrence in opinion in the days of his republicanism : and even since his apostasy to hereditary monarchy and nobility, though we differ, we differ as friends should do."

The "Jeffersonians" were, of course, delighted, and there is no knowing how much reputation for pluck the Secretary was gaining in the country at the very moment when his intimate friends were soothing his tremors. These were increased by the agitation of the British representatives in America over the affair. The following re-enforcement was sent by Madison on May 12th :

"I had seen Paine's pamphlet, with the Preface of the Philadelphia edition. It immediately occurred that you were brought into the frontispiece in the manner you explain. But I had not foreseen the particular use made of it by the British partizans. Mr. Adams can least of all complain. Under a mock defence of the Republican constitutions of his country he attacked them with all the force he possessed, and this in a book with his name to it, while he was the Representative of his country at a foreign Court. Since he has been the second magistrate in the new Republic, his pen has constantly been at work in the same Cause; and though his name has not been prefixed to his anti-republican discourses, the author has been as well known as if that formality had been observed. Surely if it be innocent and decent in one servant of the public thus to write attacks against its Government, it cannot be very criminal or indecent in another to patronize a written defence of the principles on which that Government is founded. The sensibility of Hammond [British Minister] and Bond [British Consul-General] for the indignity to the British Constitution is truly ridiculous. If offence could be justly taken in that quarter, what would France have a right to say to Burke's pamphlet, and the countenance given to it and its author, particularly by the King himself? What, in fact, might not the United States say, when revolutions and democratic Governments come in for a large charge of the scurrility lavished on those of France?"

One curious circumstance of this incident was that the fuss made by these British agents was about a book concerning which their government, under whose nose it was published, had not said a word. There was, indeed, one sting in the American edition which was not in the English, but that does not appear to have been noticed.[1] The resentment shown by the British agents was plainly meant to aid Adams and the partisans of England in their efforts to crush the republicans, and bring Washington to their side in hostility to Jefferson. Four years later they succeeded, and already it was apparent to the republican leaders that fine engineering was required to keep the Colossus on their side. Washington being at Mount Vernon, his secretary, Tobias Lear, was approached by Major Beckwith, an English agent (at Mrs. Washington's reception), who undertook to lecture through him the President and Secretary of State. He expressed surprise that Paine's pamphlet should be dedicated to the President, as it contained remarks "that could not but be offensive to the British government." The Major might have been embarrassed if asked his

[1] It has already been stated that the volume as printed by Jordan (London) in March, contained one single modification of that which Johnson had printed in February, but declined to publish. The American edition was printed from the Johnson volume; and where the English were reading "Many things," etc., the Americans read : "Every thing in the English government appears to me the reverse of what it ought to be, and of what it is said to be."

instructions on the point, but Lear only said that the President had not seen the pamphlet, nor could he be held responsible for its sentiments. "True," said Beckwith, "but I observe, in the American edition, that the Secretary of State has given a most unequivocal sanction to the book, as *Secretary of State*; it is not said as Mr. Jefferson." Lear said he had not seen the pamphlet, "but," he added, "I will venture to say that the Secretary of State has not done a thing which he would not justify." Beckwith then remarked that he had spoken only as a "private character," and Lear went off to report the conversation in a letter to Washington (May 8th) and next day to Attorney-General Randolph. Lear also reports to Washington that he had heard Adams say, with his hand upon his breast: "I detest that book and its tendency, from the bottom of my heart." Meanwhile the Attorney-General, after conversation with Beckwith, visited Jefferson, and asked if he had authorized the publication of his note in Paine's pamphlet.

"Mr. Jefferson said that, so far from having authorized it, he was exceedingly sorry to see it there : not from a disavowal of the approbation which it gave the work, but because it had been sent to the printer, with the pamphlet for republication, without the most distant idea that he would think of publishing any part of it. And Mr. Jefferson further added that he wished it might be understood, that he did not authorize the publication of any part of his note."

These words of Lear to Washington, written no doubt in Randolph's presence, suggest the delicacy of the situation. Jefferson's anxiety led him to write Vice-President Adams (July 17th) the Beckley-Smith story.

"I thought [he adds] so little of the note that I did not even keep a copy of it, nor ever heard a tittle more of it till, the week following, I was thunderstruck with seeing it come out at the head of the pamphlet. I hoped that it would not attract. But I found on my return from a journey of a month, that a writer came forward under the name of Publicola, attacking not only the author and principles of the pamphlet, but myself as its sponsor by name. Soon after came hosts of other writers, defending the pamphlet and attacking you by name as the writer of Publicola. Thus our names were thrown on the stage as public antagonists."

Then follows some effusiveness for Adams, and protestations that he has written none of these attacks. Jefferson fully believed that Publicola was the Vice-President, and had so informed Monroe, on July 10th. It was important that his lieutenants should not suspect their leader of shrinking, and Jefferson's letters to them are in a different vein. "Publicola," he tells Monroe, "in attacking all Paine's principles, is very desirous of involving me in the same censure with the author. I certainly merit the same, for I profess the same principles; but it is equally certain I never meant to have entered as a volunteer in the cause. My occupations do not permit it." To Paine he writes (July 29th): "Indeed I am glad you did not come away till you had written your Rights of Man. A writer under the signature of Publicola has attacked it, and a host of champions has entered the arena immediately in your defence." It is added that the controversy has shown the people firm in their republicanism, "contrary to the assertions of a sect here, high in name but small in numbers," who were hoping that the masses were becoming converted "to the doctrine of King, Lords, and Commons."

In the letter to which this was a reply, Paine had stated his intention of returning to America in the spring.[1] The enthusiasm for Paine and his principles elicited by the controversy was so over-whelming that Edmund Randolph and Jefferson made an effort to secure him a place in Washington's Cabinet. But, though reinforced by Madison, they failed.[2] These statesmen little knew how far Washington had committed himself to the British government. In October, 1789, Washington, with his own hand, had written to Gouverneur Morris, desiring him in "the capacity of private agent, and on the authority and credit of this letter, to converse with His Britannic Majesty's ministers on these points; viz., whether there be any, and what objections to performing those articles in the treaty which remained to be performed on his part, and whether they incline to a treaty of commerce with the United States on any, and what terms?" This was a secret between Washington, Morris, and the British Cabinet.[3] It was the deepest desire of Washington to free America from British garrisons, and his expectation was to secure this by the bribe of a liberal commercial treaty, as he ultimately did. The demonstration of the British agents in America against Paine's pamphlet, their offence at its dedication to the President and sanction by the Secretary of State, were well calculated. That it was all an American *coup*, unwarranted by any advice from England, could not occur to Washington, who was probably surprised when he presently received a

---

[1] "I enclose you a few observations on the establishment of a Mint. I have not seen your report on that subject and therefore cannot tell how nearly our opinions run together; but as it is by thinking upon and talking subjects over that we approach towards truth, there may probably be something in the enclosed that may be of use. —As the establishment of a Mint combines a portion of politics with a knowledge of the Arts, and a variety of other matters, it is a subject I shall very much like to talk with you upon. I intend at all events to be in America in the Spring, and it will please me much to arrive before you have gone thro' the arrangement."— Paine to Jefferson, dated London, September 28, 1790.

[2] Madison to Jefferson, July 13th,—"I wish you success with all my heart in your efforts for Paine. Besides the advantage to him which he deserves, an appointment for him at this moment would do public good in various ways."

Edmund Randolph to Madison, July 21st.— "I need not relate to you, that since the *standard* of republicanism has been erected, it has been resorted to by a numerous corps. The newspapers will tell you how much the crest of aristocracy has fallen. . . . But he [Adams] is impotent, and something is due to past services. Mr. J. and myself have attempted to bring Paine forward as a successor to Osgood [Postmaster-General]. It seems to be a fair opportunity for a declaration of certain sentiments. But all that I have heard has been that it would be too pointed to keep a vacancy unfilled until his return from the other side of the water."

[3] "Diary of Gouverneur Morris," i., p. 310.

letter from Paine showing that he was getting along quite comfortably under the government he was said to have aggrieved.

"LONDON, July 21, 1791—DEAR SIR.—I received your favor of last August by Col : Humphries since which I have not written to or heard from you. I mention this that you may know no letters have miscarried. I took the liberty of addressing my late work 'Rights of Man,' to you ; but tho' I left it at that time to find its way to you, I now request your acceptance of fifty copies as a token of remembrance to yourself and my Friends. The work has had a run beyond anything that has been published in this Country on the subject of Government, and the demand continues. In Ireland it has had a much greater. A letter I received from Dublin, 10th of May, mentioned that the fourth edition was then on sale. I know not what number of copies were printed at each edition, except the second, which was ten thousand. The same fate follows me here as I *at first* experienced in America, strong friends and violent enemies, but as I have got the ear of the Country, I shall go on, and at least shew them, what is a novelty here, that there can be a person beyond the reach of corruption.

"I arrived here from france about ten days ago. M. de la Fayette is well. The affairs of that Country are verging to a new crisis, whether the Government shall be Monarchical and hereditary or wholly representative? I think the latter opinion will very generally prevail in the end. On this question the people are much forwarder than the National Assembly.

"After the establishment of the American Revolution, it did not appear to me that any object could arise great enough to engage me a second time. I began to feel myself happy in being quiet ; but I now experience that principle is not confined to Time or place, and that the ardour of seventy-six is capable of renewing itself. I have another work on hand which I intend shall be my last, for I long much to return to America. It is not natural that fame should wish for a rival, but the case is otherwise with me, for I do most sincerely wish there was some person in this Country that could usefully and successfully attract the public attention, and leave me with a satisfied mind to the enjoyment of quiet life : but it is painful to see errors and abuses and sit down a senseless spectator. Of this your own mind will interpret mine.

"I have printed sixteen thousand copies ; when the whole are gone of which there remain between three and four thousand I shall then make a cheap edition, just sufficient to bring in the price of the printing and paper as I did by Common Sense.

"Mr. Green who will present you this, has been very much my friend. I wanted last October to draw for fifty pounds on General Lewis Morris who has some money of mine, but as he is unknown in the Commercial line, and American credit not very good, and my own expended, I could not succeed, especially as Gov'r Morris was then in Holland. Col : Humphries went with me to your Agent Mr. Walsh, to whom I stated the case, and took the liberty of saying that I knew you would not think it a trouble to receive it of Gen‡ Morris on Mr. Walsh's account, but he declined it. Mr. Green afterwards supplied me and I have since repaid him. He has a troublesome affair on his hands here, and is in danger of losing thirty or forty thousand pounds, embarked under the flag of the United States in East India property. The persons who have received it withhold it and shelter themselves under some law contrivance. He wishes to state the case to Congress not only on his own account, but as a matter that may be nationally interesting.

"The public papers will inform you of the riots and tumults at Birmingham, and of some disturbances at Paris, and as Mr. Green can detail them to you more particularly than I can do in a letter I leave those matters to his information. I am, etc."

Nine months elapsed before Washington answered this letter, and although important events of those months have yet to be related, the answer may be here put on record.

"PHILADELPHIA, 6 May, 1792.—DEAR SIR. —To my friends, and those who know my occupations, I am sure no apology is necessary for keeping their letters so much longer unanswered, than my inclination would lead me to do. I shall therefore offer no excuse for not having sooner acknowledged the receipt of your letter of the 21st of June [July]. My thanks, however, for the token of your remembrance, in the fifty copies of '*The Rights of Man*,' are offered with no less cordiality, than they would have been had I answered your letter in the first moment of receiving it.

"The duties of my office, which at all times, especially during the session of Congress, require an unremitting attention, naturally become more pressing towards the close of it ; and as that body have resolved to rise tomorrow, and as I have determined, in case they should, to set out for Mount Vernon on the next day, you will readily conclude that the present is a busy moment with me ; and to that I am persuaded your goodness will impute my not entering into the several points touched upon in your letter. Let it suffice, therefore, at this time, to say, that I rejoice in the information of your personal prosperity, and, as no one can feel a greater interest in the happiness of mankind than I do, that it is the first wish of my heart, that the enlightened policy of the present age may diffuse to all men those blessings, to which they are entitled, and lay the foundation of happiness for future generations.—With great esteem, I am, dear Sir &c.

" P.S. Since writing the foregoing, I have received your letter of the 13th of February, with the twelve copies of your new work, which accompanied it, and for which you must accept my additional thanks."

There is no lack of personal cordiality in this letter, but one may recognize in its ingenious vagueness, in its omission of any acknowledgment of the dedication of Paine's book, that he mistrusts the European revolution and its American allies.

CHAPTER XXI

FOUNDING THE EUROPEAN REPUBLIC

It has already been mentioned that John Adams had been proclaimed in France the author of " Common Sense." [1] The true author was now known, but, as the anti-monarchical parts of his work were expurgated, Paine, in turn, was supposed to be a kind of John Adams—a revolutionary royalist. This misunderstanding was personally distasteful, but it had the important compensation of enabling Paine to come before Europe with a work adapted to its conditions, essentially

[1] " When I arrived in France, the French naturally had a great many questions to settle. The first was, whether I was the famous Adams. ' Ah, le fameux Adams.' In order to speculate a little upon this subject, the pamphlet ' Common Sense' had been printed in the ' Affaires de l'Angleterre et de l'Amerique,' and expressly ascribed to Mr. Adams, ' the celebrated member of Congress.' It must be further known that although the pamphlet ' Common Sense' was received in France and in all Europe with rapture, yet there were certain parts of it that they did not dare to publish in France. The reasons of this any man may guess. ' Common Sense' undertakes to prove that monarchy is unlawful by the Old Testament. They therefore gave the substance of it, as they said ; and paying many compliments to Mr. Adams, his sense and rich imagination, they were obliged to ascribe some parts of it to republican zeal. When I arrived at Bordeaux all that I could say or do would not convince anybody but that I was the fameux Adams. ' C'est un homme célèbre. Votre nom est bien connu ici.' "—" Works of John Adams," vol. iii., p. 189. This was in 1779, and when Adams entered on his official duties at Paris the honors thrust upon him at Bordeaux became burdensome.

different from those of America to which " Common Sense " was addressed in 1776. It was a matter of indifference to him whether the individual executive was called " King " or " President." He objected to the thing, not the name, but as republican superstition had insisted on it in America there was little doubt that France would follow the example. Under these circumstances Paine made up his mind that the republican principle would not be lost by the harmonizing policy of preserving the nominal and ornamental king while abolishing his sovereignty. The erection of a tremendous presidential power in the United States might well suggest to so staunch a supporter of ministerial government that this substance might be secured under a show of royalty. Dr. Robinet considers it a remarkable " prophecy " that Paine should have written in 1787 of an approaching alliance of " the Majesty of the Sovereign with the Majesty of the Nation " in France. This was opposed to the theories of Jefferson, but it was the scheme of Mirabeau, the hope of Lafayette, and had not the throne been rotten this prudent policy might have succeeded. It was with an eye to France as well as to England that Paine, in his reply to Burke, had so carefully distinguished between executive sovereignty subject to law and personal monarchy.

When the last proof of his book was revised Paine sped to Paris, and placed it in the hand of his friend M. Lanthenas for translation. Mirabeau was on his death-bed, and Paine witnessed that historic procession, four miles long, which bore the orator to his shrine. Witnessed it with relief, perhaps, for he is ominously silent concerning Mirabeau. With others he strained his eyes to see the Coming Man; with others he sees formidable Danton glaring at Lafayette; and presently sees advancing softly between them the sentimental, philanthropic —Robespierre.

It was a happy hour for Paine when, on a day in May, he saw Robespierre rise in the National Assembly to propose abolition of the death penalty. How sweet this echo of the old "testimonies" of Thetford Quaker meetings. "Capital punishment," cries Robespierre, "is but a base assassination — punishing one crime by another, murder with murder. Since judges are not infallible they have no right to pronounce irreparable sentences." He is seconded by the jurist Duport, who says impressively: "Let us at least make revolutionary scenes as little tragic as possible! Let us render man honorable to man!" Marat, right man for the rôle, answered with the barbaric demand "blood for blood," and prevailed. But Paine was won over to Robespierre by this humane enthusiasm. The day was to come when he must confront Robespierre with a memory of this scene.

That Robespierre would supersede Lafayette Paine could little imagine. The King was in the charge of the great friend of America, and never had country a fairer prospect than France in those beautiful spring days. But the royal family fled. In the early morning of June 21st Lafayette burst into Paine's bedroom, before he was up, and cried: "The birds are flown!" "It is well," said Paine; "I hope there will be no attempt to recall them." Hastily dressing, he rushed out into the street, and found the people in uproar. They were clamoring as if some great loss had befallen them. At the Hôtel de Ville Lafayette was menaced by the crowd, which accused him of having assisted the King's flight, and could only answer them: "What are you complaining of? Each of you saves twenty sous tax by suppression of the Civil List." Paine encounters his friend Thomas Christie. "You see," he said, "the absurdity of monarchical governments; here will be a whole nation disturbed by the folly of one man."[1]

Here was Marat's opportunity. His journal, *L'Ami du Peuple*, clamored for a dictator, and for the head of Lafayette. Against him rose young Bonneville, who, in *La Bouche de Fer*, wrote: "No more kings! No dictator! Assemble the People in the face of the sun; proclaim that the Law alone shall be sovereign,—the Law, the Law alone, and made for all!"

Bonneville's words in his journal about that time were apt to be translations from the works of his friend Paine, with whom his life was afterwards so closely interwoven. The little group of men who had studied Paine, ardent republicans, beheld a nation suddenly become frantic to recover a king who could not be of the slightest value to any party in the state. The miserable man had left a letter denouncing all the liberal measures he had signed since October, 1789, which sealed his doom as a monarch. The appalling fact was revealed that the most powerful revolutionists—Robespierre and Marat especially—had never considered a Republic, and did not know what it was.

On June 25th, Paine was a heavy-hearted spectator of the return of the arrested king. He had personal realization that day of the folly of a people in bringing back a king who had relieved them of his presence. He had omitted to decorate his hat with a cockade, and the mob fell on him with cries of "Aris-

[1] The letter of Christie (Priestley's nephew), written June 22d, appeared in the *London Morning Chronicle*, June 29th.

tocrat! à la lanterne!" After some rough handling he was rescued by a Frenchman who spoke English, and explained the accidental character of the offence. Poor Paine's Quaker training had not included the importance of badges, else the incident had revealed to him that even the popular rage against Louis was superstitious homage to a cockade. Never did friend of the people have severer proofs that they are generally wrong. In America, while writing as with his heart's blood the first plea for its independence, he was "shadowed" as a British spy; and in France he narrowly escaped the aristocrat's lantern, at the very moment when he was founding the first republican society, and writing its declaration.

This "Société Républicaine," as yet of five members, inaugurated itself on July 1st, by placarding Paris with its manifesto, which was even nailed on the door of the National Assembly.

"Brethren and fellow citizens:
"The serene tranquillity, the mutual confidence which prevailed amongst us, during the time of the late King's escape, the indifference with which we beheld him return, are unequivocal proofs that the absence of a King is more desirable than his presence, and that he is not only a political superfluity, but a grievous burden, pressing hard on the whole nation.
"Let us not be imposed upon by sophisms; all that concerns us is reduced to four points.
"He has abdicated the throne in having fled from his post. Abdication and desertion are not characterized by the length of absence; but by the single act of flight. In the present instance, the act is everything, and the time nothing.
"The nation can never give back its confidence to a man who false to his trust, perjured to his oath, conspires a clandestine flight, obtains a fraudulent passport, conceals a King of France under the disguise of a valet, directs his course towards a frontier covered with traitors and deserters, and evidently meditates a return into our own country, with a force capable of imposing his own despotic laws.
"Whether ought his flight to be considered as his own act, or the act of those who fled with him? Was it a spontaneous resolution of his own, or was it inspired into him by others? The alternative is immaterial; whether fool or hypocrite, idiot or traitor, he has proved himself equally unworthy of the important functions that had been delegated to him.

"In every sense that the question can be considered, the reciprocal obligation which subsisted between us is dissolved. He holds no longer any authority. We owe him no longer obedience. We see in him no more than an indifferent person; we can regard him only as Louis Capet.
"The history of France présents little else than a long series of public calamity, which takes its source from the vices of the Kings; we have been the wretched victims that have never ceased to suffer either for them or by them. The catalogue of their oppressions was complete, but to complete the sum of their crimes, treason yet was wanting. Now the only vacancy is filled up, the dreadful list is full; the system is exhausted; there are no remaining errors for them to commit, their reign is consequently at an end.
"What kind of office, must that be in a government which requires for its execution neither experience nor ability? that may be abandoned to the desperate chance of birth, that may be filled by an idiot, a madman, a tyrant, with equal effect as by the good, the virtuous, and the wise? An office of this nature is a mere nonentity: it is a place of show, not of use. Let France then, arrived at the age of reason, no longer be deluded by the sound of words, and let her deliberately examine, if a King, however insignificant and contemptible in himself, may not at the same time be extremely dangerous.
"The thirty millions which it costs to support a King in the eclat of stupid brutal luxury, presents us with an easy method of reducing taxes, which reduction would at once release the people, and stop the progress of political corruption. The grandeur of nations consists, not, as Kings pretend, in the splendor of thrones, but in a conspicuous sense of their own dignity, and in a just disdain of those barbarous follies and crimes, which, under the sanction of royalty have hitherto desolated Europe.
"As to the personal safety of Louis Capet, it is so much the more confirmed, as France will not stoop to degrade herself by a spirit of revenge against a wretch who has dishonored himself. In defending a just and glorious cause, it is not possible to degrade it, and the universal tranquillity which prevails is an undeniable proof, that a free people know how to respect themselves."[1]

---

[1] "How great is a calm, couchant people! On the morrow men will say to one another, 'We have no king, yet we slept sound enough.' On the morrow Achille Duchâtelet, and Thomas Paine, the rebellious needleman, shall have the walls of Paris profusely plastered with their placard, announcing that there must be a republic."—Carlyle.
Dumont ("Recollections of Mirabeau") gives a particular account of this paper, which Duchâtelet wished him to translate. "Paine and he,

Malouet, a leading royalist member, tore down the handbill, and, having ascertained its author, demanded the prosecution of Thomas Paine and Achille Duchâtelet. He was vehemently supported by Martineau, deputy of Paris, and for a time there was a tremendous agitation. The majority, not prepared to commit themselves to anything at all, voted the order of the day, affecting, says Henri Martin, a disdain that hid embarrassment and inquietude.

This document, destined to reappear in a farther crisis, and the royalist rage, raised Paine's Republican Club to vast importance. Even the Jacobins, who had formally declined to sanction republicanism, were troubled by the discovery of a society more radical than themselves. It was only some years later that it was made known (by Paine) that this formidable association consisted of five members, and it is still doubtful who these were. Certainly Paine, Achille Duchâtelet, and Condorcet; probably also Brissot, and Nicolas Bonneville. In order to avail itself of this tide of fame, the Société Républicaine started a journal,— *The Republican*.[1] The time was not ripe, however; only one copy appeared; that, however, contained a letter by Paine, written in June, which excited considerable flutter. To the reader of to-day it is mainly interesting as showing Paine's perception that the French required instruction in the alphabet of republicanism; but, amid its studied moderation, there was a paragraph which the situation rendered pregnant :

"Whenever the French Constitution shall be rendered conformable to its declaration of rights, we shall then be enabled to give to France, and with justice, the appellation of a *Civic Empire* ; for its government will be the empire of laws, founded on the great republican principles of *elective representation* and the rights of man. But monarchy and hereditary succession are incompatible with the *basis* of its Constitution."

Now this was the very constitution which Paine, in his answer to Burke, had made comparatively presentable ; to this day it survives in human memory mainly through indulgent citations in "The Rights of Man." Those angels who, in the celestial war, tried to keep friendly with both sides, had human counterparts in France, their constitutional oracle being the Abbé Sieyès. He had entered warmly into the Revolution, invented the name "National Assembly," opposed the veto power, supported the Declaration of Rights. But he had a superstitious faith in individual executive, which, as an opportunist, he proposed to vest in the reigning house. This class of "survivals" in the constitution were the work of Sieyès, who was the brain of the Jacobins, now led by Robespierre, and with him ignoring republicanism for no better reason than that their title was "Société des Amis de la Constitution."[2] Sieyès petted his constitution maternally, perhaps because nobody else loved it, and bristled at Paine's criticism. He wrote a letter to the *Moniteur*, asserting that there was more liberty under a monarchy than under a republic. He announced his intention of maintaining monarchical executive against the new party started into life by the King's flight. In the same journal (July 8th,) Paine accepts the challenge "with pleasure."[3] Paine

---

the one an American, the other a young thoughtless member of the French nobility, put themselves forward to change the whole system of government in France." Lafayette had been sounded, but said it would take twenty years to bring freedom to maturity in France. "But some of the seed thrown out by the audacious hand of Paine began to bud forth in the minds of many leading individuals." (*E.g.*, Condorcet, Brissot, Pétion, Clavière.)

[1] "Le Républicain; on le défenseur du gouvernement Représentatif; par une Société pes Républicains. A Paris. July 1791. No. 1."

[2] The club, founded in 1789, was called "Jacobin," because they met in the hall of the Dominicans, who had been called Jacobins from the street St. Jacques in which they were first established, anno 1219.

[3] It was probably this letter that Gouverneur Morris alludes to in his "Diary," when, writing of a Fourth of July dinner given by Mr. Short (U.S. Chargé d'Affaires), he mentions the presence of Paine, "inflated to the eyes and big with a letter of Revolutions."

himself was something of an opportunist ; as in America he had favored reconciliation with George III. up to the Lexington massacre, so had he desired a *modus vivendi* with Louis XVI. up to his flight.[1] But now he unfurls the anti-monarchical flag.

"I am not the personal enemy of Kings. Quite the contrary. No man wishes more heartily than myself to see them all in a happy and honorable state of private individuals ; but I am the avowed, open, and intrepid enemy of what is called monarchy ; and I am such by principles which nothing can either alter or corrupt—by my attachment to humanity ; by the anxiety which I feel within myself for the dignity and honor of the human race ; by the disgust which I experience when I observe men directed by children and governed by brutes ; by the horror which all the evils that monarchy has spread over the earth excite within my breast ; and by those sentiments which make me shudder at the calamities, the exactions, the wars, and the massacres with which monarchy has crushed mankind : in short, it is against all the hell of monarchy that I have declared war."

In reply Sieyès used the terms "monarchy" and "republic" in unusual senses. He defines "republic" as a government in which the executive power is lodged in more than one person, "monarchy" as one where it is entrusted to one only. He asserted that while he was in this sense a monarchist Paine was a "polycrat." In a republic all action must finally lodge in an executive council deciding by majority, and nominated by the people or the National Assembly. Sieyès did not, however, care to enter the lists. "My letter does not announce that I have leisure to enter into a controversy with republican *polycrats*."

[1] In this spirit was written Part I. of "The Rights of Man," the translation of which by M. Lanthenas, with new preface, appeared in May. Sieyès agreed that "hereditaryship" was theoretically wrong, "but," he said, "refer to the histories of all elective monarchies and principalities : is there one in which the elective mode is not worse than the hereditary succession?" For notes on this incident see Professor F. A. Aulard's important work, "Les Orateurs de l'Assemblée Constituante," p. 411. Also Henri Martin's "Histoire de France," i., p. 193.

Paine now set out for London. He travelled with Lord Daer and Étienne Dumont, Mirabeau's secretary. Dumont had a pique against Paine, whose republican manifesto had upset a literary scheme of his,—to evoke Mirabeau from the tomb and make him explain to the National Assembly that the King's flight was a court plot, that they should free Louis XVI. from aristocratic captivity, and support him. But on reading the Paine placard, "I determined," says Dumont, "for fear of evil consequences to myself, to make Mirabeau return to his tomb."[2] Dumont protests that Paine was fully convinced that the world would be benefited if all other books were burned except "The Rights of Man," and no doubt the republican apostle had a sublime faith in the sacred character of his "testimonies" against kings. Without attempting to determine whether this was the self-reliance of humility or egoism, it may be safely affirmed that it was that which made Paine's strokes so effective.

It may also be remarked again that Paine showed a prudence with which he has not been credited. Thus, there is little doubt that this return to London was in pursuance of an invitation to attend a celebration of the second anniversary of the fall of the Bastille. He arrived at the White Bear, Piccadilly, the day before (July 13th), but on finding that there was much excitement about his republican manifesto in France he concluded that his presence at the meeting might connect it with movements across the Channel, and did not attend. Equal prudence was not, however, displayed by his opponents, who induced the landlord of the Crown and Anchor to close his doors against the advertised meeting. This effort to prevent the free assemblage of Englishmen, and for the humane purpose of celebrating the destruction of a prison whose horrors had excited popular indignation, caused general anger.

[2] "Souvenirs sur Mirabeau." Par Étienne Dumont.

After due consideration it was deemed opportune for those who sympathized with the movement in France to issue a manifesto on the subject. It was written by Paine, and adopted by a meeting held at the Thatched House Tavern, August 20th, being signed by John Horne Tooke, as Chairman. This "Address and Declaration of the Friends of Universal Peace and Liberty," though preceded by the vigorous "Declaration of the Volunteers of Belfast," quoted in its second paragraph, was the earliest warning England received that the revolution was now its grim guest.

"Friends and Fellow Citizens : At a moment like the present, when wilful misrepresentations are industriously spread by partizans of arbitrary power and the advocates of passive obedience and court government, we think it incumbent upon us to declare to the world our principles, and the motives of our conduct.

"We rejoice at the glorious event of the French revolution. If it be asked, 'What is the French revolution to us?' we answer as has already been answered in another place,[1] 'It is much—much to us as men ; much to us as Englishmen. As men, we rejoice in the freedom of twenty-five millions of men. We rejoice in the prospect which such a magnificent example opens to the world.'

"We congratulate the French nation for having laid the axe to the root of tyranny, and for erecting government on the sacred hereditary rights of man ; rights which appertain to all, and not to any one more than another.

"We know of no human authority superior to that of a whole nation ; and we profess and claim it as our principle that every nation has at all times an inherent and indefeasable right to constitute and establish such government for itself as best accords with its disposition, interest, and happiness.

"As Englishmen we also rejoice, because we are immediately interested in the French Revolution.

"Without inquiring into the justice, on either side, of the reproachful charges of intrigue and ambition which the English and French courts have constantly made on each other, we confine ourselves to this observation :—that if the court of France only was in fault, and the numerous wars which have distressed both countries are chargeable to her alone, that court now exists no longer, and the cause and the consequence must cease together. The French therefore, by the revolution they have made, have conquered for us as well as for themselves, if it be true that their court only was in fault, and ours never.

---

[1] Declaration of the Volunteers of Belfast.

"On this side of the case the French revolution concerns us immediately : we are oppressed with a heavy national debt, a burthen of taxes, an expensive administration of government, beyond those of any people in the world.

"We have also a very numerous poor ; and we hold that the moral obligation of providing for old age, helpless infancy, and poverty, is far superior to that of supplying the invented wants of courtly extravagance, ambition, and intrigue.

"We believe there is no instance to be produced but in England, of seven millions of inhabitants, which make but little more than one million families, paying yearly seventeen millions of taxes.

"As it has always been held out by the administrations that the restless ambition of the court of France rendered this expences necessary to us for our own defence, we consequently rejoice, as men deeply interested in the French revolution ; for that court, as we have already said, exists no longer, and consequently the same enormous expences need not continue to us.

"Thus rejoicing as we sincerely do, both as men and Englishmen, as lovers of universal peace and freedom, and as friends to our national prosperity and reduction of our public expences, we cannot but express our astonishment that any part or any members of our own government should reprobate the extinction of that very power in France or wish to see it restored, to whose influence they formerly attributed (whilst they appeared to lament) the enormous increase of our own burthens and taxes. What, then, are they sorry that the pretence for new oppressive taxes, and the occasion for continuing many old taxes, will be at an end? If so, and if it is the policy of courts and court government to prefer enemies to friends, and a system of war to that of peace, as affording more pretences for places, offices, pensions, revenue and taxation, it is high time for the people of every nation to look with circumspection to their own interests.

"Those who pay the expences, and not those who participate in the emoluments arising from them, are the persons immediately interested in inquiries of this kind. We are a part of that national body on whom this annual expence of seventeen millions falls ; and we consider the present opportunity of the French revolution as a most happy one for lessening the enormous load under which this nation groans. If this be not done we shall then have reason to conclude that the cry of intrigue and ambition against other courts is no more than the common cant of all courts.

"We think it also necessary to express our astonishment that a government desirous of being called FREE, should prefer connexion with the most despotic and arbitrary powers in Europe. We know of none more deserving this description than those of Turkey and Prussia, and the whole combination of German despots.

"Separated as we happily are by nature from the tumults of the continent, we reprobate all

F

systems and intrigues which sacrifice (and that too at a great expence) the blessings of our natural situation. Such systems cannot have a natural origin.

" If we are asked what government is, we hold it to be nothing more than a national association ; and we hold that to be the best which secures to every man his rights and promotes the greatest quantity of happiness with the least expence. We live to improve, or we live in vain ; and therefore we admit of no maxims of government or policy on the mere score of antiquity or other men's authority, the old whigs or the new.

"We will exercise the reason with which we are endued, or we possess it unworthily. As reason is given at all times, it is for the purpose of being used at all times.

"Among the blessings which the French revolution has produced to that nation we enumerate the abolition of the feudal system, of injustice, and of tyranny, on the 4th of August, 1789. Beneath the feudal system all Europe has long groaned, and from it England is not yet free. Game laws, borough tenures, and tyrannical monopolies of numerous kinds still remain amongst us ; but rejoicing as we sincerely do in the freedom of others till we shall haply accomplish our own, we intended to commemorate this prelude to the universal extirpation of the feudal system by meeting on the anniversary of that day (the 4th of August) at the Crown and Anchor : from this meeting we were prevented by the interference of certain unnamed and sculking persons with the master of the tavern, who informed us that on their representation he would not receive us. Let those who live by or countenance feudal oppressions take the reproach of this ineffectual meanness and cowardice to themselves : they cannot stifle the public declaration of our honest, open, and avowed opinions. These are our principles, and these our sentiments ; they embrace the interest and happiness of the great body of the nation of which we are a part. As to riots and tumults, let those answer for them who by wilful misrepresentations endeavour to excite and promote them ; or who seek to stun the sense of the nation, and lose the great cause of public good in the outrages of a mis-informed mob. We take our ground on principles that require no such riotous aid.

"We have nothing to apprehend from the poor for we are pleading their cause ; and we fear not proud oppression for we have truth on our side.

"We say and we repeat it that the French revolution opens to the world an opportunity in which all good citizens must rejoice, that of promoting the general happiness of man, and that it moreover offers to this country in particular an opportunity of reducing our enormous taxes. These are our objects, and we will pursue them."

A comparative study of Paine's two republican manifestoes—that placarded in Paris July 1st, and this of August 20th to the English—reveals the difference between the two nations at that period. No break with the throne in England is suggested, as none had been declared in France until the King had fled, leaving behind him a virtual proclamation of war against all the reforms he had been signing since 1789. The Thatched House address leaves it open for the King to take the side of the Republic, and be its chief. The address is simply an applied "Declaration of Rights." Paine had already maintained, in his reply to Burke, that the English monarch was an importation unrelated to the real nation, "which is left to govern itself, and does govern itself, by magistrates and juri , almost on its own charge, on republican principles." His chief complaint is that royalty is an expensive " sinecure." So far had George III. withdrawn from his attempt to govern as well as reign, which had ended so disastrously in America. The fall of the French King who had aided the American "rebellion" was probably viewed with satisfaction by the English court, so long as the revolution confined itself to France. But now it had raised its head in England, and the alarm of aristocracy was as if it were threatened with an invasion of political cholera.

The disease was brought over by Paine. He must be isolated. But he had a hold on the people, including a large number of literary men, and Nonconformist preachers. The authorities, therefore, began working cautiously, privately inducing the landlords of the Crown and Anchor and the Thatched House to refuse their rooms to the "Painites," as they were beginning to be called. But this was a confession of Paine's power. Indeed all opposition at that time was favorable to Paine. Publicola's reply to "The Rights of Man," attributed to Vice-President Adams, could only heighten Paine's fame ; for John Adams' blazing court dress, which amused us at the Centenary (1889), was not forgotten in England ; and while his influence was limited to court circles, the entrance of so high an official into the arena was accepted as homage to the author. The publication at the same time of the endorsement of Paine's "Rights of Man" by the Secretary of State, the great Jefferson, completed the triumph. The English government now had Paine on its hands, and must deal with him in one way or another.

The closing of one door after another of the usual places of assembly to sympathizers with the republican movement in France, being by hidden hands, could not be charged upon Pitt's government; it was, however, a plain indication that a free expression through public meetings could not be secured without risk of riots. And probably there would have been violent scenes in London had it not been for the moderation of the Quaker leader. At this juncture Paine held a supremacy in the constitutional clubs of England and Ireland equal to that of Robespierre over the Jacobins of Paris. He had the giant's strength, but did not use it like a giant. He sat himself down in a quiet corner of London, began another book, and from time to time consulted his Cabinet of Reformers.

His abode was with Thomas Rickman, a bookseller, his devoted friend. He had known Rickman at Lewes, as a youthful musical genius of the club there, hence called "Clio." He had then set some song of Paine's to music, and afterwards his American patriotic songs, as well as many of his own. He now lived in London with wife and children— these bearing names of the great republicans, beginning with Thomas Paine,— and with them the author resided for a time. A particular value, therefore, attaches to the following passages in Rickman's book:

"Mr. Paine's life in London was a quiet round of philosophical leisure and enjoyment. It was occupied in writing, in a small epistolary correspondence, in walking about with me to visit different friends, occasionally lounging at coffee-houses and public places, or being visited by a select few. Lord Edward Fitzgerald, the French and American ambassadors, Mr. Sharp the en-

graver, Romney the painter, Mrs. Wolstonecraft, Joel Barlow, Mr. Hull, Mr. Christie, Dr. Priestley, Dr. Towers, Col. Oswald, the walking Stewart, Captain Sampson Perry, Mr. Tuffin, Mr. William Choppin, Captain De Stark, Mr. Horne Tooke, &c. &c. were among the number of his friends and acquaintance; and of course, as he was my inmate, the most of my associates were frequently his. At this time he read but little, took his nap after dinner, and played with my family at some game in the evening, as chess, dominos, and drafts, but never at cards; in recitations, singing, music, &c.; or passed it in conversation: the part he took in the latter was always enlightened, full of information, entertainment, and anecdote. Occasionally we visited enlightened friends, indulged in domestic jaunts and recreations from home, frequently lounging at the White Bear, Picadilly, with his old friend the walking Stewart, and other clever travellers from France, and different parts of Europe and America. When by ourselves we sat very late, and often broke in on the morning hours, indulging the reciprocal interchange of affectionate and confidential intercourse. 'Warm from the heart and faithful to its fires' was that intercourse, and gave to us the 'feast of reason and the flow of soul.'"[1]

"Mr. Paine in his person was about five feet ten inches high, and rather athletic; he was broad-shouldered, and latterly stooped a little. His eye, of which the painter could not convey the exquisite meaning, was full, brilliant, and singularly piercing; it had in it the 'muse of fire.' In his dress and person he was generally very cleanly, and wore his hair cued, with side curls, and powdered, so that he looked altogether like a gentleman of the old French school. His manners were easy and gracious; his knowledge was universal and boundless; in private company and among his friends his conversation had every fascination that anecdote, novelty and truth could give it. In mixt company and among strangers he said little, and was no public speaker."[2]

Paine does not appear to have ever learned that his name had been pressed for a place in Washington's Cabinet, and apparently he did not know until long after it was over what a tempest in Jefferson's teapot his book had innocently caused. The facts came to him while he was engaged on his next work, in which they are occasionally reflected. In introducing an English friend to William Short, U.S. Chargé d'Affaires at Paris, under date of November 2d, Paine reports progress:

[1] "Life of Thomas Paine," by Thomas Clio Rickman, pp. 100–102.—H.B.B.
[2] *Id.*, p. xv.—H.B.B.

"I received your favour conveying a letter from Mr. Jefferson and the answers to Publicola for which I thank you. I had John Adams in my mind when I wrote the pamphlet and it has hit as I expected.

"M. Lenobia who presents you this is come to pass a few days at Paris. He is a bon republicain and you will oblige me much by introducing him among our friends of bon foi. I am again in the press but shall not be out till about Christmas, when the Town will begin to fill. By what I can find, the Government Gentry begin to threaten. They have already tried all the under-plots of abuse and scurrility without effect ; and have managed those in general so badly as to make the work and the author the more famous ; several answers also have been written against it which did not excite reading enough to pay the expence of printing.

"I have but one way to be secure in my next work which is, to go further than in my first. I see that *great rogues* escape by the excess of their crimes, and, perhaps, it may be the same in honest cases. However, I shall make a pretty large division in the public opinion, probably too much so to encourage the Government to put it to issue, for it will be rather like begging them than me.

"By all the accounts we have here, the french emigrants are in a hopeless condition abroad ; for my own part I never saw anything to fear from foreign courts—they are more afraid of the french Revolution than the revolution needs to be of them ; and the same caution which they take to prevent the french principles getting among their armies, will prevent their sending armies among the principles.

"We have distressing accounts here from St. Domingo. It is the natural consequence of Slavery and must be expected every where. The Negroes are enraged at the opposition made to their relief and are determined, if not to relieve themselves to punish their enemies. We have no new accounts from the East Indies, and people are in much doubt. I am, affectionately yours, THOMAS PAINE."

The "scurrility" referred to may have been that of George Chalmers, elsewhere mentioned. Two days after this letter to Short was written Paine received a notable ovation.

There was a so-called "Revolution Society" in London, originally formed by a number of prominent dissenters. The Society had manifested its existence only by listening to a sermon on the anniversary of the Revolution of 1688 (November 4th) and thereafter dining together. It had not been supposed to interest itself in any later revolution until 1789. In that year the annual sermon was delivered by Dr. Richard Price, the Unitarian whose defence of the American Revolution received the thanks of Congress. In 1776 Price and Burke stood shoulder to shoulder, but the sermon of 1789 sundered them. It was "On the Love of our Country," and affirmed the constitutional right of the English people to frame their own government, to choose their own governors, and to cashier them for misconduct. This was the "red rag" that drew Burke into the arena. Dr. Price died April 19, 1791, and his great discourse gathered new force from the tributes of Priestley and others at his grave. He had been a staunch friend of Paine, and at the November festival of this year his place was accorded to the man on whom the "Constitutionalists" beheld the mantle of Price and the wreath of Washington. The company at this dinner of 1791, at the London Tavern, included many eminent men, some of them members of Parliament. The old Society was transformed—William and Mary and 1688 passed into oblivion before Thomas Paine and 1791. It was probably for this occasion that the song was written (by whom I know not)—"Paine's Welcome to Great Britain."

"He comes—the great Reformer comes !
　Cease, cease your trumpets, cease, cease your
　　　　drums !
　Those warlike sounds offend the ear,
　Peace and Friendship now appear :
　Welcome, welcome, welcome, welcome,
　Welcome, thou Reformer, here !

"Prepare, prepare, your songs prepare,
　Freedom cheers the brow of care ;
　The joyful tidings spread around,
　Monarchs tremble at the sound !
　Freedom, freedom, freedom, freedom,—
　Rights of Man, and Paine resound !"

Mr. Dignum sang (to the tune of "The tear that bedews sensibility's shrine") :

"Unfold, Father Time, thy long records unfold,
　Of noble achievements accomplished of old ;
　When men, by the standard of Liberty led,
　Undauntedly conquered or chearfully bled :

But now 'midst the triumphs these moments
 reveal,
Their glories all fade and their lustre turns
 pale,
While France rises up, and proclaims the
 decree
That tears off their chains, and bids millions
 be free.

" As spring to the fields, or as dew to the
 flowers.
To the earth parched with heat, as the soft
 dropping showers,
As health to the wretch that lies languid and
 wan,
Or rest to the weary—is Freedom to man !
Where Freedom the light of her countenance
 gives,
There only he triumphs, there only he lives ;
Then seize the glad moment and hail the
 decree
That tears off their chains, and bids millions
 be free.

" Too long had oppression and terror entwined
Those tyrant-formed chains that enslaved the
 free mind ;
While dark superstition, with nature at strife,
For ages had locked up the fountain of life ;
But the dæmon is fled, the delusion is past,
And reason and virtue have triumphed at last ;
Then seize the glad moments, and hail the
 decree,
That tears off their chains, and bids millions
 be free.

" France, we share in the rapture thy bosom
 that fills,
While the Genius of Liberty bounds o'er thy
 hills :
Redundant henceforth may thy purple juice
 flow,
Prouder wave thy green woods, and thine olive
 trees grow !
While the hand of philosophy long shall en-
 twine,
Blest emblems, the laurel, the myrtle and
 vine,
And heaven through all ages confirm the
 decree
That tears off their chains, and bids millions
 be free ! "

Paine gave as his toast, "The Revolution of the World," and no doubt at this
point was sung " A New Song," as it was
then called, written by Paine himself to
the tune of " Rule Britannia " :

" Hail, Great Republic of the world,
 The rising empire of the West,
Where famed Columbus, with a mighty mind
 inspired,
 Gave tortured Europe scenes of rest.
 Be thou forever, forever great and free,
 The Land of Love and Liberty.

" Beneath thy spreading mantling vine,
 Beside thy flowery groves and springs,
And on thy lofty, thy lofty mountains' brow,
 May all thy sons and fair ones sing.
                                    Chorus.

" From thee may rudest nations learn
 To prize the cause thy sons began ;
From thee may future, may future tyrants
 know
 That sacred are the Rights of Man.

" From thee may hated discord fly,
 With all her dark, her gloomy train ;
And o'er thy fertile, thy fertile wide domain
 May everlasting friendship reign.

" Of thee may lisping infancy
 The pleasing wondrous story tell,
And patriot sages in venerable mood
 Instruct the world to govern well.

" Ye guardian angels watch around,
 From harm protect the new-born State ;
And all ye friendly, ye friendly nations join,
 And thus salute the Child of Fate.
 Be thou forever, forever great and free,
 The Land of Love and Liberty ! "

Notwithstanding royal tremors these
gentlemen were genuinely loyal in singing
the old anthem with new words :

" God save the Rights of Man !
 Give him a heart to scan
 Blessings so dear ;
 Let them be spread around,
 Wherever Man is found,
 And with the welcome sound
 Ravish his ear ! "

No report is preserved of Paine's
speech, but we may feel sure that in
giving his sentiment "The Revolution
of the World" he set forth his favorite
theme—that revolutions of nations should
be as quiet, lawful, and fruitful as the
revolutions of the earth.

CHAPTER XXII

THE RIGHT OF EVOLUTION

THE Abbé Sieyès did not escape by declining to stand by his challenge of the republicans. In the second part of "The Rights of Man" Paine considers the position of that gentleman, namely, that hereditary monarchy is an evil, but the elective mode historically proven worse. That both are bad Paine agrees, but "such a mode of reasoning on such a subject is inadmissible, because it finally amounts to an accusation of providence, as if she had left to man no other choice with respect to government than between two evils." Every now and then this Quaker Antæus touches his mother earth—the theocratic principle—in this way; the invigoration is recognizable in a religious seriousness, which, however, makes no allowance for the merely ornamental parts of government, always so popular. "The splendor of a throne is the corruption of a state." However, the time was too serious for the utility of bagatelles to be much considered by any. Paine engages Sieyès on his own ground, and brings historic evidence to prove that the wars of succession, civil and foreign, show hereditary a worse evil than elective headship, as illustrated by Poland, Holland, and America. But he does not defend the method of either of these countries, and clearly shows that he is, as Sieyès said, a "polycrat," so far as the numerical composition of the Executive is concerned.[1] He affirms, however, that governing is no function of a republican Executive. The law alone governs. "The sovereign authority in any country

is the power of making laws, and everything else is an official department."

More than fifty thousand copies of the first part of "The Rights of Man" had been sold, and the public hungrily awaited the author's next work. But he kept back his proofs until Burke should fulfil his promise of returning to the subject and comparing the English and French constitutions. He was disappointed, however, at finding no such comparison in Burke's "Appeal from the New to the Old Whigs." It did, however, contain a menace that was worth waiting for.

"Oldys" (Chalmers) says that Paine was disappointed at not being arrested for his first pamphlet on "The Rights of Man," and had, "while fluttering on the wing for Paris, hovered about London a whole week waiting to be taken." It is, indeed, possible that he would have been glad to elicit just then a fresh decision from the courts in favor of freedom of speech and of the press, which would strengthen faint hearts. If he had this desire he was resolved not to be disappointed a second time. A publisher (Chapman) offered him a thousand guineas for the manuscript of Part II.[2] Paine declined; "he wished to reserve it in his own hands." Facts afterwards appeared which rendered it probable that this was a ministerial effort to suppress the book.[3]

[1] "I have always been opposed to the mode of refining government up to an individual, or what is called a single Executive. Such a man will always be the chief of a party. A plurality is far better. It combines the mass of a nation better together. And besides this, it is necessary to the manly mind of a republic that it lose the debasing idea of obeying an individual."—Paine MS.

[2] At the trial of the "Rights of Man" Chapman, the printer, in his evidence stated, "I made three separate offers in the different stages of the work: the first, I believe, was 100 guineas; the second, 500; the last, 1000."—H.B.B.

[3] Paine may, indeed, only have apprehended alterations, which he always dreaded. His friends, knowing how much his antagonists had made of his grammatical faults, sometimes suggested expert revision. "He would say," says Richard Carlile, "that he only wished to be known as he was, without being decked with the plumes of another." At the time (September) when Chapman began printing Paine's Part II.,

Paine's Part Second was to appear about the first of February, or before the meeting of Parliament. But the printer (Chapman) threw up the publication, alleging its "dangerous tendencies," whereby it was delayed until February 17th, when it was published by Jordan. Meanwhile, his elaborate scheme for reducing taxes so resembled that which Pitt had just proposed in Parliament that the author appended his reasons for believing that his pages had been read by the government clerk, Chalmers, and his plan revealed to Pitt. "Be the case, however, as it may, Mr. Pitt's plan, little and diminutive as it is, would have made a very awkward appearance had this work appeared at the time the printer had engaged to finish it."

In the light of Pitt's subsequent career it is a significant fact that, in the beginning of 1792, he should be suspected of stealing Paine's thunder! And, indeed, throughout Paine's Part Second the tone towards Pitt implies some expectation of reform from him. Its severity is that which English agitators for constitutional reform have for a half century made familiar and honorable. The historical student finds mirrored in this work the rosy picture of the United States as seen at its dawn by the disfranchised people of Europe, and beside that a burdened England now hardly credible. It includes an historical statement of the

---

George Chalmers brought to the same press his libellous "Life of Pain." On learning that Chapman was printing Paine, Chalmers took his book away. As Chalmers was a government employé, and his work larger, Chapman returned Paine's work to him half printed, and the Chalmers book was restored to him. As Chapman stated in his testimony, and so wrote to Paine (January 17, 1792), that he was unwilling to go on with the printing because of the dangerous tendency of a part of it, his offer of a thousand guineas for it could only have contemplated its expurgation or total suppression. That it was the latter, and that the money was to be paid by the government, is rendered probable by the evidences in Chalmers' book, when it appeared, that he had been allowed the perusal of Paine's manuscript while in Chapman's hands. Chalmers also displays intimate knowledge of Chapman's business transactions with Paine.

powers claimed by the crown and gradually distributed among non-elective peers and class-elective commoners, the result being a combination of all three against admission of the people to any degree of self-government. Though the arraignment is heavy, the method of reform is set forth with moderation. Particular burdens are pointed out, and England is warned to escape violent revolution by accommodating itself to the new age. It is admitted that no new system need be constructed.

" Mankind (from the long tyranny of assumed power) have had so few opportunities of making the necessary trials on modes and principles of government, in order to discover the best, *that government is but now beginning to be known*, and experience is yet wanting to determine many particulars."

Paine frankly retracts an old opinion of his own, that the legislature should be unicameral. He now thinks that, though there should be but one representation, it might secure wiser deliberation to divide it, by lot, into two or three parts.

"Every proposed bill shall first be debated in those parts, by succession, that they may become hearers of each other, but without taking any vote ; after which the whole representation to assemble, for a general debate, and determination by vote."

The great necessity is that England shall gather its people, by representation, in convention and frame a constitution which shall contain the means of peaceful development in accordance with enlightenment and necessity.

In Part I. Paine stated his general principles with some reservations, in view of the survival of royalty in the French constitution. In Part II. his political philosophy is freely and fully developed, and may be summarized as follows :

1. Government is the organization of the aggregate of those natural rights which individuals are not competent to secure individually, and therefore surrender to the control of society in exchange for the protection of all rights.

2. Republican government is that in which the welfare of the whole nation is the object.

3. Monarchy is government, more or less arbitrary, in which the interests of an individual are paramount to those of the people generally.

4. Aristocracy is government, partially arbitrary, in which the interests of a class are paramount to those of the people generally.

5. Democracy is the whole people governing themselves without secondary means.

6. Representative government is the control of a nation by persons elected by the whole nation.

7. The Rights of Man mean the right of all to representation.

Democracy, simple enough in small and primitive societies, degenerates into confusion by extension to large populations. Monarchy, which originated amid such confusion, degenerates into incapacity by extension to vast and complex interests requiring "an assemblage of practical knowledges which no one individual can possess." "The aristocratical form has the same vices and defects with the monarchical, except that the chance of abilities is better from the proportion of numbers."

The representative republic advocated by Paine is different from merely epitomized democracy. "Representation is the delegated monarchy of a nation." In the early days of the American republic, when presidential electors were independent of the constituents who elected them, the filtration of democracy was a favorite principle among republicans. Paine evidently regards the representative as different from a delegate, or mere commissioner carrying out instructions. The representatives of a people are clothed with their sovereignty; that, and not opinions or orders, has been transferred to them by constituencies. Hence we find Paine, after describing the English people as "fools" (p. 106), urging representation as a sort of natural selection of wisdom.

"Whatever wisdom constituently is, it is like a seedless plant; it may be reared when it appears, but it cannot be voluntarily produced. There is always a sufficiency somewhere in the general mass of society for all purposes; but, with respect to the parts of society, it is continually changing place. It rises in one to-day, in another to-morrow, and has most probably visited in rotation every family of the earth, and again withdrawn. As this is the order of nature, the order of government must follow it, or government will, as we see it does, degenerate into ignorance. The hereditary system therefore, is as repugnant to human wisdom as to human rights; and is as absurd as unjust. As the republic of letters brings forward the best literary productions, by giving to genius a fair and universal chance, so the representative system is calculated to produce the wisest laws, by collecting wisdom where it can be found."

We have seen that "Publicola" (John Quincy Adams) in his answer to Paine's Part I. had left the people no right to alter government but the right of revolution, by violence; Erskine pointed out that Burke's pamphlet had similarly closed every other means of reform. Paine would civilize reformation:

"Formerly, when divisions arose respecting governments, recourse was had to the sword, and civil war ensued. That savage custom is exploded by the new system, and reference is had to national conventions. Discussion and the general will arbitrate the question, private opinion yields with a good grace, and order is preserved uninterrupted."

Thus he is really trying to supplant the right of revolution with the right of evolution:

"It is now towards the middle of February. Were I to take a turn in the country the trees would present a leafless wintery appearance. As people are apt to pluck twigs as they go along, I perhaps might do the same, and by chance might observe that a single bud on that twig had begun to swell. I should reason very unnaturally, or rather not reason at all to suppose this was the only bud in England which had this appearance. Instead of deciding thus, I should instantly conclude that the same appearance was beginning, or about to begin, everywhere; and though the vegetable sleep will continue longer on some trees and plants than others, and though some of them may not blossom for two or three years, all will be in leaf in the summer, except those which are rotten. What pace the political summer may keep with the natural, no human foresight can determine.

It is, however, not difficult to perceive that the Spring is begun. Thus wishing, as I sincerely do, freedom and happiness to all nations, I close the Second Part."

Apparently the publisher expected trouble. In the *Gazetteer*, January 25th, had appeared the following notice :

"MR. PAINE, it is known, is to produce another book this season. The composition of this is now past, and it was given a few weeks since to two printers, whose presses it was to go through as soon as possible. They printed about half of it, and then, being alarmed by *some intimations*, refused to go further. Some delay has thus occurred, but another printer has taken it, and in the course of the next month it will appear. Its title is to be a repetition of the former, 'The Rights of Man,' of which the words 'Part the Second' will shew that it is a continuation."

That the original printer, Chapman, impeded the publication is suggested by the fact that on February 7th, thirteen days after the above announcement, Paine writes: "Mr. Chapman, please to deliver to Mr. Jordan the remaining sheets of the Rights of Man." And that "some intimations" were received by Jordan also may be inferred from the following note and enclosure to him :

"February 16, 1792.—For your satisfaction and my own, I send you the enclosed, tho' I do not apprehend there will be any occasion to use it. If, in case there should, you will immediately send a line for me under cover to Mr. Johnson, St. Paul's Church-Yard, who will forward it to me, upon which I shall come and answer personally for the work. Send also to Mr. Horne Tooke.—T. P."

"February 16, 1792.—Sir : Should any person, under the sanction of any kind of authority, enquire of you respecting the author and publisher of the Rights of Man, you will please to mention me as the author and publisher of that work, and shew to such person this letter. I will, as soon as I am made acquainted with it, appear and answer for the work personally.— Your humble servant,

"THOMAS PAINE.
"Mr. Jordan,
   No. 166 Fleet-street."

Some copies were in Paine's hands three days before publication, as appears by a note of February 13th to Jefferson, on hearing of Morris' appointment as Minister to France:

"Mr. Kennedy, who brings this to New York, is on the point of setting out. I am therefore confined to time. I have enclosed six copies of my work for yourself in a parcel addressed to the President, and three or four for my other friends, which I wish you to take the trouble of presenting.

"I have just heard of Governeur Morris's appointment. *It is a most unfortunate one ;* and, as I shall mention the same thing to him when I see him, I do not express it to you with the injunction of confidence. He is just now arrived in London, and this circumstance has served, as I see by the french papers, to increase the dislike and suspicion of some of that nation and the National Assembly against him.

"In the present state of Europe it would be best to make no appointments."

Lafayette wrote Washington a strong private protest against Morris, but in vain. Paine spoke frankly to Morris, who mentions him on Washington's birthday :

"February 22. I read Paine's new publication today, and tell him that I am really afraid he will be punished. He seems to laugh at this, and relies on the force he has in the nation. He seems to become every hour more drunk with self-conceit. It seems, however, that his work excites but little emotion, and rather raises indignation. I tell him that the disordered state of things in France works against all schemes of reformation both here and elsewhere. He declares that the riots and outrages in France are nothing at all. It is not worth while to contest such declarations. I tell him, therefore, that as I am sure he does not mean what he says, I shall not dispute it. Visit the Duchess of Gordon, who tells me that she supposes I give Paine his information about America, and speaks very slightly of our situation, as being engaged in a civil war with the Indians. I smile, and tell her that Britain is also at war with Indians, though in another hemisphere."

In his appendix Paine alludes vaguely to the book of George Chalmers ("Oldys") .

"A ministerial bookseller in Picadilly, who has been employed, as common report says, by a clerk of one of the boards closely connected with the Ministry (the board of Trade and Plantations, of which Lord Hawkesbury is president) to publish what he calls my Life (I wish his own life and that of the Cabinet were as good,) used to have his books printed at the same printing office that I employed."

In his fifth edition Chalmers claims

that this notice of his work, unaccompanied by any denial of its statements, is an admission of their truth.   It looks as if Paine had not then seen the book, but he never further alluded to it.   There was nothing in Chalmers' political orthographical criticisms requiring answer, and its tar and feathers were so adroitly mixed, and applied with such a masterly hand, that Paine had to endure his literary lynching in silence.   "Nothing can lie like the truth."[1]   Chalmers' libels were so ingeniously interwoven with the actual stumbles and humiliations of Paine's early life, that the facts could not be told without dragging before the public his mother's corpse, and breaking treaty with his divorced wife.   Chalmers would have been more successful as a government employé in this business had he not cared more for himself than for his party.   By advertising, as we have seen (Preface, xv), his first edition as a "Defence" of Paine's writings he reaped a pecuniary harvest from the Painites before the substitution of "Review" tempted the Burkites.   This trick probably enraged more than it converted. The pompous pseudonym covered a vanity weak enough to presently drop its lion skin, revealing ears sufficiently long to expect for a government clerk the attention accorded to a reverend M.A. of the University of Pennsylvania. This degree was not only understood in England with a clerical connotation, but it competed with Paine's "M.A." from the same institution.   The pseudonym also concealed the record of Chalmers as a Tory refugee from Maryland, and an opponent of Burke, long enough to sell several editions.   But the author was known early in 1792, and was

named in an important pamphlet by no means altogether favorable to Paine. After rebuking Paine for personalities towards men whose station prevents reply, this writer also disagrees with him about the Constitution.   But he declares that Paine has collected the essence of the most venerated writers of Europe in the past, and applied the same to the executive government, which cannot stand the test.

"The Constitution will; but *the present mode of administering that Constitution* must shrink from the comparison.   And this is the reason, that foolish Mr. Rose of the Treasury trembles on the bench, and the crafty clerk in Lord Hawkesbury's office, carries on his base attacks against Paine by sap, fights him under the mask of a Philadelphia parson, fit disguise for the most impudent falsehoods that ever were published, and stabs him in the dark.   But, of this upstart clerk at the *Cockpit*, more hereafter."[2]

George Chalmers being mentioned by name in this and other pamphlets, and nothing like a repudiation coming from him or from "Oldys" in any of his ten editions, the libel recoiled on the government, while it damaged Paine.   The meanness of meeting inconvenient arguments by sniffing village gossip for private scandals was resented, and the calumnies were discounted.   Nevertheless, there was probably some weakening in the "Painite" ranks.   Although this "un-English" tracking of a man from his cradle, and masked assassination angered the republicans, it could hardly fail to intimidate some.   In every period it has been seen that the largest interests, even the liberties, of English peoples may be placed momentarily at the mercy of any incident strongly exciting the moral sentiment.   A crafty clerk accuses Paine of maltreating his wife; the leader's phalanx of friends is for one instant disconcerted; Burke perceives the opportunity and points it out to the King; Pitt must show equal jealousy of royal authority;

[1] Not that Chalmers confines himself to perversions of fact.   The book bore on its title-page five falsehoods: "Pain," instead of "Paine"; "Francis Oldys"; "A. M."; "University of Pennsylvania"; "With a Defence of his Writings."   There is a marked increase of virulence with the successive editions.   The second is in cheap form, and bears at the back of its title this note: "Read this, and then hand it to others who are requested to do likewise."

[2] "Paine's Political and Moral Maxims, etc. By a Free-Born Englishman. London. Printed for H. D. Symonds, Paternoster Row, 1792." The introductory letter is dated May 15th.

Paine is prosecuted. There is little doubt that Pitt was forced to this first step which reversed the traditions of English freedom, and gave that Minister his historic place as the English Robespierre of counter-revolution.[1]

On May 14th Paine, being at Bromley, Kent, learned that the government had issued summons against Jordan, his publisher. He hastened to London and assumed the expense of Jordan's defence. Jordan, however, privately compromised the affair by agreeing to plead guilty, surrender his notes relating to Paine, and receive a verdict to the author's prejudice—that being really the end of the government's business with the publisher. On May 21st a summons was left on Paine at his London lodgings (Rickman's house) to appear at the Court of King's Bench on June 8th. On the same day issued a royal proclamation against seditious writings. On May 25th, in the debate on the Proclamation, Secretary Dundas said in the House of Commons that the proceedings against Jordan were instituted because Mr. Paine could not be found. Thereupon Paine, detecting the unreality of the prosecution of his publisher, addressed a letter to the Attorney-General. Alluding to the remark of Dundas in Parliament, he says :

"Mr. Paine, Sir, so far from secreting himself never went a step out of his way, nor in the least instance varied from his usual conduct, to avoid any measure you might choose to adopt with respect to him. It is on the purity of his heart, and the universal utility of the principles and plans which his writings contain, that he rests the issue ; and he will not dishonor it by any kind of subterfuge. The apartments which he occupied at the time of writing the work last winter, he has continued to occupy to the present hour, and the solicitors of the prosecution know where to find him ; of which there is a proof in their own office, as far back as the 21st of May, and also in the office of my own attorney.—But

admitting, for the sake of the case, that the reason for proceeding against the publication was, as Mr. Dundas stated, that Mr. Paine could not be found, that reason can now exist no longer. The instant that I was informed that an information was preparing to be filed against me as the author of, I believe, one of the most useful and benevolent books ever offered to mankind, I directed my attorney to put in an appearance ; and as I shall meet the prosecution fully and fairly, and with a good and upright conscience, I have a right to expect that no act of littleness will be made use of on the part of the prosecution towards influencing the future issue with respect to the author. This expression may, perhaps, appear obscure to you, but I am in the possession of some matters which serve to show that the action against the publisher is not intended to be a *real* action."

He then intimates that, if his suspicions should prove well-founded, he will withdraw from his intention of defending the publisher, and proposes that the case against Jordan be given up. At the close of his letter Paine says :

"I believe that Mr. Burke, finding himself defeated, has been one of the promoters of this prosecution ; and I shall return the compliment by shewing, in a future publication, that he has been a masked pensioner at £1500 per annuim for about ten years. Thus it is that the public money is wasted, and the dread of public investigation is produced."

The secret negotiations with the publisher being thus discovered, no more was heard of Jordan, except that his papers were brought out at Paine's trial.

The Information against Paine, covering forty-one pages, octavo, is a curiosity. It recites that

"Thomas Paine, late of London, gentleman, being a wicked, malicious, seditious, and ill-disposed person, and being greatly disaffected to our said Sovereign Lord the now King, and to the happy constitution and government of this kingdom . . . and to bring them into hatred and contempt, on the sixteenth day of February, in the thirty-second year of the reign of our said present Sovereign Lord the King, with force and arms at London aforesaid, to wit, in the parish of St. Mary le Bone, in the Ward of Cheap, he, the said Thomas, wickedly, maliciously and seditiously, did write and publish, and caused to be written and published, a certain false, scandalous, malicious, and seditious libel, of and

---

[1] "Pitt 'used to say,' according to Lady Hester Stanhope, 'that Tom Paine was quite in the right, but then he would add, what am I to do? As things are, if I were to encourage Tom Paine's opinions we should have a bloody revolution.'"—Encyclop. Britannica.

concerning the said late happy Revolution, and the said settlements and limitations of the crown and regal governments of the said kingdoms and dominions . . . intituled, 'Rights of Man, Part the Second, Combining principle and practice.' . . . In one part thereof, according to the tenor and effect following, that is to say, 'All hereditary government is in its nature tyranny. An heritable crown' (meaning, amongst others, the crown of this kingdom) 'or an heritable throne,' (meaning the throne of this kingdom), 'or by what-other fanciful name such things may be called, have no other significant explanation than that mankind are heritable property. To inherit a government is to inherit the people, as if they were flocks and herds.' . . . 'The time is not very distant when England will laugh at itself for sending to Holland, Hanover, Zell, or Brunswick, for men' (meaning the said King William the Third, and King George the First) 'at the expence of a million a year, who understood neither her laws, her language, nor her interest, and whose capacities would scarcely have fitted them for the office of a parish constable. If government could be trusted to such hands, it must be some easy and simple thing indeed; and materials fit for all the purposes may be found in every town and village in England.' In contempt of our said Lord the now King and his laws, to the evil example of all others in like case offending, and against the peace of our said Lord the King, his crown and dignity. Whereupon the said Attorney General of our said Lord the King, who for our said Lord the King in this behalf, prosecuteth for our said Lord the King, prayeth the consideration of the court here in the premises, and that due process of law may be awarded against him, the said Thomas Paine, in this behalf, to make him answer to our said Lord the King, touching and concerning the premises aforesaid.

"To this information the defendant hath appeared, and pleaded Not Guilty, and thereupon issue is joined."

The specifications and quotations in the Information are reiterated twice, in one case (Paine's note on William and Mary centenary), three times.[1]   It is

marvellous that such an author, martial with "force and arms," could still walk freely about London. But the machinery for suppressing thought had always a tendency to rust in England; it had to be refurbished. To the royal proclamation against seditious writings corporations and rotten boroughs responded with loyal addresses. In the debate on that proclamation (May 25th) Secretary Dundas and Mr. Adam had arraigned Paine, and he addressed an open letter to the Secretary (June 6th) which was well received.   Mr. Adam had said that

"He had well considered the subject of constitutional publications, and was by no means ready to say that books of science upon government though recommending a doctrine or system different from the form of our constitution were fit objects of prosecution; that if he did, he must condemn Harrington for his Oceana, Sir Thomas More for his Utopia, and Hume for his Idea of a Perfect Commonwealth. But the publication of Mr. Paine reviled what was most sacred in the Constitution, destroyed every principle of subordination, and established nothing in their room."

The real difficulty was that Paine *had* put something in the room of hereditary monarchy—not a Utopia, but the representative system of the United States. He now again compares the governmental expenses of England and America and their condition.   He shows that the entire government of the United States costs less than the English pension list alone.

"Here is a form and system of government that is better organized than any other government in the world, and that for less than one hundred thousand pounds, and yet every member of Congress receives as a compensation for his time and attendance on public business, one pound seven shillings per day, which is at the rate of nearly five hundred pounds a year. This is a government that has nothing to fear. It

---

[1] "I happened to be in England at the celebration of the centenary of the Revolution of 1688. The characters of William and Mary have always appeared to me detestable; the one seeking to destroy his uncle, the other her father, to get possession of power themselves; yet, as the nation was disposed to think something of the event, I felt hurt at seeing it ascribe the whole reputation of it to a man who had undertaken it as a job; and who besides what he otherwise got, charged six hundred thousand pounds for the expense of the little fleet that brought him from Holland.   George the First acted the same close-fisted part as William had

done, and bought the Duchy of Bremen with the money he got from England, two hundred and fifty thousand pounds over and above his pay as King; and, having thus purchased it at the expense of England, added it to his Hanoverian dominions for his own private profit. In fact every nation that does not govern itself is governed as a job. England has been the prey of jobs ever since the Revolution."

needs no proclamations to deter people from writing and reading. It needs no political superstition to support it. It was by encouraging discussion and rendering the press free upon all subjects of government, that the principles of government became understood in America, and the people are now enjoying their present blessings under it. You hear of no riots, tumults and disorders in that country; because there exists no cause to produce them. Those things are never the effect of freedom, but of restraint, oppression, and excessive taxation."

On June 8th Paine appeared in court and was much disappointed by the postponement of his trial to December. Lord Onslow having summoned a meeting at Epsom of the gentry in Surrey, to respond to the proclamation, receives due notice. Paine sends for presentation to the gentlemen one hundred copies of his " Rights of Man," one thousand of his " Letter to Dundas." The bearer is Horne Tooke, who opens his speech of presentation by remarking on the impropriety that the meeting should be presided over by Lord Onslow, a bedchamber lord (sinecure) at £1,000, with a pension of £3,000. Tooke, being cut short, his speech was continued by Paine, whose two letters to Onslow (June 17th and 21st) were widely circulated.[1] On June 20th was written a respectful letter to the Sheriff of Sussex, or other presiding officer, requesting that it be read at a meeting to be held in Lewes. This interesting letter has already been quoted in connection with Paine's

early residence at Lewes. In these letters the author reinforces his accused book, reminds the assemblies of their illegal conduct in influencing the verdict in a pending matter, taunts them with their meanness in seeking to refute by brute force what forty pamphlets had failed to refute by argument.

The meeting at Lewes, his old town, to respond to the proclamation occurred on the fourth of July. That anniversary of his first cause was celebrated by Paine also. Notified by his publisher that upwards of a thousand pounds stood to his credit, he directed it to be all sent as a present to the Society for Constitutional Information.[2]

A careful tract of 1793 estimates the sales of " The Rights of Man " up to that year at 200,000 copies.[3] In the opinion of the famous publisher of such literature, Richard Carlile, the king's proclamation seriously impeded the sale. " One part of the community is afraid to sell, and another to purchase, under such conditions. It is not too much to say that, if ' Rights of Man ' had obtained two or three years' free circulation in England and Scotland, it would have produced a similar effect to that which ' Common Sense ' did in the United States." However, the reign of terror had not yet begun in France, nor the consequent reign of panic in England.

[1] To this noble pensioner and sinecurist he says: " What honor or happiness you can derive from being the principal pauper of the neighborhood, and occasioning a greater expence than the poor, the aged, and the infirm for ten miles round, I leave you to enjoy. At the same time I can see that it is no wonder you should be strenuous in suppressing a book which strikes at the root of these abuses."

[2] *The Argus*, July 6, 1792. See " Biographia Addenda," No. vii., London, 1792. To the same society Paine had given the right to publish his " Letter to Dundas," " Common Sense," and " Letter to Raynal " in new editions.

[3] " Impartial Memoirs of the Life of Thomas Paine," London, 1793. There were numbers of small " Lives " of Paine printed in these years. but most of them were mere stealings from " Oldys."

CHAPTER XXIII

THE DEPUTY FOR CALAIS IN THE CONVENTION

THE prosecution of Paine in England had its counterpart in a shrine across the channel. The *Moniteur*, June 17, 1792, announces the burning of Paine's works at "Excester," and the expulsion from Manchester of a man pointed out as Paine. Since April 16th, his "Rights of Man," sympathetically translated by M. Lanthenas, had been in every French home. Paine's portrait, just painted in England by Romney and engraved by Sharpe, was in every cottage, framed in immortelles. In this book the philosophy of visionary reformers took practical shape. From the ashes of Rousseau's "Contrat Social," burnt in Paris, rose "The Rights of Man," no phœnix, but an eagle of the new world, with eye not blinded by any royal sun.[1] It comes to tell how by union of France and America—of Lafayette and Washington — The "Contrat Social" was framed into the constitution of a happy and glorious new earth, over it a new heaven unclouded by priestly power or superstitions. By that book of Paine's (Part I), the idea of a national convention was made the purpose of the French leaders who were really inspired by an "enthusiasm of humanity." In December, 1791, when the legislature sits paralyzed under royal vetoes, Paine's panacea is proposed.[2]

On the tenth of August, 1792, after the massacre of the Marseillese by the King's Swiss guards, one book, hurled from the window of the mobbed palace, felled an American spectator—Robert Gilmor, of Baltimore—who consoled himself by carrying it home. The book, now in the collection of Dr. Thomas Addis Emmet, New York, was a copy of "The Thirteen Constitutions," translated by Franklin's order into French (1783) and distributed among the monarchs of Europe.[3] What a contrast between the peace and order amid which the thirteen peoples, when the old laws and authorities were abolished, formed new ones, and these scenes in France!

"For upwards of two years from the commencement of the American war," wrote Paine,[4] "and a longer period, in several of the American States, there were no established forms of government. The old governments had been abolished, and the country was too much occupied in defence to employ its attention in establishing new governments; yet, during this interval, order and harmony were preserved as inviolate as in any country in Europe."

When Burke pointed to the first riots in France, Paine could make a retort: the mob is what your cruel governments have made it, and only proves how necessary the overthrow of such governments. That French human nature was different from English nature he could not admit. Liberty and equality would soon end these troubles of transition. On that same tenth of August Paine's two great preliminaries are adopted: the hereditary representative is superseded and a national convention is called. The machinery for such convention, the constituencies, the objects of it, had been read in "The Rights of Man," as

[1] L'Esprit du Contrat Social; suivi de l'Esprit de Sens Commun de Thomas Paine. Présenté a la Convention. Par le Citoyen Boinvilliers, Instituteur et ci-devant Membre de plusieurs Sociétés Littéraires. L'an second.

[2] "*Veto* after *Veto*; your thumbscrew paralysed! Gods and men may see that the Legislature is in a false position. As, alas, who is in a true one? Voices already murmur for a National Convention."—Carlyle.

[3] "Constitutions des Treize États-Unis de l'Amérique." The French king's arms are on the red morocco binding, and on the title a shield, striped and winged; above this thirteen minute stars shaped into one large star, six-pointed. For the particulars of Franklin's gift to the monarchs see Sparks' "Franklin," x., p. 39. See also p. 118 of this volume.

[4] "Rights of Man." Part II. "The Writings of Thomas Paine" (Conway), vol. ii., p. 407.—H.B.B.

illustrated in the United States and Pennsylvania, by every French statesman.[1] It was the American Republic they were about to found ; and notwithstanding the misrepresentation of that nation by its surviving courtiers, these French republicans recognized their real American Minister : Paine is summoned.

On August 26, 1792, the National Assembly, on proposal of M. Guadet, in the name of the " Commission Extraordinaire," conferred the title of French citizen on " Priestley, Payne, Benthom, Wilberforce, Clarkson, Mackintosh, David Williams, Gorani, Anacharsis Clootz, Campe, Cormelle, Paw, N. Pestalozzi, Washington, Hamilton, Maddison, Klopstoc, Kosciusko, Gilleers." Schiller was afterwards added, and on September 25th the *Patriote* announces the same title conferred on Thomas Cooper, John Horne Tooke, John Oswald, George Boies, Thomas Christie, Dr. Joseph Warner, Englishmen, and Joel Barlow, American.[2]

Paine was elected to the French Convention by three different departments—Oise, Puy-de-Dôme, and Pas-de-Calais. The votes appear to have been unanimous.

Here is an enthusiastic appeal (Riom, le 8 Septembre) signed by Louvet, "auteur de la Sentinelle," and thirty-two others, representing nine communes, to Paine, that day elected representative of Puy-de-Dôme :

"Your love for humanity, for liberty and equality, the useful works that have issued from your heart and pen in their defence, have determined our choice. It has been hailed with universal and reiterated applause. Come, friend of the people, to swell the number of patriots in an assembly which will decide the destiny of a great people, perhaps of the human race. The happy period you have predicted for the nations has arrived. Come ! do not deceive their hope !"

But already Calais, which elected him September 6th, had sent a municipal officer, Achille Audibert, to London, to entreat Paine's acceptance. Paine was so eager to meet the English government in court, that he delayed his answer. But his friends had reason to fear that his martyrdom might be less mild than he anticipated, and urged his acceptance. There had been formed a society of the " Friends of Liberty," and, at its gathering of September 12th, Paine appears to have poured forth " inflammatory eloquence." At the house of his friend Johnson, on the following evening, Paine was reporting what he had said to some sympathizers, among them the mystical William Blake, who was convinced that the speech of the previous night would be followed by arrest. Gilchrist's account of what followed is here quoted :

"On Paine's rising to leave, Blake laid his hand on the orator's shoulder, saying, ' You must not go home, or you are a dead man,' and hurried him off on his way to France, whither he was now in any case bound to take his seat as a legislator. By the time Paine was at Dover, the officers were in his house, [he was staying at Rickman's, in Marylebone] and, some twenty minutes after the Custom House officials at Dover had turned over his slender baggage, narrowly escaped from the English Tories. Those were hanging days ! Blake on the occasion showed greater sagacity than Paine, whom, indeed, Fuseli affirmed to be more ignorant of the common affairs of life than himself even. Spite of unworldliness and visionary faculty, Blake never wanted for prudence and sagacity in ordinary matters."[3]

Before leaving London Paine managed to have an interview with the American Minister, Pinckney, who thought he could do good service in the Convention.

Mr. Frost, who accompanied Paine

[1] "Théorie et Pratique des Droits de l'Homme. Par Thomas Paine, Sécrétaire du Congres au Département des Affaires Étrangères pendant la guerre d'Amérique, auteur du 'Sens Commun,' et des Réponses à Burke. Traduit en Français par F. Lanthenas, D.M., et par le Traducteur du 'Sens Commun.' À Paris : Chez les Directeurs de l'Imprimerie du Cercle Social, rue du Théâtre Français, No. 4. 1792. L'an quatrième de La Liberté."

[2] "Life and Letters of Joel Barlow," etc., by Charles Burr Todd, New York, 1886, p. 97.

[3] "Life of William Blake," by Alexander Gilchrist, p. 94.

and Audibert, had information of certain plans of the officials. He guided them to Dover by a circuitous route—Rochester, Sandwich, Deal. With what emotions does our world-wanderer find himself in the old town where he married and suffered with his first love, Mary Lambert, whose grave is near! Nor is he so far from Cranbrook, where his wife receives her mysterious remittances, but since their separation "has not heard of" this said Thomas Paine, as her testimony goes some years later. Paine is parting from England and its ghosts forever. The travellers find Dover excited by the royal proclamation. The collector of customs has had general instructions to be vigilant, and searches the three men, even to their pockets. Frost pretended a desire to escape, drawing the scent from Paine. In his report (September 15th) of the search to Mr. Dundas, Paine says:

"Among the letters which he took out of my trunk were two sealed letters, given into my charge by the American minister in London [Pinckney], one of which was addressed to the American minister at Paris, the other to a private gentleman; a letter from the president of the United States, and a letter from the secretary of State in America, both directed to me, and which I had received from the American minister, now in London, and were private letters of friendship; a letter from the electoral body of the department of Calais, containing the notification of my being elected to to the National Convention; and a letter from the president of the National Assembly informing me of my being also elected for the department of the Oise [Versailles]. . . . When the collector had taken what papers and letters he pleased out of the trunks, he proceeded to read them. The first letter he took up for this purpose was that from the president of the United States to me. While he was doing this I said, that it was very extraordinary that General Washington could not write a letter of private friendship to me, without its being subject to be read by a custom-house officer. Upon this Mr. Frost laid his hand over the face of the letter, and told the collector that he should not read it, and took it from him. Mr. Frost then, casting his eyes on the concluding paragraph of the letter, said, I will read this part to you, which he did; of which the following is an exact transcript—'And as no one can feel a greater interest in the happiness of mankind than I do, it is the first wish of my

heart that the enlightened policy of the present age may diffuse to all men those blessings to which they are entitled and lay the foundation of happiness for future generations.'"

So Washington's nine months' delay (p. 123) in acknowledging Paine's letter and gift of fifty volumes had brought his letter in the nick of time. The collector quailed before the President's signature. He took away the documents, leaving a list of them, and they were presently returned. Soon afterward the packet sailed, and "twenty minutes later" the order for Paine's arrest reached Dover. Too late! Baffled pursuers gnash their teeth, and Paine passes to his ovation.

What the ovation was to be he could hardly anticipate even from the cordial, or glowing, letter of Hérault Séchelles summoning him to the Convention,—a fine translation of which by Cobbett is given in the Appendix. Ancient Calais, in its time, had received heroes from across the channel, but hitherto never with joy. That honor the centuries reserved for a Thetford Quaker. As the packet sails in a salute is fired from the battery; cheers sound along the shore. As the representative for Calais steps on French soil soldiers make his avenue, the officers embrace him, the national cockade is presented. A beautiful lady advances, requesting the honor of setting the cockade in his hat, and makes him a pretty speech, ending with Liberty, Equality, and France. As they move along the Rue de l'Égalité (late Rue du Roi) the air rings with "*Vive Thomas Paine!*" At the town hall he is presented to the Municipality, by each member embraced, by the Mayor also addressed. At the meeting of the Constitutional Society of Calais, in the *Minimes*, he sits beside the president, beneath the bust of Mirabeau and the united colors of France, England, and America. There is an official ceremony announcing his election, and plaudits of the crowd, "*Vive la Nation!*" "*Vive Thomas Paine!*" The *Minimes* proving too small, the meeting next day is held in the church, where martyred saints and miraculous Madonnas look down on this miraculous Quaker, turned savior of society. In the evening, at the theatre, a box is decorated "For the Author of 'The Rights of Man.'"

Thus for once our wayfarer, so marked by time and fate, received such welcome as hitherto had been accorded only to princes. Alas, that the aged eyes which watched over his humble cradle could not linger long enough to see a vision of this greatness, or that she who bore the name of Elizabeth Paine was too far out of his world as not even to know that her husband was in Europe. A theatrical La France must be his only bride, and in the end play the rôle of a cruel stepmother. When Washington was on his way to his inauguration in New York, passing beneath triumphal arches, amid applauding crowds, a sadness came over him as he reflected, so he wrote a friend, how easily all this enthusiasm might be reversed by a failure in the office for which he felt himself so little competent. But for Paine on his way to sit in the Convention of a People's representatives—one summoned by his own pen for objects to which his life was devoted, for which he had the training of events as well as studies,—for him there could be no black star hovering over his welcome and his triumphal pathway to Paris. For, besides his fame, there had preceded him to every town rumors of how this representative of man—of man in America, England, France—had been hunted by British oppressors down to the very edge of their coast. Those outwitted pursuers had made Paine a greater power in France than he might otherwise have been. The *Moniteur* (September 23d) told the story, and adds: "Probably M. Payne will have been indemnified for such injustices by the brilliant reception accorded him on his arrival on French soil."

Other representatives of Calais were Personne, Carnat, Bollet, Magniez, Varlet, Guffroy, Eulard, Duquesnoy, Lebas, Daunon. It could hardly be expected that there should be no jealousy of the concentration of enthusiasm on the brilliant Anglo-American. However, none of this yet appeared, and Paine glided flower-crowned in his beautiful barge, smoothly toward his Niagara rapids. He had, indeed, heard the distant roar, in such confused, hardly credited, rumors of September massacres as had reached London, but his faith in the National Convention was devout. All the riots were easily explained by the absence of that charm. He had his flask of constitutional oil, other representatives no doubt had theirs, and when they gathered on September 21st, amid equinoctial gales, the troubled waters would be still.

Paine reached White's Hotel, Paris, September 19th; on the 20th attends a gathering of the "Conventionnels"; on the 21st moves in their procession to the Tuileries, for verification of credentials by the expiring Assembly, repairing with them for work in the Salle du Manége. He was introduced by the Abbé Grégoire, and received with acclamations.

On September 21st, then, the Year One opens. It greets mankind with the decree: "Royalty is from this day abolished in France."

September 22d, on a petition from Orleans, Danton proposes removal of the entire administrative corps, municipal and judicial, to prevent their removal by popular violence. Paine (through Goupilleau) suggests postponement for more thorough discussion. Having got rid of kings they must be rid of royal hirelings; but if partial reforms are made in the judiciary system those institutions cannot possess coherence; for the present persons might be changed without altering laws; finally, justice cannot be administered by men ignorant of the laws. Danton welcomes Paine's views, and it is decreed that the administrative bodies be renewed by popular election; but the limitations on eligibility, fixed by the Constitution of

1791, are abolished—the judge need not be a lawyer, nor the municipal officer a proprietor.

On September 25th appears Paine's letter to his "Fellow Citizens," expressing his "affectionate gratitude" for his adoption and his election. "My felicity is increased by seeing the barrier broken down that divided patriotism by spots of earth, and limited citizenship to the soil, like vegetation." The letter is fairly "floreal" with optimistic felicities. "An over-ruling Providence is regenerating the old world by the principles of the new." "It is impossible to conquer a nation determined to be free." "It is now the cause of all nations against the cause of all courts." "In entering on this great scene, greater than any nation has been called to act in, let us say to the agitated mind, be calm! Let us punish by instruction, rather than by revenge. Let us begin the new era by a greatness of friendship, and hail the approach of union and success."

October 11th, a committee to frame a constitution is appointed, consisting of Sieyès, Paine, Brissot, Pétion, Vergniaud, Gensonne, Barrère, Danton, Condorcet. Supplementary — Barbaroux, Hérault Séchelles, Lanthenas, Débry, the Abbé Fauchet, Lavicourterie. Paine was placed second to his old adversary, Sieyès, only because of his unfamiliarity with French. At least four of the Committee understood English—Condorcet, Danton, Barrère, and Brissot. Paine had known Brissot in America, their friendship being caused by literary tastes in common, and the zeal of both for negro emancipation.

On October 25th was written for *Le Patriote Français* (edited by Brissot) an address by Paine arguing carefully the fallacies of royalism. He tersely expresses the view now hardly paradoxical, that "a talented king is worse than a fool."

"We are astonished at reading that the Egyptians set upon the throne a stone, which they called king. Well! such a monarch was less absurd and less mischievous than those before whom nations prostrate themselves. At least he deceived no one. None supposed that he possessed qualities or a character. They did not call him Father of his People; and yet it would have been scarcely more ridiculous than to give such a title to a blockhead (*un étourdi*) whom the right of succession crowns at eighteen. A dumb idol is better than one animated."[1]

In this letter Paine adroitly prepares the way for his purpose of saving the life of Louis XVI., for whose blood the thirst is growing. "It is little," he says, "to overthrow the idol; it is the pedestal which must especially be beaten down. It is the kingly *office*, rather than the officer, that is destructive (*meurtrière*). This is not seen by every one."

In those who sympathized with the human spirit of his views Paine inspired deep affection. A volume might be filled with the personal tributes to him. In Paris he was the centre of a loving circle, from the first. "I lodge," writes Lord Edward Fitzgerald to his mother (October 30th), "with my friend Paine— we breakfast, dine, and sup together. The more I see of his interior, the more I like and respect him. I cannot express how kind he is to me; there is a simplicity of manner, a goodness of heart, and a strength of mind in him, that I never knew a man before possess."[2]

Paine was chosen by his fellow-deputies of Calais to offer the Convention the congratulations of their department on the abolition of monarchy. This letter, written October 27th, was on that day read in Convention, in French.

[1] "Father of his People" was a title of Geo. III. "Father of his Country" was applied to Peyton Randolph, first president of Congress. Paine's essay, quoted above, which is not included in the editions of Paine's works, was printed by James Watson in London, 1843, the translation being by W. J. Linton, who, while editing the *National*, also wrote the same year, and for the same publisher, a small but useful "Life of Paine." [In the translation made direct from *Le Patriote Français* for Dr. Conway's edition of Paine's writings this passage reads somewhat differently. See vol. iii., p. 106.—H.B.B.]

[2] Moore's "Life and Death of Lord Edward Fitzgerald."

"CITIZEN PRESIDENT: In the name of the deputies of the department of Pas de Calais, I have the honor of presenting to the Convention the felicitations of the General Council of the Commune of Calais on the abolition of royalty.

"Amid the joy inspired by this event, one can not forbear some pain at the folly of our ancestors, who have placed us under the necessity of treating seriously (*solennellement*) the abolition of a phantom.

"THOMAS PAINE, Deputy, etc."[1]

The *Moniteur*, without printing the letter, says that applause followed the word "*fantôme.*" The use of this word was a resumption of Paine's effort to save the life of the king, then a prisoner of state, by a suggestion of his insignificance.[2] But he very soon realizes the power of the phantom, which lies not only in the monarchical Trade Union of Europe but in the superstition of monarchy in those who presently beheaded poor Louis. Paine was always careful to call him Louis Capet, but the French deputies took the king seriously to the last. The king's divine foot was on their necks in the moment when their axe was on his. But Paine feared a more terrible form which had arisen in place of the royal prisoner of the Temple. On the fourth day of the Convention Marat arose with the words, "It seems a great many here are my enemies," and received the shouted answer, "All! all!" Paine had seen Marat hypnotize the Convention, and hold it subdued in the hollow of his hand. Here was King Stork ready to succeed King Log.

But what has the Convention to do with deciding about Louis XVI., or about affairs, foreign or domestic? It is there like the Philadelphia Convention of 1787; its business is to frame a Constitution, then dissolve, and let the organs it created determine special affairs. So the committee work hard on

the Constitution; "Deputy Paine and France generally expect," finds Carlyle, "all finished in a few months." But, alas, the phantom is too strong for the political philosophers. The crowned heads of Europe are sinking their differences for a time and consulting about this imprisoned brother. And at the same time the subjects of those heads are looking eagerly towards the Convention.[3]

The foreign menaces had thus far caused the ferocities of the revolution, for France knew it was worm-eaten with enemies of republicanism. But now the Duke of Brunswick had retreated, the French arms were victorious everywhere; and it is just possible that the suicide of the Republic—the Reign of Terror—might never have been completed but for that discovery (November 20th) of secret papers walled up in the Tuileries. These papers compromised many, revealed foreign schemes, and made all Paris shriek "Treason!" The smith (Gamain) who revealed the locality of that invisible iron press which he had set under the wainscot, made a good deal of history that day. A cry for the king's life was raised, for to France he was the head and front of all conspiracy.

How everybody bent under the breath of those days may be seen in the fact that even Gouverneur Morris is found writing to Lord Wycombe (November 22d): "All who wish to partake thereof [freedom] will find in us (ye French) a sure and certain ally. We will chase tyranny, and, above all, *aristocracy*, off the theatre of the Universe."[4]

Paine was living in the "Passage des Pétites Pères, No. 7." There are now

---

[1] This letter I copied and translated in the Historical Exhibition of the Revolution, in Paris, 1889. This letter of the "*philosophe anglais,*" as he is described in the catalogue, is in the collection of M. Charavay, and was framed with the Bonneville portrait of Paine.

[2] In his republican manifesto at the time of the king's flight he had deprecated revenge towards the captured monarch.

[3] "That which will astonish posterity is that at Stockholm, five months after the death of Gustavus, and while the northern Powers are leaguing themselves against the liberty of France, there has been published a translation of Thomas Paine's 'Rights of Man,' the translator being one of the King's secretaries!"—*Moniteur*, Nov. 8, 1792.

[4] "Diary and Letters." The letter was probably written with knowledge of its liability to fall into the hands of the French Committee. It could not deceive Wycombe.

two narrow passages of that name, uniting near the church "Notre Dame des Victoires," which still bears the words, "Liberté, Égalité, Fraternité." No. 7 has disappeared as a number, but it may have described a part of either No. 8 or No. 9,—both ancient. Here he was close to a chapel of the Capucines, unless, indeed, it had already been replaced by this church, whose interior walls are covered with tablets set up by individuals in acknowledgment of the Virgin's miraculous benefits to them. Here he might study superstition, and no doubt did ; but on November 20th he has to deal with the madness of a populace which has broken the outer chains of superstition with a superstition of their own, one without restraints to replace the chains. Beneath his window the Place des Victoires will be crowded with revolutionists, frantic under rumors of the discovered iron press and its treasonable papers. He could hardly look out without seeing some poor human scape-goat seeking the altar's safety. Our Lady will look on him from her church the sad-eyed inquiry : "Is this, then, the new religion of Liberty, with which you supplant the Mother and Babe?"

Paine has carried to success his anti-monarchical faith. He was the first to assail monarchy in America and in France. A little more than a year before, he had founded the first Republican Society in Europe, and written its Declaration on the door of the National Assembly. Sieyès had denounced him then as a "polyarchist." Now he sat with Sieyès daily, framing a republican Constitution, having just felicitated the Convention on the abolition of the phantom—Royalty. And now, on this terrible night of November 20th, this unmaker of kings finds himself the solitary deputy ready to risk his life to save the man whose crown he had destroyed. It is not simply because the old Quaker heart in him recoils from bloodshed, but that he would save the Republic from the peril of foreign in-

vasion, which would surely follow the execution of Louis, and from disgrace in America, whose independence owed much to the fallen monarch.

In his little room, the lonely author, unable to write French, animated by sentiments which the best of the French revolutionists could not understand— Danton reminding him that " revolutions are not made of rose-water "—must have before the morrow's Convention some word that shall control the fury of the moment. Rose-water will not answer now. Louis must pass his ordeal ; his secret schemes have been revealed ; the treachery of his submissions to the people exposed. He is guilty, and the alternatives are a calm trial, or death by the hands of the mob. What is now most needed is delay, and, that secured, diversion of national rage from the individual Louis to the universal anti-republican Satan inspiring the crowned heads of Europe. Before the morning dawns, Paine has written his letter to the president. It is translated before the Convention meets, November 21st, and is read to that body the same day.[1] Louis XVI., he says, should be tried. The advice is not suggested by vengeance, but by justice and policy. If innocent, he may be allowed to prove it ; if guilty, he must be punished or pardoned by the nation. He would, however, consider Louis, individually, beneath the notice of the republic. The importance of his trial is that there is a conspiracy of "crowned brigands" against the liberties not only of France, but of all nations, and there is ground for suspecting that Louis XVI. was a partner in it. He should be utilized to ferret out the whole gang, and reveal to the various peoples what their monarchs, some of whom work in secret for fear of their subjects, are doing. Louis XVI. should not be dealt with except in the interest of all Europe.

"If seeing in Louis XVI. only a weak and narrow-minded man, badly reared, as all like

---

[1] " L'Histoire Parlémentaire," xx., p. 367.

him, subject, it is said, to intemperance, imprudently re-established by the Constituent Assembly on a throne for which he was unfit,— if we hereafter show him some compassion, this compassion should be the effect of national magnanimity, and not a result of the burlesque notion of pretended inviolability." [1]

Lamartine, in his history of the Girondists, reproaches Paine for these words concerning a king who had shown him friendship during the American war. But the facts were not well explored in Lamartine's time. Louis Blanc recognizes Paine's intent.[2] " He had learned in England that killing a monarch does

not kill monarchs." This grand revolutionary proposal to raise the inevitable trial from the low plane of popular wrath against a prisoner to the dignity of a process against European monarchy, would have secured delay and calmer counsels. If the reader, considering the newly discovered papers, and the whole situation, will examine critically Paine's words just quoted, he will find them meriting a judgment the reverse of Lamartine's. With consummate art, the hourly imperilled king is shielded from vindictive wrath by the considerations that he is *non compos*, not responsible for his bringing up, was put back on the throne by the Assembly, after he had left it, acknowledging his unfitness, and that compassion for him would be becoming to the magnanimity of France. A plea for the King's immunity from trial, for his innocence or his virtues, would at that juncture have been fatal. As it was, this ingenious document made an impression on the Convention, which ordered it to be printed.[3]

The delay which Paine's proposal would involve was, as Louis Blanc remarks, fatal to it. It remains now only to work among the members of the Convention, and secure if possible a majority that will be content, having killed the king, to save the man ; and, in saving him, to preserve him as an imprisoned hostage for the good behavior of Europe. This is now Paine's idea, and never did man toil more faithfully for another than he did for that discrowned Louis Capet.

[1] This essay has suffered in the translation found in English and American editions of Paine. The words "national magnanimity" are omitted. The phrase "brigands couronnés" becomes " crowned robbers " in England, and " crowned ruffians" in America. Both versions are commonplace, and convey an impression of haste and mere abuse. But Paine was a slow writer, and weighed his words even when " quarrelling in print." When this letter was written to the Convention its members were reading his Essay on Royalty, which filled seven columns of Brissot's *Patriote Français* three weeks before. In that he had traced royalty to the bandit-chief. " Several troops of banditti assemble for the purpose of upsetting some country, of laying contributions over it, of seizing the landed property, of reducing the people to thraldom. The expedition being accomplished, the chief of the gang assumes the title of king or monarch. Such has been the origin of royalty among all nations who live by the chase, agriculture, or the tending of flocks. A second chieftain arriving obtains by force what has been acquired by violence. He despoils his predecessor, loads him with fetters, puts him to death, and assumes his title. In the course of ages the memory of the outrage is lost ; his successors establish new forms of government ; through policy, they become the instruments of a little good ; they invent, or cause to be invented, false genealogical tables ; they employ every means to render their race sacred ; the knavery of priests steps in to their assistance ; for their body-guard they take religion itself ; then it is that Royalty, or rather Tyranny, becomes immortal. A power unjustly usurped is transformed into a hereditary right." [Both the passage in the text quoted from Paine's address to the Convention and the passage in the note taken from his essay on Royalty differ very considerably from the versions given in Dr. Conway's edition of Paine's writings. See Vol. iii., p. 118, and pp. 102-3.—H. B. B.]

[2] " Hist. de la Révolution," etc., vol. vii., p. 396.

[3] " Convention Nationale. Opinion de Thomas Payne, Deputé du Département de la Somme, concernant le jugement de Louis XVI. Précédé de sa lettre d'envoi au Président de la Convention. Imprimé par ordre de la Convention Nationale. A Paris. De l'imprimerie Nationale." It is very remarkable that, in a State paper, Paine should be described as deputy for the Somme. His votes in the Convention are all entered under Calais. Dr. John Moore, who saw much of Paine at this time, says, in his work on the French Revolution, that his (Paine's) writings for the Convention were usually translated into French by the Marchioness of Condorcet.

CHAPTER XXIV

OUTLAWED IN ENGLAND

WHILE Paine was thus, towards the close of 1792, doing the work of a humane Englishman in France, his works were causing a revolution in England—a revolution the more effectual because bloodless.

In Paine's letter to Secretary Dundas (Calais, September 15th), describing the examination of his papers at Dover, a "postscript" states that among the papers handled was "a printed proof copy of my Letter to the Addressers, which will soon be published." This must have been a thumbscrew for the Secretary when he presently read the pamphlet that escaped his officers. In humor, freedom, and force, this production may be compared with Carlyle's "Latter Day Pamphlets." Lord Stormont and Lord Grenville having made speeches about him, their services are returned by a speech which the author has prepared for them to deliver in Parliament. This satirical eulogy on the British constitution set the fashion for other radical encomiums of the wisdom of the king and of the peers, the incorruptibility of the commons, beauty of rotten boroughs, and freedom of the people from taxes, with which prosecuting attorneys were unable to deal. Having felicitated himself on the circulation of his opinions by the indictment, and the advertisements of his books by loyal " Addresses," Paine taunts the government for its method of answering argument. It had been challenging the world for a hundred years to admire the perfection of its institutions. At length the challenge is taken up, and, lo, its acceptance is turned into a crime, and the only defence of its perfection is a prosecution ! Paine points out that there was no sign of prosecution until his book was placed within reach of the poor. When cheap editions were clamored for by Sheffield, Leicester, Chester, Warwickshire, and Scotland,

he had announced that any one might freely publish it. About the middle of April he had himself put a cheap edition in the press. He knew he would be prosecuted for that, and so wrote to Thomas Walker.[1] It was the common people the government feared. He remarks that on the same day (May 21st), the prosecution was instituted and the royal proclamation issued—the latter being indictable as an effort to influence the verdict in a pending case. He calls attention to the "special jury," before which he was summoned. It is virtually selected by the Master of the Crown Office, a dependant on the Civil List assailed in his book. The special jury is treated to a dinner, and given two guineas for a conviction, and but one guinea and no dinner for acquittal. Even a fairly selected local jury could not justly determine a constitutional issue affecting every part of the empire. So Paine brings under scrutiny every part of the legal machinery sprung on him, adding new illustrations of his charges against the whole system. He begins the siege, which Bradlaugh was to carry forward in a later time, against the corrupt Pension List, introducing it with his promised exposure of Edmund Burke. Near the end of Lord North's administration Burke brought in a bill by which it was provided that a pension or annuity might be given without name, if under oath that it was not for the benefit of a member of the House of Commons. Burke's pension had been taken out under the name of another man ; but being under the necessity of

[1] At the trial the Attorney-General admitted that he had not prosecuted Part I. because it was likely to be confined to judicious readers ; but this still more reprehensible Part II. was, he said, with an industry incredible, ushered into the world in all shapes and sizes, thrust into the hands of subjects of every description, even children's sweetmeats being wrapped in it.

mortgaging it, the real pensioner had to be disclosed to the mortgagee.[1] For the rest, this "Address to the Addressers," as it was popularly called,—or "Part Third of the Rights of Man," as one publisher entitled it,—sowed broadcast through England passages that were recited in assemblies, and sentences that became proverbs.

"It is a dangerous attempt in any government to say to a Nation, *Thou shalt not read.*"

"Thought, by some means or other, is got abroad in the world, and cannot be restrained, though reading may."

"Whatever the rights of the people are, they have a right to them, and none have a right either to withhold or to grant them."

"The project of hereditary Governors and Legislatures was a treasonable usurpation over the rights of posterity."

"Put a country right, and it will soon put government right."

"When the rich plunder the poor of his rights, it becomes an example to the poor to plunder the rich of his property."

"Who are those that are frightened at reform? Are the public afraid their taxes should be lessened too much? Are they afraid that sinecure places and pensions should be abolished too fast? Are the poor afraid that their condition should be rendered too comfortable?"

"A thing moderately good is not so good as it ought to be."

"If to expose the fraud and imposition of monarchy, and every species of hereditary government—to lessen the oppression of taxes—to propose plans for the education of helpless infancy, and the comfortable support of the aged and distressed—to endeavour to conciliate

nations with each other—to extirpate the horrid practice of war—to promote universal peace, civilization, and commerce—and to break the chains of political superstition, and raise degraded man to his proper rank—if these things be libellous, let me live the life of a Libeller, and let the name of Libeller be engraven on my tomb."

Two eminent personages were burnt in effigy in Europe about this time, one in France, the other in England: Paine and the Pope.

Under date of December 19th, the American Minister (Morris) enters in his diary: "Several Americans dine with me. Paine looks a little down at the news from England; he has been burned in effigy."

This was the reply of the Addressers, the noblemen and gentry, to Paine's "Letter." It is said that on the Fifth of November it was hinted to the boys that their Guy Fawkes would extort more pennies if labelled "Tom Paine," and that henceforth the new Guy paraded with a pair of stays under his arm. The holocaust of Paines went on through December, being timed for the author's trial, set for the eighteenth. One gets glimpses in various local records and memoirs of the agitation in England. Thus in Mrs. Henry Sandford's account of Thomas Poole,[2] we read in Charlotte Poole's journal:

"December 18, 1792.—John dined with Tom Poole, and from him heard that there was a great bustle at Bridgwater yesterday—that Tom Paine was burnt in Effigy, and that he saw Richard Symes sitting on the Cornhill with a table before him, receiving the oaths of loyalty to the king, and affection to the present constitution, from the populace. I fancy this could not have been a very pleasant sight to Tom Poole, for he has imbibed some of the wild notions of liberty and equality that at present prevail so much; and it is but within these two or three days that a report has been circulated that he has distributed seditious pamphlets to the common people of Stowey. But this report is entirely without foundation. Everybody at this time talks politicks, and is looking with anxiety for fresh intelligence from France, which is a scene of guilt and confusion."

---

[1] This disclosure, though not disproved, is passed over silently by most historians. Nevertheless it was probably that which ended Burke's parliamentary career. Two years later, at the age of sixty-two, he retired with an accumulation of pensions given at the king's request, amounting to £3,700 per annum. His reputation had been built up on his supposed energy in favor of economy. The secret and illegal pension (£1,500) cast light on his sudden coalition with Lord North, whom he once proposed to impeach as a traitor. The title of "masked pensioner" given by Paine branded Burke. Writing in 1819, Cobbett says: "As my Lord Grenville introduced the name of Burke, suffer me, my Lord, to introduce that of the man [Paine] who put this Burke to shame, who drove him off the public stage to seek shelter in the pension list, and who is now named fifty million times where the name of the pensioned Burke is mentioned once."

[2] "Thomas Poole and his Friends." By Mrs. Henry Sandford. New York: Macmillan, 1888.

In Richardson's "Borderer's Table Book" is recorded : " 1792 (Dec.)— This month, Thomas Paine, author of the ' Rights of Man,' &c., &c., was burnt at most of the towns and considerable villages in Northumberland and Durham." No doubt, among the Durham towns, Wearmouth saw at the stake an effigy of the man whose iron bridge, taken down at Paddington, and sold for other benefit than Paine's, was used in spanning the Wear with the arch of his invention ; all amid shouts of " God save the King," and plaudits for the various public-spirited gentlemen and architects, who patriotically appropriated the merits and patent of the inventor. The *Bury Post* (published near Paine's birthplace) says, December 12th :

" The populace in different places have been lately amusing themselves by burning effigies. As the culprit on whom they meant to execute this punishment was Thomas Paine, they were not interrupted by any power civil or military. The ceremony has been at Croydon in Surrey, at Warrington, at Lymington, and at Plymouth."

January 9, 1793 :

" On Saturday last the effigy of Thomas Paine was carried round the town of Swaffham, and afterwards hung on a gibbet, erected on the market-hill for that purpose. In the evening his remains were committed to the flames amidst acclamations of God save the King, etc."

The trial of Paine for high treason[1] was by a Special Jury in the Court of King's Bench, Guildhall, on Tuesday, December 18, 1792, before Lord Kenyon.[2] The " Painites " had probably little hope of acquittal. In Rickman's journal (manuscript) he says : " C. Lofft

[1] Seditious libel.—H. B. B.
[2] *Special Jury :* John Campbell, John Lightfoot, Christopher Taddy, Robert Oliphant, Cornelius Donovan, Robert Rolleston, John Lubbock, Richard Tuckwell, William Porter, Thomas Bruce, Isaac Railton, Henry Evans. *Counsel for the Crown :* Sir Archibald Macdonald (Attorney-General), Solicitor-General, Mr. Bearcroft, Mr. Baldwin, Mr. Wood, Mr. Percival. *Counsel for the Defendant :* The Hon. Thomas Erskine, Mr. Piggot, Mr. Shepherd, Mr. Fitzgerald, Mr. F. Vaughan. *Solicitors :* For the Crown, Messrs. Chamberlayne and White ; for Defendant, Mr. Bonney.

told me he knew a gentleman who tried for five or six years to be on the special juries, but could not, being known to be a liberty man. He says special juries are packed to all intents and purposes." The reason for gathering such powerful counsel for defence must have been to obtain from the trial some definitive adjudication on the legal liabilities of writers and printers, and at the same time to secure, through the authority of Erskine, an affirmation of their constitutional rights. Lord Loughborough and others vainly tried to dissuade Erskine from defending Paine. For himself, Paine had given up the case some time before, and had written from Paris, November 11th, to the Attorney-General, stating that, having been called to the Convention in France, he could not stay to contest the prosecution, as he wished.

" My necessary absence from your country affords the opportunity of knowing whether the prosecution was intended against Thomas Paine, or against the Rights of the People of England to investigate systems and principles of government ; for as I cannot now be the object of the prosecution, the going on with the prosecution will show that something else was the object, and that something else can be no other than the People of England. . . . But I have other reasons than those I have mentioned for writing you this letter ; and however you chuse to interpret them they proceed from a good heart. The time, Sir, is becoming too serious to play with Court prosecutions, and sport with national rights. The terrible examples that have taken place here upon men who, less than a year ago, thought themselves as secure as any prosecuting Judge, Jury, or Attorney-General can do now in England, ought to have some weight with men in your situation. That the Government of England is as great, if not the greatest perfection of fraud and corruption that ever took place since governments began, is what you cannot be a stranger to ; unless the constant habit of seeing it has blinded your sense. But though you may not chuse to see it, the people are seeing it very fast, and the progress is beyond what you may chuse to believe. Is it possible that you or I can believe, or that reason can make any other man believe, that the capacity of such a man as Mr. Guelph, or any of his profligate sons, is necessary to the government of a nation? I speak to you as one man ought to speak to another ; and I know also that I speak what other people are beginning to think. That you cannot obtain a verdict (and if you do it will signify nothing) without *packing a Jury*, and we *both* know that such tricks are practised, is what I have very good reason to believe. . . . Do not then, Sir, be the instrument of drawing away twelve men into a situation that may be injurious to them afterwards. I do not speak this from policy, but from benevolence ; but if you chuse to go on with the process, I make it my request that you would read this letter in Court, after which the Judge and the Jury may do what they please. As I do not consider myself the object of the prosecution, neither can I be affected by the issue one way or the other, I shall, though a foreigner in your country, subscribe as much money as any other man towards supporting the right of the nation against the prosecution ; and it is for this purpose only that I shall do it. As I have not time to copy letters, you will excuse the corrections."

A month after this awful letter was written, Paine no doubt knew its imprudence. It was sprung on the Court by the Attorney-General, and must alone have settled the verdict, had it not been foregone. Erskine, Paine's leading counsel, was Attorney-General for the Prince of Wales—foremost of " Mr. Guelph's profligate sons,"—and he was compelled to treat as a forgery the letter all felt to be genuine. He endeavored to prevent the reading of it, but Lord Kenyon decided that " in prosecutions for high treason, where overt acts are laid, you may prove overt acts not laid to prove those that are laid. If it [the letter] goes to prove him the author of the book, I am bound to admit it." Authorship of the book being admitted, this was only a pretext. The Attorney-General winced a good deal at the allusion to the profligate sons, and asked :

" Is he [Paine] to teach human creatures, whose moments of existence depend upon the permission of a Being, merciful, long-suffering, and of great goodness, that those whose youthful errors, from which even royalty is not exempted, are to be treasured up in a vindictive memory, and are to receive sentence of irremissible sin at His hands ? "

It may be incidentally remarked here that the Attorney-General could hardly have failed to retort with charges against the author, had not Paine's reputation

remained proof against the libellous "biography" by the government clerk, Chalmers.

The main part of the prosecution was thus uttered by Paine himself. While reading the letter the prosecutor paused to say : " If I succeed in this prosecution he shall never return to this country otherwise than *in vinculis*, for I will outlaw him." [1]

Erskine's powerful defence of the constitutional rights of thought and speech in England is historical. He built around Paine an enduring constitutional fortress, compelling Burke and Fox to lend aid from their earlier speeches. The fable with which he closed was long remembered.

" Constraint is the natural parent of resistance, and a pregnant proof that reason is not on the side of those who use it. You must all remember, gentlemen, Lucian's pleasant story : Jupiter and a countryman were walking together, conversing with great freedom and familiarity upon the subject of heaven and earth. The countryman listened with attention and acquiescence, while Jupiter strove only to convince him ; but happening to hint a doubt, Jupiter turned hastily around and threatened him with his thunder. 'Ah, ha !' says the countryman, ' now, Jupiter, I know that you are wrong ; you are always wrong when you appeal to your thunder.' " This is the case with me. I can reason with the people of England, but I cannot fight against the thunder of authority."

Mr. Attorney-General arose immediately to reply to Mr. Erskine, when Mr. Campbell (the foreman of the jury) said : " My Lord, I am authorized by the jury here to inform the Attorney-General that

[1] 22 Howell's State Trials 357. Other reports are by Joseph Gurney and " by an eminent advocate." The brief evidence consisted mainly of the notes and statements of Paine's publishers already mentioned in connection with the publication of the indicted work. The Attorney-General cited effectively the reply to Paine which he attributed to Vice-President Adams. Publicola's pamphlet gave great comfort to Paine's prosecutors. Mr. Long writes to Mr. Miles, agent in Paris (December 1st), about this " book by the American Adams, which is admirable, proving that the American government is not founded upon the absurd doctrine of the pretended rights of man, and that if it had been it could not have stood for a week."

a reply is not necessary for them, unless the Attorney-General wishes to make it, or your Lordship." Mr. Attorney-General sat down, and the jury gave in their verdict—Guilty.

Paine was outlawed.

The eye of England followed its outlaw before and after his trial. In the English state archives is a note of G. Munro to Lord Grenville, September 8th, announcing " Mr. Payne's " election for the Département de l'Oise. Earl Gower announces, on information of Mr. Mason, that "Tom Payne is on his road to take his seat." On September 22d, a despatch mentions Paine's speech on the judiciary question. " December 17, 1792. Tom Payne is in the country unwell, or pretending to be so." The most remarkable of the secret despatches, however, are two sent from Paris on the last day of the year 1792. One of these alludes to the effect of Paine's trial and outlawry on the English radicals in Paris :

"'Tom Payne's fate and the unanimity of the English has staggered the boldest of them, and they are now dwindling into nothing. Another address was, however, proposed for the National Convention ; this motion, I understand, was made by Tom Payne and seconded by Mr. Mery ; it was opposed by Mr. Frost, seconded by Mr. McDonald."

The second allusion to Paine on December 31st deserves to be pondered by historians :

"'Tom Payne has proposed banishing the royal family of France, and I have heard is writing his opinion on the subject ; his consequence seems daily lessening in this country, and I should never be surprised if he some day receives the fate he merits."

It thus seems that whatever good deed Paine was about, he deserves death. Earl Gower, and the agents he left on his departure (September) in Paris, must have known that Paine's proposal was the only alternative of the king's execution, and that if his consequence was lessening it was solely because of labors to save the lives of the royal family. This humane man has the death-sentence

of Robespierre on him anticipated by the ambassador of a country which, while affecting grief for Louis XVI., was helping on his fate.[1]

Danton said to Count Theodore de Lameth :

" I am willing to try and save the King, but I must have a million of money to buy up the necessary votes, and the money must be on hand in eight days. I warn you that although I may save his life I shall vote for his death ; I am quite willing to save his head, but not to lose mine."

The Count and the Spanish Ambassador broached the matter to Pitt, who refused the money.[2] He was not willing to spend a few thousands to save the life of America's friend, though he made his death a pretext for exhausting his treasury to deluge Europe with blood.

Gouverneur Morris, whose dislike of Paine's republicanism was equally cynical,[3] was intimate with Earl Gower, and no doubt gave him his information. Morris was clear-headed enough to perceive that the massacres in France were mainly due to the menaces of foreign

[1] After September it was, as Talleyrand says, "no longer a question that the king should reign, but that he himself, the queen, their children, his sister, should be saved. It might have been done. It was at least a duty to attempt it. At that time France was only at war with the Emperor [Austria], the Empire [the German states], and Sardinia. Had all the other states concerted themselves to offer their mediation by proposing to recognise whatever form of government France might be pleased to adopt, with the sole condition that the prisoners in the Temple should be allowed to leave the country and retire wherever they liked, though such a proposal, as may be supposed, would not have filled the demagogues with delight, they would have been powerless to resist it."— Memoirs of the Prince de Talleyrand. New York, 1891, i., p. 168.

[2] Taine's " French Revolution " (American ed.), iii., p. 135. See also the "Correspondence of W. A. Miles on the French Revolution," London, 1890, i., p. 398. The Abbé Noel, a month before the king's death, pointed out to this British agent how he might be saved.

[3] In relating to John Randolph of Roanoke Paine's exposure of Silas Deane, Morris regards it as the prevention of a fraud, but nevertheless thinks Paine deserved punishment for his "impudence" !

monarchs, and was in hearty sympathy with Paine's plan for saving the life of Louis XVI. On December 28th he writes to Washington that a majority of the Convention

"have it in contemplation not only to refer the judgment to the electors of France, that is, to her people, but also to send him and his family to America, which Paine is to move for. He mentioned this to me in confidence, but I have since heard it from another quarter."

On January 6, 1793, Morris writes to Washington concerning Genêt, the new Minister to the United States, who had been introduced to him by Paine, and dined with him. At the close he says:

"The King's fate is to be decided next Monday the 14th. That unhappy man, conversing with one of his council on his own fate, calmly summed up the motives of every kind, and concluded that a majority of the Council [Convention] would vote for referring his case to the people, and that in consequence he should be massacred. I think he must die or reign."

Paine also feared that a reference to the populace meant death. He had counted a majority in the Convention who were opposed to the execution. Submission of the question to the masses would thus, if his majority stood firm, be risking the life of Louis again. Unfortunately this question had to be determined before the vote on life or death. At the opening of the year 1793 he felt cheerful about the situation. On January 3d he wrote to John King, a retreating comrade in England, as follows:

"Dear King,—I don't know anything, these many years, that surprised and hurt me more than the sentiments you published in the Courtly HERALD, the 12th December, signed John King, Egham Lodge. You have gone back from all you ever said. When I first knew you in Ailiffe-street, an obscure part of the city, a child, without fortune or friends, I noticed you; because I thought I saw in you, young as you was, a bluntness of temper, a boldness of

opinion, and an originality of thought, that portended some future good. I was pleased to discuss with you, under our friend Oliver's lime-tree, those political notions which I have since given the world in my 'Rights of Man.'

"You used to complain of abuses as well as me. What, then, means this sudden attachment to *Kings?* this fondness of the English Government, and hatred of the French? If you mean to curry favour, by aiding your Government, you are mistaken; they never recompence those who serve it; they buy off those who can annoy it, and let the good that is rendered it be its own reward. Believe me, KING, more is to be obtained by cherishing the rising spirit of the People, than by subduing it. Follow my fortunes, and I will be answerable that you shall make your own.—THOMAS PAINE."[1]

This last sentence may even now raise a smile. King must subsequently have reflected with satisfaction that he did not "follow the fortunes" of Paine, which led him into prison at the end of the year. A third letter from him to Paine appeared in the *Morning Herald*, April 17, 1793, in which he says:

"'If the French kill their king, it will be a signal for my departure, for I will not abide among such sanguinary men.' These, Mr. Paine, were your words at our last meeting; yet after this you are not only with them, but the chief modeller of their new Constitution."

Mr. King might have reflected that the author of the "Rights of Man," which he had admired, was personally safer in regicide France than in liberticide England, which had outlawed him.

[1] "Mr. King's Speech, at Egham, with Thomas Paine's Letter," etc. Egham, 1793. In his reply, January 11th, King says: "Such men as Frost, Barlow, and others, your associates, show the forlornness of your cause. Our respectable citizens do not go to you," etc. Writing February 11th, King expresses satisfaction at Paine's vote on the King's fate: "the imputation of cruelty will not now be added to the other censures on your character; but the catastrophe of this unhappy Monarch has shewn you the danger of putting a nation in ferment."

CHAPTER XXV

'KILL THE KING, BUT NOT THE MAN'

DUMAS' hero, Dr. Gilbert (in "Ange Pitou"), an idealization of Paine, interprets his hopes and horrors on the opening of the fateful year 1793. Dr. Gilbert's pamphlets had helped to found liberty in the New World, but sees that it may prove the germ of total ruin to the Old World.

"A new world," repeated Gilbert; "that is to say, a vast open space, a clear table to work upon,—no laws, but no abuses; no ideas, but no prejudices. In France, thirty thousand square leagues of territory for thirty millions of people; that is to say, should the space be equally divided, scarcely room for a cradle or a grave for each. Out yonder, in America, two hundred thousand square leagues for three millions of people; frontiers which are ideal, for they border on the desert, which is to say, immensity. In these two hundred thousand leagues, navigable rivers, having a course of a thousand leagues; virgin forests, of which God alone knows the limits,—that is to say, all the elements of life, of civilization, and of a brilliant future. Oh, how easy it is, Billot, when a man is called Lafayette, and is accustomed to wield a sword; when a man is called Washington, and is accustomed to reflect deeply,—how easy is it to combat against walls of wood, of earth, of stone, of human flesh! But when, instead of founding, it is necessary to destroy; when we see in the old order things that we are obliged to attack,—walls of bygone, crumbling ideas; and that behind the ruins even of these walls crowds of people and of interests still take refuge; when, after having found the idea, we find that in order to make the people adopt it, it will be necessary perhaps to decimate that people, from the old who remember to the child who has still to learn; from the recollection which is the monument to the instinct that is its germ—then, oh then, Billot, it is a task that will make all shudder who can see beneath the horizon. . . . I shall, however, persevere, for although I see obstacles, I can perceive the end; and that end is splendid, Billot. It is not the liberty of France alone that I dream of; it is the liberty of the whole world. It is not the physical equality; it is equality before the law, —equality of rights. It is not only the fraternity of our own citizens, but of all nations. . . . Forward, then, and over the heaps of our dead bodies may one day march the generations of which this boy here is in the advanced guard!"

Though Dr. Gilbert has been in the Bastille, though he barely escapes the bullet of a revolutionist, he tries to unite the throne and the people. So, as we have seen, did Paine struggle until the King took flight, and, over his own signature, branded all his pledges as extorted lies. Henceforth for the King personally he has no respect; yet the whole purpose of his life is now to save that of the prisoner. Besides his humane horror of capital punishment, especially in a case which involves the heads of thousands, Paine foresees Nemesis fashioning her wheels in every part of Europe, and her rudder across the ocean, —where America beholds in Louis XVI. her deliverer.

Paine's outlawry, announced by Kersaint in Convention, January 1st, was more eloquent for wrath than he for clemency. Under such menaces the majority for sparing Louis shrank with the New Year; French pride arose, and with Danton was eager to defy despots by tossing to them the head of a king. Poor Paine found his comrades retreating. What would a knowledge of the French tongue have been worth to this leading republican of the world, just then the one man sleeplessly seeking to save a King's life! He could not plead with his enraged republicans, who at length overpowered even Brissot, so far as to draw him into the fatal plan of voting for the King's death, coupled with submission to the verdict of the people. Paine saw that there was at the moment no people, but only an infuriated clan. He was now defending a forlorn hope, but he struggled with a heroism that would have commanded the homage of Europe had not its courts been also clans. He hit on a scheme which he hoped might, in that last extremity, save the real revolution from a suicidal inhumanity. It was the one statesmanlike proposal of the time: that the King should be held as a hostage for the peaceful behavior of other kings, and, when their war on France had ceased, banished to the United States.

On January 15th, before the vote on the King's punishment was put, Paine gave his manuscript address to the president : debate closed before it could be read, and it was printed. He argued that the Assembly, in bringing back Louis when he had abdicated and fled, was the more guilty ; and against his transgressions it should be remembered that by his aid the shackles of America were broken.

"Let then those United States be the guard and the asylum of Louis Capet. There, in the future, remote from the miseries and crimes of royalty, he may learn, from the constant presence of public prosperity, that the true system of government consists not in monarchs, but in fair, equal, and honorable representation. In recalling this circumstance, and submitting this proposal, I consider myself a citizen of both countries. I submit it as an American who feels the debt of gratitude he owes to every Frenchman. I submit it as a man, who, albeit an adversary of kings, forgets not that they are subject to human frailties. I support my proposal as a citizen of the French Republic, because it appears to me the best and most politic measure that can be adopted. As far as my experience in public life extends, I have ever observed that the great mass of people are always just, both in their intentions and their object ; but the true method of attaining such purpose does not always appear at once. The English nation had groaned under the Stuart despotism. Hence Charles I. was executed ; but Charles II. was restored to all the powers his father had lost. Forty years later the same family tried to re-establish their oppression ; the nation banished the whole race from its territories. The remedy was effectual ; the Stuart family sank into obscurity, merged itself in the masses, and is now extinct."

He reminds the Convention that the king had two brothers out of the country who might naturally desire his death : the execution of the king might make them presently plausible pretenders to the throne, around whom their foreign enemies would rally : while the man recognized by foreign powers as the rightful monarch of France was living there could be no such pretender.

"It has already been proposed to abolish the penalty of death, and it is with infinite satisfaction that I recollect the humane and excellent oration pronounced by Robespierre on the subject, in the constituent Assembly. Monarchical governments have trained the human race to sanguinary punishments, but the people should not follow the examples of their oppressors in such vengeance. As France has been the first of European nations to abolish royalty, let her also be the first to abolish the punishment of death, and to find out a milder and more effectual substitute.' [1]

This was admirable art. Under shelter of Robespierre's appeal against the death penalty, the "Mountain" [2] could not at the moment break the force of Paine's plea by reminding the Convention of his Quaker sentiments. It will be borne in mind that up to this time Robespierre was not impressed, nor Marat possessed, by the homicidal demon. Marat had felt for Paine a sort of contemptuous kindness, and one day privately said to him : "It is you, then, who believe in a republic ; you have too much sense to believe in such a dream." Robespierre, according to Lamartine, "affected for the cosmopolitan radicalism of Paine the respect of a neophite for ideas not understood." Both leaders now suspected that Paine had gone over to the "Brissotins," as the Girondists were beginning to be called. However, the Brissotins, though a majority, had quailed before the ferocity with which the Jacobins had determined on the king's death. M. Taine declares that the victory of the minority in this case was the familiar one of reckless violence over the more civilized—the wild beast over the tame. Louis Blanc denies that the Convention voted, as one of them said, under poignards ; but the signs of fear are unmistakable. Vergniaud had declared it an insult for any one to suppose he would vote for the king's

[1] Both these passages from Paine's address vary considerably from the complete version given in Dr. Conway's edition of Paine's writings. The second passage especially has suffered. See vol. iii., pp. 122–3 and 123–4. —H.B.B.
[2] So called from the high benches on which these members sat. The seats of the Girondists on the floor were called the "Plain," and after their overthrow the "Marsh."

death, but he voted for it. Villette was threatened with death if he did not vote for that of the king. Sieyès, who had attacked Paine for republicanism, voted death. "What," he afterward said— "what were the tribute of my glass of wine in that torrent of brandy?" But Paine did not withhold his cup of cold water. When his name was called he cried out: "I vote for the detention of Louis till the end of the war, and after that his perpetual banishment." He spoke his well-prepared vote in French, and may have given courage to others. For even under poignards—the most formidable being liability to a charge of royalism—the vote had barely gone in favor of death.[1]

The fire-breathing Mountain felt now that its supremacy was settled. It had learned its deadly art of conquering a thinking majority by recklessness. But suddenly another question was sprung upon the Convention: Shall the execution be immediate, or shall there be delay? The Mountain groans and hisses as the question is raised, but the dictation had not extended to this point, and the question must be discussed. Here is one more small chance for Paine's poor royal client. Can the execution only be postponed it will probably never be executed. Unfortunately Marat, whose thirst for the King's blood is almost cannibalistic, can read on Paine's face his elation. He realizes that this American, with Washington behind him, has laid before the Convention a clear and consistent scheme for utilizing the royal prisoner. The king's neck under a suspended knife, it will rest with the foreign enemies of France

whether it shall fall or not; while the magnanimity of France and its respect for American gratitude will prevail. Paine, then, must be dealt with somehow in this new debate about delay.

He might, indeed, have been dealt with summarily had not the *Moniteur* done him an opportune service; on January 17th and 18th it printed Paine's unspoken argument for mercy, along with Erskine's speech at his trial in London, and the verdict. So on the 19th, when Paine entered the Convention, it was with the prestige not only of one outlawed by Great Britain for advocating the Rights of Man, but of a representative of the best Englishmen and their principles. It would be vain to assail the author's loyalty to the republic. That he would speak that day was certain, for on the morrow (20th) the final vote was to be taken. The Mountain could not use on Paine their weapon against Girondins; they could not accuse the author of the "Rights of Man" of being royalist. When he had mounted the tribune, and the clerk (Bancal, Franklin's friend) was beginning to read his speech, Marat cried, "I submit that Thomas Paine is incompetent to vote on this question; being a Quaker his religious principles are opposed to the death-penalty." There was great confusion for a time. The anger of the Jacobins were extreme, says Guizot, and "they refused to listen to the speech of Paine, the American, till respect for his courage gained him a hearing."[2] Demands for freedom of speech gradually subdued the interruptions, and the secretary proceeded:

"Very sincerely do I regret the Convention's vote of yesterday for death. I have the advantage of some experience; it is near twenty years that I have been engaged in the cause of liberty, having contributed something to it in the revolution of the United States of America. My language has always been that of liberty *and* humanity, and I know by experience that nothing so exalts a nation as the union of these two principles, under all circumstances. I know that the public mind of France, and particularly

---

[1] Upwards of three hundred voted with Paine, who says that the majority by which death was carried, unconditionally, was twenty-five. As a witness who had watched the case, his testimony may correct the estimate of Carlyle:

"Death by a small majority of Fifty-three. Nay, if we deduct from the one side, and add to the other, a certain Twenty-six who said Death but coupled some faintest ineffectual surmise of mercy with it, the majority will be but *One*." See also Paine's "Mémoire, etc., à Monroe."

[2] "History of France," vi., p. 136.

that of Paris, has been heated and irritated by the dangers to which they have been exposed ; but could we carry our thoughts into the future, when the dangers are ended, and the irritations forgotten, what to-day seems an act of justice may then appear an act of vengeance. [*Murmurs.*] My anxiety for the cause of France has become for the moment concern for her honor. If, on my return to America, I should employ myself on a history of the French Revolution, I had rather record a thousand errors dictated by humanity, than one inspired by a justice too severe. I voted against an appeal to the people, because it appeared to me that the Convention was needlessly wearied on that point ; but I so voted in the hope that this Assembly would pronounce against death, and for the same punishment that the nation would have voted, at least in my opinion, that is, for reclusion during the war and banishment thereafter. That is the punishment most efficacious, because it includes the whole family at once, and none other can so operate. I am still against the appeal to the primary assemblies, because there is a better method. This Convention has been elected to form a Constitution, which will be submitted to the primary assemblies. After its acceptance a necessary consequence will be an election, and another Assembly. We cannot suppose that the present Convention will last more than five or six months. The choice of new deputies will express the national opinion on the propriety or impropriety of your sentence, with as much efficacy as if those primary assemblies had been consulted on it. As the duration of our functions here cannot be long, it is a part of our duty to consider the interests of those who shall replace us. If by any act of ours the number of the nation's enemies shall be needlessly increased, and that of its friends diminished,—at a time when the finances may be more strained than to-day,—we should not be justifiable for having thus unnecessarily heaped obstacles in the path of our successors. Let us therefore not be precipitate in our decisions.

"France has but one ally—the United States of America. That is the only nation that can furnish France with naval provisions, for the kingdoms of northern Europe are, or soon will be, at war with her. It happens, unfortunately, that the person now under discussion is regarded by Americans as having been the friend of their revolution. I can assure you that his execution will there spread universal sorrow, and it is in your power not thus to wound the feelings of your ally. Could I speak the French language I would descend to your bar, and in their name become your petitioner to respite the execution of the sentence on Louis."

Here were loud murmurs from the "Mountain," answered with demands for liberty of opinion. Thuriot sprang to his feet crying, "This is not the language of Thomas Paine." Marat mounted the tribune and asked Paine some questions, apparently in English, then descending he said to the Assembly in French : "I denounce the interpreter, and I maintain that such is not the opinion of Thomas Paine. It is a wicked and faithless translation." [1] These words, audacious as mendacious, caused a tremendous uproar. Garran came to the rescue of the frightened clerk, declaring that he had read the original, and the translation was correct. Paine stood silent and calm during the storm. The clerk proceeded :

"Your Executive Committee will nominate an ambassador to Philadelphia ; my sincere wish is that he may announce to America that the National Convention of France, out of pure friendship to America, has consented to respite Louis. That people, your only ally, ask you by my vote to delay the execution.

"Ah, citizens, give not the tyrant of England the triumph of seeing the man perish on the scaffold who helped my much-loved America to break his chains !"

At the conclusion of this speech Marat "launched himself into the middle of the hall" and cried out that Paine had "voted against the punishment of death because he was a Quaker." Paine replied, "I voted against it both morally and politically."

Had the vote been taken that day perhaps Louis might have escaped. Brissot, shielded from charges of royalism by Paine's republican fame, now strongly supported his cause. "A cruel precipitation," he cried, "may alienate our friends in England, Ireland, America. Take care ! The opinion of European peoples is worth to you armies !" But all this only brought out the Mountain's particular kind of courage ; they were ready to defy the world—Washington

[1] "Venant d'un démocrate tel que Thomas Paine, d'un homme qui avait vécu parmi les Américains, d'un penseur, cette déclaration parut si dangereuse à Marat que, pour en détruire l'effet, il n'hésita pas à s'écrier : 'Je dénonce le truchement. Je soutiens que ce n'est point là l'opinion de Thomas Paine. C'est une traduction infidèle.' "—Louis Blanc. See also "Histoire Parlementaire," xxiii., p. 250.

included—in order to prove that a King's neck was no more than any other man's. Marat's clan—the "Nihilists" of the time, whose strength was that they stopped at nothing—had twenty-four hours to work in ; they surrounded the Convention next day with a mob howling for "justice !" Fifty-five members were absent ; of the 690 present a majority of seventy decided that Louis XVI. should die within twenty-four hours.

A hundred years have passed since that tragedy of poor Louis ; graves have given up their dead ; secrets of the hearts that then played their part are known. The world can now judge between England's Outlaw and England's King of that day. For it is established, as we have seen, both by English and French archives, that while Thomas Paine was toiling night and day to save the life of Louis that life lay in the hand of the British Ministry. Some writers question the historic truth of the offer made by Danton, but none can question the refusal of intercession, urged by Fox and others at a time when (as Count d'Estaing told Morris) the Convention was ready to give Pitt the whole French West Indies to keep him quiet. It was no doubt with this knowledge that Paine declared from the tribune that George III. would triumph in the execution of the King who helped America to break England's chains. Brissot also knew it when with weighed words he reported for his Committee (January 12th) : "The grievance of the British Cabinet against France is not that Louis is in judgment, but that Thomas Paine wrote 'The Rights of Man.'" "The militia were armed," says Louis Blanc, "in the south-east of England troops received order to march to London, the meeting of Parliament was advanced forty days, the Tower was reinforced by a new garrison, in fine there was unrolled a formidable preparation of war against—Thomas Paine's book on the Rights of Man !" [1]

Incredible as this may appear the

debates in the House of Commons, on which it is fairly founded, would be more incredible were they not duly reported in the "Parliamentary History." [2] In the debates on the Alien Bill, permitting the King to order any foreigner out of the country at will, on making representations to the French Convention in behalf of the life of Louis, on augmenting the military forces with direct reference to France, the recent trial of Paine was rehearsed, and it was plainly shown that the object of the government was to suppress freedom of the press by Terror. Erskine was denounced for defending Paine and for afterwards attending a meeting of the "Society of Friends of the Liberty of the Press," to whose resolutions on Paine's case his name was attached. Erskine found gallant defenders in the House, among them Fox, who demanded of Pitt : "Can you not prosecute Paine without an army ?" Burke at this time enacted a dramatic scene. Having stated that three thousand daggers had been ordered at Birmingham by an Englishman, he drew from his pocket a dagger, cast it on the floor of the House of Commons, and cried : "That is what we are to get from an alliance with France !" Paine—Paine—Paine—was the burden laid on Pitt, who had said to Lady Hester Stanhope : "Tom Paine is quite right." That Thomas Paine and his "Rights of Man" were the actual cause of the English insults to which their declaration of war replied was so well understood in the French Convention that its first answer to the menaces was to appoint Paine and Condorcet to write an address to the English people. [3]

It is noticeable that on the question whether the judgment on the King's fate should be submitted to the people, Paine voted "No." His belief in the right of all to representation implied

[1] "Histoire de la Révolution," vol. viii., p. 96.

[2] Vol. xxv.

[3] "Le Département des Affaires Étrangères pendant la Révolution, 1787–1804." Par Frédéric Masson, Bibliothécaire du Ministère des Affaires Étrangères. Paris, 1877, p. 273.

distrust of the immediate voice of the masses. The King had said that if his case were referred to the people "he should be massacred." Gouverneur Morris had heard this, and no doubt communicated it to Paine, who was in consultation with him on his plan of sending Louis to America.[1] Indeed, it is probable that popular suffrage would have ratified the decree. Nevertheless, it was a fair "appeal to the people" which Paine made, after the fatal verdict, in expressing to the Convention his belief that the people would not have done so. For after the decree the helplessness of the prisoner appealed to popular compassion, and on the fatal day the tide had turned. Four days after the execution the American Minister writes to Jefferson: "The greatest care was taken to prevent a concourse of people. This proves a conviction that the majority was not favorable to that severe measure. In fact the great mass of the people mourned the fate of their unhappy prince."

To Paine, the death of an "unhappy prince" was no more a subject for mourning than that of the humblest criminal—for, with whatever extenuating circumstances, a criminal he was to the republic he had sworn to administer. But the impolicy of the execution, the resentment uselessly incurred, the loss of prestige in America, were felt by Paine as a heavy blow to his cause—always the international republic. He was, however, behind the scenes enough to know that the blame rested mainly on America's old enemy and his league of foreign courts against liberated France. The man who, when Franklin said "Where liberty is, there is my country," answered "Where liberty is not, there is mine," would not despair of the infant republic because of its blunders. Attributing these outbursts to maddening conspiracies around and within the new-born nation, he did not believe there could be peace in Europe so long as it was ruled by George III.

[1] Morris' "Diary," ii., pp. 19, 27, 32.

He therefore set himself to the struggle, as he had done in 1776. Moreover, Paine has faith in Providence.[2]

At this time, it should be remembered, opposition to capital punishment was confined to very few outside of the despised sect of Quakers. In the debate three, besides Paine, gave emphatic expression to that sentiment, Manuel, Condorcet,—Robespierre! The former, in giving his vote against death, said: "To Nature belongs the right of death. Despotism has taken it from her; Liberty will return it." As for Robespierre, his argument was a very powerful reply to Paine, who had reminded him of the bill he had introduced into the old National Assembly for the abolition of capital punishment. He did, indeed, abhor it, he said; it was not his fault if his views had been disregarded. But why should men who then opposed him suddenly revive the claims of humanity when the penalty happened to fall upon a King? Was the penalty good enough for the people, but not for a King? If there were any exception in favor of such a punishment, it should be for a royal criminal.

This opinion of Robespierre is held by some humane men. The present writer heard from Professor Francis W. Newman—second to none in philanthropy and compassionateness— a suggestion that the death penalty should be reserved for those placed at

[2] "The same spirit of fortitude that insured success to America will insure it to France, for it is impossible to conquer a nation determined to be free. . . . Man is ever a stranger to the ways by which Providence regulates the order of things. The interference of foreign despots may serve to introduce into their own enslaved countries the principles they come to oppose. Liberty and Equality are blessings too great to be the inheritance of France alone. It is honor to her to be their first champion; and she may now say to her enemies, with a mighty voice, 'O, ye Austrians, ye Prussians! ye who now turn your bayonets against us, it is for you, it is for all Europe, it is for all mankind, and not for France alone, that she raises the standard of Liberty and Equality!'"—Paine's address to the Convention (September 25, 1792) after taking his seat.

G

the head of affairs who betray their trust, or set their own above the public interests to the injury of a Commonwealth.

The real reasons for the execution of the King closely resemble those of Washington for the execution of Major André, notwithstanding the sorrow of the country, with which the Commander sympathized. The equal nationality of the United States, repudiated by Great Britain, was in question. To hang spies was, however illogically, a conventional usage among nations. Major André must die, therefore, and must be refused the soldier's death for which he petitioned. For a like reason Europe must be shown that the French Convention is peer of their scornful Parliaments; and its fundamental principle, the equality of men, could not admit a King's escape from the penalty which would be unhesitatingly inflicted on a "Citizen." The King had assumed the title of Citizen, had worn the republican cockade; the apparent concession of royal inviolability, in the moment of his betrayal of the compromise made with him, could be justified only on the grounds stated by Paine,—impolicy of slaying their hostage, creating pretenders, alienating America; and the honor of exhibiting to the world, by a salient example, the Republic's magnanimity in contrast with the cruelty of Kings.

CHAPTER XXVI

AN OUTLAWED ENGLISH AMBASSADOR

SOON after Paine had taken his seat in the Convention, Lord Fortescue wrote to Miles, an English agent in Paris, a letter fairly expressive of the feelings, fears, and hopes of his class.

"Tom Paine is just where he ought to be—a member of the Convention of Cannibals. One would have thought it impossible that any society upon the face of the globe should have been fit for the reception of such a being until the late deeds of the National Convention have shown them to be most fully qualified. His vocation will not be complete, nor theirs either, till his head finds its way to the top of a pike, which will probably not be long first." [1]

---

[1] This letter, dated September 26, 1792, appears in the Miles Correspondence (London, 1890). There are indications that Miles was favorably disposed towards Paine, and on that account, perhaps, was subjected to influence by his superiors. As an example of the way in which just minds were poisoned towards Paine, a note of Miles may be mentioned. He says he was "told by Col. Bosville, a declared friend of Paine, that his manners and conversation were coarse, and he loved the brandy bottle." But just as this Miles Correspondence was appearing in London, Dr. Grece found the

But if Paine was so fit for such a Convention, why should they behead him? The letter betrays a real perception that Paine possesses humane principles, and an English courage, which would bring him into danger. This undertone of Fortescue's invective represented the profound confidence of Paine's adherents in England. When tidings came of the King's trial and execution, whatever glimpses they gained of their outlawed leader showed him steadfast as a star caught in one wave and another of that turbid tide. Many, alas, needed

manuscript diary of Rickman, who had discovered (as two entries show) that this "declared friend of Paine," Col. Bosville, and professed friend of himself, was going about uttering injurious falsehoods concerning him (Rickman), seeking to alienate his friends at the moment when he most needed them. Rickman was a bookseller engaged in circulating Paine's works. There is little doubt that this wealthy Col. Bosville was at the time unfriendly to the radicals. He was staying in Paris on Paine's political credit, while depreciating him.

apologies, but Paine required none. That one Englishman, standing on the tribune for justice and humanity, amid three hundred angry Frenchmen in uproar, was as sublime a sight as Europe witnessed in those days. To the English radical the outlawry of Paine was as the tax on light, which was presently walling up London windows, or extorting from them the means of war against ideas.[1] The trial of Paine had elucidated nothing, except that, like Jupiter, John Bull had the thunderbolts, and Paine the arguments. Indeed, it is difficult to discover any other Englishman who at the moment pre-eminently stood for principles now proudly called English.

But Paine too presently held thunderbolts. Although his efforts to save Louis had offended the "Mountain," and momentarily brought him into the danger Lord Fortescue predicted, that party was not yet in the ascendant. The Girondists were still in power, and though some of their leaders had bent before the storm, that they might not be broken, they had been impressed both by the courage and the tactics of Paine. "The Girondists consulted Paine," says Lamartine, "and placed him on the Committee of Surveillance." At this moment many Englishmen were in France, and at a word from Paine some of their heads might have mounted on the pike which Lord Fortescue had imaginatively prepared for the head that wrote "The Rights of Man." There remained, for instance, Mr. Munro, already mentioned. This gentleman, in a note preserved in the English Archives, had written to Lord Grenville (September 8, 1792) concerning Paine: "What must a nation come to

[1] In a copy of the first edition of "The Rights of Man," which I bought in London, I found, as a sort of book-mark, a bill for 1*l.* 6*s.* 8*d.*, two quarters' window-tax, due from Mr. Williamson, Upper Fitzroy Place. Windows closed with bricks are still seen in some of the gloomiest parts of London. I have in manuscript a bitter anathema of the time:

"God made the Light, and saw that it was good :
Pitt laid a tax on it,—G— d— his blood !"

that has so little discernment in the election of their representatives, as to elect such a fellow?" But having lingered in Paris after England's formal declaration of war (February 11th), Munro was cast into prison. He owed his release to that "fellow" Paine, and must be duly credited with having acknowledged it, and changed his tone for the rest of his life,—which he probably owed to the English committeeman. Had Paine met with the fate which Lords Gower and Fortescue hoped, it would have gone hard with another eminent countryman of theirs,—Captain Grimstone, R.A. This personage, during a dinner party at the Palais Égalité, got into controversy with Paine, and, forgetting that the English Jove could not in Paris safely answer argument with thunder, called Paine a traitor to his country and struck him a violent blow. Death was the penalty of striking a deputy, and Paine's friends were not unwilling to see the penalty inflicted on this stout young Captain who had struck a man of fifty-six. Paine had much trouble in obtaining from Barrère, of the Committee of Public Safety, a passport out of the country for Captain Grimstone, whose travelling expenses were supplied by the man he had struck.

In a later instance, related by Walter Savage Landor, Paine's generosity amounted to quixotism. The story is finely told by Landor, who says in a note : "This anecdote was communicated to me at Florence by Mr. Evans, a painter of merit, who studied under Lawrence, and who knew personally (Zachariah) Wilkes and Watt. In religion and politics he differed widely from Paine."

"Sir," said he, "let me tell you what he did for me. My name is Zachariah Wilkes. I was arrested in Paris and condemned to die. I had no friend here ; and it was a time when no friend would have served me : Robespierre ruled. 'I am innocent!' I cried in desperation. 'I am innocent, so help me God ! I am condemned for the offence of another.' I wrote a statement of my case with a pencil ; thinking at first of addressing it to my judge, then of directing it to the president of the Convention. The jailer, who had been kind to me, gave me a gazette, and told me not to mind seeing my name, so many were there before it.

" 'O!' said I, 'though you would not lend me your ink, do transmit this paper to the president.'

" 'No, my friend!' answered he gaily. 'My head is as good as yours, and looks as well between the shoulders, to my liking. Why not send it (if you send it anywhere) to the deputy Paine here?' pointing to a column in the paper.

" 'O God! he must hate and detest the name of Englishman: pelted, insulted, persecuted, plundered . . .'

" 'I could give it to him,' said the jailer.

" 'Do then!' said I wildly. 'One man more shall know my innocence.' He came within the half hour. I told him my name, that my employers were Watt and Boulton of Birmingham, that I had papers of the greatest consequence, that if I failed to transmit them, not only my life was in question, but my reputation. He replied: 'I know your employers by report only; there are no two men less favorable to the principles I profess, but no two upon earth are honester. You have only one great man among you: it is Watt; for Priestley is gone to America. The church-and-king men would have japanned him. He left to these philosophers of the rival school his house to try experiments on; and you may know, better than I do, how much they found in it of carbon and calx, of silex and argilla.'

" He examined me closer than my judge had done; he required my proofs. After a long time I satisfied him. He then said, 'The leaders of the Convention would rather have my life than yours. If by any means I can obtain your release on my own security, will you promise me to return within twenty days?' I answered, 'Sir, the security I can at present give you, is trifling . . . I should say a mere nothing.'

" 'Then you do not give me your word?' said he.

" 'I give it and will redeem it.'

" He went away, and told me I should see him again when he could inform me whether he had succeeded. He returned in the earlier part of the evening, looked fixedly upon me, and said, 'Zachariah Wilkes! if you do not return in twenty-four days (four are added) you will be the most unhappy of men; for had you not been an honest one, you could not be the agent of Watt and Boulton. I do not think I have hazarded much in offering to take your place on your failure: such is the condition.' I was speechless; he was unmoved. Silence was first broken by the jailer. 'He seems to get fond of the spot now he must leave it.' I had thrown my arms upon the table towards my liberator, who sat opposite, and I rested my head and breast upon it too, for my temples ached and tears had not yet relieved them. He said, 'Zachariah! follow me to the carriage.' The soldiers paid the respect due to his scarf, presenting arms, and drawing up in file as we went along. The jailer called for a glass of wine, gave it me, poured out another, and drank to our next meeting." [1]

Another instance may be related in Paine's own words, written (March 20, 1806) to a gentleman in New York.

"SIR,—I will inform you of what I know respecting General Miranda, with whom I first became acquainted at New York, about the year 1783. He is a man of talents and enterprise, and the whole of his life has been a life of adventures.

"I went to Europe from New York in April, 1787. Mr. Jefferson was then Minister from America to France, and Mr. Littlepage, a Virginian (whom Mr. Jay knows), was agent for the king of Poland, at Paris. Mr. Littlepage was a young man of extraordinary talents, and I first met with him at Mr. Jefferson's house at dinner. By his intimacy with the king of Poland, to whom also he was chamberlain, he became well acquainted with the plans and projects of the Northern Powers of Europe. He told me of Miranda's getting himself introduced to the Empress Catharine of Russia, and obtaining a sum of money from her, four thousand pounds sterling; but it did not appear to me what the object was for which the money was given; it appeared a kind of retaining fee.

"After I had published the first part of the 'Rights of Man' in England, in the year 1791, I met Miranda at the house of Turnbull and Forbes, merchants, Devonshire Square, London. He had been a little before this in the employ of Mr. Pitt, with respect to the affair of Nootka Sound, but I did not at that time know it; and I will, in the course of this letter, inform you how this connection between Pitt and Miranda ended; for I know it of my own knowledge.

"I published the second part of the 'Rights of Man' in London, in February, 1792, and I continued in London till I was elected a member of the French Convention, in September of that year; and went from London to Paris to take my seat in the Convention, which was to meet the 20th of that month. I arrived in Paris on the 19th. After the Convention met, Miranda came to Paris, and was appointed general of the French army, under General Dumouriez. But as the affairs of that army went wrong in the beginning of the year 1793, Miranda was suspected, and was brought under arrest to Paris to take his trial. He summoned me to appear to his character, and also a Mr. Thomas

---

[1] Zachariah Wilkes did not fail to return, or Paine to greet him with safety, and the words, "There is yet English blood in England." But here Landor passes off into an imaginative picture of villages rejoicing at the fall of Robespierre. Paine himself had then been in prison seven months; so we can only conjecture the means by which Zachariah was liberated.— Landor's Works, London, 1853, i., p. 296.

Christie, connected with the house of Turnbull and Forbes. I gave my testimony as I believed, which was, that his leading object was and had been the emancipation of his country, Mexico, from the bondage of Spain; for I did not at that time know of his engagements with Pitt. Mr. Christie's evidence went to show that Miranda did not come to France as a necessitous adventurer; but believed he came from public-spirited motives, and that he had a large sum of money in the hands of Turnbull and Forbes. The house of Turnbull and Forbes was then in a contract to supply Paris with flour. Miranda was acquitted.

"A few days after his acquittal he came to see me, and in a few days afterwards I returned his visit. He seemed desirous of satisfying me that he was independent, and that he had money in the hands of Turnbull and Forbes. He did not tell me of his affair with old Catharine of Russia, nor did I tell him that I knew of it. But he entered into conversation with respect to Nootka Sound, and put into my hands several letters of Mr. Pitt's to him on that subject; amongst which was one which I believe he gave me by mistake, for when I had opened it, and was beginning to read it, he put forth his hand and said, 'O, that is not the letter I intended'; but as the letter was short I soon got through with it, and then returned it to him without making any remarks upon it. The dispute with Spain was then compromised; and Pitt compromised with Miranda for his services by giving him twelve hundred pounds sterling, for this was the contents of the letter.

"Now if it be true that Miranda brought with him a credit upon certain persons in New York for sixty thousand pounds sterling, it is not difficult to suppose from what quarter the money came; for the opening of any proposals between Pitt and Miranda was already made by the affair of Nootka Sound. Miranda was in Paris when Mr. Monroe arrived there as Minister; and as Miranda wanted to get acquainted with him, I cautioned Mr. Monroe against him, and told him of the affair of Nootka Sound, and the twelve hundred pounds.

"You are at liberty to make what use you please of this letter, and with my name to it."

Here we find a paid agent of Pitt calling on outlawed Paine for aid, by his help liberated from prison; and, when his true character is accidentally discovered, and he is at the outlaw's mercy, spared,—no doubt because this true English ambassador, who could not enter England, saw that at the moment passionate vengeance had taken the place of justice in Paris. Lord Gower had departed, and Paine must try and shield even his English enemies and their

agents, where, as in Miranda's case, the agency did not appear to affect France. This was while his friends in England were hunted down with ferocity.

In the earlier stages of the French Revolution there was much sympathy with it among literary men and in the universities. Coleridge, Southey, Wordsworth, were leaders in the revolutionary cult at Oxford and Cambridge. By 1792, and especially after the institution of Paine's prosecution, the repression became determined. The memoir of Thomas Poole, already referred to, gives the experiences of a Somerset gentleman a friend of Coleridge. After the publication of Paine's "Rights of Man" (1791) he became a "political Ishmaelite." "He made his appearance amongst the wigs and powdered locks of his kinsfolk and acquaintance, male and female, without any of the customary powder in his hair, which innocent novelty was a scandal to all beholders, seeing that it was the outward and visible sign of a love of innovation, a well-known badge of sympathy with democratic ideas."

Among Poole's friends, at Stowey, was an attorney named Symes, who lent him Paine's "Rights of Man." After Paine's outlawry Symes met a cabinet-maker with a copy of the book, snatched it out of his hand, tore it up, and, having learned that it was lent him by Poole, propagated about the country that he (Poole) was distributing seditious literature about the country. Being an influential man, Poole prevented the burning of Paine in effigy at Stowey. As time goes on this country-gentleman and scholar finds the government opening his letters, and warning his friends that he is in danger.

"It was," he writes to a friend, "the boast an Englishman was wont to make that he could think, speak, and write whatever he thought proper, provided he violated no law, nor injured any individual. But now an absolute controul exists, not indeed over the imperceptible operations of the mind, for those no power of man can controul; but, what is the same thing, over the effects of those operations, and if among these effects, that of speaking is to be checked, the soul is as much enslaved as the body in a cell of the Bastille. The man who once feels, nay fancies, this, is a slave. It shows as if the suspicious secret government of an Italian Republic had replaced the open, candid government of the English laws."

As Thomas Poole well represents the serious and cultured thought of young England in that time, it is interesting to read his judgment on the king's execution and the imminent war.

"Many thousands of human beings will be sacrificed in the ensuing contest, and for what? To support three or four individuals, called arbitrary kings, in the situation which they have usurped. I consider every Briton who loses his life in the war as much murdered as the King of France, and every one who approves the war, as signing the death-warrant of each soldier or sailor that falls. . . . The excesses in France are great; but who are the authors of them? The Emperor of Germany, the King of Prussia, and Mr. Burke. Had it not been for their impertinent interference, I firmly believe the King of France would be at this moment a happy monarch, and that people would be enjoying every advantage of political liberty. . . . The slave-trade, you will see, will not be abolished, because to be humane and honest now is to be a traitor to the constitution, a lover of sedition and licentiousness! But this universal depression of the human mind cannot last long."

It was in this spirit that the defence of a free press was undertaken in England. That thirty years' war was fought and won on the works of Paine. There were some "Lost Leaders": the king's execution, the reign of terror, caused reaction in many a fine spirit; but the rank and file followed their Thomas Paine with a faith that crowned heads might envy. The London men knew Paine thoroughly. The treasures of the world would not draw him, nor any terrors drive him, to the side of cruelty and inhumanity. Their eye was upon him. Had Paine, after the king's execution, despaired of the republic there might have ensued some demoralization among his followers in London. But they saw him by the side of the delivered prisoner of the Bastille, Brissot, an author well known in England, by the side of Condorcet and others of Franklin's honored circle, engaged in death-struggle with the fire-breathing

dragon called "the Mountain." That was the same unswerving man they had been following, and to all accusations against the revolution their answer was—Paine is still there!

A reign of terror in England followed the outlawry of Paine. Twenty-four men, at one time or another, were imprisoned, fined, or transported for uttering words concerning abuses such as now every Englishman would use concerning the same. Some who sold Paine's works were imprisoned before Paine's trial, while the seditious character of the books was not yet legally settled. Many were punished after the trial, by both fine and imprisonment. Newspapers were punished for printing extracts, and for having printed them before the trial.[1] For this kind of work

---

[1] The first trial after Paine's, that of Thomas Spence (February 26, 1793), for selling "The Rights of Man," failed through a flaw in the indictment, but the mistake did not occur again. At the same time William Holland was awarded a year's imprisonment and £100 fine for selling "Letter to the Addressers." H. D. Symonds, for publishing "Rights of Man," £20 fine and two years; for "Letter to the Addressers," one year, £100 fine, with sureties in £1,000 for three years, and imprisonment till the fine be paid and sureties given. April 17, 1793, Richard Phillips, printer, Leicester, eighteen months. May 8th, J. Ridgway, London, selling "Rights of Man," £100 and one year; "Letter to the Addressers," one year, £100 fine; in each case sureties in £1,000, with imprisonment until fines paid and sureties given. Richard Peart, "Rights" and "Letter," three months. William Belcher, "Rights" and "Letter," three months. Daniel Holt, £50, four years. Messrs. Robinson, £200. Eaton and Thompson, the latter in Birmingham, were acquitted. Clio Rickman escaped punishment by running over to Paris. Dr. Currie (1793) writes: "The prosecutions that are commenced all over England against printers, publishers, etc., would astonish you; and most of these are for offences committed many months ago. The printer of the *Manchester Herald* has had seven different indictments preferred against him for paragraphs in his paper; and six *different* indictments for selling or disposing of six different copies of Paine,—all previous to the *trial* of Paine. The man was opulent, supposed worth 20,000 *l*.; but these different actions will ruin him, as they were intended to do."—"Currie's Life," i., p. 185. See Buckle's "History of Civilization," etc., American ed., p. 352. In the cases where

old statutes passed for other purposes were impressed, new statutes framed, until Fox declared the Bill of Rights repealed, the constitution cut up by the roots, and the obedience of the people to such "despotism" no longer "a question of moral obligation and duty, but of prudence."[1]

From his safe retreat in Paris bookseller Rickman wrote his impromptu :

"Hail Briton's land ! Hail freedom's shore !
    Far happier than of old ;
For in thy blessed realms no more
    The Rights of Man are sold !"

The famous town-crier of Bolton, who reported to his masters that he had been round that place "and found in it neither the rights of man nor common sense," made a statement characteristic of the time. The aristocracy and gentry had indeed lost their humanity and their sense under a disgraceful panic. Their serfs, unable to read, were fairly represented by those who, having burned Paine in effigy, asked their employer if there was "any other gemman he would like burnt, for a glass o' beer." The White Bear (now replaced by the Criterion Restaurant) no longer knew its little circle of radicals. A symbol of how they were trampled out is discoverable in the "T. P." shoe-nails. These nails, with heads so lettered, were in great request among the gentry, who had only to hold up their boot-soles to show how they were trampling on Tom Paine and his principles. This at any rate was accurate. Manufacturers of vases also devised ceramic anathemas.[2]

"gentlemen" were found distributing the works the penalties were ferocious. Fische Palmer was sentenced to seven years' transportation. Thomas Muir, for advising persons to read "the works of that wretched outcast Paine" (the Lord Advocate's words) was sentenced to fourteen years' transportation. This sentence was hissed. The tipstaff, being ordered to take those who hissed into custody, replied : "My lord, they're all hissing."

[1] "Parl. Hist.," xxxii., p. 383.
[2] There are two Paine pitchers in the Museum at Brighton, England. Both were made at Leeds, one probably before Paine's trial, since

In all of this may be read the frantic fears of the King and aristocracy which were driving the Ministry to make good Paine's aphorism, "There is no English Constitution." An English Constitution was, however, in process of formation,—in prisons, in secret conclaves, in lands of exile, and chiefly in Paine's small room in Paris. Even in that time of Parisian turbulence and peril the hunted liberals of England found more security in France than in their native land.[3] For

---

it presents a respectable full-length portrait, holding in his hand a book, and beneath, the words : "Mr. Thomas Paine, Author of The Rights of Man." The other shows a serpent with Paine's head, two sides being adorned with the following lines :

"God save the King, and all his subjects too,
    Likewise his forces and commanders true,
    May he their rights forever hence Maintain
    Against all strife occasioned by Tom Paine."

"Prithee Tom Paine why wilt thou meddling be
    In others' business which concerns not thee ;
    For while thereon thou dost extend thy cares
    Thou dost at home neglect thine own affairs."

"God save the King !"

"Observe the wicked and malicious man
    Projecting all the mischief that he can."

[3] When William Pitt died in 1806,—crushed under disclosures in the impeachment of Lord Melville,—the verdict of many sufferers was expressed in an "Epitaph Impromptu" (MS.) found among the papers of Thomas Rickman. It has some historic interest.

"Reader ! with eye indignant view this bier ;
    The foe of all the human race lies here.
    With talents small, and those directed, too,
    Virtue and truth and wisdom to subdue,
    He lived to every noble motive blind,
    And died, the execration of mankind.

"Millions were butchered by his damnéd plan
    To violate each sacred right of man ;
    Exulting he o'er earth each misery hurled,
    And joyed to drench in tears and blood, the world.

"Myriads of beings wretched he has made
    By desolating war, his favorite trade,
    Who, robbed of friends and dearest ties, are left
    Of every hope and happiness bereft.

"In private life made up of fuss and pride,
    Not e'en his vices leaned to virtue's side ;
    Unsound, corrupt, and rotten at the core,
    His cold and scoundrel heart was black all o'er ;
    Nor did one passion ever move his mind
    That bent towards the tender, warm, and kind.

the eyes of the English reformer of that period, seeing events from prison or exile, there was a perspective such as time has now supplied to the historian. It is still difficult to distribute the burden of shame fairly. Pitt was unquestionably at first anxious to avoid war. That the King was determined on the war is certain; he refused to notice Wilberforce when he appeared at court after his separation from Pitt on that point. But the three attempts on his life, and his mental infirmity, may be pleaded for George III. Paine, in his letter to Dundas, wrote "Madjesty"; when Rickman objected, he said: "Let it stand." And it stands now as the best apology for the King, while it rolls on Pitt's memory the guilt of a twenty-two years' war for the subjugation of thought and freedom. In that last struggle of the barbarism surviving in civilization, it was shown that the madness of a populace was easily distanced by the cruelty of courts. Robespierre and Marat were humanitarian beside George and his Ministers; the Reign of Terror, and all the massacres of the French Revolution put together, were child's-play compared with the anguish and horrors spread through Europe by a war whose pretext was an execution England might have prevented.

CHAPTER XXVII

REVOLUTION *VS.* CONSTITUTION

THE French revolutionists have long borne responsibility for the first declaration of war in 1793. But from December 13, 1792, when the Painophobia Parliament began its debates, to February 1st, when France proclaimed itself at war with England, the British government had done little else than declare war— and prepare war—against France. Pitt, having to be re-elected, managed to keep away from Parliament for several days at its opening, and the onslaught was assumed by Burke. He began by heaping insults on France. On December 15th he boasted that he had not been cajoled by promise of promotion or pension, though he presently, on the same evening, took his seat for the first time on the Treasury bench. In the "Parliamentary History" (vols. xxx. and xxxi.) may be found Burke's epithets on France, —the "republic of assassins," "Cannibal Castle," "nation of murderers," "gang of plunderers," "murderous atheists," "miscreants," "scum of the earth." His vocabulary grew in grossness, of course, after the King's execution and the declaration of war, but from the first it was ribaldry and abuse. And this did not come from a private member, but from the Treasury bench. He was supported by a furious majority which stopped at no injustice. Thus the Convention was burdened with guilt of the September massacres, though it was not then in existence. Paine's works being denounced, Erskine reminded the House of the illegality of so influencing a trial not yet begun. He was not listened to. Fox and fifty other earnest men had a serious purpose of trying to save the King's life, and proposed to negotiate with the Convention. Burke fairly foamed at the motions to that end, made by Fox and Lord Lansdowne. What, negotiate with such villains! To whom is our

---

"Tyrant, and friend to war! we hail the day
  When Death, to bless mankind, made thee his prey,
  And rid the earth of all could earth disgrace,—
  The foulest, bloodiest scourge of man's oppresséd race."

agent to be accredited? Burke draws a comic picture of the English ambassador entering the Convention, and, when he announces himself as from "George Third, by the grace of God," denounced by Paine. "Are we to humble ourselves before Judge Paine?" At this point Whetstone made a disturbance and was named. There were some who found Burke's trifling intolerable. Mr. W. Smith reminded the House that Cromwell's ambassadors had been received by Louis XIV. Fox drew a parallel between the contemptuous terms used toward the French, and others about "Hancock and his crew," with whom Burke advised treaty, and with whom His Majesty did treat. All this was answered by further insults to France, these corresponding with a series of practical injuries. Lord Gower had been recalled August 17th, after the formation of a republic, and all intercourse with the French Minister in London, Chauvelin, was terminated. In violation of the treaty of 1786, the agents of France were refused permission to purchase grain and arms in England, and their vessels loaded with provisions seized. The circulation of French bonds, issued in 1790, was prohibited in England. A coalition had been formed with the enemies of France, the Emperor of Austria and the King of Prussia. Finally, on the execution of Louis XVI., Chauvelin was ordered (January 24th) to leave England in eight days. Talleyrand remained, but Chauvelin was kicked out of the country, so to say, simply because the Convention had recognized him. This appeared a plain *casus belli*, and was answered by the declaration of the Convention in that sense (February 1st), which England answered ten days later.[1]

---

[1] "It was stipulated in the treaty of commerce between France and England, concluded at Paris [1786] that the sending away an ambassador by either party, should be taken as an act of hostility by the other party. The declaration of war (February, 1793) by the Convention . . . was made in exact conformity to this article in the treaty; for it was not a declaration of war against England, but a declaration that the

In all this Paine recognized the hand of Burke. While his adherents in England, as we have seen, were finding in Pitt a successor to Satan, there is a notable absence from Paine's writings and letters of any such animosity towards that Minister. He regarded Pitt as a victim. "The father of Pitt," he once wrote, "when a member of the House of Commons, exclaiming one day, during a former war, against the enormous and ruinous expense of German connections, as the offspring of the Hanover succession, and borrowing a metaphor from the story of Prometheus, cried out: 'Thus, like Prometheus, is Britain chained to the barren rock of Hanover, whilst the imperial eagle preys upon her vitals.'" It is probable that on the intimations from Pitt, at the close of 1792, of his desire for private consultations with friendly Frenchmen, Paine entered into the honorable though unauthorized conspiracy for peace which was terminated by the expulsion of Chauvelin. In the light of later events, and the desertion of Dumouriez, these overtures of Pitt made through Talleyrand (then in London) were regarded by the French leaders, and are still regarded by French writers, as treacherous. But no sufficient reason is given for doubting Pitt's good faith in that matter. Writing to the President (Washington), December 28, 1792, the American Minister,

---

French republic is *in* war with England; the first act of hostility having been committed by England. The declaration was made on Chauvelin's return to France, and in consequence of it."—Paine's "Address to the People of France" (1797). The words of the declaration of war, following the list of injuries, are: "La Convention Nationale déclaré, au nom de la nation Française, qu'attendu les actes multipliés et d'agressions ci-dessus mentionnés, la république Française est en guerre avec le roi d'Angleterre." The solemn protest of Lords Lauderdale, Lansdowne, and Derby, February 1st, against the address in answer to the royal message, before France had spoken, regards that address as a demonstration of universal war. The facts and the situation are carefully set forth by Louis Blanc, "Histoire de la Révolution," tome viii., p. 93 *seq*.

Gouverneur Morris, states the British proposal to be :

" France shall deliver the royal family to such branch of the Bourbons as the King may choose, and shall recall her troops from the countries they now occupy. In this event Britain will send hither a Minister and acknowledge the Republic, and mediate a peace with the Emperor and King of Prussia. I have several reasons to believe that this information is not far from the truth."

It is true that Pitt had no agent in France whom he might not have disavowed, and that after the fury with which the Painophobia Parliament, under lead of Burke, inspired by the King, had opened, could hardly have maintained any peaceful terms. Nevertheless, the friends of peace in France secretly acted on this information, which Gouverneur Morris no doubt received from Paine. A grand dinner was given by Paine, at the Hôtel de Ville, to Dumouriez, where this brilliant General met Brissot, Condorcet, Santerre, and several eminent English radicals, among them Sampson Perry. At this time it was proposed to send Dumouriez secretly to London, to negotiate with Pitt, but this was abandoned. Marat went, and he found Pitt gracious and pacific. Chauvelin, however, advised the French government of this illicit negotiation, and Marat was ordered to return. Such was the situation when Louis was executed. That execution, as we have seen, might have been prevented had Pitt provided the money ; but it need not be supposed that, with Burke now on the Treasury bench, the refusal is to be ascribed to anything more than his inability to cope with his own majority, whom the King was patronizing. So completely convinced of Pitt's pacific disposition were Marat and his allies in France that the clandestine ambassador again departed for London. But on arriving at Dover, he learned that Chauvelin had been expelled, and at once returned to France.[1]

[1] See Louis Blanc's " Histoire," etc., tome viii., p. 100, for the principal authorities concerning this incident.—*Annual Register*, 1793,

Paine now held more firmly than ever the first article of his faith as to practical politics : the chief task of republicanism is to break the Anglo-German sceptre. France is now committed to war ; it must be elevated to that European aim. Lord North and America reappear in Burke and France.

Meanwhile what is said of Britain in his "Rights of Man" was now more terribly true of France — it had no Constitution. The Committee on the Constitution had declared themselves ready to report early in the winter, but the Mountaineers managed that the matter should be postponed until after the King's trial. As an American who prized his citizenship, Paine felt chagrined and compromised at being compelled to act as a legislator and a judge because of his connection with a Convention elected for the purpose of framing a legislative and judicial machinery. He and Condorcet continued to add touches to this Constitution, the Committee approving, and on the first opportunity it was reported again. This was February 15, 1793. But, says the *Moniteur*, "the struggles between the Girondins and the Mountain caused the examination and discussion to be postponed." It was, however, distributed.

Gouverneur Morris, in a letter to Jefferson (March 7th), says this Constitution "was read to the Convention, but I learnt the next morning that a Council had been held on it overnight, by which it was condemned." Here is evidence in our American archives of a meeting or "Council" condemning the Constitution on the night of its submission. It must have been secret, for it does not appear in French histories, so far as I can discover. Durand de Maillane says that "the exclusion of Robespierre and Couthon from this eminent task [framing a Constitution] was a new matter for discontent and

ch. vi. ; " Mémoires tirés des papiers d'un homme d'État.," ii., p. 157 ; " Mémoires de Dumouriez," t. iii., p. 384.

jealousy against the party of Pétion "—
a leading Girondin,—and that Robespierre and his men desired " to render
their work useless."[1] No indication of
this secret condemnation of the Paine-
Condorcet Constitution, by a conclave
appeared on March 1st, when the document was again submitted. The Convention now set April 15th for its
discussion, and the Mountaineers fixed
that day for the opening of their attack
on the Girondins. The Mayor of Paris
appeared with a petition, adopted by the
Communal Council of the thirty-five
sections of Paris, for the arrest of twenty-
two members of the Convention as
slanderers of Paris,—" presenting the
Parisians to Europe as men of blood,"—
friends of Roland, accomplices- of the
traitor Dumouriez, enemies of the clubs.
The deputies named were : Brissot,
Guadet, Vergniaud, Gensonné, Grange-
neuve, Buzot, Barbaroux, Salles, Biro-
teau, Pontécoulant, Pétion, Lanjuinais,
Valaze, Hardy, Louvet, Lehardy, Gorsas,
Abbé Fauchet, Lanthenas, Lasource,
Valady, Chambon. Of this list five
were members of the Committee on the
Constitution, and two supplementary
members.[2] Besides this, two of the
arraigned—Louvet and Lasource—had
been especially active in pressing forward the Constitution. The Mountaineers turned the discord they thus caused
into a reason for deferring discussion of
the Constitution. They declared also
that important members were absent,
levying troops, and especially that
Marat's trial had been ordered. The
discussion on the petition against the
Girondins, and whether the Constitution
should be considered, proceeded together for two days, when the Mountaineers were routed on both issues.
The Convention returned the petition to
the Mayor, pronouncing it " calumnious,"

[1] " Histoire de la Convention Nationale," p.
50. Durand-Maillane was " the silent member "
of the Convention, but a careful observer and
well-informed witness. I follow him and Louis
Blanc in relating the fate of the Paine-Condorcet
Constitution.

[2] See p. 146.

and it made the Constitution the order of
the day. Robespierre, according to
Durand-Maillane, showed much spite at
this defeat. He adroitly secured a decision that the preliminary " Declaration
of Rights" should be discussed first,
as there could be endless talk on those
generalities.[3]

[3] This Declaration, submitted by Condorcet,
April 17th, being largely the work of Paine, is
here translated : The end of all union of men in
society being maintenance of their natural rights,
civil and political, these rights should be the
basis of the social pact : their recognition and
their declaration ought to precede the Constitution which secures and guarantees them. 1.
The natural rights, civil and political, of men
are liberty, equality, security, property, social
protection, and resistance to oppression. 2.
Liberty consists in the right to do whatever is
not contrary to the rights of others ; thus, the
natural rights of each man has no limits other
than those which secure to other members of
society enjoyment of the same rights. 3. The
preservation of liberty depends on the sovereignty
of the Law, which is the expression of the
general will. Nothing unforbidden by law can
be impeached, and none may be constrained to
do what it does not command. 4. Every man
is free to make known his thought and his
opinions. 5. Freedom of the press (and every
other means of publishing one's thoughts) cannot be prohibited, suspended, or limited. 6.
Every citizen shall be free in the exercise of his
worship [*culte*]. 7. Equality consists in the
power of each to enjoy the same rights. 8.
The Law should be equal for all, whether in recompense, punishment, or restraint. 9. All
citizens are admissible to all public positions,
employments, and functions. Free peoples can
recognise no grounds of preference except
talents and virtues. 10. Security consists in
the protection accorded by society to each
citizen for the preservation of his person,
property, and rights. 11. None should be sued,
accused, arrested, or detained, save in cases determined by the law, and in accordance with
forms prescribed by it. Every other act against
a citizen is arbitrary and null. 12. Those who
solicit, promote, sign, execute or cause to be
executed such arbitrary acts are culpable, and
should be punished. 13. Citizens against
whom the execution of such acts is attempted
have the right of resistance by force. Every
citizen summoned or arrested by the authority of
law, and in the forms prescribed by it, should
instantly obey ; he renders himself guilty by
resistance. 14. Every man being presumed
innocent until declared guilty, should his arrest
be judged indispensable, all rigor not necessary
to secure his person should be severely repressed
by law. 15. None should be punished save in

It now appears plain that Robespierre, Marat, and the Mountaineers

generally were resolved that there should be no new government. The difference between them and their opponents was fundamental; to them the Revolution was an end, to the others a means. The Convention was a purely revolutionary body. It had arbitrarily absorbed all legislative and judicial functions, exercising them without responsibility to any code or constitution. For instance, in State Trials French law required three fourths of the voices for condemnation; had the rule been followed Louis XVI. would not have perished. Lanjuinais had pressed the point, and it was answered that the sentence on Louis was political, for the interest of the State; *salus populi suprema lex.* This implied that the Convention, turning aside from its appointed functions, had, in anticipation of the judicial forms it meant to establish, constituted itself into a Vigilance Committee to save the State in an emergency. But it never turned back again to its proper work. Now when the Constitution was framed, every possible obstruction was placed in the way of its adoption, which would have relegated most of the Mountaineers to private life.

Robespierre and Marat were in luck. The Paine-Condorcet Constitution omitted all mention of a Deity. Here was the immemorial and infallible recipe for discord, of which Robespierre made the most. He took the " Supreme Being " under his protection; he also took morality under his protection, insisting that the Paine-Condorcet Constitution gave liberty even to illicit traffic. While these discussions were going on Marat gained his triumphant acquittal from the charges made against him by the Girondins. This damaging blow further demoralized the majority which was eager for the Constitution. By violence, by appeals against atheism, by all crafty tactics, the Mountaineers secured recommitment of the Constitution. To the

virtue of a law established and promulgated previous to the offence, and legally applied. 16. A law that should punish offences committed before its existence would be an arbitrary Act. Retroactive effect given to any law is a crime. 17. Law should award only penalties strictly and evidently necessary to the general security ; they should be proportioned to the offence and useful to society. 18. The right of property consists in a man's being master in the disposal, at his will, of his goods, capital, income, and industry. 19. No kind of work, commerce, or culture can be interdicted for any one ; he may make, sell, and transport every species of production. 20. Every man may engage his services, and his time ; but he cannot sell himself ; his person is not an alienable property. 21. No one may be deprived of the least portion of his property without his consent, unless because of public necessity, legally determined, exacted openly, and under the condition of a just indemnity in advance. 22. No tax shall be established except for the general utility, and to relieve public needs. All citizens have the right to co-operate, personally or by their representatives, in the establishment of public contributions. 23. Instruction is the need of all, and society owes it equally to all its members. 24. Public succors are a sacred debt of society, and it is for the law to determine their extent and application. 25. The social guarantee of the rights of man rests on the national sovereignty. 26. This sovereignty is one, indivisible, imprescriptible, and inalienable. 27. It resides essentially in the whole people, and each citizen has an equal right to co-operate in its exercise. 28. No partial assemblage of citizens, and no individual may attribute to themselves sovereignty, to exercise authority and fill any public function, without a formal delegation by the law. 29. Social security cannot exist where the limits of public administration are not clearly determined by law, and where the responsibility of all public functionaries is not assured. 30. All citizens are bound to co-operate in this guarantee, and to enforce the law when summoned in its name. 31. Men united in society should have legal means of resisting oppression. In every free government the mode of resisting different acts of oppression should be regulated by the Constitution. 32. It is oppression when a law violates the natural rights, civil and political, which it should ensure. It is oppression when the law is violated by public officials in its application to individual cases. It is oppression when arbitrary acts violate the rights of citizens against the terms of the law. 33. A people has always the right to revise, reform, and change its Constitution. One generation has no right to bind future generations, and all heredity in offices is absurd and tyrannical. [The wording of the translation taken from " Œuvres Complètes de Condorcet," given in Dr. Conway's edition of Paine's Writings, vol. iii., p. 128, differs slightly from that given here.—H. B. B.].

Committee were added Hérault de Séchelles, Ramel, Mathieu, Couthon, Saint-Just,—all from the Committee of Public Safety. The Constitution as committed was the most republican document of the kind ever drafted, as remade it was a revolutionary instrument ; but its preamble read : "In the presence and under the guidance (*auspices*) of the Supreme Being, the French People declare," etc.

God was in the Constitution ; but when it was reported (June 10th) the Mountaineers had their opponents *en route* for the scaffold. The arraignment of the twenty-two, declared by the Convention " calumnious " six weeks before, was approved on June 2d. It was therefore easy to pass such a constitution as the victors desired. Some had suggested, during the theological debate, that " many crimes had been sanctioned by this King of kings,"—no doubt with emphasis on the discredited royal name. Robespierre identified his "Supreme Being" with NATURE, of whose ferocities the poor Girondins soon had tragical evidence.[1]

The Constitution was adopted by the Convention on June 25th ; it was ratified by the Communes August 10th. When it was proposed to organize a government under it, and dissolve the Convention, Robespierre remarked : *That sounds like a suggestion of Pitt!* Thereupon the Constitution was suspended until universal peace, and the Revolution superseded the Republic as end and aim of France.[2]

Some have ascribed to Robespierre a phrase he borrowed, on one occasion, from Voltaire, *Si Dieu n'existait pas, il faudrait l'inventer.* Robespierre's originality was that he did invent a god, made in his own image, and to that idol offered human sacrifices,—beginning with his own humanity. That he was genuinely superstitious is suggested by the plausibility with which his enemies connected him with the " prophetess," Catharine Théot, who pronounced him the reincarnate " Word of God." Certain it is that he revived the old forces of fanaticism, and largely by their aid crushed the Girondins, who were rationalists. Condorcet had said that in preparing a Constitution for France they had not consulted Numa's nymph or the pigeon of Mahomet; they had found human reason sufficient.

Corruption of best is worst. In the proportion that a humane deity would be a potent sanction for righteous laws, an inhuman deity is the sanction of inhuman laws. He who summoned a nature-god to the French Convention let loose the scourge on France. Nature inflicts on mankind, every day, a hundredfold the agonies of the Reign of Terror.

[1] " Les rois, les aristocrates, les tyrans qu'ils soient, sont des esclaves révoltés contre le souverain de la terre, qui est le *genre humain*, et contre le législateur de l'univers, qui est la *nature*."—Robespierre's final article of " Rights," adopted by the Jacobins, April 21, 1793. Should not slaves revolt?

[2] " I observed in the french revolutions that they always proceeded by stages, and made each stage a stepping-stone to another. The Convention, to amuse the people, voted a constitution, and then voted to suspend the practical establishment of it till after the war, and in the meantime to carry on a revolutionary government. When Robespierre fell they proposed bringing forward the *suspended* Constitution, and apparently for this purpose appointed a committee to frame what they called *organic laws*, and these organic laws turned out to be a new Constitution (the Directory Constitution which was in general a good one). When Bonaparte overthrew this Constitution he got himself appointed first *Consul* for ten years, then for life, and now Emperor with an hereditary succession."—Paine to Jefferson. MS. (Dec. 27, 1804). The Paine-Condorcet Constitution is printed in *Œuvres Complètes de Condorcet*, vol. xviii. That which superseded it may be read (the Declaration of Rights omitted) in the " Constitutional History of France. By Henry C. Lockwood." (New York, 1890). It is, *inter alia*, a sufficient reason for describing the latter as revolutionary, that it provides that a Convention, elected by a majority of the departments, and a tenth part of the primaries, to revise or alter the Constitution, shall be " formed in like manner as the legislatures, and unite in itself the highest power." In other words, instead of being limited to constitutional revision, may exercise all legislative and other functions, just as the existing Convention was doing.

Robespierre had projected into nature a sentimental conception of his own, but he had no power to master the force he had evoked. That had to take the shape of the nature-gods of all time, and straightway dragged the Convention down to the savage plane where discussion becomes an exchange of thunder-stones. Such relapses are not very difficult to effect in revolutionary times. By killing off sceptical variations, and cultivating conformity, a cerebral evolution proceeded for ages by which kind-hearted people were led to worship jealous and cruel gods, who, should they appear in human form, would be dealt with as criminals. Unfortunately, however, the nature-god does not so appear ; it is represented in euphemisms, while at the same time it coerces the social and human standard. Since the nature-god punishes hereditarily, kills every man at last, and so tortures millions that the suggestion of hell seems only too probable to those sufferers, a political system formed under the legitimacy of such a superstition must subordinate crimes to sins, regard atheism as worse than theft, acknowledge the arbitrary principle, and confuse retaliation with justice. From the time that the sheki-nah of the nature-god settled on the Mountain, offences were measured, not by their injury to man, but as insults to the Mountain-god, or to his anointed. In the mysterious counsels of the Committee of Public Safety the rewards are as little harmonious with the human standard as in the ages when sabbath-breaking and murder met the same doom. Under the paralyzing splendor of a divine authority, any such considerations as the suffering or death of men become petty. The average Mountaineer was unable to imagine that those who tried to save Louis had other than royalist motives. In this Armageddon the Girondins were far above their opponents in humanity and intelligence, but the conditions did not admit of an entire adherence to their honorable weapons of argument and eloquence. They too often used deadly threats, without meaning them ; the Mountaineers, who did mean them, took such phrases seriously, and believed the struggle to be one of life and death. Such phenomena of bloodshed, connected with absurdly inadequate causes, are known in history only where gods mingle in the fray. Reign of Terror ? What is the ancient reign of the god of battles, jealous, angry every day, with everlasting tortures of fire prepared for the unorthodox, however upright, even more than for the immoral ? In France too it was a suspicion of unorthodoxy in the revolutionary creed that plunged most of the sufferers into the lake of fire and brimstone.

From the time of Paine's speeches on the King's fate he was conscious that Marat's evil eye was on him. The American's inflexible republicanism had inspired the vigilance of the powerful journals of Brissot and Bonneville, which barred the way to any dictatorship. Paine was even propagating a doctrine against presidency, thus marring the example of the United States, on which ambitious Frenchmen, from Marat to the Napoleons, have depended for their stepping-stone to despotism. Marat could not have any doubt of Paine's devotion to the Republic, but knew well his weariness of the Revolution. In the simplicity of his republican faith Paine had made a great point of the near adoption of the Constitution, and dissolution of the Convention in five or six months, little dreaming that the Mountaineers were concentrating themselves on the aim of becoming masters of the existing Convention and then rendering it permanent. Marat regarded Paine's influence as dangerous to revolutionary government, and, as he afterwards admitted, desired to crush him. The proposed victim had several vulnerable points : he had been intimate with Gouverneur Morris, whose hostility to France was known ; he had been intimate with Dumouriez, declared a traitor ; and he had no connection with any of the Clubs, in which so many found asylum. He might have joined one of them had he known the French language, and perhaps it would have been prudent to unite himself with the "Cordeliers," in whose *esprit de corps* some of his friends found refuge.

However, the time of intimidation did not come for two months after the King's death, and Paine was busy with Condorcet on the task assigned them, of preparing an Address to the People of England concerning the war of their government against France. This work, if ever completed, does not appear to have been published. It was entrusted (February 1st) to Barrère, Paine, Condorcet, and M. Faber. As Frédéric Masson, the learned librarian and historian of the Office of Foreign Affairs, has found some trace of its being assigned to Paine and Condorcet, it may be that further research will bring to light the Address. It could hardly have been completed before the warfare broke out between the Mountain and the Girondins, when anything emanating from Condorcet and Paine would have been delayed, if not suppressed. There are one or two brief essays in Condorcet's works—notably "The French Republic to Free Men"— which suggest collaboration with Paine, and may be fragments of their Address.[1] At this time the long friendship between Paine and Condorcet, and the Marchioness too, had become very intimate.

[1] "Œuvres Complètes de Condorcet," Paris, 1804, t. xvi., p. 16: "La République Française aux hommes libres." In 1794, when Paine was in prison, a pamphlet was issued by the revolutionary government, entitled: "An Answer to the Declaration of the King of England, respecting his Motives for Carrying on the Present War, and his Conduct towards France." This anonymous pamphlet, which is in English, replies to the royal proclamation of October 29th, and bears evidence of being written while the English still occupied Toulon or early in November, 1793. There are passages in it that suggest the hand of Paine, along with others which he could not have written. It is possible that some composition of his, in pursuance of the task assigned him and Condorcet, was utilized by the Committee of Public Safety in its answer to George III.

The two men had acted together on the King's trial at every step, and their speeches on bringing Louis to trial suggest previous consultations between them.

Early in April Paine was made aware of Marat's hostility to him. General Thomas Ward reported to him a conversation in which Marat had said: "Frenchmen are mad to allow foreigners to live among them. They should cut off their ears, let them bleed a few days, and then cut off their heads." "But you yourself are a foreigner," Ward had replied, in allusion to Marat's Swiss birth.[2] The answer is not reported. At length a tragical incident occurred, just before the trial of Marat (April 13th), which brought Paine face to face with this enemy. A wealthy young Englishman, named Johnson, with whom Paine had been intimate in London, had followed him to Paris, where he lived in the same house with his friend. His love of Paine amounted to worship. Having heard of Marat's intention to have Paine's life taken, such was the young enthusiast's despair, and so terrible the wreck of his republican dreams, that he resolved on suicide. He made a will bequeathing his property to Paine, and stabbed himself. Fortunately he was saved by some one who entered just as he was about to give himself the third blow. It may have been Paine himself who then saved his friend's life; at any rate, he did so eventually.

The decree for Marat's trial was made amid galleries crowded with his adherents, male and female ("Dames de la Fraternité"), who hurled cries of wrath on every one who said a word against him. All were armed, the women ostentatious of their poignards. The trial before the Revolutionary Tribunal was already going in Marat's favor, when it was determined by the Girondins to bring forward this affair of Johnson. Paine was not, apparently, a party to this

[2] "Englishmen in the French Revolution." By John G. Alger. London, 1889, p. 176. (A book of many blunders.)

move, though he had enjoined no secrecy in telling his friend Brissot of the incident, which occurred before Marat was accused. On April 16th there appeared in Brissot's journal *Le Patriote Français*, the following paragraph :

"A sad incident has occurred to apprise the anarchists of the mournful fruits of their frightful teaching. An Englishman, whose name I reserve, had abjured his country because of his detestation of kings ; he came to France hoping to find there liberty; he saw only its mask on the hideous visage of anarchy. Heart-broken by this spectacle, he determined on self-destruction. Before dying, he wrote the following words, which we have read, as written by his own trembling hand, on a paper which is in the possession of a distinguished foreigner :—'I had come to France to enjoy liberty, but Marat has assassinated it. Anarchy is even more cruel than despotism. I am unable to endure this grievous sight, of the triumph of imbecility and inhumanity over talent and virtue.'"

The acting editor of *Le Patriote Français*, Girey-Dupré, was summoned before the Tribunal, where Marat was on trial, and testified that the note published had been handed to him by Brissot, who assured him that it was from the original, in the hands of Thomas Paine. Paine deposed that he had been unacquainted with Marat before the Convention assembled ; that he had not supposed Johnson's note to have any connection with the accusations against Marat.

President.—Did you give a copy of the note to Brissot ?
Paine.—I showed him the original.
President.—Did you send it to him as it is printed ?
Paine.—Brissot could only have written this note after what I read to him, and told him. I would observe to the tribunal that Johnson gave himself two blows with the knife after he had understood that Marat would denounce him.
Marat.—Not because I would denounce the youth who stabbed himself, but because I wish to denounce Thomas Paine.[1]
Paine (continuing).—Johnson had for some time suffered mental anguish. As for Marat, I never

spoke to him but once. In the lobby of the Convention he said to me that the English people are free and happy ; I replied, they groan under a double despotism.[2]

No doubt it had been resolved to keep secret the fact that young Johnson was still alive. The moment was critical ; a discovery that Brissot had written or printed "avant de mourir" of one still alive might have precipitated matters.

It came out in the trial that Marat, addressing a club ("Friends of Liberty and Equality "), had asked them to register a vow to recall from the Convention "all of those faithless members who had betrayed their duties in trying to save a tyrant's life," such deputies being "traitors, royalists, or fools."

Meanwhile the Constitution was undergoing discussion in the Convention, and to that Paine now gave his entire attention. On April 20th the Convention, about midnight, when the Moderates had retired and the Mountaineers found themselves masters of the field, voted to entertain the petition of the Parisian sections against the Girondins. Paine saw the star of the Republic sinking. On "April 20th, 2d year of the Republic," he wrote as follows to Jefferson :

"My dear Friend,—The gentleman (Dr. Romer) to whom I entrust this letter is an intimate acquaintance of Lavater ; but I have not had the opportunity of seeing him, as he had sett off for Havre prior to my writing this letter, which I forward to him under cover from one of his friends, who is also an acquaintance of mine.

"We are now in an extraordinary crisis, and it is not altogether without some considerable faults here. Dumouriez, partly from having no fixed principles of his own, and partly from the continual persecution of the Jacobins, who act without either prudence or morality, has gone off to the Enemy, and taken a considerable part of the Army with him. The expedition to Holland has totally failed and all Brabant is again in the hands of the Austrians.

"You may suppose the consternation which such a sudden reverse of fortune has occasioned, but it has been without commotion. Dumouriez threatened to be in Paris in three weeks. It is now three weeks ago ; he is still on the frontier near to Mons with the Enemy, who do not make

---

[1] It would appear that Paine had not been informed until Marat declared it. and was confirmed by the testimony of Choppin, that the attempted suicide was on his account.

[2] *Moniteur*, April 24, 1793.

any progress. Dumouriez has proposed to re-establish the former Constitution, in which plan the Austrians act with him. But if France and the National Convention act prudently this project will not succeed. In the first place there is a popular disposition against it, and there is force sufficient to prevent it. In the next place, a great deal is to be taken into the calculation with respect to the Enemy. There are now so many powers accidentally jumbled together as to render it exceedingly difficult to them to agree upon any common object.

"The first object, that of restoring the old Monarchy, is evidently given up by the proposal to re-establish the late Constitution. The object of England and Prussia was to preserve Holland, and the object of Austria was to recover Brabant ; while those separate objects lasted, each party having one, the Confederation could hold together, each helping the other ; but after this I see not how a common object is to be formed. To all this is to be added the probable disputes about opportunity, the expense, and the projects of reimbursements. The Enemy has once adventured into France, and they had the permission or the good fortune to get back again. On every military calculation it is a hazardous adventure, and armies are not much disposed to try a second time the ground upon which they have been defeated.

"Had this revolution been conducted consistently with its principles, there was once a good prospect of extending liberty through the greatest part of Europe ; but I now relinquish that hope. Should the Enemy by venturing into France put themselves again in a condition of being captured, the hope will revive ; but this is a risk that I do not wish to see tried, lest it should fail.

"As the prospect of a general freedom is now much shortened, I begin to contemplate returning home. I shall await the event of the proposed Constitution, and then take my final leave of Europe. I have not written to the President, as I have nothing to communicate more than in this letter. Please to present to him my affection and compliments, and remember me among the circle of my friends. Your sincere and affectionate friend,

"THOMAS PAINE.

"P. S. I just now received a letter from General Lewis Morris, who tells me that the house and Barn on my farm at N. Rochelle are burnt down. I assure you I shall not bring money enough to build another."

Four days after this letter was written Marat, triumphant, was crowned with oak leaves. Foufrede in his speech (April 16th) had said : "Marat has formally demanded dictatorship." This was the mob's reply : *Bos locutus est.*

With Danton, Paine had been on friendly terms, though he described as "rose water" the author's pleadings against the guillotine. On May 6th, Paine wrote to Danton a letter brought to light by Taine, who says : "Compared with the speeches and writings of the time, it produces the strangest effect by its practical good sense."[1] Dr. Robinet also finds here evidence of "a lucid and wise intellect."[2]

"PARIS, May 6th, 2nd year of the Republic (1793).

"CITOYEN DANTON :

"As you read English, I write this letter to you without passing it through the hands of a translator. I am exceedingly disturbed at the distractions, jealousies, discontents and uneasiness that reign among us, and which, if they continue, will bring ruin and disgrace on the Republic. When I left America in the year 1787, it was my intention to return the year following, but the French Revolution, and the prospect it afforded of extending the principles of liberty and fraternity through the greater part of Europe, have induced me to prolong my stay upwards of six years. I now despair of seeing the great object of European liberty accomplished, and my despair arises not from the combined foreign powers, not from the intrigues of aristocracy and priestcraft, but from the tumultuous misconduct with which the internal affairs of the present revolution is conducted.

"All that now can be hoped for is limited to France only, and I agree with your motion of not interfering in the government of any foreign country, nor permitting any foreign country to interfere in the government of France. This decree was necessary as a preliminary toward terminating the war. But while these internal contentions continue, while the hope remains to the enemy of seeing the Republic fall to pieces, while not only the representatives of the departments but representation itself is publicly insulted, as it has lately been and now is by the people of Paris, or at least by the tribunes, the enemy will be encouraged to hang about the frontiers and await the issue of circumstances.

"I observe that the confederated powers have not yet recognised Monsieur, or D'Artois, as regent, nor made any proclamation in favour of any of the Bourbons ; but this negative conduct admits of two different conclusions. The one is that of abandoning the Bourbons and the war together ; the other is that of changing the object of the war and substituting a partition scheme in the place of their first object, as they have done by Poland. If this should be their

---

[1] "La Révolution," ii., pp. 382, 413, 414.
[2] "Danton Emigré," p. 177.

object, the internal contentions that now rage will favour that object far more than it favoured their former object. The danger every day increases of a rupture between Paris and the departments. The departments did not send their deputies to Paris to be insulted, and every insult shown to them is an insult to the departments that elected and sent them. I see but one effectual plan to prevent this rupture taking place, and that is to fix the residence of the Convention, and of the future assemblies, at a distance from Paris.

"I saw, during the American Revolution, the exceeding inconvenience that arose by having the government of Congress within the limits of any Municipal Jurisdiction. Congress first resided in Philadelphia, and after a residence of four years it found it necessary to leave it. It then adjourned to the State of Jersey. It afterwards removed to New York ; it again removed from New York to Philadelphia, and after experiencing in every one of these places the great inconvenience of a government, it formed the project of building a Town, not within the limits of any municipal jurisdiction, for the future residence of Congress. In any one of the places where Congress resided, the municipal authority privately or openly opposed itself to the authority of Congress, and the people of each of those places expected more attention from Congress than their equal share with the other States amounted to. The same thing now takes place in France, but in a far greater excess.

"I see also another embarrassing circumstance arising in Paris of which we have had full experience in America. I mean that of fixing the price of provisions. But if this measure is to be attempted it ought to be done by the Municipality. The Convention has nothing to do with regulations of this kind ; neither can they be carried into practice. The people of Paris may say they will not give more than a certain price for provisions, but as they cannot compel the country people to bring provisions to market the consequence will be directly contrary to their expectations, and they will find dearness and famine instead of plenty and cheapness. They may force the price down upon the stock in hand, but after that the market will be empty.

"I will give you an example. In Philadelphia we undertook, among other regulations of this kind, to regulate the price of Salt ; the consequence was that no Salt was brought to market, and the price rose to thirty-six shillings sterling per Bushel. The price before the war was only one shilling and sixpence per Bushel ; and we regulated the price of flour (farine) till there was none in the market, and the people were glad to procure it at any price.

"There is also a circumstance to be taken into the account which is not much attended to. The assignats are not of the same value they were a year ago, and as the quantity increases the value of them will diminish. This gives the appearance of things being dear when they are not so in fact, for in the same proportion that any kind of money falls in value articles rise in price. If it were not for this the quantity of assignats would be too great to be circulated. Paper money in America fell so much in value from this excessive quantity of it, that in the year 1781 I gave three hundred paper dollars for one pair of worsted stockings. What I write you upon this subject is experience, and not merely opinion.

"I have no personal interest in any of these matters, nor in any party disputes. I attend only to general principles.

"As soon as a constitution shall be established I shall return to America ; and be the future prosperity of France ever so great, I shall enjoy no other part of it than the happiness of knowing it. In the mean time I am distressed to see matters so badly conducted, and so little attention paid to moral principles. It is these things that injure the character of the Revolution and discourage the progress of liberty all over the world.

"When I began this letter I did not intend making it so lengthy, but since I have gone thus far I will fill up the remainder of the sheet with such matters as occur to me.

"There ought to be some regulation with respect to the spirit of denunciation that now prevails. If every individual is to indulge his private malignacy or his private ambition, to denounce at random and without any kind of proof, all confidence will be undermined and all authority be destroyed. Calumny is a species of Treachery that ought to be punished as well as any other kind of Treachery. It is a private vice productive of public evils ; because it is possible to irritate men into disaffection by continual calumny who never intended to be disaffected. It is therefore, equally as necessary to guard against the evils of unfounded or malignant suspicion as against the evils of blind confidence. It is equally as necessary to protect the characters of public officers from calumny as it is to punish them for treachery or misconduct. For my own part I shall hold it a matter of doubt, until better evidence arises than is known at present, whether Dumouriez has been a traitor from policy or from resentment. There was certainly a time when he acted well, but it is not every man whose mind is strong enough to bear up against ingratitude, and I think he experienced a great deal of this before he revolted. Calumny becomes harmless and defeats itself when it attempts to act upon too large a scale. Thus the denunciation of the Sections [of Paris] against the twenty-two deputies [Girondists] falls to the ground. The departments that elected them are better judges of their moral and political characters than those who have denounced them. This denunciation will injure Paris in the opinion of the departments because it has the appearance of dictating to them what sort of deputies they shall elect. Most of the acquaintances that I have in the convention are among those who are in that list, and I know there are not better men nor better patriots than what they are.

"I have written a letter to Marat of the same date as this but not on the same subject. He may show it to you if he chuse.

"Votre Ami,
"THOMAS PAINE.

" Citoyen Danton."

It is to be hoped that Paine's letter to Marat may be discovered in France; it is shown by the Cobbett papers, printed in the Appendix, that he kept a copy, which there is reason to fear perished with General Bonneville's library in St. Louis. Whatever may be the letter's contents, there is no indication that thereafter Marat troubled Paine. Possibly Danton and Marat compared their letters, and the latter got it into his head that hostility to this American, anxious only to cross the ocean, could be of no advantage to him. Or perhaps he remembered that if a hue and cry were raised against "foreigners" it could not stop short of his own leaf-crowned Neufchatel head. He had shown some sensitiveness about that at his trial. Samson-Pegnet had testified that, at conversations in Paine's house, Marat had been reported as saying that it was necessary to massacre all the foreigners, especially the English. This Marat pronounced an "atrocious calumny, a device of the statesmen [his epithet for Girondins] to render me odious." Whatever his motives, there is reason to believe that Marat no longer included Paine in his proscribed list. Had it been otherwise a fair opportunity of striking down Paine presented itself on the occasion, already alluded to, when Paine gave his testimony in favor of General Miranda. Miranda was tried before the Revolutionary Tribunal on May 12th, and three days following. He had served under Dumouriez, was defeated, and was suspected of connivance with his treacherous commander. Paine was known to have been friendly with Dumouriez, and his testimony in favor

of Miranda might naturally have been used against both men. Miranda was, however, acquitted, and that did not make Marat better disposed towards that adventurer's friends, all Girondins, or, like Paine, who belonged to no party, hostile to Jacobinism. Yet when, on June 2d, the doomed Girondins were arrested, there were surprising exceptions: Paine and his literary collaborateur, Condorcet. Moreover, though the translator of Paine's works, Lanthenas, was among the proscribed, his name was erased on Marat's motion.

On June 7th Robespierre demanded a more stringent law against foreigners, and one was soon after passed ordering their imprisonment. It was understood that this could not apply to the two foreigners in the Convention—Paine and Anacharsis Clootz,—though it was regarded as a kind of warning to them. I have seen it stated, but without authority, that Paine had been admonished by Danton to stay away from the Convention on June 2d, and from that day there could not be the slightest utility in his attendance. The Mountaineers had it all their own way. For simply criticising the Constitution they brought forward in place of that of the first committee, Condorcet had to fly from prosecution. Others also fled, among them Brissot and Duchatel. What with the arrestations and flights Paine found himself, in June, almost alone. In the Convention he was sometimes the solitary figure left on the Plain, where but now sat the brilliant statesmen of France. They, his beloved friends, have started in procession towards the guillotine, for even flight must end there ; daily others are pressed into their ranks ; his own summons, he feels, is only a question of a few weeks or days. How Paine loved those men—Brissot, Condorcet, Lasource, Duchatel, Vergniaud, Gensonné ! Never was man more devoted to his intellectual comrades. Even across a century one may realize what it meant to him, that march of some of his best friends to the scaffold, while others were hunted through France, and the agony of their families, most of whom he well knew.

Alas, even this is not the worst ! For what were the personal fate of himself or any compared with the fearful fact that the harvest is past and the republic not saved ! Thus had ended all his labors, and his visions of the Commonwealth of Man. The time had come when many besides poor Johnson sought peace in annihilation. Paine, heartbroken, sought oblivion in brandy. Recourse to such anæsthetic, of which any affectionate man might fairly avail himself under such incredible agony as the ruin of his hopes and the approaching murder of his dearest friends, was hitherto unknown in Paine's life. He drank freely, as was the custom of his time ; but with the exception of the evidence of an enemy at his trial in England,[1] that he once saw him under the influence of wine after a dinner party (1792), which he admitted was "unusual," no intimation of excess is discoverable in any contemporary record of Paine until this his fifty-seventh year. He afterwards told his friend Rickman that, "borne down by public and private affliction, he had been driven to excesses in Paris " ; and, as it was about this time that Gouverneur Morris and Colonel Bosville, who had reasons for disparaging Paine, reported stories of his drunkenness (growing ever since), we may assign the

[1] Evidence of Chapman, the printer, at the trial for seditious libel (" Rights of Man "), Dec., 1792.—H.B.B.

excesses mainly to June. It will be seen by comparison of the dates of events and documents presently mentioned that Paine could not have remained long in this pardonable refuge of mental misery. Charlotte Corday's poignard cut a rift in the black cloud. After that tremendous July 13th there is positive evidence not only of sobriety, but of life and work on Paine's part that make the year memorable.

Marat dead, hope springs up for the arrested Girondins. They are not yet in prison, but under " arrestation in their homes " ; death seemed inevitable while Marat lived, but Charlotte Corday has summoned a new leader. Why may Paine's imperilled comrades not come forth again ? Certainly they will if the new chieftain is Danton, who under his radical rage hides a heart. Or if Marat's mantle falls on Robespierre, would not that scholarly lawyer, who would have abolished capital punishment, reverse Marat's cruel decrees ? Robespierre had agreed to the new Constitution (reported by Paine's friend, Hérault de Séchelles) and when even that dubious instrument returns with the popular sanction, all may be well. The Convention, which is doing everything except what it was elected to do, will then dissolve, and the happy Republic remember it only as a nightmare. So Paine takes heart again, abandons the bowl of forgetfulness, and becomes a republican Socrates instructing disciples in an old French garden.

CHAPTER XXVIII

A GARDEN IN THE FAUBOURG ST. DENIS

Sir George Trevelyan has written a pregnant passage, reminding the world of the moral burden which radicals in England had to bear a hundred years ago.

"When to speak or write one's mind on politics is to obtain the reputation, and render one's self liable to the punishment of a criminal, social discredit, with all its attendant moral dangers, soon attaches itself to the more humble opponents of a ministry. To be outside the law as a publisher or a pamphleteer is only less trying to conscience and conduct than to be outside the law as a smuggler or a poacher ; and those who, ninety years ago, placed themselves within the grasp of the penal statutes as they were administered in England and barbarously perverted in Scotland were certain to be very bold men, and pretty sure to be unconventional up to the uttermost verge of respectability. As an Italian Liberal was sometimes half a bravo, and a Spanish patriot often more than half a brigand, so a British Radical under George the Third had generally, it must be confessed, a dash of the Bohemian. Such, in a more or less mitigated form, were Paine and Cobbett, Hunt, Hone, and Holcroft; while the same causes in part account for the elfish vagaries of Shelley and the grim improprieties of Godwin. But when we recollect how these, and the like of these, gave up every hope of worldly prosperity, and set their life and liberty in continual hazard for the sake of that personal and political freedom which we now exercise as unconsciously as we breathe the air, it would be too exacting to require that each and all of them should have lived as decorously as Perceval, and died as solvent as Bishop Tomline." [1]

To this right verdict it may be added that, even at the earlier period when it was most applicable, the radicals could only produce one rival in profligacy (John Wilkes) to their aristocratic oppressors. It may also be noted as a species of homage that the slightest failings of eminent reformers become historic. The vices of Burke and Fox are forgotten. Who remembers that the younger Pitt was brought to an early grave by the bottle? But every fault of those who resisted his oppression is placed under a solar microscope. Although, as Sir George affirms, the oppressors largely caused the faults, this homage to the higher moral standard of the reformers may be accepted. [2]

[1] "Early History of Charles James Fox," American ed., p. 440.

[2] The following document was found among the papers of Mr. John Hall, originally of Leicester, England, and has been forwarded to me by his descendant, J. Dutton Steele, Jr., of Philadelphia:

"A Copy of a Letter from the chairman of a meeting of the Gentry and Clergy at Atherstone, written in consequence of an envious schoolmaster and two or three others who informed the meeting that the Excise Officers of Polesworth were employed in distributing the Rights of Man; but which was very false.

"Sir: I should think it unnecessary to inform you, that the purport of his Majesty's proclamation in the Month of May last, and the numerous meetings which are daily taking

It was, indeed, a hard time for reformers in England. Among them were many refined gentlemen who felt that it was no country for a thinker and scholar to live in. Among the pathetic pictures of the time was that of the twelve scholars, headed by Coleridge and Southey, and twelve ladies, who found the atmosphere of England too impure for any but slaves to breathe, and proposed to seek in America some retreat where their pastoral "pantisocrasy" might be realized. Lack of funds prevented the fulfilment of this dream, but that it should have been an object of concert and endeavor, in that refined circle at Bristol, is a memorable sign of that dreadful time. In the absence of means to form such communities, preserving the culture and charm of a society evolved out of barbarism, apart from the walls of a remaining political barbarism threatening it with their ruins, some scholars were compelled, like Coleridge, to rejoin the feudalists, and help them to buttress the crumbling castle. They secured themselves from the social deterioration of living on wild "honey-dew" in a wilderness, at cost of wearing intellectual masks. Some fled to America, like Cobbett. But others fixed their abode in Paris, where radicalism was

place both in Town and Country, are for the avowed purpose of suppressing treasonable and seditious writings amongst which Mr. Payne's Rights of Man ranks most conspicuous. Were I not informed you have taken some pains in spreading that publication, I write to say If you don't from this time adopt a different kind of conduct you will be taken notice of in such way as may prove very disagreeable.

"The Eyes of the Country are upon you and you will do well in future to shew yourself faithful to the Master who employs you.

"I remain,

"Your Hble servant,

"(Signed) Jos. Boultbee.

"Baxterby, Decr. 15th, '92.

"N. B. The letter was written the next morning after the Meeting where most of the Loyal souls got drunk to an uncommon degree. They drank his Majesty's health so often the reckoning amounted to 7s. 6d. each. One of the informers threw down a shilling and ran away."

fashionable, and invested with the charm of the *salon* and the theatre.

Before the declaration of war Paine had been on friendly terms with some eminent Englishmen in Paris : he dined every week with Lord Lauderdale, Dr. John Moore, an author, and others in some restaurant. After most of these had followed Lord Gower to England he had to be more guarded. A British agent, Major Semple, approached him under the name of Major Lisle. He professed to be an Irish patriot, wore the green cockade, and desired introduction to the Minister of War. Paine fortunately knew too many Irishmen to fall into this snare.[1] But General Miranda, as we have seen, fared better. Paine was, indeed, so overrun with visitors and adventurers that he appropriated two mornings of each week at the Philadelphia House for levees. These, however, became insufficient to. stem the constant stream of visitors, including spies and lion-hunters, so that he had little time for consultation with the men and women whose co-operation he needed in public affairs. He therefore leased an out-of-the-way house, reserving knowledge of it for particular friends, while still retaining his address at the Philadelphia Hotel, where the levees were continued.

The irony of fate had brought an old mansion of Madame de Pompadour to become the residence of Thomas Paine and his half-dozen English disciples. It was then, and still is, No. 63 Faubourg St. Denis. Here, where a King's mistress held her merry fêtes, and issued the decrees of her reign—sometimes of terror,—the little band of English humanitarians read and conversed, and sported in the garden. In a little essay on "Forgetfulness," addressed to his friend, Lady Smith, Paine described these lodgings.

"They were the most agreeable, for situation, of any I ever had in Paris, except that they were too remote from the Convention, of which I was then a member. But this was recompensed by their being also remote from the alarms and confusion into which the interior of Paris was then often thrown. The news of those things used to arrive to us, as if we were in a state of tranquillity in the country. The house, which was enclosed by a wall and gateway from the street, was a good deal like an old mansion farm-house, and the court-yard was like a farm yard, stocked with fowls,—ducks, turkies, and geese ; which, for amusement, we used to feed out of the parlor window on the ground floor. There were some hutches for rabbits, and a sty with two pigs. Beyond was a garden of more than an acre of ground, well laid out, and stocked with excellent fruit trees. The orange, apricot, and greengage plum were the best I ever tasted ; and it is the only place where I saw the wild cucumber. The place had formerly been occupied by some curious person.

"My apartments consisted of three rooms ; the first for wood, water, etc. ; the next was the bedroom ; and beyond it the sitting room, which looked into the garden through a glass door ; and on the outside there was a small landing place railed in, and a flight of narrow stairs almost hidden by the vines that grew over it, by which I could descend into the garden without going down stairs through the house. . . . I used to find some relief by walking alone in the garden, after dark, and cursing with hearty good will the authors of that terrible system that had turned the character of the Revolution I had been proud to defend. I went but little to the Convention, and then only to make my appearance, because I found it impossible to join in their tremendous decrees, and useless and dangerous to oppose them. My having voted and spoken extensively, more so than any other member, against the execution of the king, had already fixed a mark upon me ; neither dared any of my associates in the Convention to translate and speak in French for me anything I might have dared to have written. . . . Pen and ink were then of no use to me ; no good could be done by writing, and no printer dared to print ; and whatever I might have written, for my private amusement, as anecdotes of the times, would have been continually exposed to be examined, and tortured into any meaning that the rage of party might fix upon it. And as to softer subjects, my heart was in distress at the fate of my friends, and my harp hung upon the weeping willows.

"As it was summer, we spent most of our time in the garden, and passed it away in those childish amusements that serve to keep reflection from the mind,—such as marbles, Scotch hops, battledores, etc., at which we were all pretty expert. In this retired manner we remained about six or seven weeks, and our landlord went every evening into the city to bring us the news of the day and the evening journal."[2]

---

[1] Rickman, p. 129.

[2] "The Writings of Thomas Paine" (Conway), vol. iii., pp. 316–18.—H. B. B.

The "we" included young Johnson, Mr. and Mrs. Christie, Mr. Choppin, probably Mr. Shapworth, an American, and M. Laborde, a scientific friend of Paine. These appear to have entered with Paine into co-operative housekeeping, though taking their chief meals at the restaurants. In the evenings they were joined by others,—the Brissots (before the arrest), Nicholas Bonneville, Joel Barlow, Captain Imlay, Mary Wollstonecraft, the Rolands. Mystical Madame Roland dreaded Paine's power, which she considered more adapted to pull down than to build, but has left a vivid impression of "the boldness of his conceptions, the originality of his style, the striking truths he throws out bravely among those whom they offend." The Mr. Shapworth alluded to is mentioned in a manuscript journal of Daniel Constable, sent me by his nephew, Clair J. Grece, LL.D. This English gentleman visited Baton Rouge and Shapworth's plantation in 1822. "Mr. S.," he says, "has a daughter married to the Governor [Robinson], has travelled in Europe, married a French lady. He is a warm friend of Thomas Paine, as is his son-in-law. He lived with Paine many months at Paris. He [Paine] was then a sober, correct gentleman in appearance and manner." The English refugees, persecuted for selling the "Rights of Man," were, of course, always welcomed by Paine, and poor Rickman was his guest during this summer of 1793.[1] The

following reminiscence of Paine, at a time when Gouverneur Morris was (for reasons that presently appear) reporting him to his American friends as generally drunk, was written by Rickman:

"He usually rose about seven. . . . After breakfast he usually strayed an hour or two in the garden, where he one morning pointed out the kind of spider whose web furnished him with the first idea of constructing his iron bridge; a fine model of which, in mahogany, is preserved in Paris. The little happy circle who lived with him will ever remember those days with delight: with these select friends he would talk of his boyish days, played at chess, whist, piquet, or cribbage, and enliven the moments by many interesting anecdotes: with these he would play at marbles, scotch hops, battledores, etc.: on the broad and fine gravel walk at the upper end of the garden, and then retire to his boudoir, where he was up to his knees in letters and papers of various descriptions. Here he remained till dinner time; and unless he visited Brissot's family, or some particular friend, in the evening, which was his frequent custom, he joined again the society of his favorites and fellow-boarders, with whom his conversation was often witty and cheerful, always acute and improving, but never frivolous. Incorrupt, straightforward, and sincere, he pursued his political course in France, as everywhere else, let the government or clamor or faction of the day be what it might, with firmness, with clearness, and without a shadow of turning."[2]

In the spring of 1890 the present writer visited the spot. The lower front of the old mansion is divided into shops, —a Fruiterer being appropriately next the gateway, which now opens into a wide thoroughfare. Above the rooms once occupied by Paine was the sign "Ecrivain Publique,"—placed there by a Mademoiselle who wrote letters and

---

[1] Rickman appears to have escaped from England in 1792, according to the following sonnet sent me by Dr. Grece. It is headed: "Sonnet to my Little Girl, 1792. Written at Calais, on being pursued by cruel prosecution and persecution."

"Farewell, sweet babe! and mayst thou never know,
Like me, the pressure of exceeding woe.
Some griefs (for they are human nature's right)
On life's eventful stage will be thy lot;
Some generous cares to clear thy mental sight,
Some pains, in happiest hours, perhaps, begot;

But mayst thou ne'er be, like thy father, driven
From a loved partner, family, and home,
Snatched from each heart-felt bliss, domestic heaven!
From native shores, and all that's valued, roam.
Oh, may bad governments, the source of human woe,
Ere thou becom'st mature, receive their deadly blow;
Then mankind's greatest curse thou ne'er wilt know."

[2] Rickman, pp. 134-36.—H. B. B.

advertisements for humble neighbors not expert in penmanship. At the end of what was once the garden is a Printer's office, in which was a large lithograph portrait of Victor Hugo. The printer, his wife, and little daughter were folding publications of the " Extreme Left." Near the door remains a veritable survival of the garden and its living tenants which amused Paine and his friends. There were two ancient fruit trees, of which one was dying, but the other budding in the spring sunshine. There were ancient coops with ducks, and pigeon-houses with pigeons, also rabbits, and some flowers. This little nook, of perhaps forty square feet, and its animals, had been there—so an old inhabitant told me—time out of mind. They belonged to nobody in particular ; the pigeons were fed by the people around; the fowls were probably kept there by some poultryman. There were eager groups attending every stage of the investigation. The exceptional antiquity of the mansion had been recognized by its occupants,—several families,—but without curiosity, and perhaps with regret. Comparatively few had heard of Paine.

Shortly before I had visited the garden near Florence which Boccaccio's immortal tales have kept in perennial beauty through five centuries. It may be that in the far future some brother of Boccace will bequeath to Paris as sweet a legend of the garden where beside the plague of blood the prophet of the universal Republic realized his dream in microcosm. Here gathered sympathetic spirits from America, England, France, Germany, Holland, Switzerland, freed from prejudices of race, rank, or nationality, striving to be mutually helpful, amusing themselves with Arcadian sports, studying nature, enriching each other by exchange of experiences. It is certain that in all the world there was no group of men and women more disinterestedly absorbed in the work of benefiting their fellow-beings. They could not, however, like Boccaccio's ladies and gentlemen " kill Death " by their witty tales ; for

presently beloved faces disappeared from their circle, and the cruel axe was gleaming over them.

And now the old hotel became the republican capitol of Europe. There sat an international Premier with his Cabinet, concentrated on the work of saving the Girondins. He was indeed treated by the Executive government as a Minister. It was supposed by Paine and believed by his adherents that Robespierre had for him some dislike. Paine in later years wrote of Robespierre as a "hypocrite," and the epithet may have a significance not recognized by his readers. It is to me probable that Paine considered himself deceived by Robespierre with professions of respect, if not of friendliness before being cast into prison ; a conclusion naturally based on requests from the Ministers for opinions on public affairs. The archives of the Revolution contain various evidences of this, and several papers by Paine evidently in reply to questions. We may feel certain that every subject propounded was carefully discussed in Paine's little cosmopolitan Cabinet before his opinion was transmitted to the revolutionary Cabinet of Committees. In reading the subjoined documents it must be borne in mind that Robespierre had not yet been suspected of the cruelty presently associated with his name. The Queen and the Girondist leaders were yet alive. Of these leaders Paine was known to be the friend, and it was of the utmost importance that he should be suavely loyal to the government that had inherited these prisoners from Marat's time.

The first of these papers is erroneously endorsed " January 1793. Thom. Payne. Copie," in the French State Archives.[1] Its reference to the defeat of the Duke of York at Dunkirk assigns its date to the late summer. It is headed, " Observations on the situation of the Powers joined against France."

" It is always useful to know the position and the designs of one's enemies. It is much easier

---

[1] États Unis. Vol. 37. Document 39.

to do so by combining and comparing the events, and by examining the consequences which result from them, than by forming one's judgment by letters found or intercepted. These letters could be fabricated with the intention of deceiving, but events or circumstances have a character which is proper to them. If in the course of our political operations we mistake the designs of our enemy, it leads us to do precisely that which he desired we should do, and it happens, by the fact, but against our intentions, that we work for him.

"It appears at first sight that the coalition against France is not of the nature of those which form themselves by a treaty. It has been the work of circumstances. It is a heterogeneous mass, the parts of which dash against each other, and often neutralise themselves. They have but one single point of reunion, the re-establishment of the monarchical government in France. Two means can conduct them to the execution of this plan. The first is, to re-establish the Bourbons, and with them the Monarchy; the second, to make a division similar to that which they have made in Poland, and to reign themselves in France. The political questions to be solved are, then, to know on which of these two plans it is most probable, the united Powers will act; and which are the points of these plans on which they will agree or disagree.

"Supposing their aim to be the re-establishment of the Bourbons, the difficulty which will present itself, will be, to know who will be their Allies?

"Will England consent to the re-establishment of the compact of family in the person of the Bourbons, against whom she has machinated and fought since her existence? Will Prussia consent to re-establish the alliance which subsisted between France and Austria, or will Austria wish to re-establish the ancient alliance between France and Prussia, which was directed against her? Will Spain, or any other maritime Power, allow France and her Marine to ally themselves to England? In fine, will any of these Powers consent to furnish forces which could be directed against herself? However, all these cases present themselves in the hypothesis of the restoration of the Bourbons.

"If we suppose that their plan be the dismemberment of France, difficulties will present themselves under another form, but not of the same nature. It will no longer be question, in this case, of the Bourbons, as their position will be worse; for if their preservation is a part of their first plan, their destruction ought to enter in the second; because it is necessary for the success of the dismembering that not a single pretendant to the Crown of France should exist.

"As one must think of all the probabilities in political calculations, it is not unlikely that some of the united Powers, having in view the first of these plans, and others the second,—that this may be one of the causes of their disagreement. It is to be remembered that Russia recognised a Regency from the beginning of Spring; not one of the other Powers followed her example. The distance of Russia from France, and the different countries by which she is separated from her, leave no doubt as to her dispositions with regard to the plan of division; and as much as one can form an opinion on the circumstances, it is not her scheme.

"The coalition directed against France, is composed of two kinds of Powers. The Maritime Powers, not having the same interest as the others, will be divided, as to the execution of the project of division.

"I do not hesitate to believe that the politic of the English Government is to foment the scheme of dismembering, and the entire destruction of the Bourbon family.

"The difficulty which must arise, in this last hypothesis, between the united Maritime Powers proceeds from their views being entirely opposed.

"The trading vessels of the Northern Nations, from Holland to Russia, must pass through the narrow Channel, which lies between Dunkirk and the coasts of England; and consequently not one of them, will allow this latter Power to have forts on both sides of this Strait. The audacity with which she has seized the neutral vessels ought to demonstrate to all Nations how much her schemes increase their danger, and menace the security of their present and future commerce.

"Supposing then that the other Nations oppose the plans of England, she will be forced to cease the war with us; or, if she continues it, the Northern Nations will become interested in the safety of France.

"There are three distinct parties in England at this moment: the Government party, the Revolutionary party, and an intermedial party, —which is only opposed to the war on account of the expense it entails, and the harm it does commerce and manufacture. I am speaking of the People, and not of the Parliament. The latter is divided into two parties: the Ministerial, and the Anti-Ministerial. The Revolutionary party, the intermedial party and the Anti-Ministerial party will all rejoice, publicly or privately, at the defeat of the Duke of York's army, at Dunkirk. The intermedial party, because they hope that this defeat will finish the war. The Anti-Ministerial party, because they hope it will overthrow the Ministry. And all the three because they hate the Duke of York. Such is the state of the different parties in England.

"Signed: THOMAS PAINE."

In the same volume of the State Archives (Paris) is the following note by Paine, with its translation:

"You mentioned to me that saltpetre was becoming scarce. I communicate to you a project of the late Captain Paul Jones, which, if successfully put in practice, will furnish you with that article.

"All the English East India ships put into St. Helena, off the coast of Africa, on their return from India to England. A great part of their ballast is saltpetre. Captain Jones, who had been at St. Helena, says that the place can be very easily taken. His proposal was to send off a small squadron for that purpose, to keep the English flag flying at port. The English vessels will continue coming in as usual. By this means it will be a long time before the Government of England can have any knowledge of what has happened. The success of this depends so much upon secrecy that I wish you would translate this yourself, and give it to Barrère."

In the next volume (38) of the French Archives, marked "États Unis, 1793," is a remarkable document (No. 39), entitled "A Citizen of America to the Citizens of Europe." The name of Paine is only pencilled on it, and it was probably written by him; but it purports to have been written in America, and is dated "Philadelphia, July 28, 1793; 18th Year of Independence." It is a clerk's copy, so that it cannot now be known whether the ruse of its origin in Philadelphia was due to Paine or to the government. It is an extended paper, and repeats to some extent, though not literally, what is said in the "Observations" quoted above. Possibly the government, on receiving that paper (Document 39 also), desired Paine to write it out as an address to the "Citizens of Europe." It does not appear to have been published. The first four paragraphs of this paper, combined with the "Observations," will suffice to show its character.

"Understanding that a proposal is intended to be made at the ensuing meeting of the Congress of the United States of America, to send Commissioners to Europe to confer with the Ministers of all the Neutral Powers, for the purpose of negociating preliminaries of Peace, I address this letter to you on that subject, and on the several matters connected therewith.

"In order to discuss this subject through all its circumstances, it will be necessary to take a review of the state of Europe, prior to the French revolution. It will from thence appear, that the powers leagued against France are fighting to attain an object, which, were it possible to be attained, would be injurious to themselves.

"This is not an uncommon error in the history of wars and governments, of which the conduct of the English government in the war against America is a striking instance. She commenced that war for the avowed purpose of subjugating America ; and after wasting upwards of one hundred millions sterling, and then abandoning the object, she discovered in the course of three or four years, that the prosperity of England was increased, instead of being diminished, by the independence of America. In short, every circumstance is pregnant with some natural effect, upon which intentions and opinions have no influence ; and the political error lies in misjudging what the effect will be. England misjudged it in the American war, and the reasons I shall now offer will shew, that she misjudges it in the present war.—In discussing this subject, I leave out of the question every thing respecting forms and systems of government ; for as all the governments of Europe differ from each other, there is no reason that the government of France should not differ from the rest.

"The clamors continually raised in all the countries of Europe were, that the family of the Bourbons was become too powerful ; that the intrigues of the court of France endangered the peace of Europe. Austria saw with a jealous eye the connection of France with Prussia ; and Prussia, in her turn became jealous of the connection of France with Austria ; England had wasted millions unsuccessfully in attempting to prevent the family compact with Spain ; Russia disliked the alliance between France and Turkey ; and Turkey became apprehensive of the inclination of France towards an alliance with Russia. Sometimes the quadruple alliance alarmed some of the powers, and at other times a contrary system alarmed others, and in all those cases the charge was always made against the intrigues of the Bourbons."[1]

In each of these papers a plea for the imperilled Girondins is audible. Each is a reminder that he, Thomas Paine, friend of the Brissotins, is continuing their anxious and loyal vigilance for the Republic. And during all this summer Paine had good reason to believe that his friends were safe. Robespierre was eloquently deprecating useless effusion of blood. As for Paine himself, he was not only consulted on public questions, but trusted in practical affairs. He was still able to help Americans and Englishmen who invoked his aid. Writing to Lady Smith concerning two applications of that kind, he says :

[1] The full text of this pamphlet is published in the "Writings of Thomas Paine" (Conway), vol. iii., p. 140.—H.B.B.

"I went into my chamber to write and sign a certificate for them, which I intended to take to the guard house to obtain their release. Just as I had finished it, a man came into my room, dressed in the Parisian uniform of a captain, and spoke to me in good English, and with a good address. He told me that two young men, Englishmen, were arrested and detained in the guard house, and that the section (meaning those who represented and acted for the section) had sent him to ask me if I knew them, in which case they would be liberated. This matter being soon settled between us, he talked to me about the Revolution, and something about the 'Rights of Man,' which he had read in English ; and at parting offered me, in a polite and civil manner, his services. And who do you think the man was who offered me his services? It was no other than the public executioner, Samson, who guillotined the King and all who were guillotined in Paris, and who lived in the same street with me."[1]

There appeared no reason to suppose this a domiciliary visit, or that it had any relation to anything except the two Englishmen. Samson was not a detective. It soon turned out, however, that there was a serpent creeping into Paine's little garden in the Faubourg St. Denis. He and his guests knew it not, however, until all their hopes fell with the leaves and blossoms amid which they had passed a summer to which Paine, from his prison, looked back with fond recollection.

[1] Forgetfulness. "Writings of Thomas Paine" (Conway), vol. iii., p. 317.—H.B.B.

CHAPTER XXIX

A CONSPIRACY

"HE suffered under Pontius Pilate." Pilate's gallant struggle to save Jesus from lynchers survives in no kindly memorial save among the peasants of Oberammergau. It is said that the impression once made in England by the Miracle Play has left its relic in the miserable puppet-play Punch and Judy (*Pontius cum Judæis*) ; but meanwhile the Church repeats, throughout Christendom, "He suffered under Pontius Pilate." It is almost normal in history that the brand of infamy falls on the wrong man. This is the penalty of personal eminence, and especially of eloquence. In the opening years of the French Revolution the two men in Europe who seemed omnipotent were Pitt and Robespierre. By reason of their eloquence, their ingenious defences, their fame, the columns of credit and discredit were begun in their names, and have so continued. English liberalism, remembering the imprisoned and flying writers, still repeats, "They suffered under William Pitt." French republics transmit their legend of Condorcet, Camille Desmoulins, Brissot, Malesherbes, "They suffered under Robespierre." The friends, disciples, biographers, of Thomas Paine have it in their creed that he suffered under both Pitt and Robespierre. It is certain that neither Pitt nor Robespierre was so strong as he appeared. Their hands cannot be cleansed, but they are historic scapegoats of innumerable sins they never committed.

Unfortunately for Robespierre's memory, in England and America especially, those who for a century might have been the most ready to vindicate a slandered revolutionist have been confronted by the long imprisonment of the author of the "Rights of Man," and by the discovery of his virtual death-sentence in Robespierre's handwriting. Louis Blanc, Robespierre's great vindicator, could not, we may assume, explain this ugly fact, which he passes by in silence. He has proved, conclusively as I think, that Robespierre was among the revolutionists least guilty of the Terror ; that he was murdered by a conspiracy of those whose cruelties he was trying to restrain; that, when no longer alive to answer, they burdened him with their crimes, as the only means of saving their heads. Robespierre's doom was sealed when he had real power, and used it to prevent any organization of the constitutional government which might have checked revolutionary excesses. He then, because of a superstitious faith in the auspices of the Supreme Being, threw the reins upon the neck of the revolution he afterwards vainly tried to curb. Others, who did not wish to restrain it, seized the reins and when the precipice was reached took care that Robespierre should be hurled over it.

Many allegations against Robespierre have been disproved. He tried to save Danton and Camille Desmoulins, and did save seventy-three deputies whose death the potentates of the Committee of Public Safety had planned. But against him still lies that terrible sentence found in his Note Book, and reported by a Committee to the Convention: "Demand that Thomas Paine be decreed of accusation for the interests of America as much as of France."[1]

The Committee on Robespierre's papers, and especially Courtois its Chairman, suppressed some things favorable to him (published long after), and it can never be known whether they found anything further about Paine. They made a strong point of the sentence found, and added: "Why Thomas Payne more than another? Because he helped to establish the liberty of both worlds."

An essay by Paine on Robespierre has been lost, and his opinion of the man can be gathered only from occasional remarks. After the Courtois report he had to accept the theory of Robespierre's malevolence and hypocrisy. He then, for the first time, suspected the same hand in a previous act of hostility towards him. In August, 1793, an address had been sent to the Convention

from Arras, a town in his constituency, saying that they had lost confidence in Paine. This failed of success because a counter-address came from St. Omer. Robespierre being a native of Arras, it now seemed clear that he had instigated the address. It was, however, almost certainly the work of Joseph Lebon, who, as Paine once wrote, "made the streets of Arras run with blood." Lebon was his *suppléant*, and could not sit in the Convention until Paine left it.

But although Paine would appear to have ascribed his misfortunes to Robespierre at the time, he was evidently mystified by the whole thing. No word against him had ever fallen from Robespierre's lips, and if that leader had been hostile to him why should he have excepted him from the accusations of his associates, have consulted him through the summer, and even after imprisonment, kept him unharmed for months? There is a notable sentence in Paine's letter (from prison) to Monroe, elsewhere considered, showing that while there he had connected his trouble rather with the Committee of Public Safety than with Robespierre.

"However discordant the late American Minister Gouvernoeur Morris, and the late French Committee of Public Safety, were, it suited the purposes of both that I should be continued in arrestation. The former wished to prevent my return to America, that I should not expose his misconduct; and the latter lest I should publish to the world the history of its wickedness. Whilst that Minister and that Committee continued, I had no expectation of liberty. I speak here of the Committee of which Robespierre was a member."[2]

Paine wrote this letter on September 10, 1794. Robespierre, three months before that, had ceased to attend the Committee, disavowing responsibility for its actions: Paine was not released. Robespierre, when the letter to Monroe was written, had been dead more than six months:[3] Paine was not released.

---

[1] "Demander que Thomas Payne soit décr-éte d'accusation pour les intérêts de l'Amerique autant que de la France."

[2] Memorial to Monroe. "Writings of Thomas Paine" (Conway), vol. iii., p. 180.—H.B.B.

[3] This should be "weeks": Robespierre was guillotined on July 28, 1794.—H.B.B.

The prisoner had therefore good reason to look behind Robespierre for his enemies; and although the fatal sentence found in the Note Book, and a private assurance of Barrère, caused him to ascribe his wrongs to Robespierre, farther reflection convinced him that hands more hidden had also been at work. He knew that Robespierre was a man of measured words, and pondered the sentence that he should "be decreed of accusation for the interests of America as much as of France." In a letter written in 1802, Paine said:

"There must have been a coalition in sentiment, if not in fact, between the terrorists of America and the terrorists of France, and Robespierre must have known it, or he could not have had the idea of putting America into the bill of accusation against me." [1]

Robespierre, he remarks, assigned no reason for his imprisonment.

The secret for which Paine groped has remained hidden for a hundred years. It is painful to reveal it now, but historic justice, not only to the memory of Paine, but to that of some eminent contemporaries of his, demands that the facts be brought to light.

The appointment of Gouverneur Morris to be Minister to France, in 1792, passed the Senate by 16 to 11 votes. The President did not fail to advise him of this reluctance, and admonish him to be more cautious in his conduct. In the same year Paine took his seat in the Convention. Thus the royalist and republican tendencies, whose struggles made chronic war in Washington's Cabinet, had their counterpart in Paris, where our Minister Morris wrote royalist, and Paine republican, manifestoes. It will have been seen, by quotations from his diary already given, that Gouverneur Morris harbored a secret hostility towards Paine; and it is here assumed that those entries and incidents are borne in mind. The Diary shows an appearance of friendly terms between

the two; Morris dines Paine and receives information from him. The royalism of Morris and humanity of Paine brought them into a common desire to save the life of Louis.

But about the same time the American Minister's own position became a subject of anxiety to him. He informs Washington (December 28, 1792) that Genêt's appointment as Minister to the United States had not been announced to him (Morris). "Perhaps the Ministry think it is a trait of republicanism to omit those forms which were anciently used to express good will." His disposition towards Paine was not improved by finding that it was to him Genêt had reported. "I have not yet seen M. Genêt," writes Morris again, "but Mr. Paine is to introduce him to me." Soon after this Morris became aware that the French Ministry had asked his recall, and had Paine also known this the event might have been different. The Minister's suspicion that Paine had instigated the recall gave deadliness to his resentment when the inevitable break came between them.

The occasion of this arose early in the spring. When war had broken out between England and France, Morris, whose sympathies were with England, was eager to rid America of its treaty obligations to France. He so wrote repeatedly to Jefferson, Secretary of State. An opportunity presently occurred for acting on this idea. In reprisal for the seizure by British cruisers of American ships conveying provisions to France, French cruisers were ordered to do the like, and there were presently ninety-two captured American vessels at Bordeaux. They were not allowed to re-load and go to sea lest their cargoes should be captured by England. Morris pointed out to the French Government this violation of the treaty with America, but wrote to Jefferson that he would leave it to them in Philadelphia to insist on the treaty's observance, or to accept the "unfettered" condition in which its violation

[1] Letters to American Citizens. "Writings of Thomas Paine" (Conway), vol. iii., p. 393. —H.B.B.

by France left them. Consultation with Philadelphia was a slow business, however, and the troubles of the American vessels were urgent. The captains, not suspecting that the American Minister was satisfied with the treaty's violation, were angry at his indifference about their relief, and applied to Paine. Unable to move Morris, Paine asked him " if he did not feel ashamed to take the money of the country and do nothing for it." It was, of course, a part of Morris' scheme for ending the treaty to point out its violation and the hardships resulting, and this he did; but it would defeat his scheme to obtain the practical relief from those hardships which the untheoretical captains demanded. On August 20th, the captains were angrily repulsed by the American Minister, who, however, after they had gone, must have reflected that he had gone too far, and was in an untenable position; for on the same day he wrote to the French Minister a statement of the complaint.

" I do not [he adds] pretend to interfere in the internal concerns of the French Republic, and I am persuaded that the Convention has had weighty reasons for laying upon Americans the restriction of which the American captains complain. The result will nevertheless be that this prohibition will severely aggrieve the parties interested, and put an end to the commerce between France and the United States."

The note is half-hearted, but had the captains known it was written they might have been more patient. Morris owed his subsequent humiliation partly to his bad manners. The captains went off to Paine, and proposed to draw up a public protest against the American Minister. Paine advised against this, and recommended a petition to the Convention. This was offered on August 22d. In this the captains said . "We, who know your political situation, do not come to you to demand the rigorous execution of the treaties of alliance which unite us to you. We confine ourselves to asking for the present, to carry provisions to your colonies." To this the Convention promptly and favorably responded.

It was a double humiliation to Morris that the first important benefit gained by Americans since his appointment should be secured without his help, and that it should come through Paine. And it was a damaging blow to his scheme of transferring to England our alliance with France. A "violation" of the treaty excused by the only sufferers could not be cited as "releasing" the United States. A cruel circumstance for Morris was that the French Minister wrote (October 14th): "You must be satisfied, sir, with the manner in which the request presented by the American captains from Bordeaux, has been received"—and so forth. Four days before, Morris had written to Jefferson, speaking of the thing as mere "mischief," and belittling the success, which "only served an ambition so contemptible that I shall draw over it the veil of oblivion."

The "contemptible ambition" thus veiled from Paine's friend, Jefferson, was revealed by Morris to others. Some time before (June 25th), he had written to Robert Morris:

" I suspected that Paine was intriguing against me, although he put on a face of attachment. Since that period I am confirmed in the idea, for he came to my house with Col. Oswald, and being a little more drunk than usual, behaved extremely ill, and through his insolence I discovered clearly his vain ambition."

This was probably written after Paine's rebuke already quoted. It is not likely that Colonel Oswald would have taken a tipsy man eight leagues out to Morris' retreat, Sainport, on business, or that the tipsy man would remember the words of his rebuke two years after, when Paine records them in his letter to Washington. At any rate, if Morris saw no deeper into Paine's physical than into his mental condition, the "insolent" words were those of soberness. For Paine's private letters prove him ignorant of any intrigue against Morris, and under an impression that the Minister had himself asked for recall; also that, instead of being ambitious to succeed Morris, he was eager to get out of France and back to America. The first expression of French dissatisfaction with Morris had been made through De Ternant, (February 20, 1793,) whom he had himself been the means of sending as Minister to the United States. The positive recall was made through Genêt.[1] It would appear that Morris must have had sore need of a scapegoat to fix on poor Paine, when his intrigues with the King's agents, his trust of the King's money, his plot for a second attempt of the King to escape, his concealment of royalist leaders in his house, had been his main ministerial performances for some time after his appointment. Had the French known half as much as is now revealed in Morris' "Diary," not even his office could have shielded him from arrest. That the executive there knew much of it, appears in the revolutionary archives. There is reason to believe that Paine, instead of intriguing against Morris, had, in ignorance of his intrigues, brought suspicion on himself by continuing his intercourse with the Minister. The following letter of Paine to Barrère, chief Committeeman of Public Safety, dated September 5th, shows him protecting Morris while he is trying to do something for the American captains.

[1] On September 1, 1792, Morris answered a request of the executive of the republic that he could not comply until he had received " orders from his Court," (*les ordres de ma cour*). The representatives of the new-born republic were scandalized by such an expression from an American Minister, and also by his intimacy with Lord and Lady Gower. They may have suspected what Morris' " Diary " now suggests, that he (Morris) owed his appointment to this English Ambassador and his wife. On August 17, 1792, Lord Gower was recalled, in hostility to the republic, but during the further weeks of his stay in Paris the American Minister frequented their house. From the recall Morris was saved for a year by the intervention of Edmund Randolph. (See my " Omitted Chapters of History," etc., p. 149.) Randolph met with a Morrisian reward. Morris (" Diary," ii., p. 98) records an accusation of Randolph, to which he listened in the office of Lord Grenville, Secretary of State, which plainly meant his (Randolph's) ruin, which followed. He knew it to be untrue, but no defence is mentioned.

" I send you the papers you asked me for.

" The idea you have to send Commissioners to Congress, and of which you spoke to me yesterday, is excellent, and very necessary at this moment. Mr. Jefferson, formerly Minister of the United States in France, and actually Minister for Foreign Affairs at Congress, is an ardent defender of the interests of France. Gouverneur Morris, who is here now, is badly disposed towards you. I believe he has expressed the wish to be recalled. The reports which he will make on his arrival will not be to the advantage of France. This event necessitates the sending direct of Commissioners from the Convention. Morris is not popular in America. He has set the Americans who are here against him, as also the Captains of that Nation who have come from Bordeaux, by his negligence with regard to the affair they had to treat about with the Convention. *Between us* [*sic*] he told them : ' That they had thrown themselves into the lion's mouth, and it was for them to get out of it as best they could.' I shall return to America on one of the vessels which will start from Bordeaux in the month of October. This was the project I had formed, should the rupture not take place between America and England ; but now it is necessary for me to be there as soon as possible. The Congress will require a great deal of information, independently of this. It will soon be seven years that I have been absent from America, and my affairs in that country have suffered considerably through my absence. My house and farm buildings have been entirely destroyed through an accidental fire.

" Morris has many relations in America, who are excellent patriots. I enclose you a letter which I received from his brother, General Louis Morris, who was a member of the Congress at the time of the Declaration of Independence. You will see by it that he writes like a good patriot. I only mention this so that you may know the true state of things. It will be fit to have respect for Gouverneur Morris, on account of his relations, who, as I said above, are excellent patriots.

" There are about 45 American vessels at Bordeaux, at the present moment. If the English Government wished to take revenge on the Americans, these vessels would be very much exposed during their passage. The American Captains left Paris yesterday. I advised them, on leaving, to demand a convoy of the Convention, in case they heard it said that the English had begun reprisals against the Americans, if only to conduct as far as the Bay of Biscay, at the expense of the American Government. But if the Convention determines to send Commissioners to Congress, they will be sent in a ship of the line. But it would be better for the Commissioners to go in one of the best American sailing vessels, and for the ship of the line to serve as a convoy ; it could also serve to convoy the ships that will return to France charged with flour. I am sorry that we cannot converse together, but if you could give me a rendezvous, where I could see Mr. Otto, I shall be happy and ready to be there. If events force the American captains to demand a convoy, it will be to me that they will write on the subject, and not to Morris, against whom they have grave reasons of complaint. Your friend, etc.

THOMAS PAINE."[1]

This is the only letter written by Paine to any one in France about Gouverneur Morris, so far as I can discover, and not knowing French he could only communicate in writing. The American Archives are equally without anything to justify the Minister's suspicion that Paine was intriguing against him, even after his outrageous conduct about the captains. Morris had laid aside the functions of a Minister to exercise those of a treaty-making government. During this excursion into presidential and senatorial power, for the injury of the country to which he was commissioned, his own countrymen in France were without an official Minister, and in their distress imposed ministerial duties on Paine. But so far from wishing to supersede Morris, Paine, in the above letter to Barrère, gives an argument for his retention, namely, that if he goes home he will make reports disadvantageous to France. He also asks respect for Morris on account of his relations, " excellent patriots."

Barrère, to whom Paine's letter is written, was chief of the Committee of Public Safety, and had held that powerful position since its establishment, April 6, 1793. To this all-powerful Committee of Nine Robespierre was added July 27th. On the day that Paine wrote the letter, September 5th, Barrère opened the Terror by presenting a report in which it is said, " Let us make terror the order of the day ! " This Barrère was a sensualist, a crafty orator, a sort of eel which in danger turned into a snake. His " supple

genius," as Louis Blanc expresses it, was probably appreciated by Morris, who was kept well informed as to the secrets of the Committee of Public Safety. This omnipotent Committee had supervision of foreign affairs and appointments. At this time the Minister of Foreign Affairs was Deforgues, whose secretary was the M. Otto alluded to in Paine's letter to Barrère. Otto spoke English fluently ; he had been in the American Legation. Deforgues became Minister June 5th, on the arrest of his predecessor (Lebrun), and was anxious lest he should follow Lebrun to prison also,—as he ultimately did. Deforgues and his secretary, Otto, confided to Morris their strong desire to be appointed to America, Genêt having been recalled.[2]

Despite the fact that Morris' hostility to France was well known, he had become an object of awe. So long as his removal was daily expected in reply to a request twice sent for his recall, Morris was weak, and even insulted. But when ship after ship came in without such recall, and at length even with the news that the President had refused the Senate's demand for Morris' entire correspondence, everything was changed.[3] " So long," writes Morris to Washington, " as they believed in the success of their demand, they treated my representations with indifference and contempt ; but at last, hearing nothing from their minister on that subject, or, indeed, on any other, they took it into their heads that I was immovable, and made overtures for conciliation." It must be borne in mind that at this time America was the only ally of France ; that already there were fears that Washington was feeling his way towards a treaty with England. Soon after the overthrow of the monarchy Morris had hinted that the treaty between the United States and France, having been made with the King, might be

---

[1] State Archives, Paris. États Unis, Vol. 38, No. 93. Endorsed : " No. 6. Translation of a letter from Thomas Payne to Citizen Barrère." It may be noted that Paine and Barrère, though they could read each other's language, could converse only in their own tongue.

[2] Morris' letter to Washington, Oct. 18, 1793. The passage is omitted from the letter as quoted in his " Diary and Letters," ii., p. 53.

[3] See my " Life of Edmund Randolph," p. 214.

represented by the English Ministry in America as void under the revolution ; and that "it would be well to evince a degree of good will to America." When Robespierre first became a leader he had particular charge of diplomatic affairs. It is stated by Frédéric Masson that Robespierre was very anxious to recover for the republic the initiative of the alliance with the United States, which was credited to the King ; and "although their Minister Gouverneur Morris was justly suspected, and the American republic was at that time aiming only to utilize the condition of its ally, the French republic cleared it at a cheap rate of its debts contracted with the King."[1] Such were the circumstances which, when Washington seemed determined to force Morris on France, made this Minister a power. Lebrun, the ministerial predecessor of Deforgues, may indeed have been immolated to placate Morris, who having been, under his administration, subjected to a domiciliary visit, had gone to reside in the country. That was when Morris' removal was supposed near ; but now his turn came for a little reign of terror on his own account. In addition to Deforgues' fear of Lebrun's fate, should he anger Washington's immovable representative, he knew that his hope of succeeding Genêt in America must depend on Morris. The terrors and schemes of Deforgues and Otto brought them to the feet of Morris.

About the time when the chief of the Committee of Public Safety, Barrère, was consulting Paine about sending Commissioners to America, Deforgues was consulting Morris on the same point. The interview was held shortly after the humiliation which Morris had suffered, in the matter of the captains, and the defeat of his scheme for utilizing their grievance to release the United States from their alliance. The American captains had appointed Paine their Minister, and he had been successful.

[1] "Le Département des Affaires Étrangères pendant la Révolution," p. 295.

Paine and his clients had not stood in awe of Morris; but he now had the strength of a giant, and proceeded to use it like a giant.

The interview with Deforgues was not reported by Morris to the Secretary of State (Paine's friend, Jefferson), but in a confidential letter to Washington,—so far as was prudent.

" I have insinuated [he writes] the advantages which might result from an early declaration on the part of the new minister that, as France has announced the determination not to meddle with the interior affairs of other nations, he can know only the *government* of America. In union with this idea, I told the minister that I had observed an overruling influence in their affairs which seemed to come from the other side of the channel, and at the same time had traced the intention to excite a seditious spirit in America ; that it was impossible to be on a friendly footing with such persons, but that at present a different spirit seemed to prevail, etc. This declaration produced the effect I intended."[2]

In thus requiring that the new minister to America shall recognize only the "government" (and not negotiate with Kentucky, as Genêt had done), notice is also served on Deforgues that the Convention must in future deal only with the American Minister, and not with Paine or sea-captains in matters affecting his countrymen. The reference to an influence from the other side of the channel could only refer to Paine, as there were then no Englishmen in Paris outside his garden in the Faubourg St. Denis. By this ingenious phrase Morris already disclaims jurisdiction over Paine, and suggests that he is an Englishman worrying Washington through Genêt. This was a clever hint in another way. Genêt, now recalled, evidently for the guillotine, had been introduced to Morris by Paine, who no doubt had given him letters to eminent Americans. Paine had sympathized warmly with the project of the Kentuckians to expel the Spanish from the Mississippi, and this was patriotic American doctrine even after Kentucky was admitted into the Union (June 1, 1792). He had

[2] Letter to Washington, Oct. 18, 1793.

H

corresponded with Dr. O'Fallon, a leading Kentuckian on the subject. But things had changed, and when Genêt went out with his blank commissions he found himself confronted with a proclamation of neutrality which turned his use of them to sedition. Paine's acquaintance with Genêt, and his introductions, could now be plausibly used by Morris to involve him. The French Minister is shown an easy way of relieving his country from responsibility for Genêt, by placing it on the deputy from "the other side of the channel."

"This declaration produced the effect I intended," wrote Morris. The effect was indeed swift. On October 3d, Amar, after the doors of the Convention were locked, read the memorable accusation against the Girondins, four weeks before their execution. In that paper he denounced Brissot for his effort to save the King, for his intimacy with the English, for injuring the colonies by his labors for negro emancipation! In this denunciation Paine had the honor to be included.

"At that same time the Englishman Thomas Paine, called by the faction [Girondin] to the honor of representing the French nation, dishonored himself by supporting the opinion of Brissot, and by promising us in his fable the dissatisfaction of the United States of America, our natural allies, which he did not blush to depict for us as full of veneration and gratitude for the tyrant of France."

On October 19th the Minister of Foreign Affairs, Deforgues, writes to Morris:

"I shall give the Council an account of the punishable conduct of their agent in the United States [Genêt], and I can assure you beforehand that they will regard the strange abuse of their confidence by this agent, as I do, with the liveliest indignation. The President of the United States has done justice to our sentiments in attributing the deviations of the citizen Genêt to causes entirely foreign to his instructions, and we hope that the measures to be taken will more and more convince the head and members of your Government that so far from having authorized the proceedings and manœuvres of Citizen Genêt our only aim has been to maintain between the two nations the most perfect harmony."

One of "the measures to be taken" was the imprisonment of Paine, for which Amar's denunciation had prepared the way. But this was not so easy. For Robespierre had successfully attacked Amar's report for extending its accusations beyond the Girondins. How then could an accusation be made against Paine, against whom no charge could be brought, except that he had introduced a French minister to his friends in America! A deputy must be formally accused by the Convention before he could be tried by the Revolutionary Tribunal. An indirect route must be taken to reach the deputy secretly accused by the American Minister, and the latter had pointed it out by ‥ading to Paine as an influence "‥ ‥ across the channel." There was a law passed in June for the imprisonment of foreigners belonging to countries at war with France. This was administered by the Committees. Paine had not been liable to this law, being a deputy, and never suspected of citizenship in the country which had outlawed him, until Morris suggested it. Could he be got out of the Convention the law might be applied to him without necessitating any public accusation and trial, or anything more than an announcement to the Deputies.

Such was the course pursued. Christmas day was celebrated by the terrorist Bourdon de l'Oise with a denunciation of Paine: "They have boasted the patriotism of Thomas Paine. *Eh bien !* Since the Brissotins disappeared from the bosom of this Convention he has not set foot in it. And I know that he has intrigued with a former agent of the bureau of Foreign Affairs." This accusation could only have come from the American Minister and the Minister of Foreign Affairs—from Gouverneur Morris and Deforgues. Genêt was the only agent of Deforgues' office with whom Paine could possibly have been connected; and what that connection was the reader knows. That accusation is associated with the terrorist's charge that Paine had declined to unite with the murderous decrees of the Convention.

After the speech of Bourdon de l'Oise, Bentabole moved the "exclusion of foreigners from every public function during the war." Bentabole was a leading member of the Committee of General Surety. "The Assembly," adds *The Moniteur*, " decreed that no foreigner should be admitted to represent the French people." The Committee of General Surety assumed the right to regard Paine as an Englishman ; and as such out of the Convention, and consequently under the law of June against aliens of hostile nations. He was arrested next day, and on December 28th committed to the Luxembourg prison.

CHAPTER XXX

A TESTIMONY UNDER THE GUILLOTINE

WHILE Paine was in prison the English gentry were gladdened by a rumor that he had been guillotined, and a libellous leaflet of " The Last Dying Words of Thomas Paine " appeared in London. Paine was no less confident than his enemies that his execution was certain— after the denunciation in Amar's report, October 3d—and did indeed utter what may be regarded as his dying words— " The Age of Reason." This was the task which he had from year to year adjourned to his maturest powers, and to it he dedicates what brief remnant of life may await him. That completed, it will be time to die with his comrades, awakened by his pen to a dawn now red with their blood.

The last letter I find written from the old Pompadour mansion is to Jefferson, under date of October 20th :

"DEAR SIR, — I wrote you by Captain Dominick who was to sail from Havre about the 20th of this month. This will probably be brought you by Mr. Barlow or Col. Oswald. Since my letter by Dominick I am every day more convinced and impressed with the propriety of Congress sending Commissioners to Europe to confer with the Ministers of the Jesuitical Powers on the means of terminating the war. The enclosed printed paper will shew there are a variety of subjects to be taken into consideration which did not appear at first, all of which have some tendency to put an end to the war. I see not how this war is to terminate if some intermediate power does not step forward.

There is now no prospect that France can carry revolutions thro' Europe on the one hand, or that the combined powers can conquer France on the other hand. It is a sort of defensive War on both sides. This being the case how is the War to close ? Neither side will ask for peace though each may wish it. I believe that England and Holland are tired of the war. Their Commerce and Manufactures have suffered most exceedingly—and besides this it is to them a war without an object. Russia keeps herself at a distance. I cannot help repeating my wish that Congress would send Commissioners, and I wish also that yourself would venture once more across the Ocean as one of them. If the Commissioners rendezvous at Holland they would then know what steps to take. They could call Mr. Pinckney to their Councils, and it would be of use, on many accounts, that one of them should come over from Holland to France. Perhaps a long truce, were it proposed by the neutral Powers, would have all the effects of a Peace, without the difficulties attending the adjustment of all the forms of Peace.—Yours affectionately

"THOMAS PAINE." [1]

Thus has finally faded the dream of Paine's life—an international republic.

It is notable that in this letter Paine makes no mention of his own danger. He may have done so in the previous letter, unfound, to which he alludes. Why he made no attempt to escape after Amar's report seems a mystery, especially as he was assisting others to

[1] I am indebted for this letter to Dr. John S. H. Fogg, of Boston. The letter is endorsed by Jefferson, " Rec'd Mar. 3." [1794.]

H 2

leave the country. Two of his friends, Johnson and Choppin—the last to part from him in the old garden,—escaped to Switzerland. Johnson will be remembered as the young man who attempted suicide on hearing of Marat's menaces against Paine. Writing to Lady Smith of these two friends, he says :

" He [Johnson] recovered, and being anxious to get out of France, a passport was obtained for him and Mr. Choppin ; they received it late in the evening, and set off the next morning for Basle, before four, from which place I had a letter from them, highly pleased with their escape from France, into which they had entered with an enthusiasm of patriotic devotion. Ah, France ! thou hast ruined the character of a revolution virtuously begun, and destroyed those who produced it. I might also say like Job's servant, 'and I only am escaped.'

" Two days after they were gone I heard a rapping at the gate, and looking out of the window of the bedroom I saw the landlord going with the candle to the gate, which he opened ; and a guard with muskets and fixed bayonets entered. I went to bed again and made up my mind for prison, for I was the only lodger. It was a guard to take up Johnson and Choppin, but, I thank God, they were out of their reach.

" The guard came about a month after, in the night, and took away the landlord, Georgeit. And the scene in the house finished with the arrestation of myself. This was soon after you called on me, and sorry I was that it was not in my power to render to Sir [Robert Smith] the service that you asked." [1]

All then had fled. Even the old landlord had been arrested. In the wintry garden this lone man—in whose brain and heart the republic and the religion of humanity have their abode—moves companionless. In the great mansion, where once Madame de Pompadour glittered amid her courtiers, where in the past summer gathered the Round Table of great-hearted gentlemen and ladies, Thomas Paine sits through the watches of the night at his devout task.[2]

[1] Forgetfulness. "Writings of Thomas Paine" (Conway), vol. iii., p. 318.—H. B. B.
[2] It was a resumed task. Early in the year Paine had brought to his colleague Lanthenas a manuscript on religion, probably entitled "The Age of Reason." Lanthenas translated it, and had it printed in French, though no trace of its circulation appears. At that time Lanthenas

" My friends were falling as fast as the guillotine could cut their heads off, and as I expected every day, the same fate, I resolved to begin my work. I appeared to myself to be on my death bed, for death was on every side of me, and I had no time to lose. This accounts for my writing at the time I did, and so nicely did the time and intention meet, that I had not finished the first part of the work more than six hours before I was arrested and taken to prison. The people of France were running headlong into atheism, and I had the work translated in their own language, to stop them in that career, and fix them to the first article of every man's creed, who has any creed at all—*I believe in God*." [3]

The second Christmas of the new republican era dawns. Where is the vision that has led this wayworn pilgrim ? Where the star he has followed so long, to find it hovering over the new birth of humanity ? It may have been on that day that, amid the shades of his slain friends, he wrote, as with blood about to be shed, the tribute to one that was pierced in trying to benefit mankind.

" Nothing that is here said can apply, even with the most distant disrespect, to the real character of Jesus Christ. He was a virtuous and amiable man. The morality that he preached and practised was of the most benevolent kind ; and though similar systems of morality had been preached by Confucius, and by some of the Greek philosophers, many years before, by the Quakers since, and by good men in all ages, it has not been exceeded by any. . . . He preached most excellent morality, and the equality of man ; but he preached also against the corruption and avarice of the Jewish priests,

may have apprehended the proscription which fell on him, with the other Girondins, in May, and took the precaution to show Paine's essay to Couthon, who, with Robespierre, had religious matters particularly in charge. Couthon frowned on the work and on Paine, and reproached Lanthenas for translating it. There was no frown more formidable than that of Couthon, and the essay (printed only in French) seems to have been suppressed. At the close of the year Paine wrote the whole work *de novo*. The first edition in English, now before me, was printed in Paris, by Barrois, 1794. In his preface to Part II., Paine implies a previous draft in saying : "I had not finished it more than six hours, *in the state it has since appeared*, before a guard came," etc. (The italics are mine.) The fact of the early translation appears in a letter of Lanthenas to Merlin de Thionville.
[3] Letter to Samuel Adams. The execution of the Girondins took place on October 31st.

and this brought upon him the hatred and vengeance of the whole order of priesthood. The accusation which those priests brought against him was that of sedition and conspiracy against the Roman government, to which the Jews were then subject and tributary ; and it is not improbable that the Roman government might have some secret apprehension of the effect of his doctrine, as well as the Jewish priests ; neither is it improbable that Jesus Christ had in contemplation the delivery of the Jewish nation from the bondage of the Romans. Between the two however, this virtuous reformer and religionist lost his life. . . . He was the son of God in like manner that every other person is—for the Creator is the Father of All. . . . Jesus Christ founded no new system. He called men to the practice of moral virtues, and the belief of one God. The great trait in his character is philanthropy."

Many Christmas sermons were preached in 1793, but probably all of them together do not contain so much recognition of the humanity of Jesus as these paragraphs of Paine. The Christmas bells ring in the false, but shall also ring in the true. While he is writing, on that Christmas night, word comes that he has been denounced by Bourdon de l'Oise, and expelled from the Convention. He now enters the Dark Valley. "Conceiving, after this, that I had but a few days of liberty I sat down, and brought the work to a close as speedily as possible."

In the "Age of Reason" there is a page of personal recollections.[1] I have a feeling that this little episode marks the hour when Paine was told of his doom. From this overshadowed Christmas, likely to be his last, the lonely heart—as loving a heart as ever beat—here wanders across tempestuous years to his early Norfolkshire home. There is a grateful remembrance of the Quaker meeting, the parental care, the Grammar School ; of his pious aunt who read him a printed sermon, and the garden steps where he pondered what he had just heard,—a Father demanding his Son's death for the sake of making mankind happier and better. He "perfectly recollects the spot" in the garden where,

[1] "Writings of Thomas Paine" (Conway), vol. iv., pp. 62–5.—H.B.B.

even then, but seven or eight years of age, he felt sure a man would be executed for doing such a thing, and that God was too good to act in that way. So clearly come out the scenes of childhood under the shadow of death.

He probably had an intimation on December 27th that he would be arrested that night. The place of his abode, though well known to the authorities, was not in the Convention's Almanach. Officially, therefore, his residence was still in the Passage des Petits Pères. There the officers would seek him, and there he should be found. "For that night only he sought a lodging there," reported the officers afterwards. He may have feared, too, that his manuscript would be destroyed if he were taken in his residence.

His hours are here traceable. On the evening of December 27th, in the old mansion, Paine reaches the last page of the "Age of Reason." They who have supposed him an atheist, may search as far as Job, who said, "Though He slay me I will trust in Him," before finding an author who, caught in the cruel machinery of destructive nature, could write that last page.

"The creation we behold is the real and ever existing word of God, in which we cannot be deceived. It proclaimeth his power, it demonstrates his wisdom, it manifests his goodness and beneficence. The moral duty of man consists in imitating the moral goodness and beneficence of God manifested in the creation towards all his creatures. That seeing, as we daily do, the goodness of God to all men, it is an example calling upon all men to practise the same towards each other, and consequently that everything of persecution and revenge between man and man, and everything of cruelty to animals, is a violation of moral duty."

In what "Israel" is greater faith found ? Having written these words, the pen drops from our world-wanderer's hand. It is nine o'clock of the night. He will now go and bend his neck under the decree of the Convention—provided by "the goodness of God to all men." Through the Faubourg, past Porte St. Martin, to the Rue Richelieu, to the

Passage des Petits Pères, he walks in the wintry night. In the house where he wrote his appeal that the Convention would slay not the man in destroying the monarch, he asks a lodging "for that night only."

As he lays his head on the pillow, it is no doubt with a grateful feeling that the good God has prolonged his freedom long enough to finish a defence of true religion from its degradation by superstition or destruction by atheism,—these, as he declares, being the two purposes of his work. It was providently if not providentially timed.

"I had not finished it more than six hours, in the state it has since appeared, before a guard came, about three in the morning, with an order, signed by the two Committees of Public Safety and Surety General, for putting me in arrestation as a foreigner, and conveying me to the prison of the Luxembourg."[1]

The following documents are translated for this work from the originals in the National Archives of France.

"NATIONAL CONVENTION.
"Committee of General Surety and Surveillance of the National Convention.
"On the 7th Nivose [December 27th] of the 2d year of the French Republic, one and indivisible.

"TO THE DEPUTIES :
"The Committee resolves, that the persons named Thomas Paine and Anacharsis Clootz, formerly Deputies to the National Convention, be arrested and imprisoned, as a measure of General Surety ; that an examination be made of their papers, and those found suspicious put under seal and brought to the Committee of General Surety.

"Citizens Jean Baptiste Martin and Lamy, bearers of the present decree are empowered to execute it,—for which they ask the help of the Civil authorities and, if need be, of the army.
"The representatives of the nation, members of the Committee of General Surety—Signed : M. Bayle, Voulland, Jagot, Amar, Vadier, Élie Lacoste, Guffroy, Louis (du bas Rhin) La Vicomterie, Panis."
"This day, the 8th Nivose of the 2d year of the French Republic, one and indivisible, to execute and fulfil the order given us, we have gone to the residence of Citizen Thomas Paine, Passage des Petits Pères, number seven, Philadelphia House. Having requested the

Commander of the [Police] post, William Tell Section, to have us escorted, according to the order we showed him, he obeyed by assigning us four privates and a corporal, to search the above-said lodging ; where we requested the porter to open the door, and asked him whether he knew all who lodged there ; and as he did not affirm it, we desired him to take us to the principal agent, which he did ; having come to the said agent, we asked him if he knew by name all the persons to whom he rented lodgings; after having repeated to him the name mentioned in our order, he replied to us, that he had come to ask him a lodging for that night only ; which being ascertained, we asked him to conduct us to the bedroom of Citizen Thomas Paine, where he arrived ; then seeing we could not be understood by him, an American, we begged the manager of the house, who knows his language, to kindly interpret for him, giving him notice of the order of which we were bearers ; whereupon the said Citizen Thomas Paine submitted to be taken to Rue Jacob, Great Britain Hotel, which he declared through his interpreter to be the place where he had his papers ; having recognized that his lodging contained none of them, we accompanied the said Thomas Paine and his interpreter to Great Britain Hotel, Rue Jacob, Unity Section ; the present minutes closed, after being read before the undersigned.
"(Signed) :
    THOMAS PAINE.   J. B. MARTIN.
    DORLÉ, Commissary.
    GILLET, Commissary.
    F. DELLANAY.
    ACHILLE AUDIBERT, Witness.[2]
    LAMY."

"And as it was about seven or eight o'clock in the morning of this day 8th Nivose, being worn out with fatigue, and forced to take some food, we postponed the end of our proceeding till eleven o'clock of the same day, when, desiring to finish it, we went with Citizen Thomas Paine to Britain House, where we found Citizen Barlow, whom Citizen Thomas Paine informed that we, the Commissaries, were come to look into the papers, which he said were at his house, as announced in our preceding paragraph through Citizen Dellanay, his interpreter ; We, Commissary of the Section of the Unity, undersigned, with the Citizens order-bearers, requested Citizen Barlow to declare whether there were in his house, any papers or correspondence belonging to Citizen Thomas Paine ; on which, complying with our request, he declared there did not exist any ; but wishing to leave no doubt on our way of conducting the matter, we did not think it right to rely on what he said ; resolving, on the contrary, to ascertain by all legal ways that

---

[1] Preface to Part II.—H.B.B.

[2] It will be remembered that Audibert had carried to London Paine's invitation to the Convention.

there did not exist any, we requested Citizen Barlow to open for us all his cupboards ; which he did, and after having visited them, we, the above said Commissary, always in the presence of Citizen Thomas Paine, recognized that there existed no papers belonging to him ; we also perceived that it was a subterfuge on the part of Citizen Thomas Paine who wished only to transfer himself to the house of Citizen Barlow, his native friend (*son ami natal*) whom we invited to ask of Citizen Thomas Paine his usual place of abode ; and the latter seemed to wish that his friend might accompany him and be present at the examination of his papers. Which we, the said Commissary granted him, as Citizen Barlow could be of help to us, together with Citizen Etienne Thomas Dessous, interpreter for the English language, and Deputy Secretary to the Committee of General Surety of the National Convention, whom we called, in passing by the said Committee, to accompany us to the true lodging of the said Paine, Faubourg du Nord, Nro. 63. At which place we entered his rooms, and gathered in the Sitting-room all the papers found in the other rooms of the said apartment. The said Sitting-room receives light from three windows, looking, one on the Garden and the two others on the Courtyard ; and after the most scrupulous examination of all the papers, that we had there gathered, none of them has been found suspicious, neither in French nor in English, according to what was affirmed to us by Citizen Dessous our interpreter who signed with us, and Citizen Thomas Paine ; and we, the undersigned Commissary, resolved that no seal should be placed, after the examination mentioned, and closed the said minutes, which we declare to contain the truth. Drawn up at the residence, and closed at 4 p.m. in the day and year above-named ; and we have all signed after having read the minutes.

"(Signed) :

THOMAS PAINE.   JOEL BARLOW.
DORLÉ, Commissary. GILLET, Commissary.
DESSOUS.   J. B. MARTIN.   LAMY.

" And after having signed we have requested, according to the order of the Committee of General Surety of the National Convention, Citizen Thomas Paine to follow us, to be led to jail ; to which he complied without any difficulty, and he has signed with us :

THOMAS PAINE.   J. B. MARTIN.
DORLÉ, Commissary.   LAMY.
GILLETT, Commissary."

" I have received from the Citizens Martin and Lamy, Deputy-Secretaries to the Committee of General Surety of the National Convention, the Citizens Thomas Paine and Anacharsis Clootz, formerly Deputies ; by order of the said Committee.

" At the Luxembourg, this day 8th Nivose, 2nd year of the French Republic, One and Indivisible.

"Signed :   BENOIT, *Concierge.*"

" FOREIGN OFFICE—Received the 12th Ventose [March 2d]. Sent to the Committees of General Surety and Public Safety the 8th Pluviose [January 27th] this 2d year of the French Republic, One and indivisible.

"Signed :   BASSOL, *Secretary.*"

"CITIZENS LEGISLATORS !—The French nation has, by a universal decree, invited to France one of our countrymen, most worthy of honor, namely, Thomas Paine, one of the political founders of the independence and of the Republic of America.

"Our experience of twenty years has taught America to know and esteem his public virtues and the invaluable services he rendered her.

" Persuaded that his character of foreigner and ex-Deputy is the only cause of his provisional imprisonment, we come in the name of our country (and we feel sure she will be grateful to us for it), we come to you, Legislators, to reclaim our friend, our countryman, that he may sail with us for America, where he will be received with open arms.

" If it were necessary to say more in support of the Petition which, as friends and allies of the French Republic, we submit to her representatives, to obtain the liberation of one of the most earnest and faithful apostles of liberty, we would beseech the National Convention, for the sake of all that is dear to the glory and to the heart of freemen, not to give a cause of joy and triumph to the allied tyrants of Europe, and above all to the despotism of Great Britain, which did not blush to outlaw this courageous and virtuous defender of Liberty.

" But their insolent joy will be of short duration ; for we have the intimate persuasion that you will not keep longer in the bonds of painful captivity the man whose courageous and energetic pen did so much to free the Americans, and whose intentions we have no doubt whatever were to render the same services to the French Republic. Yes, we feel convinced that his principles and views were pure, and in that regard he is entitled to the indulgence due to human fallibility, and to the respect due to rectitude of heart ; and we hold all the more firmly our opinion of his innocence, inasmuch as we are informed that after a scrupulous examination of his papers, made by order of the Committee of General Surety, instead of anything to his charge, enough has been found rather to corroborate the purity of his principles in politics and morals.

" As a countryman of ours, as a man above all so dear to the Americans, who like yourselves are earnest friends of Liberty, we ask you, in the name of that goddess cherished of the only two Republics of the World, to give back Thomas Paine to his brethren and permit us to take him to his country which is also ours.

" If you require it, Citizens Representatives, we shall make ourselves warrant and security for his conduct in France during the short stay he may make in this land.

" Signed :
W. JACKSON, of Philadelphia.   J. RUSSELL, of Boston.   PETER WHITESIDE, of Philadelphia. HENRY JOHNSON, of Boston.   THOMAS CARTER, of Newbury Port.   JAMES COOPER of Philadelphia.   JOHN WILLERT BILLOPP, of New York.   THOMAS WATERS GRIFFITH, of Baltimore.   TH. RAMSDEN, of Boston.   SAMUEL P. BROOME, of New York.   A. MEADENWORTH, of Connecticut.   JOEL BARLOW, of Connecticut. MICHAEL ALCORN, of Philadelphia.   M. ONEALY, of Baltimore.   JOHN MCPHERSON, of Alexandria [Va.].   WILLIAM HASKINS, of Boston.   J. GREGORY, of Petersburg, Virginia.   JAMES INGRAHAM, of Boston." [1]

The following answer to the petitioning Americans was giving by Vadier, then president of the Convention.

" CITIZENS : The brave Americans are our brothers in liberty ; like us they have broken the chains of despotism : like us they have sworn the destruction of kings and vowed an eternal hatred to tyrants and their instruments.   From this identity of principles should result a union of the two nations forever unalterable.   If the tree of liberty already flourishes in the two hemispheres, that of commerce should, by this happy alliance, cover the poles with its fruitful branches.   It is for France, it is for the United States, to combat and lay low, in concert, these proud islanders, these insolent dominators of the sea and the commerce of nations.   When the sceptre of despotism is falling from the criminal hand of the tyrants of the earth, it is necessary also to break the trident which emboldens the insolence of these corsairs

of Albion, these modern Carthaginians.   It is time to repress the audacity and mercantile avarice of these pirate tyrants of the sea, and of the commerce of nations.

" You demand of us, citizens, the liberty of Thomas Paine ; you wish to restore to your hearths this defender of the rights of man.   One can only applaud this generous movement. Thomas Paine is a native of England ; this is undoubtedly enough to apply to him the measures of security prescribed by the revolutionary laws. It may be added, citizens, that if Thomas Paine has been the apostle of liberty, if he has powerfully co-operated with the American Revolution, his genius has not understood that which has regenerated France ; he has regarded the system only in accordance with the illusions with which the false friends of our revolution have invested it.   You must with us deplore an error little reconcilable with the principles admired in the justly esteemed works of this republican author.

" The National Convention will take into consideration the object of your petition, and invites you to its sessions."

A memorandum adds : " Reference of this petition is decreed to the Committees of Public Safety and General Surety, united."

It is said that Paine sent an appeal for intervention to the Cordeliers Club, and that their only reply was to return to him a copy of his speech in favor of preserving the life of Louis XVI.   This I have not been able to verify.

On leaving his house for prison, Paine entrusted to Joel Barlow the manuscript of the " Age of Reason," to be conveyed to the printer.   This was with the knowof the guard, whose kindness is mentioned by Paine.

---

[1] The preceding documents connected with the arrest are in the Archives Nationales, F. 4641.

CHAPTER XXXI

A MINISTER AND HIS PRISONER

BEFORE resuming the history of the conspiracy against Paine it is necessary to return a little on our steps.   For a year after the fall of monarchy in France (August 10, 1792), the real American Minister there was Paine, whether for Americans or for the French Executive. The Ministry would not confer with a

hostile and presumably decapitated agent, like Morris.   The reader has (Chaps. XXVIII. and XXIX.) evidence of their consultations with Paine.   Those communications of Paine were utilized in Robespierre's report to the Convention, November 17, 1793, on the foreign relations of France.   It was inspired by the humiliating tidings that Genêt in America had reinforced the European intrigues to detach Washington from France. The President had demanded Genêt's recall, had issued a proclamation of "impartiality" between France and her foes, and had not yet decided whether the treaty formed with Louis XVI. should survive his death. And Morris was not recalled !

In his report Robespierre makes a solemn appeal to the "brave Americans." Was it "that crowned automaton called Louis XVI." who helped to rescue them from the oppressor's yoke, or our arm and armies? Was it his money sent over or the taxes of French labor? He declares that the Republic has been treacherously compromised in America.

"By a strange fatality the Republic finds itself still represented among their allies by agents of the traitors she has punished : Brissot's brother-in-law is Consul-General there ; another man, named Genêt, sent by Lebrun and Brissot to Philadelphia as plenipotentiary agent, has faithfully fulfilled the views and instructions of the faction that appointed him."

The result is that "parallel intrigues" are observable — one aiming to bring France under the league, the other to break up the American republic into parts.[1]

In this idea of "parallel intrigues" the irremovable Morris is discoverable. It is the reappearance of what he had said to Deforgues about the simultaneous sedition in America (Genêt's) and "influence in their affairs from the other side of the channel" (Paine's). There was not, however, in Robespierre's report any word that might be construed into a suspicion of Paine; on the contrary, he declares the Convention now pure. The Convention instructed the Committee of Public Safety to provide for strictest fulfilment of its treaties with America, and caution to its agents to respect the government and territory of its allies. The first necessary step was to respect the President's Minister, Gouverneur Morris, however odious he

might be, since it would be on his representations that the continuance of France's one important alliance might depend. Morris played cleverly on that string ; he hinted dangers that did not exist, and dangled promises never to be fulfilled. He was master of the situation. The unofficial Minister who had practically superseded him for a year was now easily locked up in the Luxembourg.

But why was not Paine executed? The historic paradox must be ventured that he owed his reprieve—his life—to Robespierre. Robespierre had Morris' intercepted letters and other evidences of his treachery, yet as Washington insisted on him, and the alliance was at stake, he must be obeyed. On the other hand were evidences of Washington's friendship for Paine, and of Jefferson's intimacy with him. Time must therefore be allowed for the prisoner to communicate with the President and Secretary of State. They must decide between Paine and Morris. It was only after ample time had passed, and no word about Paine came from Washington or Jefferson, while Morris still held his position, that Robespierre entered his memorandum that Paine should be tried before the revolutionary tribunal.

Meanwhile a great deal happened, some of which, as Paine's experiences in the Luxembourg, must be deferred to a further chapter. The American Minister had his triumph. The Americans in Paris, including the remaining sea-captains, who had been looking to Paine as their Minister, were now to discover where the power was lodged. Knowing Morris' hatred for Paine, they repaired to the Convention with their petition. Major Jackson, a well known officer of the American Revolution, who headed the deputation (which included every unofficial American in Paris), utilized a letter of introduction he had brought from Secretary Jefferson to Morris by giving it to the Committee of General Surety, as an evidence of his right to act in the emergency.

[1] "Hist. Parl.," xxx., p. 224.

Action was delayed by excitement over the celebration of the first anniversary of the King's execution. On that occasion (January 21st) the Convention joined the Jacobin Club in marching to the "Place de la Révolution," with music and banners; there the portraits of kings were burned, an act of accusation against all the kings of the earth adopted, and a fearfully realistic drama enacted. By a prearrangement unknown to the Convention four condemned men were guillotined before them. The Convention recoiled, and instituted an inquisition as to the responsibility for this scene. It was credited to the Committee of General Surety, justly no doubt, but its chief, Vadier, managed to relieve it of the odium. This Vadier was then president of the Convention. He was appropriately selected to give the first anniversary oration on the King's execution. A few days later it fell to Vadier to address the eighteen Americans at the bar of the Convention on their petition for Paine's release. The petition and petitioners being referred to the Committees of Public Safety and General Surety in joint session, the Americans were there answered, by Billaud-Varennes it was said, "that their reclamation was only the act of individuals, without any authority from the American government."

This was a plain direction. The American government, whether in Paris or Philadelphia, had Paine's fate in its hands.

At this time it was of course not known that Jefferson had retired from the Cabinet. To him Paine might have written, but — sinister coincidence! immediately after the committees had referred the matter to the American government an order was issued cutting off all communication between prisoners and the outside world. That Morris had something to do with this is suggested by the fact that he was allowed to correspond with Paine in prison, though this was not allowed to his successor, Monroe. However, there is, unfor-

tunately, no need to repair to suspicions for the part of Gouverneur Morris in this affair. His first ministerial mention of the matter to Secretary Jefferson is dated on the tragical anniversary, January 21st. "Lest I should forget it," he says of this small incident, the imprisonment of one whom Congress and the President had honored—

"Least I should forget it, I must mention that Thomas Paine is in prison, where he amuses himself with publishing a pamphlet against Jesus Christ. I do not recollect whether I mentioned to you that he would have been executed along with the rest of the Brissotins if the advance party had not viewed him with contempt. I incline to think that if he is quiet in prison he may have the good luck to be forgotten, whereas, should he be brought much into notice, the long suspended axe might fall on him. I believe he thinks that I ought to claim him as an American citizen; but considering his birth, his naturalization in this country, and the place he filled, I doubt much the right, and I am sure that the claim would be, for the present at least, inexpedient and ineffectual."

Although this paragraph is introduced in such a casual way, there is calculation in every word. First of all, however, be it observed, Morris knows precisely how the authorities will act several days before they have been appealed to. It also appears that if Paine was not executed with the Brissotins on October 31st, it was not due to any interference on his part. The "contempt" which saved Paine may be estimated by a reference to the executive consultations with him, and to Amar's bitter denunciation of him (October 3d) after Morris had secretly accused this contemptible man of influencing the Convention and helping to excite sedition in the United States. In the next place, Jefferson is admonished that if he would save his friend's head he must not bring the matter into notice. The government at Philadelphia must, in mercy to Paine, remain silent. As to the "pamphlet against Jesus Christ," my reader has already perused what Paine wrote on that theme in the "Age of Reason." But as that may not be so likely to affect freethinking Jefferson, Morris adds the falsehood that Paine had been naturalized in France. The reader need hardly be reminded that if an application by the American Minister for the release would be "ineffectual," it must be because the said Minister would have it so. Morris had already found, as he tells Washington, that the Ministry, supposing him immovable, were making overtures of conciliation ; and none can read the obsequious letter of the Foreign Minister, Deforgues (October 19, 1793), without knowing that a word from Morris would release Paine. The American petitioners had indeed been referred to their own Government—that is, to Morris.

The American Minister's version of what had occurred is given in a letter to Secretary Jefferson, dated March 6th :

"I have mentioned Mr. Paine's confinement. Major Jackson—who, by the by, has not given me a letter from you which he says was merely introductory, but left it with the Comité de Sûreté Générale, as a kind of letter of credence —-Major Jackson, relying on his great influence with the leaders here, stepped forward to get Mr. Paine out of jail, and with several other Americans, has presented a petition to that effect, which was referred to that Committee and the Comité de Salut Public. This last, I understand, slighted the application as totally irregular ; and some time afterwards Mr. Paine wrote me a note desiring I would claim him as an American, which I accordingly did, though contrary to my judgment, for reasons mentioned in my last. The Minister's letter to me of the 1st Ventose, of which I enclose a copy, contains the answer to my reclamation. I sent a copy to Mr. Paine, who prepared a long answer, and sent it to me by an Englishman, whom I did not know. I told him, as Mr. Paine's friend, that my present opinion was similar to that of the Minister, but I might, perhaps, see occasion to change it, and in that case, if Mr. Paine wished it, I would go on with the claim, but that it would be well for him to consider the result ; that, if the Government meant to release him, they had already a sufficient ground ; but if not, I could only push them to bring on his trial for the crimes imputed to him ; seeing that whether he be considered as a Frenchman, or as an American, he must be amenable to the tribunals of France for his conduct while he was a Frenchman, and he may see in the fate of the Brissotins, that to which he is exposed. I have heard no more of the affair since ; but it is not impossible that he may force on a decision, which, as far as I can judge, would be fatal

to him : for in the best of times he had a larger share of every other sense than common sense, and lately the intemperate use of ardent spirits has, I am told, considerably impaired the small stock he originally possessed."

In this letter the following incidental points suggest comment :

1. "Several other Americans." The petitioners for Paine's release were eighteen in number, and seem to have comprised all the Americans then left in Paris, some of them eminent.

2. "The crimes imputed to him." There were none. Paine was imprisoned under a law against "foreigners." Those charged with his arrest reported that his papers were entirely innocent. The archives of France, now open to exploration, prove that no offence was ever imputed to him, showing his arrest due only to Morris' insinuation of his being objectionable to the United States. By this insinuation ("crimes imputed to him") Paine was asserted to be amenable to French laws for matters with which the United States would of course have nothing to do, and of which nothing could be known in Philadelphia.

3. "While he was a Frenchman." Had Paine ever been a Frenchman, he was one when Morris pretended that he had claimed him as an American. But Paine had been excluded from the Convention and imprisoned expressly because he was not a Frenchman. No word of the Convention's published action was transmitted by Morris.

4. "The fate of the Brissotins," etc. This of course would frighten Paine's friends by its hint of a French hostility to him which did not exist, and might restrain them from applying to America for interference. Paine was already restrained by the new order preventing him from communicating with any one except the American Minister.

5. "Intemperate," etc. This is mere calumny. Since the brief lapse in June, 1793, when overwhelmed by the arrest of his friends, Paine's daily life is known from those who dwelt with him. During the months preceding his arrest he wrote the "Age of Reason"; its power, if

alcoholic, might have recommended his cellar to Morris, or to any man living.

So much for the insinuations and *suggestiones falsi* in Morris' letter. The suppressions of fact are more deadly. There is nothing of what had really happened; nothing of the eulogy of Paine by the President of the Convention, which would have been a commentary on what Morris had said of the contempt in which he was held; not a word of the fact that the petitioners were reminded by the Committee that their application was unofficial,—in other words, that the determination on Paine's fate rested with Morris himself. This Morris hides under the phrase: "slighted the application as totally irregular."

But the fatal far-reaching falsehood of Morris' letter to Jefferson was his assertion that he had claimed Paine as an American. This falsehood, told to Washington, Jefferson, Edmund Randolph, paralyzed all action in America in Paine's behalf; told to the Americans in Paris, it paralyzed further effort of their own.

The actual correspondence between Morris and Deforgues is now for the first time brought to light.

MORRIS TO DEFORGUES.

"PARIS, 14th February 1794.

"SIR,—Thomas Paine has just applied to me to claim him as a Citizen of the United States. These (I believe) are the facts which relate to him. He was born in England. Having become a citizen of the United States, he acquired great celebrity there through his revolutionary writings. In consequence he was adopted as French Citizen, and then elected Member of the Convention. His behaviour since that epoch is out of my jurisdiction. I am ignorant of the reason for his present detention in the Luxembourg prison, but I beg you, Sir, if there be reasons which prevent his liberation, and which are unknown to me, be so good as to inform me of them, so that I may communicate them to the Government of the United States.— I have the honour to be, Sir, Your very humble servant,

"GOUV. MORRIS." [1]

---

[1] "Etats Unis," vol. xl., Doc. 54. Endorsed: "Received the 28th of same [Pluviose,

DEFORGUES TO MORRIS.

"PARIS, 1st Ventose, 2nd year of the Republic. [February 19, 1794.]

"The Minister of Foreign Affairs to the Minister of the United States.

"In your letter of the 26th of last month you reclaim the liberty of Thomas Payne, as an American Citizen. Born in England, this co-deputy has become successively an American and a French Citizen. In accepting this last title, and in occupying a place in the Legislative Corps, he submitted himself to the laws of the Republic, and has renounced the protection which the right of the people and treaties concluded with the United States could have assured him.

"I am ignorant of the motives of his detention, but I must presume they are well founded. I shall nevertheless submit the demand you have addressed me to the Committee of Public Safety, and I shall lose no time in letting you know its decision.

"DEFORGUES."

The opening assertion of the French Minister's note reveals the collusion. Careful examination of the American Minister's letter, to find where he "reclaims the liberty of Thomas Payne as an American citizen," forces me to the conclusion that the Frenchman only discovered such reclamation there by the assistance of Morris.

The American Minister distinctly declares Paine to be a French citizen, and disclaims official recognition of his conduct as "*pas de mon ressort.*"

It will be borne in mind that this French Minister is the same Deforgues who had confided to Morris his longing to succeed Genêt in America, and to whom Morris had whispered his design against Paine. Morris resided at Sainport, twenty-seven miles away, but his note is written in Paris. Four days elapse before the reply. Consultation is further proved by the French Minister's speaking of Paine as "occupying a place in the Legislative Corps." No uninspired Frenchman could have so described the Convention, any more than an American would have described the

---

i. e., Feb. 16th]. To declare reception and to tell him that the Minister will take the necessary steps." The French Minister's reply is Doc. 61 of the same volume.

Convention of 1787 as "Congress." Deforgues' phrase is calculated for Philadelphia, where it might be supposed that the recently adopted Constitution had been followed by the organization of a legislature, whose members must of course take an oath of allegiance, which the Convention had not required.[1] Deforgues also makes bold to delare— as far away as Philadelphia—that Paine is a French citizen, though he was excluded from the Convention and imprisoned because he was a "foreigner." The extreme ingenuity of the letter was certainly not original with this Frenchman. The American Minister, in response to his note declaring Paine a French citizen, and disclaiming jurisdiction over him, returns to Sainport with his official opiate for Paine's friends in America and Paris—a certificate that he has "reclaimed the liberty of Thomas Paine as an American citizen." The alleged reclamation suppressed, the certificate sent to Secretary Jefferson and to Paine, the American Minister is credited with having done his duty. In Washington's Cabinet, where the technicalities of citizenship had become of paramount importance, especially as regarded France, Deforgues' claim that Paine was not an American must be accepted—Morris consenting—as final.

It may be wondered that Morris should venture on so dangerous a game. But he had secured himself in anything he might choose to do. So soon as he discovered, in the previous summer, that he was not to be removed, and had fresh thunderbolts to wield, he veiled himself from the inspection of Jefferson. This he did in a letter of September 22, 1793. In the quasi-casual way characteristic of him when he is particular deep, Morris then wrote : "*By the bye, I shall cease to send you copies*

[1] Deforgues' phrase "laws of the Republic" is also a deception. The Constitution had been totally suspended by the Convention ; no government or law had been or ever was established under or by it. There was as yet no Republic, and only revolutionary or martial laws.

of my various applications in particular cases, for they will cost you more in postage than they are worth." I put in italics this sentence, as one which merits memorable record in the annals of diplomacy.

The French Foreign Office being secret as the grave, Jefferson facile, and Washington confiding, there was no danger that Morris' letter to Deforgues would ever appear. Although the letter of Deforgues,—his certificate that Morris had reclaimed Paine as an American,— was a little longer than the pretended reclamation, postal economy did not prevent the American Minister from sending *that*, but his own was never sent to his government, and to this day is unknown to its archives.

It cannot be denied that Morris' letter to Deforgues is masterly in its way. He asks the Minister to give him such reasons for Paine's detention as may not be known to him (Morris), there being no such reasons. He sets at rest any timidity the Frenchman might have, lest Morris should be ensnaring him also, by begging—not demanding—such knowledge as he may communicate to his government. Philadelphia is at a safe distance in time and space. Deforgues is complacent enough, Morris being at hand, to describe it as a "demand," and to promise speedy action on the matter —which was then straightway buried, for a century's slumber.

Paine was no doubt right in his subsequent belief that Morris was alarmed at his intention of returning to America. Should Paine ever reach Jefferson and his adherents, Gouverneur Morris must instantly lose a position which, sustained by Washington, made him a power throughout Europe. Moreover, there was a Nemesis lurking near him. The revolutionists, aware of his relations with their enemies, were only withheld from laying hands on him by awe of Washington and anxiety about the alliance. The moment of his repudiation by his government would have been a perilous one. It so proved, indeed, when Monroe supplanted him. For the present, however, he is powerful. As the French Executive could have no interest merely to keep Paine, for six months, without suggestion of trial, it is difficult to imagine any reason, save the wish of Morris, why he was not allowed to depart with the Americans, in accordance with their petition.

Thus Thomas Paine, recognized by every American statesman and by Congress as a founder of their Republic, found himself a prisoner, and a man without a country. Outlawed by the rulers of his native land—though the people bore his defender, Erskine, from the court on their shoulders—imprisoned by France as a foreigner, disowned by America as a foreigner, and prevented by its Minister from returning to the country whose President had declared his services to it pre-eminent!

Never dreaming that his situation was the work of Morris, Paine (February 24th) appealed to him for help.

"I received your letter enclosing a copy of a letter from the Minister of foreign affairs. You must not leave me in the situation in which this letter places me. You know I do not deserve it, and you see the unpleasant situation in which I am thrown. I have made an essay in answer to the Minister's letter, which I wish you to make ground of a reply to him. They have nothing against me—except that they do not choose I should be in a state of freedom to write my mind freely upon things I have seen. Though you and I are not on terms of the best harmony, I apply to you as the Minister of America, and you may add to that service whatever you think my integrity deserves. At any rate I expect you to make Congress acquainted with my situation, and to send to them copies of the letters that have passed on the subject. A reply to the Minister's letter is absolutely necessary, were it only to continue the reclamation. Otherwise your silence will be a sort of consent to his observations."

Supposing, from the French Minister's opening assertion, that a reclamation had really been made, Paine's simplicity led him into a trap. He sent his argument to be used by the Minister in an answer of his own, so that Minister was able to do as he pleased with it, the result being that it was buried among his private papers, to be partly brought to light by

Jared Sparks, who is candid enough to remark on the Minister's indifference and the force of Paine's argument. Not a word to Congress was ever said on the subject.

Jefferson, without the knowledge or expectation of Morris, had resigned the State Secretaryship at the close of 1793. Morris' letter of March 6th reached the hands of Edmund Randolph, Jefferson's successor, late in June. On June 25th Randolph writes Washington, at Mount Vernon, that he has received a letter from Morris, of March 6th, saying "that he has demanded Paine as an American citizen, but that the Minister holds him to be amenable to the French laws." Randolph was a just man and an exact lawyer; it is certain that if he had received a copy of the fictitious "reclamation" the imprisonment would have been curtailed. Under the false information before him, nothing could be done but await the statement of the causes of Paine's detention, which Deforgues would "lose no time" in transmitting. It was impossible to deny, without further knowledge, the rights over Paine apparently claimed by the French government.

And what could be done by the Americans in Paris, whom Paine alone had befriended? Joel Barlow, who had best opportunities of knowing the facts, says: "He [Paine] was always charitable to the poor beyond his means, a sure friend and protector to all Americans in distress that he found in foreign countries; and he had frequent occasions to exert his influence in protecting them during the Revolution in France."[1] They were grateful and deeply moved, these Americans, but thoroughly deceived about the situation. Told that they must await the action of a distant government, which itself was waiting for

[1] Written on Aug. 11, 1809, in reply to Cheetham, who began to prepare his life of Paine immediately after the death of the latter. He wrote for information to various persons; if the answers suited his purpose, he used them; if they did not he suppressed them. See Vale, p. 134.—H.B.B.

action in Paris, alarmed by the American Minister's hints of danger that might ensue on any misstep or agitation, assured that he was proceeding with the case, forbidden to communicate with Paine, they were reduced to helplessness. Meanwhile, between silent America and these Americans, all so cunningly disabled, stood the remorseless French Committee, ready to strike or to release in obedience to any sign from the alienated ally, to soothe whom no sacrifice would be too great. Genêt had been demanded for the altar of sacred Alliance, but (to Morris' regret) refused by the American government. The Revolution would have preferred Morris as a victim, but was quite ready to offer Paine.

Six or seven months elapsed without bringing from President or Cabinet a word of sympathy for Paine. But they brought increasing indications that America was in treaty with England, and Washington disaffected towards France. Under these circumstances Robespierre resolved on the accusation and trial of Paine. It does not necessarily follow that Paine would have been condemned ; but there were some who did not mean that he should escape, among whom Robespierre may or may not have been included. The probabilities, to my mind, are against that theory. Robespierre having ceased to attend the Committee of Public Safety when the order issued for Paine's death.

CHAPTER XXXII

SICK AND IN PRISON

It was a strange world into which misfortune had introduced Paine. There was in prison a select and rather philosophical society, mainly persons of refinement, more or less released from conventional habit by the strange conditions under which they found themselves. There were gentlemen and ladies, no attempt being made to separate them until some scandal was reported. The Luxembourg was a special prison for the French nobility and the English, who had a good opportunity for cultivating democratic ideas. The gaoler, Benoit, was good-natured, and cherished his unwilling guests as his children, according to a witness. Paine might even have been happy there but for the ever recurring tragedies—the cries of those led forth to death. He was now and then in strange juxtapositions. One day Deforgues came to join him, he who had conspired with Morris. Instead of receiving for his crime diplomatic security in America he found

himself beside his victim. Perhaps if Deforgues and Paine had known each other's language a confession might have passed. There were horrors on horrors. Paine's old friend, Hérault de Séchelles, was imprisoned for having humanely concealed in his house a poor officer who was hunted by the police ; he parted from Paine for the scaffold. So also he parted from the brilliant Camille Desmoulins, and the fine dreamer, Anacharsis Clootz. One day came Danton, who, taking Paine's hand, said : "That which you did for the happiness and liberty of your country, I tried in vain to do for mine. I have been less fortunate, but not less innocent. They will send me to the scaffold ; very well, my friends, I shall go gaily." Even so did Danton meet his doom.[1]

All of the English prisoners became Paine's friends. Among these was General O'Hara,—that same general who had fired the American heart at

[1] "Mémoires sur les prisons," t. ii., p. 153.

Yorktown by offering the surrendered sword of Cornwallis to Rochambeau instead of Washington. O'Hara's captured suite included two physicians— Bond and Graham—who attended Paine during an illness, as he gratefully records. What money Paine had when arrested does not appear to have been taken from him, and he was able to assist General O'Hara with £200 to return to his country; though by this and similar charities he was left without means when his own unexpected deliverance came.[1]

The first part of "The Age of Reason" was sent out with final revision at the close of January. In the second edition appeared the following inscription :

"To my fellow citizens of the United States of America.—I put the following work under your protection. It contains my opinion upon Religion. You will do me the justice to remember, that I have always strenuously supported the Right of every man to his opinion, however different that opinion might be to mine. He who denies to another this right, makes a slave of himself to his present opinion, because he precludes himself the right of changing it. The most formidable weapon against errors of every kind is Reason. I have never used any other, and I trust I never shall.—Your affectionate friend and fellow citizen,
"Thomas Paine.'

This dedication is dated, "Luxembourg (Paris), 8th Pluviose, Second year of the French Republic, one and indivisible. January 27, O. S. 1794." Paine now addressed himself to the second part of "The Age of Reason," concerning which the following anecdote is told in the manuscript memoranda of Thomas Rickman :

"Paine, while in the Luxembourg prison and expecting to die hourly, read to Mr. Bond (surgeon of Brighton, from whom this anecdote came) parts of his *Age of Reason;* and every night, when Mr. Bond left him, to be separately

---

[1] Among the anecdotes told of O'Hara in prison, one is related of an argument he held with a Frenchman, on the relative degrees of liberty in England and France. "In England," he said, "we are perfectly free to write and print, *George is a good King;* but you—why you are not even permitted to write, *Robespierre is a tiger!* "

locked up, and expecting not to see Paine alive in the morning, he [Paine] always expressed his firm belief in the principles of that book, and begged Mr. Bond should tell the world such were his dying sentiments. Paine further said, if he lived he should further prosecute the work and print it. Bond added, Paine was the most conscientious man he ever knew."

In after years, when Paine was undergoing persecution for "infidelity," he reminded the zealots that they would have to "accuse Providence of infidelity," for having "protected him in all his dangers." Incidentally he gives reminiscences of his imprisonment.

"I was one of the nine members that composed the first Committee of Constitution. Six of them have been destroyed. Sieyès and myself have survived—he by bending with the times, and I by not bending. The other survivor [Barrère] joined Robespierre ; he was seized and imprisoned in his turn, and sentenced to transportation. He has since apologized to me for having signed the warrant, by saying he felt himself in danger and was obliged to do it. Hèrault Séchelles, an acquaintance of Mr. Jefferson, and a good patriot, was my *suppleant* as member of the Committee of Constitution. . . . He was imprisoned in the Luxembourg with me, was taken to the tribunal and guillotined, and I, his principal, left. There were two foreigners in the Convention, Anacharsis Clootz and myself. We were both put out of the Convention by the same vote, arrested by the same order, and carried to prison together the same night. He was taken to the guillotine, and I was again left. . . . Joseph Lebon, one of the vilest characters that ever existed, and who made the streets of Arras run with blood, was my *suppleant*, as member of the Convention for the Pas de Calais. When I was put out of the Convention he came and took my place. When I was liberated from prison and voted again into the Convention, he was sent to the same prison and took my place there, and he was sent to the guillotine instead of me. He supplied my place all the way through.
"One hundred and sixty-eight persons were taken out of the Luxembourg in one night, and a hundred and sixty of them guillotined next day, of which I knew I was to be one ; and the manner I escaped that fate is curious, and has all the appearance of accident. The room in which I lodged was on the ground floor, and one of a long range of rooms under a gallery, and the door of it opened outward and flat against the wall ; so that when it was open the inside of the door appeared outward, and the contrary when it was shut. I had three comrades, fellow prisoners with me, Joseph Vanhuile of Bruges, since president of the municipality of that town,

Michael and Robbins Bastini of Louvain. When persons by scores and by hundreds were to be taken out of the prison for the guillotine it was always done in the night, and those who performed that office had a private mark or signal by which they knew what rooms to go to, and what number to take. We, as I have said, were four, and the door of our room was marked, unobserved by us, with that number in chalk ; but it happened, if happening is the proper word, that the mark was put on when the door was open and flat against the wall, and thereby came on the inside when we shut it at night ; and the destroying angel passed by it." [1]

Paine did not hear of this chalk mark until afterwards. In his letter to Washington he says :

"I had been imprisoned seven months, and the silence of the executive part of the government of America (Mr. Washington) upon the case, and upon every thing respecting me, was explanation enough to Robespierre that he might proceed to extremities. A violent fever which had nearly terminated my existence was, I believe, the circumstance that preserved it. I was not in a condition to be removed, or to know of what was passing, or of what had passed, for more than a month. It makes a blank in my remembrance of life. The first thing I was informed of was the fall of Robespierre."

The probabilities are that the prison physician Marhaski, whom Paine mentions with gratitude, was with him when the chalk mark was made, and that there was some connivance in the matter. In the same letter he says :

"From about the middle of March (1794) to the fall of Robespierre, July 29, (9th of Thermidor,) the state of things in the prisons was a continued scene of horror. No man could count upon life for twenty-four hours. To such a pitch of rage and suspicion were Robespierre and his committee arrived, that it seemed as if they feared to leave a man to live. Scarcely a night passed in which ten, twenty, thirty, forty, fifty or more were not taken out of the prison, carried before a pretended tribunal in the morning, and guillotined before night. One hundred and sixty-nine were taken out of the Luxembourg one night in the month of July, and one hundred and sixty of them guillotined. A list of two hundred more, according to the report in the prison, was preparing a few days before Robespierre fell. In this last list I have good reason to believe I was included."

To this Paine adds the memorandum for his accusation found in Robespierre's note-book. Of course it was natural, especially with the memorandum, to accept the Robespierre mythology of the time without criticism. The massacres of July were not due to Robespierre, who during that time was battling with the Committee of Public Safety, at whose hands he fell on the 29th. At the close of June there was an alarm at preparations for an insurrection in Luxembourg prison, which caused a union of the Committee of Public Safety and the police, resulting in indiscriminate slaughter of prisoners. But Paine was discriminated. Barrère, long after, apologized to him for having signed "the warrant," by saying he felt himself in danger and was obliged to do it. Paine accepted the apology, and when Barrère had returned to France, after banishment, Paine introduced him to the English author, Lewis Goldsmith.[2] As Barrère did not sign the warrant for Paine's imprisonment, it must have been a warrant for his death, or for accusation at a moment when it was equivalent to a death sentence. Whatever danger Barrère had to fear, so great as to cause him to sacrifice Paine, it was not from Robespierre ; else it would not have continued to keep Paine in prison three months after Robespierre's death. As Robespierre's memorandum was for a "decree of accusation" against Paine, separately, which might not have gone against him, but possibly have dragged to light the conspiracy against him, there would seem to be no ground for connecting that "demand" with the warrant signed by a Committee he did not attend.

Paine had good cause for writing as he did in praise of "Forgetfulness." During the period in which he was unconscious with fever the horrors of the prison reached their apogee. On June 19th the kindly gaoler, Benoit, was

---

[1] Letters to American Citizens. "Writings of Thomas Paine" (Conway), vol. iii., p. 394.— H.B.B.

[2] "Mémoires de B. Barrère," t. i., p. 80. Lewis Goldsmith was the author of "Crimes of the Cabinets."

removed and tried; he was acquitted but not restored. His place was given to a cruel fellow named Gayard, who instituted a reign of terror in the prison.

There are many evidences that the good Benoit, so warmly remembered by Paine, evaded the rigid police regulations as to communications of prisoners with their friends outside, no doubt with precaution against those of a political character. It is pleasant to record an instance of this which was the means of bringing beautiful rays of light into Paine's cell. Shortly before his arrest an English lady had called on him, at his house in the Faubourg St. Denis, to ask his intervention in behalf of an Englishman of rank who had been arrested. Paine had now, however, fallen from power, and could not render the requested service. This lady was the last visitor who preceded the officers who arrested him. But while he was in prison there was brought to him a communication, in a lady's handwriting, signed "A little corner of the World." So far as can be gathered, this letter was of a poetical character, perhaps tinged with romance. It was followed by others, all evidently meant to beguile the weary and fearful hours of a prisoner whom she had little expectation of ever meeting again. Paine, by the aid of Benoit, managed to answer his "contemplative correspondent," as he called her, signing, "The Castle in the Air." These letters have never seen the light, but the sweetness of this sympathy did, for many an hour, bring into Paine's *oubliette* the oblivion of grief described in the letter on "Forgetfulness," sent to the lady after his liberation.

"Memory, like a beauty that is always present to hear herself flattered, is flattered by every one. But the absent and silent goddess, Forgetfulness, has no votaries, and is never thought of: yet we owe her much. She is the goddess of ease, though not of pleasure. When the mind is like a room hung with black, and every corner of it crowded with the most horrid images imagination can create, this kind, speechless maid, Forgetfulness, is following us night and day with her opium wand, and gently touching first one and then another, benumbs

them into rest, and then glides away with the silence of a departing shadow."

Paine was not forgotten by his old friends in France. So soon as the excitement attending Robespierre's execution had calmed a little, Lanthenas (August 7th) sent Merlin de Thionville a copy of the "Age of Reason," which he had translated, and made his appeal.

"I think it would be in the well-considered interest of the Republic, since the fall of the tyrants we have overthrown, to re-examine the motives of Thomas Paine's imprisonment. That re-examination is suggested by too many and sensible grounds to be related in detail. Every friend of liberty familiar with the history of our Revolution, and feeling the necessity of repelling the slanders with which despots are loading it in the eyes of nations, misleading them against us, will understand these grounds. Should the Committee of Public Safety, having before it no founded charge or suspicion against Thomas Paine, retain any scruples, and think that from my occasional conversation with that foreigner, whom the people's suffrage called to the national representation, and some acquaintance with his language, I might perhaps throw light upon their doubt, I would readily communicate to them all that I know about him. I request Merlin de Thionville to submit these considerations to the Committee."

Merlin was now a leading member of the Committee. On the following day Paine sent (in French) the following letters:

"CITIZENS, REPRESENTATIVES, AND MEMBERS OF THE COMMITTEE OF PUBLIC SAFETY: I address you a copy of a letter which I have to-day written to the Convention. The singular situation in which I find myself determines me to address myself to the whole Convention, of which you are a part.
"THOMAS PAINE.
" Maison d'Arrèt du Luxembourg,
Le 19 Thermidor, l'an 2 de la République, une et indivisible."

"CITIZEN REPRESENTATIVES: If I should not express myself with the energy I used formerly to do, you will attribute it to the very dangerous illness I have suffered in the prison of the Luxembourg. For several days I was insensible of my own existence; and though I am much recovered, it is with exceeding great difficulty that I find power to write you this letter.
" But before I proceed further, I request the Convention to observe: that this is the first line that has come from me, either to the Convention,

or to any of the Committees, since my imprisonment,—which is approaching to Eight months. —Ah, my friends, eight months' loss of Liberty seems almost a life-time to a man who has been, as I have been, the unceasing defender of Liberty for twenty years.

"I have now to inform the Convention of the reason of my not having written before. It is a year ago that I had strong reason to believe that Robespierre was my inveterate enemy, as he was the enemy of every man of virtue and humanity. The address that was sent to the Convention some time about last August from Arras, the native town of Robespierre, I have always been informed was the work of that hypocrite and the partizans he had in the place. The intention of that address was to prepare the way for destroying me, by making the People declare (though without assigning any reason) that I had lost their confidence ; the Address, however, failed of success, as it was immediately opposed by a counter-address from St. Omer which declared the direct contrary. But the strange power that Robespierre, by the most consummate hypocrisy and the most hardened cruelties, had obtained rendered any attempt on my part to obtain justice not only useless but even dangerous ; for it is the nature of Tyranny always to strike a deeper blow when any attempt has been made to repel a former one. This being my situation I submitted with patience to the hardness of my fate and waited the event of brighter days. I hope they are now arrived to the nation and to me.

"Citizens, when I left the United States in the year 1787, I promised to all my friends that I would return to them the next year ; but the hope of seeing a Revolution happily established in France, that might serve as a model to the rest of Europe, and the earnest and disinterested desire of rendering every service in my power to promote it, induced me to defer my return to that country, and to the society of my friends, for more than seven years. This long sacrifice of private tranquillity, especially after having gone through the fatigues and dangers of the American Revolution which continued almost eight years, deserved a better fate than the long imprisonment I have silently suffered. But it is not the nation but a faction that has done me this injustice, and it is to the national representation that I appeal against that injustice, Parties and Factions, various and numerous as they have been, I have always avoided. My heart was devoted to all France, and the object to which I applied myself was the Constitution. The Plan which I proposed to the Committee, of which I was a member, is now in the hands of Barrère, and it will speak for itself.

"It is perhaps proper that I inform you of the cause assigned in the order for my imprisonment. It is that I am 'a Foreigner'; whereas, the *Foreigner* thus imprisoned was invited into France by a decree of the late national Assembly, and that in the hour of her greatest danger, when invaded by Austrians and Prussians. He was, moreover, a citizen of the United States of America, an ally of France, and not a subject of any country in Europe, and consequently not within the intentions of any of the decrees concerning Foreigners. But any excuse can be made to serve the purpose of malignity when it is in power.

"I will not intrude on your time by offering any apology for the broken and imperfect manner in which I have expressed myself. I request you to accept it with the sincerity with which it comes from my heart ; and I conclude with wishing Fraternity and prosperity to France, and union and happiness to her representatives.

"Citizens, I have now stated to you my situation, and I can have no doubt but your justice will restore me to the Liberty of which I have been deprived.

"THOMAS PAINE.
"Luxembourg, Themidor 19th, 2d year of the French Republic, one and indivisible."

No doubt this touching letter would have been effectual had it reached the Convention. But the Committee of Public Safety took care that no whisper even of its existence should be heard. Paine's participation in their fostered dogma, that *Robespierre le veut* explained all crimes, probably cost him three more months in prison. The lamb had confided its appeal to the wolf. Barrère, Billaud-Varennes, and Collot d'Herbois, by skilful use of the dead scapegoat, maintained their places on the Committee until September 1st, and after that influenced its counsels. At the same time Morris, as we have seen, was keeping Monroe out of his place. There might have been a serious reckoning for these men had Paine been set free, or his case inquired into by the Convention. And Thuriot was now on the Committee of Public Safety ; he was eager to lay his own crimes on Robespierre, and to conceal those of the Committee. Paine's old friend, Achille Audibert, unsuspicious as himself of the real facts, sent an appeal (August 20th) to "Citizen Thuriot, member of the Committee of Public Safety."

"REPRESENTATIVE :—A friend of mankind is groaning in chains,—Thomas Paine, who was not so politic as to remain silent in regard to a man unlike himself, but dared to say that Robespierre was a monster to be erased from the list of men. From that moment he became a criminal; the despot marked him as his victim, put him into prison, and doubtless prepared the way to the scaffold for him, as for others who knew him and were courageous enough to speak out.[1]

"Thomas Paine is an acknowledged citizen of the United States. He was the secretary of the Congress for the department of foreign affairs during the Revolution. He has made himself known in Europe by his writings, and especially by his ' Rights of Man.' The electoral assembly of the department of Pas-de-Calais elected him one of its representatives to the Convention, and commissioned me to go to London, inform him of his election, and bring him to France. I hardly escaped being a victim to the English Government with which he was at open war ; I performed my mission ; and ever since friendship has attached me to Paine. This is my apology for soliciting you for his liberation.

"I can assure you, Representative, that America was by no means satisfied with the imprisonment of a strong column of its Revolution. Please to take my prayer into consideration. But for Robespierre's villainy this friend of man would now be free. Do not permit liberty longer to see in prison a victim of the wretch who lives no more but by his crimes ; and you will add to the esteem and veneration I feel for a man who did so much to save the country amidst the most tremendous crisis of our Revolution.

"Greeting, respect, and brotherhood,
"ACHILLE AUDIBERT, of Calais.
"No. 216 Rue de Bellechase, Fauborg St. Germaine."

Audibert's letter, of course, sank under the burden of its Robespierre myth to a century's sleep beside Paine's, in the Committee's closet.

Meanwhile, the regulation against any communication of prisoners with the outside world remaining in force, it was some time before Paine could know that his letter had been suppressed on its way to the Convention. He was thus late in discovering his actual enemies.

An interesting page in the annals of diplomacy remains to be written on the closing weeks of Morris in France. On August 14th he writes to Robert Morris : "I am preparing for my departure, but as yet can take no step, as there is a kind of interregnum in the government and Mr. Monroe is not yet received, at

which he grows somewhat impatient." There was no such interregnum, and no such explanation was given to Monroe, who writes :

"I presented my credentials to the commissary of foreign affairs soon after my arrival [August 2d] ; but more than a week had elapsed, and I had obtained no answer, when or whether I should be received. A delay beyond a few days surprised me, because I could discern no adequate or rational motive for it." [2]

It is plain that the statement of Paine, who was certainly in communication with the Committees a year later, is true, that Morris was in danger on account of the interception of compromising letters written by him. He needed time to dispose of his house and horses, and ship his wines, and felt it important to retain his protecting credentials. At any moment his friends might be expelled from the Committee, and their papers be examined. While the arrangements for Monroe's reception rested with Morris and this unaltered Committee, there was little prospect of Monroe's being installed at all. The new Minister was therefore compelled, as other Americans had been, to appeal directly to the Convention. That assembly reponded at once, and he was received (August 28th) with highest honors. Morris had nothing to do with the arrangement. The historian Frédéric Masson, alluding to the "unprecedented" irregularity of Morris in not delivering or receiving letters of recall, adds that Monroe found it important to state that he had acted without consultation with his predecessor.[3] This was necessary for a cordial reception by the Convention, but it invoked the cordial hatred of Morris, who marked him for his peculiar guillotine set up in Philadelphia.

So completely had America and Congress been left in the dark about

---

[1] It must be remembered that at this time it seemed the strongest recommendation of any one to public favor to describe him a victim of Robespierre ; and Paine's friends could conceive no other cause for the detention of a man they knew to be innocent.

[2] "View of the Conduct of the Executive in the Foreign Affairs of the United States," by James Monroe, p. 7.

[3] "Le Départément des Affaires Étrangères," etc., p. 345.

Paine that Monroe was surprised to find him a prisoner. When at length the new Minister was in a position to consult the French Minister about Paine, he found the knots so tightly tied around this particular victim—almost the only one left in the Luxembourg of those imprisoned during the Terror—that it was difficult to untie them. The Minister of Foreign Affairs was now M. Bouchot, a weak creature who, as Morris said, would not wipe his nose without permission of the Committee of Public Safety. When Monroe opened Paine's case he was asked whether he had brought instructions. Of course he had none, for the administration had no suspicion that Morris had not, as he said, attended to the case.

When Paine recovered from his fever he heard that Monroe had superseded Morris.

" As soon as I was able to write a note legible enough to be read, I found a way to convey one to him [Monroe] by means of the man who lighted the lamps in the prison, and whose unabated friendship to me, from whom he never received any service, and with difficulty accepted any recompense, puts the character of Mr. Washington to shame. In a few days I received a message from Mr. Monroe, conveyed in a note from an intermediate person, with assurance of his friendship, and expressing a desire that I should rest the case in his hands. After a fortnight or more had passed, and hearing nothing farther, I wrote to a friend [Whiteside], a citizen of Philadelphia, requesting him to inform me what was the true situation of things with respect to me. I was sure that something was the matter ; I began to have hard thoughts of Mr. Washington, but I was unwilling to encourage them. In about ten days I received an answer to my letter, in which the writer says : ' Mr. Monroe told me he had no order (meaning from the president, Mr. Washington) respecting you, but that he (Mr. Monroe) will do everything in his power to liberate you, but, from what I learn from the Americans lately arrived in Paris, you are not considered, either by the American government or by individuals, as an American citizen.' "

As the American government did regard Paine as an American citizen, and approved Monroe's demanding him as such, there is no difficulty in recognizing the source from which these statements were diffused among Paine's newly arriving countrymen. Morris was still in Paris.

On the receipt of Whiteside's note, Paine wrote a Memorial to Monroe, of which important parts—amounting to eight printed pages—are omitted from American and English editions of his works. In quoting this Memorial, I select mainly the omitted portions.[1] Paine says that before leaving London for the Convention, he consulted Minister Pinckney, who agreed with him that "it was for the interest of America that the system of European governments should be changed and placed on the same principle with her own"; and adds : "I have wished to see America the mother church of government, and I have done my utmost to exalt her character and her condition." He points out that he had not accepted any title or office under a foreign government, within the meaning of the United States Constitution, because there was no government in France, the Convention being assembled to frame one ; that he was a citizen of France only in the honorary sense in which others in Europe and America were declared such; that no oath of allegiance was required or given. The following paragraphs are from various parts of the Memorial.

"They who propagate the report of my not being considered as a citizen of America by government, do it to the prolongation of my imprisonment, and without authority ; for Congress, as a government, has neither decided upon it, nor yet taken the matter into consideration ; and I request you to caution such persons against spreading such reports. . . .

"I know not what opinions have been circulated in America. It may have been supposed there, that I had voluntarily and intentionally abandoned America, and that my citizenship had ceased by my own choice. I can easily conceive that there are those in that Country who would take such a proceeding on my part somewhat in disgust. The idea of forsaking old friendships for new acquaintances

[1] The whole is published in French : "Mémoire de Thomas Payne, autographé et signé de sa main : addressé à M. Monroe, ministre des États-unis en France, pour réclamer sa mise en liberté comme Citoyen Américain, 10 Septembre, 1794. Villeneuve."

is not agreeable. I am a little warranted in making this supposition by a letter I received some time ago from the wife of one of the Georgia delegates, in which she says, 'your friends on this side the water cannot be reconciled to the idea of your abandoning America.' I have never abandoned America in thought, word, or deed, and I feel it incumbent upon me to give this assurance to the friends I have in that country, and with whom I have always intended, and am determined, if the possibility exists, to close the scene of my life. It is there that I have made myself a home. It is there that I have given the services of my best days. America never saw me flinch from her cause in the most gloomy and perilous of her situations: and I know there are those in that Country who will not flinch from me. If I have Enemies (and every man has some) I leave them to the enjoyment of their ingratitude. . . .

"It is somewhat extraordinary, that the Idea of my not being a Citizen of America should have arisen only at the time that I am imprisoned in France because, or on the pretence that, I am a foreigner. The case involves a strange contradiction of Ideas. None of the Americans who came to France whilst I was in liberty, had conceived any such idea or circulated any such opinion; and why it should arise now is a matter yet to be explained. However discordant the late American Minister, Gouverneur Morris, and the late French Committee of Public Safety were, it suited the purpose of both that I should be continued in arrestation. The former wished to prevent my return to America, that I should not expose his misconduct; and the latter, lest I should publish to the world the history of its wickedness. Whilst that Minister and that Committee continued, I had no expectation of liberty. I speak here of the Committee of which Robespierre was a member. . . .

"I here close my Memorial and proceed to offer you a proposal, that appears to me suited to all the circumstances of the case; which is, that you reclaim me conditionally, until the opinion of Congress can be obtained upon the subject of my Citizenship of America, and that I remain in liberty under your protection during that time. I found this proposal upon the following grounds:

"First, you say you have no orders respecting me; consequently you have no orders *not* to reclaim me; and in this case you are left discretionary judge whether to reclaim or not. My proposal therefore unites a consideration of your situation with my own.

"Secondly, I am put in arrestation because I am a foreigner. It is therefore necessary to determine to what Country I belong. The right of determining this question cannot appertain exclusively to the committee of public safety or general surety; because I appear to the Minister of the United States, and shew that my citizenship of that Country is good and valid, referring at the same time, through the

agency of the Minister, my claim of Right to the opinion of Congress,—it being a matter between two governments.

"Thirdly, France does not claim me for a citizen; neither do I set up any claim of citizenship in France. The question is simply, whether I am or am not a citizen of America. I am imprisoned here on the decree for imprisoning Foreigners, because, say they, I was born in England. I say in answer, that, though born in England, I am not a subject of the English Government any more than any other American is who was born, as they all were, under the same government, or that the citizens of France are subjects of the French monarchy, under which they were born. I have twice taken the oath of abjuration to the British king and government, and of Allegiance to America. Once as a citizen of the State of Pennsylvania in 1776; and again before Congress, administered to me by the President, Mr. Hancock, when I was appointed Secretary in the office of foreign affairs in 1777. . . .

"Painful as the want of liberty may be, it is a consolation to me to believe that my imprisonment proves to the world that I had no share in the murderous system that then reigned. That I was an enemy to it, both morally and politically, is known to all who had any knowledge of me; and could I have written French as well as I can English, I would publicly have exposed its wickedness, and shown the ruin with which it was pregnant. They who have esteemed me on former occasions, whether in America or in England, will, I know, feel no cause to abate that esteem when they reflect, that imprisonment with preservation of character, is preferable to liberty with disgrace."

In a postscript Paine adds that "as Gouverneur Morris could not inform Congress of the cause of my arrestation, as he knew it not himself, it is to be supposed that Congress was not enough acquainted with the case to give any directions respecting me when you left." Which to the reader of the preceding pages will appear sufficiently naïve.

To this Monroe responded (September 18th) with a letter of warm sympathy, worthy of the high-minded gentleman that he was. After ascribing the notion that Paine was not an American to mental confusion, and affirming his determination to maintain his rights as a citizen of the United States, Monroe says:

"It is unnecessary for me to tell you how much all your countrymen, I speak of the great mass of the people, are interested in your welfare. They have not forgotten the history of their own revolution, and the difficult scenes through which they passed; nor do they review its several stages without reviving in their bosoms a due sensibility of the merits of those who served them in that great and arduous conflict. The crime of ingratitude has not yet stained, and I trust never will stain, our national character. You are considered by them, as not only having rendered important services in our own revolution, but as being on a more extensive scale, the friend of human rights, and a distinguished and able advocate in favor of public liberty. To the welfare of Thomas Paine the Americans are not and cannot be indifferent. Of the sense which the President has always entertained of your merits, and of his friendly disposition towards you, you are too well assured to require any declaration of it from me. That I forward his wishes in seeking your safety is what I well know; and this will form an additional obligation on me to perform what I should otherwise consider as a duty.

"You are, in my opinion, menaced by no kind of danger. To liberate you will be an object of my endeavors, and as soon as possible. But you must, until that event shall be accomplished, face your situation with patience and fortitude; you will likewise have the justice to recollect, that I am placed here upon a difficult theatre, many important objects to attend to, and with few to consult. It becomes me in pursuit of those, to regulate my conduct in respect to each, as to the manner and the time, as will, in my judgment, be best calculated to accomplish the whole.

"With great esteem and respect consider me personally your friend,

"JAMES MONROE."

Monroe was indeed "placed upon a difficult theatre." Morris was showing a fresh letter from the President expressing unabated confidence in him, apologizing for his recall; he still had friends in the Committee of Public Safety, to which Monroe had appealed in vain. The continued dread the conspirators had of Paine's liberation appears in the fact that Monroe's letter, written September 18th, did not reach Paine until October 18th, when Morris had reached the boundary line of Switzerland, which he entered on the 19th. He had left Paris (Sainport) October 14th, when Barrère, Billaud-Varennes, and Collot d'Herbois, no longer on the Committee, were under accusation, and their papers under investigation,—a search that resulted in their exile. Morris got across the line on an irregular passport.

While Monroe's reassuring letter to Paine was taking a month to penetrate his prison walls, he vainly grappled with the subtle obstacles. All manner of delays impeded the correspondence, the principal one being that he could present no instructions from the President concerning Paine. Of course he was fighting in the dark, having no suspicion that the imprisonment was due to his predecessor. At length, however, he received from Secretary Randolph a letter (dated July 30th), from which, though Paine was not among its specifications, he could select a sentence as basis of action: "We have heard with regret that several of our citizens have been thrown into prison in France, from a suspicion of criminal attempts against the government. If they are guilty we are extremely sorry for it; if innocent we must protect them." What Paine had said in his Memorial of collusion between Morris and the Committee of Public Safety probably determined Monroe to apply no more in that quarter; so he wrote (November 2d) to the Committee of General Surety. After stating the general principles and limitations of ministerial protection to an imprisoned countryman, he adds:

"The citizens of the United States cannot look back upon the time of their own revolution without recollecting among the names of their most distinguished patriots that of Thomas Paine; the services he rendered to his country in its struggle for freedom have implanted in the hearts of his countrymen a sense of gratitude never to be effaced as long as they shall deserve the title of a just and generous people.

"The above-named citizen is at this moment languishing in prison, affected with a disease growing more intense from his confinement. I beg, therefore, to call your attention to his condition and to request you to hasten the moment when the law shall decide his fate, in case of any accusation against him, and if none, to restore him to liberty.

"Greeting and fraternity, "MONROE."

At this the first positive assertion of Paine's American citizenship the prison door flew open. He had been kept there solely "pour les interêts de l'Amérique," as embodied in Morris, and two days after Monroe undertook, without instructions, to affirm the real interests of America in Paine he was liberated.

"Brumaire, 13th. Third year of the French Republic.—The Committee of General Surety ordeis that the Citizen Thomas Paine be set at liberty, and the seals taken from his papers, on sight of these presents.
"Members of the Committee (signed) : Clauzel, Lesage, Senault, Bentabole, Reverchon Goupilleau de Fontenai, Rewbell.
"Delivered to Clauzel, as Commissioner."

There are several interesting points about this little decree. It is signed by Bentabole, who had moved Paine's expulsion from the Convention. It orders that the seals be removed from Paine's papers, whereas none had been placed on them, the officers reporting them innocent. This same authority, which had ordered Paine's arrest, now, in ordering his liberation, shows that the imprisonment had never been a subject of French inquiry. It had ordered the seals but did not know whether they were on the papers or not. It was no concern of France, but only of the American Minister. It is thus further evident that when Monroe invited a trial of Paine there was not the least trace of any charge against him. And there was precisely the same absence of any accusation against Paine in the new Committee of Public Safety, to which Monroe's letter was communicated the same day.

Writing to Secretary Randolph (November 7th) Monroe says :

"He was actually a citizen of the United States, and of the United States only ; for the Revolution which parted us from Great Britain broke the allegiance which was before due to the Crown, of all who took our side. He was, of course, not a British subject ; nor was he strictly a citizen of France, for he came by invitation for the temporary purpose of assisting in the formation of their government only, and meant to withdraw to America when that should be completed. And what confirms this is the act of the Convention itself arresting him, by which he is declared a foreigner. Mr. Paine pressed my interference. I told him I had hoped getting him enlarged without it ; but, if I did interfere, it could only be by requesting that he be tried, in case there was any charge against him, and liberated in case there was not. This was admitted. His correspondence with me is lengthy and interesting, and I may probably be able hereafter to send you a copy of it. After some time had elapsed, without producing any change in his favor, I finally resolved to address the Committee of General Surety in his behalf, resting my application on the above principle. My letter was delivered by my Secretary in the Committee to the president, who assured him he would communicate its contents immediately to the Committee of Public Safety, and give me an answer as soon as possible. The conference took place accordingly between the two Committees, and, as I presume, on that night, or on the succeeding day ; for on the morning of the day after, which was yesterday, I was presented by the Secretary of the Committee of General Surety with an order for his enlargement. I forwarded it immediately to the Luxembourg, and had it carried into effect ; and have the pleasure now to add that he is not only released to the enjoyment of liberty, but is in good spirits."

In reply, the Secretary of State (Randolph) in a letter to Monroe of March 8, 1795, says : "Your observations on our commercial relations to France, and your conduct as to Mr. Gardoqui's letter, prove your judgment and assiduity. Nor are your measures as to Mr. Paine, and the lady of our friend [Lafayette] less approved."

Thus, after an imprisonment of ten months and nine days, Thomas Paine was liberated from the prison into which he had been cast by a Minister of the United States.

CHAPTER XXXIII

A RESTORATION

As in 1792 Paine had left England with the authorities at his heels, so in 1794 escaped Morris from France. The ex-Minister went off to play courtier to George III. and write for Louis XVIII. the despotic proclamation with which monarchy was to be restored in France ;[1] Paine sat in the house of a real American Minister, writing proclamations of republicanism to invade the empires. So passed each to his own place.

While the American Minister in Paris and his wife were nursing their predecessor's victim back into life, a thrill of joy was passing through European courts, on a rumor that the dreaded author had been guillotined. Paine had the satisfaction of reading, at Monroe's fireside, his own last words on the scaffold,[2] and along with it an invitation of the Convention to return to its bosom. On December 7, 1794, Thibaudeau had spoken to that assembly in the following terms :

" It yet remains for the Convention to perform an act of justice. I reclaim one of the most zealous defenders of liberty—Thomas Paine. (*Loud applause.*) My reclamation is for a man who has honored his age by his energy in defence of the rights of humanity, and who is so gloriously distinguished by his part in the American revolution. A naturalized Frenchman[3] by a decree of the legislative assembly, he was nominated by the people. It was only by an intrigue that he was driven from the Convention, the pretext being a decree excluding foreigners from representing the French people. There were only two foreigners in the Convention ; one [Anacharsis Clootz] is dead, and I speak not of him, but of Thomas Paine, who powerfully contributed to establish liberty in a country allied with the French Republic. I demand that he be recalled to the bosom of the Convention." (*Applause.*)

The *Moniteur*, from which I translate, reports the unanimous adoption of Thibaudeau's motion. But this was not enough. The Committee of Public Instruction, empowered to award pensions for literary services, reported (January 3, 1795) as the first name on their list, Thomas Paine. Chenier, in reading the report, claimed the honor of having originally suggested Paine's name as an honorary citizen of France, and denounced, amid applause, the decree against foreigners under which the great author had suffered.

" You have revoked that inhospitable decree, and we again see Thomas Paine, the man of genius without fortune, our colleague, dear to all friends of humanity,—a cosmopolitan, persecuted equally by Pitt and by Robespierre. Notable epoch in the life of this philosopher, who opposed the arms of Common Sense to the sword of Tyranny, the Rights of Man to the machiavelism of English politicians ; and who, by two immortal works, has deserved well of the human race, and consecrated liberty in the two worlds."

Poor as he was, Paine declined this literary pension. He accepted the honors paid him by the Convention,

---

[1] Morris' royal proclamations are printed in full in his biography by Jared Sparks.

[2] "The last dying words of Thomas Paine. Executed at the Guillotine in France on the 1st of September, 1794." The dying speech begins ; "Ye numerous spectators gathered around, pray give ear to my last words ; I am determined to speak the Truth in these my last moments, altho' I have written and spoke nothing but lies all my life." There is nothing in the witless leaflet worth quoting. When Paine was burnt in effigy, in 1792, it appears to have been with accompaniments of the same kind. Before me is a small placard, which reads thus : " The Dying Speech and Confession of the Arch-Traitor Thomas Paine. Who was executed at Oakham on Thursday the 27th of December 1792. This morning the Officers usually attending on such occasions went in procession on Horseback to the County Gaol, and demanded the Body of the Arch-Traitor, and from thence proceeded with the Criminal drawn in a Cart by an Ass to the usual place of execution with his Pamphlet called the 'Rights of Man' in his right hand."

[3] Here Thibaudeau was inexact. In the next sentence but one he rightly describes Paine as a foreigner. The allusion to "an intrigue" is significant.

no doubt with a sorrow at the contrasted silence of those who ruled in America. Monroe, however, encouraged him to believe that he was still beloved there, and, as he got stronger, a great home-sickness came upon him. The kindly host made an effort to satisfy him. On January 4th he (Monroe) wrote to the Committee of Public Safety:

"CITIZENS: The Decree just passed, bearing on the execution of Articles 23 and 24 of the Treaty of Friendship and Commerce between the two Republics, is of such great importance to my country, that I think it expedient to send it there officially, by some particularly confidential hand; and no one seems to be better fitted for this errand than Thomas Paine. Having resided a long time in France, and having a perfect knowledge of the many vicissitudes which the Republic has passed, he will be able to explain and compare the happy lot she now enjoys. As he has passed the same himself, remaining faithful to his principles, his reports will be the more trustworthy, and consequently produce a better effect. But as Citizen Paine is a member of the Convention, I thought it better to submit this subject to your consideration. If this affair can be arranged, the Citizen will leave for America, immediately, *via* Bordeaux, on an American vessel which will be prepared for him. As he has reason to fear the persecution of the English government, should he be taken prisoner, he desires that his departure may be kept a secret.

"JAS. MONROE."

The Convention alone could give a passport to one of its members, and as an application to it would make Paine's mission known, the Committee returned next day a negative answer.

"CITIZEN: We see with satisfaction and without surprise, that you attach some interest to sending officially to the United States the Decree which the National Convention has just made, in which are recalled and confirmed the reports of Friendship and Commerce existing between the two Republics.

"As to the design you express of confiding this errand to Citizen Thomas Paine, we must observe to you that the position he holds will not permit him to accept it. Salutation and Friendship.

"CAMBACÉRÈS." [1]

---

[1] State Archives of France. Etats Unis, vol. xliii. Monroe dates his letter, "19th year of the American Republic."

Liberty's great defender gets least of it! The large seal of the Committee—mottoed "Activity, Purity, Attention"—looks like a wheel of fortune; but one year before it had borne from the Convention to prison the man it now cannot do without. France now especially needs the counsel of shrewd and friendly American heads. There are indications that Jay in London is carrying the United States into Pitt's combination against the Republic, just as it is breaking up on the Continent.

Monroe's magnanimity towards Paine found its reward. He brought to his house, and back into life, just the one man in France competent to give him the assistance he needed. Comprehending the history of the Revolution, knowing the record of every actor in it, Paine was able to revise Monroe's impressions, and enable him to check calumnies circulated in America. The despatches of Monroe are of high historic value, largely through knowledge derived from Paine.

Nor was this all. In Monroe's instructions emphasis was laid on the importance to the United States of the free navigation of the Mississippi and its ultimate control.[2] Paine's former enthusiasm in this matter had possibly been utilized by Gouverneur Morris to connect him, as we have seen, with Genêt's proceedings. The Kentuckians consulted Paine at a time when expulsion of the Spaniard was a patriotic American scheme. This is shown in a letter written by the Secretary of State (Randolph) to the President, February 27, 1794.

"Mr. Brown [Senator of Kentucky] has shown me a letter from the famous Dr. O'Fallon to Captain Herron, dated Oct. 18, 1793. It was intercepted, and he has permitted me to

---

[2] "The conduct of Spain towards us is unaccountable and injurious. Mr. Pinckney is by this time gone over to Madrid as our envoy extraordinary to bring matters to a conclusion some way or other. But you will seize any favorable moment to execute what has been entrusted to you respecting the Mississippi."— *Randolph to Monroe*, February 15, 1795.

take the following extract :—' This plan (an attack on Louisiana) was digested between Gen. Clarke and me last Christmas. I framed the whole of the correspondence in the General's name, and corroborated it by a private letter of my own to Mr. Thomas Paine, of the National Assembly, with whom during the late war I was very intimate. His reply reached me but a few days since, enclosed in the General's despatches from the Ambassador." [1]

That such letters (freely written as they were at the beginning of 1793) were now intercepted indicates the seriousness of the situation time had brought on. The administration had soothed the Kentuckians by pledges of pressing the matter by negotiations. Hence Monroe's instructions, in carrying out which Paine was able to lend a hand.

In the State Archives at Paris (*États Unis*, vol. xliii.) there are two papers marked "Thomas Payne." The first urges the French Ministry to seize the occasion of a treaty with Spain to do a service to the United States : let the free navigation of the Mississippi be made by France a condition of peace. The second paper (endorsed " 3 Ventose, February 21, 1795") proposes that, in addition to the condition made to Spain, an effort should be made to include American interests in the negotiation with England, if not too late. The negotiation with England was then finished, but the terms unpublished. Paine recommended that the Convention should pass a resolution that freedom of the Mississippi should be a condition of peace with Spain, which would necessarily accept it ; and that,

in case the arrangement with England should prove unsatisfactory, any renewed negotiations should support the just reclamations of their American ally for the surrender of the frontier posts and for depredations on their trade. Paine points out that such a declaration could not prolong the war a day, nor cost France an obole ; whereas it might have a decisive effect in the United States, especially if Jay's treaty with England should be reprehensible, and should be approved in America. That generosity "would certainly raise the reputation of the French Republic to the most eminent degree of splendour, and lower in proportion that of her enemies." It would undo the bad effects of the depredations of French privateers on American vessels, which rejoiced the British party in the United States and discouraged the friends of liberty and humanity there. It would acquire for France the merit which is her due, supply her American friends with strength against the intrigues of England, and cement the alliance of the Republics.

This able paper might have been acted on, but for the anger in France at the Jay treaty.

While writing in Monroe's house, the invalid, with an abscess in his side and a more painful sore in his heart—for he could not forget that Washington had forgotten him,—receives tidings of new events through cries in the street. In the month of his release they had been resonant with yells as the Jacobins were driven away and their rooms turned to a Normal School. Then came shouts, when, after trial, the murderous committeemen were led to execution or exile. In the early weeks of 1795 the dread sounds of retribution subside, and there is a cry from the street that comes nearer to Paine's heart—"Bread and the Constitution of Ninety-three !" He knows that it is his Constitution for which they are really calling, for they cannot understand the Robespierrian adulteration of it given out, as one said, as an opiate to keep the country asleep. The

[1] Two important historical works have recently appeared relating to the famous Senator Brown. The first is a publication of the Filson Club : "The Political Beginnings of Kentucky," by John Mason Brown. The second is : "The Spanish Conspiracy," by Thomas Marshall Green (Cincinnati, Robert Clarke & Co., 1891). The intercepted letter quoted above has some bearing on the controversy between these authors. Apparently, Senator Brown, like many other good patriots, favored independent action in Kentucky when that seemed for the welfare of the United States, but, when the situation had changed, Brown is found cooperating with Washington and Randolph.

people are sick of revolutionary rule. These are the people in whom Paine has ever believed,—the honest hearts that summoned him, as author of "The Rights of Man," to help form their Constitution. They, he knows, had to be deceived when cruel deeds were done, and heard of such deeds with as much horror as distant peoples. Over that Constitution for which they were clamoring he and his lost friend Condorcet had spent many a day of honest toil. Of the original Committee of Nine appointed for the work, six had perished by the revolution, one was banished, and two remained—Sieyès and Paine. That original Committee had gradually left the task to Paine and Condorcet,— Sieyès, because he had no real sympathy with republicanism, though he honored Paine.[1] When afterwards asked how he had survived the Terror, Sieyès answered, "I lived." He lived by bending, and now leads a Committee of Eleven on the Constitution, while Paine, who did not bend, is disabled. Paine knows Sieyès well. The people will vainly try for the "Constitution of Ninety-three." They shall have no Constitution but of Sieyès' making, and in it will be some element of monarchy. Sieyès presently seemed to retire from the Committee, but old republicans did not doubt that he was all the more swaying it.

So once more Paine seizes his pen; his hand is feeble, but his intellect has lost no fibre of force, nor his heart its

[1] "Mr. Thomas Paine is one of those men who have contributed the most to establish the liberty of America. His ardent love of humanity, and his hatred of every sort of tyranny, have induced him to take up in England the defence of the French revolution, against the amphigorical declamation of Mr. Burke. His work has been translated into our language, and is universally known. What French patriot is there who has not already, from the bottom of his heart, thanked this foreigner for having strengthened our cause by all the powers of his reason and reputation? It is with pleasure that I observe an opportunity of offering him the tribute of my gratitude and my esteem for the truly philosophical application of talents so distinguished as his own."—Sieyès in the *Moniteur*, July 6, 1791.

old faith. His trust in man has passed through the ordeal of seeing his friends —friends of man—murdered by the people's Convention, himself saved by accident; it has survived the apparent relapse of Washington into the arms of George the Third. The ingratitude of his faithfully-served America is represented by an abscess in his side, which may strike into his heart—in a sense has done so—but will never reach his faith in liberty, equality, and humanity.

Early in July the Convention is reading Paine's "Dissertation on First Principles of Government." His old arguments against hereditary right, or investing even an elective individual with extraordinary power, are repeated with illustrations from the passing Revolution.

"Had a Constitution been established two years ago (as ought to have been done), the violences that have since desolated France and injured the character of the revolution, would, in my opinion, have been prevented. The nation would then have had a bond of union, and every individual would have known the line of conduct he was to follow. But, instead of this, a revolutionary government, a thing without either principle or authority, was substituted in its place; virtue or crime depended upon accident; and that which was patriotism one day, became treason the next. All these things have followed from the want of a Constitution; for it is the nature and intention of a Constitution to prevent governing by party, by establishing a common principle that shall limit and control the power and impulse of party, and that says to all parties, *Thus far shalt thou go, and no farther.* But in the absence of a Constitution men look entirely to party; and instead of principle governing party, party governs principle.
"An avidity to punish is always dangerous to liberty. It leads men to stretch, to misinterpret and to misapply even the best of laws. He that would make his own liberty secure, must guard even his enemy from oppression; for if he violates this duty, he establishes a precedent that will reach to himself."

Few of Paine's pamphlets better deserve study than this. In writing it, he tells us, he utilized the fragment of a work begun at some time not stated, which he meant to dedicate to the people of Holland, then contemplating a revolution. It is a condensed statement of the principles underlying the Constitution written by himself and Condorcet, now included among Condorcet's works. They who imagine that Paine's political system was that of the democratic demagogues may undeceive themselves by pondering this pamphlet. It has been pointed out, on a previous page of this work, that Paine held the representative to be not the voter's mouthpiece, but his delegated sovereignty. The representatives of a people are therefore its supreme power. The executive, the ministers, are merely as chiefs of the national police engaged in enforcing the laws. They are mere employés, without any authority at all, except of superintendence. "The executive department is official, and is subordinate to the legislative as the body is to the mind." The chief of these official departments is the judicial. In appointing officials the most important rule is, "never to invest any individual with extraordinary power; for besides being tempted to misuse it, it will excite contention and commotion in the nation for the office."

All of this is in logical conformity with the same author's "Rights of Man," which James Madison declared to be an exposition of the principles on which the United States government is based. It would be entertaining to observe the countenance of a President should our House of Representatives address him as a chief of national police.

Soon after the publication of Paine's "Dissertation" a new French Constitution was textually submitted for popular consideration. Although in many respects it accorded fairly well with Paine's principles, it contained one provision which he believed would prove fatal to the Republic. This was the limitation of citizenship to payers of direct taxes, except soldiers who had fought in one or more campaigns for the Republic, this being a sufficient qualification. This revolutionary disfranchisement of near half the nation brought Paine to the Convention (July 7th) for the first time since the fall of the Brissotins, two years

before. The scene at his return was impressive. A special motion was made by Lanthenas and unanimously adopted, "that permission be granted Thomas Paine to deliver his sentiments on the declaration of rights and the Constitution." With feeble step he ascended the tribune, and stood while a secretary read his speech. Of all present this man had suffered most by the confusion of the mob with the people, which caused the reaction on which was floated the device he now challenged. It is an instance of idealism rare in political history. The speech opens with words that caused emotion.

"CITIZENS, The effects of a malignant fever, with which I was afflicted during a rigorous confinement in the Luxembourg, have thus long prevented me from attending at my post in the bosom of the Convention; and the magnitude of the subject under discussion, and no other consideration on earth, could induce me now to repair to my station. A recurrence to the vicissitudes I have experienced, and the critical situations in which I have been placed in consequence of the French Revolution, will throw upon what I now propose to submit to the Convention the most unequivocal proofs of my integrity, and the rectitude of those principles which have uniformly influenced my conduct. In England I was proscribed for having vindicated the French Revolution, and I have suffered a rigorous imprisonment in France for having pursued a similar line of conduct. During the reign of terrorism I was a prisoner for eight long months, and remained so above three months after the era of the 10th Thermidor. I ought, however, to state, that I was not persecuted by the *people*, either of England or France. The proceedings in both countries were the effects of the despotism existing in their respective governments. But, even if my persecution had originated in the people at large, my principles and conduct would still have remained the same. Principles which are influenced and subject to the control of tyranny have not their foundation in the heart."

Though they slay him Paine will trust in the people. There seems a slight slip of memory; his imprisonment, by revolutionary calendar, lasted ten and a half months, or 315 days; but there is no failure of conviction or of thought. He points out the inconsistency of the disfranchisement of indirect tax-payers with the Declaration of Rights, and the opportunity afforded partisan majorities to influence suffrage by legislation on the mode of collecting taxes. The soldier, enfranchised without other qualification, would find his children slaves.

"If you subvert the basis of the Revolution, if you dispense with principles and substitute expedients, you will extinguish that enthusiasm which has hitherto been the life and soul of the revolution ; and you will substitute in its place nothing but a cold indifference and self-interest, which will again degenerate into intrigue, cunning, and effeminacy."

There was an educational test of suffrage to which he did not object. "Where knowledge is a duty, ignorance is a crime." But in his appeal to pure principle simple-hearted Paine knew nothing of the real test of the Convention's votes. This white-haired man was the only eminent member of the Convention with nothing in his record to cause shame or fear. He almost alone among them had the honor of having risked his head rather than execute Louis, on whom he had looked as one man upon another. He alone had refused to enter the Convention when it abandoned the work for which it was elected and became a usurping tribunal. During two fearful years the true Republic had been in Paine's house and garden, where he conversed with his disciples ; or in Luxembourg prison, where he won all hearts, as did imprisoned George Fox, who reappeared in him, and where, beneath the knife whose fall seemed certain, he criticised consecrated dogmas. With this record Paine spoke that day to men who feared to face the honest sentiment of the harried peasantry. Some of the members had indeed been terrorized, but a majority shared the disgrace of the old Convention. They were jeered at on the streets. The heart of France was throbbing again, and what would become of these "Conventionnels," when their assembly should die in giving birth to a government? They must from potentates become pariahs. Their aim now was to prolong their political existence. The constitutional narrowing of the suffrage was in anticipation of the decree presently appended, that two-thirds of the new legislature should be chosen from the Convention.

Paine's speech was delivered against a foregone conclusion. This was his last appearance in the Convention. Out of it he naturally dropped when it ended (October 26, 1795), with the organization of the Directory. Being an American he would not accept candidature in a foreign government.

CHAPTER XXXIV

THE SILENCE OF WASHINGTON

MONROE, in a letter of September 15th to his relative, Judge Joseph Jones, of Fredericksburg, Virginia, after speaking of the Judge's son and his tutor at St. Germain, adds :

"As well on his account as that of our child, who is likewise at St. Germain, we had taken rooms there, with the intention of occupying for a month or two in the course of the autumn, but fear it will not be in our power to do so, on account of the ill-health of Mr. Paine, who has lived in my house for about ten months past. He was upon my arrival confined in the Luxembourg, and released on my application ; after which, being ill, he has remained with me. For some time the prospect of his recovery was good ; his malady being an abscess in his side, the consequence of a severe fever in the Luxembourg. Latterly his symptoms have become worse, and the prospect now is that he will not be able to hold out more than a month or two at the furthest. I shall certainly pay the utmost attention to this gentleman, as he is one of those whose merits in our Revolution were most distinguished." [1]

Paine's speech in the Convention told sadly on his health. Again he had to face death. As when, in 1793, the guillotine rising over him, he had set about writing his last bequest, the "Age of Reason," he now devoted himself to its completion. The manuscript of the second part, begun in prison, had been in the printer's hands some time before Monroe wrote of his approaching end. When the book appeared, he was so low that his death was again reported.

So far as France was concerned, there was light about his eventide.

"Almost as suddenly," so he wrote, "as the morning light dissipates darkness, did the establishment of the Constitution change the face of affairs in France. Security succeeded to terror, prosperity to distress, plenty to famine, and confidence increased as the days multiplied." [2]

This may now seem morbid optimism, but it was shared by the merry youth, and the pretty dames, whose craped arms did not prevent their sandalled feet and Greek-draped-forms from dancing in their transient Golden Age. Of all this, we may be sure, the invalid hears many a beguiling story from Madame Monroe.

But there is a grief in his heart more cruel than death. The months have come and gone,—more than eighteen,— since Paine was cast into prison, but as yet no word of kindness or inquiry had come from Washington. Early in the year, on the President's sixty-third birthday, Paine had written him a letter of sorrowful and bitter reproach, which Monroe persuaded him not to send, probably because of its censures on the ministerial failures of Morris, and "the pusillanimous conduct of Jay in England." It now seems a pity that Monroe did not encourage Paine to

[1] I am indebted to Mrs. Gouverneur, of Washington, for this letter, which is among the invaluable papers of her ancestor, President Monroe, which surely should be secured for our national archives.
[2] The Eighteenth Fructidor. "Writings of Paine" (Conway), vol. iii., p. 351.—H.B.B.

send Washington, in substance, the personal part of his letter, which was in the following terms :

"As it is always painful to reproach those one would wish to respect, it is not without some difficulty that I have taken the resolution to write to you. The danger to which I have been exposed cannot have been unknown to you, and the guarded silence you have observed upon that circumstance, is what I ought not to have expected from you, either as a friend or as a President of the United States.

"You knew enough of my character to be assured that I could not have deserved imprisonment in France, and, without knowing anything more than this, you had sufficient ground to have taken some interest for my safety. Every motive arising from recollection ought to have suggested to you the consistency of such a measure. But I cannot find that you have so much as directed any enquiry to be made whether I was in prison or at liberty, dead or alive ; what the cause of that imprisonment was, or whether there was any service or assistance you could render. Is this what I ought to have expected from America after the part I had acted towards her ? Or, will it redound to her honor or to your's that I tell the story ?

"I do not hesitate to say that you have not served America with more fidelity, or greater zeal, or greater disinterestedness, than myself, and I know not if with better effect. After the revolution of America was established, you rested at home to partake its advantages, and I ventured into new scenes of difficulty to extend the principles which that revolution had produced. In the progress of events you beheld yourself a president in America and me a prisoner in France : you folded your arms, forgot your friend, and became silent.

"As everything I have been doing in Europe was connected with my wishes for the prosperity of America, I ought to be the more surprised at this conduct on the part of her government. It leaves me but one mode of explanation, which is, that everything is not as it ought to be amongst you, and that the presence of a man who might disapprove, and who had credit enough with the country to be heard and believed, was not wished for. This was the operating motive of the despotic faction that imprisoned me in France (though the pretence was, that I was a foreigner) ; and those that have been silent towards me in America, appear to me to have acted from the same motive. It is impossible for me to discover any other."

Unwilling as all are to admit anything disparaging to Washington, justice requires the fair consideration of Paine's complaint. There were in his hands many letters proving Washington's friendship, and his great appreciation of Paine's services. Paine had certainly done nothing to forfeit his esteem. The "Age of Reason" had not appeared in America early enough to affect the matter, even should we suppose it offensive to a deist like Washington. The dry approval, forwarded by the Secretary of State, of Monroe's reclamation of Paine, enhanced the grievance. It admitted Paine's American citizenship. It was not then an old friend unhappily beyond his help, but a fellow-citizen whom he could legally protect, whom the President had left to languish in prison, and in hourly danger of death. During six months he saw no visitor, he heard no word, from the country for which he had fought. To Paine it could appear only as a sort of murder. And, although he kept back the letter, at his friend's desire, he felt that it might yet turn out to be murder. Even so it seemed, six months later, when the effects of his imprisonment, combined with his grief at Washington's continued silence (surely Monroe must have written on the subject), brought him to death's door. One must bear in mind also the disgrace, the humiliation of it, for a man who had been reverenced as a founder of the American Republic, and its apostle in France. This, indeed, had made his last three months in prison, after there had been ample time to hear from Washington, heavier than all the others. After the fall of Robespierre the prisons were rapidly emptied —from twenty to forty liberations daily, —the one man apparently forgotten being he who wrote, "in the times that tried men's souls," the words that Washington ordered to be read to his dispirited soldiers.

And now death approaches. If there can be any explanation of this long neglect and silence, knowledge of it would soothe the author's dying pillow; and though there be little probability that he can hold out so long, a letter (September 20th) is sent to Washington, under cover to Franklin Bache.

"SIR—I had written you a letter by Mr. Letombe, French consul, but, at the request of Mr. Monroe, I withdrew it, and the letter is still by me. I was the more easily prevailed upon to do this, as it was then my intention to have returned to America the latter end of the present year (1795;) but the illness I now suffer prevents me. In case I had come, I should have applied to you for such parts of your official letters (and your private ones, if you had chosen to give them) as contained any instructions or directions either to Mr. Monroe, to Mr. Morris, or to any other person, respecting me : for after you were informed of my imprisonment in France it was incumbent on you to make some enquiry into the cause, as you might very well conclude that I had not the opportunity of informing you of it. I cannot understand your silence upon this subject upon any other ground, than as connivance at my imprisonment ; and this is the manner in which it is understood here, and will be understood in America, unless you will give me authority for contradicting it. I therefore write you this letter, to propose to you to send me copies of any letters you have written, that I may remove this suspicion. In the Second Part of the *Age of Reason*, I have given a memorandum from the handwriting of Robespierre, in which he proposed a decree of accusation against me 'for the interest of America as well as of France.' He could have no cause for putting America in the case, but by interpreting the silence of the American government into connivance and consent. I was imprisoned on the ground of being born in England ; and your silence in not inquiring the cause of that imprisonment, and reclaiming me against it, was tacitly giving me up. I ought not to have suspected you of treachery ; but whether I recover from the illness I now suffer, or not, I shall continue to think you treacherous, till you give me cause to think otherwise. I am sure you would have found yourself more at your ease had you acted by me as you ought ; for whether your desertion of me was intended to gratify the English government, or to let me fall into destruction in France that you might exclaim the louder against the French Revolution ; or whether you hoped by my extinction to meet with less opposition in mounting up the American government ; either of these will involve you in reproach you will not easily shake off.

"THOMAS PAINE."

This is a bitter letter, but it is still more a sorrowful one. In view of what Washington had written of Paine's services, and for the sake of twelve years of *camaraderie*, Washington should have overlooked the sharpness of a deeply wronged and dying friend, and written to him what his Minister in France had reported. My reader already knows, what the sufferer knew not, that a part of Paine's grievance against Washington was unfounded. Washington could not know that the only charge against Paine was one trumped up by his own Minister in France. But, if he ever saw the letter just quoted, he must have perceived that Paine was laboring under an error in supposing that no inquiry had been made into his case. There are facts antecedent to the letter showing that his complaint had a real basis. For instance, in a letter to Monroe (July 30th), the President's interest was expressed in two other American prisoners in France—Archibald Hunter and Shubael Allen,—but no word was said of Paine. There was certainly a change in Washington towards Paine, and the following may have been its causes.

1. Paine had introduced Genêt to Morris, and probably to public men in America. Genêt had put an affront on Morris, and taken over a demand for his recall, with which Morris connected Paine. In a letter to Washington (private) Morris falsely insinuated that Paine had incited the actions of Genêt which had vexed the President.

2. Morris, perhaps in fear that Jefferson, influenced by Americans in Paris, might appoint Paine to his place, had written to Robert Morris in Philadelphia slanders of Paine, describing him as a sot and an object of contempt. This he knew would reach Washington without passing under the eye of Paine's friend, Jefferson.

3. In a private letter Morris related that Paine had visited him with Colonel Oswald, and treated him insolently. Washington particularly disliked Oswald, an American journalist actively opposing his administration.

4. Morris had described Paine as intriguing against him, both in Europe and America, thus impeding his mission, to which the President attached great importance.

5. The President had set his heart on bribing England with a favorable treaty of commerce to give up its six military posts in America. The most obnoxious man in the world to England was Paine. Any interference in Paine's behalf would not only have offended England, but appeared as a sort of repudiation of Morris' intimacy with the English court. The (alleged) reclamation of Paine by Morris had been kept secret by Washington even from friends so intimate (at the time) as Madison, who writes of it as having never been done. So carefully was avoided the publication of anything that might vex England.

6. Morris had admonished the Secretary of State that if Paine's imprisonment were much noticed it might endanger his life. So conscience was free to jump with policy.

What else Morris may have conveyed to Washington against Paine can be only matter for conjecture; but what he was capable of saying about those he wished to injure may be gathered from various letters of his. In one (December 19, 1795) he tells Washington that he had heard from a trusted informant that his Minister, Monroe, had told various Frenchmen that "he had no doubt but that, if they would do what was proper here, he and his friends would turn out Washington."

Liability to imposition is the weakness of strong natures. Many an Iago of canine cleverness has made that discovery. But, however Washington's mind may have been poisoned towards Paine, it seems unaccountable that, after receiving the letter of September 20th, he did not mention to Monroe, or to somebody, his understanding that the prisoner had been promptly reclaimed. His silence looks as if he had not received the letter. After Edmund Randolph's resignation his successor, Pickering, suppressed a document that would have exculpated him in Washington's eyes, and it is now among the Pickering papers. Paine had an enemy in Pickering. The letter of Paine was sent under cover to Benjamin Franklin Bache, of the *General Advertiser*, with whom as with other republicans

I

Washington had no intercourse. Pickering may therefore have had official opportunity to intercept it. The President was no longer visited by his old friends, Madison and others, and they could not discuss with him the intelligence they were receiving about Paine. Madison, in a letter to Jefferson (dated at Philadelphia, January 10, 1796), says:

"I have a letter from Thomas Paine which breathes the same sentiments, and contains some keen observations on the administration of the government here. It appears that the neglect to claim him as an American citizen when confined by Robespierre, or even to interfere in any way whatever in his favor, has filled him with an indelible rancor against the President, to whom it appears he has written on the subject [September 20, 1795]. His letter to me is in the style of a dying one, and we hear that he is since dead of the abscess in his side, brought on by his imprisonment. His letter desires that he may be remembered to you."

Whatever the explanation may be, no answer came from Washington. After waiting a year Paine employed his returning strength in embodying the letters of February 22d and September 20th, with large additions, in a printed *Letter to George Washington*. The story of his imprisonment and death sentence here for the first time really reached the American people. His personal case is made preliminary to an attack on Washington's whole career. The most formidable part of the pamphlet was the publication of Washington's letter to the Committee of Public Safety, which, departing from its rule of secrecy (in anger at the British Treaty), thus delivered a blow not easily answerable. The President's letter was effusive about the "alliance," "closer bonds of friendship," and so forth,—phrases which, just after the virtual transfer of our alliance to the enemy of France, smacked of perfidy. Paine attacks the treaty, which is declared to have put American commerce under foreign dominion. "The sea is not free to her. Her right to navigate is reduced to the right of escaping; that is, until some ship of England or France stops her vessels and carries them into port."

The ministerial misconduct of Gouverneur Morris, and his neglect of American interests, are exposed in a sharp paragraph. Washington's military mistakes are relentlessly raked up, with some that he did not commit, and the credit given him for victories won by others heavily discounted.

That Washington smarted under this pamphlet appears by a reference to it in a letter to David Stuart, January 8, 1797. Speaking of himself in the third person, he says: "Although he is soon to become a private citizen, his opinions are to be knocked down, and his character reduced as low as they are capable of sinking it, even by resorting to absolute falsehoods. As an evidence whereof, and of the plan they are pursuing, I send you a letter of Mr. Paine to me, printed in this city [Philadelphia], and disseminated with great industry." In the same letter he says: "Enclosed you will receive also a production of Peter Porcupine, alias William Cobbett. Making allowances for the asperity of an Englishman, for some of his strong and coarse expressions, and a want of official information as to many facts, it is not a bad thing."[1] Cobbett's answer to Paine's personal grievance was really an arraignment of the President. He undertakes to prove that the French Convention was a real government, and that by membership in it Paine had forfeited his American citizenship. But Monroe had formally claimed Paine as an American citizen, and the President had officially endorsed that claim. That this approval was unknown to Cobbett is a remarkable fact, showing that even such small and tardy action in Paine's favor was kept secret from the President's new British and Federalist allies.

For the rest it is a pity that Washington did not specify the "absolute falsehoods" in Paine's pamphlet, if he meant the phrase to apply to that. It might assist us in discovering just how the case stood

[1] "Porcupine's Political Censor, for December, 1796. A Letter to the Infamous Tom. Paine, in answer to his letter to General Washington."

in his mind. He may have been indignant at the suggestion of his connivance with Paine's imprisonment; but, as a matter of fact, the President had been brought by his Minister into the conspiracy which so nearly cost Paine his life.

On a review of the facts, my own belief is that the heaviest part of Paine's wrong came indirectly from Great Britain. It was probably one more instance of Washington's inability to weigh any injustice against an interest of this country. He ignored compacts of capitulation in the cases of Burgoyne and Asgill, in the Revolution; and when convinced that this nation must engage either in war or commercial alliance with England he virtually broke faith with France.[1] To the new alliance he sacrificed his most faithful friends Edmund Randolph and James Monroe; and to it, mainly, was probably due his failure to express any interest in England's outlaw, Paine. For this might gain publicity and offend the government with which Jay was negotiating. Such was George Washington. Let justice add that he included himself in the list of patriotic martyrdoms. By sacrificing France and embracing George III. he lost his old friends, lost the confidence of his own State, incurred denunciations that, in his own words, "could scarcely be applied to a Nero, a notorious defaulter, or even to a common pickpocket." So he wrote before Paine's pamphlet appeared, which, save in the personal matter, added nothing to the

[1] In a marginal note on Monroe's "View, etc.," found among his papers, Washington writes: "Did then the situation of our affairs admit of any other alternative than negotiation or war?" (Sparks' "Washington," xi., p. 505). Since writing my "Life of Randolph," in which the history of the British treaty is followed, I found in the French Archives (États-Unis, vol. ii., doc. 12) Minister Fauchet's report of a conversation with Secretary Randolph in which he (Randolph) said: "What would you have us do? We could not end our difficulties with the English but by a war or a friendly treaty. We were not prepared for war; it was necessary to negotiate." It is now tolerably certain that there was "bluff" on the part of the British players, in London and Philadelphia, but it won.

general accusations. It is now forgotten that with one exception—Johnson—no President ever went out of office so loaded with odium as Washington. It was the penalty of Paine's power that, of the thousand reproaches, his alone survived to recoil on his memory when the issues and the circumstances that explain if they cannot justify his pamphlet, are forgotten. It is easy for the Washington worshipper of to-day to condemn Paine's pamphlet, especially as he is under no necessity of answering it. But could he imagine himself abandoned to long imprisonment and imminent death by an old friend and comrade, whose letters of friendship he cherished, that friend avowedly able to protect him, with no apparent explanation of the neglect but deference to an enemy against whom they fought as comrades, an unprejudiced reader would hardly consider Paine's letter unpardonable even where unjust. Its tremendous indignation is its apology so far as it needs apology. A man who is stabbed cannot be blamed for crying out. It is only in poetry that dying Desdemonas exonerate even their deluded slayers. Paine, who when he wrote these personal charges felt himself dying of an abscess traceable to Washington's neglect, saw not Iago behind the President. His private demand for explanation, sent through Bache, was answered only with cold silence. "I have long since resolved," wrote Washington to Governor Stone (December 6, 1795), "for the present time at least, to let my calumniators proceed without any notice being taken of their invectives by myself, or by any others with my participation or knowledge." But now, nearly a year later, comes Paine's pamphlet, which is not made up of invectives, but of statements of fact. If, in this case, Washington sent, to one friend at least, Cobbett's answer to Paine, despite its errors which he vaguely mentions, there appears no good reason why he should not have specified those errors, and Paine's also. By his silence, even in the confidence of friendship, the truth which might have come to light was suppressed beyond his grave. For such silence the best excuse to me imaginable is that, in ignorance of the part Morris had acted, the President's mind may have been in bewilderment about the exact facts.

As for Paine's public letter, it was an answer to Washington's unjustifiable refusal to answer his private one. It was the natural outcry of an ill and betrayed man to one whom we now know to have been also betrayed. Its bitterness and wrath measure the greatness of the love that was wounded. The mutual personal services of Washington and Paine had continued from the beginning of the American revolution to the time of Paine's departure for Europe in 1787. Although he recognized, as Washington himself did, the commander's mistakes Paine had magnified his successes; his all-powerful pen defended him against loud charges on account of the retreat to the Delaware, and the failures near Philadelphia. In those days what " Common Sense " wrote was accepted as the People's verdict. It is even doubtful whether the proposal to supersede Washington might not have succeeded but for

Paine's fifth *Crisis*.[1] The personal relations between the two had been even affectionate. We find Paine consulting him about his projected publications at little oyster suppers in his own room ; and Washington giving him one of his two overcoats, when Paine's had been stolen. Such incidents imply many others never made known ; but they are represented in a terrible epigram found among Paine's papers,— " Advice to the statuary who is to execute the statue of Washington.

" Take from the mine the coldest, hardest stone,
　It needs no fashion : it is Washington.
　But if you chisel, let the stroke be rude,
　And on his heart engrave—Ingratitude."

Paine never published the lines. Washington being dead, old memories may have risen to restrain him ; and he had learned more of the treacherous influences around the great man which had poisoned his mind towards other friends besides himself. For his pamphlet he had no apology to make. It was a thing inevitable, volcanic, and belongs to the history of a period prolific in intrigues, of which both Washington and Paine were victims.

CHAPTER XXXV

' THE AGE OF REASON '

THE reception which " The Age of Reason" met is its sufficient justification. The chief priests and preachers answered it with personal abuse and slander, revealing by such fruits the

nature of their tree, and confessing the feebleness of its root, either in reason or human affection.

Lucian, in his " $Z\epsilon\acute{\upsilon}\varsigma$ $\tau\rho\alpha\gamma\omega\delta\acute{o}\varsigma$," represents the gods as invisibly present

---

[1] " When a party was forming, in the latter end of seventy-seven and beginning of seventy-eight, of which John Adams was one, to remove Mr. Washington from the command of the army, on the complaint that *he did nothing*, I wrote the fifth number of the *Crisis*, and published it at Lancaster (Congress then being at Yorktown, in Pennsylvania), to ward off that meditated blow ; for though I well knew that the black times of seventy-six were the natural consequence of his want of military judgment in the choice of positions into which the army was put about New York and New Jersey, I could see no possible advantage, and nothing but mischief, that could arise by distracting the army into parties, which would have been the case had the intended motion gone on."—Paine's Letter iii. to the People of the United States (1802).

at a debate, in Athens, on their existence. Damis, who argues from the
evils of the world that there are no
gods, is answered by Timocles, a theological professor with large salary. The
gods feel doleful, as the argument
goes against them, until their champion
breaks out against Damis,—" You blasphemous villain, you! Wretch! Accursed
monster !" The chief of the gods takes
courage, and exclaims : " Well done,
Timocles ! give him hard words. That
is your strong point. Begin to reason
and you will be dumb as a fish."

So was it in the age when the Twilight of the Gods was brought on by
faith in the Son of Man. Not very
different was it when this Son of Man,
dehumanized by despotism, made to
wield the thunderbolts of Jove, reached
in turn his inevitable Twilight. The
man who pointed out the now admitted
survivals of Paganism in the despotic
system then called Christianity, who
said, " the church has set up a religion
of pomp and revenue in the pretended
imitation of a person whose life was
humility and poverty," was denounced
as a sot and an adulterer. These
accusations, proved in this work unquestionably false, have accumulated
for generations, so that a mountain of
prejudice must be tunnelled before any
reader can approach " The Age of
Reason" as the work of an honest
and devout mind.

It is only to irrelevant personalities
that allusion is here made. Paine was
vehement in his arraignment of Church
and Priesthood, and it was fair enough
for them to strike back with animad-
versions on Deism and Infidelity. But
it was no answer to an argument against
the antiquity of Genesis to call Paine a
drunkard, had it been true. This kind
of reply was heard chiefly in America.
In England it was easy for Paine's chief
antagonist, the Bishop of Llandaff, to
rebuke Paine's strong language, when
his lordship could sit serenely in the
House of Peers with knowledge that
his opponent was answered with handcuffs for every Englishman who sold his
book. But in America, slander had to
take the place of handcuffs.

Paine is at times too harsh and
militant. But in no case does he
attack any person's character. Nor is
there anything in his language, where-
ever objectionable, which I have heard
censured when uttered on the side
of orthodoxy. It is easily forgotten
that Luther desired the execution of a
rationalist, and that Calvin did burn a
Socinian. The furious language of Protestants against Rome, and of Presbyterians against the English Church, is
considered even heroic, like the invective ascribed to Christ, " Generation of
vipers, how can you escape the damnation of hell ! " Although vehement
language grates on the ear of an age
that understands the real forces of
evolution, the historic sense remembers
that moral revolutions have been made
with words hard as cannon-balls. It
was only when soft phrases about the
evil of slavery, which " would pass away
in God's good time," made way for the
abolitionist denunciation of the Constitution as " an agreement with hell,"
that the fortress began to fall. In other
words, reforms are wrought by those
who are in earnest.[1] It is difficult in
our time to place one's self in the situation of a heretic of Paine's time. Darwin,
who is buried in Westminster, remembered the imprisonment of some educated men for opinions far less heretical
than his own. George III.'s egoistic
insanity appears (1892) to have been
inherited by an imperial descendant,
and should Germans be presently
punished for their religion, as Paine's
early followers were in England, we
shall again hear those words that are
the "half-battles" preceding victories.

1 " In writing upon this, as upon every other
subject, I speak a language plain and intelligible. I deal not in hints and intimations. I
have several reasons for this : first, that I may
be clearly understood ; secondly, that it may
be seen I am in earnest ; and thirdly, because
it is an affront to truth to treat falsehood with
complaisance."—Paine's reply to Bishop Watson.

There is even greater difficulty in the appreciation by one generation of the inner sense of the language of a past one. The common notion that Paine's "Age of Reason" abounds in "vulgarity" is due to the lack of literary culture in those—probably few—who have derived that impression from its perusal. It is the fate of all genius potent enough to survive a century that its language will here and there seem coarse. The thoughts of Boccaccio, Rabelais, Shakespeare, — whose works are commonly expurgated, — are so modern that they are not generally granted the allowances conceded to writers whose ideas are as antiquated as their words. Only the instructed minds can set their classic nudities in the historic perspective that reveals their innocency and value. Paine's book has done as much to modify human belief as any ever written. It is one of the very few religious works of the last century which survive in unsectarian circulation. It requires a scholarly perception to recognize in its occasional expressions, by some called " coarse," the simple Saxon of Norfolk. Similar expressions abound in pious books of the time ; they are not censured, because they are not read. His refined contemporary antagonists—Dr. Watson and Dr. Priestley—found no fault with Paine's words, though the former twice accuses his assertions as "indecent." In both cases, however, Paine is pointing out some biblical triviality or indecency —or what he conceived such. I have before me original editions of both Parts of " The Age of Reason" printed from Paine's manuscripts. Part First may be read by the most prudish parent to a daughter, without an omission. In Part Second six or seven sentences might be omitted by the parent, where the writer deals, without the least prurience, with biblical narratives that can hardly be daintily touched. Paine would have been astounded at the suggestion of any impropriety in his expressions. He passes over four-fifths of the passages in the Bible whose grossness he might have cited in support of his objection to its immorality. "Obscenity," he says, " in matters of faith, however wrapped up, is always a token of fable and imposture ; for it is necessary to our serious belief in God that we do not connect it with stories that run, as this does, into ludicrous interpretations. The story [of the miraculous conception] is, upon the face of it, the same kind of story as that of Jupiter and Leda."

Another fostered prejudice supposes " The Age of Reason" largely made up of scoffs. The Bishop of Llandaff, in his reply to Paine, was impressed by the elevated Theism of the work, to portions of which he ascribed "a philosophical sublimity." [1] Watson apparently tried to constrain his ecclesiastical position into English fair play, so that his actual failures to do so were especially misleading, as many knew Paine only as represented by this eminent antagonist. For instance, the Bishop says, "Moses you term a coxcomb, etc." But Paine, commenting on Numbers xii., 3, "Moses was very meek, above all men," had argued that Moses could not have written the book, for "If Moses said this of himself he was a coxcomb." Again the Bishop says Paine terms Paul "a fool." But Paine had quoted from Paul, " 'Thou fool, that which thou sowest is not quickened except it die.' To which [he says] one might reply in his own language, and say, 'Thou fool, Paul, that which thou sowest is not quickened except it die not."

No intellect that knows the law of literature, that deep answers only unto deep, can suppose that the effect of Paine's "Age of Reason," on which book the thirty years' war for religious freedom in England was won, after many martyrdoms, came from a scoffing or scurrilous work. It is never Paine's object to raise a laugh ; if he does so it is because of the miserable baldness of the dogmas, and the ignorant literalism,

[1] "An Apology for the Bible. By R. Llandaff" [Dr. Richard Watson].

consecrated in the popular mind of his time. Through page after page he peruses the Heavens, to him silently declaring the glory of God, and it is not laughter but awe when he asks, "From whence then could arise the solitary and strange conceit, that the Almighty, who had millions of worlds equally dependent on his protection, should quit the care of all the rest, and come to die in our world, because, they say, one man and one woman had eaten an apple!"

In another work Paine finds allegorical truth in the legend of Eden. The comparative mythologists of to-day, with many sacred books of the East, can find mystical meaning and beauty in many legends of the Bible wherein Paine could see none, but it is because of their liberation by the rebels of last century from bondage to the pettiness of literalism. Paine sometimes exposes an absurdity with a taste easily questionable by a generation not required like his own to take such things under foot of the letter. But his spirit is never flippant, and the sentences that might so seem to a casual reader are such as Browning defended in his "Christmas Eve."

> "If any blames me,
> Thinking that merely to touch in brevity
> The topics I dwell on, were unlawful—
> Or, worse, that I trench, with undue levity,
> On the bounds of the Holy and the awful,
> I praise the heart, and pity the head of him,
> And refer myself to THEE, instead of him ;
> Who head and heart alike discernest,
> Looking below light speech we utter,
> When the frothy spume and frequent sputter
> Prove that the soul's depths boil in earnest!"

Even Dr. James Martineau, whose reverential spirit no one can question, once raised a smile in his audience, of which the present writer was one, by saying that the account of the temptation of Jesus, if true, must have been reported by himself, or "by the only other party present." Any allusion to the devil in our day excites a smile. But it was not so in Paine's day, when many crossed themselves while speaking of this dark prince. Paine has "too much respect for the moral character of Christ" to

suppose that he told the story of the devil showing him all the kingdoms of the world. "How happened it that he did not discover America; or is it only with *kingdoms* that his sooty highness has any interest?" This is not flippancy; it was by following the inkstand Luther threw at the devil with equally vigorous humor that the grotesque figure was eliminated, leaving the reader of to-day free to appreciate the profound significance of the Temptation.

How free Paine is from any disposition to play to pit or gallery, any more than to dress circle, is shown in his treatment of the Book of Jonah. It is not easy to tell the story without exciting laughter; indeed the proverbial phrases for exaggeration,—"a whale," "a fish story," —probably came from Jonah. Paine's smile is slight. He says, "it would have approached nearer to the idea of a miracle if Jonah had swallowed the whale"; but this is merely in passing to an argument that miracles, in the early world, would hardly have represented Divinity. Had the fish cast up Jonah in the streets of Nineveh the people would probably have been affrighted, and fancied them both devils. But in the second Part of the work there is a very impressive treatment of the Book of Jonah. This too is introduced with a passing smile—"if credulity could swallow Jonah and the whale it could swallow anything." But it is precisely to this supposed "scoffer" that we owe the first interpretation of the profound and pathetic significance of the book, lost sight of in controversies about its miracle. Paine anticipates Baur in pronouncing it a poetical work of Gentile origin. He finds in it the same lesson against intolerance contained in the story of the reproof of Abraham for piously driving the suffering fire-worshipper from his tent. (This story is told by the Persian Saadi, who also refers to Jonah: "And now the whale swallowed Jonah: the sun set.") In the prophet mourning for his withered gourd, while desiring the destruction of a city, Paine finds a satire; in the divine rebuke he hears the voice of a true God, and one very different from the deity to whom the Jews ascribed massacres. The same critical acumen is shown in his treatment of the Book of Job, which he believes to be also of Gentile origin, and much admires.

The large Paine Mythology cleared aside, he who would learn the truth about this religious teacher will find in his way a misleading literature of uncritical eulogies. Indeed the pious prejudices against Paine have largely disappeared, as one may see by comparing the earlier with the later notices of him in religious encyclopædias. But though he is no longer placed in an infernal triad as in the old hymn—"The world, the devil, and Tom Paine"—and his political services are now candidly recognized, he is still regarded as the propagandist of a bald illiterate deism. This, which is absurdly unhistorical, Paine having been dealt with by eminent critics of his time as an influence among the educated, is a sequel to his long persecution. For he was relegated to the guardianship of an unlearned and undiscriminating radical-ism, little able to appreciate the niceties of his definitions, and was gilded by its defensive commonplaces into a figure-head. Paine therefore has now to be saved from his friends more perhaps than from his enemies. It has been shown on a former page that his governmental theories were of a type peculiar in his time. Though such writers as Spencer, Frederic Harrison, Bagehot, and Dicey have familiarized us with his ideas, few of them have the historic perception which enables Sir George Trevelyan to recognize Paine's connection with them. It must now be added that Paine's religion was of a still more peculiar type. He cannot be classed with deists of the past or theists of the present. Instead of being the mere iconoclast, the militant assailant of Christian beliefs, the "infidel" of pious slang, which even men who should know better suppose, he was an exact thinker, a slow and careful writer, and his religious ideas, developed through long years, require and repay study.

The dedication of "The Age of Reason" places the work under the "protection" of its author's fellow-citizens of the United States. To-day the trust comes to many who really are such as Paine supposed all of his countrymen to be,—just and independent lovers of truth and right. We shall see that his trust was not left altogether unfulfilled by a multitude of his contemporaries, though they did not venture to do justice to the man. Paine had idealized his country-men, looking from his prison across three thousand miles. But, to that vista of space, a century of time had to be added before the book which fanatical Couthon suppressed, and the man whom murder-ous Barrère sentenced to death, could both be fairly judged by educated America.

"The Age of Reason" is in two Parts, published in successive years. These divisions are interesting as memorials of the circumstances under which they were written and published,—in both cases with death apparently at hand. But taking the two Parts as one work, there appears to my own mind a more real division : a part written by Paine's cen-tury, and another originating from him-self. Each of these has an important and traceable evolution.

I. The first of these divisions may be considered, fundamentally, as a continua-tion of the old revolution against arbitrary authority. Carlyle's humor covers a pro-found insight when he remarks that Paine, having freed America with his "Common Sense," was resolved to free this whole world, and perhaps the other ! All the authorities were and are interde-pendent. "If thou release this man thou art not Cæsar's friend," cried the Priest to Pilate. The proconsul must face the fact that in Judea Cæsarism rests on the same foundation with Jahvism. Authority leans on authority ; none can stand alone. It is still a question whether political revolutions cause or are caused by religious revolutions. Buckle maintained that the French revo-lution was chiefly due to the previous overthrow of spiritual authority; Rocquain, that the political *régime* was shaken before the philosophers arose.[1] In England religious changes seem to have usually followed those of a political character, not only in order of time, but in character. In beginning "The Age of Reason," Paine says:

"Soon after I had published the pamphlet 'Common Sense' in America I saw the exceeding probability that a revolution in the system of government would be followed by a revolution in the system of religion. The adulterous connection of church and state, wherever it had taken place, whether Jewish, Christian, or Turkish, had so effectually prohibited by pains and penalties every discussion upon established creeds, and upon first principles of religion, that until the system of government should be changed those subjects could not be brought fairly and openly before the world; but that whenever this should be done a revolution in the system of religion would follow. Human inventions and priestcraft would be detected; and man would return to the pure, unmixed, and unadulterated belief of one God and no more."

The historical continuity of the critical negations of Paine with the past is represented in his title. The Revolution of 1688,—the secular arm transferring the throne from one family to another,—brought the monarchical superstition into doubt; straightway the Christian authority was shaken. One hundred years before Paine's book, appeared Charles Blount's "Oracles of Reason." Macaulay describes Blount as the head of a small school of "infidels," troubled with a desire to make converts; his delight was to worry the priests by asking them how light existed before the sun was made, and where Eve found thread to stitch her fig-leaves. But to this same Blount, Macaulay is constrained to attribute emancipation of the press in England.

Blount's title was taken up in America by Ethan Allen, leader of the "Green Mountain Boys." Allen's "Oracles of

Reason" is forgotten; he is remembered by his demand (1775) for the surrender of Fort Ticonderoga, "in the name of Jehovah and the Continental Congress." The last five words of this famous demand would have been a better title for the book. It introduces the nation to a Jehovah qualified by the Continental Congress. Ethan Allen's deity is no longer a King of kings: arbitrariness has disappeared; men are summoned to belief in a governor administering laws inherent in the constitution of a universe co-eternal with himself, and with which he is interdependent. His administration is not for any divine glory, but, in anticipation of our constitutional preamble, to "promote the general welfare." The old Puritan alteration in the Lord's Prayer, "Thy Commonwealth come!" would in Allen's church have been "Thy Republic come!" That is, had he admitted prayer, which to an Executive is of course out of place. It must not, however, be supposed that Ethan Allen is conscious that his system is inspired by the Revolution. His book is a calm, philosophical analysis of New England theology and metaphysics; an attempt to clear away the ancient biblical science and set Newtonian science in its place; to found what he conceives "Natural Religion."

In editing his "Account of Arnold's Campaign in Quebec," John Joseph Henry says in a footnote that Paine borrowed from Allen. But the aged man was, in his horror of Paine's religion, betrayed by his memory. The only connection between the books runs above the consciousness of either writer. There was necessarily some resemblance between negations dealing with the same narratives, but a careful comparison of the books leaves me doubtful whether Paine ever read Allen. His title may have been suggested by Blount, whose "Oracles of Reason" was in the library of his assistant at Bordentown, John Hall. The works are distinct in aim, products of different religious climes. Allen is occupied mainly with the meta-

[1] Felix Rocquain's fine work, "L'Esprit révolutionnaire avant la Révolution," though not speculative, illustrates the practical nature of revolution,—an uncivilized and often retrograde form of evolution.

physical, Paine with quite other, aspects of their common subject. There is indeed a conscientious originality in the freethinkers who successively availed themselves of the era of liberty secured by Blount. Collins, Bolingbroke, Hume, Toland, Chubb, Woolston, Tindal, Middleton, Annet, Gibbon,—each made an examination for himself, and represents a distinct chapter in the religious history of England. Annet's "Free Inquirer," aimed at enlightenment of the lower classes, proved that free thought was tolerated only as an aristocratic privilege ; the author was pilloried, just thirty years before the cheapening of "The Rights of Man" led to Paine's prosecution. Probably Morgan did more than any of the deists to prepare English ground for Paine's sowing, by severely criticising the Bible by a standard of civilized ethics, so far as ethics were civilized in the early eighteenth century. But none of these writers touched the deep chord of religious feeling in the people. The English-speaking people were timid about venturing too much on questions which divided the learned, and were content to express their protest against the worldliness of the Church, and faithlessness to the lowly Saviour, by following pietists and enthusiasts. The learned clergy, generally of the wealthy classes, were largely deistical, but conservative. They gradually perceived that the political and the theological authority rested on the same foundation. So between the deists and the Christians there was, as Leslie Stephen says, a "comfortable compromise, which held together till Wesley from one side, and Thomas Paine from another, forced more serious thoughts on the age."[1]

While "The Age of Reason" is thus, in one aspect, the product of its time, the renewal of an old siege—begun far back indeed as Celsus,—its intellectual originality is none the less remarkable. Paine is more complete master of the

[1] "History of English Thought in the Eighteenth Century."

comparative method than Tindal in his "Christianity as old as the Creation" In his studies of "Christian Mythology" (his phrase), one is surprised by anticipations of Baur and Strauss. These are all the more striking by reason of his homely illustrations. Thus, in discussing the liabilities of ancient manuscripts to manipulation, he mentions in his second Part that in the first, printed less than two years before, there was already a sentence he never wrote ; and contrasts this with the book of nature wherein no blade of grass can be imitated or altered.[2] He distinguishes the historical Jesus from the mythical Christ with nicety, though none had previously done this. He is more discriminating than the early deists in his explanations of the scriptural marvels which he discredits. There was not the invariable alternative of imposture with which the orthodoxy of his time had been accustomed to deal. He does indeed suspect Moses with his rod of conjuring, and thinks no better of those who pretended knowledge of future events ; but the incredible narratives are traditions, fables, and occasionally "downright lies." "It is not difficult to discover the progress by which even simple supposition, with the aid of credulity, will in time grow into a lie, and at last be told as a fact ; and wherever we can find a charitable reason for a thing of this kind we ought not to indulge a severe one." Paine's use of the word "lies" in this connection is an archaism. Carlyle told me that his father always

[2] The sentence imported into Paine's Part First is : "The book of Luke was carried by one voice only." I find the words added as a footnote in the Philadelphia edition, 1794, p. 33. While Paine in Paris was utilizing the ascent of the footnote to his text, Dr. Priestley in Pennsylvania was using it to show Paine's untrustworthiness. ("Letters to a Philosophical Unbeliever," p. 73.) But it would appear, though neither discovered it, that Paine's critic was the real offender. In quoting the page, before answering it, Priestley incorporated in the text the footnote of an American editor. Priestley could not of course imagine such editorial folly, but all the same the reader may here see the myth-insect already building the Paine Mythology.

spoke of such tales as "The Arabian Nights" as "downright lies"; by which he no doubt meant fables without any indication of being such, and without any moral. Elsewhere Paine uses "lie" as synonymous with "fabulous"; when he means by the word what it would now imply, "wilful" is prefixed. In the Gospels he finds "inventions" of Christian Mythologists—tales founded on vague rumors, relics of primitive works of imagination mistaken for history, —fathered upon disciples who did not write them.

His treatment of the narrative of Christ's resurrection may be selected as an example of his method. He rejects Paul's testimony, and his five hundred witnesses to Christ's reappearance, because the evidence did not convince Paul himself, until he was struck by lightning, or otherwise converted. He finds disagreements in the narratives of the gospels, concerning the resurrection, which, while proving there was no concerted imposture, show that the accounts were not written by witnesses of the events ; for in this case they would agree more nearly. He finds in the narratives of Christ's reappearances,—" suddenly coming in and going out when doors are shut, vanishing out of sight and appearing again,"—and the lack of details, as to his dress, etc., the familiar signs of a ghost-story, which is apt to be told in different ways.

"Stories of this kind had been told of the assassination of Julius Cæsar, not many years before, and they generally have their origin in violent deaths, or in the execution of innocent persons. In cases of this kind compassion lends its aid, and benevolently stretches the story. It goes on a little and a little further, till it becomes a most certain truth. Once start a ghost, and credulity fills up its life and assigns the cause of its appearance."

The moral and religious importance of the resurrection would thus be an afterthought. The secrecy and privacy of the alleged appearances of Christ after death are, he remarks, repugnant to the supposed end of convincing the world.[1]

[1] In 1778 Lessing set forth his "New Hypo-

Paine admits the power of the deity to make a revelation. He therefore deals with each of the more notable miracles on its own evidence, adhering to his plan of bringing the Bible to judge the Bible. Such an investigation, written with lucid style and quaint illustration, without one timid or uncandid sentence, coming from a man whose services and sacrifices for humanity were great, could not have failed to give "The Age of Reason " long life, even had these been its only qualities. Four years before the book appeared, Burke said in Parliament : "Who, born within the last forty years, has read one word of Collins, and Toland, and Tindal, and Chubb, and Morgan, and the whole race who call themselves freethinkers?" Paine was, in one sense, of this intellectual pedigree ; and had his book been only a digest and expansion of previous negative criticisms, and a more thorough restatement of theism, these could have given it but a somewhat longer life ; "The Age of Reason" must have swelled Burke's list of forgotten freethinking books. But there was an immortal soul in Paine's book. It is to the consideration of this its unique life, which has defied the darts of criticism for a century, and survived its own faults and limitations, that we now turn.

II. Paine's book is the uprising of the human HEART against the Religion of Inhumanity.

This assertion may be met with a chorus of denials that there was, or is, in Christendom any Religion of Inhumanity. And, if Thomas Paine is

thesis of the Evangelists," that they had independently built on a basis derived from some earlier Gospel of the Hebrews,—a theory now confirmed by the recovered fragments of that lost Memoir, collected by Dr. Nicholson of the Bodleian Library. It is tolerably certain that Paine was unacquainted with Lessing's work, when he became convinced, by variations in the accounts of the resurrection, that some earlier narrative " became afterwards the foundation of the four books ascribed to Matthew, Mark, Luke, and John,"—these being, traditionally, eye-witnesses.

enjoying the existence for which he hoped, no heavenly anthem would be such music in his ears as a chorus of stormiest denials from earth reporting that the Religion of Inhumanity is so extinct as to be incredible. Nevertheless, the Religion of Inhumanity did exist, and it defended against Paine a god of battles, of pomp, of wrath ; an instigator of race hatreds and exterminations; an establisher of slavery ; a commander of massacres in punishment of theological beliefs ; a sender of lying spirits to deceive men, and of destroying angels to afflict them with plagues ; a creator of millions of human beings under a certainty of their eternal torture by devils and fires of his own creation. This apotheosis of Inhumanity is here called a religion, because it managed to survive from the ages of savagery by violence of superstition, to gain a throne in the Bible by killing off all who did not accept its authority to the letter, and because it was represented by actual inhumanities. The great obstruction of Science and Civilization was that the Bible was quoted in sanction of war, crusades against alien religions, murders for witchcraft, divine right of despots, degradation of reason, exaltation of credulity, punishment of opinion and unbiblical discovery, contempt of human virtues and human nature, and costly ceremonies before an invisible majesty, which, exacted from the means of the people, were virtually the offering of human sacrifices.

There had been murmurs against this consecrated Inhumanity through the ages, dissentients here and there ; but the Revolution began with Paine. Nor was this accidental. He was just the one man in the world who had undergone the training necessary for this particular work.

The higher clergy, occupied with the old textual controversy, proudly instructing Paine in Hebrew or Greek idioms, little realized their ignorance in the matter now at issue. Their ignorance had been too carefully educated to even imagine the University in which words are things, and things the word, and the many graduations passed between Thetford Quaker meeting and the French Convention. What to scholastics, for whom humanities meant ancient classics, were the murders and massacres of primitive tribes, declared to be the word and work of God? Words, mere words. They never saw these things. But Paine had seen that war-god at his work. In childhood he had seen the hosts of the Defender of the Faith as, dripping with the blood of Culloden and Inverness, they marched through Thetford ; in manhood he had seen the desolations wrought "by the grace of" that deity to the royal invader of America ; he had seen the massacres ascribed to Jahve repeated in France, while Robespierre and Couthon were establishing worship of an infrahuman deity. By sorrow, poverty, wrong, through long years, amid revolutions and death-agonies, the stay-maker's needle had been forged into a pen of lightning. No Oxonian conductor could avert that stroke, which was not at mere irrationalities, but at a huge idol worshipped with human sacrifices.

The creation of the heart of Paine, historically traceable, is so wonderful, its outcome seems so supernatural, that in earlier ages he might have been invested with fable, like some Avatar. Of some such man, no doubt, the Hindu poets dreamed in their picture of young Arguna (in the *Bhagavatgîtâ*). The warrior, borne to the battlefield in his chariot, finds arrayed against him his kinsmen, friends, preceptors. He bids his charioteer pause ; he cannot fight those he loves. His charioteer turns: 't is the radiant face of divine Chrishna, his Saviour ! Even He has led him to this grievous contention with kinsmen, and those to whose welfare he was devoted. Chrishna instructs his disciple that the war is an illusion ; it is the conflict by which, from age to age, the divine life in the world is preserved. "This imperishable devotion I declared to the sun, the sun delivered it to Manu, Manu to Ikshâku; handed down from one to another it was studied by the royal sages. In the lapse of time that devotion was lost. It is even the same discipline which I this day communicate to thee, for thou art my servant and my friend. Both thou and I have passed through many births. Mine are known to me; thou knowest not of thine. I am made evident by my own power: as often as there is a decline of virtue, and an insurrection of wrong and injustice in the world, I appear."

Paine could not indeed know his former births; and, indeed, each former self of his—Wycliffe, Fox, Roger Williams—was sectarianized beyond recognition. He could hardly see kinsmen in the Unitarians, who were especially eager to disown the heretic affiliated on them by opponents; nor in the Wesleyans, though in him was the blood of their apostle, who declared salvation a present life, free to all. In a profounder sense, Paine was George Fox. Here was George Fox disowned, freed from his accidents, naturalized in the earth and humanized in the world of men. Paine is explicable only by the intensity of his Quakerism, consuming its own traditions as once the church's ceremonies and sacraments. On him, in Thetford meeting-house, rolled the burden of that Light that enlighteneth every man, effacing distinctions of rank, race, sex, making all equal, clearing away privilege, whether of priest or mediator, subjecting all scriptures to its immediate illumination.

This faith was a fearful heritage to carry, even in childhood, away from the Quaker environment which, by mixture with modifying "survivals," in habit and doctrine, cooled the fiery gospel for the average tongue. The intermarriage of Paine's father with a family in the English Church brought the precocious boy's Light into early conflict with his kindred, his little lamp being still fed in the meeting-house. A child brought up without respect for the conventional symbols of religion, or even with pious antipathy to them, is as if born with only one spiritual skin; he will bleed at a touch.

"I well remember, when about seven or eight years of age, hearing a sermon read by a relation of mine, who was a great devotee of the Church, upon the subject of what is called *redemption by the death of the Son of God*. After the sermon was ended I went into the garden, and as I was going down the garden steps, (for I perfectly remember the spot), I revolted at the recollection of what I had heard, and thought to myself that it was making God Almighty act like a passionate man, that killed his son when he could not revenge himself in any other way; and, as I was sure a man would be hanged that did such a thing, I could not see for what purpose they preached such sermons. This was not one of that kind of thoughts that had anything in it of childish levity; it was to me a serious reflection, arising from the idea I had, that God was too good to do such an action, and also too almighty to be under any necessity of doing it. I believe in the same manner at this moment; and I moreover believe that any system of religion that has anything in it which shocks the mind of a child, cannot be a true system."

The child took his misgivings out into the garden; he would not by a denial shock his aunt Cocke's faith as his own had been shocked. For many years he remained silent in his inner garden, nor ever was drawn out of it until he found the abstract dogma of the death of God's Son an altar for sacrificing men, whom he reverenced as all God's sons. What he used to preach at Dover and Sandwich cannot now be known. His ignorance of Greek and Latin, the scholastic "humanities," had prevented his becoming a clergyman, and introduced him to humanities of another kind. His mission was then among the poor and ignorant.[1] Sixteen years later he is in Philadelphia, attending the English Church, in which he had been confirmed. There were many deists in that Church, whose laws then as now were sufficiently liberal to include them. In his "Common Sense" (published January 10, 1776) Paine used the

[1] "Old John Berry, the late Col. Hay's servant, told me he knew Paine very well when he was at Dover—had heard him preach there—thought him a staymaker by trade."—W. Weedon, of Glynde, quoted in *Notes and Queries* (London), December 29, 1866.

reproof of Israel (I. Samuel) for desiring a King. John Adams, a Unitarian and monarchist, asked him if he really believed in the inspiration of the Old Testament. Paine said he did not, and intended at a later period to publish his opinions on the subject. There was nothing inconsistent in Paine's believing that a passage confirmed by his own Light was a divine direction, though contained in a book whose alleged inspiration throughout he did not accept. Such was the Quaker principle. Before that, soon after his arrival in the country, when he found African Slavery supported by the Old Testament, Paine had repudiated the authority of that book; he declares it abolished by "Gospel light," which includes man-stealing among the greatest crimes. When, a year later, on the eve of the Revolution, he writes "Common Sense," he has another word to say about religion, and it is strictly what the human need of the hour demands. Whatever his disbeliefs, he could never sacrifice human welfare to them, any more than he would suffer dogmas to sacrifice the same. It would have been a grievous sacrifice of the great cause of republican independence, consequently of religious liberty, had he introduced a theological controversy at the moment when it was of vital importance that the sects should rise above their partition-walls and unite for a great common end. The Quakers, deistical as they were, preserved religiously the "separatism" once compulsory; and Paine proved himself the truest Friend among them when he was "moved" by the Spirit of Humanity, for him at length the Holy Spirit, to utter (1776) his brave cheer for Catholicity.

"As to religion, I hold it to be the indispensable duty of government to protect all conscientious professors thereof, and I know of no other business which government hath to do therewith. Let a man throw aside that narrowness of soul, that selfishness of principle, which the niggards of all professions are so unwilling to part with, and he will be at once delivered of his fears on that head. Suspicion is the companion of mean souls, and the bane of all good society. For myself, I fully and conscientiously believe, that it is the will of the Almighty that there should be a diversity of religious opinions amongst us: it affords a larger field for our Christian kindness. Were we all of one way of thinking, our religious dispositions would want matter for probation; and, on this liberal principle, I look on the various denominations among us to be like children of the same family, differing only in what is called their Christian names." [1]

There was no pedantry whatever about Paine, this obedient son of Humanity. He would defend Man against men, against sects and parties; he would never quarrel about the botanical label of a tree bearing such fruits as the Declaration of Independence. But no man better knew the power of words, and that a botanical error may sometimes result in destructive treatment of the tree. For this reason he censured the Quakers for opposing the Revolution on the ground that, in the words of their testimony (1776), "the setting up and putting down kings and governments is God's peculiar prerogative." Kings, he answers, are not removed by miracles, but by just such means as the Americans were using.

"Oliver Cromwell thanks you. Charles, then, died not by the hands of man; and should the present proud imitator of him come to the same untimely end, the writers and publishers of the Testimony are bound, by the doctrine it contains, to applaud the fact." [2]

Paine was a Christian. In his "Epistle to Quakers" he speaks of the dispersion of the Jews as "foretold by our Saviour." In his famous first *Crisis* he exhorts the Americans not to throw "the burden of the day upon Providence, but 'show your faith by your works,' that God may bless you." For in those days there was visible to such eyes as his, as to antislavery eyes in our civil war,

"A fiery Gospel writ in burnished rows of steel."

The Republic, not American but Human, became Paine's religion. "Divine

[1] Common Sense. "Writings of Paine" (Conway), vol. i., p. 108.—H. B. B.
[2] Epistle to Quakers. "Writings of Paine" (Conway), vol. i., p. 125.—H. B. B.

Providence intends this country to be the asylum of persecuted virtue from every quarter of the globe." So he had written before the Declaration of Independence. In 1778 he finds that there still survives some obstructive superstition among English churchmen in America about the connection of Protestant Christianity with the King. In his seventh *Crisis* (November 21, 1778) he wrote sentences inspired by his new conception of religion.

"In a Christian and philosophical sense, mankind seem to have stood still at individual civilization, and to retain as nations all the original rudeness of nature. . . . As individuals we profess ourselves Christians, but as nations we are heathens, Romans, and what not. I remember the late Admiral Saunders declaring in the House of Commons, and that in the time of peace, ' That the city of Madrid laid in ashes was not a sufficient atonement for the Spaniards taking off the rudder of an English sloop of war.' . . . The arm of Britain has been spoken of as the arm of the Almighty, and she has lived of late as if she thought the whole world created for her diversion. Her politics, instead of civilizing, has tended to brutalize mankind, and under the vain unmeaning title of ' Defender of the Faith,' she has made war like an Indian on the Religion of Humanity." [1]

Thus, forty years before Auguste Comte sat, a youth of twenty, at the feet of Saint Simon, learning the principles now known as "The Religion of Humanity," Thomas Paine had not only minted the name, but with it the idea of international civilization, in which nations are to treat each other as gentlemen in private life. National honor was, he said, confused with "bullying"; but "that which is the best character for an individual is the best character for a nation." The great and pregnant idea was, as in the previous instances, occasional. It was a sentence passed upon the "Defender-of-the-Faith" superstition, which detached faith from humanity, and had pressed the Indian's tomahawk into the hands of Jesus.

At the close of the American Revolu-

[1] Mr. Thaddeus B. Wakeman, an eminent representative of the "Religion of Humanity," writes me that he has not found this phrase in any work earlier than Paine's *Crisis*, vii.

tion there appeared little need for a religious reformation. The people were happy, prosperous, and, there being no favoritism toward any sect under the new state constitutions, but perfect equality and freedom, the Religion of Humanity meant sheathing of controversial swords also. It summoned every man to lend a hand in repairing the damages of war, and building the new nationality. Paine therefore set about constructing his iron bridge of thirteen symbolic ribs, to overleap the ice-floods and quicksands of rivers. His assistant in this work, at Bordentown, New Jersey, John Hall, gives us in his journal, glimpses of the religious ignorance and fanaticism of that region. But Paine showed no aggressive spirit towards them. "My employer," writes Hall (1786), has *Common Sense* enough to disbelieve most of the common systematic theories of Divinity, but does not seem to establish any for himself." In all of his intercourse with Hall (a Unitarian just from England), and his neighbors, there is no trace of any disposition to deprive any one of a belief, or to excite any controversy. Humanity did not demand it, and by that direction he left the people to their weekly toils and Sunday sermons.

But when (1787) he was in England, Humanity gave another command. It was obeyed in the eloquent pages on religious liberty and equality in "The Rights of Man." Burke had alarmed the nation by pointing out that the Revolution in France had laid its hand on religion. The cry was raised that religion was in danger. Paine then uttered his impressive paradox:

"Toleration is not the opposite of intoleration, but the counterfeit of it. Both are despotisms. The one assumes the right of withholding liberty of conscience, and the other of granting it. The one is the pope armed with fire and faggot, the other is the pope selling or granting indulgences. . . . Toleration by the same assumed authority by which it tolerates a man to pay his worship, presumptuously and blasphemously sets itself up to tolerate the Almighty to receive it. . . . Who then art thou, vain dust and ashes, by whatever name thou art called, whether a king, a bishop, a church or a state, a parliament or anything else, that obtrudest thine insignificance between the soul of man and his maker? Mind thine own concerns. If he believes not as thou believest, it is a proof that thou believest not as he believeth, and there is no earthly power can determine between you. . . . Religion, without regard to names, as directing itself from the universal family of mankind to the divine object of all adoration, is man bringing to his maker the fruits of his heart; and though these fruits may differ like the fruits of the earth, the grateful tribute of every one is accepted.

This, which I condense with reluctance, was the affirmation which the Religion of Humanity needed in England. But when he came to sit in the French Convention a new burden rolled upon him. There was Marat with the Bible always before him, picking out texts that justified his murders: there were Robespierre and Couthon invoking the God of Nature to sanction just such massacres as Marat found in his Bible; and there were crude "atheists" consecrating the ferocities of nature more dangerously than if they had named them Siva, Typhon, or Satan. Paine had published the rights of man for men; but here human hearts and minds had been buried under the superstitions of ages. The great mischief had ensued, to use his own words, "by the possession of power before they understood principles: they earned liberty in words but not in fact." Exhumed suddenly, as if from some Nineveh, resuscitated into semi-conscious strength, they remembered only the methods of the allied inquisitors and tyrants they were overthrowing; they knew no justice but vengeance; and when on crumbled idols they raised forms called "Nature" and "Reason," old idols gained life in the new forms. These were the gods which had but too literally created, by the slow evolutionary force of human sacrifices, the new revolutionary priesthood. Their massacres could not be questioned by those who acknowledged the divine hand in the slaughter of Canaanites.[1]

The Religion of Humanity again issued its command to its minister. "The Age of Reason" was written, in its first form, and printed in French. "Couthon," says Lanthenas, "to whom I sent it, seemed offended with me for having translated it."[2] Couthon raged against the priesthood, but could not tolerate a work which showed vengeance to be atheism, and compassion—not merely for men, but for animals—true worship of God. On the other hand, Paine's opposition to atheism would appear to have brought him into danger from another quarter, in which religion could not be distinguished from priestcraft. In a letter to Samuel Adams Paine says that he endangered his life by opposing the king's execution, and "a second time by opposing atheism." Those who denounce "The Age of Reason" may thus learn that red-handed Couthon, who hewed men to pieces before his Lord, and those who acknowledged no Lord, agreed with them. Under these menaces the original work was as I have inferred, suppressed. But

---

[1] On August 10, 1793, there was a sort of communion of the Convention around the statue of Nature, whose breasts were fountains of water. Hérault de Séchelles, at that time president, addressed the statue: "Sovereign of the savage and of the enlightened nations, O Nature, this great people, gathered at the first beam of day before thee, is free! It is in thy bosom, it is in thy sacred sources, that it has recovered its rights, that it has regenerated itself after traversing so many ages of error and servitude: it must return to the simplicity of thy ways to rediscover liberty and equality. O Nature! receive the expression of the eternal attachment of the French people for thy laws; and may the teeming waters gushing from thy breasts, may this pure beverage which refreshed the first human beings, consecrate in this Cup of Fraternity and Equality the vows that France makes thee this day,—the most beautiful that the sun has illumined since it was suspended in the immensity of space." The cup passed around from lip to lip, amid fervent ejaculations. Next year Nature's breasts issued Hérault's blood.

[2] The letter of Lanthenas to Merlin de Thionville, of which the original French is before me, is quoted in an article in *Scribner*, September, 1880, by Hon. E. B. Washburne (former Minister to France); it is reprinted in Remsburg's compilation of testimonies: "Thomas Paine, the Apostle of Religious and Political Liberty" (1880). See also p. 210.

the demand of Humanity was peremptory, and Paine re-wrote it all, and more. When it appeared he was a prisoner; his life was in Couthon's hands. He had personally nothing to gain by its publication—neither wife, child, nor relative to reap benefit by its sale. It was published as purely for the good of mankind as any work ever written. Nothing could be more simply true than his declaration, near the close of life:

"As in my political works my motive and object have been to give man an elevated sense of his own character, and free him from the slavish and superstitious absurdity of monarchy and hereditary government, so, in my publications on religious subjects, my endeavors have been directed to bring man to a right use of the reason that God has given him; to impress on him the great principles of divine morality, justice, and mercy, and a benevolent disposition to all men, and to all creatures; and to inspire in him a spirit of trust, confidence and consolation, in his Creator, unshackled by the fables of books pretending to be the word of God."

It is misleading at the present day to speak of Paine as an opponent of Christianity. This would be true were Christianity judged by the authorized formulas of any church; but nothing now acknowledged as Christianity by enlightened Christians of any denomination was known to him. In our time, when the humanizing wave, passing through all churches, drowns old controversies, floats the dogmas, till it seems ungenerous to quote creeds and confessions in the presence of our "orthodox" lovers of man—even "totally depraved" and divinely doomed man—the theological eighteenth century is inconceivable. Could one wander from any of our churches, unless of the Christian Pagans or remote villagers (*pagani*), into those of the last century, he would find himself moving in a wilderness of cinders, with only the plaintive song of John and Charles Wesley to break the solitude. If he would hear recognition of the human Jesus, on whose credit the crowned Christ is now maintained, he would be sharply told that it were a sin to "know Christ after

the flesh," and must seek such recognition among those stoned as infidels. Three noble and pathetic tributes to the Man of Nazareth are audible from the last century—those of Rousseau, Voltaire, and Paine. From its theologians and its pulpits not one! Should the tribute of Paine be to-day submitted, without his name, to our most eminent divines, even to leading American and English Bishops, beside any theological estimate of Christ from the same century, the Jesus of Paine would be surely preferred.

Should our cultured Christian of to-day press beyond those sectarian, miserable controversies of the eighteenth century, known to him now as cold ashes, into the seventeenth century, he would find himself in a comparatively embowered land; that is, in England, and in a few oases in America—like that of Roger Williams in Rhode Island. In England he would find brain and heart still in harmony, as in Tillotson and South; still more in Bishop Jeremy Taylor, "Shakespeare of divines." He would hear this Jeremy reject the notions of original sin and transmitted guilt, maintain the "liberty of prophesying," and that none should suffer for conclusions concerning a book so difficult of interpretation as the Bible. In those unsophisticated years Jesus and the disciples and the Marys still wore about them the reality gained in miracle-plays. What Paine need arise where poets wrote the creed, and men knew the Jesus of whom Thomas Dekker wrote:

"The best of men
That e'er wore earth about him was a sufferer;
A soft, meek, patient, humble, tranquil spirit,
The first true gentleman that ever breathed."

Dean Swift, whose youth was nourished in that living age, passed into the era of dismal disputes, where he found the churches "dormitories of the living as well as of the dead." Some ten years before Paine's birth the Dean wrote: "Since the union of Divinity and Humanity is the great Article of our

Religion, 't is odd to see some clergymen, in their writings of Divinity, wholly devoid of Humanity." Men have, he said, enough religion to hate, but not to love. Had the Dean lived to the middle of the eighteenth century he might have discovered exceptions to this holy heartlessness, chiefly among those he had traditionally feared — the Socinians. These, like the Magdalene, were seeking the lost humanity of Jesus. He would have sympathized with Wesley, who escaped from "dormitories of the living" far enough to publish the Life of a Socinian (Firmin), with the brave apology, "I am sick of opinions, give me the life." But Socinianism, in eagerness to disown its bolder children, presently lost the heart of Jesus, and when Paine was recovering it the best of them could not comprehend his separation of the man from the myth. So came on the desiccated Christianity of which Emerson said, even among the Unitarians of fifty years ago, "The prayers and even the dogmas of our church are like the zodiac of Denderah, wholly insulated from anything now extant in the life and business of the people." Emerson may have been reading Paine's idea that Christ and the Twelve were mythically connected with Sun and Zodiac, this speculation being an indication of their distance from the Jesus he tenderly revered. If Paine rent the temple-veils of his time, and revealed the stony images behind them, albeit with rudeness, let it not be supposed that those forms were akin to the Jesus and the Marys whom skeptical criticism is re-incarnating, so that they dwell with us. Outside Paine's heart the Christ of his time was not more like the Jesus of our time than Jupiter was like the Prometheus he bound on a rock. The English Christ was then not a Son of Man, but a Prince of Dogma, bearing handcuffs for all who reasoned about him ; a potent phantasm that tore honest thinkers from their families and cast them into outer darkness, because they circulated the works of Paine, which

reminded the clergy that the Jesus even of their own Bible sentenced those only who ministered not to the hungry and naked, the sick and in prison. Paine's religious culture was English. There the brain had retreated to deistic caves, the heart had gone off to "Salvationism" of the time ; the churches were given over to the formalist and the politician, who carried divine sanction to the repetition of biblical oppressions and massacres by Burke and Pitt. And in all the world there had not been one to cry *Sursum Corda* against the consecrated tyranny until that throb of Paine's heart which brought on it the vulture. But to-day, were we not swayed by names and prejudices, it would bring on that prophet of the divine humanity, even the Christian dove.

Soon after the appearance of Part First of "The Age of Reason" it was expurgated of its negative criticisms, probably by some English Unitarians, and published as a sermon, with text from Job xi., 7: "Canst thou by searching find out God? Canst thou find out the Almighty to perfection?" It was printed anonymously ; and were its sixteen pages read in any orthodox church to-day it would be regarded as admirable. It might be criticized by left wings as somewhat old-fashioned in the warmth of its theism. It is fortunate that Paine's name was not appended to this doubtful use of his work, for it would have been a serious misrepresentation.[1] That his Religion of Humanity took the deistical form was an evolutionary necessity. English deism was not a religion, but at first a philosophy, and afterwards a scientific generalization. Its founder, as a philosophy,

[1] "A Lecture on the Existence and Attributes of the Deity, as Deduced from a Contemplation of His Works. M,DCC,XCV." The copy in my possession is inscribed with pen : "This was J. Joyce's copy, and noticed by him as Paine's work." Mr. Joyce was a Unitarian minister. It is probable that the suppression of Paine's name was in deference to his outlawry, and to the dread, by a sect whose legal position was precarious, of any suspicion of connection with "Painite" principles.

Herbert of Cherbury, had created the matrix in which was formed the Quaker religion of the "inner light," by which Paine's childhood was nurtured ; its founder as a scientific theory of creation, Sir Isaac Newton, had determined the matrix in which all unorthodox systems should originate. The real issue was between a sanctified ancient science and a modern science. The utilitarian English race, always the stronghold of science, had established the freedom of the new deism, which thus became the mould into which all unorthodoxies ran. From the time of Newton, English and American thought and belief have steadily become Unitarian. The dualism of Jesus, the thousand years of faith which gave every soul its post in a great war between God and Satan, without which there would have been no church, has steadily receded before a monotheism which, under whatever verbal disguises, makes the deity author of all evil. English Deism prevailed only to be reconquered into alliance with a tribal god of antiquity, developed into the tutelar deity of Christendom. And this evolution involved the transformation of Jesus into Jehovah, deity of a "chosen" or "elect" people. It was impossible for an apostle of the international republic, of the human brotherhood, whose Father was degraded by any notion of favoritism to a race, or to a "first-born son," to accept a name in which foreign religions had been harried, and Christendom established on a throne of thinkers' skulls. The philosophical and scientific deism of Herbert and Newton had grown cold in Paine's time, but it was detached from all the internecine figure-heads called gods ; it appealed to the reason of all mankind ; and in that manger, amid the beasts, royal and revolutionary, was cradled anew the divine humanity.

Paine wrote "Deism" on his banner in a militant rather than an affirmative way. He was aiming to rescue the divine Idea from traditional degradations in order that he might with it confront a revolutionary Atheism defying the celestial monarchy. In a later work, speaking of a theological book, "An Antidote to Deism," he remarks : "An antidote to Deism must be Atheism." So far as it is theological, "The Age of Reason" was meant to combat Infidelity. It raised before the French the pure deity of Herbert, of Newton, and other English deists whose works were unknown in France. But when we scrutinize Paine's positive Theism we find a distinctive nucleus forming within the nebulous mass of deistical speculations. Paine recognizes a deity only in the astronomic laws and intelligible order of the universe, and in the corresponding reason and moral nature of man. Like Kant, he was filled with awe by the starry heavens and man's sense of right.[1] The first part of "The Age of Reason" is chiefly astronomical ; with those celestial wonders he contrasts such stories as that of Samson and the foxes. "When we contemplate the immensity of that Being who directs and governs the incomprehensible Whole, of which the utmost ken of human sight can discover but a part, we ought to feel shame at calling such paltry stories the word of God." Then turning to the Atheist he says : "We did not make ourselves ; we did not make the principles of science, which we discover and apply but cannot alter." The only revelation of God in which he believes is "the universal display of himself in the works of creation, and that repugnance we feel in ourselves to bad actions, and disposition to do good ones." "The only idea we can have of serving God, is that of contributing to the happiness of the living creation that God has made."

[1] Astronomy, as we know, he had studied profoundly. In early life he had studied astronomic globes, purchased at the cost of many a dinner, and the orrery, and attended lectures. In "The Age of Reason" he writes, twenty-one years before Herschel's famous paper on the Nebulæ : "The probability is that each of those fixed stars is also a sun, round which another system of worlds or planets, though too remote for us to discover, performs its revolutions."

It thus appears that in Paine's Theism the deity is made manifest, not by omnipotence, a word I do not remember in his theories, but in this correspondence of universal order and bounty with reason and conscience, and the humane heart. In later works this speculative side of his Theism presented a remarkable Zoroastrian variation. When pressed with Bishop Butler's terrible argument against previous Deism,—that the God of the Bible is no more cruel than the God of Nature,—Paine declared his preference for the Persian religion, which exonerated the deity from responsibility for natural evils, above the Hebrew which attributed such things to God. He was willing to sacrifice God's omnipotence to his humanity. He repudiates every notion of a devil, but was evidently unwilling to ascribe the unconquered realms of chaos to the divine Being in whom he believed.

Thus, while theology was lowering Jesus to a mere King, glorying in baubles of crown and throne, pleased with adulation, and developing him into an authorizor of all the ills and agonies of the world, so depriving him of his humanity, Paine was recovering from the universe something like the religion of Jesus himself. "Why even of yourselves judge ye not what is right." In affirming the Religion of Humanity, Paine did not mean what Comte meant, a personification of the continuous life of our race [1]; nor did he merely mean benevolence towards all living creatures. He affirmed a Religion based on the authentic divinity of that which is supreme in human nature and distinctive of it. The sense of right, justice, love, mercy, is God himself in man ; this spirit judges all things,—all alleged revelations, all gods. In affirming a deity too good, loving, just, to do what is ascribed to Jahve, .Paine was animated by the same spirit that led the early believer to turn from heartless elemental gods to one born of

[1] Paine's friend and fellow-prisoner, Anacharsis Clootz, was the first to describe Humanity as "L'Être Suprême."

woman, bearing in his breast a human heart. Pauline theology took away this human divinity, and effected a restoration, by making the Son of Man Jehovah, and commanding the heart back from its seat of judgment, where Jesus had set it. "Shall the clay say to the potter, why hast thou formed me thus ? " " Yes," answered Paine, " if the thing felt itself hurt, and could speak." He knew as did Emerson, whom he often anticipates, that " no god dare wrong a worm."

The force of " The Age of Reason " is not in its theology, though this ethical variation of Deism in the direction of humanity is of exceeding interest to students who would trace the evolution of avatars and incarnations. Paine's theology was but gradually developed, and in this work is visible only as a tide beginning to rise under the fiery orb of his religious passion. For abstract theology he cares little. " If the belief of errors not morally bad did no mischief, it would make no part of the moral duty of man to oppose and remove them." He evinces regret that the New Testament, containing so many elevated moral precepts, should, by leaning on supposed prophecies in the Old Testament, have been burdened with its barbarities. " It must follow the fate of its foundation." This fatal connection, he knows, is not the work of Jesus ; he ascribes it to the church which evoked from the Old Testament a crushing system of priestly and imperial power reversing the benign principles of Jesus. It is this oppression, the throne of all oppressions, that he assails. His affirmations of the human deity are thus mainly expressed in his vehement denials.

This long chapter must now draw to a close. It would need a volume to follow thoroughly the argument of this epoch-making book, to which I have here written only an introduction, calling attention to its evolutionary factors, historical and spiritual. Such then was the new Pilgrim's Progress. As in that earlier prison, at Bedford, there shone in Paine's cell in the Luxembourg a great and imperishable vision, which multitudes are still following. The book is accessible in many editions. The Christian teacher of to-day may well ponder this fact. The atheists and secularists of our time are printing, reading, revering a work that opposes their opinions. For above its arguments and criticisms they see the faithful heart contending with a mighty Apollyon, girt with all the forces of revolutionary and royal Terrorism. Just this one Englishman, born again in America, confronting George III. and Robespierre on earth and tearing the like of them from the throne of the universe! Were it only for the grandeur of this spectacle in the past Paine would maintain his hold on thoughtful minds. But in America the hold is deeper than that. In this self-forgetting insurrection of the human heart against deified Inhumanity there is an expression of the inarticulate wrath of humanity against continuance of the same wrong. In the circulation throughout the earth of the Bible as the Word of God, even after its thousand serious errors of translation are turned, by exposure, into falsehoods; in the deliverance to savages of a scriptural sanction of their tomahawks and poisoned arrows; in the diffusion among cruel tribes of a religion based on human sacrifice, after intelligence has abandoned it; in the preservation of costly services to a deity who "needs nothing at men's hands," beside hovels of the poor who need much; in an exemption of sectarian property from taxation which taxes every man to support the sects, and continues the alliance of church and state; in these things, and others—the list is long— there is still visible, however refined, the sting and claw of the Apollyon against whom Paine hurled his far-reaching dart. "The Age of Reason" was at first published in America by a religious house, and as a religious book. It was circulated in Virginia by Washington's old friend, Parson Weems. It is still circu-lated, though by supposed unbelievers, as a religious book, and such it is.

Its religion is expressed largely in those same denunciations which theologians resent. I have explained them; polite agnostics apologize for them, or cast Paine over as a Jonah of the rationalistic ship. But to make one expression more gentle would mar the work. As it stands, with all its violences and faults, it represents, as no elaborate or polite treatise could, the agony and bloody sweat of a heart breaking in the presence of crucified Humanity. What dear heads, what noble hearts had that man seen laid low; what shrieks had he heard in the desolate homes of the Condorcets, the Brissots; what Canaanite and Midianite massacres had he seen before the altar of Brotherhood, erected by himself! And all because every human being had been taught from his cradle that there is something more sacred than humanity, and to which man should be sacrificed. Of all those massacred thinkers not one voice remains: they have gone silent: over their reeking guillotine sits the gloating Apollyon of Inhumanity. But here is one man, a prisoner, preparing for his long silence. He alone can speak for those slain between the throne and the altar. In these outbursts of laughter and tears, these outcries that think not of literary style, these appeals from surrounding chaos to the starry realm of order, from the tribune of vengeance to the sun shining for all, this passionate horror of cruelty in the powerful which will brave a heartless heaven or hell with its immortal indignation,—in all these the unfettered mind may hear the wail of enthralled Europe, sinking back choked with its blood, under the chain it tried to break. So long as a link remains of the same chain, binding reason or heart, Paine's "Age of Reason" will live. It is not a mere book —it is a man's heart.

CHAPTER XXXVI

FRIENDSHIPS

BARON PICHON, who had been a sinuous Secretary of Legation in America under Genêt and Fauchet, and attached to the Foreign Office in France under the Directory, told George Ticknor, in 1837, that "Tom Paine, who lived in Monroe's house at Paris, had a great deal too much influence over Monroe."[1] The Baron, apart from his prejudice against republicanism (Talleyrand was his master), knew more about American than French politics at the time of Monroe's mission in France. The agitation caused in France by Jay's negotiations in England, and rumors set afloat by their secrecy,—such secrecy being itself felt as a violation of good faith—rendered Monroe's position unhappy and difficult. After Paine's release from prison, his generous devotion to France, undiminished by his wrongs, added to the painful illness that reproached the Convention's negligence, excited a chivalrous enthusiasm for him. The tender care of Mr. and Mrs. Monroe for him, the fact that this faithful friend of France was in their house, were circumstances of international importance. Of Paine's fidelity to republican principles, and his indignation at their probable betrayal in England, there could be no doubt in any mind. He was consulted by the French Executive, and was virtually the most important *attaché* of the United States Legation. The "intrigue" of which Thibaudeau had spoken, in Convention, as having driven Paine from that body, was not given to the public, but it was well understood to involve the American President. If Paine's suffering represented in London Washington's deference to England, all the more did he stand to France as a representative of those who in America were battling for the Alliance. He was therefore a tower

1 "Life of George Ticknor," ii., p. 113.

of strength to Monroe. It will be seen by the subjoined letter that while he was Monroe's guest it was to him rather than the Minister that the Foreign Office applied for an introduction of a new Consul to Samuel Adams, Governor of Massachusetts—a Consul with whom Paine was not personally acquainted. The general feeling and situation in France at the date of this letter (March 6th), and the anger at Jay's secret negotiations in England, are reflected in it :

"MY DEAR FRIEND,—Mr. Mozard, who is appointed Consul, will present you this letter. He is spoken of here as a good sort of man, and I can have no doubt that you will find him the same at Boston. When I came from America it was my intention to return the next year, and I have intended the same every year since. The case I believe is, that as I am embarked in the revolution, I do not like to leave it till it is finished, notwithstanding the dangers I have run. I am now almost the only survivor of those who began this revolution, and I know not how it is that I have escaped. I know however that I owe nothing to the government of America. The executive department has never directed either the former or the present Minister to enquire whether I was dead or alive, in prison or in liberty, what the cause of the imprisonment was, and whether there was any service or assistance it could render. Mr. Monroe acted voluntarily in the case, and reclaimed me as an American citizen ; for the pretence for my imprisonment was that I was a foreigner, born in England.

" The internal scene here from the 31st of May 1793 to the fall of Robespierre has been terrible. I was shut up in the prison of the Luxembourg eleven months, and I find by the papers of Robespierre that have been published by the Convention since his death, that I was designed for a worse fate. The following memorandum is in his own handwriting : 'Démander que Thomas Paine soit décrété d'accusation pour les interêts de l'Amérique autant que de la France.'

" You will see by the public papers that the successes of the French arms have been and continue to be astonishing, more especially since the fall of Robespierre, and the suppression of the system of Terror. They have fairly beaten all the armies of Austria, Prussia, England, Spain, Sardignia, and Holland. Holland is entirely conquered, and there is now a revolution in that country.

" I know not how matters are going on your side the water, but I think everything is not as it ought to be. The appointment of G. Morris to be Minister here was the most unfortunate and the most injudicious appointment that could be made. I wrote this opinion to Mr. Jefferson at the time, and I said the same to Morris. Had he not been removed at the time he was I think the two countries would have been involved in a quarrel, for it is a fact, that he would either have been ordered away or put in arrestation ; for he gave every reason to suspect that he was secretly a British Emissary.

" What Mr. Jay is about in England I know not ; but is it possible that any man who has contributed to the Independence of America, and to free her from the tyranny of the British Government, can read without shame and indignation the note of Jay to Grenville ? That the United States has no other resource than in the justice and magnanimity of his Majesty, is a satire upon the Declaration of Independence, and exhibits [such] a spirit of meanness on the part of America, that, were it true, I should be ashamed of her. Such a declaration may suit the spaniel character of Aristocracy, but it cannot agree with manly character of a Republican.

" Mr. Mozard is this moment come for this letter, and he sets off directly.—God bless you, remember me among the circle of our friends, and tell them how much I wish to be once more among them.

" Thomas Paine."[1]

There are indications of physical feebleness as well as haste in this letter. The spring and summer brought some vigor, but, as we have seen by Monroe's letter to Judge Jones, he sank again, and in the autumn seemed nearing his end. Once more the announcement of his death appeared in England, this time bringing joy to the orthodox. From the same quarter, probably, whence issued in 1793, " Intercepted Correspondence from Satan to Citizen Paine," came now (1795) a folio sheet : " Glorious News for Old England. The British Lyon rous'd ; or John Bull for ever.

" The Fox has lost his Tail
The Ass has done his Braying,
The Devil has got Tom Paine."

Good-hearted as Paine was, it must be admitted that he was cruelly persistent

[1] Mr. Spofford, Librarian of Congress, has kindly copied this letter for me from the original, among the papers of George Bancroft.

in disappointing these British obituaries. Despite anguish, fever, and abscess— this for more than a year eating into his side,—he did not gratify those prayerful expectations by becoming a monument of divine retribution. Nay, amid all these sufferings he had managed to finish Part Second of " The Age of Reason," write the " Dissertation on Government," and give the Address before the Convention. Nevertheless when, in November, he was near death's door, there came from England tidings grievous enough to crush a less powerful constitution. It was reported that many of his staunchest old friends had turned against him on account of his heretical book. This report seemed to find confirmation in the successive volumes of Gilbert Wakefield in reply to the two Parts of Paine's book. Wakefield held Unitarian opinions, and did not defend the real fortress besieged by Paine. He was enraged that Paine should deal with the authority of the Bible, and the orthodox dogmas, as if they were Christainity, ignoring unorthodox versions altogether. This, however, hardly explains the extreme and coarse vituperation of these replies, which shocked Wakefield's friends.[2] Although in his thirty-eighth year at this time, Wakefield was not old enough to escape the sequelæ of his former clericalism. He had been a Fellow of Jesus College, Cambridge, afterwards had a congregation, and had continued his connection with the English Church after he was led, by textual criticism, to adopt Unitarian opinions. He had great reputation as a linguist, and wrote Scriptural expositions and retranslations. But few read his books, and he became a tutor in a dissenting college at Hackney, mainly under

[2] " The office of ' castigation' was unworthy of our friend's talents, and detrimental to his purpose of persuading others. Such a contemptuous treatment, even of an unfair disputant, was also too well calculated to depreciate in the public estimation that benevolence of character by which Mr. Wakefield was so justly distinguished."—" Life of Gilbert Wakefield," 1804, ii., p. 33.

influence of the Unitarian leaders, Price and Priestley. Wakefield would not condescend to any connection with a dissenting society, and his career at Hackney was marked by arrogant airs towards Unitarians, on account of a university training, then not open to dissenters. He attacked Price and Priestley, his superiors in every respect, apart from their venerable position and services, in a contemptuous way; and, in fact, might be brevetted a prig, with a fondness for coarse phrases, sometimes printed with blanks. He flew at Paine as if he had been waiting for him; his replies, not affecting any vital issue, were displays of linguistic and textual learning, set forth on the background of Paine's page, which he blackened. He exhausts his large vocabulary of vilification on a book whose substantial affirmations he concedes; and it is done in the mean way of appropriating the credit of Paine's arguments.

Gilbert Wakefield was indebted to the excitement raised by Paine for the first notice taken by the general public of anything he ever wrote. Paine, however, seems to have been acquainted with a sort of autobiography which he had published in 1792. In this book Wakefield admitted with shame that he had subscribed the Church formulas when he did not believe them, while indulging in flings at Price, Priestley, and others, who had suffered for their principles. At the same time there were some things in Wakefield's autobiography which could not fail to attract Paine: it severely attacked slavery, and also the whole course of Pitt towards France. This was done with talent and courage. It was consequently a shock when Gilbert Wakefield's outrageous abuse of himself came to the invalid in his sick-room. It appeared to be an indication of the extent to which he was abandoned by the Englishmen who had sympathized with his political principles, and to a large extent with his religious views. This acrimonious repudiation added groans to Paine's sick and sinking heart,

some of which were returned upon his Socinian assailant, and in kind. This private letter my reader must see, though it was meant for no eye but that of Gilbert Wakefield. It is dated at Paris, November 19, 1795.

"DEAR SIR,—When you prudently chose, like a starved apothecary, to offer your eighteen-penny antidote to those who had taken my two-and-sixpenny Bible-purge,[1] you forgot that although my dose was rather of the roughest, it might not be the less wholesome for possessing that drastick quality; and if I am to judge of its salutary effects on your infuriate polemic stomach, by the nasty things it has made you bring away, I think you should be the last man alive to take your own panacea. As to the collection of words of which you boast the possession, nobody, I believe, will dispute their amount, but every one who reads your answer to my 'Age of Reason' will wish there were not so many scurrilous ones among them; for though they may be very usefull in emptying your gall-bladder they are too apt to move the bile of other people.

"Those of Greek and Latin are rather foolishly thrown away, I think, on a man like me, who, you are pleased to say, is '*the greatest ignoramus in nature*': yet I must take the liberty to tell you, that wisdom does not consist in the mere knowledge of language, but of things.

"You recommended me to *know myself*,—a thing very easy to advise, but very difficult to practice, as I learn from your own book; for you take yourself to be a meek disciple of Christ, and yet give way to passion and pride in every page of its composition.

"You have raised an ant-hill about the roots of my sturdy oak, and it may amuse idlers to see your work; but neither its body nor its branches are injured by you; and I hope the shade of my Civic Crown may be able to preserve your little contrivance, at least for the season.

"When you have done as much service to the world by your writings, and suffered as much for them, as I have done, you will be better entitled to dictate: but although I know you to be a keener politician than Paul, I can assure you, from my experience of mankind, that you do not much commend the Christian doctrines to them by announcing that it requires the labour of a learned life to make them understood.

"May I be permitted, after all, to suggest that your truly vigorous talents would be best employed in teaching men to preserve their liberties exclusively,—leaving to that God who made their immortal souls the care of their eternal welfare.

"I am, dear Sir,
"Your true well-wisher,
"THO. PAINE.
"TO GILBERT WAKEFIELD, A. B."

---

[1] These were the actual prices of the books.

After a first perusal of this letter has made its unpleasant impression, the reader will do well to read it again. Paine has repaired to his earliest Norfolkshire for language appropriate to the coarser tongue of his Nottinghamshire assailant; but it should be said that the offensive paragraph, the first, is a travesty of one written by Wakefield. In his autobiography, after groaning over his books that found no buyers, a veritable " starved apothecary," Wakefield describes the uneasiness caused by his pamphlet on " Religious Worship " as proof that the disease was yielding to his " potion." He says that " as a physician of spiritual maladies " he had seconded " the favorable operation of the first prescription,"—and so forth. Paine, in using the simile, certainly allows the drugs and phials of his sickroom to enter it to a disagreeable extent, but we must bear in mind that we are looking over his shoulder. We must also, by the same consideration of its privacy, mitigate the letter's egotism. Wakefield's ant-hill protected by the foliage, the " civic crown," of Paine's oak which it has attacked,—gaining notice by the importance of the work it belittles,—were admirable if written by another; and the egotism is not without some warrant. It is the rebuke of a scarred veteran of the liberal army to the insults of a subaltern near twenty years his junior. It was no doubt taken to heart. For when the agitation which Gilbert Wakefield had contributed to swell, and to lower, presently culminated in handcuffs for the circulators of Paine's works, he was filled with anguish. He vainly tried to resist the oppression, and to call back the Unitarians, who for twenty-five years continued to draw attention from their own heresies by hounding on the prosecution of Paine's adherents.[1] The prig perished; in his

[1] " But I would not forcibly suppress this book [" Age of Reason "]; much less would I punish (O my God, be such wickedness far from me, or leave me destitute of thy favour in the midst of this perjured and sanguinary generation !) much less would I punish, by fine or im-

place stood a martyr of the freedom bound up with the work he had assailed. Paine's other assailant, the Bishop of Llandaff, having bent before Pitt, and episcopally censured the humane side he once espoused, Gilbert Wakefield answered him with a boldness that brought on him two years' imprisonment. When he came out of prison (1801) he was received with enthusiasm by all of Paine's friends, who had forgotten the wrong so bravely atoned for. Had he not died in the same year, at the age of forty-five, Gilbert Wakefield might have become a standard-bearer of the freethinkers.

Paine's recovery after such prolonged and perilous suffering was a sort of resurrection. In April (1796) he leaves Monroe's house for the country, and with the returning life of nature his strength is steadily recovered. What to the man whose years of anguish, imprisonment, disease, at last pass away, must have been the paths and hedgerows of Versailles, where he now meets the springtide, and the more healing sunshine of affection ! Risen from his thorny bed of pain—

" The meanest floweret of the vale,
    The simplest note that swells the gale,
    The common sun, the air, the skies,
    To him are opening paradise."

prisonment, from any possible consideration, the publisher or author of these pages."—Letter of Gilbert Wakefield to Sir John Scott, Attorney General, 1798. For evidence of Unitarian intolerance see the discourse of W. J. Fox on " The Duties of Christians towards Deists " (Collected Works, vol. i.). In this discourse, October 24, 1819, on the prosecution of Carlile for publishing " The Age of Reason," Mr. Fox expresses his regret that the first prosecution should have been conducted by a Unitarian. " Goaded," he says, " by the calumny which would identify them with those who yet reject the Saviour, they have, in repelling so unjust an accusation, caught too much of the tone of their opponents, and given the most undesirable proof of their affinity to other Christians by that unfairness towards the disbeliever which does not become any Christian." Ultimately Mr. Fox became the champion of all the principles of " The Age of Reason " and " The Rights of Man."

So had it been even if nature alone had surrounded him. But Paine had been restored by the tenderness and devotion of friends. Had it not been for friendship he could hardly have been saved. We are little able, in the present day, to appreciate the reverence and affection with which Thomas Paine was regarded by those who saw in him the greatest apostle of liberty in the world. Elihu Palmer spoke a very general belief when he declared Paine "probably the most useful man that ever existed upon the face of the earth." This may sound wild enough on the ears of those to whom Liberty has become a familiar drudge. There was a time when she was an ideal Rachel, to win whom many years of terrible service were not too much; but now in the garish day she is our prosaic Leah,—a serviceable creature in her way, but quite unromantic. In Paris there were ladies and gentlemen who had known something of the cost of Liberty,—-Colonel and Mrs. Monroe, Sir Robert and Lady Smith, Madame Lafayette, Mr. and Mrs. Barlow, M. and Madame De Bonneville. They had known what it was to watch through anxious nights with terrors surrounding them. He who had suffered most was to them a sacred person. He had come out of the succession of ordeals, so weak in body, so wounded by American ingratitude, so sore at heart, that no delicate child needed more tender care. Set those ladies and their charge a thousand years back in the poetic past, and they become Morgan le Fay, and the Lady Nimue, who bear the wounded warrior away to their Avalon, there to be healed of his grievous hurts. Men say their Arthur is dead, but their love is stronger than death. And though the service of these friends might at first have been reverential, it had ended with attachment, so great was Paine's power, so wonderful and pathetic his memories, so charming the play of his wit, so full his response to kindness.

One especially great happiness awaited him when he became convalescent. Sir Robert Smith, a wealthy banker in Paris, made his acquaintance, and he discovered that Lady Smith was no other than "The Little Corner of the World," whose letters had carried sunbeams into his prison.[1] An intimate friendship was at once established with Sir Robert and his lady, in whose house, probably at Versailles, Paine was a guest after leaving the Monroes. To Lady Smith, on discovering her, Paine addressed a poem, —"The Castle in the Air to the Little Corner of the World":

" In the region of clouds, where the whirlwinds arise,
    My Castle of Fancy was built ;
The turrets reflected the blue from the skies,
    And the windows with sunbeams were gilt.

" The rainbow sometimes, in its beautiful state,
    Enamelled the mansion around ;
And the figures that fancy in clouds can create
    Supplied me with gardens and ground.

" I had grottos, and fountains, and orange-tree groves,
    I had all that enchantment has told ;
I had sweet shady walks for the gods and their loves,
    I had mountains of coral and gold.

" But a storm that I felt not had risen and rolled,
    While wrapped in a slumber I lay ;
And when I looked out in the morning, behold,
    My Castle was carried away.

" It passed over rivers and valleys and groves,
    The world it was all in my view ;
I thought of my friends, of their fates, of their loves,
    And often, full often, of YOU.

" At length it came over a beautiful scene,
    That nature in silence had made ;
The place was but small, but 't was sweetly serene,
    And chequered with sunshine and shade.

" I gazed and I envied with painful good will,
    And grew tired of my seat in the air ;
When all of a sudden my Castle stood still,
    As if some attraction were there.

" Like a lark from the sky it came fluttering down,
    And placed me exactly in view,
When whom should I meet in this charming retreat,
    This corner of calmness, but—YOU.

[1] Sir Robert Smith (Smythe in the Peerage List) was born in 1744, and married, first, Miss Blake of London (1776). The name of the second Lady Smith, Paine's friend, before her marriage I have not ascertained.

" Delighted to find you in honor and ease,
  I felt no more sorrow nor pain ;
But the wind coming fair, I ascended the
  breeze,
  And went back with my Castle again."

Paine was now a happy man. The kindness that rescued him from death was followed by the friendship that beguiled him from horrors of the past. From gentle ladies he learned that beyond the Age of Reason lay the forces that defeat Giant Despair.

" To reason [so he writes to Lady Smith] against feelings is as vain as to-reason against fire : it serves only to torture the torture, by adding reproach to horror. All reasoning with ourselves in such cases acts upon us like the reasoning of another person, which, however kindly done, serves but to insult the misery we suffer. If Reason could remove the pain, Reason would have prevented it. If she could not do the one, how is she to perform the other ? In all such cases we must look upon Reason as dispossessed of her empire, by a revolt of the mind. She retires to a distance to weep, and the ebony sceptre of Despair rules alone. All that Reason can do is to suggest, to hint a thought, to signify a wish, to cast now and then a kind of bewailing look, to hold up, when she can catch the eye, the miniature shaded portrait of Hope; and though dethroned, and can dictate no more, to wait upon us in the humble station of a handmaid." [1]

The mouth of the rescued and restored captive was filled with song. Several little poems were circulated among his friends, but not printed ; among them the following :

" CONTENTMENT ; OR, IF YOU PLEASE, CONFESSION. *To Mrs. Barlow, on her pleasantly telling the author that, after writing against the superstition of the Scripture religion, he was setting up a religion capable of more bigotry and enthusiasm, and more dangerous to its votaries— that of making a religion of Love.*

" O could we always live and love,
  And always be sincere,
I would not wish for heaven above,
  My heaven would be here.

" Though many countries I have seen,
  And more may chance to see,
My *Little Corner of the World*
  Is half the world to me.

" The other half, as you may guess,
  America contains ;
And thus, between them, I possess
  The whole world for my pains.

" I 'm then contented with my lot,
  I can no happier be ;
For neither world I'm sure has got
  So rich a man as me.

" Then send no fiery chariot down
  To take me off from hence,
But leave me on my heavenly ground—
  This prayer is *common sense.*

" Let others choose another plan,
  I mean no fault to find ;
The true theology of man
  Is happiness of mind."

Paine gained great favor with the French government and fame throughout Europe by his pamphlet, "The Decline and Fall of the English System of Finance," in which he predicted the suspension of the Bank of England, which followed the next year. He dated the pamphlet April 8th, and the Minister of Foreign Affairs is shown, in the Archives of that office, to have ordered, on April 27th, a thousand copies. It was translated in all the languages of Europe, and was a terrible retribution for the forged assignats whose distribution in France the English government had considered a fair mode of warfare. This translation "into all the languages of the continent" is mentioned by Ralph Broome, to whom the British government entrusted the task of answering the pamphlet.[2] As Broome's answer is dated June 4th, this circulation in six or seven weeks is remarkable. The proceeds were devoted by Paine to the relief of prisoners for debt in Newgate, London.[3]

[1] Forgetfulness. "Writings of Paine" (Conway), vol. iii., p. 320.

[2] "Observations on Mr. Paine's Pamphlet," etc. Broome escapes the charge of prejudice by speaking of "Mr. Paine, whose abilities I admire and deprecate in a breath." Paine's pamphlet was also replied to by George Chalmers ("Oldys"), who had written the slanderous biography.

[3] Richard Carlile's sketch of Paine, p. 20. This large generosity to English sufferers appears the more characteristic beside the closing paragraph of Paine's pamphlet, "As an individual citizen of America, and as far as an individual can go, I have revenged (if I may use the

The concentration of this pamphlet on its immediate subject, which made it so effective, renders it of too little intrinsic interest in the present day to delay us long, especially as it is included in all editions of Paine's works. It possesses, however, much biographical interest as proving the intellectual power of Paine while still but a convalescent. He never wrote any work involving more study and mastery of difficult details. It was this pamphlet, written in Paris, while "Peter Porcupine," in America, was rewriting the slanders of "Oldys," which revolutionized Cobbett's opinion of Paine, and led him to try and undo the injustice he had wrought.

It now so turned out that Paine was able to repay all the kindnesses he had received. The relations between the French government and Monroe, already strained, as we have seen, became in the spring of 1796 almost intolerable. The Jay treaty seemed to the French so incredible that, even after it was ratified, they believed that the Representatives would refuse the appropriation needed for its execution. But when tidings came that this effort of the House of Representatives had been crushed by a menaced *coup d'état*, the ideal America fell in France, and was broken in fragments. Monroe could now hardly have remained save on the credit of Paine with the French. There was, of course, a fresh accession of wrath towards England for this appropriation of the French alliance. Paine had been only the first sacrifice on the altar of the new alliance; now all English families and all Americans in Paris except himself were likely to become its victims.

expression without any immoral meaning) the piratical depredations committed on American commerce by the English government. I have retaliated for France on the subject of finance : and I conclude with retorting on Mr. Pitt the expression he used against France, and say, that the English system of finance 'is on the verge, nay even in the gulf of bankruptcy.'"
Concerning the false French assignats forged in England, see Louis Blanc's "History of the Revolution," vol. xii., p. 101.

The English-speaking residents there made one little colony, and Paine was sponsor for them all. His blow at English credit proved the formidable power of the man whom Washington had delivered up to Robespierre in the interest of Pitt. So Paine's popularity reached its climax; the American Legation found through him a *modus vivendi* with the French government; the families which had received and nursed him in his weakness found in his intimacy their best credential. Mrs. Joel Barlow especially, while her husband was in Algeria, on the service of the American government, might have found her stay in Paris unpleasant but for Paine's friendship. The importance of his guarantee to the banker, Sir Robert Smith, appears by the following note, written at Versailles, August 13th:

"CITIZEN MINISTER: The citizen Robert Smith, a very particular friend of mine, wishes to obtain a passport to go to Hamburg, and I will be obliged to you to do him that favor. Himself and family have lived several years in France, for he likes neither the government nor the climate of England. He has large property in England, but his Banker in that country has refused sending him remittances. This makes it necessary for him to go to Hamburg, because from there he can draw his money out of his Banker's hands, which he cannot do whilst in France. His family remains in France.— *Salut et fraternité.*

"THOMAS PAINE."[1]

Amid his circle of cultured and kindly friends Paine had dreamed of a lifting of the last cloud from his life, so long overcast. His eyes were strained to greet that shining sail that should bring him a response to his letter of September to Washington, in his heart being a great hope that his apparent wrong would be explained as a miserable mistake, and that old friendship restored. As the reader knows, the hope was grievously disappointed. The famous public letter to Washington (August 3d), which was not published in France, has

[1] Soon after Jefferson became President Paine wrote to him, suggesting that Sir Robert's firm might be safely depended on as the medium of American financial transactions in Europe.

already been considered, in advance of its chronological place. It will be found, however, of more significance if read in connection with the unhappy situation, in which all of Paine's friends, and all Americans in Paris, had been brought by the Jay treaty. From their point of view the deliverance of Paine to prison and the guillotine was only one incident in a long-planned and systematic treason, aimed at the life of the French republic. Jefferson in America, and Paine in France, represented the faith and hope of republicans that the treason would be overtaken by retribution and reversal.

CHAPTER XXXVII

THEOPHILANTHROPY

IN the ever-recurring controversies concerning Paine and his "Age of Reason" we have heard many triumphal claims. Christianity and the Church, it is said, have advanced and expanded, unharmed by such criticisms. This is true. But there are several fallacies implied in this mode of dealing with the religious movement caused by Paine's work. It assumes that Paine was an enemy of all that now passes under the name of Christianity—a title claimed by nearly a hundred and fifty different organizations, with some of which (as the Unitarians, Universalists, Broad Church, and Hicksite Friends) he would largely sympathize. It further assumes that he was hostile to all churches, and desired or anticipated their destruction. Such is not the fact. Paine desired and anticipated their reformation, which has steadily progressed. At the close of "The Age of Reason" he exhorts the clergy to "preach something that is edifying, and from texts that are known to be true."

" The Bible of the creation is inexhaustible in texts. Every part of science, whether connected with the geometry of the universe, with the systems of animal and vegetable life, or with the properties of inanimate matter, is a text for devotion as well as for philosophy—for gratitude as for human improvement. It will perhaps be said, that, if such a revolution in the system of religion takes place, every preacher ought to be a philosopher. *Most certainly*. And every house of devotion a school of science. It has been by wandering from the immutable laws of science, and the right use of reason, and setting up an invented thing called revealed religion, that so many wild and blasphemous conceits have been formed of the Almighty. The Jews have made him the assassin of the human species, to make room for the religion of the Jews. The Christians have made him the murderer of himself, and the founder of a new religion, to supersede and expel the Jewish religion. And to find pretence and admission for these things they must have supposed his power and his wisdom imperfect, or his will changeable ; and the changeableness of the will is the imperfection of the judgment. The philosopher knows that the laws of the Creator have never changed with respect either to the principles of science, or the properties of matter. Why then is it to be supposed they have changed with respect to man ? "

To the statement that Christianity has not been impeded by "The Age of Reason," it should be added that its advance has been largely due to modifications rendered necessary by that work. The unmodified dogmas are represented in small and eccentric communities. The advance has been under the Christian name, with which Paine had no concern ; but to confuse the word "Christianity" with the substance it labels is inadmissible. England wears the device of St. George and the Dragon ; but English culture has reduced the saint and dragon to a fable.

The special wrath with which Paine is still visited, above all other deists put together, or even atheists, is a tradition from a so-called Christianity which his work compelled to capitulate. That system is now nearly extinct, and the *vendetta* it bequeathed should now end. The capitulation began immediately with the publication of the Bishop of Llandaff's "Apology for the Bible," a title that did not fail to attract notice when it appeared (1796). There were more than thirty replies to Paine, but they are mainly taken out of the Bishop's "Apology," to which they add nothing. It is said in religious encyclopedias that Paine was "answered" by one and another writer, but in a strict sense Paine was never answered, unless by the successive surrenders referred to. As Bishop Watson's "Apology" is adopted by most authorities as the sufficient "answer," it may be here accepted as a representative of the rest. Whether Paine's points dealt with by the Bishop are answerable or not, the following facts will prove how uncritical is the prevalent opinion that they were really answered.

Dr. Watson concedes generally to Paine the discovery of some "real difficulties" in the Old Testament, and the exposure, in the Christian grove, of "a few unsightly shrubs, which good men had wisely concealed from public view" (p. 44).[1] It is not Paine that here calls some "sacred" things unsightly, and charges the clergy with concealing them—it is the Bishop. Among the particular and direct concessions made by the Bishop are the following:

1. That Moses may not have written every part of the Pentateuch. Some passages were probably written by later hands, transcribers or editors (pp. 9–11, 15). [If human reason and scholarship are admitted to detach any portions, by what authority can they be denied the right to bring all parts of the Pentateuch, or even the whole Bible, under their human judgment?]

2. The law in Deuteronomy giving parents the right, under certain circumstances, to have their children stoned to death, is excused only as a "humane restriction of a power improper to be

[1] Carey's edition, Philadelphia, 1796.

lodged with any parent" (p. 13). [Granting the Bishop's untrue assertion, that the same "improper" power was arbitrary among the Romans, Gauls, and Persians, why should it not have been abolished in Israel? And if Dr. Watson possessed the right to call any law established in the Bible "improper," how can Paine be denounced for subjecting other things in the book to moral condemnation? The moral sentiment is not an episcopal prerogative.]

3. The Bishop agrees that it is "the opinion of many learned men and good Christians" that the Bible, though authoritative in religion, is fallible in other respects, "relating the ordinary history of the times" (p. 23). [What but human reason, in the absence of papal authority, is to draw the line between the historical and religious elements in the Bible?]

4. It is conceded that "Samuel did not write any part of the second book bearing his name, and only a part of the first" (p. 24). [One of many blows dealt by this prelate at confidence in the Bible.]

5. It is admitted that Ezra contains a contradiction in the estimate of the numbers who returned from Babylon; it is attributed to a transcriber's mistake of one Hebrew figure for another (p. 30). [Paine's question here had been: "What certainty then can there be in the Bible for anything?" It is no answer to tell him how an error involving a difference of 12,542 people may perhaps have occurred.]

6. It is admitted that David did not write some of the Psalms ascribed to him (p. 131).

7. "It is acknowledged that the order of time is not everywhere observed" [in Jeremiah]; also that this prophet, fearing for his life, suppressed the truth [as directed by King Zedekiah]. "He was under no obligation to tell the whole [truth] to men who were certainly his enemies and no good subjects of the king" (pp. 36, 37). [But how can it be determined how much in Jeremiah

is the "word of God," and how much uttered for the casual advantage of himself or his king?]

8. It is admitted that there was no actual fulfilment of Ezekiel's prophecy, "No foot of man shall pass through it [Egypt], nor foot of beast shall pass through it, for forty years" (p. 42).

9. The discrepancies between the genealogies of Christ, in Matthew and Luke, are admitted : they are explained by saying that Matthew gives the genealogy of Joseph, and Luke that of Mary ; and that Matthew commits "an error" in omitting three generations between Joram and Ozias (p. 48). [Paine had asked, why might not writers mistaken in the natural genealogy of Christ be mistaken also in his celestial genealogy ? To this no answer was attempted.]

Such are some of the Bishop's direct admissions. There are other admissions in his silences and evasions. For instance, having elaborated a theory as to how the error in Ezra might occur, by the close resemblance of Hebrew letters representing widely different numbers, he does not notice Nehemiah's error in the same matter, pointed out by Paine,— a self-contradiction, and also a discrepancy with Ezra, which could not be explained by his theory. He says nothing about several other contradictions alluded to by Paine. The Bishop's evasions are sometimes painful, as when he tries to escape the force of Paine's argument, that Paul himself was not convinced by the evidences of the resurrection which he adduces for others. The Bishop says : "That Paul had so far resisted the evidence which the apostles had given of the resurrection and ascension of Jesus, as to be a persecutor of the disciples of Christ, is certain ; but I do not remember the place where he declares that he had not believed them." But when Paul says, "I verily thought with myself that I ought to do many things contrary to the name of Jesus of Nazareth," surely this is inconsistent with his belief in the resurrection and ascension. Paul declares that when it was the good pleasure of God "to reveal his Son in me," immediately he entered on his mission. He "was not disobedient to the heavenly vision." Clearly then Paul had not been convinced of the resurrection and ascension until he saw Christ in a vision.

In dealing with Paine's moral charges against the Bible the Bishop has left a confirmation of all that I have said concerning the Christianity of his time. An "infidel" of to-day could need no better moral arguments against the Bible than those framed by the Bishop in its defence. He justifies the massacre of the Canaanites on the ground that they were sacrificers of their own children to idols, cannibals, addicted to unnatural lust. Were this true it would be no justification ; but as no particle of evidence is adduced in support of these utterly unwarranted and entirely fictitious accusations, the argument now leaves the massacre without any excuse at all. The extermination is not in the Bible based on any such considerations, but simply on a divine command to seize the land and slay its inhabitants. No legal right to the land is suggested in the record ; and, as for morality, the only persons spared in Joshua's expedition were a harlot and her household, she having betrayed her country to the invaders, to be afterwards exalted into an ancestress of Christ. Of the cities destroyed by Joshua it is said : "It was of Jehovah to harden their hearts, to come against Israel in battle, that he might utterly destroy them, that they might have no favor, but that he might destroy them, as Jehovah commanded Moses" (Joshua xi., 20). As their hearts were thus in Jehovah's power for hardening, it may be inferred that they were equally in his power for reformation, had they been guilty of the things alleged by the Bishop. With these things before him, and the selection of Rahab for mercy above all the women in Jericho—every woman slain save the harlot who delivered them up to slaughter—the Bishop says : "The destruction of the Canaanites exhibits to all nations, in all ages, a signal proof of God's displeasure against sin."

The Bishop rages against Paine for supposing that the commanded preservation of the Midianite maidens, when all males and married women were slain, was for their " debauchery."

" Prove this, and I will allow that Moses was the horrid monster you make him—prove this, and I will allow that the Bible is what you call it—' a book of lies, wickedness, and blasphemy ' —prove this, or excuse my warmth if I say to you, as Paul said to Elymas the sorcerer, who sought to turn away Sergius Paulus from the faith, 'O full of all subtilty, and of all mischief, thou child of the devil, thou enemy of all righteousness, wilt thou not cease to pervert the right ways of the Lord?'—I did not, when I began these letters, think that I should have been moved to this severity of rebuke, by anything you could have written ; but when so gross a misrepresentation is made of God's proceedings, coolness would be a crime."

And what does my reader suppose is the alternative claimed by the prelate's foaming mouth? The maidens, he declares, were not reserved for debauchery, but for slavery !

Little did the Bishop foresee a time when, of the two suppositions, Paine's might be deemed the more lenient. The subject of slavery was then under discussion in England, and the Bishop is constrained to add, concerning this enslavement of thirty-two thousand maidens, from the massacred families, that slavery is "a custom abhorrent from our manners, but everywhere practised in former times, and still practised in countries where the benignity of the Christian religion has not softened the ferocity of human nature." Thus, Jehovah is represented as not only ordering the wholesale murder of the worshippers of another deity, but an adoption of their "abhorrent" and inhuman customs.

This connection of the deity of the Bible with "the ferocity of human nature" in one place, and its softening in another, justified Paine's solemn rebuke to the clergy of his time.

" Had the cruel and murderous orders with which the Bible is filled, and the numberless torturing executions of men, women, and children, in consequence of those orders, been ascribed to some friend whose memory you revered, you would have glowed with satisfaction at detecting the falsehood of the charge, and gloried in defending his injured fame. It is because ye are sunk in the cruelty of superstition, or feel no interest in the honor of your Creator, that ye listen to the horrid tales of the Bible, or hear them with callous indifference."

This is fundamentally what the Bishop has to answer, and of course he must resort to the terrible *Tu quoque* of Bishop Butler. Dr. Watson says he is astonished that " so acute a reasoner " should reproduce the argument.

" You profess yourself to be a deist, and to believe that there is a God, who created the universe, and established the laws of nature, by which it is sustained in existence. You profess that from a contemplation of the works of God you derive a knowledge of his attributes ; and you reject the Bible because it ascribes to God things inconsistent (as you suppose) with the attributes which you have discovered to belong to him ; in particular, you think it repugnant to his moral justice that he should doom to destruction the crying and smiling infants of the Canaanites. Why do you not maintain it to be repugnant to his moral justice that he should suffer crying or smiling infants to be swallowed up by an earthquake, drowned by an inundation, consumed by fire, starved by a famine, or destroyed by a pestilence ? "

Dr. Watson did not, of course, know that he was following Bishop Butler in laying the foundations of atheism, though such was the case. As was said in my chapter on the " Age of Reason," this dilemma did not really apply to Paine. His deity was inferred, despite all the disorders in nature, exclusively from its apprehensible order without, and from the reason and moral nature of man. He had not dealt with the problem of evil, except implicitly, in his defence of the divine goodness, which is inconsistent with the responsibility of his deity for natural evils, or for anything that would be condemned by reason and conscience if done by man. It was thus the Christian prelate who had abandoned the primitive faith in the divine humanity for a natural deism, while the man he calls a " child of the devil " was defending the divine humanity.

This then was the way in which Paine was "answered," for I am not aware of any important addition to the Bishop's "Apology" by other opponents. I cannot see how any Christian of the present time can regard it otherwise than as a capitulation of the system it was supposed to defend, however secure he may regard the Christianity of to-day. It subjects the Bible to the judgment of human reason for the determination of its authorship, the integrity of its text, and the correction of admitted errors in authorship, chronology, and genealogy; it admits the fallibility of the writers in matters of fact; it admits that some of the moral laws of the Old Testament are "improper" and others, like slavery, belong to "the ferocity of human nature"; it admits the non-fulfilment of one prophet's prediction, and the self-interested suppression of truth by another; and it admits that "good men" were engaged in concealing these "unsightly" things. Here are gates thrown open for the whole "Age of Reason."

The unorthodoxy of the Bishop's "Apology" does not rest on the judgment of the present writer alone. If Gilbert Wakefield presently had to reflect on his denunciations of Paine from the inside of a Prison, the Bishop of Llandaff had occasion to appreciate Paine's ideas on "mental lying" as the Christian infidelity. The Bishop, born in the same year (1737) with the two heretics he attacked—Gibbon and Paine —began his career as a professor of chemistry at Cambridge (1764), but seven years later became Regius professor of divinity there. His posthumous papers present a remarkable picture of the church in his time. In replying to Gibbon he studied first principles, and assumed a brave stand against all intellectual and religious coercion. On the episcopal bench he advocated a liberal policy toward France. In undertaking to answer Paine he became himself unsettled; and at the very moment when unsophisticated orthodoxy was hailing

him as its champion, the sagacious magnates of Church and State proscribed him. He learned that the king had described him as "impracticable"; with bitterness of soul he saw prelates of inferior rank and ability promoted over his head. He tried the effect of a political recantation, in one of his charges; and when Williams was imprisoned for publishing the "Age of Reason," and Gilbert Wakefield for rebuking his "Charge," this former champion of free speech dared not utter a protest. But by this servility he gained nothing. He seems to have at length made up his mind that if he was to be punished for his liberalism he would enjoy it. While preaching on "Revealed Religion" he saw the Bishop of London shaking his head. In 1811, five years before his death, he writes this significant note: "I have treated my divinity as I, twenty-five years ago, treated my chemical papers: I have lighted my fire with the labor of a great portion of my life." [1]

Next to the "Age of Reason," the book that did most to advance Paine's principles in England was, as I believe, Dr. Watson's "Apology for the Bible." Dean Swift had warned the clergy that if they began to reason with objectors to the creeds they would awaken skepticism. Dr. Watson fulfilled this pre-

[1] Patrick Henry's Answer to the "Age of Reason" shared the like fate. "When, during the first two years of his retirement, Thomas Paine's 'Age of Reason' made its appearance, the old statesman was moved to write out a somewhat elaborate treatise in defence of the truth of Christianity. This treatise it was his purpose to have published. 'He read the manuscript to his family as he progressed with it, and completed it a short time before his death' [1799]. When it was finished, however, 'being diffident about his own work,' and impressed also by the great ability of the replies to Paine which were then appearing in England, 'he directed his wife to destroy' what he had written. She 'complied literally with his directions,' and thus put beyond the chance of publication a work which seemed, to some who heard it, 'the most eloquent and unanswerable argument in defence of the Bible which was ever written.'"—Fontaine MS. quoted in Tyler's "Patrick Henry."

K

diction. He pointed out, as Gilbert Wakefield did, some exegetical and verbal errors in Paine's book, but they no more affected its main purpose and argument than the grammatical mistakes in "Common Sense." diminished its force in the American Revolution. David Dale, the great manufacturer at Paisley, distributed three thousand copies of the "Apology" among his workmen. The books carried among them extracts from Paine, and the Bishop's admissions. Robert Owen married Dale's daughter, and presently found the Paisley workmen a ripe harvest for his rationalism and radicalism.

Thus, in the person of its first clerical assailant, began the march of the "Age of Reason" in England. In the Bishop's humiliations for his concessions to truth, were illustrated what Paine had said of his system's falsity and fraudulence. After the Bishop had observed the Bishop of London manifesting disapproval of his sermon on "Revealed Religion" he went home and wrote: "What is this thing called Orthodoxy, which mars the fortunes of honest men? It is a sacred thing to which every denomination of Christians lays exclusive claim, but to which no man, no assembly of men, since the apostolic age, can prove a title." There is now a Bishop of London who might not acknowledge the claim even for the apostolic age. The principles, apart from the particular criticisms, of Paine's book have established themselves in the English Church. They were affirmed by Bishop Wilson in clear language: "Christian duties are founded on reason, not on the sovereignty of God commanding what he pleases : God cannot command us what is not fit to be believed or done, all his commands being founded in the necessities of our nature." It was on this principle that Paine declared that things in the Bible "not fit to be believed or done," could not be divine commands. His book, like its author, was outlawed, but men more heretical are now buried in Westminster Abbey, and the lost bones of Thomas Paine are really reposing in those tombs. It was he who compelled the hard and

heartless Bibliolatry of his time to repair to illiterate conventicles, and the lovers of humanity, true followers of the man of Nazareth, to abandon the crumbling castle of dogma, preserving its creeds as archaic bric-a-brac. As his "Rights of Man" is now the political constitution of England, his "Age of Reason" is in the growing constitution of its Church,—the most powerful organization in Christendom because the freest and most inclusive.

The excitement caused in England by the "Age of Reason," and the large number of attempted replies to it, were duly remarked by the *Moniteur* and other French journals. The book awakened much attention in France, and its principles were reproduced in a little French book entitled : "Manuel des Théoantropophiles." This appeared in September, 1796. In January, 1797, Paine, with five families, founded in Paris the church of Theophilanthropy, —a word, as he stated in a letter to Erskine, "compounded of three Greek words, signifying God, Love, and Man. The explanation given to this word is *Lovers of God and Man*, or *Adorers of God and Friends of Man*." The society opened "in the street Denis, No. 34, corner of Lombard Street." "The Theophilanthropists believe in the existence of God, and the immortality of the soul." The inaugural discourse was given by Paine. It opens with these words : "Religion has two principal enemies, Fanaticism and Infidelity, or that which is called atheism. The first requires to be combated by reason and morality, the other by natural philosophy." The discourse is chiefly an argument for a divine existence based on motion, which, he maintains, is not a property of matter. It proves a Being "at the summit of all things." At the close he says :

"The society is at present in its infancy, and its means are small ; but I wish to hold in view the subject I allude to, and instead of teaching the philosophical branches of learning as ornamental branches only, as they have hitherto been taught, to teach them in a manner that shall combine theological knowledge with scientific instruction. To do this to the best advantage, some instruments will be necessary for the purpose of explanation, of which the society is not yet possessed. But as the views of the Society extend to public good, as well as to that of the individual, and as its principles can have no enemies, means may be devised to procure them. If we unite to the present instruction a series of lectures on the ground I have mentioned, we shall, in the first place, render theology the most entertaining of all studies. In the next place, we shall give scientific instruction to those who could not otherwise obtain it. The mechanic of every profession will there be taught the mathematical principles necessary to render him proficient in his art. The cultivator will there see developed the principles of vegetation ; while, at the same time, they will be led to see the hand of God in all these things."

A volume of 214 pages put forth at the close of the year shows that the Theophilanthropists sang theistic and humanitarian hymns, and read Odes ; also that ethical readings were introduced from the Bible, and from the Chinese, Hindu, and Greek authors. A library was established ("rue Neuve-Etienne-l'Estrapade, No. 25) at which was issued (1797), "Instruction Élémentaire sur la Morale religieuse,"— this being declared to be morality based on religion.

Thus Paine, pioneer in many things, helped to found the first theistic and ethical society.

It may now be recognized as a foundation of the Religion of Humanity. It was a great point with Paine that belief in the divine existence was the one doctrine common to all religions. On this rock the Church of Man was to be built. Having vainly endeavoured to found the international Republic he must repair to an ideal moral and human world. Robespierre and Pitt being unfraternal he will bring into harmony the sages of all races. It is a notable instance of Paine's unwillingness to bring a personal grievance into the sacred presence of Humanity that one of the four festivals of Theophilanthropy was in honor of Washington, while its catholicity was represented in a like honor to St. Vincent de Paul. The others so honored were Socrates and Rousseau. These selections were no doubt mainly due to the French members, but they could hardly have been made without Paine's agreement. It is creditable to them all that, at a time when France believed itself wronged by Washington, his services to liberty should alone have been remembered. The flowers of all races, as represented in literature or in history, found emblematic association with the divine life in nature through the flowers that were heaped on a simple altar, as they now are in many churches and chapels. The walls were decorated with ethical mottoes, enjoining domestic kindness and public benevolence.

Paine's pamphlet of this year (1797) on "Agrarian Justice" should be considered part of the theophilanthropic movement. It was written as a proposal to the French government, at a time when readjustment of landed property had been rendered necessary by the Revolution.[1] It was suggested by a sermon printed by the Bishop of Llandaff, on "The wisdom and goodness of God in having made both rich and poor." Paine denies that God made rich and poor : "he made only male and female, and gave them the earth for their inheritance." The earth, though naturally the equal possession of all, has been necessarily appropriated by individuals, because their improvements, which alone render its productiveness adequate to human needs, cannot be detached from the soil. Paine maintains that these private owners do nevertheless owe mankind ground-rent. He therefore proposes a tithe,—not for God, but for man. He advises that at the time when the owner will feel it least,—when property is passing by inheritance from one to another, —the tithe shall be taken from it. Personal property also owes a debt to society, without which wealth could not exist,—as in the case of one alone on an island. By a careful estimate he

[1] " Thomas Payne à la Législature et au Directoire : ou la Justice Agraire Opposée à la Loi et aux Privilèges Agraires."

estimates that a tithe on inheritances would give every person, on reaching majority, fifteen pounds, and after the age of fifty an annuity of ten pounds, leaving a substantial surplus for charity. The practical scheme submitted is enforced by practical rather than theoretical considerations. Property is always imperilled by poverty, especially where wealth and splendor have lost their old fascinations, and awaken emotions of disgust.

"To remove the danger it is necessary to remove the antipathies, and this can only be done by making property productive of a national blessing, extending to every individual. When the riches of one man above another shall increase the national fund in the same proportion; when it shall be seen that the prosperity of that fund depends on the prosperity of individuals; when the more riches a man acquires, the better it shall be for the general mass; it is then that antipathies will cease, and property be placed on the permanent basis of national interest and protection.

"I have no property in France to become subject to the plan I propose. What I have, which is not much, is in the United States of America. But I will pay one hundred pounds sterling towards this fund in France, the instant it shall be established; and I will pay the same sum in England, whenever a similar establishment shall take place in that country."

The tithe was to be given to rich and poor alike, including owners of the property tithed, in order that there should be no association of alms with this "agrarian justice."

About this time the priesthood began to raise their heads again. A report favorable to a restoration to them of the churches, the raising of bells, and some national recognition of public worship, was made by Camille Jordan for a committee on the subject. The jesuitical report was especially poetical about church bells, which Paine knew would ring the knell of the Republic. He wrote a theophilanthropic letter to Camille Jordan, from which I quote some paragraphs.

"You claim a privilege incompatible with the Constitution, and with rights. The Constitution protects equally, as it ought to do, every profession of religion; it gives no exclusive privilege

to any. The churches are the common property of all the people; they are national goods, and cannot be given exclusively to any one profession, because the right does not exist of giving to any one that which appertains to all. It would be consistent with right that the churches should be sold, and the money arising therefrom be invested as a fund for the education of children of poor parents of every profession, and, if more than sufficient for this purpose, that the surplus be appropriated to the support of the aged poor. After this every profession can erect its own place of worship, if it choose—support its own priests, if it choose to have any—or perform its worship without priests, as the Quakers do."

"It is a want of feeling to talk of priests and bells whilst so many infants are perishing in the hospitals, and aged and infirm poor in the streets. The abundance that France possesses is sufficient for every want, if rightly applied; but priests and bells, like articles of luxury, ought to be the least articles of consideration."

"No man ought to make a living by religion. It is dishonest to do so. Religion is not an act that can be performed by proxy. One person cannot act religion for another. Every person must perform it for himself; and all that a priest can do is to take from him; he wants nothing but his money, and then to riot in the spoil and laugh at his credulity. The only people who, as a professional sect of Christians, provide for the poor of their society, are people known by the name of Quakers. These men have no priests. They assemble quietly in their places of worship, and do not disturb their neighbors with shows and noise of bells. Religion does not unite itself to show and noise. True religion is without either."

"One good schoolmaster is of more use than a hundred priests. If we look back at what was the condition of France under the *ancien régime*, we cannot acquit the priests of corrupting the morals of the nation."

"Why has the Revolution of France been stained with crimes, while the Revolution of the United States of America was not? Men are physically the same in all countries; it is education that makes them different. Accustom a people to believe that priests, or any other class of men, can forgive sins, and you will have sins in abundance."

While Thomas Paine was thus founding in Paris a religion of love to God expressed in love to man, his enemies in England were illustrating by characteristic fruits the dogmas based on a human sacrifice. The ascendency of the priesthood of one church over others, which he was resisting in France, was exemplified across the channel in the prosecution of his publisher, and the confiscation of a thousand pounds which had somehow fallen due to Paine.[1] The "Age of Reason," amply advertised by its opponents, had reached a vast circulation, and a prosecution of its publisher, Thomas Williams, for blasphemy, was instituted in the King's Bench. Williams being a poor man, the defence was sustained by a subscription.[2] The trial occurred June 24th. The extent to which the English reign of terror had gone was shown in the fact that Erskine was now the prosecutor; he who five years before had defended the "Rights of Man," who had left the court in a carriage drawn by the people, now stood in the same room to assail the most sacred of rights. He began with a menace to the defendant's counsel (S. Kyd) on account of a notice served on the prosecution, foreshadowing a search into the Scriptures.[3] "No man," he cried, "deserves to be upon the Rolls of the Court who dares, as an Attorney, to put his name to such a notice. It is an insult to the authority and dignity of the Court of which he is an officer; since it seems to call in question the very foundations of its jurisdiction." So soon did Erskine point the satire of the fable he quoted from Lucian, in Paine's defence, of Jupiter answering arguments with thunderbolts. Erskine's argument was that the King had taken a solemn oath "to maintain the Christian Religion as it is promulgated by God in the Holy Scriptures." "Every man has a right to investigate, with modesty and decency, controversial points of the Christian religion; but no man, consistently with a law which only exists under its sanction, has a right not only broadly to deny its very existence, but to pour forth a shocking and insulting invective, etc." The law, he said, permits, by a like principle, the intercourse between the sexes to be set forth in plays and novels, but punishes such as "address the imagination in a manner to lead the passions into dangerous excesses." Erskine read several passages from the "Age of Reason," which, their main point being omitted, seemed mere aimless abuse. In his speech, he quoted as Paine's words of his own collocation, representing the author as saying, "The Bible teaches nothing but 'lies, obscenity, cruelty, and injustice.'" This is his entire and inaccurate rendering of what Paine,—who always distinguishes the "Bible" from the "New Testament,"—says at the close of his comment on the massacre of the Midianites and appropriation of their maidens:

"People in general know not what wickedness there is in this pretended word of God. Brought up in habits of superstition, they take it for granted that the Bible [Old Testament] is true, and that it is good; they permit themselves not to doubt it; and they carry the ideas they form of the benevolence of the Almighty to the book they have been taught to believe was written by his authority. Good heavens! it is quite another thing! it is a book of lies, wickedness, and blasphemy; for what can be greater blasphemy than to ascribe the wickedness of man to the orders of the Almighty?"

Erskine argued that the sanction of Law was the oath by which judges, juries, witnesses administered law and justice under a belief in "the revelation of the unutterable blessings which shall attend their observances, and the awful punishments which shall await upon their transgressions." The rest of his opening argument was, mainly, that great men had believed in Christianity.

Mr. Kyd, in replying, quoted from the Bishop of Llandaff's "Answer to Gibbon": "I look upon the right of private judgment, in every respect concerning

---

[1] This loss, mentioned by Paine in a private note, occurred about the time when he had devoted the proceeds of his pamphlet on English Finance, a very large sum, to prisoners held for debt in Newgate. I suppose the thousand pounds were the proceeds of the "Age of Reason."

[2] "Subscriptions (says his circular) will be received by J. Ashley, Shoemaker, No. 6 High Holborn; C. Cooper, Grocer, New Compton-st., Soho; G. Wilkinson, Printer, No. 115 Shoreditch; J. Rhynd, Printer, Ray-st., Clerkenwell; R. Hodgson, Hatter, No. 29 Brook-st., Holborn." It will be observed that the defence of free printing had fallen to humble people.

[3] "The King *v.* Thomas Williams for Blasphemy.—Take notice that the Prosecutors of the Indictment against the above-named Defendant will upon the Trial of this cause be required to produce a certain Book described in the said Indictment to be the Holy Bible.—John Martin, Solicitor for the Defendant. Dated the 17th day of June 1797."

God and ourselves, as superior to the control of human authority"; and his claim that the Church of England is distinguished from Mahometanism and Romanism by its permission of every man to utter his opinion freely.   He also cites Dr. Lardner, and Dr. Waddington, the Bishop of Chichester, who declared that Woolston "ought not to be punished for being an infidel, nor for writing against the Christian religion." He quoted Paine's profession of faith on the first page of the incriminated book: "I believe in one God and no more; I hope for happiness, beyond this life; I believe in the equality of men, and I believe that religious duties consist in doing justice, loving mercy, and endeavoring to make our fellow creatures happy." He also quoted Paine's homage to the character of Jesus. He defied the prosecution to find in the "Age of Reason" a single passage "inconsistent with the most chaste, the most correct system of morals," and declared the very passages selected for indictment pleas against obscenity and cruelty.   Mr. Kyd pointed out fourteen narratives in the Bible (such as Sarah giving Hagar to Abraham, Lot and his daughters, etc.) which, if found in any other book, would be pronounced obscene.   He was about to enumerate instances of cruelty when the judge, Lord Kenyon, indignantly interrupted him, and with consent of the jury said he could only allow him to cite such passages without reading them. (Mr. Kyd gratefully acknowledged this release from the painful task of reading such horrors from the "Word of God"!) One of the interesting things about this trial was the disclosure of the general reliance on Butler's "Analogy," used by Bishop Watson in his reply to Paine,—namely, that the cruelties objected to in the God of the Bible are equally found in nature, through which deists look up to their God.   When Kyd, after quoting from Bishop Watson, said, "Gentlemen, observe the weakness of this answer," Lord Kenyon exclaimed: "I cannot sit in this place and hear this kind of discussion." Kyd said: "My Lord, I stand here

on the privilege of an advocate in an English Court of Justice: this man has applied to me to defend him; I have undertaken his defence; and I have often heard your Lordship declare, that every man had a right to be defended. I know no other mode by which I can seriously defend him against this charge, than that which I am now pursuing; if your Lordship wish to prevent me from pursuing it, you may as well tell me to abandon my duty to my client at once." Lord Kenyon said: "Go on, Sir." Returning to the analogy of the divinely ordered massacres in the Bible with the like in nature, Kyd said:

"Gentlemen, this is reasoning by comparison; and reasoning by comparison is often fallacious. On the present occasion the fallacy is this: that, in the first case, the persons perish by the operation of the general laws of nature, not suffering punishment for a crime; whereas, in the latter, the general laws of nature are suspended or transgressed, and God commands the slaughter to avenge his offended will. Is this then a satisfactory answer to the objection? I think it is not; another may think so too; which it may be fairly supposed the Author did; and then the objection, as to him, remains in full force, and he cannot, from insisting upon it, be fairly accused of malevolent intention."

In his answer Erskine said: "The history of man is the history of man's vices and passions, which could not be censured without adverting to their existence; many of the instances that have been referred to were recorded as memorable warnings and examples for the instruction of mankind." But for this argument Erskine was indebted to his old client, Paine, who did not argue against the things being recorded, but against the belief "that the inhuman and horrid butcheries of men, women, and children, told of in those books, were done, as those books say they were done, at the command of God." Paine says: "Those accounts are nothing to us, nor to any other persons, unless it be to the Jews, as a part of the history of their nation; and there is just as much of the word of God in those books as there is in any of the histories of France, or Rapin's 'History of England,' or the history of any other country."

As in Paine's own trial in 1792, the nfallible scheme of a special jury was used against Williams. Lord Kenyon closed his charge with the words: " Unless it was for the most malignant purposes, I cannot conceive how it was published. It is, however, for you to judge of it, and to do justice between the Public and the Defendant."

"The jury instantly found the Defendant—Guilty."

Paine at once wrote a letter to Erskine, which was first printed in Paris. He calls attention to the injustice of the special jury system, in which all the jurymen are nominated by the crown. In London a special jury generally consists of merchants.

" Talk to some London merchants about scripture, and they will understand you mean scrip, and tell you how much it is worth at the Stock Exchange. Ask them about Theology, and they will say they know no such gentleman upon 'Change."

He also declares that Lord Kenyon's course in preventing Mr. Kyd from reading passages from the Bible was irregular, and contrary to words, which he cites, used by the same judge in another case.

This Letter to Erskine contains some effective passages. In one of these he points out the sophistical character of the indictment in declaring the "Age of Reason" a blasphemous work, tending to bring in contempt the holy scriptures. The charge should have stated that the work was intended to prove certain books not the holy scriptures.

"It is one thing if I ridicule a work as being written by a certain person ; but it is quite a different thing if I write to prove that such a work was not written by such person. In the first case I attack the person through the work ; in the other case I defend the honor of the person against the work."

After alluding to the two accounts in Genesis of the creation of man, according to one of which there was no Garden of Eden and no forbidden tree, Paine says :

" Perhaps I shall be told in the cant language of the day, as I have often been told by the Bishop of Llandaff and others, of the great and laudable pains that many pious and learned men have taken to explain the obscure, and reconcile the contradictory, or, as they say, the seemingly contradictory, passages of the Bible. It is because the Bible needs such an undertaking, that is one of the first causes to suspect it is *net* the word of God : this single reflection, when carried home to the mind, is in itself a volume. What ! does not the Creator of the Universe, the Fountain of all Wisdom, the Origin of all Science, the Author of all Knowledge, the God of Order and of Harmony, know how to write ? When we contemplate the vast economy of the creation, when we behold the unerring regularity of the visible solar system, the perfection with which all its several parts revolve, and by corresponding assemblage form a whole ;—when we launch our eye into the boundless ocean of space, and see ourselves surrounded by innumerable worlds, not one of which varies from its appointed place—when we trace the power of a Creator, from a mite to an elephant, from an atom to a universe, can we suppose that the mind which could conceive such a design, and the power that executed it with incomparable perfection, cannot write without inconsistence ; or that a book so written can be the work of such a power ? The writings of Thomas Paine, even of Thomas Paine, need no commentator to explain, compound, arrange, and re-arrange their several parts, to render them intelligible— he can relate a fact, or write an essay, without forgetting in one page what he has written in another ; certainly then, did the God of all perfection condescend to write or dictate a book, that book would be as perfect as himself is perfect: The Bible is not so, and it is confessedly not so, by the attempts to amend it."

Paine admonishes Erskine that a prosecution to preserve God's word, were it really God's word, would be like a prosecution to prevent the sun from falling out of heaven; also that he should be able to comprehend that the motives of those who declare the Bible not God's word are religious. He then gives him an account of the new church of Theophilanthropists in Paris, and appends his discourse before that society.

In the following year, Paine's discourse to the Theophilanthropists was separately printed by Clio Rickman, with a sentence from Shakespeare in the title-page : " I had as lief have the foppery of freedom as the morality of imprisonment." There was also the following dedication :

" The following little Discourse is dedicated to the enemies of Thomas Paine, by one who has known him long and intimately, and who is convinced that he is the enemy of no man. It is printed to do good, by a well wisher to the world. By one who thinks that discussion should be unlimited, that all coercion is error ; and that human beings should adopt no other conduct towards each other but an appeal to truth and reason."

Paine wrote privately, in the same sense as to Erskine, to his remonstrating friends. In one such letter (May 12th) he goes again partly over the round.

" You," he says, " believe in the Bible from the accident of birth, and the Turks believe in the Koran from the same accident, and each calls the other *infidel*. This answer to your letter is not written for the purpose of changing your opinion. It is written to satisfy you, and some other friends whom I esteem, that my disbelief of the Bible is founded on a pure and religious belief in God." " All are infidels who believe falsely of God." " Belief in a cruel God makes a cruel man." [1]

Paine had for some time been attaining unique fame in England. Some publisher had found it worth while to issue a book, entitled " Tom Paine's Jests : Being an entirely new and select Collection of Patriotic Bons Mots, Repartees, Anecdotes, Epigrams, &c., on Political Subjects. By Thomas Paine." There are hardly a half dozen items by Paine in the book (72 pages), which shows that his name was considered marketable. The government had made the author a cause. Erskine, who had lost his office as Attorney-General for the Prince of Wales by becoming Paine's counsel in 1792, was at once taken back into favor after prosecuting the " Age of Reason, " and put on his way to become

Lord Erskine. The imprisonment of Williams caused a reaction in the minds of those who had turned against Paine. Christianity suffered under royal patronage. The terror manifested at the name of Paine—some were arrested even for showing his portrait—was felt to be political. None of the aristocratic deists, who wrote for the upper classes, were dealt with in the same way. Paine had proclaimed from the housetops what, as Dr. Watson confessed, scholars were whispering in the ear. There were lampoons of Paine, such as those of Peter Pindar (Rev. John Wolcott), but they only served to whet popular curiosity concerning him. [2] The " Age of Reason " had passed through several editions before it was outlawed, and every copy of it passed through many hands. From the prosecution and imprisonment of Williams may be dated the consolidation of the movement for the " Rights of Man," with antagonism to the kind of Christianity which that injustice illustrated. Political liberalism and heresy thenceforth progressed in England, hand in hand.

[1] " Writings of Paine " (Conway), vol. iv., p. 199.—H.B.B.

[2] " I have preserved," says Royall Tyler, "an epigram of Peter Pindar's, written originally in a blank leaf of a copy of Paine's 'Age of Reason,' and not inserted in any of his works.

" ' Tommy Paine wrote this book to prove that the bible
Was an old woman's dream of fancies most idle ;
That Solomon's proverbs were made by low livers,
That prophets were fellows who sang semiquavers ;
That religion and miracles all were a jest,
And the devil in torment a tale of the priest.
Though Beelzebub's absence from hell I'll maintain,
Yet we all must allow that the Devil's in Paine."

CHAPTER XXXVIII

THE REPUBLICAN ABDIEL

The sight of James Monroe and Thomas Paine in France, representing Republican America, was more than

Gouverneur Morris could stand. He sent to Washington the abominable slander of Monroe already quoted

(p. 225), and the Minister's recall came at the close of 1796.[1] Monroe could not sail in midwinter with his family, so they remained until the following spring. Paine made preparations to return to America with them, and accompanied them to Havre ; but he found so many "british frigates cruising in sight" (so he writes Jefferson) that he did not "trust [himself] to their discretion, and the more so as [he] had no confidence in the Captain of the Dublin Packet." Sure enough this Captain Clay was friendly enough with the British cruiser which lay in wait to catch Paine, but only succeeded in finding his letter to Jefferson. Before returning from Havre to Paris he wrote another letter to Vice-President Jefferson.

"HAVRE, May 14, 1797.

"DEAR SIR,—I wrote to you by the Ship Dublin Packet, Captain Clay, mentioning my intention to have returned to America by that Vessel, and to have suggested to some Member of the House of Representatives the propriety of calling Mr. Monroe before them to have enquired into the state of their affairs in France. This might have laid the foundation for some resolves on their part that might have led to an accomodation with France, for that House is the only part of the American Government that have any reputation here. I apprised Mr. Monroe of my design, and he wishes to be called up.

"You will have heard before this reaches you that the Emperor has been obliged to sue for peace, and to consent to the establishment of the new republic in Lombardy. How France will proceed with respect to England, I am not,

at this distance from Paris, in the way of knowing, but am inclined to think she meditates a descent upon that Country, and a revolution in its Government. If this should be the plan, it will keep me in Europe at least another year.

"As the british party has thrown the American commerce into wretched confusion, it is necessary to pay more attention to the appointment of Consuls in the ports of france, than there was occasion to do in time of peace ; especially as there is now no Minister, and Mr. Skipwith, who stood well with the Government here, has resigned. Mr. Cutting, the Consul for Havre, does not reside at it, and the business is altogether in the hands of De la Motte, the Vice Consul, who is a frenchman, [and] cannot have the full authority proper for the office in the difficult state matters are now in. I do not mention this to the disadvantage of Mr. Cutting, for no man is more proper than himself if he thought it an object to attend to.

"I know not if you are acquainted with Captain Johnson of Massachusetts—he is a staunch man and one of the oldest American Captains in the American employ. He is now settled at Havre and is a more proper man for a Vice Consul than La Motte. You can learn his character from Mr. Monroe. He has written to some of his friends to have the appointment and if you can see an opportunity of throwing in a little service for him, you will do a good thing. We have had several reports of Mr. Madison's coming. He would be well received as an individual, but as an Envoy of John Adams he could do nothing.

"THOMAS PAINE."

The following, in Paine's handwriting, is copied from the original in the Morrison papers, at the British Museum. It was written in the summer of 1797, when Lord Malmsbury was at Lille in negotiation for peace. The negotiations were broken off because the English commissioners were unauthorized to make the demanded restorations to Holland and Spain. Paine's essay was no doubt sent to the Directory in the interests of peace, suggesting as it does a compromise, as regards the Cape of Good Hope.

"CAPE OF GOOD HOPE.—It is very well known that Dundas, the English Minister for Indian affairs, is tenacious of holding the Cape of Good Hope, because it will give to the English East India Company a monopoly of the commerce of India ; and this, on the other hand, is the very reason that such a claim is inadmissible by France, and by all the nations trading in India and to Canton, and would also be injurious to Canton itself.—We pretend not

---

[1] This sudden recall involved Monroe in heavy expenses, which Congress afterwards repaid. I am indebted to Mr. Frederick McGuire, of Washington, for the manuscript of Monroe's statement of his expenses and annoyances caused by his recall, which he declares due to "the representations which were made to him [Washington] by those in whom he confided." He states that Paine remained in his house a year and a half, and that he advanced him 250 louis d'or. For these services to Paine, he adds, "no claims were ever presented on my part, nor is any indemnity now desired." This money was repaid ($1,188) to Monroe by an Act of Congress, April 7, 1831. The advances are stated in the Act to have been made "from time to time," and were no doubt regarded by both Paine and Monroe as compensated by the many services rendered by the author to the Legation.

to know anything of the negociations at Lille, but it is very easy to see, from the nature of the case, what ought to be the condition of the Cape. It ought to be a free port open to the vessels of all nations trading to any part of the East Indias. It ought also to be a neutral port at all times, under the guarantee of all nations; the expense of keeping the port in constant repair to be defrayed by a tonnage tax to be paid by every vessel, whether of commerce or of war, and in proportion to the time of their stay.—Nothing then remains but with respect to the nation who shall be the port-master; and this ought to be the Dutch, because they understand the business best. As the Cape is a half-way stage between Europe and India, it ought to be considered as a tavern, where travellers on a long journey put up for rest and refreshment.—T. P."

The suspension of peace negotiations,[1] and the bloodless defeat of Pichigru's conspiracy of 18 Fructidor (September 4th) were followed by a pamphlet addressed to "The People of France and the French Armies." This little work is of historical value, in connection with 18 Fructidor, but it was evidently written to carry two practical points. The first was, that if the war with England must continue it should be directed to the end of breaking the Anglo-Germanic compact. England has the right to her internal arrangements, but this is an external matter. While "with respect to England it has been the cause of her immense national debt, the ruin of her finances, and the insolvency of her bank," English intrigues on the continent "are generated by, and act through, the medium of this Anglo-Germanic compound. It will be necessary to dissolve it. Let the elector retire to his electorate, and the world will have peace."

[1] In a letter to Duane, many years later, Paine relates the following story concerning the British Union: "When Lord Malmsbury arrived in Paris, in the time of the Directory Government, to open a negociation for a peace, his credentials ran in the old style of 'George, by the grace of God, of Great Britain, *France*, and Ireland, king.' Malmsbury was informed that although the assumed title of king of France, in his credentials, would not prevent France opening a negociation, yet that no treaty of peace could be concluded until that assumed title was removed. Pitt then hit on the Union Bill, under which the assumed title of king of France was discontinued."

Paine's other main point is, that the neutral nations should secure, in time of war, an unarmed neutrality.

"Were the neutral nations to associate, under an honorable injunction of fidelity to each other, and publickly declare to the world, that if any belligerent power shall seize or molest any ship or vessel belonging to the citizens or subjects of any of the powers composing that association, that the whole association will shut its ports against the flag of the offending nation, and will not permit any goods, wares, or merchandize, produced or manufactured in the offending nation, or appertaining thereto, to be imported into any of the ports included in the association, until reparation be made to the injured party; the reparation to be three times the value of the vessel and cargo; and moreover that all remittances in money, goods, and bills of exchange, do cease to be made to the offending nation, until the said reparation be made. Were the neutral nations only to do this, which it is their direct interest to do, England, as a nation depending on the commerce of neutral nations in time of war, dare not molest them, and France would not. But whilst, from want of a common system, they individually permit England to do it, because individually they cannot resist it, they put France under the necessity of doing the same thing. The supreme of all laws, in all cases, is that of self-preservation."

It is a notable illustration of the wayward course of political evolution, that the English republic—for it is such—grew largely out of the very parts of its constitution once so oppressive. The foreign origin of the royal family helped to form its wholesome timidity about meddling with politics, allowing thus a development of ministerial government. The hereditary character of the throne, which George III.'s half-insane condition associated with the recklessness of irresponsibility, was by his complete insanity made to serve ministerial independence. Regency is timid about claiming power, and childhood cannot exercise it. The decline of royal and aristocratic authority in England secured freedom to commerce, which necessarily gave hostages to peace. The protection of neutral commerce at sea, concerning which Paine wrote so much, ultimately resulted from English naval strength, which formerly scourged the world.

To Paine, England, at the close of 1797, could appear only as a dragon-guarded prison of fair Humanity. The press was paralyzed, thinkers and publishers were in prison, some of the old orators like Erskine were bought up, and the forlorn hope of liberty rested only with Fox and his fifty in Parliament, overborne by a majority made brutal by strength. The groans of imprisoned thought in his native land reached its outlawed representative in Paris. And at the same time the inhuman decree went forth from that country that there should be no peace with France. It had long been his conviction that the readiness of Great Britain to go to war was due to an insular position that kept the horrors at a distance. War never came home to her. This conviction, which we have several times met in these pages, returned to him with new force when England now insisted on more bloodshed. He was convinced that the right course of France would be to make a descent on England, ship the royal family to Hanover, open the political prisons, and secure the people freedom to make a Constitution. These views, freely expressed to his friends of the Directory and Legislature, reached the ears of Napoleon on his triumphal return from Italy. The great man called upon Paine in his little room and invited him to dinner. He made the eloquent professions of republicanism so characteristic of Napoleons until they became pretenders. He told Paine that he slept with the "Rights of Man" under his pillow, and that its author ought to have a statue of gold.[1] He consulted Paine about a descent on England, and adopted the plan. He invited the author to accompany the expedition, which was to consist of a thousand gun-boats, with a hundred men each. Paine consented, "as [so he wrote Jefferson] the intention of the expedition was to give the people of England an opportunity of forming a government for themselves, and thereby bring about peace." One of the points to be aimed at was Norfolk, and no doubt Paine indulged a happy vision of standing once more in Thetford

[1] Rickman, p. 164.

and proclaiming liberty throughout the land!

The following letter (December 29, 1797) from Paine to Barras is in the archives of the Directory, with a French translation :

" CITIZEN PRESIDENT,—A very particular friend of mine, who had a passport to go to London upon some family affairs and to return in three months, and whom I had commissioned upon some affairs of my own (for I find that the English government has seized upon a thousand pounds sterling which I had in the hands of a friend), returned two days ago and gave me the memorandum which I enclose :—the first part relates only to my publication on the event of the 18 Fructidor, and to a letter to Erskine (who had been counsel for the prosecution against a former work of mine the 'Age of Reason') both of which I desired my friend to publish in London. The other part of the memorandum respects the state of affairs in that country, by which I see they have little or no idea of a descent being made upon them ; tant mieux— but they will be guarded in Ireland, as they expect a descent there.

"I expect a printed copy of the letter to Erskine in a day or two. As this is in English, and on a subject that will be amusing to the Citizen Revellière Le Peaux, I will send it to him. The friend of whom I speak was a pupil of Dessault the surgeon, and whom I once introduced to you at a public audience in company with Captain Cooper on his plan respecting the Island of Bermuda.—Salut et Respect."

Thus once again did the great hope of a liberated, peaceful, and republican Europe shine before simple-hearted Paine. He was rather poor now, but gathered up all the money he had, and sent it to the Council of Five Hundred. The accompanying letter was read by Coupè at the sitting of January 28, 1798 :

" CITIZENS REPRESENTATIVES,—Though it is not convenient to me, in the present situation of my affairs, to subscribe to the loan towards the descent upon England, my economy permits me to make a small patriotic donation. I send a hundred livres, and with it all the wishes of my heart for the success of the descent, and a voluntary offer of any service I can render to promote it.

"There will be no lasting peace for France, nor for the world, until the tyranny and corruption of the English government be abolished, and England, like Italy, become a sister republic. As to those men, whether in England, Scotland, or Ireland, who, like Robespierre in France, are covered with crimes, they, like him, have no other resource than in committing more. But the mass of the people are the friends of liberty : tyranny and taxation oppress them, but they deserve to be free.

"Accept, Citizens Representatives, the congratulations of an old colleague in the dangers we have passed, and on the happy prospect before us. Salut et respect.

"THOMAS PAINE."

Coupè added : " The gift which Thomas Paine offers you appears very trifling, when it is compared with the revolting injustice which this faithful friend of liberty has experienced from the English government; but compare it with the state of poverty in which our former colleague finds himself, and you will then think it considerable." He moved that the notice of this gift and Thomas Paine's letter be printed. " Mention honorable et impression," adds the *Moniteur*.

The President of the Directory at this time was Larevéllière-Lépeaux, a friend of the Theophilanthropic Society. To him Paine gave, in English, which the president understood, a plan for the descent, which was translated into French, and adopted by the Directory. Two hundred and fifty gun-boats were built, and the expedition abandoned. To Jefferson, Paine intimates his suspicion that it was all "only a feint to cover the expedition to Egypt, which was then preparing." He also states that the British descent on Ostend, where some two thousand of them were made prisoners, "was in search of the gun-boats, and to cut the dykes, to prevent their being assembled." This he was told by Vanhuile, of Bruges, who heard it from the British officers.

After the failure of his attempt to return to America with the Monroes, Paine was for a time the guest of Nicolas de Bonneville, in Paris, and the visit ended in an arrangement for his abode with that family. Bonneville was an editor, thirty-seven years of age, and had been one of the five members of Paine's Republican Club, which placarded Paris with its manifesto after the king's flight in 1791. An enthusiastic devotee of Paine's principles from youth, he had advocated them in his successive jour-

nals, *Le Tribun du Peuple*, *Bouche de Fer*, and *Bien Informé*. He had resisted Marat and Robespierre, and suffered imprisonment during the Terror. He spoke English fluently, and was well known in the world of letters by some striking poems, also by his translation into French of German tales, and parts of Shakespeare. He had set up a printing office at No. 4 Rue du Théâtre-Français, where he published liberal pamphlets, also his *Bien Informé*. Then, in 1794, he printed in French the "Age of Reason." He also published, and probably translated into French, Paine's letter to the now exiled Camille Jordan, —"Lettre de Thomas Paine, sur les Cultes." Paine, unable to converse in French, found with the Bonnevilles a home he needed. M. and Madame Bonneville had been married three years, and their second child had been named after Thomas Paine, who stood as his godfather. Paine, as we learn from Rickman, who knew the Bonnevilles, paid board, but no doubt he aided Bonneville more by his pen.

With public affairs, either in France or America, Paine now mingled but little. The election of John Adams to the presidency he heard of with dismay. He wrote to Jefferson that since he was not president, he was glad he had accepted the vice-presidency, "for John Adams has such a talent for blundering and offending, it will be necessary to keep an eye over him." Finding, by the abandonment of a descent on England for one on Egypt, that Napoleon was by no means his ideal missionary of republicanism, he withdrew into his little study, and now remained so quiet that some English papers announced his arrival and cool reception in America. He was, however, fairly bored with visitors from all parts of the world, curious to see the one international republican left. It became necessary for Madame Bonneville, armed with polite prevarications, to defend him from such sight-seers. For what with his visits to and from the Barlows, the Smiths, and his friends of the Directory,

Paine had too little time for the inventions in which he was again absorbed, —his "Saints." Among his intimate friends at this time was Robert Fulton, then residing in Paris. Paine's extensive studies of the steam-engine, and his early discovery of its adaptability to navigation, had caused Rumsey to seek him in England, and Fitch to consult him both in America and Paris. Paine's connection with the invention of the steamboat was recognized by Fulton, as indeed by all of his scientific contemporaries.[1] To Fulton he freely gave his ideas, and may perhaps have had some hope that the steamboat might prove a missionary of international republicanism, though Napoleon had failed.

It will not be forgotten that in the same year in which Paine startled William Henry with a plan for steam-navigation, namely in 1778, he wrote his sublime sentence about the "Religion of Humanity." The steamships which Emerson described as enormous shuttles weaving the races of men into the woof of humanity, have at length rendered possible that

[1] Sir Richard Phillips says: "In 1778 Thomas Paine proposed, in America, this application of steam." ("Million of Facts," p. 776.) As Sir Richard assisted Fulton in his experiments on the Thames, he probably heard from him the fact about Paine, though, indeed, in the controversy between Rumsey and Fitch, Paine's priority to both was conceded. In America, however, the priority really belonged to the eminent mechanician William Henry, of Lancaster, Pa. When Fitch visited Henry, in 1785, he was told by him that he was not the first to devise steam-navigation; that he himself had thought of it in 1776, and mentioned it to Andrew Ellicott; and that Thomas Paine, while a guest at his house in 1778, had spoken to him on the subject. I am indebted to Mr. John W. Jordan, of the Historical Society of Pennsylvania, for notes from the papers of Henry, his ancestor, showing that Paine's scheme was formed without knowledge of others, and that it contemplated a turbine application of steam to a wheel. Both he and Henry, as they had not published their plans, agreed to leave Fitch the whole credit. Fitch publicly expressed his gratitude to Paine. Thurston adds that Paine, in 1788, proposed that Congress should adopt the whole matter for the national benefit. ("History of the Growth of the Steam Engine," pp. 252, 253.)

universal human religion which Paine foresaw. In that old Lancaster mansion of the Henrys, which still stands, Paine left his spectacles, now in our National Museum; they are strong and far-seeing; through them looked eyes held by visions that the world is still steadily following. One cannot suppress some transcendental sentiment in view of the mystical harmony of this man's inventions for human welfare,—mechanical, political, religious. Of his gunpowder motor, mention has already been made (p. 98). On this he was engaged about the time that he was answering Bishop Watson's book on the "Age of Reason." The two occupations are related. He could not believe, he said, that the qualities of gunpowder — the small and light grain with maximum of force—were meant only for murder, and his faith in the divine humanity is in the sentence. To supersede destroying gunpowder with beneficent gunpowder, and to supersede the god of battles with the God of Love, were kindred aims in Paine's heart. Through the fiery furnaces of his time he had come forth with every part of his being welded and beaten and shaped together for this Human Service. Patriotism, in the conventional sense, race-pride, sectarianism, partizanship, had been burnt out of his nature. The universe could not have wrung from his tongue approval of a wrong because it was done by his own country.

It might be supposed that there were no heavier trials awaiting Paine's political faith than those it had undergone. But it was becoming evident that liberty had not the advantage he once ascribed to truth over error,—"it cannot be unlearned." The United States had unlearned it as far as to put into the President's hands a power of arbitrarily crushing political opponents, such as even George III. hardly aspired to. The British Treaty had begun to bear its natural fruits. Washington signed the Treaty to avoid war, and rendered war inevitable with both France and England. The affair with France was happily a transient squall, but it was sufficient to again bring on Paine the offices of an American Minister in France. Many an American in that country had occasion to appreciate his powerful aid and unfailing kindness. Among these was Captain Rowland Crocker of Massachusetts, who had sailed with a letter of marque. His vessel was captured by the French, and its wounded commander brought to Paris, where he was more agreeably conquered by kindness. Freeman's "History of Cape Cod" (of which region Crocker was a native) has the following :

"His [Captain Crocker's] reminiscences of his residence in that country, during the most extraordinary period of its history, were of a highly interesting character. He had taken the great Napoleon by the hand ; he had familiarly known Paine, at a time when his society was sought for and was valuable. Of this noted individual, we may in passing say, with his uniform and characteristic kindness, he always spoke in terms which sounded strange to the ears of a generation which has been taught, with or without justice, to regard the author of 'The Age of Reason' with loathing and abhorrence. He remembered Paine as a well-dressed and most gentlemanly man, of sound and orthodox republican principles, of a good heart, a strong intellect, and a fascinating address."

The *coup d'état* in America, which made President Adams virtual emperor, pretended constitutionality, and was reversible. That which Napoleon and Sieyès — who had his way at last — effected in France (November 9, 1799) was lawless and fatal. The peaceful Bonneville home was broken up. Bonneville, in his *Bien Informé*, described Napoleon as "a Cromwell," and was promptly imprisoned. Paine, either before or soon after this catastrophe, went to Belgium, on a visit to his old friend Vanhuile, who had shared his cell in the Luxembourg prison. Vanhuile was now president of the municipality of Bruges, and Paine got from him information about European affairs. On his return he found Bonneville released from prison, but under severe surveillance, his journal being suppressed. The family was thus reduced to penury and anxiety, but there was all the more reason that Paine should stand by them. He continued his abode in their house, now probably supported by drafts on his resources in America, to which country they turned their thoughts.

The European Republic on land having become hopeless, Paine turned his attention to the seas. He wrote a pamphlet on "Maritime Compact," including in it ten articles for the security of neutral commerce, to be signed by the nations entering the "Unarmed Association," which he proposed. This scheme was substantially the same as that already quoted from his letter "To the People of France, and to the French Armies." It was translated by Bonneville, and widely circulated in Europe. Paine sent it in manuscript to Jefferson, who at once had it printed. His accompanying letter to Jefferson (October 1, 1800) is of too much biographical interest to be abridged.

"DEAR SIR,—I wrote to you from Havre by the ship Dublin Packet in the year 1797. It was then my intention to return to America ; but there were so many British frigates cruising in sight of the port, and which after a few days knew that I was at Havre waiting to go to America, that I did not think it best to trust myself to their discretion, and the more so, as I had no confidence in the Captain of the Dublin Packet (Clay). I mentioned to you in that letter, which I believe you received thro' the hands of Colonel [Aaron] Burr, that I was glad since you were not President that you had accepted the nomination of Vice President.

"The Commissioners Ellsworth & Co.[1] have been here about eight months, and three more useless mortals never came upon public business. Their presence appears to me to have been rather an injury than a benefit. They set themselves up for a faction as soon as they arrived. I was then in Belgia. Upon my return to Paris I learned they had made a point of not returning the visits of Mr. Skipwith and Barlow, because,

[1] Oliver Ellsworth, William V. Murray, and William R. Davie, were sent by President Adams to France to negotiate a treaty. There is little doubt that the famous letter of Joel Barlow to Washington, October 2, 1798, written in the interest of peace, was composed after consultation with Paine. Adams, on reading the letter, abused Barlow. "Tom Paine," he said, " is not a more worthless fellow." But he obeyed the letter. The Commissioners he sent were associated with the anti-French and British party in America, but peace with America was of too much importance to the new despot of France for the opportunity to be missed of forming a Treaty.

they said, they had not the confidence of the executive. Every known republican was treated in the same manner. I learned from Mr. Miller of Philadelphia, who had occasion to see them upon business, that they did not intend to return my visit, if I made one. This I supposed it was intended I should know, that I might not make one. It had the contrary effect. I went to see Mr. Ellsworth. I told him, I did not come to see him as a commissioner, nor to congratulate him upon his mission; that I came to see him because I had formerly known him in Congress. I mean not, said I, to press you with any questions, or to engage you in any conversation upon the business you are come upon, but I will nevertheless candidly say that I know not what expectations the Government or the people of America may have of your mission, or what expectations you may have yourselves, but I believe you will find you can do but little. The treaty with England lies at the threshold of all your business. The American Government never did two more foolish things than when it signed that Treaty and recalled Mr. Monroe, who was the only man could do them any service. Mr. Ellsworth put on the dull gravity of a Judge, and was silent. I added, you may perhaps make a treaty like that you have now made with England, which is a surrender of the rights of the American flag; for the principle that neutral ships make neutral property must be general or not at all. I then changed the subject, for I had all the talk to myself upon this topic, and enquired after Sam. Adams, (I asked nothing about John,) Mr. Jefferson, Mr. Monroe, and others of my friends, and the melancholy case of the yellow fever,—of which he gave me as circumstantial an account as if he had been summing up a case to a Jury. Here my visit ended, and had Mr. Ellsworth been as cunning as a statesman, or as wise as a Judge, he would have returned my visit that he might appear insensible of the intention of mine.

" I now come to the affairs of this country and of Europe. You will, I suppose, have heard before this arrives to you, of the battle of Marengo in Italy, where the Austrians were defeated—of the armistice in consequence thereof, and the surrender of Milan, Genoa, etc., to the french—of the successes of the french army in Germany—and the extension of the armistice in that quarter—of the preliminaries of peace signed at Paris—of the refusal of the Emperor [of Austria] to ratify these preliminaries—of the breaking of the armistice by the french Government in consequence of that refusal—of the 'gallant' expedition of the Emperor to put himself at the head of his Army—of his pompous arrival there—of his having made his will —of prayers being put in all his churches for the preservation of the life of this Hero—of General Moreau announcing to him, immediately on his arrival at the Army, that hostilities would commence the day after the next at sunrise, unless he signed the treaty or gave security that he would sign within 45 days—of his surrendering

up three of the principal keys of Germany (Ulm, Philipsbourg, and Ingolstad), as security that he would sign them. This is the state things [they] are now in, at the time of writing this letter; but it is proper to add that the refusal of the Emperor to sign the preliminaries was motived upon a note from the King of England to be admitted to the Congress for negociating Peace, which was consented to by the french upon the condition of an armistice at Sea, which England, before knowing of the surrender the Emperor had made, had refused. From all which it appears to me, judging from circumstances, that the Emperor is now so compleatly in the hands of the french, that he has no way of getting out but by a peace. The Congress for the peace is to be held at Luneville, a town in france. Since the affair of Rastadt the french commissioners will not trust themselves within the Emperor's territory.

"I now come to domestic affairs. I know not what the Commissioners have done, but from a paper I enclose to you, which appears to have some authority, it is not much. The paper as you will perceive is considerably prior to this letter. I knew that the Commissioners before this piece appeared intended setting off. It is therefore probable that what they have done is conformable to what this paper mentions, which certainly will not atone for the expence their mission has incurred, neither are they, by all the accounts I hear of them, men fitted for the business.

" But independently of these matters there appears to be a state of circumstances rising, which if it goes on, will render all partial treaties unnecessary. In the first place I doubt if any peace will be made with England; and in the second place, I should not wonder to see a coalition formed against her, to compel her to abandon her insolence on the seas. This brings me to speak of the manuscripts I send you.

"The piece No. 1, without any title, was written in consequence of a question put to me by Bonaparte. As he supposed I knew England and English Politics he sent a person to me to ask, that in case of negociating a Peace with Austria, whether it would be proper to include England. This was when Count St. Julian was in Paris, on the part of the Emperor negociating the preliminaries :—which as I have before said the Emperor refused to sign on the pretence of admitting England.

"The piece No. 2, entitled *On the Jacobinism of the English at Sea*, was written when the English made an insolent and impolitic expedition to Denmark, and is also an auxiliary to the politic of No. 1. I shewed it to a friend [Bonneville] who had it translated into french, and printed in the form of a Pamphlet, and distributed gratis among the foreign Ministers, and persons in the Government. It was immediately copied into several of the french Journals, and into the official Paper, the Moniteur. It appeared in this paper one day before the last dispatch arrived from Egypt; which agreed perfectly with what I had said respecting Egypt. It hit the two cases of Denmark and Egypt in the exact proper moment.

"The piece No. 3, entitled *Compact Maritime*, is the sequel of No. 2 digested in form. It is translating at the time I write this letter, and I am to have a meeting with the Senator Garat upon the subject. The pieces 2 and 3 go off in manuscript to England, by a confidential person, where they will be published.

"By all the news we get from the North there appears to be something meditating against England. It is now given for certain that Paul has embargoed all the English vessels and English property in Russia till some principle be established for protecting the Rights of neutral Nations, and securing the liberty of the Seas. The preparations in Denmark continue, notwithstanding the convention that she has made with England, which leaves the question with respect to the right set up by England to stop and search Neutral vessels undecided. I send you the paragraphs upon the subject.

"The tumults are great in all parts of England on account of the excessive price of corn and bread, which has risen since the harvest. I attribute it more to the abundant increase of paper, and the non-circulation of cash, than to any other cause. People in trade can push the paper off as fast as they receive it, as they did by continental money in America; but as farmers have not this opportunity they endeavour to secure themselves by going considerably in advance.

"I have now given you all the great articles of intelligence, for I trouble not myself with little ones, and consequently not with the Commissioners, nor any thing they are about, nor with John Adams, otherwise than to wish him safe home, and a better and wiser man in his place.

"In the present state of circumstances and the prospects arising from them, it may be proper for America to consider whether it is worth her while to enter into any treaty at this moment, or to wait the event of those circumstances which if they go on will render partial treaties useless by deranging them. But if, in the mean time, she enters into any treaty it ought to be with a condition to the following purpose: Reserving to herself the right of joining in an association of Nations for the protection of the Rights of Neutral Commerce and the security of the liberty of the Seas.

"The pieces 2, 3, may go to the press. They will make a small pamphlet and the printers are welcome to put my name to it. It is best it should be put from thence; they will get into the newspapers. I know that the faction of John Adams abuses me pretty heartily. They are welcome. It does not disturb me, and they lose their labor; and in return for it I am doing America more service, as a neutral nation, than their expensive Commissioners can do, and she has that service from me for nothing. The piece No. 1 is only for your own amusement and that of your friends.

"I come now to speak confidentially to you on a private subject. When Mr. Ellsworth and Davie return to America, Murray will return to Holland, and in that case there will be nobody in Paris but Mr. Skipwith that has been in the habit of transacting business with the french Government since the revolution began. He is on a good standing with them, and if the chance of the day should place you in the presidency you cannot do better than appoint him for any purpose you may have occasion for in France. He is an honest man and will do his country Justice, and that with civility and good manners to the government he is commissioned to act with; a faculty which that Northern Bear Timothy Pickering wanted, and which the Bear of that Bear, John Adams, never possessed.

"I know not much of Mr. Murray, otherwise than of his unfriendliness to every American who is not of his faction, but I am sure that Joel Barlow is a much fitter man to be in Holland than Mr. Murray. It is upon the fitness of the man to the place that I speak, for I have not communicated a thought upon the subject to Barlow, neither does he know, at the time of my writing this (for he is at Havre), that I have intention to do it.

"I will now, by way of relief, amuse you with some account of the progress of Iron Bridges. The french revolution and Mr. Burke's attack upon it, drew me off from any pontifical Works. Since my coming from England in '92, an Iron Bridge of a single arch 236 feet span versed sine 34 feet, has been cast at the Iron Works of the Walkers where my model was, and erected over the river Wear at Sunderland in the county of Durham in England. The two members in Parliament for the County, Mr. Bourdon and Mr. Milbank, were the principal subscribers; but the direction was committed to Mr. Bourdon. A very sincere friend of mine, Sir Robert Smyth, who lives in france, and whom Mr. Monroe well knows, supposing they had taken their plan from my model wrote to Mr. Milbank upon the subject. Mr. Milbank answered the letter, which answer I have by me and I give you word for word the part concerning the Bridge: 'With respect to the Bridge over the river Wear at Sunderland it certainly is a Work well deserving admiration both for its structure, durability and utility, and I have good grounds for saying that the first Idea was taken from Mr. Paine's bridge exhibited at Paddington. But with respect to any compensation to Mr. Paine, however desirous of rewarding the labors of an ingenious man, I see not how it is in my power, having had nothing to do with his bridge after the payment of my subscription, Mr. Bourdon being accountable for the whole. But if you can point out any mode by which I can be instrumental in procuring for Mr. P. any compensation for the advantages which the public may have derived from his ingenious model, from which certainly the outlines of the Bridge at Sunderland was taken, be assured it will afford me very great satisfaction.'

"I have now made two other models, one is pasteboard, five feet span and five inches of height from the cords. It is in the opinion of every person who has seen it one of the most beautifull objects the eye can behold. I then cast a model in Metal following the construction of that in pasteboard and of the same dimensions. The whole was executed in my own Chamber. It is far superior in strength, elegance, and readiness in execution to the model I made in America, and which you saw in Paris. I shall bring those Models with me when I come home, which will be as soon as I can pass the seas in safety from the piratical John Bulls.

"I suppose you have seen, or have heard of the Bishop of Landaff's answer to my second part of the Age of reason. As soon as I got a copy of it I began a third part, which served also as an answer to the Bishop; but as soon as the clerical Society for promoting *Christian Knowledge* knew of my intention to answer the Bishop, they prosecuted, as a Society, the printer of the first and second parts, to prevent that answer appearing. No other reason than this can be assigned for their prosecuting at the time they did, because the first part had been in circulation above three years and the second part more than one, and they prosecuted immediately on knowing that I was taking up their Champion. The Bishop's answer, like Mr. Burke's attack on the french revolution, served me as a background to bring forward other subjects upon, with more advantage than if the background was not there. This is the motive that induced me to answer him, otherwise I should have gone on without taking any notice of him. I have made and am still making additions to the manuscript, and shall continue to do so till an opportunity arrive for publishing it.

"If any American frigate should come to france, and the direction of it fall to you, I will be glad you would give me the opportunity of returning. The abscess under which I suffered almost two years is entirely healed of itself, and I enjoy exceeding good health. This is the first of October, and Mr. Skipwith has just called to tell me the Commissioners set off for Havre to-morrow. This will go by the frigate but not with the knowledge of the Commissioners. Remember me with much affection to my friends and accept the same to yourself."

As the Commissioners did not leave when they expected, Paine added several other letters to Jefferson, on public affairs. In one (October 1st) he says he has information of increasing aversion in the English people to their govern-ment. "It was the hope of conquest, and is now the hope of peace that keeps it [Pitt's administration] up." Pitt is anxious about his paper money. "The credit of Paper is suspicion asleep. When suspicion wakes the credit vanishes as the dream would." "England has a large Navy, and the expense of it leads to her ruin." The English nation is tired of war, longs for peace, "and calculates upon defeat as it would upon victory." On October 4th, after the Commissioners had concluded a treaty, Paine alludes to an article said to be in it, requiring certain expenditures in France, and says that if he, Jefferson, be "in the chair, and not otherwise," he should offer himself for this business, should an agent be required. "It will serve to defray my expenses until I can return, but I wish it may be with the condition of returning. I am not tired of working for nothing, but I cannot afford it. This appointment will aid me in promoting the object I am now upon of a law of nations for the protection of neutral commerce." On October 6th he reports to Jefferson that at an enter-tainment given the American envoys, Consul Le Brun gave the toast: "A l'union de l'Amérique avec les puissances du Nord pour faire respecter la liberté des mers." On October 15th the last of his enclosures to Jefferson is written. He says that Napoleon, when asked if there would be more war, replied: "Nous n'aurions plus qu'une guerre d'écritoire." In all of Paine's writing about Napoleon, at this time, he seems as if watching a thundercloud, and trying to make out meteorologically its drift, and where it will strike.

CHAPTER XXXIX

THE LAST YEAR IN EUROPE

ON July 15, 1801, Napoleon concluded with Pius VII. the Concordat. Naturally, the first victim offered on the restored altar was Theophilanthropy. I have called Paine the founder of this Society, because it arose amid the controversy excited by the publication of " Le Siècle de la Raison," its manual and tracts reproducing his ideas and language ; and because he gave the inaugural discourse. Theism was little known in France save as iconoclasm, and an assault on the Church : Paine treated it as a Religion. But, as he did not speak French, the practical organization and management of the Society were the work of others, and mainly of a Russian named Hauëy. There had been a good deal of odium incurred at first by a society which satisfied neither the pious nor the freethinkers, but it found a strong friend on the Directory. This was Larevéllière-Lépeaux, whose secretary, Antoine Vallée, and young daughter, had become interested in the movement. This statesman never joined the Society, but he had attended one of its meetings, and, when a distribution of religious edifices was made, Theophilanthropy was assigned ten parish churches. It is said that when Larevéllière-Lépeaux mentioned to Talleyrand his desire for the spread of this Society, the diplomat said : " All you have to do is to get yourself hanged, and revive the third day." Paine, who had pretty nearly fulfilled that requirement, saw the Society spread rapidly, and he had great hopes of its future. But Pius VII. also had an interested eye on it, and though the Concordat did not go into legal operation until 1802, Theophilanthropy was offered as a preliminary sacrifice in October, 1801.

The description of Paine by Walter Savage Landor, and representations of his talk, in the " Imaginary Conversations," so mix up persons, times, and places, that I was at one time inclined to doubt whether the two had met. But Mr. J. M. Wheeler, a valued correspondent in London, writes me : "Landor told my friend Mr. Birch of Florence that he particularly admired Paine, and that he visited him, having first obtained an interview at the house of General Dumouriez. Landor declared that Paine was always called ' Tom,' not out

of disrespect, but because he was a jolly good fellow." An interview with Paine at the house of Dumouriez could only have occurred when the General was in Paris, in 1793. This would account for what Landor says of Paine taking refuge from trouble in brandy. There had been, as Rickman testifies, and as all the facts show, nothing of this kind since that period. It would appear therefore that Landor must have mixed up at least two interviews with Paine, one in the time of Dumouriez, the other in that of Napoleon. Not even such an artist as Landor could invent the language ascribed to Paine concerning the French and Napoleon.

" The whole nation may be made as enthusiastic about a salad as about a constitution ; about the colour of a cockade as about a consul or a king. You will shortly see the real strength and figure of Bonaparte. He is wilful, headstrong, proud, morose, presumptuous ; he will be guided no longer ; he has pulled the pad from his forehead, and will break his nose or bruise his cranium against every table, chair, and brick in the room, until at last he must be sent to the hospital."

Paine prophesies that Napoleon will make himself emperor, and that "by his intemperate use of power and thirst of dominion" he will cause the people to "wish for their old kings, forgetting what beasts they were." Possibly under the name "Mr. Normandy" Landor disguises Thomas Poole, referred to on a preceding page. Normandy's sufferings on account of one of Paine's books are not exaggerated. In Mrs. Sanford's work is printed a letter from Paris, July 20, 1802, in which Poole says : "I called one morning on Thomas Paine. He is an original, amusing fellow. Striking, strong physiognomy. Said a great many quaint things, and read us part of a reply which he intends to publish to Watson's ' Apology.'"[1]

Paine seems to have had no relation with the ruling powers at this time, though an Englishman who visited him is quoted by Rickman (p. 198) as remarking his manliness and fearlessness, and that he spoke as freely as ever after

[1] " Thomas Poole and His Friends," ii., p. 85.

Bonaparte's supremacy. One communication only to any member of the government appears; this was to the Minister of the Interior concerning a proposed iron bridge over the Seine.[1] Political France and Paine had parted.

Under date of March 18, 1801, President Jefferson informs Paine that he had sent his manuscripts (Maritime Compact) to the printer to be made into a pamphlet, and that the American people had returned from their frenzy against France. He adds:

"You expressed a wish to get a passage to this country in a public vessel. Mr. Dawson is charged with orders to the captain of the Maryland to receive and accommodate you back if you can be ready to depart at such short warning. Rob. R. Livingston is appointed minister plenipotentiary to the republic of France, but will not leave this till we receive the ratification of the convention by Mr. Dawson.[2] I am in hopes you will find us returned generally to sentiments worthy of former times. In these it will be your glory to have steadily labored, and with as much effect as any man living. That you may long live to continue your useful labors and to reap the reward in the thankfulness of nations, is my sincere prayer. Accept assurances of my high esteem and affectionate attachment."

The subjoined notes are from letters of Paine to Jefferson:

Paris, June 9, 1801. "Your very friendly letter by Mr. Dawson gave me the real sensation of happy satisfaction, and what served to increase it was that he brought it to me himself before I knew of his arrival. I congratulate America on your election. There has been no circumstance with respect to America since the times of her revolution that excited so much attention and expectation in France, England, Ireland, and Scotland as the pending election for President of the United States, nor any of which the event has given more general joy:

"I thank you for the opportunity you give me of returning by the Maryland, but I shall wait the return of the vessel that brings Mr. Livingston."

Paris, June 25, 1801. " The Parliamentaire, from America to Havre, was taken in going out, and carried into England. The pretence, as the papers say, was that a Swedish Minister was on board for America. If I had happened to have been there, I suppose they would have made no ceremony in conducting me on shore.

Paris, March 17, 1802. "As it is now Peace, though the definitive Treaty is not yet signed, I shall set off by the first opportunity from Havre or Dieppe, after the equinoctial gales are over. I continue in excellent health, which I know your friendship will be glad to hear of.—Wishing you and America every happiness, I remain your former fellow-labourer and much obliged fellow-citizen.

Paine's determination not to return to America in a national vessel was owing to a paragraph he saw in a Baltimore paper, headed " Out at Last." It stated that Paine had written to the President, expressing a wish to return by a national ship, and that " permission was given." There was here an indication that Jefferson's invitation to Paine by the Hon. John Dawson had become known to the President's enemies, and that Jefferson, on being attacked, had apologized by making the matter appear an act of charity. Paine would not believe that the President was personally responsible for the apologetic paragraph, which seemed inconsistent with the cordiality of the letter brought by Dawson; but, as he afterwards wrote to Jefferson, " it determined me not to come by a national ship."[1] His re-

---

[1] "THE MINISTER OF THE INTERIOR TO THOMAS PAINE: I have received, Citizen, the observations that you have been so good as to address to me upon the construction of iron bridges. They will be of the greatest utility to us when the new kind of construction goes to be executed for the first time. With pleasure, I assure you, Citizen, that you have rights of more than one kind to the gratitude of nations, and I give you, cordially, the expression of my particular esteem.—CHAPTAL."
It is rather droll, considering the appropriation of his patent in England, and the confiscation of a thousand pounds belonging to him, to find Paine casually mentioning that at this time a person came from London with plans and drawings to consult with him about an iron arch of 600 feet, over the Thames, then under consideration by a committee of the House of Commons.

[2] "Beau Dawson," an eminent Virginia Congressman.

[1] It was cleared up afterwards. Jefferson had been charged with sending a national ship to France for the sole purpose of bringing Paine home, and Paine himself would have been the first to condemn such an assumption of power. Although the President's adherents thought it right to deny this, Jefferson wrote to Paine that he had nothing to do with the paragraph. "With respect to the letter [offering the ship] I never hesitate to avow and justify it in conversation. In no other way do I trouble myself to contradict anything which is said. At that time,

quest had been made at a time when any other than a national American ship was pretty certain to land him in an English prison. There was evidently no thought of any *éclat* in the matter, but no doubt a regard for economy as well as safety.

The following to the eminent deist lecturer in New York, Elihu Palmer, bears the date, "Paris, February 21, 1802, since the Fable of Christ":

"DEAR FRIEND, I received, by Mr. Livingston, the letter you wrote me, and the excellent work you have published ["The Principles of Nature"]. I see you have thought deeply on the subject, and expressed your thoughts in a strong and clear style. The hinting and intimating manner of writing that was formerly used on subjects of this kind, produced skepticism, but not conviction. It is necessary to be bold. Some people can be reasoned into sense, and others must be shocked into it. Say a bold thing that will stagger them, and they will begin to think.

"There is an intimate friend of mine, Colonel Joseph Kirkbride of Bordentown, New Jersey, to whom I would wish you to send your work. He is an excellent man, and perfectly in our sentiments. You can send it by the stage that goes partly by land and partly by water, between New York and Philadelphia, and passes through Bordentown.

"I expect to arrive in America in May next. I have a third part of the Age of Reason to publish when I arrive, which, if I mistake not, will make a stronger impression than anything I have yet published on the subject.

"I write this by an ancient colleague of mine in the French Convention, the citizen Lequinio, who is going [as] Consul to Rhode Island, and who waits while I write.[1] Yours in friendship."

The following, dated July 8, 1802, to Consul Rotch, is the last letter I find written by Paine from Paris:

"MY DEAR FRIEND,—The bearer of this is a young man that wishes to go to America. He is willing to do anything on board a ship to lessen the expense of his passage. If you know any captain to whom such a person may be usefull I will be obliged to you to speak to him about it.

"As Mr. Otte was to come to Paris in order to go to America, I wanted to take a passage

however, there were anomalies in the motions of some of our friends which events have at length reduced to regularity."

[1] J. M. Lequinio, author of "Prejudices Destroyed," and other rationalistic works, especially dealt with in Priestley's "Letters to the Philosophers of France."

with him, but as he stays in England to negociate some arrangements of Commerce, I have given up that idea. I wait now for the arrival of a person from England whom I want to see,[2] after which, I shall bid adieu to restless and wretched Europe. I am with affectionate esteem to you and Mrs. Rotch,
　　　　"Yours,
　　　　　　"THOMAS PAINE."

The President's cordial letter had raised a happy vision before the eyes of one sitting amid the ruins of his republican world. As he said of Job, he had "determined, in the midst of accumulating ills, to impose upon himself the hard duty of contentment." Of the comrades with whom he began the struggle for liberty in France but a small circle remained. As he wrote to Lady Smith,— from whom he must now part,—"I might almost say like Job's servant, 'and I only am escaped.'" Of the American and English friends who cared for him when he came out of prison few remain.

The President's letter came to a poor man in a small room, furnished only with manuscripts and models of inventions. Here he was found by an old friend from England, Henry Redhead Yorke, who, in 1795, had been tried in England for sedition. Yorke has left us a last glimpse of the author in "wretched and restless Europe." The "rights of man" had become so antiquated in Napoleon's France, that Yorke found Paine's name odious on account of his antislavery writings, the people "ascribing to his espousal of the rights of the negroes of St. Domingo the resistance which Leclercq had experienced from them." He found Paine in No. 4 Rue du Théâtre Français. A "jolly-looking woman" (in whom we recognize Madame Bonneville) scrutinized Yorke severely, but was smiling enough on learning that he was Paine's old friend. He was ushered into a little room heaped with boxes of documents, a chaos of pamphlets and journals. While Yorke was meditating on the contrast between this habitation of a founder of two great republics and the mansions of their rulers, his old friend entered, dressed in a long flannel gown.

[2] No doubt Clio Rickman.

" Time seemed to have made dreadful ravages over his whole frame, and a settled melancholy was visible on his countenance. He desired me to be seated, and although he did not recollect me for a considerable time, he conversed with his usual affability. I confess I felt extremely surprised that he should have forgotten me ; but I resolved not to make myself known to him, as long as it could be avoided with propriety. In order to try his memory, I referred to a number of circumstances which had occurred while we were in company, but carefully abstained from hinting that we had ever lived together. He would frequently put his hand to his forehead, and exclaim, 'Ah! I know that voice, but my recollection fails !' At length I thought it time to remove his suspense, and stated an incident which instantly recalled me to his mind. It is impossible to describe the sudden change which this effected ; his countenance brightened, he pressed me by the hand, and a silent tear stole down his cheek. Nor was I less affected than himself. For some time we sat without a word escaping from our lips. ' Thus are we met once more, Mr. Paine,' I resumed, 'after a long separation of ten years, and after having been both of us severely weather-beaten.' ' Aye,' he replied, 'and who would have thought that we should meet in Paris?' He then enquired what motive had brought me here, and on my explaining myself, he observed with a smile of contempt, 'They have shed blood enough for liberty, and now they have it in perfection. This is not a country for an honest man to live in ; they do not understand any thing at all of the principles of free government, and the best way is to leave them to themselves. You see they have conquered all Europe, only to make it more miserable than it was before.' Upon this, I remarked that I was surprised to hear him speak in such desponding language of the fortune of mankind, and that I thought much might yet be done for the Republic. 'Republic!' he exclaimed, 'do you call this a Republic? Why they are worse off than the slaves of Constantinople ; for there, they expect to be bashaws in heaven by submitting to be slaves below, but here they believe neither in heaven nor hell, and yet are slaves by choice. I know of no Republic in the world except America, which is the only country for such men as you and I. It is my intention to get away from this place as soon as possible, and I hope to be off in the autumn ; you are a young man and may see better times, but I have done with Europe, and its slavish politics.'

" I have often been in company with Mr. Paine, since my arrival here, and I was not a little surprised to find him wholly indifferent about the public spirit in England, or the remaining influence of his doctrines among its people. Indeed he seemed to dislike the mention of the subject ; and when, one day, in order to provoke discussion, I told him I had altered my opinions upon many of his principles, he answered, 'You certainly have the right to do so ; but you cannot alter the nature of things ;

the French have alarmed all honest men ; but still truth is truth. Though you may not think that my principles are practicable in England, without bringing on a great deal of misery and confusion, you are, I am sure, convinced of their justice.' Here he took occasion to speak in terms of the utmost severity of Mr. ——, who had obtained a seat in parliament, and said that 'parsons were always mischievous fellows when they turned politicians.' This gave rise to an observation respecting his 'Age of Reason,' the publication of which I said had lost him the good opinion of numbers of his English advocates. He became uncommonly warm at this remark, and in a tone of singular energy declared that he would not have published it if he had not thought it calculated to 'inspire mankind with a more exalted idea of the Supreme Architect of the Universe, and to put an end to villainous imposture.' He then broke out with the most violent invectives against our received opinions, accompanying them at the same time with some of the most grand and sublime conceptions of an Omnipotent Being, that I ever heard or read of. In the support of his opinion, he avowed himself ready to lay down his life, and said 'the Bishop of Llandaff may roast me in Smithfield if he likes, but human torture cannot shake my conviction.' . . . He reached down a copy of the Bishop's work, interleaved with remarks upon it, which he read me ; after which he admitted the liberality of the Bishop, and regretted that in all controversies among men a similar temper was not maintained. But in proportion as he appeared listless in politics, he seemed quite a zealot in his religious creed ; of which the following is an instance. An English lady of our acquaintance, not less remarkable for her talents than for elegance of manners, entreated me to contrive that she might have an interview with Mr. Paine. In consequence of this I invited him to dinner on a day when we were to be favored with her company. But as she is a very rigid Roman Catholic I cautioned Mr. Paine, beforehand, against touching upon religious subjects, assuring him at the same time that she felt much interested to make his acquaintance. With much good nature he promised to be *discreet*. . . . For above four hours he kept every one in astonishment and admiration of his memory, his keen observation of men and manners, his numberless anecdotes of the American Indians, of the American war, of Franklin, Washington, and even of his Majesty, of whom he told several curious facts of humor and benevolence. His remarks on genius and taste can never be forgotten by those present. Thus far everything went on as I could wish ; the sparkling champagne gave a zest to his conversation, and we were all delighted. But alas ! alas ! an expression relating to his ' Age of Reason' having been mentioned by one of the company, he broke out immediately. He began with Astronomy—addressing himself to Mrs. Y.,—he declared that the least inspection of the motion of the stars was a convincing proof that Moses was a liar.

Nothing could stop him. In vain I attempted to change the subject, by employing every artifice in my power, and even attacking with vehemence his political principles. He returned to the charge with unabated ardor. I called upon him for a song though I never heard him sing in my life. He struck up one of his own composition; but the instant he had finished it he resumed his favorite topic. I felt extremely mortified, and remarked that he had forgotten his promise, and that it was not fair to wound so deeply the opinions of the ladies. 'Oh!' said he, 'they'll come again. What a pity it is that people should be so prejudiced!' To which I retorted that their prejudices might be virtues. 'If so,' he replied, 'the blossoms may be beautiful to the eye, but the root is weak.' . . . One of the most extraordinary properties belonging to Mr. Paine is his power of retaining everything he has written in the course of his life. It is a fact that he can repeat word for word every sentence in his 'Common Sense,' 'Rights of Man,' etc., etc. The Bible is the only book which he has studied, and there is not a verse in it that is not familiar to him. . . . In shewing me one day the beautiful models of two bridges he had devised he observed that Dr. Franklin once told him that 'books are written to please, houses built for great men, churches for priests, but no bridges for the people.' These models exhibit an extraordinary degree not only of skill but of taste; and are wrought with extreme delicacy entirely by his own hands. The largest is nearly four feet in length; the iron works, the chains, and every other article belonging to it, were forged and manufactured by himself. It is intended as the model of a bridge which is to be constructed across the Delaware, extending 480 feet with only one arch. The other is to be erected over a lesser river, whose name I forget, and is likewise a single arch, and of his own workmanship, excepting the chains, which, instead of iron, are cut out of pasteboard, by the fair hand of his correspondent the 'Little Corner of the World,' whose indefatigable perseverance is extraordinary. He was offered £3000 for these models and refused it. The iron bars, which I before mentioned that I noticed in a corner of his room, were also forged by himself, as the model of a crane, of a new description. He put them together, and exhibited the power of the lever to a most surprising degree."[1]

About this time Sir Robert Smith died, and another of the ties to Paris was snapped. His beloved Bonnevilles promised to follow him to the New World. His old friend Rickman has come over to see him off, and observed that "he did not drink spirits, and wine he took moderately; he even objected

to any spirits being laid in as a part of his sea-stock." These two friends journeyed together to Havre, where, on September 1st, the way-worn man begins his homeward voyage. Poor Rickman, the perpetually prosecuted, strains his eyes till the sail is lost, then sits on the beach and writes his poetical tribute to Jefferson and America for recalling Paine, and a touching farewell to his friend:

"Thus smooth be thy waves, and thus gentle
　　the breeze,
　　As thou bearest my Paine far away;
O waft him to comfort and regions of ease,
Each blessing of freedom and friendship to
　　seize,
　　And bright be his setting sun's ray."

Who can imagine the joy of those eyes when they once more beheld the distant coast of the New World! Fifteen years have passed,—years in which all nightmares became real, and liberty's sun had turned to blood,—since he saw the happy land fading behind him. Oh, America, thine old friend who first claimed thy republican independence, who laid aside his Quaker coat and fought for thy cause, believing it sacred, is returning to thy breast! This is the man of whom Washington wrote: "His writings certainly had a powerful effect on the public mind,—ought they not then to meet an adequate return? He is poor! He is chagrined!" It is not money he needs now, but tenderness, sympathy; for he comes back from an old world that has plundered, outlawed, imprisoned him for his love of mankind. He has seen his dear friends sent to the guillotine, and others are pining in British prisons for publishing his "Rights of Man,"—principles pronounced by President Jefferson and Secretary Madison to be those of the United States. Heartsore, scarred, white-haired, there remains to this veteran of many struggles for humanity but one hope, a kindly welcome, a peaceful haven for his tempest-tossed life. Never for an instant has his faith in the heart of America been shaken. Already he sees his friend Jefferson's arms extended: he sees his old comrades welcoming him

---

[1] "Letters from France," etc., London, 1804, 2 vols., 8vo. Thirty-three pages of the last letter are devoted to Paine.

to their hearths ; he sees his own house and sward at Bordentown, and the beautiful Kirkbride mansion beside the Delaware,—river of sacred memories, soon to be spanned by his graceful arch. How the ladies he left girls,—Fanny, Kitty, Sally,—will come with their husbands to greet him ! How will they admire the latest bridge-model, with Lady Smith's delicate chainwork for which (such is his estimate of friendship) he refused three thousand pounds, though it would have made his mean room palatial ! Ah, yes, poor heart, America will soothe your wounds, and pillow your sinking head on her breast ! America, with Jefferson in power, is herself again. They do not hate men in America for not believing in a celestial Robespierre. Thou stricken friend of man, who hast appealed from the god of wrath to the God of Humanity, see

in the distance that Maryland coast, which early voyagers called Avalon, and sing again your song when first stepping on that shore twenty-seven years ago :

"I come to sing that summer is at hand,
  The summer time of wit, you 'll understand ;
  Plants, fruits, and flowers, and all the smiling race
That can the orchard or the garden grace ;
  The Rose and Lily shall address the fair,
  And whisper sweetly out, 'My dears, take care :'
With sterling worth the Plant of Sense shall rise,
  And teach the curious to philosophize !'
The frost returns? We 'll garnish out the scenes
  With stately rows of Evergreens,
Trees that will bear the frost, and deck their tops
  With everlasting flowers, like diamond drops." [1]

---

[1] "The Snowdrop and Critic," *Pennsylvania Magazine*, 1775. Couplets are omitted between those given.

CHAPTER XL

THE AMERICAN INQUISITION

On October 30th Paine landed at Baltimore. More than two and a half centuries had elapsed since the Catholic Lord Baltimore appointed a Protestant Governor of Maryland, William Stone, who proclaimed in that province (1648) religious freedom and equality. The Puritans, crowding thither, from regions of oppression, grew strong enough to exterminate the religion of Lord Baltimore who had given them shelter, and imprisoned his Protestant Governor. So, in the New World, passed the Inquisition from Catholic to Protestant hands.

In Paine's first American pamphlet, he had repeated and extolled the principle of that earliest proclamation of religious liberty. "Diversity of religious opinions affords a larger field for Christian kindness." The Christian kindness now consists in a cessation of sectarian strife that they may unite in stretching the author of the "Age of Reason" on their common rack, so far as was possible

under a Constitution acknowledging no deity. This persecution began on the victim's arrival.

Soon after landing Paine wrote to President Jefferson :

"I arrived here on Saturday from Havre, after a passage of sixty days. I have several cases of models, wheels, etc., and as soon as I can get them from the vessel and put them on board the packet for Georgetown I shall set off to pay my respects to you. Your much obliged fellow-citizen,—THOMAS PAINE."

On reaching Washington City Paine found his dear friend Monroe starting off to resume his ministry in Paris, and by him wrote to Mr. Este, banker in Paris (Sir Robert Smith's son-in-law), enclosing a letter to Rickman, in London. "You can have no idea," he tells Rickman, "of the agitation which my arrival occasioned." Every paper is "filled with applause or abuse."

"My property in this country has been taken care of by my friends, and is now worth six thousand pounds sterling; which put in the funds will bring me £400 sterling a year. Remember me in friendship and affection to your wife and family, and in the circle of our friends. I am but just arrived here, and the minister sails in a few hours, so that I have just time to write you this. If he should not sail this tide I will write to my good friend Col. Bosville, but in any case I request you to wait on him for me.[1] Yours in friendship."

The defeated Federalists had already prepared their batteries to assail the President for inviting Paine to return on a national ship, under escort of a Congressman. It required some skill for these adherents of John Adams, a Unitarian, to set the Inquisition in motion. It had to be done, however, as there was no chance of breaking down Jefferson but by getting preachers to sink political differences and hound the President's favorite author. Out of the North, stronghold of the "British Party," came this partisan crusade under a pious

flag. In Virginia and the South the "Age of Reason" was fairly discussed, its influence being so great that Patrick Henry, as we have seen, wrote and burnt a reply. In Virginia, Deism, though largely prevailing, had not prevented its adherents from supporting the Church as an institution. It had become their habit to talk of such matters only in private. Jefferson had not ventured to express his views in public, and was troubled at finding himself mixed up with the heresies of Paine.[2] The author on reaching Lovell's Hotel, Washington, had made known his arrival to the President, and was cordially received; but as the newspapers came in with their abuse, Jefferson may have been somewhat intimidated. At any rate Paine so thought. Eager to disembarrass the administration, Paine published a letter in the *National Intelligencer*, which had cordially welcomed him, in which he said that he should not ask or accept any office.[3] He meant to continue writing

---

[1] Paine still had faith in Bosville. He was slow in suspecting any man who seemed enthusiastic for liberty. In this connection it may be mentioned that it is painful to find in the "Diary and Letters of Gouverneur Morris" (ii., p. 426), a confidential letter to Robert R. Livingston, Minister in France, which seems to assume that Minister's readiness to receive slanders of Jefferson, who appointed him, and of Paine whose friendship he seemed to value. Speaking of the President, Morris says: "The employment of and confidence in adventurers from abroad will sooner or later rouse the pride and indignation of this country." Morris' editor adds: "This was probably an allusion to Thomas Paine, who had recently returned to America and was supposed to be an intimate friend of Mr. Jefferson, who, it was said, received him warmly, dined him at the White House, and could be seen walking arm in arm with him on the street any fine afternoon." The allusion to "adventurers" was no doubt meant for Paine, but not to his reception by Jefferson, for Morris' letter was written on August 27th, some two months before Paine's arrival. It was probably meant by Morris to damage Paine in Paris, where it was known that he was intimate with Livingston, who had been introduced by him to influential men, among others to Sir Robert Smith and Este, bankers. It is to be hoped that Livingston resented Morris' assumption of his treacherous character. Morris, who had shortly before dined at the White House, tells Livingston that Jefferson " is descending to a condition which I find no decent word to designate." Surely Livingston's descendants should discover his reply to that letter.

[2] To the Rev. Dr. Waterhouse (Unitarian) who had asked permission to publish a letter of his, Jefferson, with a keen remembrance of Paine's fate, wrote (July 19, 1822): "No, my dear Sir, not for the world. Into what a hornet's nest would it thrust my head!—The *genus irritabile vatum*, on whom argument is lost, and reason is by themselves disdained in matters of religion. Don Quixote undertook to redress the bodily wrongs of the world, but the redressment of mental vagaries would be an enterprise more than Quixotic. I should as soon undertake to bring the crazy skulls of Bedlam to sound understanding as to inculcate reason into that of an Athanasian. I am old, and tranquillity is now my *summum bonum*. Keep me therefore from the fire and faggot of Calvin and his victim Servetus. Happy in the prospect of a restoration of a primitive Christianity, I must leave to younger athletes to lop off the false branches which have been engrafted into it by the mythologists of the middle and modern ages."—MS. belonging to Dr. Fogg of Boston.

[3] The *National Intelligencer* (Nov. 3d), announcing Paine's arrival at Baltimore, said, among other things: "Be his religious sentiments what they may, it must be their [the American people's] wish that he may live in the undisturbed possession of our common blessings, and enjoy them the more from his active participation in their attainment." The same paper said, Nov. 10th: "Thomas Paine has arrived in this city [Washington] and has received a cordial reception from the Whigs of Seventy-six,

and bring forward his mechanical projects. None the less did the "federalist" press use Paine's infidelity to belabour the President, and the author had to write defensive letters from the moment of his arrival. On October 29th, before Paine had landed, the *National Intelligencer* had printed (from a Lancaster, Pa., journal) a vigorous letter, signed "A Republican," showing that the denunciations of Paine were not religious, but political, as John Adams was also unorthodox. The "federalists" must often have wished that they had taken this warning, for Paine's pen was keener than ever, and the opposition had no writer to meet him. His eight "Letters to the Citizens of the United States" were scathing, eloquent, untrammelled by partisanship, and made a profound impression on the country,—for even the opposition press had to publish them as part of the news of the day.[1]

On Christmas Day Paine wrote the President a suggestion for the purchase of Louisiana. The French, to whom Louisiana had been ceded by Spain, closed New Orleans (November 26th) against foreign ships (including American), and prohibited deposits there by way of the Mississippi This caused much excitement, and the "federalists" showed eagerness to push the administration into a belligerent attitude towards France. Paine's "common sense" again came to the front, and he sent Jefferson the following paper :

"OF LOUISIANA.

"Spain has ceded Louisiana to france, and france has excluded the Americans from N. Orleans and the navigation of the Mississippi : the people of the Western Territory have complained of it to their Government, and the governt. is of consequence involved and inter-

and the republicans of 1800, who have the independence to feel and avow a sentiment of gratitude for his eminent revolutionary services."

[1] They were published in the *National Intelligencer* of November 15th, 22d, 29th, December 6th, January 25th, and February 2d, 1803. Of the others one appeared in the *Aurora* (Philadelphia), dated from Bordentown, N. J., March 12th, and the last in the Trenton *True American*, dated April 21st.

ested in the affair. The question then is—What is the best step to be taken ?

"The one is to begin by memorial and remonstrance against an infraction of a right. The other is by accommodation, still keeping the right in view, but not making it a groundwork.

"Suppose then the Government begin by making a proposal to france to repurchase the cession, made to her by Spain, of Louisiana, provided it be with the consent of the people of Louisiana or a majority thereof.

"By beginning on this ground any thing can be said without carrying the appearance of a threat,—the growing power of the western territory can be stated as matter of information, and also the impossibility of restraining them from seizing upon New Orleans, and the equal impossibility of france to prevent it.

"Suppose the proposal attended to, the sum to be given comes next on the carpet. This, on the part of America, will be estimated between the value of the Commerce, and the quantity of revenue that Louisiana will produce.

"The french treasury is not only empty, but the Government has consumed by anticipation a great part of the next year's revenue. A monied proposal will, I believe, be attended to ; if it should, the claims upon france can be stipulated as part of the payment, and that sum can be paid here to the claimants.

"——I congratulate you on the *birthday of the New Sun*, now called christmas-day ; and I make you a present of a thought on Louisiana.

"T. P."

Jefferson next day told Paine, what was as yet a profound secret, that he was already contemplating the purchase of Louisiana.[2]

The "New Sun" was destined to

[2] "The idea occurred to me," Paine afterwards wrote to the President, "without knowing it had occurred to any other person, and I mentioned it to Dr. Leib who lived in the same house (Lovell's) ; and, as he appeared pleased with it, I wrote the note and showed it to him before I sent it. The next morning you said to me that measures were already taken in that business. When Leib returned from Congress I told him of it. 'I knew that,' said he. 'Why then,' said I, 'did you not tell me so, because in that case I would not have sent the note.' 'That is the very reason,' said he ; 'I would not tell you, because two opinions concurring on a case strengthen it.' I do not, however, like Dr. Leib's motion about Banks. Congress ought to be very cautious how it gives encouragement to this speculating project of banking, for it is now carried to an extreme. It is but another kind of striking paper money. Neither do I like the notion respecting the recession of the territory [District of Columbia.]." Dr. Michael Leib was a representative from Pennsylvania.

bring his sunstrokes on Paine. The pathetic story of his wrongs in England, his martyrdom in France, was not generally known, and, in reply to attacks, he had to tell it himself. He had returned for repose and found himself a sort of battlefield. One of the most humiliating circumstances was the discovery that in this conflict of parties the merits of his religion were of least consideration. The outcry of the country against him, so far as it was not merely political, was the mere ignorant echo of pulpit vituperation. His well-considered theism, fruit of so much thought, nursed amid glooms of the dungeon, was called infidelity or atheism. Even some from whom he might have expected discriminating criticism accepted the vulgar version and wrote him in deprecation of a work they had not read. Samuel Adams, his old friend, caught in this *schwärmerei*, wrote him from Boston (November 30th) that he had "heard" that he had "turned his mind to a defence of infidelity." Paine copied for him his creed from the "Age of Reason," and asked, "My good friend, do you call believing in God infidelity?"

This letter to Samuel Adams (January 1, 1803) has indications that Paine had developed farther his theistic ideal.

"We cannot serve the Deity in the manner we serve those who cannot do without that service. He needs no service from us. We can add nothing to eternity. But it is in our power to render a service acceptable to him, and that is, not by praying, but by endeavoring to make his creatures happy. A man does not serve God by praying, for it is himself he is trying to serve; and as to hiring or paying men to pray, as if the Deity needed instruction, it is in my opinion an abomination. I have been exposed to and preserved through many dangers, but instead of buffeting the Deity with prayers, as if I distrusted him, or must dictate to him, I reposed myself on his protection; and you, my friend, will find, even in your last moments, more consolation in the silence of resignation than in the murmuring wish of a prayer."

Paine must have been especially hurt by a sentence in the letter of Samuel Adams in which he said: "Our friend, the President of the United States, has been calumniated for his liberal senti-

ments, by men who have attributed that liberality to a latent design to promote the cause of infidelity." To this he did not reply, but it probably led him to feel a deeper disappointment at the postponement of the interviews he had hoped to enjoy with Jefferson after thirteen years of separation. A feeling of this kind no doubt prompted the following note (January 12th) sent to the President:

"I will be obliged to you to send back the Models, as I am packing up to set off for Philadelphia and New York. My intention in bringing them here in preference to sending them from Baltimore to Philadelphia, was to have some conversation with you on those matters and others I have not informed you of. But you have not only shown no disposition towards it, but have, in some measure, by a sort of shyness, as if you stood in fear of federal observation, precluded it. I am not the only one, who makes observations of this kind."

Jefferson at once took care that there should be no misunderstanding as to his regard for Paine. The author was for some days a guest in the President's family, where he again met Maria Jefferson (Mrs. Eppes) whom he had known in Paris. Randall says the devout ladies of the family had been shy of Paine, as was but natural, on account of the President's reputation for rationalism, but "Paine's discourse was weighty, his manners sober and inoffensive; and he left Mr. Jefferson's mansion the subject of lighter prejudices than he entered it." [1]

Paine's defamers have manifested an eagerness to ascribe his maltreatment to personal faults. This is not the case. For some years after his arrival in the country no one ventured to hint anything disparaging to his personal habits or sobriety. On January 1, 1803, he wrote to Samuel Adams: "I have a good state of health and a happy mind; I take care of both by nourishing the first with temperance, and the latter with abundance." Had not this been true the

[1] "Life of Jefferson," ii., 642 *seq.* Randall is mistaken in some statements. Paine, as we have seen, did not return on the ship placed at his service by the President; nor did the President's letter appear until long after his return, when he and Jefferson felt it necessary in order to disabuse the public mind of the most absurd rumors on the subject.

"federal" press would have noised it abroad. He was neat in his attire. In all portraits, French and American, his dress is in accordance with the fashion. There was not, so far as I can discover, a suggestion while he was at Washington, that he was not a suitable guest for any drawing-room in the capital. On February 23, 1803, probably, was written the following which I find among the Cobbett papers:

From Mr. Paine to Mr. Jefferson, on the occasion of a toast being given at a federal dinner at Washington, of "MAY THEY NEVER KNOW PLEASURE WHO LOVE PAINE."

"I send you, Sir, a tale about some Feds,
Who, in their wisdom, got to loggerheads.
The case was this, they felt so flat and sunk,
They took a glass together and got drunk.
Such things, you know, are neither new nor rare,
For some will hary themselves when in despair.
It was the natal day of Washington,
And that they thought a famous day for fun ;
For with the learned world it is agreed,
The better day the better deed.
They talked away, and as the glass went round
They grew, in point of wisdom, more profound ;
For at the bottom of the bottle lies
That kind of sense we overlook when wise.
Come, here 's a toast, cried one, with roar
   immense,
May none know pleasure who love Common
   Sense.
Bravo ! cried some,—no, no ! some others cried,
But left it to the waiter to decide.
I think, said he, the case would be more plain,
To leave out Common Sense, and put in Paine.
On this a mighty noise arose among
This drunken, bawling, senseless throng.
Some said that Common Sense was all a curse,
That making people wiser made them worse ;
It learned them to be careful of their purse,
And not be laid about like babes at nurse,
Nor yet believe in stories upon trust,
Which all mankind, to be well governed must :
And that the toast was better at the first,
And he that did n't think so might be cursed.
So on they went, till such a fray arose
As all who know what Feds are may suppose."

On his way northward, to his old home in Bordentown, Paine passed many a remembered spot, but found little or no greeting on his journey. In Baltimore a "New Jerusalemite," as the Swedenborgian was then called, the Rev. Mr. Hargrove, accosted him with the information that the key to scripture was found, after being lost 4,000 years. "Then it must be very rusty," answered

Paine. In Philadelphia his old friend Dr. Benjamin Rush never came near him. "His principles," wrote Rush to Cheetham, "avowed in his 'Age of Reason,' were so offensive to me that I did not wish to renew my intercourse with him." Paine made arrangements for the reception of his bridge models at Peale's Museum, but if he met any old friend there no mention of it appears. Most of those who had made up the old circle—Franklin, Rittenhouse, Muhlenberg—were dead, some were away in Congress ; but no doubt Paine saw George Clymer. However, he did not stay long in Philadelphia, for he was eager to reach the spot he always regarded as his home, Bordentown. And there, indeed, his hope, for a time, seemed to be fulfilled. It need hardly be said that his old friend Colonel Kirkbride gave him hearty welcome. John Hall, Paine's bridge mechanician, "never saw him jollier," and he was full of mechanical "whims and schemes" they were to pursue together. Jefferson was candidate for the presidency, and Paine entered heartily into the canvass ; which was not prudent, but he knew nothing of prudence. The issue not only concerned an old friend, but was turning on the question of peace with France. On March 12th he writes against the "federalist" scheme for violently seizing New Orleans. At a meeting in April, over which Colonel Kirkbride presides, Paine drafts a reply to an attack on Jefferson's administration, circulated in New York. On April 21st he writes the refutation of an attack on Jefferson, *àpropos* of the national vessel offered for his return, which had been coupled with a charge that Paine had proposed to the Directory an invasion of America ! In June he writes about his bridge models (then at Peale's Museum, Philadelphia), and his hope to span the Delaware and the Schuylkill with iron arches.

Here is a letter written to Jefferson from Bordentown (August 2d) containing suggestions concerning the beginning of government in Louisiana, from which it would appear that Paine's faith in the natural inspiration of *vox populi* was still imperfect:

"I take it for granted that the present inhabitants know little or nothing of election and representation as constituting government. They are therefore not in an immediate condition to exercise those powers, and besides this they are perhaps too much under the influence of their priests to be sufficiently free.

"I should suppose that a Government *provisoire* formed by Congress for three, five, or seven years would be the best mode of beginning. In the meantime they may be initiated into the practice by electing their Municipal government, and after some experience they will be in train to elect their State government. I think it would not only be good policy but right to say, that the people shall have the right of electing their Church Ministers, otherwise their Ministers will hold by authority from the Pope. I do not make it a compulsive article, but to put it in their power to use it when they please. It will serve to hold the priests in a stile of good behavior, and also to give the people an idea of elective rights. Anything, they say, will do to learn upon, and therefore they may as well begin upon priests.

"The present prevailing language is french and spanish, but it will be necessary to establish schools to teach english as the laws ought to be in the language of the Union.

"As soon as you have formed any plan for settling the Lands I shall be glad to know it. My motive for this is because there are thousands and tens of thousands in England and Ireland and also in Scotland who are friends of mine by principle, and who would gladly change their present country and condition. Many among them, for I have friends in all ranks of life in those countries, are capable of becoming monied purchasers to any amount.

"If you can give me any hints respecting Louisiana, the quantity in square miles, the population, and amount of the present Revenue I will find an opportunity of making some use of it. When the formalities of the cession are compleated, the next thing will be to take possession, and I think it would be very consistent for the President of the United States to do this in person.

"What is Dayton gone to New Orleans for? Is he there as an Agent for the British as Blount was said to be?"

Of the same date is a letter to Senator Breckenridge, of Kentucky, forwarded through Jefferson:

"MY DEAR FRIEND,—Not knowing your place of Residence in Kentucky I send this under cover to the President desiring him to fill up the direction.

"I see by the public papers and the Proclamation for calling Congress, that the cession of Louisiana has been obtained. The papers state the purchase to be 11,250,000 dollars in the six per cents and 3,750,000 dollars to be paid to American claimants who have furnished supplies to France and the french Colonies and are yet unpaid, making on the whole 15,000,000 dollars.

"I observe that the faction of the Feds who last Winter were for going to war to obtain possession of that country and who attached so much importance to it that no expense or risk ought to be spared to obtain it, have now altered their tone and say it is not worth having, and that we are better without it than with it. Thus much for their consistency. What follows is for your private consideration.

"The second section of the 2d article of the constitution says, The 'President shall have Power by and with the consent of the senate to make Treaties provided two thirds of the senators present concur.'

"A question may be supposed to arise on the present case, which is, under what character is the cession to be considered and taken up in congress, whether as a treaty, or in some other shape? I go to examine this point.

"Though the word, Treaty, as a Word, is unlimited in its meaning and application, it must be supposed to have a defined meaning in the constitution. It there means Treaties of alliance or of navigation and commerce—Things which require a more profound deliberation than common acts do, because they entail on the parties a future reciprocal responsibility and become afterwards a supreme law on each of the contracting countries which neither can annull. But the cession of Louisiana to the United States has none of these features in it. It is a sale and purchase. A sole act which when finished, the parties have no more to do with each other than other buyers and sellers have. It has no future reciprocal consequences (which is one of the marked characters of a Treaty) annexed to it; and the idea of its becoming a supreme law to the parties reciprocally (which is another of the characters of a Treaty) is inapplicable in the present case. There remains nothing for such a law to act upon.

"I love the restriction in the constitution which takes from the Executive the power of making treaties of his own will: and also the clause which requires the consent of two thirds of the Senators, because we cannot be too cautious in involving and entangling ourselves with foreign powers; but I have an equal objection against extending the same power to the senate in cases to which it is not strictly and constitutionally applicable, because it is giving a nullifying power to a minority. Treaties, as already observed, are to have future consequences and whilst they remain, remain always in execution externally as well as internally, and therefore it is better to run the risk of losing a good treaty for the want of two thirds of the senate than be exposed to the danger of ratifying a bad one by a small majority. But in the present case no operation is to follow but what acts itself within our own Territory and under our own laws. We are the sole power concerned after the cession is accepted and the money paid, and therefore the cession is not a Treaty in the constitutional meaning of the word subject to be rejected by a minority in the senate.

"The question whether the cession shall be accepted and the bargain closed by a grant of money for the purpose, (which I take to be the sole question) is a case equally open to both houses of congress, and if there is any distinction of *formal right*, it ought according to the constitution, as a money transaction, to begin in the house of Representatives.

"I suggest these matters that the senate may not be taken unawares, for I think it not improbable that some Fed, who intends to negative the cession, will move to take it up as if it were a Treaty of Alliance or of Navigation and Commerce.

"The object here is an increase of territory for a valuable consideration. It is altogether a home concern—a matter of domestic policy. The only real ratification is the payment of the money, and as all verbal ratification without this goes for nothing, it would be a waste of time and expense to debate on the verbal ratification distinct from the money ratification. The shortest way, as it appears to me, would be to appoint a committee to bring in a report on the President's Message, and for that committee to report a bill for the payment of the money. The french Government, as the seller of the property, will not consider anything ratification but the payment of the money contracted for.

"There is also another point, necessary to be aware of, which is, to accept it in toto. Any alteration or modification in it, or annexed as a condition is so far fatal, that it puts it in the power of the other party to reject the whole and propose new Terms. There can be no such thing as ratifying in part, or with a condition annexed to it and the ratification to be binding. It is still a continuance of the negociation.

"It ought to be presumed that the American ministers have done to the best of their power and procured the best possible terms, and that being immediately on the spot with the other party they were better Judges of the whole, and of what could, or could not be done, than any person at this distance, and unacquainted with many of the circumstances of the case, can possibly be.

"If a treaty, a contract, or a cession be good upon the whole, it is ill policy to hazard the whole, by an experiment to get some trifle in it altered. The right way of proceeding in such case is to make sure of the whole by ratifying it, and then instruct the minister to propose a clause to be added to the Instrument to obtain the amendment or alteration wished for. This was the method Congress took with respect to the Treaty of Commerce with France in 1778. Congress ratified the whole and pro-

posed two new articles which were agreed to by France and added to the Treaty.

"There is according to newspaper account an article which admits french and spanish vessels on the same terms as American vessels. But this does not make it a commercial Treaty. It is only one of the Items in the payment : and it has this advantage, that it joins Spain with France in making the cession and is an encouragement to commerce and new settlers.

"With respect to the purchase, admitting it to be 15 millions dollars, it is an advantageous purchase. The revenue alone purchased as an annuity or rent roll is worth more—at present I suppose the revenue will pay five per cent. for the purchase money.

"I know not if these observations will be of any use to you. I am in a retired village and out of the way of hearing the talk of the great world. But I see that the Feds, at least some of them, are changing their tone and now reprobating the acquisition of Louisiana ; and the only way they can take to lose the affair will be to take it up as they would a Treaty of Commerce and annull it by a Minority ; or entangle it with some condition that will render the ratification of no effect.

" I believe in this state (Jersey) we shall have a majority at the next election. We gain some ground and lose none anywhere. I have half a disposition to visit the Western World next spring and go on to New Orleans. They are a new people and unacquainted with the principles of representative government and I think I could do some good among them.

"As the stage-boat which was to take this letter to the Post-office does not depart till to-morrow, I amuse myself with continuing the subject after I had intended to close it.

"I know little and can learn but little of the extent and present population of Louisiana. After the cession be compleated and the territory annexed to the United States it will, I suppose, be formed into states, one, at least, to begin with. The people, as I have said, are new to us and we to them and a great deal will depend on a right beginning. As they have been transferred backward and forward several times from one European Government to another it is natural to conclude they have no fixed prejudices with respect to foreign attachments, and this puts them in a fit disposition for their new condition. The established religion is roman ; but in what state it is as to exterior ceremonies (such as processions and celebrations), I know not. Had the cession to france continued with her, religion I suppose would have been put on the same footing as it is in that country, and there no ceremonial of religion can appear on the streets or highways ; and the same regulation is particularly necessary now or there will soon be quarrells and tumults between the old settlers and the new. The Yankees will not move out of the road for a little wooden Jesus stuck on a stick and carried in procession nor kneel in the dirt to a wooden Virgin Mary.

As we do not govern the territory as provinces but incorporated as states, religion there must be on the same footing it is here, and Catholics have the same rights as Catholics have with us and no others. As to political condition the Idea proper to be held out is, that we have neither conquered them, nor bought them, but formed a Union with them and they become in consequence of that union a part of the national sovereignty.

"The present Inhabitants and their descendants will be a majority for some time, but new emigrations from the old states and from Europe, and intermarriages, will soon change the first face of things, and it is necessary to have this in mind when the first measures shall be taken. Everything done as an expedient grows worse every day, for in proportion as the mind grows up to the full standard of sight it disclaims the expedient. America had nearly been ruined by expedients in the first stages of the revolution, and perhaps would have been so, had not 'Common Sense' broken the charm and the Declaration of Independence sent it into banishment.

"Yours in friendship

"remember me in
the circle of your friends." "THOMAS PAINE.[1]

Mr. E. M. Woodward, in his account of Bordentown, mentions among the "traditions" of the place, that Paine used to meet a large number of gentlemen at the "Washington House," kept by Debora Applegate, where he conversed freely "with any proper person who approached him."

"Mr. Paine was too much occupied in literary pursuits and writing to spend a great deal of his time here, but he generally paid several visits during the day. His drink was invariably brandy. In walking he was generally absorbed in deep thought, seldom noticed any one as he passed, unless spoken to, and in going from his home to the tavern was frequently observed to cross the street several times. It is stated that several members of the church were turned from their faith by him, and on this account, and the general feeling of the community against him for his opinions on religious subjects, he was by the mass of the people held in odium, which feeling to some extent was extended to Col. Kirkbride."

These "traditions" were recorded in 1876. Paine's "great power of conversation" was remembered. But among the traditions, even of the religious, there is none of any excess in drinking.

Possibly the turning of several church-members from their faith may not have

[1] The original is in possession of Mr. William F. Havermeyer, Jr.

been so much due to Paine as to the parsons, in showing their "religion" as a gorgon turning hearts to stone against a benefactor of mankind. One day Paine went with Colonel Kirkbride to visit Samuel Rogers, the Colonel's brother-in-law, at Bellevue, across the river. As he entered the door Rogers turned his back, refusing his old friend's hand, because it had written the "Age of Reason." Presently Bordentown was placarded with pictures of the Devil flying away with Paine. The pulpits set up a chorus of vituperation. Why should the victim spare the altar on which he is sacrificed, and justice also? Dogma had chosen to grapple with the old man in its own way. That it was able to break a driven leaf Paine could admit as truly as Job; but he could as bravely say: Withdraw thy hand from me, and I will answer thee, or thou shalt answer me! In Paine too it will be proved that such outrages on truth and friendship, on the rights of thought, proceed from no God, but from the destructive forces once personified as the adversary of man.

Early in March Paine visited New York, to see Monroe before his departure for France. He drove with Kirkbride to Trenton; but so furious was the pious mob, he was refused a seat in the Trenton stage. They dined at Government House, but when starting for Brunswick were hooted. These were the people for whose liberties Paine had marched that same road on foot, musket in hand. At Trenton insults were heaped on the man who by camp-fires had written the *Crisis*, which animated the conquerors of the Hessians at that place, in "the times that tried men's souls." These people he helped to make free,—free to cry *Crucify!*

Paine had just written to Jefferson that the Louisianians were "perhaps too much under the influence of their priests to be sufficiently free." Probably the same thought occurred to him about people nearer home, when he presently heard of Colonel Kirkbride's sudden unpopularity, and death. On October 3d Paine lost this faithful friend.[2]

[2] It should be stated that Burlington County,

CHAPTER XLI

NEW ROCHELLE AND THE BONNEVILLES

THE Bonnevilles, with whom Paine had resided in Paris, were completely impoverished after his departure. They resolved to follow Paine to America, depending on his promise of aid should they do so. Foreseeing perils in France, Nicolas, unable himself to leave at once, hurried off his wife and children—Benjamin, Thomas, and Louis. Madame Bonneville would appear to have arrived in August, 1803. I infer this because Paine writes, September 23d, to Jefferson from Stonington, Connecticut; and later letters show that he had been in New York, and afterwards placed Thomas Paine Bonneville with the Rev. Mr. Foster (Universalist) of Stonington for education. Madame Bonneville was placed in his house at Bordentown, where she was to teach French.

At New York, Paine found both religious and political parties sharply divided

in which Bordentown is situated, was preponderantly Federalist, and that Trenton was in the hands of a Federalist mob of young well-to-do rowdies. The editor of the *True American*, a Republican paper to which Paine had contributed, having commented on a Fourth of July orgie of those rowdies in a house associated with the revolution, was set upon with bludgeons on July 12th, and suffered serious injuries. The Grand Jury refused to present the Federalist ruffians, though the evidence was clear, and the mob had free course.

The facts of the Paine mob are these: after dining at Government House, Trenton, Kirkbride applied for a seat on the New York stage for Paine. The owner, Voorhis, cursed Paine as "a deist," and said, "I'll be damned if he shall go in my stage." Another stage-owner also refused, saying, "My stage and horses were once struck by lightning, and I don't want them to suffer again." When Paine and Kirkbride had entered their carriage a mob surrounded them with a drum, playing the "rogue's march." The local reporter (*True American*) says, "Mr. Paine discovered not the least emotion of fear or anger, but calmly observed that such conduct had no tendency to hurt his feelings or injure his fame." The mob then tried to frighten the horse with the drum, and succeeded, but the two gentlemen reached a friend's house in Brunswick in safety. A letter from Trenton had been written to the stage-master there also, to prevent Paine from securing a seat, whether with success does not appear.

over him. At Lovett's Hotel, where he stopped, a large dinner was given him, March 18th, seventy being present. One of the active promoters of this dinner was James Cheetham, editor of the *American Citizen*, who, after seriously injuring Paine by his patronage, became his malignant enemy.

In the summer of 1803 the political atmosphere was in a tempestuous condition, owing to the widespread accusation that Aaron Burr had intrigued with the Federalists against Jefferson to gain the presidency. There was a Society in New York called "Republican Greens," who, on Independence Day, had for a toast "Thomas Paine, the Man of the People," and who seem to have had a piece of music called the "Rights of Man." Paine was also apparently the hero of that day at White Plains, where a vast crowd assembled, "over 1,000," among the toasts being: "Thomas Paine—the bold advocate of rational liberty—the People's friend." He probably reached New York again in August. A letter for "Thomas Payne" is in the advertised Letter-list of August 6th, and in the *American Citizen* (August 9th) are printed (and misprinted) "Lines, extempore, by Thomas Paine, July, 1803."[1] The verses, crudely expressing the contrast between President Jefferson and King George—or Napoleon, it is not clear which,—sufficiently show that Paine's genius was not extempore. His

[1] "Quick as the lighting's vivid flash
   The poet's eye o'er Europe rolls;
   Sees battles rage, hears tempests crash,
   And dims at horror's threatening scowls.

"Mark ambition's ruthless king,
   With crimsoned banners scathe the globe;
   While trailing after conquest's wing,
   Man's festering wounds his demons probe.

"Palléd with streams of reeking gore
   That stain the proud imperial day,
   He turns to view the western shore,
   Where freedom holds her boundless sway.

"'T is here her sage triumphant sways
   An empire in the people's love;
   'T is here the sovereign will obeys
   No king but Him who rules above."

reputation as a patriotic minstrel was high; his " Hail, great Republic," to the tune of " Rule, Britannia," was the established Fourth-of-July song, and it was even sung at the dinner of the American consul in London (Erving) March 4, 1803, the anniversary of Jefferson's election. Possibly the extempore lines were sung on some Fourth-of-July occasion. I find "Thomas Paine" and the "Rights of Man" favorite toasts at republican celebrations in Virginia also at this time. In New York we may discover Paine's coming and going by rancorous paragraphs concerning him in the *Evening Post*.[1] Perhaps the most malignant wrong done Paine in this paper was the adoption of his signature, "Common Sense," by one of its contributors!

The most learned physician in New York, Dr. Nicholas Romayne, invited Paine to dinner, where he was met by John Pintard, and other eminent citizens. Pintard said to Paine: "I have read and re-read your 'Age of Reason,' and any doubts which I before entertained of the truth of revelation have been removed by your logic. Yes, sir, your very arguments against Christianity have convinced me of its truth." "Well then,"

answered Paine, "I may return to my couch to-night with the consolation that I have made at least one Christian."[2] This authentic anecdote is significant. John Pintard, thus outdone by Paine in politeness, founded the Tammany Society, and organized the democratic party. When the "Rights of Man" appeared, the book and its author were the main toasts of the Tammany celebrations; but it was not so after the "Age of Reason" had appeared. For John Pintard was all his life a devotee of Dutch Reformed orthodoxy. Tammany, having begun with the populace, had by this time got up somewhat in society. As a rule the "gentry" were Federalists, though they kept a mob in their back yard to fly at the democrats on occasion. But with Jefferson in the presidential chair, and Clinton vice-president, Tammany was in power. To hold this power Tammany had to court the clergy. So there was no toast to Paine in the Wigwam of 1803.[3]

President Jefferson was very anxious about the constitutional points involved in his purchase of Louisiana, and solicited Paine's views on the whole subject. Paine wrote to him extended communications, among which was the letter of September 23d, from Stonington. The interest of the subject is now hardly sufficient to warrant publication of the whole of this letter, which, however, possesses much interest.

[1] On July 12th the *Evening Post* (edited by William Coleman) tries to unite republicanism and infidelity by stating that Part I. of the "Age of Reason" was sent in MS. to Mr. Fellows of New York, and in the following year Part II. was gratuitously distributed "from what is now the office of the Aurora." On September 24th that paper publishes a poem about Paine, ending :

"And having spent a lengthy life in evil,
Return again unto thy parent Devil ! "

Another paragraph says that Franklin hired Paine in London to come to America and write in favor of the Revolution,—a remarkable example of federalist heredity from "Toryism." On September 27th the paper prints a letter purporting to have been found by a waiter in Lovett's Hotel after Paine's departure,—a long letter to Paine, by some red-revolutionary friend, of course gloating over the exquisite horrors filling Europe in consequence of the "Rights of Man." The pretended letter is dated "Jan. 12, 1803," and signed "J. Oldney." The paper's correspondent pretends to have found out Oldney, and conversed with him. No doubt many simple people believed the whole thing genuine.

[2] Dr. Francis' "Old New York," p. 140.
[3] *The New York Daily Advertiser* published the whole of Part I. of the "Rights of Man" in 1791 (May 6–27), the editor being then John Pintard. At the end of the publication a poetical tribute to Paine was printed. Four of the lines run :

" Rous'd by the reason of his manly page,
Once more shall Paine a listening world
engage ;
From reason's source a bold reform he brings,
By raising up mankind he pulls down
kings."

At the great celebration (October 12, 1792) of the third Centenary of the discovery of America, by the sons of St. Tammany, New York, the first man toasted after Columbus was Paine, and next to Paine "The Rights of Man." They were also extolled in an ode composed for the occasion, and sung.

"Your two favors of the 10th and 18th ult. reached me at this place on the 14th inst.; also one from Mr. Madison. I do not suppose that the framers of the Constitution thought anything about the acquisition of new territory, and even if they did it was prudent to say nothing about it, as it might have suggested to foreign Nations the idea that we contemplated foreign conquest. It appears to me to be one of those cases with which the Constitution had nothing to do, and which can be judged of only by the circumstances of the times when such a case shall occur. The Constitution could not foresee that Spain would cede Louisiana to France or to England, and therefore it could not determine what our conduct should be in consequence of such an event. The cession makes no alteration in the Constitution; it only extends the principles of it over a larger territory, and this certainly is within the morality of the Constitution, and not contrary to, nor beyond, the expression or intention of any of its articles. . . . Were a question to arise it would apply, not to the Cession, because it violates no article of the Constitution, but to Ross and Morris's motion. The Constitution empowers Congress to *declare* war, but to make war without declaring it is anti-constitutional. It is like attacking an unarmed man in the dark. There is also another reason why no such question should arise. The english Government is but in a tottering condition and if Bonaparte succeeds, that Government will break up. In that case it is not improbable we may obtain Canada, and I think that Bermuda ought to belong to the United States. In its present condition it is a nest for piratical privateers. This is not a subject to be spoken of, but it may be proper to have it in mind.

"The latest news we have from Europe in this place is the insurrection in Dublin. It is a disheartening circumstance to the english Government, as they are now putting arms into the hands of people who but a few weeks before they would have hung had they found a pike in their possession. I think the probability is in favor of the descent [on England by Bonaparte] . . .

"I shall be employed the ensuing Winter in cutting two or three thousand Cords of Wood on my farm at New Rochelle for the New York market distant twenty miles by water. The Wood is worth 3½ dollars per load as it stands. This will furnish me with ready money, and I shall then be ready for whatever may present itself of most importance next spring. I had intended to build myself a house to my own taste, and a workshop for my mechanical operations, and make a collection, as authors say, of my works, which with what I have in manuscript will make four, or five octavo volumes, and publish them by subscription, but the prospects that are now opening with respect to England hold me in suspence.

"It has been customary in a President's discourse to say something about religion. I offer you a thought on this subject. The word, religion, used as a word *en masse* has no application to a country like America. In catholic countries it would mean exclusively the religion of the romish church: with the Jews, the jewish religion; in England, the protestant religion or in the sense of the english church, the established religion; with the Deists it would mean Deism; with the Turks, Mahometism &c., &c., As well as I recollect it is *Lego, Relego, Relegio, Religion,* that is to say, tied or bound by an oath or obligation. The french use the word properly; when a woman enters a convent, she is called a novitiate; when she takes the oath, she is a *religieuse,* that is, she is bound by an oath. Now all that we have to do, as a Government with the word religion, in this country, is with the civil rights of it, and not at all with its *creeds.* Instead therefore of using the word religion, as a word *en masse,* as if it meant a creed, it would be better to speak only of its civil rights; *that all denominations of religion are equally protected, that none are dominant, none inferior, that the rights of conscience are equal to every denomination and to every individual and that it is the duty of Government to preserve this equality of conscientious rights.* A man cannot be called a hypocrite for defending the civil rights of religion, but he may be suspected of insincerity in defending its creeds.

"I suppose you will find it proper to take notice of the impressment of American seamen by the Captains of British vessels, and procure a list of such captains and report them to their government. This pretence of searching for british seamen is a new pretence for visiting and searching American vessels. . . .

"I am passing some time at this place at the house of a friend till the wood cutting time comes on, and I shall engage some cutters here and then return to New Rochelle. I wrote to Mr. Madison concerning the report that the british Government had cautioned ours not to pay the purchase money for Louisiana, as they intended to take it for themselves. I have received his [negative] answer, and I pray you make him my compliments.

"We are still afflicted with the yellow fever, and the Doctors are disputing whether it is an imported or a domestic disease. Would it not be a good measure to prohibit the arrival of all vessels from the West Indies from the last of June to the middle of October. If this was done this session of Congress, and we escaped the fever next summer, we should always know how to escape it. I question if performing quarantine is a sufficient guard. The disease may be in the cargo, especially that part which is barrelled up, and not in the persons on board, and when that cargo is opened on our wharfs, the hot steaming air in contact with the ground imbibes the infection. I can conceive that infected air can be barrelled up, not in a hogshead of rum, nor perhaps sucre, but in a barrel of coffee. I am badly off in this place for pen and Ink, and short of paper. I heard yesterday from Boston that our old friend

L

S. Adams was at the point of death. Accept my best wishes."

When Madame Bonneville left France it was understood that her husband would soon follow, but he did not come, nor was any letter received from him. This was probably the most important allusion in a letter of Paine, dated New York, March 1, 1804, to Citizen Skipwith, Agent Commercial d'Amerique, Paris."

"DEAR FRIEND—I have just a moment to write you a line by a friend who is on the point of sailing for Bordeaux. The Republican interest is now compleatly triumphant. The change within this last year has been great. We have now 14 States out of 17,—N. Hampshire, Mass. and Connecticut stand out. I much question if any person will be started against Mr. Jefferson. Burr is rejected for the vice-presidency; he is now putting up for Governor of N. York. Mr. Clinton will be run for vice-president. Morgan Lewis, Chief Justice of the State of N. Y., is the Republican candidate for Governor of that State.

"I have not received a line from Paris, except a letter from Este, since I left it. We have now been nearly 80 days without news from Europe. What is Barlow about? I have not heard anything from him except that he is *always* coming. What is Bonneville about? Not a line has been received from him. Respectful compliments to Mr. Livingston and family. Yours in friendship."

Madame Bonneville, unable to speak English, found Bordentown dull, and soon turned up in New York. She ordered rooms in Wilburn's boarding-house, where Paine was lodging, and the author found the situation rather complicated. The family was absolutely without means of their own, and Paine, who had given them a comfortable home at Bordentown, was annoyed by their coming on to New York. Anxiety is shown in the following letter written at 16 Gold St., New York, March 24th, to "Mr. Hyer, Bordenton, N. J."

"DEAR SIR,—I received your letter by Mr. Nixon, and also a former letter, but I have been so unwell this winter with a fit of gout, tho' not so bad as I had at Bordenton about twenty years ago, that I could not write, and after I got better I got a fall on the ice in the garden where I lodge that threw me back for above a month. I was obliged to get a person to copy off the letter to the people of England, published in the Aurora, March 7th, as I dictated it verbally, for all the time my complaint continued. My health and spirits were as good as ever. It was my intention to have cut a large quantity of wood for the New York market, and in that case you would have had the money directly, but this accident and the gout prevented my doing anything. I shall now have to take up some money upon it, which I shall do by the first of May to put Mrs. Bonneville into business, and I shall then discharge her bill. In the mean time I wish you to receive a quarter's rent due on the 1st of April from Mrs. Richardson, at $25 per ann., and to call on Mrs. Read for 40 or 50 dollars, or what you can get, and to give a receipt in my name. Col. Kirkbride should have discharged your bill, it was what he engaged to do. Mrs. Wharton owes for the rent of the house while she lived in it, unless Col. Kirkbride has taken it into his accounts. Samuel Hileyar owes me 84 dollars lent him in hard money. Mr. Nixon spake to me about hiring my house, but as I did not know if Mrs. Richardson intended to stay in it or quit it I could give no positive answer, but said I would write to you about it. Israel Butler also writes me about taking at the same rent as Richardson pays. I will be obliged to you to let the house as you may judge best. I shall make a visit to Bordenton in the spring, and I shall call at your house first.

"There have been several arrivals here in short passages from England. P. Porcupine, I see, is become the panegyrist of Bonaparte. You will see it in the Aurora of March 19th, and also the message of Bonaparte to the french legislature. It is a good thing.

"Mrs. Bonneville sends her compliments. She would have wrote, but she cannot yet venture to write in English. I congratulate you on your new appointment.

"Yours in friendship."[1]

Paine's letter alluded to was printed in the *Aurora* with the following note:

"TO THE EDITOR.—As the good sense of the people in their elections has now put the affairs of America in a prosperous condition at home and abroad, there is nothing immediately important for the subject of a letter. I therefore send you a piece on another subject."

The piece presently appeared as a pamphlet of sixteen pages with the following title: "Thomas Paine to the People of England, on the Invasion of England. Philadelphia: Printed at the Temple of Reason Press, Arch Street, 1804." Once more the hope had risen in Paine's breast that Napoleon was to

[1] I am indebted for this letter to the N. Y. Hist. Society, which owns the original.

turn liberator, and that England was to be set free.

"If the invasion succeed I hope Bonaparte will remember that this war has not been provoked by the people. It is altogether the act of the government without their consent or knowledge; and though the late peace appears to have been insidious from the first, on the part of the government, it was received by the people with a sincerity of joy."

He still hopes that the English people may be able to end the trouble peacefully, by compelling Parliament to fulfil the Treaty of Amiens, naïvely informing them that "a Treaty ought to be fulfilled." The following passages may be quoted:

"In casting my eye over England and America, and comparing them together, the difference is very striking. The two countries were created by the same power, and peopled from the same stock. What then has caused the difference? Have those who emigrated to America improved, or those whom they left behind degenerated? . . . We see America flourishing in peace, cultivating friendship with all nations, and reducing her public debt and taxes, incurred by the revolution. On the contrary we see England almost perpetually in war, or warlike disputes, and her debt and taxes continually increasing. Could we suppose a stranger, who knew nothing of the origin of the two nations, he would from observation conclude that America was the old country, experienced and sage, and England the new, eccentric and wild. Scarcely had England drawn home her troops from America, after the revolutionary war, than she was on the point of plunging herself into a war with Holland, on account of the Stadtholder; then with Russia; then with Spain on account of the Nootka catskins; and actually with France to prevent her revolution. Scarcely had she made peace with France, and before she had fulfilled her own part of the Treaty, than she declared war again, to avoid fulfilling the Treaty. In her Treaty of peace with America, she engaged to evacuate the western posts within six months; but, having obtained peace, she refused to fulfil the conditions, and kept possession of the posts, and embroiled herself in an Indian war.[1] In her Treaty of peace with France, she engaged to evacuate Malta within three months; but, having obtained peace, she refused to evacuate Malta, and began a new war."

Paine points out that the failure of the French Revolution was due to "the provocative interference of foreign

[1] Paine's case is not quite sound at this point. The Americans had not, on their side, fulfilled the condition of paying their English debts.

powers, of which Pitt was the principal and vindictive agent," and affirms the success of representative government in the United States after thirty years' trial.

"The people of England have now two revolutions before them,—the one as an example, the other as a warning. Their own wisdom will direct them what to choose and what to avoid; and in everything which regards their happiness, combined with the common good of mankind, I wish them honor and success."

During this summer, Paine wrote a brilliant paper on a memorial sent to Congress from the French inhabitants of Louisiana. They demanded immediate admission to equal Statehood, also the right to continue the importation of negro slaves. Paine reminds the memorialists of the "mischief caused in France by the possession of power before they understood principles." After explaining their position, and the freedom they have acquired by the merits of others, he points out their ignorance of human "rights" as shown in their guilty notion that to enslave others is among them.

"Dare you put up a petition to Heaven for such a power, without fearing to be struck from the earth by its justice? Why, then, do you ask it of man against man? Do you want to renew in Louisiana the horrors of Domingo?"

This article (dated September 22d) produced great effect. John Randolph of Roanoke, in a letter to Albert Gallatin (October 14th), advises "the printing of . . . thousand copies of Tom Paine's answer to their remonstrance, and transmitting them by as many thousand troops, who can speak a language perfectly intelligible to the people of Louisiana, whatever that of their governor may be."

Nicolas Bonneville still giving no sign, and Madame being uneconomical in her notions of money, Paine thought it necessary—morally and financially—to let it be known that he was not responsible for her debts. When, therefore, Wilburn applied to him for her board ($35), Paine declined to pay, and was sued. Paine pleaded *non assumpsit*, and, after gaining the case, paid Wilburn the money.

It presently turned out that the surveillance of Nicolas Bonneville did not permit him to leave France, and, as he was not permitted to resume his journal or publications, he could neither join his family nor assist them.

Paine now resolved to reside on his farm. The following note was written to Col. John Fellows. It is dated at New Rochelle, July 9th :

"FELLOW CITIZEN,—As the weather is now getting hot at New York, and the people begin to get out of town, you may as well come up here and help me settle my accounts with the man who lives on the place. You will be able to do this better than I shall, and in the mean time I can go on with my literary works, without having my mind taken off by affairs of a different kind. I have received a packet from Governor Clinton, enclosing what I wrote for. If you come up by the stage you will stop at the post-office, and they will direct you the way to the farm. It is only a pleasant walk. I send a price for the Prospect ; if the plan mentioned in it is pursued, it will open a way to enlarge and give establishment to the deistical church ; but of this and some other things we will talk when you come up, and the sooner the better. Yours in friendship."

Paine was presently enjoying himself on his farm at New Rochelle, and Madame Bonneville began to keep house for him.

"It is a pleasant and healthy situation [he wrote to Jefferson somewhat later], commanding a prospect always green and peaceable, as New Rochelle produces a great deal of grass and hay. The farm contains three hundred acres, about one hundred of which is meadow land, one hundred grazing and village land, and the remainder woodland. It is an oblong about a mile and a half in length. I have sold off sixty-one acres and a half for four thousand and twenty dollars. With this money I shall improve the other part, and build an addition 34 feet by 32 to the present dwelling."

He goes on into an architectural description, with drawings, of the arched roof he intends to build, the present form of roof being "unpleasing to the eye." He also draws an oak floor such as they make in Paris, which he means to imitate.

With a black cook, Rachel Gidney, the family seemed to be getting on with fair comfort ; but on Christmas Eve an event occurred which came near bringing Paine's plans to an abrupt conclusion.

This is related in a letter to William Carver, New York, dated January 16th, at New Rochelle.

"ESTEEMED FRIEND,—I have recd. two letters from you, one giving an account of your taking Thomas to Mr. Foster [1]—the other dated Jany. 12—I did not answer the first because I hoped to see you the next Saturday or the Saturday after. What you heard of a gun being fired into the room is true—Robert and Rachel were both gone out to keep Christmas Eve and about eight o'clock at Night the gun were fired. I ran immediately out, one of Mr. Dean's boys with me, but the person that had done it was gone. I directly suspected who it was, and I halloed to him by name, that *he was discovered*. I did this that the party who fired might know I was on the watch. I cannot find any ball, but whatever the gun was charged with passed through about three or four inches below the window making a hole large enough to a finger to go through—the muzzle must have been very near as the place is black with the powder, and the glass of the window is shattered to pieces. Mr. Shute, after examining the place and getting what information could be had, issued a warrant to take up Derrick, and after examination committed him.

"He is now on bail (five hundred dollars) to take his trial at the supreme Court in May next. Derrick owes me forty-eight dollars for which I have his note, and he was to work it out in making stone fence which he has not even begun, and besides this I have had to pay forty-two pounds eleven shillings for which I had passed my word for him at Mr. Pelton's store. Derrick borrowed the Gun under pretence of giving Mrs. Bayeaux a Christmas Gun. He was with Purdy about two hours before the attack on the house was made and he came from thence to Dean's half drunk and brought with him a bottle of Rum, and Purdy was with him when he was taken up.

"I am exceedingly well in health and shall always be glad to see you. Hubbs tells me that your horse is getting better. Mrs. Shute sent for the horse and took him when the first snow came but he leaped the fences and came back. Hubbs says there is a bone broke. If this be the case I suppose he has broke or cracked it in leaping a fence when he was lame on the other hind leg, and hung with his hind legs in the fence. I am glad to hear what you tell me of Thomas. He shall not want for anything that is necessary if he be a good boy for he has no friend but me. You have not given me any account about the meeting house. Remember me to our Friends. Yours in friendship." [2]

---

[1] Thomas Bonneville, Paine's godson, at school in Stonington.

[2] I am indebted for this letter to Dr. Clair J. Grece, of England, whose uncle, Daniel Constable, probably got it from Carver.

The window of the room said to have been Paine's study is close to the ground, and it is marvellous that he was not murdered.[1]

The most momentous change which had come over America during Paine's absence was the pro-slavery reaction. This had set in with the first Congress. An effort was made by the Virginia representatives to check the slave traffic by imposing a duty of $10 on each negro imported, but was defeated by an alliance of members from more Southern States and professedly antislavery men of the North. The Southern leader in this first victory of slavery in Congress was Major Jackson of Georgia, who defended the institution as scriptural and civilizing. The aged Dr. Franklin published (*Federal Gazette*, March 25, 1790) a parody of Jackson's speech, purporting to be a speech uttered in 1687 by a Divan of Algiers in defence of piracy and slavery, against a sect of Erika, or Purists, who had petitioned for their suppression. Franklin was now president of the American Antislavery Society, founded in Philadelphia in 1775, five weeks after the appearance of Paine's scheme of emancipation (March 8, 1775). Dr. Rush was also active in the cause, and to him Paine wrote (March 16, 1790) the letter on the subject elsewhere quoted (p. 111). This letter was published by Rush (*Columbian Magazine*, vol. ii., p. 318) while the country was still agitated by the debate which was going on in Congress at the time when it was written, on a petition of the Antislavery Society, signed by Franklin, —his last public act. Franklin died

April 17, 1790, twenty-five days after the close of the debate, in which he was bitterly denounced by the proslavery party. Washington had pronounced the petition "inopportune,"—his presidential mansion in New York was a few steps from the slave-market,—Jefferson (now Secretary of State) had no word to say for it, Madison had smoothed over the matter by a compromise. Thenceforth slavery had become a suppressed subject, and the slave trade, whenever broached in Congress, had maintained its immunity. In 1803, even under Jefferson's administration, the negroes fleeing from oppression in Domingo were forbidden asylum in America, because it was feared that they would incite servile insurrections. That the United States, under presidency of Jefferson, should stand aloof from the struggle of the negroes in Domingo for liberty, cut Paine to the heart. Unperturbed by the attempt made on his own life a few days before, he wrote to Jefferson on New Year's Day, 1805, (from New Rochelle,) what may be regarded as an appeal :

"DEAR SIR,—I have some thoughts of coming to Washington this winter, as I may as well spend a part of it there as elsewhere. But lest bad roads or any other circumstance should prevent me I suggest a thought for your consideration, and I shall be glad if in this case, as in that of Louisiana, we may happen to think alike without knowing what each other had thought of.

"The affair of Domingo will cause some trouble in either of the cases in which it now stands. If armed merchantmen·force their way through the blockading fleet it will embarrass us with the french Government ; and, on the other hand, if the people of Domingo think that we show a partiality to the french injurious to them there is danger they will turn Pirates upon us, and become more injurious on account of vicinity than the barbary powers, and England will encourage it, as she encourages the Indians. Domingo is lost to France either as to the Government or the possession of it. But if a way could be found out to bring about a peace between france and Domingo through the mediation, and under the guarantee of the United States, it would be beneficial to all parties, and give us a great commercial and political standing, not only with the present people of Domingo but with the West Indies generally. And when we have gained their confidence by acts of justice and friendship, they will listen to our advice in matters of Civilization and Government, and prevent the danger

---

[1] Derrick (or Dederick) appears by the records at White Plains to have been brought up for trial May 19, 1806, and to have been recognized in the sum of $500 for his appearance at the next Court of Oyer and Terminer and General Gaol Delivery, and in the meantime to keep the peace towards the People, and especially towards Thomas Payne (*sic*). Paine, Christopher Hubbs, and Andrew A. Dean were recognized in $50 to appear and give evidence against Derrick. Nothing further appears in the records (examined for me by Mr. B. D. Washburn up to 1810). It is pretty certain that Paine did not press the charge.

of their becoming pirates, which I think they will be, if driven to desperation.

"The United States is the only power that can undertake a measure of this kind. She is now the Parent of the Western world, and her knowledge of the local circumstances of it gives her an advantage in a matter of this kind superior to any European Nation. She is enabled by situation, and grow[ing] importance to become a guarantee, and to see, as far as her advice and influence can operate, that the conditions on the part of Domingo be fulfilled. It is also a measure that accords with the humanity of her principles, with her policy, and her commercial interest.

"All that Domingo wants of France, is, that France agree to let her alone, and withdraw her forces by sea and land; and in return for this Domingo to give her a monopoly of her commerce for a term of years,—that is, to import from France all the utensils and manufactures she may have occasion to use or consume (except such as she can more conveniently procure from the manufactories of the United States), and to pay for them in produce. France will gain more by this than she can expect to do even by a conquest of the Island, and the advantage to America will be that she will become the carrier of both, at least during the present war.

"There was considerable dislike in Paris against the Expedition to Domingo; and the events that have since taken place were then often predicted. The opinion that generally prevailed at that time was that the commerce of the Island was better than the conquest of it,— that the conquest could not be accomplished without destroying the negroes, and in that case the Island would be of no value.

"I think it might be signified to the french Government, yourself is the best judge of the means, that the United States are disposed to undertake an accommodation so as to put an end to this otherwise endless slaughter on both sides, and to procure to France the best advantages in point of commerce that the state of things will admit of. Such an offer, whether accepted or not, cannot but be well received, and may lead to a good end.

"There is now a fine snow, and if it continues I intend to set off for Philadelphia in about eight days, and from thence to Washington. I congratulate your constituents on the success of the election for President and Vice-President.

"Yours in friendship,
"THOMAS PAINE."

The journey to Washington was given up, and Paine had to content himself with his pen. He took in several newspapers, and was as keenly alive as ever to the movements of the world. His chief anxiety was lest some concession might be made to the Louisianians about the slave trade, that region being an emporium of the traffic which grew more enterprising and brutal as its term was at hand. Much was said of the great need of the newly acquired region for more laborers, and it was known that Jefferson was by no means so severe in his opposition to slavery as he was once supposed to be. The President repeatedly invited Paine's views, and they were given fully and freely. The following extracts are from a letter dated New York, January 25, 1805:

"Mr. Levy Lincoln and Mr. Wingate called on me at N. York, where I happened to be when they arrived on their Journey from Washington to the Eastward: I find by Mr. Lincoln that the Louisiana Memorialists will have to return as they came and the more decisively Congress put an end to this business the better. The Cession of Louisiana is a great acquisition; but great as it is it would be an incumbrance on the Union were the prayer of the petitioners to be granted, nor would the lands be worth settling if the settlers are to be under a french jurisdiction. . . . When the emigrations from the United States into Louisiana become equal to the number of french inhabitants it may then be proper and right to erect such part where such equality exists into a constitutional state; but to do it now would be sending the american settlers into exile. . . . For my own part, I wish the name of Louisiana to be lost, and this may in a great measure be done by giving names to the new states that will serve as descriptive of their situation or condition. France lost the names and almost the remembrance of provinces by dividing them into departments with appropriate names.

"Next to the acquisition of the territory and the Government of it is that of settling it. The people of the Eastern States are the best settlers of a new country, and of people from abroad the German Peasantry are the best. The Irish in general are generous and dissolute. The Scotch turn their attention to traffic, and the English to manufactures. These people are more fitted to live in cities than to be cultivators of new lands. I know not, if in Virginia they are much acquainted with the importation of German redemptioners, that is, servants indented for a term of years. The best farmers in Pennsylvania are those who came over in this manner or the descendants of them. The price before the war used to be twenty pounds pennsylvania currency for an indented servant for four years, that is, the ship-owner, got twenty pounds per head passage money, so that upon two hundred persons he would receive after their arrival four thousand pounds paid by the persons who purchased the time of their indentures which was generally four years. These would be the best people, of foreigners, to bring into Louisiana— because they would grow to be citizens. Whereas bringing poor negroes to work the lands in a state of slavery and wretchedness, is, besides the immorality of it, the certain way of preventing population and consequently of preventing revenue. I question if the revenue arising from ten Negroes in the consumption of imported articles is equal to that of one white citizen. In the articles of dress and of the table it is almost impossible to make a comparison.

"These matters though they do not belong to the class of principles are proper subjects for the consideration of Government; and it is always fortunate when the interests of Government and that of humanity act unitedly. But I much doubt if the Germans would come to be under a french Jurisdiction. Congress must frame the laws under which they are to serve out their time; after which Congress might give them a few acres of land to begin with for themselves and they would soon be able to buy more. I am inclined to believe that by adopting this method the Country will be more peopled in about twenty years from the present time than it has been in all the times of the french and Spaniards. Spain, I believe, held it chiefly as a barrier to her dominions in Mexico, and the less it was improved the better it agreed with that policy; and as to france she never shewed any great disposition or gave any great encouragement to colonizing. It is chiefly small countries, that are straitened for room at home, like Holland and England, that go in quest of foreign settlements. . . .

"I have again seen and talked with the gentleman from Hamburg. He tells me that some Vessels under pretence of shipping persons to America carried them to England to serve as soldiers and sailors. He tells me he has the Edict or Proclamation of the Senate of Hamburg forbidding persons shipping themselves without the consent of the Senate, and that he will give me a copy of it, which if he does soon enough I will send with this letter. He says that the American Consul has been spoken to respecting this kidnapping business under American pretences, but that he says he has no authority to interfere. The German members of Congress, or the Philadelphia merchants or ship-owners who have been in the practice of importing German redemptioners, can give you better information respecting the business of importation than I can. But the redemptioners thus imported must be at the charge of the Captain or shipowner till their time is sold. Some of the quaker Merchants of Philadelphia went a great deal into the importation of German servants or redemptioners. It agreed with the morality of their principles that of bettering people's condition, and to put an end to the practice of importing slaves. I think it not an unreasonable estimation to suppose that the population of Louisiana may be increased ten thousand souls every year. What retards the settlement of it is the want of laborers, and until laborers can be had the sale of the lands will be slow. Were I twenty years younger, and my name and reputation as well known in European countries as it is now, I would contract for a quantity of land in Louisiana and go to Europe and bring over settlers. . . .

"It is probable that towards the close of the session I may make an excursion to Washington. The piece on Gouverneur Morris's Oration on Hamilton and that on the Louisiana Memorial are the last I have published; and as every thing of public affairs is now on a good ground I shall do as I did after the War, remain a quiet spectator and attend now to my own affairs.

"I intend making a collection of all the pieces I have published, beginning with Common Sense, and of what I have by me in manuscript, and publish them by subscription. I have deferred doing this till the presidential election should be over, but I believe there was not much occasion for that caution. There is more hypocrisy than bigotry in America. When I was in Connecticut the summer before last, I fell in company with some Baptists among whom were three Ministers. The conversation turned on the election for President, and one of them who appeared to be a leading man said 'They cry out against Mr. Jefferson because, they say he is a Deist. Well, a Deist may be a good man, and if he think it right, it is right to him. For my own part,' said he, 'I had rather vote for a Deist than for a blue-skin presbyterian.' 'You judge right,' said I, 'for a man that is not of any of the sectaries will hold the balance even between all; but give power to a bigot of any sectary and he will use it to the oppression of the rest, as the blue-skins do in connection.' They all agree in this sentiment, and I have always found it assented to in any company I have had occasion to use it.

"I judge the collection I speak of will make five volumes octavo of four hundred pages each at two dollars a volume to be paid on delivery; and as they will be delivered separately, as fast as they can be printed and bound the subscribers may stop when they please. The three first volumes will be political and each piece will be accompanied with an account of the state of affairs at the time it was written, whether in America, france, or England, which will also shew the occasion of writing it. The first expression in the first No· of the Crisis published the 19th December '76 is '*These are the times that try men's souls.*' It is therefore necessary as explanatory to the expression in all future times to shew what those times were. The two last volumes will be theological and those who do not chuse to take them may let them alone. They will have the right to do so, by the conditions of the subscription. I shall also make a miscellaneous Volume of correspondence, Essays, and some pieces of Poetry, which I believe will have some claim to originality. . . .

"I find by the Captain [from New Orleans] above mentioned that several Liverpool ships have been at New Orleans. It is chiefly the people of Liverpool that employ themselves in the slave trade and they bring cargoes of those unfortunate Negroes to take back in return the hard money and the produce of the country. Had I the command of the elements I would blast Liverpool with fire and brimstone. It is the Sodom and Gomorrah of brutality. . . .

"I recollect when in France that you spoke of a plan of making the Negroes tenants on a plantation, that is, alotting each Negroe family a quantity of land for which they were to pay to the owner a certain quantity of produce. I think that numbers of our free negroes might be provided for in this manner in Louisiana. The best way that occurs to me is for Congress to give them their passage to New Orleans, then for them to hire themselves out to the planters for one or two years ; they would by this means learn plantation business, after which to place them on a tract of land as before mentioned. A great many good things may now be done ; and I please myself with the idea of suggesting my thoughts to you.

"Old Captain Landais who lives at Brooklyn on Long Island opposite New York calls sometimes to see me. I knew him in Paris. He is a very respectable old man. I wish something had been done for him in Congress on his petition ; for I think something is due to him, nor do I see how the Statute of limitation can consistently apply to him. The law in John Adams's administration, which cut off all commerce and communication with france, cut him off from the chance of coming to America to put in his claim. I suppose that the claims of some of our merchants on England, france and Spain is more than 6 or 7 years standing yet no law of limitation, that I know of take place between nations or between individuals of different nations. I consider a statute of limitation to be a domestic law, and can only have a domestic opperation. Dr. Miller, one of the New York Senators in Congress, knows Landais and can give you an account of him.

"Concerning my former letter, on Domingo, I intended had I come to Washington to have talked with Pichon about it—if you had approved that method, for it can only be brought forward in an indirect way. The two *Emperors* are at too great a distance in objects and in colour to have any intercourse but by Fire and Sword, yet something I think might be done. It is time I should close this long epistle. Yours in friendship."

Paine made but a brief stay in New York (where he boarded with William Carver). His next letter (April 22d) is from New Rochelle, written to John Fellows, an auctioneer in New York City, one of his most faithful friends.

"CITIZEN : I send this by the N. Rochelle boat and have desired the boatman to call on you with it. He is to bring up Bebia and Thomas and I will be obliged to you to see them safe on board. The boat will leave N. Y. on friday.

"I have left my pen knife at Carver's. It is, I believe, in the writing desk. It is a small french pen knife that slides into the handle. I wish Carver would look behind the chest in-the bed room. I miss some papers that I suppose are fallen down there. The boys will bring up with them one pair of the blankets Mrs. Bonneville took down and also my best blanket which is at Carver's.—I send enclosed three dollars for a ream of writing paper and one dollar for some letter paper, and porterage to the boat. I wish you to give the boys some good advice when you go with them, and tell them that the better they behave the better it will be for them. I am now their only dependance, and they ought to know it. Yours in friendship."

"All my Nos. of the Prospect, while I was at Carver's, are left there. The boys can bring them. I have received no No. since I came to New Rochelle." [1]

The Thomas mentioned in this letter was Paine's godson, and "Bebia" was Benjamin,—the late Brigadier-General Bonneville, U.S.A. The third son, Louis, had been sent to his father in France. The *Prospect* was Elihu Palmer's rationalistic paper.

Early in this year a series of charges affecting Jefferson's public and private character were published by one Hulbert, on the authority of Thomas Turner of Virginia. Beginning with an old charge of cowardice, while Governor (of which Jefferson had been acquitted by the Legislature of Virginia), the accusation proceeded to instances of immorality, persons and places being named. The following letter from New Rochelle, July 19th, to John Fellows enclosed Paine's reply, which appeared in the *American Citizen*, July 23d and 24th :

"CITIZEN—I inclose you two pieces for Cheetham's paper, which I wish you to give to him yourself. He may publish one No. in one daily paper, and the other number in the next daily paper, and then both in his country paper. There has been a great deal of anonimous abuse thrown out in the federal papers against Mr. Jefferson, but until some names could be got hold of it was fighting the air to take any notice of them. We have now got hold of two names, your townsman Hulbert, the hypocritical Infidel of Sheffield, and Thomas Turner of Virginia, his correspondent. I have already given Hulbert a basting with my name

---

[1] This letter is in the possession of Mr. Grenville Kane, Tuxedo, N. Y.

to it, because he made use of my name in his speech in the Mass. legislature. Turner has not given me the same cause in the letter he wrote (and evidently) to Hulbert, and which Hulbert, (for it could be no other person) has published in the Repertory to vindicate himself. Turner has detailed his charges against Mr. Jefferson, and I have taken them up one by one, which is the first time the opportunity has offered for doing it; for before this it was promiscuous abuse. I have not signed it either with my name or signature (Common Sense) because I found myself obliged, in order to make such scoundrels feel a little smart, to go somewhat out of my usual manner of writing, but there are some sentiments and some expressions that will be supposed to be in my stile, and I have no objection to that supposition, but I do not wish Mr. Jefferson to be *obliged* to know it is from me.

"Since receiving your letter, which contained no direct information of any thing I wrote to you about, I have written myself to Mr. Barrett accompanied with a piece for the editor of the Baltimore Evening Post, who is an acquaintance of his, but I have received no answer from Mr. B., neither has the piece been published in the Evening Post. I will be obliged to you to call on him & to inform me about it. You did not tell me if you called upon Foster; but at any rate do not delay the enclosed.—I do not trouble you with any messages or compliments, for you never deliver any. Yours in friendship."[1]

By a minute comparison of the two alleged specifications of immorality, Paine proved that one was intrinsically absurd, and the other without trustworthy testimony. As for the charge of cowardice, Paine contended that it was the duty of a civil magistrate to move out of danger, as Congress had done in the Revolution. The article was signed "A Spark from the Altar of '76," but the writer was easily recognized. The service thus done Jefferson was greater than can now be easily realized.

Another paper by Paine was on "Constitutions, Governments, and Charters." It was an argument to prove the unconstitutionality in New York of the power assumed by the legislature to grant charters. This defeated the object of annual elections, by placing the act of one legislature beyond the reach of its successor. He proposes that all matters of "extra-

[1] I am indebted for this letter to Mr. John M. Robertson, editor of the *National Reformer*, London.

ordinary legislation," such as those involving grants of land and incorporations of companies, shall be passed only by a legislature succeeding the one in which it was proposed.

"Had such an article been originally in the Constitution [of New York] the bribery and corruption employed to seduce and manage the members of the late legislature, in the affair of the Merchants' Bank, could not have taken place. It would not have been worth while to bribe men to do what they had no power of doing."

Madame Bonneville hated country life, and insisted on going to New York. Paine was not sorry to have her leave, as she could not yet talk English, and did not appreciate Paine's idea of plain living and high thinking. She apparently had a notion that Paine had a mint of money, and, like so many others, might have attributed to parsimony efforts the unpaid author was making to save enough to give her children, practically fatherless, some start in life. The philosophic solitude in which he was left at New Rochelle is described in a letter (July 31st) to John Fellows, in New York.

"It is certainly best that Mrs. Bonneville go into some family as a teacher, for she has not the least talent of managing affairs for herself. She may send Bebia up to me. I will take care of him for his own sake and his father's, but that is all I have to say. . . . I am master of an empty house, or nearly so. I have six chairs and a table, a straw-bed, a feather-bed, and a bag of straw for Thomas, a tea kettle, an iron pot, an iron baking pan, a frying pan, a gridiron, cups, saucers, plates and dishes, knives and forks, two candlesticks and a pair of snuffers. I have a pair of fine oxen and an ox-cart, a good horse, a Chair, and a one-horse cart; a cow, and a sow and 9 pigs. When you come you must take such fare as you meet with, for I live upon tea, milk, fruit-pies, plain dumplins, and a piece of meat when I get it; but I live with that retirement and quiet that suit me. Mrs. Bonneville was an encumbrance upon me all the while she was here, for she would not do anything, not even make an apple dumplin for her own children. If you cannot make yourself up a straw bed, I can let you have blankets, and you will have no occasion to go over to the tavern to sleep.

"As I do not see any federal papers, except by accident, I know not if they have attempted any remarks or criticisms on my Eighth Letter, [or] the piece on Constitutional Governments and Charters, the two numbers on Turner's letter, and also the piece on Hulbert. As to anonymous paragraphs, it is not worth noticing them. I consider the generality of such editors only as a part of their press, and let them pass. —I want to come to Morrisania, and it is probable I may come on to N. Y., but I wish you to answer this letter first.—Yours in friendship." [1]

It must not be supposed from what Paine says of Madame Bonneville that there was anything acrimonious in their relations. She was thirty-one years younger than Paine, fond of the world, handsome. The old gentleman, all day occupied with writing, could give her little companionship, even if he could have conversed in French. But he indulged her in every way, gave her more money than he could afford, devoted his ever decreasing means to her family. She had boundless reverence for him, but, as we have seen, had no taste for country life. Probably, too, after Dederick's attempt on Paine's life she became nervous in the lonely house. So she had gone to New York, where she presently found good occupation as a teacher of French in several families. Her sons, however, were fond of New Rochelle, and of Paine, who had a knack of amusing children, and never failed to win their affection. [2]

The spring of 1805 at New Rochelle was a pleasant one for Paine. He wrote his last political pamphlet, which was printed by Duane, Philadelphia, with the title: "Thomas Paine to the Citizens of Pennsylvania, on the Proposal for Calling a Convention." It opens with a reference to his former life and work in Philadelphia. "Removed as I now am from the place, and detached from everything of personal party, I address

[1] I am indebted for an exact copy of the letter from which this is extracted to Dr. Garnett of the British Museum, though it is not in that institution.

[2] In the Tarrytown *Argus*, October 18, 1890, appeared an interesting notice of the Rev. Alexander Davis (Methodist), by C. K. B[uchanan] in which it is stated that Davis, a native of New Rochelle, remembered the affection of Paine, who "would bring him round-hearts and hold him on his knee." Many such recollections of his little neighbors have been reported.

this token to you on the ground of principle, and in remembrance of former times and friendship." He gives an historical account of the negative or veto-power, finding it the English Parliament's badge of disgrace under William of Normandy, a defence of personal prerogative that ought to find no place in a republic. He advises that in the new Constitution the principle of arbitration, outside of courts, should be established. The governor should possess no power of patronage; he should make one in a Council of Appointments. The Senate is an imitation of the House of Lords. The Representatives should be divided by lot into two equal parts, sitting in different chambers. One half, by not being entangled in the debate of the other on the issue submitted, nor committed by voting, would become silently possessed of the arguments, and be in a calm position to review the whole. The votes of the two houses should be added together, and the majority decide. Judges should be removable by some constitutional mode, without the formality of impeachment at "stated periods." (In 1807 Paine wrote to Senator Mitchell of New York suggesting an amendment to the Constitution of the United States by which judges of the Supreme Court might be removed by the President for reasonable cause, though insufficient for impeachment, on the address of a majority of both Houses of Congress.)

In this pamphlet was included the paper already mentioned (on Charters, etc.), addressed to the people of New York. The two essays prove that there was no abatement in Paine's intellect, and that despite occasional "flings" at the "Feds,"—retorts on their perpetual naggings,—he was still occupied with the principles of political philosophy.

At this time Paine had put the two young Bonnevilles at a school in New Rochelle, where they also boarded. He had too much solitude in the house, and too little nourishment for so much work. So the house was let and he was taken in as a boarder by Mrs. Bayeaux, in the old Bayeaux House, which is still standing,[1]—but Paine's pecuniary situation now gave him anxiety. He was earning nothing, his means were found to be far less than he supposed, the needs of the Bonnevilles increasing. Considering the important defensive articles he had written for the President, and their long friendship, he ventured (September 30th) to allude to his situation and to remind him that his State, Virginia, had once proposed to give him a tract of land, but had not done so. He suggests that Congress should remember his services.

" But I wish you to be assured that whatever event this proposal may take it will make no alteration in my principles or my conduct. I have been a volunteer to the world for thirty years without taking profits from anything I have published in America or Europe. I have relinquished all profits that those publications might come cheap among the people for whom they were intended.—Yours in friendship."

This was followed by another note (November 14th) asking if it had been received. What answer came from the President does not appear.

About this time Paine published an essay on "The cause of the Yellow Fever, and the means of preventing it in places not yet infected with it. Addressed to the Board of Health in America." The treatise, which he dates June 27th, is noticed by Dr. Francis as timely. Paine points out that the epidemic which almost annually afflicted New York, had been unknown to the Indians; that it began around the

¹ Mrs. Bayeaux is mentioned in Paine's letter about Dederick's attempt on his life.

wharves, and did not reach the higher parts of the city. He does not believe the disease certainly imported from the West Indies, since it is not carried from New York to other places. He thinks that similar filthy conditions of the wharves and the water about them generate the miasma alike in the West Indies and in New York. It would probably be escaped if the wharves were built on stone or iron arches, permitting the tides to cleanse the shore and carry away the accumulations of vegetable and animal matter decaying around every ship and dock. He particularly proposes the use of arches for wharves about to be constructed at Corlder's Hook and on the North River.

Dr. Francis justly remarks, in his " Old New York," that Paine's writings were usually suggested by some occasion. Besides this instance of the essay on the yellow fever, he mentions one on the origin of Freemasonry, there being an agitation in New York concerning that fraternity. But this essay—in which Paine, with ingenuity and learning, traces Freemasonry to the ancient solar mythology also identified with Christian mythology—was not published during his life. It was published by Madame Bonneville with the passages affecting Christianity omitted. The original manuscript was obtained, however, and published with an extended preface, criticizing Paine's theory, the preface being in turn criticized by Paine's editor. The preface was probably written by Colonel Fellows, author of a large work on Freemasonry.

CHAPTER XLII

A NEW YORK PROMETHEUS

When Paine left Bordentown, on March 1st, 1803, driving past placards of the devil flying away with him, and hooted by a pious mob at Trenton, it was with hope of a happy reunion with old friends in more enlightened New York. Col. Few, formerly senator from Georgia, his friend of many years, married Paine's correspondent, Kitty Nicholson, to whom was written the beautiful letter from London (p. 101). Col. Few had become a leading man in New York, and his home, and that of the Nicholsons, were of highest social distinction. Paine's arrival at Lovett's Hotel was well known, but not one of those former friends came near him. "They were actively as well as passively religious," says Henry Adams, "and their relations with Paine after his return to America in 1802 were those of compassion only, for his intemperate and offensive habits, and intimacy was impossible."[1] But Mr. Adams will vainly search his materials for any intimation at that time of the intemperate or offensive habits.

The "compassion" is due to those devotees of an idol requiring sacrifice of friendship, loyalty, and intelligence. What a mistake they made! The old author was as a grand organ from which a cunning hand might bring music to be remembered through the generations. In that brain were stored memories of the great Americans, Frenchmen, Englishmen who acted in the revolutionary dramas, and of whom he loved to talk. What would a diary of interviews with Paine, written by his friend Kitty Few, be now worth? To intolerance, the least pardonable form of ignorance, must be credited the failure of those former friends, who supposed themselves educated, to make more of Thomas Paine than a scarred monument of an Age of Unreason.

But the ostracism of Paine by the society which, as Henry Adams states, had once courted him "as the greatest literary genius of his day," was not due merely to his religious views, which were those of various statesmen who had incurred no such odium. There was at work a lingering dislike and distrust of the common people. Deism had been rather aristocratic. From the scholastic study, where heresies once written only in Latin were daintily wrapped up in metaphysics, from drawing-rooms where cynical smiles went round at Methodism, and other forms of "Christianity in earnest," Paine carried heresy to the

people. And he brought it as a religion, —as fire from the fervid heaven that orthodoxy had monopolized. The popularity of his writing, the revivalistic earnestness of his protest against dogmas common to all sects, were revolutionary; and while the vulgar bigots were binding him on their rock of ages, and tearing his vitals, most of the educated, the social leaders, were too prudent to manifest any sympathy they may have felt.[2]

It were unjust to suppose that Paine met with nothing but abuse and maltreatment from ministers of serious orthodoxy in New York. They had warmly opposed his views, even denounced them, but the controversy seems to have died away until he took part in the deistic propaganda of Elihu Palmer.[3] The following to Col. Fellows (July 31st) shows Paine much interested in the "cause":

"I am glad that Palmer and Foster have got together. It will greatly help the cause on. I enclose a letter I received a few days since from Groton, in Connecticut. The letter is well written, and with a good deal of sincere enthusiasm. The publication of it would do good, but there is an impropriety in publishing a man's name to a private letter. You may show the letter to Palmer and Foster. . . . Remember me to my much respected friend Carver and tell him I am sure we shall succeed if we hold on. We have already silenced the clamor of the priests. They act now as if they would say, let us alone and we will let you alone. You do not tell me if the Prospect goes on. As Carver will want pay he may have it from me, and pay when it suits him; but I expect he will take a ride up some Saturday, and then he can chuse for himself."

The result of this was that Paine passed the winter in New York, where he threw himself warmly into the theistic movement, and no doubt occasionally spoke from Elihu Palmer's platform.

---

[1] "Life of Albert Gallatin." Gallatin continued to visit Paine.

[2] When Paine first reached New York, 1803, he was (March 5th) entertained at supper by John Crauford. For being present Eliakim Ford, a Baptist elder, was furiously denounced, as were others of the company.

[3] An exception was the leading Presbyterian, John Mason, who lived to denounce Channing as "the devil's disciple." Grant Thorburn was psalm-singer in this Scotch preacher's church. Curiosity to see the lion led Thorburn to visit Paine, for which he was "suspended." Thorburn afterwards made amends by fathering Cheetham's slanders of Paine after Cheetham had become too infamous to quote.

The rationalists who gathered around Elihu Palmer in New York were called the "Columbian Illuminati." The pompous epithet looks like an effort to connect them with the Columbian Order (Tammany) which was supposed to represent Jacobinism and French ideas generally. Their numbers were considerable, but they did not belong to fashionable society. Their lecturer, Elihu Palmer, was a scholarly gentleman of the highest character. A native of Canterbury, Connecticut, (born 1754,) he had graduated at Dartmouth. He was married by the Rev. Mr. Watt to a widow, Mary Powell, in New York (1803), at the time when he was lecturing in the Temple of Reason (Snow's Rooms, Broadway). This suggests that he had not broken with the clergy altogether. Somewhat later he lectured at the Union Hotel, William Street. He had studied divinity, and turned against the creeds what was taught him for their support.

"I have more than once [says Dr. Francis] listened to Palmer; none could be weary within the sound of his voice; his diction was classical; and much of his natural theology attractive by variety of illustration. But admiration of him sank into despondency at his assumption, and his sarcastic assaults on things most holy. His boldest philippic was his discourse on the title-page of the Bible, in which, with the double shield of jacobinism and infidelity, he warned rising America against confidence in a book authorised by the monarchy of England. Palmer delivered his sermons in the Union Hotel in William Street."

Dr. Francis does not appear to have known Paine personally, but had seen him. Palmer's chief friends in New York were, he says, John Fellows; Rose, an unfortunate lawyer; Taylor, a philanthropist; and Charles Christian. Of Rev. John Foster, another rationalist lecturer, Dr. Francis says he had a noble presence and great eloquence. Foster's exordium was an invocation to the goddess of Liberty. He and Palmer called each other Brother. No doubt Paine completed the Triad.

Col. John Fellows, always the devoted friend of Paine, was an auctioneer, but in later life was a constable in the city courts. He has left three volumes which show considerable literary ability, and industrious research; but these were unfortunately bestowed on such extinct subjects as Freemasonry, the secret of Junius, and controversies concerning General Putnam. It is much to be regretted that Colonel Fellows should not have left a volume concerning Paine, with whom he was in especial intimacy, during his last years.

Other friends of Paine were Thomas Addis Emmet, Walter Morton, a lawyer, and Judge Hertell, a man of wealth, and a distinguished member of the State Assembly. Fulton also was much in New York, and often called on Paine. Paine was induced to board at the house of William Carver (36 Cedar Street), which proved a grievous mistake. Carver had introduced himself to Paine, saying that he remembered him when he was an exciseman at Lewes, England, he (Carver) being a young farrier there. He made loud professions of deism, and of devotion to Paine. The farrier of Lewes had become a veterinary practitioner and shopkeeper in New York. Paine supposed that he would be cared for in the house of this active rationalist, but the man and his family were illiterate and vulgar. His sojourn at Carver's probably shortened Paine's life. Carver, to anticipate the narrative a little, turned out to be a bad-hearted man and a traitor.

Paine had accumulated a mass of fragmentary writings on religious subjects, and had begun publishing them in a journal started in 1804 by Elihu Palmer, —*The Prospect; or View of the Moral World*. This succeeded the paper called *The Temple of Reason*. One of Paine's objects was to help the new journal, which attracted a good deal of attention. His first communication (February 18, 1804), was on a sermon by Robert Hall, on "Modern Infidelity," sent him by a gentleman in New York. The following are some of its trenchant paragraphs:

"Is it a fact that Jesus Christ died for the sins of the World, and how is it proved? If a God he could not die, and as a man he could not redeem: how then is this redemption proved to be fact? It is said that Adam eat of the for-bidden fruit, commonly called an apple, and thereby subjected himself and all his posterity forever to eternal damnation. This is worse than visiting the sins of the fathers upon the children unto the third and fourth generations. But how was the death of Jesus Christ to affect or alter the case? Did God thirst for blood? If so, would it not have been better to have crucified Adam upon the forbidden tree, and made a new man?"

"Why do not the Christians, to be consistent, make Saints of Judas and Pontius Pilate, for they were the persons who accomplished the act of salvation. The merit of a sacrifice, if there can be any merit in it, was never in the thing sacrificed, but in the persons offering up the sacrifice—and therefore Judas and Pilate ought to stand first in the calendar of Saints."

Other contributions to the *Prospect* were: "Of the word Religion"; "Cain and Abel"; "The Tower of Babel"; "Of the religion of Deism compared with the Christian Religion"; "Of the Sabbath Day in Connecticut"; "Of the Old and New Testaments"; "Hints towards forming a Society for inquiring into the truth or falsehood of ancient history, so far as history is connected with systems of religion ancient and modern"; "To the members of the Society styling itself the Missionary Society"; "On Deism, and the writings of Thomas Paine"; "Of the Books of the New Testament." There were several communications without any heading. Passages and sentences from these little essays have long been a familiar currency among freethinkers.

"We admire the wisdom of the ancients, yet they had no bibles, nor books, called revelation. They cultivated the reason that God gave them, studied him in his works, and rose to eminence."

"The Cain and Abel of Genesis appear to be no other than the ancient Egyptian story of Typhon and Osiris, the darkness and the light, which answered very well as allegory without being believed as fact."

"Those who most believe the Bible are those who know least about it."

"Another observation upon the story of Babel is, the inconsistence of it with respect to the opinion that the bible is the word of God given for the information of mankind; for nothing could so effectually prevent such a word being known by mankind as confounding their language."

"God has not given us reason for the purpose of confounding us."

"Jesus never speaks of Adam, of the Garden of Eden, nor of what is called the fall of man."

"Is not the Bible warfare the same kind of warfare as the Indians themselves carry on?" [On the presentation of a Bible to some Osage chiefs in New York.]

"The remark of the Emperor Julian is worth observing. 'If,' said he, 'there ever had been or could be a Tree of Knowledge, instead of God forbidding man to eat thereof, it would be that of which he would order him to eat the most.'"

"Do Christians not see that their own religion is founded on a human sacrifice? Many thousands of human sacrifices have since been offered on the altar of the Christian Religion."

"For several centuries past the dispute has been about doctrines. It is now about fact."

"The Bible has been received by Protestants on the authority of the Church of Rome."

"The same degree of hearsay evidence, and that at third and fourth hand, would not, in a court of justice, give a man title to a cottage, and yet the priests of this profession presumptuously promise their deluded followers the kingdom of Heaven."

"Nobody fears for the safety of a mountain, but a hillock of sand may be washed away. Blow then, O ye priests, 'the Trumpet in Zion,' for the Hillock is in danger."

The force of Paine's negations was not broken by any weakness for speculations of his own. He constructed no system to invite the missiles of antagonists. It is, indeed, impossible to deny without affirming. The basis of Paine's denials being the divine wisdom and benevolence, there was in his use of such expressions an implication of limitation in the divine nature. Wisdom implies the necessity of dealing with difficulties, and benevolence the effort to make all sentient creatures happy. Neither quality is predicable of an omniscient and omnipotent being, for whom there could be no difficulties or evils to over-come. Paine did not confuse the world with his doubts or with his mere opinions. He stuck to his certainties, that the scriptural deity was not the true one, nor the dogmas called Christian reason-able. But he felt some of the moral difficulties surrounding theism, and these were indicated in his reply to the Bishop of Llandaff.

"The Book of Job belongs either to the ancient Persians, the Chaldeans, or the Egyp-tians; because the structure of it is consistent with the dogma they held, that of a good and evil spirit, called in Job *God* and *Satan*, existing as distinct and separate beings, and it is not consistent with any dogma of the Jews. . . . The God of the Jews was the God of everything. All good and evil came from him. According to Exodus it was God, and not the Devil, that hardened Pharaoh's heart. According to the Book of Samuel it was an evil spirit from God that troubled Saul. And Ezekiel makes God say, in speaking of the Jews, 'I gave them statutes that were not good, and judgments by which they should not live.' . . . As to the precepts, principles, and maxims in the Book of Job, they show that the people abusively called the heathen, in the books of the Jews, had the most sublime ideas of the Creator, and the most exalted devotional morality. It was the Jews who dishonoured God. It was the Gentiles who glorified him."

Several passages in Paine's works show that he did not believe in a personal devil; just what he did believe was no doubt written in a part of his reply to the Bishop, which, unfortunately, he did not live to carry through the press. In the part that we have he expresses the opinion that the Serpent of Genesis is an allegory of winter, necessitating the " coats of skins " to keep Adam and Eve warm, and adds : " Of these things I shall speak fully when I come in another part to speak of the ancient religion of the Persians, and compare it with the modern religion of the New Testament." But this part was never published. The part published was transcribed by Paine and given, not long before his death, to the widow of Elihu Palmer, who published it in the *Theophilanthropist* in 1810. Paine had kept the other part, no doubt for revision, and it passed with his effects into the hands of Madame Bonneville, who eventually became a devotee. She either suppressed it or sold it to some one who destroyed it. We can therefore only infer from the above extract the author's belief on this momentous point. It seems clear that he did not attribute any evil to the divine Being. In the last article Paine published he rebukes the " Predestinarians " for dwelling mainly on God's " physical attribute " of power. " The Deists, in addition to this, believe in his moral attributes, those of justice and goodness."

Among Paine's papers was found one entitled " My private thoughts of a Future State," from which his editors have dropped important sentences.

"'I have said in the first part of the Age of Reason that 'I hope for happiness after this life.' This hope is comfortable to me, and I presume not to go beyond the comfortable idea of hope, with respect to a future state. I consider myself in the hands of my Creator, and that he will dispose of me after this life, consistently with his justice and goodness. I leave all these matters to him as my Creator and friend, and I hold it to be presumption in man to make an article of faith as to what the Creator will do with us hereafter. I do not believe, because a man and a woman make a child, that it imposes on the Creator the unavoidable obligation of keeping the being so made in eternal existence hereafter. It is in his power to do so, or not to do so, and it is not in our power to decide which he will do." [After quoting from Matthew 25th the figure of the sheep and goats he continues :] "The world cannot be thus divided. The moral world, like the physical world, is composed of numerous degrees of character, running imperceptibly one into the other, in such a manner that no fixed point can be found in either. That point is nowhere, or is everywhere. The whole world might be divided into two parts numerically, but not as to moral character ; and therefore the metaphor of dividing them, as sheep and goats can be divided, whose difference is marked by their external figure, is absurd. All sheep are still sheep ; all goats are still goats ; it is their physical nature to be so. But one part of the world are not all good alike, nor the other part all wicked alike. There are some exceedingly good, others exceedingly wicked. There is another description of men who cannot be ranked with either the one or the other—they belong neither to the sheep nor the goats. And there is still another description of them who are so very insignificant, both in character and conduct, as not to be worth the trouble of damning or saving, or of raising from the dead. My own opinion is, that those whose lives have been spent in doing good, and endeavoring to make their fellow mortals happy, for this is the only way in which we can serve God, will be happy hereafter ; and that the very wicked will meet with some punishment. But those who are neither good nor bad, or are too insignificant for notice, will be drop entirely. This is my opinion. It is consistent with my idea of God's justice, and with the reason that God has given me, and I gratefully know that he has given me a large share of that divine gift."

The closing tribute to his own reason, written in privacy, was, perhaps pardonably, suppressed by the modern editor, and also the reference to the insignificant who " will be dropt entirely." This sentiment is not indeed democratic, but it is significant. It seems plain that Paine's conception of the universe was dualistic. Though he discards the notion of a devil, I do not find that he ever ridicules it. No doubt he would, were he now living, incline to a division of nature into organic and inorganic, and find his deity, as Zoroaster did, in the living as distinguished from, and sometimes in antagonism with, the "not-living." In this belief he would now find himself in harmony with some of the ablest modern philosophers.[1]

The opening year 1806 found Paine in New Rochelle. By insufficient nourishment in Carver's house his health was impaired. His means were getting low, insomuch that to support the Bonnevilles he had to sell the Bordentown house and property.[2] Elihu Palmer had gone off to Philadelphia for a time; he died there of yellow fever in 1806. The few intelligent people whom Paine knew were much occupied, and he was almost without congenial society. His hint to Jefferson of his impending poverty, and his reminder that Virginia had not yet given him the honorarium he and Madison approved, had brought no result. With all this, and the loss of early friendships, and the theological hornet-nest he had found in New York, Paine began to feel that his return to America was a mistake.

The air-castle that had allured him to his beloved land had faded. His little room with the Bonnevilles in Paris, with its chaos of papers, was preferable; for there at least he could enjoy the society of educated persons, free from bigotry. He dwelt a stranger in his Land of Promise.

So he resolved to try and free himself from his depressing environment. He

[1] John Stuart Mill, for instance. See also the Rev. Dr. Abbott's " Kernel and Husk " (London), and the great work of Samuel Laing, " A Modern Zoroastrian."

[2] It was bought for $300 by his friend John Oliver, whose daughter, still residing in the house, told me that her father to the end of his life "thought everything of Paine." John Oliver, in his old age, visited Colonel Ingersoll in order to testify against the aspersions on Paine's character and habits.

would escape to Europe again. Jefferson had offered him a ship to return in, perhaps he would now help him to get back. So he writes (Jan. 30th) a letter to the President, pointing out the probabilities of a crisis in Europe which must result in either a descent on England by Bonaparte, or in a treaty. In the case that the people of England should be thus liberated from tyranny, he (Paine) desired to share with his friends there the task of framing a republic. Should there be, on the other hand, a treaty of peace, it would be of paramount interest to American shipping that such treaty should include that maritime compact, or safety of the seas for neutral ships, of which Paine had written so much, and which Jefferson himself had caused to be printed in a pamphlet. Both of these were, therefore, Paine's subjects. " I think," he says, " you will find it proper, perhaps necessary, to send a person to France in the event of either a treaty or a descent, and I make you an offer of my services on that occasion to join Mr. Monroe. . . . As I think that the letters of a friend to a friend have some claim to an answer, it will be agreeable to me to receive an answer to this, but without any wish that you should commit yourself, neither can you be a judge of what is proper or necessary to be done till about the month of April or May."

This little dream must also vanish. Paine must face the fact that his career is ended.

It is probable that Elihu Palmer's visit to Philadelphia was connected with some theistic movement in that city. How it was met, and what annoyances Paine had to suffer, are partly intimated in the following letter, printed in the Philadelphia *Commercial Advertiser*, February 10, 1806.

" TO JOHN INSKEEP, MAYOR OF THE CITY OF PHILADELPHIA.

" I saw in the *Aurora* of January the 30th a piece addressed to you and signed Isaac Hall. It contains a statement of your malevolent conduct in refusing to let him have Vine-st. Wharf after he had bid fifty dollars more rent for it than another person had offered, and had been unanimously approved of by the Commissioners appointed by law for that purpose. Among the reasons given by you for this refusal, one was, that ' *Mr. Hall was one of Paine's disciples.*' If those whom you may chuse to call my disciples follow my example in doing good to mankind, they will pass the confines of this world with a happy mind, while the hope of the hypocrite shall perish and delusion sink into despair.

"I do not know who Mr. Inskeep is, for I do not remember the name of Inskeep at Philadelphia in ' *the time that tried men's souls.*' He must be some mushroom of modern growth that has started up on the soil which the generous services of Thomas Paine contributed to bless with freedom ; neither do I know what profession of religion he is of, nor do I care, for if he is a man malevolent and unjust, it signifies not to what class or sectary he may hypocritically belong.

"As I set too much value on my time to waste it on a man of so little consequence as yourself, I will close this short address with a declaration that puts hypocrisy and malevolence to defiance. Here it is : My motive and object in all my political works, beginning with Common Sense, the first work I ever published, have been to rescue man from tyranny and false systems and false principles of government, and enable him to be free and establish government for himself ; and I have borne my share of danger in Europe and in America in every attempt I have made for this purpose. And my motive and object in all my publications on religious subjects, beginning with the first part of the Age of Reason, have been to bring man to a right reason that God has given him ; to impress on him the great principles of divine morality, justice, mercy, and a benevolent disposition to all men and to all creatures ; and to excite in him a spirit of trust, confidence and consolation in his creator, unshackled by the fable and fiction of books, by whatever invented name they may be called. I am happy in the continual contemplation of what I have done, and I thank God that he gave me talents for the purpose and fortitude to do it. It will make the continual consolation of my departing hours, whenever they finally arrive.

"THOMAS PAINE."

"' *These are the times that try men's souls.*' Crisis No. 1, written while on the retreat with the army from fort Lee to the Delaware and published in Philadelphia in the dark days of 1776 December the 19th, six days before the taking of the Hessians at Trenton."

But the year 1806 had a heavier blow yet to inflict on Paine, and it naturally came, though in a roundabout way, from his old enemy Gouverneur Morris. While at New Rochelle, Paine offered his vote at the election, and it was refused, on the ground that he was not an American citizen ! The supervisor declared that the former American Minister, Gouverneur Morris, had refused to reclaim him from a French prison because he was not an American, and that Washington had also refused to reclaim him. Gouverneur Morris had just lost his seat in Congress, and was politically defunct, but his ghost thus rose on poor Paine's pathway. The supervisor who disfranchised the author of "Common Sense" had been a "Tory" in the Revolution ; the man he disfranchised was one to whom the President of the United States had written, five years before : "I am in hopes you will find us returned generally to sentiments worthy of former times. In these it will be your glory to have steadily labored, and with as much effect as any man living." There was not any question of Paine's qualification as a voter on other grounds than the supervisor (Elisha Ward) raised. More must presently be said concerning this incident. Paine announced his intention of suing the inspectors, but meanwhile he had to leave the polls in humiliation. It was the fate of this founder of republics to be a monument of their ingratitude.

And now Paine's health began to fail. An intimation of this appears in a letter to Andrew A. Dean, to whom his farm at New Rochelle was let, dated from New York, August, 1806. It is in reply to a letter from Dean on a manuscript which Paine had lent him.[1]

"RESPECTED FRIEND : I received your friendly letter, for which I am obliged to you. It is three weeks ago to-day (Sunday, Aug. 15th) that I was struck with a fit of an apoplexy, that

---

[1] "I have read," says Dean, "with good attention your manuscript on Dreams, and Examination of the Prophecies in the Bible. I am now searching the old prophecies, and comparing the same to those said to be quoted in the New Testament. I confess the comparison is a matter worthy of our serious attention ; I know not the result till I finish ; then, if you be living, I shall communicate the same to you. I hope to be with you soon." Paine was now living with Jarvis, the artist. One evening he fell as if by apoplexy, and, as he lay, his first word was (to Jarvis) : "My corporeal functions have ceased ; my intellect is clear ; this is a proof of immortality."

deprived me of all sense and motion. I had neither pulse nor breathing, and the people about me supposed me dead. I had felt exceedingly well that day, and had just taken a slice of bread and butter for supper, and was going to bed. The fit took me on the stairs, as suddenly as if I had been shot through the head ; and I got so very much hurt by the fall, that I have not been able to get in and out of bed since that day, otherwise than being lifted out in a blanket, by two persons ; yet all this while my mental faculties have remained as perfect as I ever enjoyed them. I consider the scene I have passed through as an experiment on dying, and I find death has no terrors for me. As to the people called Christians, they have no evidence that their religion is true. There is no more proof that the Bible is the word of God, than that the Koran of Mahomet is the word of God. It is education makes all the difference. Man, before he begins to think for himself, is as much the child of habit in Creeds as he is in ploughing and sowing. Yet creeds, like opinions, prove nothing. Where is the evidence that the person called Jesus Christ is the begotten Son of God ? The case admits not of evidence either to our senses or our mental faculties : neither has God given to man any talent by which such a thing is comprehensible. It cannot therefore be an object for faith to act upon, for faith is nothing more than an assent the mind gives to something it sees cause to believe is fact. But priests, preachers, and fanatics, put imagination in the place of faith, and it is the nature of the imagination to believe without evidence. If Joseph the carpenter dreamed (as the book of Matthew, chapter 1st, says he did,) that his betrothed wife, Mary, was with child by the Holy Ghost, and that an angel told him so, I am not obliged to put faith in his dream ; nor do I put any, for I put no faith in my own dreams, and I should be weak and foolish indeed to put faith in the dreams of others.—The Christian religion is derogatory to the Creator in all its articles. It puts the Creator in an inferior point of view, and places the Christian Devil above him. It is he, according to the absurd story in Genesis, that outwits the Creator, in the garden of Eden, and steals from him his favorite creature, man ; and, at last, obliges him to beget a son, and put that son to death, to get man back again. And this the priests of the Christian religion call redemption.

" Christian authors exclaim against the practice of offering human sacrifices, which, they say, is done in some countries ; and those authors make those exclamations without ever reflecting that their own doctrine of salvation is founded on a human sacrifice. They are saved, they say, by the blood of Christ. The Christian religion begins with a dream and ends with a murder.

" As I am well enough to sit up some hours in the day, though not well enough to get up without help, I employ myself as I have always done, in endeavoring to bring man to the right use of the reason that God has given him, and to direct his mind immediately to his Creator, and not to fanciful secondary beings called mediators, as if God was superannuated or ferocious.

"As to the book called the Bible, it is blasphemy to call it the word of God. It is a book of lies and contradictions, and a history of bad times and bad men. There are but a few good characters in the whole book. The fable of Christ and his twelve apostles, which is a parody on the sun and the twelve signs of the Zodiac, copied from the ancient religions of the eastern world, is the least hurtful part. Every thing told of Christ has reference to the sun. His reported resurrection is at sunrise, and that on the first day of the week ; that is, on the day anciently dedicated to the sun, and from thence called Sunday ; in latin Dies Solis, the day of the sun ; as the next day, Monday, is Moon Day. But there is no room in a letter to explain these things. While man keeps the belief of one God, his reason unites with his creed. He is not shocked with contradictions and horrid stories. His bible is the heavens and the earth. He beholds his Creator in all his works, and every thing he beholds inspires him with reverence and gratitude. From the goodness of God to all, he learns his duty to his fellow-man, and stands self-reproved when he transgresses it. Such a man is no persecutor. But when he multiplies his creed with imaginary things, of which he can have neither evidence nor conception, such as the tale of the garden of Eden, the talking serpent, the fall of man, the dreams of Joseph the carpenter, the pretended resurrection and ascension, of which there is even no historical relation, for no historian of those times mentions such a thing, he gets into the pathless region of confusion, and turns either frantic or hypocrite. He forces his mind, and pretends to believe what he does not believe. This is in general the case with the Methodists. Their religion is all creed and no morals.

" I have now my friend given you a fac-simile of my mind on the subject of religion and creeds, and my wish is, that you may make this letter as publicly known as you find opportunities of doing. Yours in friendship."

The "Essay on Dream" was written early in 1806 and printed in May, 1807. It was the last work of importance written by Paine. In the same pamphlet was included a part of his reply to the Bishop of Llandaff, which was written in France: "An Examination of the Passages in the New Testament, quoted from the Old, and called Prophecies of the Coming of Jesus Christ." The Examination is widely known and is among Paine's characteristic works,—a continuation of the "Age of Reason." The "Essay on Dream" is a fine specimen of the author's literary art. Dream is the imagination awake while the judgment is asleep. "Every person is mad once in twenty-four hours; for were he to act in the day as he dreams in the night, he would be confined for a lunatic." Nathaniel Hawthorne thought spiritualism "a sort of dreaming awake." Paine explained in the same way some of the stories on which popular religion is founded. The incarnation itself rests on what an angel told Joseph in a dream, and others are referred to.

"This story of dreams has thrown Europe into a dream for more than a thousand years. All the efforts that nature, reason, and conscience have made to awaken man from it have been ascribed by priestcraft and superstition to the workings of the devil, and had it not been for the American revolution, which by establishing the universal right of conscience, first opened the way to free discussion, and for the French revolution which followed, this religion of dreams had continued to be preached, and that after it had ceased to be believed."

But Paine was to be reminded that the revolution had not made conscience free enough in America to challenge waking dreams without penalties. The following account of his disfranchisement at New Rochelle was written from Broome St., New York, May 4, 1807, to Vice-President Clinton.

"RESPECTED FRIEND,—Elisha Ward and three or four other Tories who lived within the british lines in the revolutionary war, got in to be inspectors of the election last year at New Rochelle. Ward was supervisor. These men refused my vote at the election, saying to me: 'You are not an American: our minister at Paris, Gouverneur Morris, would not reclaim you when you were emprisoned in the Luxembourg prison at Paris, and General Washington refused to do it.' Upon my telling him that the two cases he stated were falsehoods, and that if he did me injustice I would prosecute him, he got up, and calling for a constable, said to me, 'I will commit you to prison.' He chose, however, to sit down and go no farther with it.

"I have written to Mr. Madison for an attested copy of Mr. Munro's letter to the then Secretary of State Randolph, in which Mr. Munro gives the government an account of his reclaiming me and my liberation in consequence of it; and also for an attested copy of Mr. Randolph's answer, in which he says: 'The President approves what you have done in the case of Mr. Paine.' The matter I believe is, that, as I had not been guillotined, Washing-

ton thought best to say what he did. As to Gouverneur Morris, the case is that he did reclaim me; but his reclamation did me no good, and the probability is, he did not intend it should. Joel Barlow and other Americans in Paris had been in a body to reclaim me, but their application, being unofficial, was not regarded. I then applied to Morris. I shall subpœna Morris, and if I get attested copies from the Secretary of State's office it will prove the lie on the inspectors.

"As it is a new generation that has risen up since the declaration of independence, they know nothing of what the political state of the country was at the time the pamphlet 'Common Sense' appeared; and besides this there are but few of the old standers left, and none that I know of in this city.

"It may be proper at the trial to bring the mind of the Court and the Jury back to the times I am speaking of, and if you see no objection in your way, I wish you would write a letter to some person, stating from your own knowledge, what the condition of those times were, and the effect which the work 'Common Sense' and the several members of the 'Crisis' had upon the country. It would, I think, be best that the letter should begin directly on the subject in this manner: Being informed that Thomas Paine has been denied his rights of citizenship by certain persons acting as inspectors at an election at New Rochelle, &c.

"I have put the prosecution into the hands of Mr. Riker, district attorney, who can make use of the letter in his address to the Court and Jury. Your handwriting can be sworn to by persons here, if necessary. Had you been on the spot I should have subpœnaed you, unless it had been too inconvenient to you to have attended. Yours in friendship."

To this Clinton replied from Washington, 12th May, 1807:

"DEAR SIR,—I had the pleasure to receive your letter of the 4th instant, yesterday; agreeably to your request I have this day written a letter to Richard Riker, Esquire, which he will show you. I doubt much, however, whether the Court will admit it to be read as evidence.

"I am indebted to you for a former letter. I can make no other apology for not acknowledging it before than inability to give you such an answer as I could wish. I constantly keep the subject in mind, and should any favorable change take place in the sentiments of the Legislature, I will apprize you of it.

"I am, with great esteem, your sincere friend."

In the letter to Madison Paine tells the same story. At the end he says that Morris's reclamation was not out of any good will to him. "I know not what he wrote to the french minister; whatever it was he concealed it from me." He also says Morris could hardly keep himself out of prison.[1]

A letter was also written to Joel Barlow, at Washington, dated Broome Street, New York, May 4th. He says in this:

"I have prosecuted the Board of Inspectors for disfranchising me. You and other Americans in Paris went in a body to the Convention to reclaim me, and I want a certificate from you, properly attested, of this fact. If you consult with Gov. Clinton he will in friendship inform you who to address it to.

"Having now done with business I come to meums and tuums. What are you about? You sometimes hear of me but I never hear of you. It seems as if I had got to be master of the feds and the priests. The former do not attack my political publications; they rather try to keep them out of sight by silence. And as to the priests, they act as if they would say, let us alone and we will let you alone. My Examination of the passages called prophecies is printed, and will be published next week. I have prepared it with the Essay on Dream. I do not believe that the priests will attack it, for it is not a book of opinions but of facts. Had the Christian Religion done any good in the world I would not have exposed it, however fabulous I might believe it to be. But the delusive idea of having a friend at court whom they call a redeemer, who pays all their scores, is an encouragement to wickedness.

"What is Fulton about? Is he taming a whale to draw his submarine boat? I wish you would desire Mr. Smith to send me his country National Intelligencer. It is printed twice a week without advertisement. I am somewhat at a loss for want of authentic intelligence. Yours in friendship."

It will be seen that Paine was still in ignorance of the conspiracy which had thrown him in prison, nor did he suspect that Washington had been deceived by Gouverneur Morris, and that his private letter to Washington might have been suppressed by Pickering.[2] It will be

seen, by Madame Bonneville's and Jarvis's statements elsewhere, that Paine lost his case against Elisha Ward, on what ground it is difficult to imagine. The records of the Supreme Court, at Albany, and the Clerk's office at White Plains, have been vainly searched for any trace of this trial. Mr. John H. Riker, son of Paine's counsel, has examined the remaining papers of Richard Riker (many were accidentally destroyed) without finding anything related to the matter. It is so terrible to think that with Jefferson, Clinton, and Madison at the head of the government, and the facts so clear, the federalist Elisha Ward could vindicate his insult to Thomas Paine, that it may be hoped the publi-

---

[1] The letter is in Mr. Frederick McGuire's collection of Madison papers.

[2] It has been already surmised (p. 226) that Washington's Secretary of State might have kept Paine's letter from the President, and thus prevented an answer, which might have led to an explanation. I had not then observed a reference to that letter by Madison, in writing to Monroe (April 7, 1796), which proves that Paine's communication to Washington had been read by Pickering. Monroe was anxious lest some attack on the President should be written by Paine while under his roof,—an impropriety avoided by Paine, as we have seen,—

and had written to Madison on the subject. Madison answers: "I have given the explanation you desired to F. A. M[uhlenberg], who has not received any letter as yet, and has promised to pay due regard to your request. It is proper you should know that Thomas Paine wrote some time ago a severe letter to the President which Pickering mentioned to me in harsh terms when I delivered a note from Thomas Paine to the Secretary of State, inclosed by T. P. in a letter to me. Nothing passed, however, that betrayed the least association of your patronage or attention to Thomas Paine with the circumstance; nor am I apprehensive that any real suspicion can exist of your countenancing or even knowing the steps taken by T. P. under the influence of his personal feelings or political principles. At the same time the caution you observe is by no means to be disapproved. Be so good as to let T. P. know that I have received his letter and handed his note to the Secretary of State, which requested copies of such letters as might have been written hence in his behalf. The note did not require any answer either to me or through me, and I have heard nothing of it since I handed it to Pickering." At this time the Secretary of State's office contained the President's official recognition of Paine's citizenship; but this application for the papers relating to his imprisonment by a foreign power received no reply, though it was evidently couched in respectful terms; as the letter was open for the eye of Madison, who would not have conveyed it otherwise. It is impossible that Washington could have sanctioned such an outrage on one he had recognized as an American citizen. There is thus reason to believe that Timothy Pickering, as he had kept back a letter in the case of Randolph, intercepted that of Paine to Washington (Sept. 20, 1795), whose silence brought on him the public letter.

cation of these facts will bring others to light that may put a better face on the matter.[1] Madame Bonneville may have misunderstood the procedure for which she had to pay costs, as Paine's legatee. Whether an ultimate decision was reached or not, the sufficiently shameful fact remains that Thomas Paine was practically disfranchised in the country to which he had rendered services pronounced pre-eminent by Congress, by Washington, and by every soldier and statesman of the Revolution.

Paine had in New York the most formidable of enemies,—an enemy with a newspaper. This was James Cheetham, of whom something has been said in the preface to this work (p. xiii). In addition to what is there stated, it may be mentioned that Paine had observed, soon after he came to New York, the shifty course of this man's paper, *The American Citizen*. But it was the only republican paper in New York, supported Governor Clinton, for which it had reason, since it had the State printing,—and Colonel Fellows advised that Cheetham should not be attacked. Cheetham had been an attendant at Elihu Palmer's lectures, and after his participation in the dinner to Paine,

his federalist opponent, the *Evening Post*, alluded to his being at Palmer's. Thereupon Cheetham declared that he had not heard Palmer for two years. In the winter of 1804 he casually spoke of Paine's "mischievous doctrines." In the following year, when Paine wrote the defence of Jefferson's personal character already alluded to, Cheetham omitted a reference in it to Alexander Hamilton's pamphlet, by which he escaped accusation of official defalcation by confessing an amorous intrigue.[2] Cheetham having been wont to write of Hamilton as "the gallant of Mrs. Reynolds," Paine did not give much credit to the pretext of respect for the dead, on which the suppression was justified. He was prepared to admit that his allusion might be fairly suppressed, but perceived that the omission was made merely to give Cheetham a chance for vaunting his superior delicacy, and casting a suspicion on Paine. "Cheetham," wrote Paine, "might as well have put the part in, as put in the reasons for which he left it out. Those reasons leave people to suspect that the part suppressed related to some new discovered immorality in Hamilton worse than the old story."

About the same time with Paine, an Irishman came to America, and, after travelling about the country a good deal, established a paper in New York called *The People's Friend*. This paper began a furious onslaught on the French, professed to have advices that Napoleon meant to retake New Orleans, and urged an offensive alliance of the United States

[1] Gilbert Vale relates an anecdote which suggests that a reaction may have occurred in Elisha Ward's family: "At the time of Mr. Paine's residence at his farm, Mr. Ward, now a coffee-roaster in Gold Street, New York, and an assistant alderman, was then a little boy and residing at New Rochelle. He remembers the impressions his mother and some religious people made on him by speaking of *Tom* Paine, so that he concluded that *Tom* Paine must be a very bad and brutal man. Some of his elder companions proposed going into Mr. Paine's orchard to obtain some fruit, and he, out of fear, kept at a distance behind, till he beheld, with surprise, Mr. Paine come out and assist the boys in getting apples, patting one on the head and caressing another, and directing them where to get the best. He then advanced and received his share of encouragement, and the impression this kindness made on him determined him at a very early period to examine his writings. His mother at first took the books from him, but at a later period restored them to him, observing that he was then of an age to judge for himself; perhaps she had herself been gradually undeceived, both as to his character and writings."

[2] "I see that Cheetham has left out the part respecting Hamilton and Mrs. Reynolds, but for my own part I wish it had been in. Had the story never been publicly told I would not have been the first to tell it; but Hamilton had told it himself, and therefore it was no secret; but my motive in introducing it was because it was applicable to the subject I was upon, and to show the revilers of Mr. Jefferson that while they are affecting a morality of horror at an unproved and unfounded story about Mr. Jefferson, they had better look at home and give vent to their horror, if they had any, at a real case of their own Dagon (*sic*) and his Delilah." —Paine to Colonel Fellows, July 31, 1805.

with England against France and Spain. These articles appeared in the early autumn of 1806, when, as we have seen, Paine was especially beset by personal worries. They made him frantic. His denunciations, merited as they were, of this assailant of France reveal the unstrung condition of the old author's nerves. Duane, of the Philadelphia *Aurora*, recognized in Carpenter a man he had seen in Calcutta, where he bore the name of Cullen. It was then found that he had on his arrival in America borne the *alias* of Maccullen. Paine declared that he was an "emissary" sent to this country by Windham, and indeed most persons were at length satisfied that such was the case. Paine insisted that loyalty to our French alliance demanded Cullen's expulsion. His exposures of "the emissary Cullen" (who disappeared) were printed in a new republican paper in New York, *The Public Advertiser*, edited by Mr. Frank. The combat drew public attention to the new paper, and Cheetham was probably enraged by Paine's transfer of his pen to Frank. In 1807, Paine had a large following in New York, his friends being none the less influential among the masses because not in the fashionable world. Moreover, the very popular Mayor of New York, De Witt Clinton, was a hearty admirer of Paine. So Cheetham's paper suffered sadly, and he opened his guns on Paine, declaring that in the Revolution he (Paine) "had stuck very correctly to his pen in a safe retreat," that his "Rights of Man" merely repeated Locke, and so forth. He also began to denounce France and applaud England, which led to the belief that, having lost republican

patronage, Cheetham was aiming to get that of England.

In a "Reply to Cheetham" (August 21st), Paine met personalities in kind. "Mr. Cheetham, in his rage for attacking everybody and everything that is not his own (for he is an ugly-tempered man, and he carries the evidence of it in the vulgarity and forbiddingness of his countenance—God has set a mark upon Cain), has attacked me, etc." In reply to further attacks, Paine printed a piece headed "Cheetham and his Tory Paper." He said that Cheetham was discovering symptoms of being the successor of Cullen, *alias* Carpenter. "Like him he is seeking to involve the United States in a quarrel with France for the benefit of England." This article caused a duel between the rival editors, Cheetham and Frank, which seems to have been harmless. Paine wrote a letter to the *Evening Post*, saying that he had entreated Frank to answer Cheetham's challenge by declaring that he (Paine) had written the article and was the man to be called to account. In company Paine mentioned an opinion expressed by the President in a letter just received. This got into the papers, and Cheetham declared that the President could not have so written, and that Paine was intoxicated when he said so. For this Paine instituted a suit against Cheetham for slander, but died before any trial.

Paine had prevailed with his pen, but a terrible revenge was plotted against his good name. The farrier William Carver, in whose house he had lived, turned Judas, and concocted with Cheetham the libels against Paine that have passed as history.

CHAPTER XLIII

PERSONAL TRAITS

On July 1, 1806, two young English gentlemen, Daniel and William Constable, arrived in New York, and for some years travelled about the country. The Diary kept by Daniel Constable has been shown me by his nephew, Clair J.

Grece, LL.D. It contains interesting allusions to Paine, to whom they brought an introduction from Rickman.

"July 1st. To the Globe, in Maiden Lane, to dine. Mr. Segar at the Globe offered to send for Mr. Paine, who lived only a few doors off: He seemed a true Painite.

"3d. William and I went to see Thomas Paine. When we first called he was taking a nap. . . . Back to Mr. Paine's about 5 o'clock, sat about an hour with him. . . . I meant to have had T. Paine in a carriage with me to-morrow, and went to inquire for one. The price was $1 per hour, but when I proposed it to T.P. he declined it on account of his health.

"4th. Friday. Fine clear day. The annual Festival of Independence. We were up by five o'clock, and on the battery saw the cannons fired, in commemoration of liberty, which had been employed by the English against the sacred cause. The people seemed to enter into the spirit of the day : stores &c. were generally shut. . . . In the fore part of the day I had the honour of walking with T. Paine along the Broadway. The day finished peaceably, and we saw no scenes of quarreling or drunkenness.

"14th. A very hot day. Evening, met T. Paine in the Broadway and walked with him to his house.

"Oct. 29th [on returning from a journey]. Called to see T. Paine, who was walking about Carver's shop."

"Nov. 1st. Changed snuff-boxes with T. Paine at his lodgings.[1] The old philosopher, in bed at 4 o'clock afternoon, seems as talkative and well as when we saw him in the summer."

In a letter written jointly by the brothers to their parents, dated July 6th, they say that Paine "begins to feel the effects of age. The print I left at Horley is a very strong likeness. He lives with a small family who came from Lewes [Carvers] quite retired, and but little known or noticed." They here also speak of "the honor of walking with our old friend T. Paine in the midst of the bustle on Independence Day." There is no suggestion, either here or in the Diary, that these gentlemen of culture and position observed anything in the appearance or habits of Paine that diminished the pleasure of meeting him. In November they travelled down the Mississippi, and on their return to New

York, nine months later, they heard (July 20, 1807) foul charges against Paine from Carver. "Paine has left his house, and they have had a violent disagreement. Carver charges Paine with many foul vices, as debauchery, lying, ingratitude, and a total want of common honor in all his actions, says that he drinks regularly a quart of brandy per day." But next day they call on Paine, in "the Bowery road," and William Constable writes :

"He looks better than last year. He read us an essay on national defence, comparing the different expenses and powers of gunboats and ships of war and batteries in protecting a sea coast ; and gave D. C., [Daniel Constable] a copy of his Examination of the texts of scriptures called prophecies, etc., which he published a short time since. He says that this work is of too high a cut for the priests and that they will not touch it."

These brothers Constable met Fulton, "a friend of Paine's," just then experimenting with his steamboat on the Hudson. They also found that a scandal had been caused by a report brought to the British Consul that thirty passengers on the ship by which they (the Constables) came, had "the Bible bound up with the 'Age of Reason,' and that they spoke in very disrespectful terms of the mother country." Paine had left his farm at New Rochelle, at which place the travellers heard stories of his slovenliness, also that he was penurious, though nothing was said of intemperance.

Inquiry among aged residents of New Rochelle has been made from time to time for a great many years. The Hon. J. B. Stallo, late U. S. Minister to Italy, told me that in early life he visited the place and saw persons who had known Paine, and declared that Paine resided there without fault. Paine lived for a time with Mr. Staple, brother of the influential Captain Pelton, and the adoption of Paine's religious views by some of these persons caused the odium.[2] Paine sometimes preached at New Rochelle.

---

[1] Dr. Grece showed me Paine's papier-maché snuff-box, which his uncle had fitted with silver plate, inscription, decorative eagle, and banner of "Liberty, Equality." It is kept in a jewel-box with an engraving of Paine on the lid.

[2] Mr. Burger, Pelton's clerk, used to drive Paine about daily. Vale says :

"He [Burger] describes Mr. Paine as really abstemious, and when pressed to drink by those on whom he called during his rides, he usually

Cheetham publishes a correspondence purporting to have passed between Paine and Carver, in November, 1806, in which the former repudiates the latter's bill for board (though paying it), saying he was badly and dishonestly treated in Carver's house, and had taken him out of his Will. To this a reply is printed, signed by Carver, which he certainly never wrote; specimens of his composition, now before me, prove him hardly able to spell a word correctly or to frame a sentence.[1] The letter in Cheetham shows a practised hand, and was evidently written for Carver by the "biographer." This ungenuineness of Carver's letter and expressions not characteristic in that of Paine render the correspondence mythical. Although Carver passed many penitential years hanging about Paine celebrations, deploring the wrong he had done Paine, he could not squarely repudiate the correspondence, to which Cheetham had compelled him to swear

in court. He used to declare that Cheetham had obtained under false pretences and printed without authority letters written in anger. But thrice in his letter to Paine Carver says he means to publish it. Its closing words are : "There may be many grammatical errours in this letter. To you I have no apologies to make ; but I hope a candid and impartial public will not view them 'with a critick's eye.'" This is artful; besides the fling at Paine's faulty grammar, which Carver could not discover, there is a pretence to faults in his own letter which do not exist, but certainly would have existed had he written it. The style throughout is transparently Cheetham's.

In the book at Concord the unassisted Carver writes : "The libel for wich [*sic*] he [Cheetham] was sued was contained in the letter I wrote to Paine." This was the libel on Madame Bonneville, Carver's antipathy to whom arose from his hopes of Paine's property. In reply to Paine's information, that he was excluded from his Will, Carver says : "I likewise have to inform you, that I totally disregard the power of your mind and pen ; for should you, by your conduct, permit this letter to appear in public, in vain may you attempt to print or publish any thing afterwards." This is plainly an attempt at blackmail. Carver's letter is dated December 2, 1806. It was not published during Paine's life, for the farrier hoped to get back into the Will by frightening Madame Bonneville and other friends of Paine with the stories he meant to tell. About a year before Paine's death he made another blackmailing attempt. He raked up the scandalous stories published by "Oldys" concerning Paine's domestic troubles in Lewes, pretending that he knew the facts personally. "Of these facts Mr. Carver has offered me an affidavit," says Cheetham. "He stated them all to Paine in a private letter which he wrote to him a year before his death ; to which no answer was returned. Mr. Carver showed me the letter soon after it was written." On this plain evidence of long conspiracy with Cheetham, and attempt to

refused with great firmness, but politely. In one of these rides he was met by De Witt Clinton, and their mutual greetings were extremely hearty. Mr. Paine at this time was the reverse of morose, and though careless of his dress and prodigal of his snuff, he was always clean and well clothed. Mr. Burger describes him as familiar with children and humane to animals, playing with the neighboring children, and communicating a friendly pat even to a passing dog." Our frontispiece shows Paine's dress in 1803.

[1] In the Concord (Mass.) Public Library there is a copy of Cheetham's book, which belonged to Carver, by whom it was filled with notes. He says: "Cheetham was a hypocrate turned Tory." "Paine was not Drunk when he wrote the thre pedlars for me, I sold them to a gentleman, a Jew for a dollar—Cheetham knew that he told a lie saying Paine was drunk—any person reading Cheetham's life of Paine that [*sic*] his pen was guided by prejudice that was brought on by Cheetham's altering a peice that Paine had writen as an answer to a peice that had apeared in his paper, I had careyd the peice to Cheetham, the next Day the answer was printed with the alteration, Paine was angry, sent me to call Cheetham I then asked how he undertook to mutilate the peice, if aney thing was rong he knew ware to find him & sad he never permitted a printer to alter what he had wrote, that the sence of the peice was spoiled—by this means their freind ship was broken up through life——" (The marginalia in this volume have been copied for me with exactness by Miss E. G. Crowell, of Concord.)

blackmail Paine when he was sinking in mortal illness, Carver never made any comment. When Paine was known to be near his end Carver made an effort at conciliation. "I think it a pity," he wrote, "that you or myself should depart this life with envy in our hearts against each other—and I firmly believe that no difference would have taken place between us, had not some of your pretended friends endeavored to have caused a separation of friendship between us." [1] But abjectness was not more effectual than blackmail. The property went to the Bonnevilles, and Carver, who had flattered Paine's "great mind," in the letter just quoted, proceeded to write a mean one about the dead author for Cheetham's projected biography. He did not, however, expect Cheetham to publish his slanderous letter about Paine and Madame Bonneville, which he meant merely for extortion; nor could Cheetham have got the letter had he not written it. All of Cheetham's libels on Paine's life in New York are amplifications of Carver's insinuations. In describing Cheetham as "an abominable liar," Carver passes sentence upon himself. On this blackmailer, this confessed libeller, rest originally and fundamentally the charges relating to Paine's last years.

It has already been stated that Paine boarded for a time in the Bayeaux mansion. With Mrs. Bayeaux lived her daughter, Mrs. Badeau. In 1891 I visited, at New Rochelle, Mr. Albert Badeau, son of the lady last named, finding him, as I hope he still is, in good health and memory. Seated in the arm-chair given him by his mother, as that in which Paine used to sit by their fireside, I took down for publication some words of his. "My mother would never tolerate the aspersions on Mr. Paine. She declared steadfastly to the end of her life that he was a perfect gentleman, and a most faithful friend, amiable, gentle, never intemperate in eating or drinking. My mother declared that my grandmother equally pro-

nounced the disparaging reports about Mr. Paine slanders. I never remember to have seen my mother angry except when she heard such calumnies of Mr. Paine, when she would almost insult those who uttered them. My mother and grandmother were very religious, members of the Episcopal Church." What Mr. Albert Badeau's religious opinions are I do not know, but no one acquainted with that venerable gentleman could for an instant doubt his exactness and truthfulness. It certainly was not until some years after his return to America that any slovenliness could be observed about Paine, and the contrary was often remarked in former times.[2] After he had come to New York, and was neglected, by the pious ladies and gentlemen with whom he had once associated, he neglected his personal appearance. "Let those dress who need it," he said to a friend.

Paine was prodigal of snuff, but used tobacco in no other form. He had aversion to profanity, and never told or listened to indecent anecdotes.

With regard to the charges of excessive drinking made against Paine, I have sifted a vast mass of contrarious testimonies, and arrived at the following conclusions. In earlier life Paine drank spirits, as was the custom in England and America; and he unfortunately selected brandy, which causes alcoholic indigestion, and may have partly produced the oft-quoted witness against him—his somewhat red nose. His nose was prominent, and began to be red when he was fifty-five. That was just after he had been dining a good deal with rich people in England, and at

[1] "A Bone to Gnaw for Grant Thorburn." By W. Carver (1836).

[2] "He dined at my table," said Aaron Burr. "I always considered Mr. Paine a gentleman, a pleasant companion, and a good-natured and intelligent man; decidedly temperate, with a proper regard for his personal appearance, whenever I have seen him." (Quoted in *The Beacon*, No. 30, May, 1837.) "In his dress," says Joel Barlow, "he was generally very cleanly, though careless, and wore his hair queued with side curls, and powdered, like a gentleman of the old French School. His manners were easy and gracious, his knowledge universal."

public dinners. During his early life in England (1737–1774) no instance of excess was known, and Paine expressly pointed the Excise Office to his record. "No complaint of the least dishonesty or intemperance has ever appeared against me." His career in America (1774–1787) was free from any suspicion of intemperance. John Hall's daily diary while working with Paine for months is minute, mentioning everything, but in no case is a word said of Paine's drinking. This was in 1785-7. Paine's enemy, Chalmers ("Oldys"), raked up in 1791 every charge he could against Paine, but intemperance is not included. Paine told Rickman that in Paris, when borne down by public and private affliction, he had been driven to excess. That period I have identified on a former page (p. 180) as a few weeks in 1793, when his dearest friends were on their way to the guillotine, whither he daily expected to follow them. After that Paine abstained altogether from spirits, and drank wine in moderation. Mr. Lovett, who kept the City Hotel, New York, where Paine stopped in 1803 and 1804 for some weeks, wrote a note to Caleb Bingham, of Boston, in which he says that Paine drank less than any of his boarders. Gilbert Vale, in preparing his biography, questioned D. Burger, the clerk of Pelton's store at New Rochelle, and found that Paine's liquor supply while there was one quart of rum per week. Brandy he had entirely discarded. He also questioned Jarvis the artist, in whose house Paine resided in New York (Church Street) five months, who declared that what Cheetham had reported about Paine and himself was entirely false. Paine, he said, "did not and could not drink much." In July, 1809, just after Paine's death, Cheetham wrote Barlow for information concerning Paine, "useful in illustrating his character," and said: "He was a great drunkard here, and Mr. M., a merchant of this city, who lived with him when he was arrested by order of Robespierre, tells me he was intoxicated when that event happened." Barlow,

recently returned from Europe, was living just out of Washington; he could know nothing of Cheetham's treachery, and fell into his trap; he refuted the story of "Mr. M.," of course, but took it for granted that a supposed republican editor would tell the truth about Paine in New York, and wrote of the dead author as having "a mind, though strong enough to bear him up and to rise elastic under the heaviest hand of oppression, yet unable to endure the contempt of his former friends and fellow-laborers, the rulers of the country that had received his first and greatest services; a mind incapable of looking down with serene compassion, as it ought, on the rude scoffs of their imitators, a new generation that knows him not; a mind that shrinks from their society, and unhappily seeks refuge in low company, or looks for consolation in the sordid, solitary bottle, etc." [1] Barlow, misled as he was, well knew Paine's nature, and that if he drank to excess it was not from appetite, but because of ingratitude and wrong. The man was not a stock or a stone. If any can find satisfaction in the belief that Paine found no Christian in America so merciful as rum, they may perhaps discover some grounds for it in a brief period of his sixty-ninth year. While living in the house of Carver, Paine was seized with an illness that threatened to be mortal, and from which he never fully recovered. It is probable that he was kept alive for a time by spirits during the terrible time, but this ceased when in the latter part of 1806 he left Carver's to live with Jarvis. In the spring of 1808 he resided in the house of Mr. Hitt, a baker, in Broome Street, and there remained ten months. Mr. Hitt reports that Paine's weekly supply then—his seventy-second year, and his last—was three quarts of rum per week.

After Paine had left Carver's he became acquainted with more people. The late Judge Tabor's recollections have

[1] Todd's "Joel Barlow," p. 236. The "Mr. M." was one Murray, an English speculator in France, where he never resided with Paine at all.

been sent me by his son, Mr. Stephen Tabor, of Independence, Iowa.

"I was an associate editor of the *New York Beacon* with Col. John Fellows, then (1836) advanced in years, but retaining all the vigor and fire of his manhood. He was a ripe scholar, a most agreeable companion, and had been the correspondent and friend of Jefferson, Madison, Monroe and John Quincy Adams, under all of whom he held a responsible office. One of his productions was dedicated, by permission, to [J. Q.] Adams, and was republished and favorably received in England. Col. Fellows was the soul of honor and inflexible in his adherence to truth. He was intimate with Paine during the whole time he lived after returning to this country, and boarded for a year in the same house with him.

"I also was acquainted with Judge Hertell, of New York City, a man of wealth and position, being a member of the New York Legislature, both in the Senate and Assembly, and serving likewise on the judicial bench. Like Col. Fellows, he was an author, and a man of unblemished life and irreproachable character.

"These men assured me of their own knowledge derived from constant personal intercourse during the last seven years of Paine's life, that he never kept any company but what was entirely respectable, and that all accusations of drunkenness were grossly untrue. They saw him under all circumstances and *knew* that he was never intoxicated. Nay, more, they said, for that day, he was even abstemious. That was a drinking age and Paine, like Jefferson, could 'bear but little spirit,' so that he was constitutionally temperate.

"Cheetham refers to William Carver and the portrait painter Jarvis. I visited Carver, in company with Col. Fellows, and naturally conversed with the old man about Paine. He said that the allegation that Paine was a drunkard was altogether without foundation. In speaking of his letter to Paine which Cheetham published, Carver said that he was angry when he wrote it and that he wrote unwisely, as angry men generally do; that Cheetham obtained the letter under false pretences and printed it without authority.

"Col. Fellows and Judge Hertell visited Paine throughout the whole course of his last illness. They repeatedly conversed with him on religious topics and they declared that he died serenely, philosophically and resignedly. This information I had directly from their own lips, and their characters were so spotless, and their integrity so unquestioned, that more reliable testimony it would be impossible to give."

During Paine's life the world heard no hint of sexual immorality connected with him, but after his death Cheetham published the following: "Paine brought with him from Paris, and from her husband in whose house he had lived, Margaret Brazier Bonneville, and her three sons. *Thomas* has the features, countenance, and temper of Paine." Madame Bonneville promptly sued Cheetham for slander. Cheetham had betrayed his "pal," Carver, by printing the letter concocted to blackmail Paine, for whose composition the farrier no doubt supposed he had paid the editor with stories borrowed from "Oldys," or not actionable. Cheetham probably recognized, when he saw Madame Bonneville in court, that he too had been deceived, and that any illicit relation between the accused lady and Paine, thirty years her senior, was preposterous. Cheetham's lawyer (Griffin) insinuated terrible things that his witnesses were to prove, but they all dissolved into Carver. Mrs. Ryder, with whom Paine had boarded, admitted trying to make Paine smile by saying Thomas was like him, but vehemently repudiated the slander. "Mrs. Bonneville often came to visit him. She never saw but decency with Mrs. Bonneville. She never staid there but one night, when Paine was very sick." Mrs. Dean was summoned to support one of Carver's lies that Madame Bonneville tried to cheat Paine, but denied the whole story (which has unfortunately been credited by Vale and other writers). The Rev. Mr. Foster, who had a claim against Paine's estate for tuition of the Bonnevilles, was summoned. "Mrs. Bonneville," he testified, "might possibly have said as much as that but for Paine she would not have come here, and that he was under special obligations to provide for her children." A Westchester witness, Peter Underhill, testified that "he one day told Mrs. Bonneville that her child resembled Paine, and Mrs. Bonneville said it was Paine's child." But, apart from the intrinsic incredibility of this statement (unless she meant "godson"), Underhill's character broke down under the testimony of his neighbors, Judge Sommerville and Captain Pelton. Cheetham had thus no dependence but Carver, who actually tried to support his slanders from the dead lips of Paine! But in doing so he ruined Cheetham's case by saying that Paine told him Madame Bonneville was never the wife of M. Bonneville; the charge being that she was seduced from her husband. It was extorted from Carver that Madame Bonneville, having seen his scurrilous letter to Paine, threatened to prosecute him; also that he had taken his wife to visit Madame Bonneville. Then it became plain to Carver that Cheetham's case was lost, and he deserted it on the witness-stand; declaring that " he had never seen the slightest indication of any meretricious or illicit commerce between Paine and Mrs. Bonneville, that they never were alone together, and that all the three children were alike the objects of Paine's care." Counsellor Sampson (no friend to Paine) perceived that Paine's Will was at the bottom of the business. " That is the key to this mysterious league of apostolic slanderers, mortified expectants and disappointed speculators." Sampson's invective was terrific: Cheetham rose and claimed protection of the court, hinting at a duel. Sampson took a pinch of snuff, and pointing his finger at the defendant, said:

"If he complains of personalities, he who is hardened in every gross abuse, he who lives reviling and reviled, who might construct himself a monument with no other materials but those records to which he is a party, and in which he stands enrolled as an offender [1]: if he cannot sit still to hear his accusation, but calls for the protection of the court against a counsel whose duty it is to make his crimes appear, how does *she* deserve protection, whom he has driven to the sad necessity of coming here to vindicate her honor, from those personalities he has lavished on her?"

The editor of Counsellor Sampson's speech says that the jury, "although composed of men of different political sentiments, returned in a few minutes a verdict of guilty." It is added:

"The court, however, when the libeller came up the next day to receive his sentence, highly commended the book which contained the libellous publication, declared that it tended to serve the cause of religion, and imposed no other punishment on the libeller than the payment of

---

[1] Cheetham was at the moment a defendant in nine or ten cases for libel.

$150, with a direction that the costs be taken out of it. It is fit to remark, lest foreigners who are unacquainted with our political condition should receive erroneous impressions, that Mr. Recorder Hoffman does not belong to the Republican party in America, but has been elevated to office by men in hostility to it, who obtained a temporary ascendency in the councils of state." [2]

Madame Bonneville had in court eminent witnesses to her character,— Thomas Addis Emmet, Fulton, Jarvis, and ladies whose children she had taught French. Yet the scandal was too tempting an illustration of the " Age of Reason " to disappear with Cheetham's defeat. Americans in their peaceful habitations were easily made suspicious of a French woman who had left her husband in Paris and followed Paine; they could little realize the complications into which ten tempestuous years had thrown thousands of families in France, and how such poor radicals as the Bonnevilles had to live as they could. The scandal branched into variants. Twenty-five years later pious Grant Thorburn promulgated that Paine had run off from Paris with the wife of a tailor named Palmer. " Paine made no scruples of living with this woman openly." (Mrs. Elihu Palmer, in her penury, was employed by Paine to attend to his rooms, etc., during a few months of illness.) As to Madame Bonneville, whose name Grant Thorburn seems not to have heard, she was turned into a romantic figure. Thorburn says that Paine escaped the guillotine by the execution of another man in his place.

"The man who suffered death for Paine left a widow, with two young children in poor circumstances. Paine brought them all to this country, supported them while he lived, and, it is said, left most of his property to them when he died. The widow and children lived in apartments up town by themselves. He then boarded with Carver. I believe his conduct

---

[2] "Speech of Counsellor Sampson; with an Introduction to the Trial of James Cheetham, Esq., for a libel on Margaret Brazier Bonneville, in his Memoirs of Thomas Paine. Philadelphia: Printed by John Sweeny, No. 357 Arch Street, 1810." I am indebted for the use of this rare pamphlet, and for other information, to the industrious collector of *causes célèbres*, Mr. E. B. Wynn, of Watertown, N. Y.

was disinterested and honorable to the widow. She appeared to be about thirty years of age, and was far from being handsome." [1]

Grant Thorburn was afterwards led to doubt whether this woman was the widow of the man guillotined, but declares that when "Paine first brought her out, he and his friends passed her off as such." As a myth of the time (1834), and an indication that Paine's generosity to the Bonneville family was well known in New York, the story is worth quoting. But the Bonnevilles never escaped from the scandal. Long years afterward, when the late Gen. Bonneville was residing in St. Louis, it was whispered about that he was the natural son of Thomas Paine, though he was born before Paine ever met Madame Bonneville. Of course it has gone into the religious encyclopædias. The best of them, that of McClintock and Strong, says: "One of the women he supported [in France] followed him to this country." After the fall of Napoleon, Nicolas Bonneville, relieved of his surveillance,

[1] "Forty Years' Residence in America."

hastened to New York, where he and his family were reunited, and enjoyed the happiness provided by Paine's self-sacrificing economy.

The present writer, having perused some thousands of documents concerning Paine, is convinced that no charge of sensuality could have been brought against him by any one acquainted with the facts, except out of malice. Had Paine held, or practised, any latitudinarian theory of sexual liberty, it would be recorded here, and his reasons for the same given. I have no disposition to suppress anything. Paine was conservative in such matters. And as to his sacrificing the happiness of a home to his own pleasure, nothing could be more inconceivable.

Above all, Paine was a profoundly religious man,—one of the few in our revolutionary era of whom it can be said that his delight was in the law of his Lord, and in that law did he meditate day and night. Consequently, he could not escape the immemorial fate of the great believers, to be persecuted for unbelief—by unbelievers.

CHAPTER XLIV

DEATH AND RESURRECTION

THE blow that Paine received by the refusal of his vote at New Rochelle was heavy. Elisha Ward, a Tory in the Revolution, had dexterously gained power enough to give his old patrons a good revenge on the first advocate of independence. The blow came at a time when his means were low, and Paine resolved to apply to Congress for payment of an old debt. The response would at once relieve him, and overwhelm those who were insulting him in New York. This led to a further humiliation, and one or two letters to Congress, of which Paine's enemies did not fail to make the most.[1] The letters

[1] Paine had always felt that Congress was in

are those of a broken-hearted man, and it seems marvellous that Jefferson, Madi-

his debt for his voyage to France for supplies with Col. Laurens (p. 70). In a letter (Feb. 20, 1782) to Robert Morris, Paine mentions that when Col. Laurens proposed that he should accompany him, as secretary, he was on the point of establishing a newspaper. He had purchased twenty reams of paper, and Mr. Izard had sent to St. Eustatia for seventy more. This scheme, which could hardly fail of success, was relinquished for the voyage. It was undertaken at the urgent solicitation of Laurens, and Paine certainly regarded it as official. He had ninety dollars when he started, in bills of exchange; when Col. Laurens left him, after their return, he had but two louis d'or. The Memorial sent by Paine to Congress (Jan. 21, 1808) recapitulated facts known to my reader. It was presented by the Hon. George Clinton, Jr., son, and the Clintons did not intervene and see that some recognition of Paine's former services, by those who should not have forgotten them, was made without the ill-judged memorial. While they were enjoying their grandeur the man who, as Jefferson wrote, "steadily labored, and with as much effect as any man living," to secure America freedom, was living—or rather dying—in a miserable lodging-house, 63 Partition Street. He had gone there for economy; for he was exhibiting that morbid apprehension about his means which is a well-known symptom of decline in those who have suffered poverty in early life. Washington, with 40,000 acres, wrote in his last year as if facing ruin. Paine had only a little farm at New Rochelle. He had for some time suffered from want of income, and at last had to sell the farm he meant for the Bonnevilles for $10,000, but the purchaser died, and at his widow's appeal the contract was cancelled. It was at this time that he appealed to Congress. It appears, however, that Paine was not anxious for himself, but for the family of Madame Bonneville, whose statement on this point is important.

The last letter that I can find of

February 4th, and referred to the Committee of Claims. On February 14th Paine wrote a statement concerning the $3,000 given him (1785) by Congress, which he maintained was an indemnity for injustice done him in the Deane case. Laurens had long been dead. The Committee consulted the President, whose reply I know not. Vice-President Clinton wrote (March 23, 1808) that "from the information I received at the time I have reason to believe that Mr. Paine accompanied Col. Laurens on his mission to France in the course of our revolutionary war, for the purpose of negotiating a loan, and that he acted as his secretary on that occasion; but although I have no doubt of the truth of this fact, I cannot assert it from my own actual knowledge." There was nothing found on the journals of Congress to show Paine's connection with the mission. The old author was completely upset by his longing to hear the fate of his memorial, and he wrote two complaints of the delay, showing that his nerves were shattered. "If," he says, March 7th, "my memorial was referred to the Committee of Claims for the purpose of losing it, it is unmanly policy. After so many years of service my heart grows cold towards America."

Paine's was written to Jefferson, July 8, 1808:

"The british Ministry have out-schemed themselves. It is not difficult to see what the motive and object of that Ministry were in issuing the orders of Council. They expected those orders would force all the commerce of the United States to England, and then, by giving permission to such cargoes as they did not want for themselves to depart for the Continent of Europe, to raise a revenue out of those countries and America. But instead of this they have lost revenue; that is, they have lost the revenue they used to receive from American imports, and instead of gaining all the commerce they have lost it all.

"This being the case with the british Ministry it is natural to suppose they would be glad to tread back their steps, if they could do it without too much exposing their ignorance and obstinacy. The Embargo law empowers the President to suspend its operation whenever he shall be satisfied that our ships can pass in safety. It therefore includes the idea of empowering him to use means for arriving at that event. Suppose the President were to authorise Mr. Pinckney to propose to the british Ministry that the United States would negociate with France for rescinding the Milan Decree, on condition the English Ministry would rescind their orders of Council; and in that case the United States would recall their Embargo. France and England stand now at such a distance that neither can propose any thing to the other, neither are there any neutral powers to act as mediators. The U. S. is the only power that can act.

"Perhaps the british Ministry if they listen to the proposal will want to add to it the Berlin decree, which excludes english commerce from the continent of Europe; but this we have nothing to do with, neither has it any thing to do with the Embargo. The british Orders of Council and the Milan decree are parallel cases, and the cause of the Embargo. Yours in friendship."

Paine's last letters to the President are characteristic. One pleads for American intervention to stay the hand of French oppression among the negroes in St. Domingo; for the colonization of Louisiana with free negro laborers; and his very last letter is an appeal for mediation between France and England for the sake of peace.

Nothing came of these pleadings of Paine; but perhaps on his last stroll along the Hudson, with his friend Fulton, to watch the little steamer, he may have recognized the real mediator beginning its labors for the federation of the world.

Early in July, 1808, Paine removed to a comfortable abode, that of Mrs. Ryder, near which Madame Bonneville and her two sons resided. The house was on Herring Street (afterwards 293 Bleecker), and not far, he might be pleased to find, from " Reason Street." Here he made one more attempt to wield his pen,—the result being a brief letter " To the Federal Faction," which he warns that they are endangering American commerce by abusing France and Bonaparte, provoking them to establish a navigation act that will exclude American ships from Europe. "The United States have flourished, unrivalled in commerce, fifteen or sixteen years. But it is not a permanent state of things. It arose from the circumstances of the war, and most probably will change at the close of the present war. The Federalists give provocation enough to promote it."

Apparently this is the last letter Paine ever sent to the printer. The year passed peacefully away ; indeed there is reason to believe that from the middle of July, 1808, to the end of January, 1809, he fairly enjoyed existence. During this time he made acquaintance with the worthy Willett Hicks, watchmaker, who was a Quaker preacher. His conversations with Willett Hicks—whose cousin, Elias Hicks, became such an important figure in the Quaker Society twenty years later—were fruitful.

Seven serene months then passed away. Towards the latter part of January, 1809, Paine was very feeble. On the 18th he wrote and signed his Will, in which he reaffirms his theistic faith. On February 1st the Committee of Claims reported unfavorably on his memorial, while recording, "That Mr. Paine rendered great and eminent services to the United States during their struggle for liberty and independence cannot be doubted by any person acquainted with his labors in the cause, and attached to the principles of the contest." On February 25th he had some fever, and a doctor was sent for. Mrs. Ryder attributed the attack to Paine's having

stopped taking stimulants, and their resumption was prescribed. About a fortnight later symptoms of dropsy appeared. Towards the end of April Paine was removed to a house on the spot now occupied by No. 59 Grove Street, Madame Bonneville taking up her abode under the same roof. The owner was William A. Thompson, once a law partner of Aaron Burr, whose wife, *née* Maria Holdron, was a niece of Elihu Palmer. The whole of the back part of the house (which was in a lot, no street being then cut) was given up to Paine.[1] Reports of neglect of Paine by Madame Bonneville have been credited by some, but are unfounded. She gave all the time she could to the sufferer, and did her best for him. Willett Hicks sometimes called, and his daughter (afterwards Mrs. Cheeseman) used to take Paine delicacies. The only procurable nurse was a woman named Hedden, who combined piety and artfulness. Paine's physician was the most distinguished in New York, Dr. Romaine, but nurse Hedden managed to get into the house one Dr. Manly, who turned out to be Cheetham's spy. Manly afterwards contributed to Cheetham's book a lying letter, in which he claimed to have been Paine's physician. It will be seen, however, by Madame Bonneville's narrative to Cobbett, that Paine was under the care of his friend, Dr. Romaine. As Manly, assuming that he called as many did, never saw Paine alone, he was unable to assert that Paine recanted, but he converted the exclamations of the sufferer into prayers to Christ.[2]

[1] The topographical facts were investigated by John Randel, Jr., Civil Engineer, at the request of David C. Valentine, Clerk of the Common Council, New York, his report being rendered April 6, 1864.

[2] Another claimant to have been Paine's physician has been cited. In 1876 (*N. Y. Observer*, Feb. 17th) Rev. Dr. Wickham reported from a late Dr. Matson Smith, of New Rochelle, that he had been Paine's physician, and witnessed his drunkenness. Unfortunately for Wickham he makes Smith say it was on his farm where Paine "spent his latter days." Paine was not on his farm for two years before his death. Smith could never have attended

The god of wrath who ruled in New York a hundred years, through the ministerial prerogatives, was guarded by a Cerberean legend. The three alternatives of the heretic were, recantation, special judgment, terrible death. Before Paine's arrival in America, the excitement on his approach had tempted a canny Scot, Donald Fraser, to write an anticipated "Recantation" for him, the title-page being cunningly devised so as to imply that there had been an actual recantation. On his arrival in New York, Paine found it necessary to call Fraser to account. The Scotchman pleaded that he had vainly tried to earn a living as fencing-master, preacher, and school-teacher, but had got eighty dollars for writing the "Recantation." Paine said : " I am glad you found the expedient a successful shift for your needy family ; but write no more concerning Thomas Paine. I am satisfied with your acknowledgment—try something more worthy of a man."[1] The second mouth of Cerberus was noisy throughout the land ; revivalists were describing in New Jersey how some "infidel" had been struck blind in Virginia, and in Virginia how one was struck dumb in New Jersey. But here was the very head and front of what they called "infidelity," Thomas Paine, who ought to have gathered in his side a sheaf of thunderbolts, preserved by more marvellous "providences" than any sectarian saint. Out of one hundred and sixty carried to the guillotine from his prison, he alone was saved, by the accident of a chalk mark affixed to the wrong side of his cell door. On two ships he prepared to return to America, but was prevented ; one sank at sea, the other was searched by the British for him particularly. And at the very moment when New Rochelle disciples were calling down fire on his head, Christopher Dederick tried vainly to answer the imprecation ; within a few feet of Paine, his gun only shattered the window at which the author sat. " Providence must be as bad as Thomas Paine," wrote the old deist. This amounted to a sort of contest like that of old between the prophets of Baal and those of Jehovah. The deists were crying to their antagonists : "Perchance he sleepeth." It seemed a test case. If Paine was spared, what heretic need tremble ? But he reached his threescore years and ten in comfort ; and the placard of Satan flying off with him represented a last hope.

Skepticism and rationalism were not understood by pious people a hundred years ago. In some regions they are not understood yet. Renan thinks he will have his legend in France modelled after Judas. But no educated Christian conceives of a recantation or extraordinary death bed for a Darwin, a Parker, an Emerson. The late Mr. Bradlaugh had some fear that he might be a posthumous victim of the "infidel's legend." In 1875, when he was ill in St. Luke's Hospital, New York, he desired me to question the physicians and nurses, that I might, if necessary, testify to his fearlessness and fidelity to his views in the presence of death. But he has died without the "legend," whose decline dates from Paine's case ; that was its crucial challenge.[2]

The whole nation had recently been thrown into a wild excitement by the fall of Alexander Hamilton in a duel with Aaron Burr. Hamilton's worldliness had been notorious, but the clergymen (Bishop Moore and the Presbyterian John Mason) reported his dying words of unctuous piety and orthodoxy. In

---

Paine unless in 1803, when he had a slight trouble with his hands,—the only illness he ever had at New Rochelle,—while the guest of a neighbor, who attests his sobriety. Finally, a friend of Dr. Smith is living, Mr. Albert Willcox, who writes me his recollection of what Smith told him of Paine. Neither drunkenness, nor any item of Wickham's report is mentioned. He said Paine was afraid of death, but could only have heard it.

[1] Dr. Francis' "Old New York," p. 139.

[2] Dr. Conway was under a misapprehension on this point. The "legend" was started immediately after Mr. Bradlaugh's death in 1891, and in spite of repeated contradictions is continually revived.—H. B. B.

a public letter to the Rev. John Mason Paine said:

"Between you and your rival in communion ceremonies, Dr. Moore of the Episcopal church, you have, in order to make yourselves appear of some importance, reduced General Hamilton's character to that of a feeble-minded man, who in going out of the world wanted a passport from a priest. Which of you was first applied to for this purpose is a matter of no consequence. The man, sir, who puts his trust and confidence in God, that leads a just and moral life, and endeavors to do good, does not trouble himself about priests when his hour of departure comes, nor permit priests to trouble themselves about him."

The words were widely commented on, and both sides looked forward, almost as if to a prize-fight, to the hour when the man who had unmade thrones, whether in earth or heaven, must face the King of Terrors. Since Michael and Satan had their legendary combat for the body of Moses, there was nothing like it. In view of the pious raids on Paine's death-bed, freethinkers have not been quite fair. To my own mind, some respect is due to those humble fanatics, who really believed that Paine was approaching eternal fires, and had a frantic desire to save him.[1]

Paine had no fear of death; Madame Bonneville's narrative shows that his fear was rather of living too long. But he had some such fear as that of Voltaire when entering his house at Fernay after it began to lighten. He was not afraid of the lightning, he said, but of what the neighboring priest would make of it should he be struck. Paine had some reason to fear that the zealots who had placarded the devil flying away with him might fulfil their prediction by body-snatching. His unwillingness to be left alone, ascribed to superstitious terror, was due to efforts to get a recantation from him, so determined that he dare not be without witnesses. He had foreseen this. While living with Jarvis, two years before, he desired him to bear witness that he maintained his theistic convictions to the last. Jarvis merrily proposed that he should make a sensation by a mock recantation, but the author said, "Tom Paine never told a lie." When he knew that his illness was mortal he solemnly reaffirmed these opinions in the presence of Madame Bonneville, Dr. Romaine, Mr. Haskin, Captain Pelton, and Thomas Nixon.[2] The nurse Hedden, if the Catholic Bishop of Boston (Fenwick) remembered accurately thirty-seven years later, must have conspired to get him into the patient's room, from which, of course, he was stormily expelled. But the Bishop's story is so like a pious novelette that, in the absence of any mention of his visit by Madame Bonneville, herself a Catholic, one cannot be sure that the interview he waited so long to report did not take place in some slumberous episcopal chamber in Boston.[3] It was rumoured that Paine's adherents were keeping him under the influence of liquor in order that he might not recant,—so convinced, at heart, or enamoured of Calvinism was this martyr of Theism, who had published his "Age of Reason" from the prison where he awaited the guillotine.[4]

[1] Nor should it be forgotten that several liberal Christians, like Hicks, were friendly towards Paine at the close of his life, whereas his most malignant enemies were of his own "Painite" household, Carver and Cheetham. Mr. William Erving tells me that he remembers an English clergyman in New York, named Cunningham, who used to visit his (Erving's) father. He heard him say that Paine and he were friends; and that "the whole fault was that people hectored Paine, and made him say things he would never say to those who treated him as a gentleman."

[2] See the certificate of Nixon and Pelton to Cobbett (Vale, p. 177).

[3] Bishop Fenwick's narrative (*U. S. Catholic Magazine*, 1846) is quoted in the *N. Y. Observer*, September 27, 1877. (Extremes become friends when a freethinker is to be crucified.)

[4] Engineer Randel (orthodox), in his topographical report to the Clerk of the City Council (1864), mentions that the "very worthy mechanic," Amasa Wordsworth, who saw Paine daily, told him "there was no truth in such report, and that Thomas Paine had declined saying anything on that subject [religion]." "Paine," testifies Dr. Francis, "clung to his infidelity to the last moment of his natural life." Dr. Francis (orthodox) heard that Paine yielded to King Alcohol, but says Cheetham wrote with "settled malignity," and suspects "sinister motives" in his "strictures on the fruits of unbelief in the degradation of the wretched Paine."

M

Of what his principles had cost him Paine had near his end a reminder that cut him to the heart. Albert Gallatin had remained his friend, but his connections, the Fews and Nicholsons, had ignored the author they once idolized. The woman for whom he had the deepest affection, in America, had been Kitty Nicholson, now Mrs. Few. Henry Adams, in his biography of Gallatin, says: " When confined to his bed with his last illness he [Paine] sent for Mrs. Few, who came to see him, and when they parted she spoke some words of comfort and religious hope. Poor Paine only turned his face to the wall, and kept silence." What is Mr. Adams' authority for this? According to Rickman, Sherwin, and Vale, Mr. and Mrs. Few came of their own accord, and "Mrs. Few expressed a wish to renew their former friendship." Paine said to her, "very impressively, 'You have neglected me, and I beg that you will leave the room.' Mrs. Few went into the garden and wept bitterly." I doubt this tradition also, but it was cruelly tantalizing for his early friend, after ignoring him six years, to return with Death.

If, amid tortures of this kind, the annoyance of fanatics and the "Painites" who came to watch them, and the paroxysms of pain, the sufferer found relief in stimulants, the present writer can only reflect with satisfaction that such resource existed. For some time no food would stay on his stomach. In such weakness and helplessness he was for a week or so almost as miserable as the Christian spies could desire, and his truest friends were not sorrowful when the peace of death approached. After the years in which the stories of Paine's wretched end have been accumulating, now appears the testimony of the Catholic lady,—persons who remember Madame Bonneville assure me that she was a perfect lady,—that Paine's mind was active to the last, that shortly before death he made a humorous retort to Dr. Romaine, that he died after a tranquil night.

Paine died at eight o'clock on the morning of June 8, 1809. Shortly

before, two clergymen had invaded his room, and so soon as they spoke about his opinions Paine said: "Let me alone; good morning!" Madame Bonneville asked if he was satisfied with the treatment he had received in her house, and he said "Oh yes." These were the last words of Thomas Paine.

On June 10th Paine's friends assembled to look on his face for the last time. Madame Bonneville took a rose from her breast and laid it on that of her dead benefactor. His adherents were busy men, and mostly poor, they could not undertake the then difficult journey (nearly twenty-five miles) to the grave beyond New Rochelle. Of the *cortége* that followed Paine a contemptuous account was printed (Aug. 7th) in the London *Packet:*

"Extract of a letter dated June 20th, Philadelphia, written by a gentleman lately returned from a tour: 'On my return from my journey, when I arrived near Harlem, on York island, I met the funeral of Tom Paine on the road. It was going on to East Chester. The followers were two negroes, the next a carriage with six drunken Irishmen, then a riding chair with two men in it, one of whom was asleep, and then an Irish Quaker on horseback. I stopped my sulkey to ask the Quaker what funeral it was; he said it was Paine, and that his friends as well as his enemies were all glad that he was gone, for he had tired his friends out by his intemperance and frailties. I told him that Paine had done a great deal of mischief in the world, and that, if there was any purgatory, he certainly would have a good share of it before the devil would let him go. The Quaker replied, he would sooner take his chance with Paine than any man in New York, on that score. He then put his horse on a trot, and left me.'"

The funeral was going to West Chester; one of the vehicles contained Madame Bonneville and her children; and the Quaker was not an Irishman. I have ascertained that a Quaker did follow Paine, and that it was Willett Hicks. Hicks, who has left us his testimony that Paine was "a good man, and an honest man," may have said that Paine's friends were glad that he was gone, for it was only humane to so feel, but all said about "intemperance and frailties" is doubtless a gloss of the correspondent, like the "drunken Irishmen" substituted for Madame Bonneville and her family.

Could the gentleman of the sulky have appreciated the historic dignity of that little *cortége* he would have turned his horse's head and followed it. Those two negroes, travelling twenty-five miles on foot, represented the homage of a race for whose deliverance Paine had pleaded from his first essay written in America to his recent entreaty for the President's intervention in behalf of the slaughtered negroes of Domingo.[1] One of those vehicles bore the wife of an oppressed French author, and her sons, one of whom was to do gallant service to this country in the War of 1812, the other to explore the unknown West. Behind the Quaker preacher, who would rather take his chance in the next world with Paine than with any man in New York, was following invisibly another of his family and name, who presently built up Hicksite Quakerism, the real monument of Paine, to whom unfriendly Friends refused a grave.

The grand people of America were not there, the clergy were not there; but beside the negroes stood the Quaker preacher and the French Catholic woman. Madame Bonneville placed her son Benjamin—afterwards General in the United States army—at one end of the grave, and standing herself at the other end, cried, as the earth fell on the coffin: "Oh, Mr. Paine, my son stands here as testimony of the gratitude of America, and I for France!"[2]

[1] "On the last day men shall wear
On their heads the dust,
As ensign and as ornament
Of their lowly trust."—*Hafiz*.

[2] No sooner was Paine dead than the ghoul sat gloating upon him. I found in the Rush papers a letter from Cheetham (July 31st) to Benjamin Rush: "Since Mr. Paine's arrival in this city from Washington, when on his way you very properly avoided him, his life, keeping the lowest company, has been an uninterrupted scene of filth, vulgarity, and drunkenness. As to the reports, that on his deathbed he had something like compunctious visitings of conscience with regard to his deistical writings and opinions, they are altogether groundless. He resisted very angrily, and with a sort of triumphant and obstinate pride, all attempts to draw him from those doctrines. Much as you must have seen in the course of your professional

The day of Paine's death was a day of judgment. He had not been struck blind or dumb; Satan had not carried him off; he had lived beyond his three-score years and ten and died peacefully in his bed. The self-appointed messengers of Zeus had managed to vex this Prometheus who brought fire to men, but could not persuade him to whine for mercy, nor did the predicted thunderbolts come. This immunity of Thomas Paine brought the deity of dogma into a dilemma. It could be explained only on the theory of an apology made and accepted by the said deity. Plainly there had to be a recantation somewhere. Either Paine had to recant or Dogma had to recant.

The excitement was particularly strong among the Quakers, who regarded Paine as an apostate Quaker, and perhaps felt compromised by his desire to be buried among them. Willett Hicks told Gilbert Vale that he had been beset by pleading questions. "Did thee never hear him call on Christ?" "As for money," said Hicks, "I could have had any sum." There was found, later on, a Quakeress, formerly a servant in the family of Willett

practice of everything that is offensive in the poorest and most depraved of the species, perhaps you have met with nothing excelling the miserable condition of Mr. Paine. He had scarcely any visitants. It may indeed be said that he was totally neglected and forgotten. Even Mrs. Bournville [*sic*], a woman, I cannot say a Lady, whom he brought with him from Paris, the wife of a Parisian of that name, seemed desirous of hastening his death. He died at Greenwich, in a small room he had hired in a very obscure house. He was hurried to his grave with hardly an attending person. An ill-natured epitaph, written on him in 1796, when it was supposed he was dead, very correctly describes the latter end of his life. He

"Blasphemes the Almighty, lives in filth like a hog,
Is abandoned in death and interr'd like a dog."

The object of this letter was to obtain from Rush, for publication, some abuse of Paine; but the answer honored Paine, save for his heresy, and is quoted by freethinkers as a tribute.

Within a year the grave opened for Cheetham also, and he sank into it branded by the law as the slanderer of a woman's honor, and scourged by the community as a traitor in public life.

Hicks, not proof against such temptations. She pretended that she was sent to carry some delicacy to Paine, and heard him cry "Lord Jesus have mercy upon me"; she also heard him declare "if the Devil has ever had any agency in any work he has had it in my writing that book [the 'Age of Reason']."[1] Few souls are now so belated as to credit such stories; but my readers may form some conception of the mental condition of the community in which Paine died from the fact that such absurdities were printed, believed, spread through the world. The Quaker servant became a heroine, as the one divinely appointed witness of Tom Paine's recantation.

But in the end it was that same Mary that hastened the resurrection of Thomas Paine. The controversy as to whether Mary was or was not a calumniator; whether orthodoxy was so irresistible that Paine must needs surrender at last to a servant-girl who told him she had thrown his book into the fire; whether she was to be believed against her employer, who declared she never saw Paine at all; all this kept Paine alive. Such boiling up from the abysses, of vulgar credulity, grotesque superstition, such commanding illustrations of the

Age of Unreason, disgusted thoughtful Christians.[2]

Such was the religion which was supposed by some to have won Paine's heart at last, but which, when mirrored in the controversy over his death, led to a tremendous reaction. The division in the Quaker Society swiftly developed. In December, 1826, there was an afternoon meeting of Quakers of a critical kind, some results of which led directly to the separation. The chief speaker was Elias Hicks, but it is also recorded that "Willet Hicks was there, and had a short testimony, which seemed to be impressive on the meeting." He had stood in silence beside the grave of the man whose chances in the next world he had rather take than those of any man in New York; but now the silence is broken.[3]

---

[1] "Life and Gospel Labors of Stephen Grellet." This "valuable young Friend," as Stephen Grellet calls her, had married a Quaker named Hinsdale. Grellet, a native of France, convert from Voltaire, led the anti-Hicksites, and was led by his partisanship to declare that Elias promised him to suppress his opinions! The cant of the time was that "deism might do to live by but not to die by." But it had been announced in Paine's obituaries that "some days previous to his demise he had an interview with some Quaker gentlemen on the subject [of burial in their graveyard] but as he declined a renunciation of his deistical opinions his anxious wishes were not complied with." But ten years later, when Hicks' deism was spreading, death-bed terrors seemed desirable, and Mary (Roscoe) Hinsdale, formerly Grellet's servant also, came forward to testify that the recantation refused by Paine to the "Quaker gentlemen," even for a much desired end, had been previously confided to her for no object at all! The story was published by one Charles Collins, a Quaker, who afterwards admitted to Gilbert Vale his doubts of its truth, adding "some of our *friends* believe she indulges in opiates" (Vale, p. 186).

[2] The excitement of the time was well illustrated in a notable caricature by the brilliant artist John Wesley Jarvis. Paine is seen dead, his pillow "Common Sense," his hand holding a manuscript, "A rap on the knuckles for John Mason." On his arm is the label, "Answer to Bishop Watson." Under him is written: "A man who devoted his whole life to the attainment of two objects—rights of man and freedom of conscience—had his vote denied when living, and was denied a grave when dead!" The Catholic Father O'Brian (a notorious drunkard), with very red nose, kneels over Paine, exclaiming, "Oh, you ugly drunken beast!" The Rev. John Mason (Presbyterian) stamps on Paine, exclaiming, "Ah, Tom! Tom! thou'lt get thy frying in hell; they'll roast thee like a herring.

"They'll put thee in the furnace hot,
    And on thee bar the door:
How the devils all will laugh
    To hear thee burst and roar!"

The Rev. Dr. Livingston kicks at Paine's head, exclaiming, "How are the mighty fallen, Right fol-de-riddle-lol!" Bishop Hobart kicks the feet, singing:

"Right fol-de-rol, let's dance and sing,
    Tom is dead, God save the king—
The infidel now low doth lie—
    Sing Hallelujah—hallelujah!"

A Quaker turns away with a shovel, saying, "I'll not bury thee."

[3] Curiously enough, Mary (Roscoe) Hinsdale turned up again. She had broken down under the cross-examination of William Cobbett, but he had long been out of the country when the Quaker separation took place. Mary now reported that a distinguished member of the Hicksite Society, Mary Lockwood, had recanted

I told Walt Whitman, himself partly
a product of Hicksite Quakerism, of the
conclusion to which I had been steadily
drawn, that Thomas Paine rose again in
Elias Hicks, and was in some sort the
origin of our one American religion. I
said my visit was mainly to get his
"testimony" on the subject for my book,
as he was born in Hicks' region, and
mentions in "Specimen Days" his
acquaintance with Paine's friend, Colonel
Fellows. Walt said, for I took down his
words at the time:

"In my childhood a great deal was said of
Paine in our neighborhood, in Long Island.
My father, Walter Whitman, was rather favorable to Paine. I remember hearing Elias Hicks
preach; and his look, slender figure, earnestness,
made an impression on me, though I was only
about eleven. He died in 1830. He is well
represented in the bust there, one of my treasures.
I was a young man when I enjoyed the friendship of Col. Fellows,—then a constable of the
courts; tall, with ruddy face, blue eyes, snowy
hair, and a fine voice; neat in dress, an old-
school gentleman, with a military air, who used
to awe the crowd by his looks; they used to call
him 'Aristides.' I used to chat with him in
Tammany Hall. It was a time when, in religion,
there was as yet no philosophical middle-ground;
people were very strong on one side or the other;
there was a good deal of lying, and the liars
were often well paid for their work. Paine and
his principles made the great issue. Paine was
double-damnably lied about. Col. Fellows was
a man of perfect truth and exactness; he assured
me that the stories disparaging to Paine personally were quite false. Paine was neither drunken
nor filthy; he drank as other people did, and was
a high-minded gentleman. I incline to think
you right in supposing a connection between
the Paine excitement and the Hicksite movement. Paine left a deep, clear-cut impression
on the public mind. Col. Fellows told me that
while Paine was in New York he had a much
larger following than was generally supposed.
After his death a reaction in his favor appeared
among many who had opposed him, and this reaction became exceedingly strong between 1820
and 1830, when the division among the Quakers

in the same way as Paine. This being proved
false, the hysterical Mary sank and remained in
oblivion, from which she is recalled only by the
Rev. Rip Van Winkle. It was the unique sentence on Paine to recant and yet be damned.
This honor belies the indifference expressed in
the rune taught children sixty years ago:

"Poor Tom Paine! there he lies:
Nobody laughs and nobody cries:
Where he has gone or how he fares,
Nobody knows and nobody cares!"

developed. Probably William Cobbett's conversion to Paine had something to do with it.
Cobbett lived in the neighborhood of Elias
Hicks, in Long Island, and probably knew him.
Hicks was a fair-minded man, and no doubt
read Paine's books carefully and honestly. I
am very glad you are writing the Life of Paine.
Such a book has long been needed. Paine was
among the best and truest of men."

Paine's risen soul went marching on
in England also. The pretended recantation proclaimed there was exploded by
William Cobbett, and the whole controversy over Paine's works renewed.
One after another deist was sent to
prison for publishing Paine's works, the
last being Richard Carlile and his wife.
In 1819, the year in which William Cobbett carried Paine's bones to England,
Richard Carlile and his wife, solely for
this offence, were sent to prison,—he for
three years, with fine of £1,500, she
for two years, with fine of £500.[1] This
was a suicidal victory for bigotry. When
these two came out of prison they found
that wealthy gentlemen had provided for
them an establishment in Fleet Street,
where these books were thenceforth sold
unmolested. Mrs. Carlile's petition to
the House of Commons awakened that
body and the whole country. When
Richard Carlile entered prison it was
as a captive deist; when he came out
the freethinkers of England were generally atheists.[2]

[1] I have before me an old fly-leaf picture,
issued by Carlile in the same year. It shows
Paine in his chariot advancing against Superstition. Superstition is a snaky-haired demoness,
with poison-cup in one hand and dagger in the
other, surrounded by instruments of torture, and
treading on a youth. Behind her are priests,
with mask, crucifix, and dagger. Burning fag-
gots surround them with a cloud, behind which
are worshippers around an idol, with a priest
near by, upholding a crucifix before a man burning at the stake. Attended by fair genii, who
uphold a banner inscribed, "Moral Rectitude."
Paine advances, uplifting in one hand the mirror
of Truth, in the other his "Age of Reason."
There are ten stanzas describing the conflict,
Superstition being described as holding

"in vassalage a doating World,
Till Paine and Reason burst upon the mind,
And Truth and Deism their flag unfurled."

[2] Richard Carlile was sentenced to three
years' imprisonment with a fine of £1500. The

But what was this atheism? Merely another Declaration of Independence. Common sense and common justice were entering into religion as they were entering into government. Such epithets as "atheism," "infidelity," were but labels of outlawry which the priesthood of all denominations pronounced upon men who threatened their throne, precisely as "sedition" was the label of outlawry fixed by Pitt on all hostility to George III. In England, atheism was an insurrection of justice against any deity diabolical enough to establish the reign of terror in that country or any deity worshipped by a church which imprisoned men for their opinions. Paine was a theist, but he arose legitimately in his admirer Shelley, who was punished for atheism. Knightly service was done by Shelley in the struggle for the Englishman's right to read Paine. If any enlightened religious man of to-day had to choose between the godlessness of Shelley and the godliness that imprisoned good men for their opinions, he would hardly select the latter. The genius of Paine was in every word of Shelley's letter to Lord Ellenborough on the punishment of Eaton for publishing the "Age of Reason." [1]

In America "atheism" was never anything but the besom which again and again has cleared the human mind of phantasms represented in outrages on honest thinkers. In Paine's time the phantasm which was called Jehovah represented a grossly ignorant interpretation of the Bible; the revelation of its monstrous character, represented in the hatred, slander, falsehood, meanness, and superstition, which Jarvis represented as crows and vultures hovering near the preachers kicking Paine's dead body, necessarily destroyed the phantasm, whose pretended power was proved nothing more than that of certain men to injure a man who out-reasoned them. Paine's fidelity to his unanswered argument was fatal to the consecrated phantasm. It was confessed to be ruling without reason, right, or humanity, like the King from whom "Common Sense," mainly, had freed America, and not by any "Grace of God" at all, but through certain reverend Lord Norths and Lord Howes. Paine's peaceful death, the benevolent distribution of his property by a will affirming his Theism, represented a posthumous and potent conclusion to the "Age of Reason."

Paine had aimed to form in New York a Society for Religious Inquiry, also a Society of Theophilanthropy. The latter was formed, and his posthumous works first began to appear, shortly after his death, in an organ called *The Theophil-*

---

fine he could not pay if he would, and would not if he could; in default therefore he was kept a further three years in Dorchester Gaol, making six years in all. His wife, Jane Carlile, was sentenced to two years' imprisonment; his sister, Mary Ann Carlile, to one year with a fine of £500, which, as she was without means and unable to pay in cash, had to be paid by a further year in gaol. In addition to the three Carliles, Carlile's shopmen were also arrested and imprisoned, and as they were arrested, volunteers came from all parts of the country to take their places, first behind the counter in the shop, then in the dock, and finally in the prison. The gallant stand made by these devoted men and women purchased immunity for the "Age of Reason" in England, where it has been freely sold in edition after edition ever since.—H. B. B.

[1] "Whence is any right derived, but that which power confers, for persecution? Do you think to convert Mr. Eaton to your religion by embittering his existence? You might force him by torture to profess your tenets, but he could not believe them except you should make them credible, which perhaps exceeds your power. Do you think to please the God you

worship by this exhibition of your zeal? If so the demon to whom some nations offer human hecatombs is less barbarous than the Deity of civilized society. . . . Does the Christian God, whom his followers eulogize as the deity of humility and peace—he, the regenerator of the world, the meek reformer—authorise one man to rise against another, and, because lictors are at his beck, to chain and torture him as an infidel? When the Apostles went abroad to convert the nations, were they enjoined to stab and poison all who disbelieved the divinity of Christ's mission? . . . The time is rapidly approaching —I hope that you, my Lord, may live to behold its arrival—when the Mahometan, the Jew, the Christian, the Deist, and the Atheist will live together in one community, equally sharing the benefits which arrive from its association, and united in the bonds of charity and brotherly love."

anthropist. But his movement was too cosmopolitan to be contained in any local organization. "Thomas Paine," said President Andrew Jackson to Judge Hertell, "Thomas Paine needs no monument made by hands; he has erected a monument in the hearts of all lovers of liberty." The like may be said of his religion : Theophilanthropy, under a hundred translations and forms, is now the fruitful branch of every religion and every sect. The real cultivators of skepticism,—those who ascribe to deity biblical barbarism, and the savagery of nature,—have had their day.

The removal and mystery of Paine's bones appear like some page of Mosaic mythology.[1] An English caricature pictured Cobbett seated on Paine's coffin, in a boat named RIGHTS OF MAN, rowed by NEGRO SLAVES.

"A singular coincidence [says Dr. Francis] led me to pay a visit to Cobbett at his country seat, within a couple of miles of the city, on the island, on the very day that he had exhumed the bones of Paine, and shipped them for England. I will here repeat the words which Cobbett gave utterance to at the friendly interview our party had with him. 'I have just performed a duty, gentlemen, which has been too long delayed : you have neglected too long the remains of Thomas Paine. I have done myself the honour to disinter his bones. I have removed them from New Rochelle. I have dug them up ; they are now on their way to England. When I myself return, I shall cause them to speak the common sense of the great man ; I shall gather together the people of Liverpool and Manchester in one assembly with those of London, and those bones will effect the reformation of England in Church and State.'"

Mr. Badeau, of New Rochelle, remembers standing near Cobbett's workmen while they were digging up the bones, about dawn. There is a legend that Paine's little finger was left in America, a fable, perhaps, of his once small movement, now stronger than the loins of the bigotry that refused him a vote or a grave in the land he so greatly served. As to his bones, no man knows the place of their rest to this day. His principles rest not. His thoughts, untraceable like his dust, are blown about the world which he held in his heart. For a hundred years no human being has been born in the civilized world without some spiritual tincture from that heart whose every pulse was for humanity, whose last beat broke a fetter of fear, and fell on the throne of thrones.

---

[1] The bones of Thomas Paine were landed in Liverpool, November 21, 1819. The monument contemplated by Cobbett was never raised. There was much parliamentary and municipal excitement. A Bolton town-crier was imprisoned nine weeks for proclaiming the arrival. In 1836 the bones passed with Cobbett's effects into the hands of a Receiver (West). The Lord Chancellor refusing to regard them as an asset, they were kept by an old day-laborer until 1844, when they passed to B. Tilley, 13 Bedford Square, London, a furniture dealer. In 1849 the empty coffin was in possession of J. Chennell, Guildford. The silver plate bore the inscription "Thomas Paine, died June 8, 1809, aged 72." In 1854, Rev. R. Ainslie (Unitarian) told E. Truelove that he owned " the skull and the right hand of Thomas Paine," but evaded subsequent inquiries. The removal caused excitement in America. Of Paine's gravestone the last fragment was preserved by his friends of the Bayeaux family, and framed on their wall. In November, 1839, the present marble monument at New Rochelle was erected. [The monument, erected in 1839 by Gilbert Vale and other Freethinkers, and since that date kept in repair and supplied with a bronze bust of Paine by the Freethinkers of New York and elsewhere, was on October 14, 1905, taken over with great ceremony by the Mayor on behalf of the people of New Rochelle. The occasion was made a great demonstration at which the United States was officially represented by several battalions of infantry and a battery of five guns ; representatives from the National Guard and War Veterans were also present. The monument has been moved about fifty feet from its original position to a much better situation on more elevated ground ; it is placed in the middle of an avenue, called "Paine Avenue." Buried beneath the monument is a box containing a fragment of Paine's brain and hair, which after wandering about the world ever since Cobbett brought Paine's remains to England, was purchased in 1900 by Dr. Moncure Conway, and which through his devotion has, we may hope, found at last a final resting-place.—H. B. B.]

APPENDIX A

THE COBBETT PAPERS

IN the autumn of 1792 William Cobbett arrived in America. Among the papers preserved by the family of Thomas Jefferson is a letter from Cobbett, enclosing an introduction from Mr. Short, U. S. Secretary of Legation at Paris. In this letter, dated at Wilmington, Delaware, November 2, 1792, the young Englishman writes: "Ambitious to become the citizen of a free state I have left my native country, England, for America. I bring with me youth, a small family, a few useful literary talents, and that is all."

Cobbett had been married in the same year, on February 5th, and visited Paris, perhaps with an intention of remaining, but becoming disgusted with the revolution he left for America. He had conceived a dislike of the French revolutionary leaders, among whom he included Paine. He thus became an easy victim of the libellous Life of Paine, by George Chalmers, which had not been reprinted in America, and reproduced the statements of that work in a brief biographical sketch published in Philadelphia, 1796. In later life Cobbett became convinced that he had been deceived into giving fresh currency to a tissue of slanders. In the very year of this publication, afterwards much lamented, Paine published in Europe a work that filled Cobbett with admiration. This was "The Decline and Fall of the English System of Finance," which predicted the suspension of gold payments by the Bank of England that followed the next year. The pamphlet became Cobbett's text-book, and his *Register* was eloquent in Paine's praise, the more earnestly, he confessed, because he had "been one of his most violent assailants." "Old age having laid his hand upon this truly great man, this truly philosophical politician, at his expiring flambeau I lighted my taper."

A sketch of Thomas Paine and some related papers of Cobbett are generously confided to me by his daughter, Eleanor Cobbett, through her nephew, William Cobbett, Jr., of Woodlands, near Manchester, England. The public announcement (1818) by Cobbett, then in America, of his intention to write a Life of Paine, led to his negotiation with Madame Bonneville, who, with her husband, resided in New York. Madame Bonneville had been disposing of some of Paine's manuscripts, such as that on "Freemasonry," and the reply to Bishop Watson, printed in *The Theophilanthropist* (1810). She had also been preparing, with her husband's assistance, notes for a biography of Paine, because of the "unjust efforts to tarnish the memory of Mr. Paine;" adding, "*Et l'indignation m'a fait prendre la plume.*" Cobbett agreed to give her a thousand dollars for the manuscript, which was to contain important letters from and to eminent men. She stated (September 30, 1819) her conditions, that it should be published in England, without any addition, and separate from any other writings. I suppose it was one or all of these conditions that caused the non-completion of the bargain. Cobbett re-wrote the whole thing, and it is now all in his writing except a few passages by Madame Bonneville, which I indicate by brackets, and two or three by his son, J. P. Cobbett. Although Madame Bonneville gave some revision to Cobbett's manuscript, most of the letters to be supplied are merely indicated. No trace of them exists among the Cobbett papers. Soon afterward the Bonnevilles went to Paris, where they kept a small book shop. Nicolas died in 1828. His biography in Michaud's Dictionary is annotated by the widow, and states that in 1829 she had begun to edit for publication the Life and posthumous papers of Thomas Paine. From this it would appear that she had retained the manuscript, and the original letters. In 1833 Madame Bonneville emigrated to St. Louis, where her son, the late General Bonneville, lived. Her Catholicism became, I believe, devout with advancing years, and to that cause, probably also to a fear of reviving the old scandal Cheetham had raised, may be due the suppression of the papers, with the result mentioned in the introduction to this work. She died in St. Louis, October 30, 1846, at the age of 79. Probably William Cobbett did not feel entitled to publish the manuscript obtained under such conditions, or he might have waited for the important documents that were never sent. He died in 1835.

The recollections are those of both M. and Madame Bonneville. The reader will find no difficulty in making out the parts that represent Madame's personal knowledge and reminiscences, as Cobbett has preserved her speech in the first person, and, with characteristic literary acumen, her expressions in such important points. His manuscript is perfect, and I have little editing to do beyond occasional correction of a date, supplying one or two letters indicated, which I have found, and omitting a few letters, extracts, etc., already printed in the body of this work, where unaccompanied by any comment or addition from either Cobbett or the Bonnevilles.

At the time when this Cobbett-Bonneville sketch was written New York was still a provincial place. Nicolas Bonneville, as Irving describes him, seated under trees at the Battery, absorbed in his classics, might have been regarded with suspicion had it been known that his long separation from his family was due to detention by the police. Madame Bonneville is reserved on that point. The following incident, besides illustrating the characters of Paine and Bonneville, may suggest a cause for the rigor of Bonneville's surveillance. In 1797, while Paine and Bonneville were editing the *Bien Informé*, a "suspect" sought asylum with them. This was Count Barruel-Beauvert, an author whose writings alone had caused his denunciation as a royalist. He had escaped from the Terror, and now wandered back in disguise, a pauper Count, who knew well the magnanimity of the two men whose protection he asked. He remained, as proof-reader, in the Bonneville house for some time, safely; but when the conspiracy of 18 Fructidor (September 4, 1797) exasperated the Republic against

royalists, the Count feared that he might be the means of compromising his benefactors, and disappeared. When the royalist conspiracy against Bonaparte was discovered, Barruel-Beauvert was again hunted, and arrested (1802). His trial probably brought to the knowledge of the police his former sojourn with Paine and Bonneville. Bonaparte sent by Fouché a warning to Paine that the eye of the police was upon him, and that "on the first complaint he would be sent to his own country, America." Whether this, and the closer surveillance on Bonneville, were connected with the Count, who also suffered for a time, or whether due to their anti-slavery writings on Domingo, remains conjectural. Towards the close of life Bonneville received a pension, which was continued to his widow. So much even a monarchy with an established church could do for a republican author, and a freethinker; for Bonneville had published heresies like those of Paine.

THOMAS PAINE
A SKETCH OF HIS LIFE AND CHARACTER

[More exactly than any other author Thomas Paine delineates every Circumstantial Events, private or Public in his Writings; nevertheless, since many pretended Histories of the Life of T. P. have been published, tracing him back to the day of his][1] birth, we shall shortly observe, that, as was never denied by himself, he was born at Thetford, in the County of Norfolk, England on the 29th January, in the year 1737; that his father Joseph Paine was a stay-maker, and by religion a Quaker; that his mother was the daughter of a country-attorney, and that she belonged to the Church of England; but, it appears, that she also afterwards became a Quaker; for these parents both belonged to the Meeting in 1787, as appears from a letter of the father to the son. The above-mentioned histories relate (and the correctness of the statement has

---

[1] The bracketed words, Madame Bonneville's, are on a separate slip. An opening paragraph by Cobbett is crossed out by her pen: "The early years of the life of a Great Man are of little consequence to the world. Whether Paine made stays or gauged barrels before he became a public character, is of no more importance to us than whether he was swaddled with woollen or with linen. It is the man, in conjunction with those labours which have produced so much effect in the world, whom we are to follow and contemplate. Nevertheless, since many pretended histories of the life of Paine have been published, etc."

not been denied by him), that Paine was educated at the free-school of Thetford ; that he left it in 1752, when he was fifteen years of age, and then worked for some time with his father : that in a year afterwards, he went to London : that from London he went to Dover : that about this time he was on the eve of becoming a sailor : that he afterwards did embark on board a privateer : that, between the years 1759 and 1774 he was a stay-maker, an excise officer, a grocer, and an usher to a school ; and that, during the period he was twice married, and seperated by mutual consent, from his second wife.[1]

In this year 1774 and in the month of September, Paine sailed from England for Philadelphia, where he arrived safe ; and now we *begin* his history ; for here we have him in connection with his literary labours.

It being an essential part of our plan to let Thomas Paine speak in his own words, and explain himself the reason for his actions, whenever we find written papers in his own hand, though in incomplete notes or fragments, we shall insert such, in order to enable the reader to judge for himself, and to estimate the slightest circumstances. *Souvent d'un grand dessin un mot nous fait juger*. " A word often enables us to judge of a great design."

"I happened to come to America a few months before the breaking out of hostilities. I found the disposition of the people such that they might have been led by a thread and governed by a reed. Their suspicion was quick and penetrating, but their attachment to Britain was obstinate, and it was at that time a kind of treason to speak against it. They disliked the Ministry, but they esteemed the Nation. Their idea of grievance operated without resentment, and their single object was reconciliation. Bad as I believed the Ministry to be, I never conceived them capable of a measure so rash and wicked as the commencing of hostilities ; much less did I imagine the Nation would encourage it. I viewed the dispute as a kind of law-suit, in which I supposed the parties would find a way either to decide or settle it. I had no thoughts of independence or of arms. The world could not then have persuaded me that I should be either a soldier or an author. If I had any talents for either they were buried in me, and might ever have continued so had not the necessity of the times dragged and driven them into action. I had formed my plan of life, and conceiving myself happy wished everybody else so. But when the country, into which I had just set my foot, was set on fire about my ears, it was time to stir. It was time for every man to stir."[2]

His first intention at Philadelphia was to establish an Academy for young ladies, who were to be taught many branches of learning then little known in the education of young American ladies. But, in 1775, he undertook the management of the Pennsylvania Magazine

About this time he published, in Bradford's journal, an essay on the slavery of the negroes, which was universally well received ; and also stanzas on the death of General Wolfe.

In 1776, January 10, he published Common Sense. In the same year he joined the army as aid-de-camp to General Greene. Gordon, in his history of the Independence of the United States (vol. ii. p. 78), says : [*Wanting.*]—Ramsay (Lond. ed. i. p. 336) says : [*Wanting.*] Anecdote of Dr. Franklin preserved by Thomas Paine : [*Wanting, but no doubt one elsewhere given, in the Hall manuscripts.*]

When Washington had made his retreat from New York Thomas Paine published the first number of the *Crisis*, which was read to every corporal's guard in the camp. It revived the army, reunited the members of the [New York] Convention, when despair had reduced them to nine in number, while the militia were abandoning their standards and flying in all directions. The success of the army at Trenton was, in some degree, owing to this first number of the Crisis. In 1778 he discovered the robberies of Silas Deane, an agent of the United States in France. He gave in his resignation as Secretary, which was accepted by the Congress. In 1779 he was appointed Clerk to the General Assembly of Pennsylvania, which office he retained until 1780. In 1780 he departed for France with Col. John Laurens, commissioned especially by the Congress to the Court at Versailles to obtain the aid that was wanted. (See Gordon's Hist. v. iii., p. 154.) After his return from France he received the following letter from Col. Laurens :

"CAROLINA, April 18, 1782.—I received the letter wherein you mention my horse and trunk, (the latter of which was left at Providence). The misery which the former has suffered at different times, by mismanagement, has greatly distressed me. He was wounded in service, and I am much attached to him. If he can be of any service to you, I entreat your acceptance of him, more especially if you will make use of him in bringing you to a country (Carolina) where you will be received with open arms, and all that affection and respect which our citizens are anxious to testify to the author of Common Sense, and the Crisis.

"Adieu! I wish you to regard this part of America (Carolina) as your particular home— and everything that I can command in it to be in common between us."

On the 10th of April, 1783, the definitive treaty of peace was received and published. Here insert the letter from Gen. Nathaniel Greene :

"ASHLEY-RIVES (Carolina), Nov. 18, 1782. —Many people wish to get you into this country. " I see you are determined to follow your genius and not your fortune. I have always been in hopes that Congress would have made some

---

[1] The dates given by Cobbett from contemporary histories require revision by the light of the careful researches made by myself and others, as given at the beginning of this biography.

[2] From *Crisis vii.*, dated Philadelphia, November 21, 1778. In Cobbett's MS. the extract is only indicated.

handsome acknowledgement to you for past services. I must confess that I think you have been shamefully neglected ; and that America is indebted to few characters more than to you. But as your passion leads to fame, and not to wealth, your mortification will be the less. Your fame for your writings, will be immortal. At present my expenses are great ; nevertheless, if you are not conveniently situated, I shall take a pride and pleasure in contributing all in my power to render your situation happy."[1]

Then letter from his father.—"Dear Son, &c." [*Lost.*]

The following letter from William Livingston (Trenton, 4th November, 1784) will show that Thomas Paine was not only honored with the esteem of the most famous persons, but that they were all convinced that he had been useful to the country.[2]

At this time Thomas Paine was living with Colonel Kirkbride, Bordentown, where he remained till his departure for France. He had bought a house [in], and five acres of marshy land over against, Bordentown, near the Delaware, which overflowed it frequently. He sold the land in 1787.

Congress gave an order for three thousand dollars, which Thomas Paine received in the same month.

Early in 1787 he departed for France. He carried with him the model of a bridge of his own invention and construction, which he submitted, in a drawing, to the French Academy, by whom it was approved. From Paris he went to London on the 3d of September 1787 ; and in the same month he went to Thetford, where he found his father was dead, from the small-pox ; and where he settled an allowance on his mother of 9 shillings a week.

A part of 1788 he passed in Rotherham, in Yorkshire, where his bridge was cast and erected, chiefly at the expense of the ingenious Mr. Walker. The experiment, however, cost Thomas Paine a considerable sum.

When Burke published his *Reflexions on the French Revolution*, Thomas Paine answered him in his *First Part of the Rights of Man*. In January, 1792, appeared the *Second Part of the Rights of Man*. The sale of the *Rights of Man* was prodigious, amounting in the course of one year to about a hundred thousand copies.

In 1792 he was prosecuted for his Rights of Man by the Attorney General, McDonald, and was defended by Mr. Erskine, and found guilty of libel. But he was now in France, and could not be brought up for judgment.

Each district of France sent electors to the principal seat of the Department, where the Deputies to the National Assembly were chosen. Two Departments appointed Thomas Paine their Deputy, those of *Oise* and of *Pas de Calais*, of which he accepted the latter. He received

the following letter from the President of the National Assembly, Hérault de Séchelles :

"To THOMAS PAINE :

"France calls you, Sir, to its bosom, to perform one of the most useful and most honorable functions, that of contributing, by wise legislation, to the happiness of a people, whose destinies interest all who think and are united with the welfare of all who suffer in the world.

"It becomes the nation that has proclaimed the *Rights of Man*, to desire among her legislators him who first dared to estimate the consequences of those Rights, and who has developed their principles with that *Common Sense*, which is the only genius inwardly felt by all men, and the conception of which springs forth from nature and truth.

"The National Assembly gave you the title of Citizen, and had seen with pleasure that its decree was sanctioned by the only legitimate authority, that of the people, who had already claimed you, even before you were nominated.

"Come, Sir, and enjoy in France the most interesting of scenes for an observer and a philosopher,—that of a confiding and generous people who, infamously betrayed for three years, and wishing at last to end the struggle between slavery and liberty, between sincerity and perfidy, at length arises in its resolute and gigantic force, gives up to the sword of the law those guilty crowned things who betrayed them, resists the barbarians whom they raised up to destroy the nation. Her citizens turned soldiers, her territory into camp and fortress, she yet calls and collects in congress the lights scattered through the universe. Men of genius, the most capable for their wisdom and virtue, she now calls to give to her people a government the most proper to insure their liberty and happiness.

"The Electoral Assembly of the Department of Oise, anxious to be the first to elect you, has been so fortunate as to insure to itself that honour ; and when many of my fellow citizens desired me to inform you of your election, I remembered, with infinite pleasure, having seen you at Mr. Jefferson's, and I congratulated myself on having had the pleasure of knowing you.

"HÉRAULT,
"President of the National Assembly."

At the trial of Louis XVI. before the National Convention Thomas Paine at the Tribune, with the deputy Bancal for translator and interpreter, gave his opinion, written, on the capital sentence on Louis :—That, though a Deputy of the National Convention of France, he could not forget, that, previous to his being that, he was a citizen of the United States of America, which owed their liberty to Louis, and that gratitude would not allow him to vote for the death of the benefactor of America. On the 21st of January, 1793, Louis XVI. was beheaded in the Square of Louis XV. (Letter to Marat. Letter to Marat.)[3]

---

[1] This and the preceding letter supplied by the author.

[2] Not found. Referred to in this work, p. 81.

[3] Both missing. Possibly the second should be to Danton. See p. 177.

Thomas Paine was named by the Assembly as one of the Committee of Legislation, and, as he could not discuss article by article without the aid of an interpreter, he drew out a plan of a constitution.[1]

The reign of terror began on the night of the 10th of March 1793, when the greatest number and the best part of the real friends to freedom had retired [from the Convention]. But, as the intention of the conspiracy against the Assembly had been suspected, as the greatest part of the Deputies they wished to sacrifice had been informed of the threatening danger, as, moreover, a mutual fear [existed] of the cunning tyrany of some usurper, the conspirators, alarmed, could not this night consummate their horrible machinations. They therefore, for this time, confined themselves to single degrees of accusation and arrestation against the most valuable part of the National Convention. Robespiere had placed himself at the head of a conspiring Common-Hall, which dared to dictate *laws of blood* and proscription to the Convention. All those whom he could not make bend under a Dictatorship, which a certain number of anti-revolutionists feigned to grant him, as a tool which they could destroy at pleasure, were guilty of being suspected, and secretly destined to disappear from among the living. Thomas Paine, as his marked enemy and rival, by favour of the *decree on the suspected* was classed among the *suspected*, and, as a *foreigner*, was imprisoned in the Luxembourg in December 1793. (See Letter to Washington.)[2]

From this document it will be seen, that, while in the prison, he was, for a month, afflicted with an illness that deprived him of his memory. It was during this illness of Thomas Paine that the fall of Robespierre took place. Mr. Monroe, who arrived at Paris some days afterwards, wrote to Mr. Paine, assuring him of his friendship, as appears from the letter to Washington. Fifteen days afterwards Thomas Paine received a letter from Peter Whiteside.[3] In consequence of this letter Thomas Paine wrote a memorial to Mr. Monroe. Mr. Monroe now claimed Thomas Paine, and he *came out of the prison on the 6th of November,* 1794, *after ten months of imprisonment.* He went to live with Mr. Monroe, who had cordially offered him his house. In a short time after, the Convention called him to take his seat in that Assembly ; which he did, for the reasons he alleges in his letter to Washington.

The following two pieces Thomas Paine wrote while in Prison: "Essay on Aristocracy." "Essay on the character of Robespierre." [*Both missing.*]

Thomas Paine received the following letter from Madame Lafayette, whose husband was then a prisoner of war in Austria :

"19 BRUMAIRE, PARIS.—I was this morning so much agitated by the kind visit from Mr. Monroe, that I could hardly find words to to speak ; but, however, I was, my dear Sir, desirous to tell you, that the news of your being set at liberty, which I this morning learnt from General Kilmaine, who arrived here at the same time with me, has given me a moment's consolation in the midst of this abyss of misery, where I shall all my life remain plunged. Gen. Kilmaine has told me that you recollected me, and have taken great interest in my situation ; for which I am exceedingly grateful.

"Accept, along with Mr. Monroe, my congratulations upon your being restored to each other, and the assurances of these sentiments from her who is proud to proclaim them, and who well deserved the title of citizen of *that* second country, though I have assuredly never failed, nor shall ever fail, to the former. Salut and friendship.

"With all sincerity of my heart,
"N. LAFAYETTE."

On the 27th of January, 1794, Thomas Paine published in Paris, the First Part of the "Age of Reason."

Seeing the state of things in America, Thomas Paine wrote a letter to Gen. Washington 22d February 1795. Mr. Monroe entreated him not to send it, and, accordingly it was not sent to Washington ; but it was afterwards published.

A few months after his going out of prison, he had a violent fever. Mrs. Monroe showed him all possible kindness and attention. She provided him with an excellent nurse, who had for him all the anxiety and assiduity of a sister. She neglected nothing to afford him ease and comfort, when he was totally unable to help himself. He was in the state of a helpless child who has its face and hands washed by its mother. The surgeon was the famous Dessault, who cured him of an abscess which he had in his side. After the horrible 13 Brumaire, a friend of Thomas Paine being very sick, he, who was in the house, went to bring his own excellent nurse to take care of his sick friend : a fact of little account in itself, but a sure evidence of ardent and active friendship and kindness.

The Convention being occupied with a discussion of the question of what Constitution ought to be adopted, that of 1791 or that of 1793, Thomas Paine made a speech (July 7, 1795) as a member of the [original] Committee [on the Constitution] and Lanthénas translated it and read it in the Tribune. This speech has been translated into English, and published in London ; but, the language of the author has been changed by the two translations. It is now given as written by the author. [*Missing.*]

In April, 1796, he wrote his *Decline and Fall of the British System of Finance ;* and, on the 30th of July of that year he sent his letter to Washington off for America by Mr. ——— who sent it to Mr. Bache, a newspaper printer of Philadelphia, to be published, and it was published the same year. The name of the

---

[1] See p. 170 *seq.* of this work.

[2] This is the bitter letter of which when it appeared Cobbett had written such a scathing review.

[3] The letter telling him of the allegations made by some against his American citizenship.

gentleman who conveyed the letter, and who wrote the following to Thomas Paine, is not essential and therefore we suppress it. [*Missing.*]

We here insert a letter from Talleyrand, the Minister of Foreign Affairs, to show that Thomas Paine was always active and attentive in doing every thing which would be useful to America. [*Missing.*]

Thomas Paine after he came out of prison and had re-entered the Convention wrote the following letter. [*Missing.*]

The following is essentially connected with the foregoing : " Paris, October 4, 1796." [*Missing.*]

In October, 1796, Thomas Paine published the *Second Part of the Age of Reason.*

This year Mr. Monroe departed from France, and soon after Thomas Paine went to Havre de Grace, to embark for the United States. But, he did not, upon inquiry, think it prudent to go, on account of the great number of English vessels then cruizing in the Channel. He therefore came back to Paris ; but, while at Havre, wrote the following letter, 13th April 1797, to a friend at Paris. [*Missing.*]

The following letter will not, we hope, seem indifferent to the reader : " Dear Sir, I wrote to you etc." [*Missing.*]

At this time it was that Thomas Paine took up his abode at Mr. Bonneville's, who had known him at the Minister Roland's, and as Mr. B. spoke English, Thomas Paine addressed himself to him in a more familiar and friendly manner than to any other persons of the society. It was a reception of Hospitality which was here given to Thomas Paine for a week or a fortnight ; but, the visit lasted till 1802, when he and Mr. Bonneville parted,—alas never to meet again !

Our house was at No. 4 Rue du Théatre François. All the first floor was occupied as a printing office. The whole house was pretty well filled ; and Mr. Bonneville gave up his study, which was not a large one, and a bed-chamber to Thomas Paine. He was always in his apartments excepting at meal times. He rose late. He then used to read the newspapers, from which, though he understood but little of the French language when spoken, he did not fail to collect all the material information relating to politics, in which subject he took most delight. When he had his morning's reading, he used to carry back the journals to Mr. Bonneville, and they had a chat upon the topicks of the day.

If he had a short jaunt to take, as for instance, to Puteaux just by the bridge of Neuilly, where Mr. Skipwith lived, he always went on foot, after suitable preparations for the journey in that way. I do not believe he ever hired a coach to go out on pleasure during the whole of his stay in Paris. He laughed at those who, depriving themselves of a wholesome exercise, could make no other excuse for the want of it than that they were able to take it whenever they pleased. He was never idle in the house. If not writing he was busily employed on some mechanical invention, or else entertaining his visitors. Not a day escaped without his receiving many visits.

Mr. Barlow, Mr. Fulton, Mr. Smith [Sir Robert] came very often to see him. Many travellers also called on him ; and, often, having no other affair, talked to him only of his great reputation and their admiration of his works. He treated such visitors with civility, but with little ceremony, and, when their conversation was mere chit-chat, and he found they had nothing particular to say to him, he used to retire to his own pursuits, leaving them to entertain themselves with their own ideas.

He sometimes spent his evenings at Mr. Barlow's, where Mr. Fulton lived, or at Mr. Smith's [Sir Robert], and sometimes at an Irish Coffee-house in Condé Street, where Irish, English, and American people met. He here learnt the state of politics in England and America. He never went out after dinner without first taking a nap, which was always of two or three hours' length. And, when he went out to a dinner of *parade*, he often came home for the purpose of taking his accustomed sleep. It was seldom he went into the society of French people ; except when, by seeing some one in office or power, he could obtain some favour for his countrymen who might be in need of his good offices. These he always performed with pleasure, and he never failed to adopt the most likely means to secure success. But in one instance he failed. He wrote as follows to Lord Cornwallis ; but, he did not save Napper Tandy. Letter to Lord Cornwallis. Letter 27 Brumaire, 4 year. Letter 23 Germinal 4 year. [*The three letters missing.*]

C. Jourdan made a report to the Convention on the re-establishment of *Bells*, which had been suppressed, and, in great part melted. Paine published, on this occasion, a letter to C. Jourdan.[1]

He had brought with him from America, as we have seen, a model of a bridge of his own construction and invention, which model had been adopted in England *for building bridges* under his own direction. He employed part of his time, while at our house, in bringing this model to high perfection, and this he accomplished to his wishes. He afterwards, and according to the model, made a bridge of lead, which he accomplished by moulding different blocks of lead, which, when joined together, made the form that he required. This was most pleasant amusement for him. Though he fully relied on the strength of his new bridge, and would produce arguments enough in proof of its infallible strength, he often demonstrated the proof by blows of the sledge-hammer, not leaving any one in doubt on the subject. One night he took off the scaffold of his bridge and seeing that it stood firm under the repeated strokes of hammer, he was so ravished that an enjoyment so great was not to be sufficiently felt if confined to his own bosom. He was not satisfied without admirers of his success. One night we had just gone to bed, and were sur-

---

[1] The words "which will find a place in the Appendix" are here crossed out by Madame Bonneville. See p. 260 concerning Jourdan.

prised at hearing repeated strokes of the hammer. Paine went into Mr. Bonneville's room and besought him to go and see his bridge : come and look, said he, it bears all my blows and stands like a rock. Mr. Bonneville arose, as well to please himself by seeing a happy man as to please him by looking at his bridge. Nothing would do, unless I saw the sight as well as Mr. Bonneville. After much exultation : "nothing, in the world," said he, "is so fine as my bridge" ; and, seeing me standing by without uttering a word, he added, "*except a woman!*" which happy compliment to the sex he seemed to think, a full compensation for the trouble caused by this nocturnal visit to the bridge.

A machine for planing boards was his next invention, which machine he had executed partly by one blacksmith and partly by another. The machine being put together by him, he placed it on the floor, and with it planed boards to any number that he required, to make some models of *wheels*. Mr. Bonneville has two of these wheels now. There is a specification of the wheels, given by Mr. Paine himself. This specification, together with a drawing of the model, made by Mr. Fulton, were deposited at Washington, in February 1811 ; and the other documents necessary to obtain a patent as an invention of Thomas Paine, for the benefit of Madame Bonneville. To be presented to the Directory of France, a memorial on the progress and construction of iron bridges. On this subject the two pieces here subjoined will throw sufficient light. (Memoir upon Bridges.—Upon Iron Bridges.—To the Directory.—Memoir on the Progress and Construction &c.)

Preparations were made, real or simulated, for a Descent upon England. Thomas Paine was consulted by B. 8, who was then in the house of Talma, and he wrote the following notes and instructions. Letter at Brussells.—The Ça-ira of America.—To the Consul Lépeaux.[1]

Chancellor Livingston, after his arrival in France, came a few times to see Paine. One morning we had him at breakfast, Dupuis, the author of the Origin of Worship, being of the party ; and Mr. Livingston, when he got up to go away, said to Mr. Paine smiling, "Make your Will ; leave the mechanics, the iron bridge, the wheels, etc. to America, and your religion to France."

Thomas Paine, while at our house, published in Mr. Bonneville's journal (the *Bien Informé*) several articles on passing events.[2]

A few days before his departure for America, he said, at Mr. Smith's [Sir Robert] that he had

---

[1] This paragraph is in the writing of Madame Bonneville. "B. 8." means Bonaparte, and seems to be some cipher. All of the pieces by Paine mentioned are missing ; also that addressed "To the Directory," for the answer to which see p. 275.

[2] The following words are here crossed out : "Also several pieces of poetry, which will be published hereafter, with his miscellaneous prose."

nothing to detain him in France ; for that he was neither in love, debt nor difficulty. Some lady observed, that it was not, in the company of ladies, gallant to say he was not in love. Upon this occasion he wrote the *New Covenant*, from the *Castle in the Air* to the *Little Corner of the World*, in three stanzas, and sent it with the following words : "As the ladies are better judges of gallantry than the men are, I will thank you to tell me, whether the enclosed be gallantry. If it be, it is truly original ; and the merit of it belongs to the person who inspired it." The following was the answer of Mrs. Smith. "If the usual style of gallantry was as clever as your new covenant, many a fair ladies heart would be in danger, but the *Little Corner of the World* receives it from the Castle in the Air ; it is agreeable to her as being the elegant fancy of a friend.—C. Smith." [*Stanzas missing.*]

At this time, 1802, public spirit was at end in France. The real republicans were harrassed by eternal prosecutions. Paine was a truly grateful man : his friendship was active and warm, and steady. During the six years that he lived in our house, he frequently pressed us to go to America, offering us all that he should be able to do for us, and saying that he would bequeath his property to our children. Some affairs of great consequence made it impracticable for Mr. Bonneville to quit France ; but, foreseeing a new revolution, that would strike, personally, many of the Republicans, it was resolved, soon after the departure of Mr. Paine for America, that I should go thither with my children, relying fully on the good offices of Mr. Paine, whose conduct in America justified that reliance.

In 1802 Paine left France, regretted by all who knew him. He embarked at Havre de Grace on board a stout ship, belonging to Mr. Patterson, of Baltimore, he being the only passenger. After a very stormy passage, he landed at Baltimore on the 30th of October, 1802. He remained there but a few days, and then went to Washington, where he published his Letters to the Americans.

A few months afterwards, he went to Bordentown, to his friend Col. Kirkbride, who had invited him, on his return, by the following letter of 12th November, 1802. [*Missing.*]

He staid at Bordentown about two months, and then went to New York, where a great number of patriots gave him a splendid dinner at the City Hotel. In June, 1803, he went to Stonington, New England, to see some friends ; and in the autumn he went to his farm at New Rochelle. (The letter of Thomas Paine to Mr. Bonneville, 20 Nov., 1803.) [*Missing.*]

An inhabitant of this village offered him an apartment, of which he accepted, and while here he was taken ill. His complaint was a sort of paralytic affection, which took away the use of his hands. He had had the same while at Mr. Monroe's in Paris, after he was released from prison. Being better, he went to his farm, where he remained a part of the winter, and he came to New York to spend the rest of it ; but in the spring (1804) he went back to his farm. The farmer who had had his farm for 17 or 18 years, instead of paying his rent, brought Mr. Paine a bill for fencing, which made Paine his debtor ! They had a law-suit by which Paine got nothing but the right of paying the law-expenses ! This and other necessary expenses compelled him to sell sixty acres of his land. He then gave the honest farmer notice to quit the next April (1805).

Upon taking possession of the farm himself, he hired *Christopher Derrick* to cultivate it for him. He soon found that Derrick was not fit for his place, and he, therefore, discharged him. This was in the summer; and, on Christmas Eve ensuing, about six o'clock, Mr. Paine being in his room, on the ground floor, reading, a gun was fired a few yards from the window. The contents of the gun struck the bottom part of the window, and all the charge, which was of small shot, lodged, as was next day discovered, in the window sill and wall. The shooter, in firing the gun, *fell;* and the barrel of the gun had entered the ground where he fell, and left an impression, which Thomas Paine observed the next morning. Thomas Paine went immediately to the house of a neighbouring farmer, and there (seeing a gun, he took hold of it, and perceived that the muzzle of the gun was filled with fresh earth. And then he heard that Christopher Derrick had borrowed the gun about five o'clock the evening before, and had returned it again before six o'clock the same evening. Derrick was arrested, and Purdy, his brother farmer, became immediately and voluntarily his bail. The cause was brought forward at New Rochelle; and Derrick was acquitted.[1]

In 1806 Thomas Paine offered to vote at New Rochelle for the election. But his vote was not admitted; on the pretence only of his not being a citizen of America; whereon he wrote the following letters. [*The letters are here missing, but no doubt the same as those in pp. 307–8.*] This case was pleaded before the Supreme Court of New York by Mr. Riker, then Attorney General, and, though Paine *lost his cause,* I as his legatee, did not lose the having to *pay for it.* It is however, an undoubted fact, that Mr. Paine was an American Citizen.

He remained at New Rochelle till June 1807: till disgust of every kind, occasioned by the gross and brutal conduct of some of the people there, made him resolve to go and live at New York.

On the 4th of April, 1807, he wrote the following letter to Mr. Bonneville [in Paris]:

"MY DEAR BONNEVILLE: Why don't you come to America? Your wife and two boys, Benjamin and Thomas, are here, and in good health. They all speak English very well; but Thomas has forgot his French. I intend to provide for the boys, but I wish to see you here. We heard of you by letters by Madget and Captain Hailey. Mrs. Bonneville, and Mrs. Thomas, an English woman, keep an academy for young ladies.

"I send this by a friend, Mrs. Champlin, who will call on Mercier at the Institute, to know where you are. Your affectionate friend."

And some time after the following letter :

"MY DEAR BONNEVILLE: I received your letter by Mrs. Champlin, and also the letter for Mrs. Bonneville, and one from her sister. I have written to the American Minister in Paris, Mr. Armstrong, desiring him to interest himself to have your *surveillance* taken off *on condition of your coming to join your family in the United States.*

"This letter, with Mrs. Bonneville's, comes to you under cover to the American Minister from Mr. Madison, Secretary of State. As soon as you receive it I advise you to call on General Armstrong and inform him of the proper method to have your surveillance taken off. Mr. Champagny, who succeeds Talleyrand, is, I suppose, the same who was Minister of the Interior, from whom I received a handsome friendly letter, respecting the iron bridge. I think you once went with me to see him.

"Call on Mr. Skipwith with my compliments. He will inform you what vessels will sail for New York and where from. Bordeaux will be the best place to sail from. I believe Mr. Lee is American Consul at Bordeaux. When you arrive there, call on him, with my compliments. You may contrive to arrive at New York in April or May. The passages, in the Spring, are generally short; seldom more than five weeks, and often less.

"Present my respects to Mercier, Bernardin St. Pierre, Dupuis, Grégoire.—When you come, I intend publishing all my works, and those I have yet in manuscript, by subscription. They will make 4 or 5 vol. 4⁰, or 5 vol. 8⁰, about 400 pages each. Yours in friendship.—T. P."[2]

While Paine was one day taking his usual after-dinner nap, an old woman called, and, asking for Mr. Paine, said she had something of great importance to communicate to him. She was shown into his bed-chamber; and Paine, raising himself on his elbow, and turning towards the woman, said : "What do you want with me?" "I came," said she, "from God, to tell you, that if you don't repent, and believe in Christ, you'll be damned." "Poh, poh, it's not true," said Paine; "you are not sent with such an impertinent message. Send her away.

---

[1] See pp. 292–3. Several paragraphs here are in the writing of J. P. Cobbett, then with his father in New York.

[2] This letter is entirely in the writing of Madame Bonneville. Beneath it is written : "The above is a true copy of the original; I have compared the two together. James P. Cobbett." The allusion to Champagny is either a slip of Madame's pen or Paine's memory. The minister who wrote him about his bridge was Chaptal. See p. 275. The names in the last paragraph show what an attractive literary circle Paine had left in France, for a country unable to appreciate him.

Pshaw ! God would not send such a foolish ugly old woman as you. Turn this messenger out. Get away ; be off : shut the door." And so the old woman packed herself off.

After his arrival Paine published several articles in the newspapers of New York and Philadelphia. Subsequent to a short illness which he had in 1807, he could not walk without pain, and the difficulty of walking increased every day. On the 21st of January, 1808, he addressed a memorial to the Congress of the United States, asking remuneration for his services ; and, on the 14th of February, the same year, another on the same subject. These documents and his letter to the Speaker are as follows.[1]

The Committee of Claims, to which the memorial had been submitted, passed the following resolution : " Resolved, that Thomas Paine has leave to withdraw his memorial and the papers accompanying the same." He was deeply grieved at this refusal ; some have blamed him for exposing himself to it. But, it should be recollected, that his expenses were greatly augmented by his illness, and he saw his means daily diminish, while he feared a total palsy ; and while he expected to live to a very great age, as his ancestors had before him. His money yielded no interest, always, having been unwilling to place money out in that way.

He had made his will in 1807, during the short illness already noticed. But three months later, he assembled his friends, and read to them another will ; saying that he had believed such and such one to be his friend, and that now having altered his belief in them, he had also altered his will. From motives of the same kind, he, three months before his death, made another will, which he sealed up and directed *to me*, and gave it me to keep, observing to me, that I was more interested in it than any body else.

He wished to be buried in the Quaker burying ground, and sent for a member of the committee [Willett Hicks] who lived in the neighborhood. The interview took place on the 19th of March, 1809. Paine said, when we were looking out for another lodging, we had to put in order the affairs of our present abode. This was precisely the case with him ; all his affairs were settled, and he had only to provide his burying-ground ; his father had been a Quaker, and he hoped they would not refuse him a grave ; " I will," added he, "pay for the digging of it."

The committee of the Quakers refused to receive his body, at which he seemed deeply moved, and observed to me, who was present at the interview, that their refusal was foolish. "You will," said I, "be buried on your *farm*." "I have no objection to that," said he "but the farm will be sold, and they will dig my bones up before they be half rotten." "Mr.

Paine," I replied, "have confidence in your friends. I assure you, that the place where you will be buried, shall never be sold." He seemed satisfied ; and never spoke upon this subject again. I have been as good as my word.

Last December [1818] the land of the farm having been divided between my children, I gave fifty dollars to keep apart and to myself, the place whereon the grave was.

Paine, doubtless, considered me and my children as strangers in America. His affection for us was, at any rate, great and sincere. He anxiously recommended us to the protection of Mr. Emmet, saying to him, " when I am dead, Madam Bonneville will have no friend here." And a little time after, obliged to draw money from the Bank, he said, with an air of sorrow, "you will have nothing left." [2]

---

[1] " Are as follows " in Madame B.'s writing, after striking out Cobbett's words, " will be found in the Appendix." The documents and letters are not given, but they are well known. See p. 317.

[2] Paine's Will appoints Thomas Addis Emmet, Walter Morton (with $200 each), and Madame Bonneville executors ; gives a small bequest to the widow of Elihu Palmer, and a considerable one to Rickman of London, who was to divide with Nicolas Bonneville proceeds of the sale of the North part of his farm. To Madame Bonneville went his manuscripts, movable effects, stock in the N. Y. Phœnix Insurance Company estimated at $1500, and money in hand. The South part of the New Rochelle farm, over 100 acres, were given Madame Bonneville in trust for her children, Benjamin and Thomas, "their education and maintenance, until they come to the age of twenty-one years, in order that she may bring them well up, give them good and useful learning, and instruct them in their duty to God, and the practice of morality." At majority they were to share and share alike in fee simple. He desires to be buried in the Quaker ground,—"my father belonged to that profession, and I was partly brought up in it,"—but if this is not permitted, to be buried on his farm. " The place where I am to be buried to be a square of twelve feet, to be enclosed with rows of trees, and a stone or post and railed fence, with a head-stone with my name and age engraved upon it, author of "Common Sense." He confides Mrs. Bonneville and her children to the care of Emmet and Morton. "Thus placing confidence in their friendship, I herewith take my final leave of them and of the world. I have lived an honest and useful life to mankind ; my time has been spent in doing good ; and I die in perfect composure and resignation to the will of my Creator God." The Will, dated January 18, 1809, opens with the words, "The last Will and Testament of me, the subscriber, Thomas Paine, reposing confidence in my Creator God, and in no other being, for I know of no other, and I believe in no other."

Mr. William Fayel, to whom I am indebted for much information concerning the Bonnevilles in St. Louis, writes me that so little is known of Paine's benefactions, that "an ex-senator of the United States recently asserted that Gen. Bonneville was brought over by Jefferson and

He was now become extremely weak. His strength and appetite daily departed from him; and in the day-time only he was able, when not in bed, to sit up in his arm-chair to read the newspapers, and sometimes write. When he could no longer quit his bed, he made some one read the newspapers to him. His mind was always active. He wrote nothing for the press after writing his last will, but he would converse, and took great interest in politics. The vigor of his mind, which had always so strongly characterized him, did not leave him to the last moment. He never complained of his bodily sufferings, though they became excessive. His constitution was strong. The want of exercise alone was the cause of his sufferings. Notwithstanding the great inconveniences he was obliged to sustain during his illness, in a carman's house [Ryder's], in a small village [Greenwich], without any bosom friend in whom he could repose confidence, without any society he liked, he still did not complain of his sufferings. I indeed, went regularly to see him twice a week; but, he said to me one day: "I am here alone, for all these people are nothing to me, day after day, week after week, month after month, and you don't come to see me."

In a conversation between him and Mr. [Albert] Gallatin, about this time, I recollect his using these words: "*I am very sorry that I ever returned to this country.*" As he was thus situated and paying a high price for his lodgings[1] he expressed a wish to come to my house. This must be a great inconvenience to me from the frequent visits to Mr. Thomas Paine; but, I, at last, consented; and hired a house in the neighborhood, in May 1809, to which he was carried in an arm-chair, after which he seemed calm and satisfied, and gave himself no trouble about anything. He had no disease that required a Doctor, though Dr. Romaine came to visit him twice a week. The swelling, which had commenced at his feet, had now reached his body, and some one had been so officious as to tell him that he ought to be *tapped*. He asked me if this was necessary. I told him, that I did not know; but, that, unless he was likely to derive great good from it, it should not be done. The next [day] Doctor Romaine came and brought a physician with him, and they resolved that the tapping need not take place.

He now grew weaker and weaker very fast. A very few days before his death, Dr. Romaine said to me, "I don't think he can live till night." Paine, hearing some one speak, opens his eyes, and said: "'T is you Doctor: what news?" "Mr. such an one is gone to France on such business.' "He will do nothing there," said

Paine. "Your belly diminishes," said the Doctor. "And yours augments," said Paine.

When he was near his end, two American clergymen came to see him, and to talk with him on religious matters. "Let me alone," said he; "good morning." He desired they should be admitted no more. One of his friends came to New York; a person for whom he had a great esteem, and whom he had not seen for a long while. He was overjoyed at seeing him; but, this person began to speak upon religion, and Paine turned his head on the other side, and remained silent, even to the adieu of the person.[2]

Seeing his end fast approaching, I asked him, in presence of a friend, if he felt satisfied with the treatment he had received at our house, upon which he could only exclaim, *O! yes!* He added other words, but they were incoherent. It was impossible for me not to exert myself to the utmost in taking care of a person to whom I and my children owed so much. He now appeared to have lost all kind of feeling. He spent the night in tranquillity, and expired in the morning at eight o'clock, after a short oppression, at my house in Greenwich, about two miles from the city of New York. Mr. Jarvis, a Painter, who had formerly made a portrait of him, moulded his head in plaster, from which a bust was executed.

He was, according to the American custom, deposited in a mahogany coffin, with his name and age engraved on a silver-plate, put on the coffin. His corpse was dressed in a shirt, a muslin gown tied at neck and wrists with black ribbon, stockings, drawers; and a cap was put under his head as a pillow. (He never slept in a night-cap.) Before the coffin was placed on the carriage, I went to see him; and having a rose in my bosom, I took it out, and placed on his breast. Death had not disfigured him. Though very thin, his bones were not protuberant. He was not wrinkled, and had lost very little hair.

His voice was very strong even to his last moments. He often exclaimed, oh, lord help me! An exclamation the involuntary effect of pain. He groaned deeply, and when a question was put to him, calling him by his name, he opened his eyes, as if waking from a dream. He never answered the question, but asked one himself; as, what is it o'clock, &c.

On the ninth of June my son and I, and a few of Thomas Paine's friends, set off with the corpse to New Rochelle, a place 22 miles from New York. It was my intention to have him buried in the Orchard of his own farm; but the farmer who lived there at that time said, that Thomas Paine, walking with him one day, said, pointing to another part of the land, he was desirous of being buried there. "Then," said I, "that shall be the place of his burial." And, my instructions were accordingly put in execution. The head-stone was put up about a week afterwards with the following inscription: "Thomas Paine, Author of 'Common Sense,' died the

---

a French lady; and a French lady, who was intimate with the Bonnevilles, assured me that General Bonneville was sent to West Point by Lafayette."

[1] The sentence thus far is struck out by Madame Bonneville.

[2] Cobbett's words erased: "and Paine could no longer bear the sight of him."

eighth of June, 1809, aged 72 years." According to his will, a wall twelve feet square was erected round his tomb. Four trees have been planted outside the wall, two weeping willows and two cypresses. Many persons have taken away pieces of the tombstone and of the trees, in memory of the deceased; foreigners especially have been eager to obtain these memorials, some of which have been sent to England.[1] They have been put in frames and preserved. Verses in honor of Paine have been written on the head stone. The grave is situated at the angle of the farm, by the entrance to it.

This interment was a scene to affect and to wound any sensible heart. Contemplating who it was, what man it was, that we were committing to an obscure grave on an open and disregarded bit of land, I could not help feeling most acutely. Before the earth was thrown down upon the coffin, I, placing myself at the east end of the grave, said to my son Benjamin, "stand you there, at the other end, as a witness for grateful America." Looking round me, and beholding the small group of spectators, I exclaimed, as the earth was tumbled into the grave, " Oh ! Mr. Paine ! My son stands here as testimony of the gratitude of America, and I, for France ! " This was the funeral ceremony of this great politician and philosopher !²

The eighty-eight acres of the north part were sold at 25 dollars an acre. The half of the south (the share of Thomas de Bonneville) has been sold for the total sum of 1425 dollars. The other part of the south, which was left to Benjamin de Bonneville, has just (1819) been sold in lots, reserving the spot in which Thomas Paine was buried, being a piece of land 45 feet square.

Thomas Paine's posthumous works. He left the manuscript of his answer to Bishop Watson; the Third Part of his Age of Reason; several pieces on Religious subjects, prose and verse. The great part of his posthumous political works will be found in the Appendix. Some correspondences cannot be, as yet, published.[3]

---

[1] The breaking of the original gravestone has been traditionally ascribed to pious hatred. A fragment of it, now in New York, is sometimes shown at celebrations of Paine's birthday as a witness of the ferocity vented on Paine's grave. It is satisfactory to find another interpretation.

[2] Paine's friends, as we have said, were too poor to leave their work in the city, which had refused Paine a grave. The Rev. Robert Bolton, in his history of Westchester County, introduces Cheetham's slanders of Paine with the words: "as his own biographer remarks." His own ! But even Cheetham does not lie enough for Bolton, who says: "His [Paine's] body was brought up from New York in a hearse used for carrying the dead to Potter's Field; a white man drove the vehicle, accompanied by a negro to dig the grave." The whole Judas legend is in that allusion to Potter's Field. Such is history, where Paine is concerned !

[3] All except the first two MSS., of which fragments exist, and some poems, were no doubt

In *Mechanics* he has left two models of wheels for carriages, and of a machine to plane boards. Of the two models of bridges, left at the Philadelphia Museum, only one has been preserved, and that in great disorder, one side being taken entirely off. But, I must say here, that it was then out of the hands of Mr. Peale.[4]

Though it is difficult, at present, to make some people believe that, instead of being looked on as a *deist* and a *drunkard,* Paine ought to be viewed as a philosopher and a truly benevolent man, future generations will make amends for the errors of their forefathers, by regarding him as a most worthy man, and by estimating his talents and character according to their real worth.

Thomas Paine was about five feet nine inches high, English measure, and about five feet six French measure. His bust was well proportioned; and his face oblong. Reflexion was the great expression of his face ; in which was always seen the calm proceeding from a conscience void of reproach. His eye, which was black, was lively and piercing, and told us that he saw into the very heart of hearts [of any one who wished to deceive him].[5] A most benignant smile expressed what he felt upon receiving an affectionate salutation, or praise delicately conveyed. His leg and foot were elegant, and he stood and walked upright, without stiffness or affectation. [He never wore a sword nor cane], but often walked with his hat in one hand and with his other hand behind his back. His countenance, when walking, was generally thoughtful. In receiving salutations he bowed very gracefully, and, if from an acquaintance, he did not begin with "how d' ye do?" but, with a "what news?" If they had none, he gave them his. His beard, his lips, his head, the motion of his eye-brow, all aided in developing his mind.

Was he where he got at the English or American newspapers, he hastened to over-run them all, like those who read to make extracts for their paper. His first glance was for the funds, which, in spite of jobbing and the tricks of government, he always looked on as the sure thermometer of public affairs. Parliamentary Debates, the Bills, concealing a true or sham opposition of such or such orators, the secret pay and violent theatrical declamation, or the revelations of public or private meetings at the taverns ; these interested him so much that he longed for an ear and a heart to pour forth all his soul. When he added that he knew the Republican or the hypocrite, he would affirm, beforehand, that such or such a bill, such or such a measure, would take place ; and very seldom, in such a case, the cunning politic or the clear-sighted observer was mistaken in his assertions ;

---

consumed at St. Louis, as stated in the Introduction to this work.

[4] I have vainly searched in Philadelphia for some relic of Paine's bridges.

[5] Bracketed words marked out. In this paragraph and some that follow the hand of Nicolas Bonneville is, I think, discernible.

for they were not for him mere conjectures. He spoke of a future event as of a thing past and consummated. In a country where the slightest steps are expanded to open day, where the feeblest connexions are known from their beginning, and with all the views of ambition, of interest or rivalship, it is almost impossible to escape the eye of such an observer as Thomas Paine, whom no private interest could blind or bewitch, as was said by the clear-sighted Michael Montaigne.

His writings are generally perspicuous and full of light, and often they discover the sardonic and sharp smile of Voltaire. One may see that he wishes to wound to the quick ; and that he hugs himself in his success. But Voltaire all at once overruns an immense space and resumes his vehement and dramatic step : Paine stops you, and points to the place where you ought to smile with him at the ingenious traits ; a gift to envy and stupidity.

Thomas Paine did not like to be questioned. He used to say, that he thought nothing more impertinent, than to say to any body : "What do you think of that ? " On his arrival at New York, he went to see General Gates. After the usual words of salutation, the General said : " I have always had it in mind, if I ever saw you again, to ask you whether you were married, as people have said." Paine not answering, the General went on : " Tell me how it is." " I never," said Paine, "answer impertinent questions."

Seemingly insensible and hard to himself, he was not so to the just wailings of the unhappy. Without any vehement expression of his sorrow, you might see him calling up all his powers, walking silently, thinking of the best means of consoling the unfortunate applicant ; and never did they go from him without some rays of hope. And as his will was firm and settled, his efforts were always successful. The man hardened in vice and in courts [of law], yields more easily than one imagines to the manly entreaties of a disinterested benefactor.

Thomas Paine loved his friends with sincere and tender affection. His simplicity of heart and that happy kind of openness, or rather, carelessness, which charms our hearts in reading the fables of the good Lafontaine, made him extremely amiable. If little children were near him he patted them, searched his pockets for the store of cakes, biscuits, sugar-plums, pieces of sugar, of which he used to take possession as of

a treasure belonging to them, and the distribution of which belonged to him.[1] His conversation was unaffectedly simple and frank ; his language natural ; always abounding in curious anecdotes. He justly and fully seized the characters of all those of whom he related any singular traits. For his conversation was satyrick, instructive, full of witticisms. If he related an anecdote a second time, it was always in the same words and the same tone, like a comic actor who knows the place where he is to be applauded. He neither cut the tale short nor told it too circumstantially. It was real conversation, enlivened by digressions well brought in. The vivacity of his mind, and the numerous scenes of which he had been a spectator, or in which he had been an actor, rendered his narrations the more animated, his conversation more endearing. His memory was admirable. Politics were his favorite subject. He never spoke on religious subjects, unless pressed to it, and never disputed about such matters. He could not speak French : he could understand it tolerably well when spoken to him, and he understood it when on paper perfectly well. He never went to the theatre : never spoke on dramatic subjects. He rather delighted in ridiculing poetry. He did not like it : he said it was not a serious thing, but a sport of the mind, which often had not common sense. His common reading was the affairs of the day ; not a single newspaper escaped him ; not a political discussion : he knew how to strike while the iron was hot ; and, as he was always on the watch, he was always ready to write. Hence all his pamphlets have been popular and powerful. He wrote with composure and steadiness, as if under the guidance of a tutelary genius. If, for an instant, he stopped, it was always in the attitude of a man who listens. The Saint Jerome of Raphael would give a perfect idea of his contemplative recollection, to listen to the voice from on high which makes itself heard in the heart.

[It will be proper, I believe, to say here, that shortly after the Death of Thomas Paine a book appeared, under the *Title* of : *The Life of Thomas Paine*, by *Cheetham*. In this libel my character was calumniated. I cited the Author before the Criminal Court of New York. He was tried and in spite of all his manœuvres, he was found *guilty*.—M. B. de Bonneville.]

This last paragraph, in brackets, is in the writing of Madame Bonneville.

APPENDIX B

THE HALL MANUSCRIPTS

IN 1785, John Hall, an able mechanician and admirable man, emigrated from Leicester, England, to Philadelphia. He carried letters to Paine, who found him a man after his own heart. I am indebted to his relatives, Dr. Dutton Steele of

[1] At this point are the words : " Barlow's letter [*i. e.* to Cheetham] we agreed to suppress."

Philadelphia and the Misses Steele, for Hall's journals, which extend over many years. It will be seen that the papers are of historical importance apart from their records concerning Paine. Hall's entries of his daily intercourse with Paine, which he never dreamed would see the light, represent a portraiture such as has rarely been secured of any character in history. The extent already reached by this work compels me to omit much that would impress the reader with the excellent work of John Hall himself, who largely advanced ironwork in New Jersey, and whose grave at Flemmington, surrounded by those of the relatives that followed him, and near the library and workshop he left, merits a noble monument.

Letter. Philadelphia, August 30, 1785.

" I went a day or two past with the Captain and his lady to see the exhibition of patriotic paintings. Paine the author of Common Sense is amongst them. He went from England (had been usher to a school) on board the same vessel that our Captain [Coltman] went in last time ; their acquaintance then commenced and has continued ever since. He resides now in Bordentown in the Jerseys, and it is probable that I may see him before it be long as when he comes to town the Captain says he is sure to call on him. It is supposed the various States have made his circumstances easy—General Washington, said if they did not provide for him he would himself. I think his services were as useful as the sword."

Journal, 1785.

Nov. 16th. Received a Letter from Mr. Pain by his Boy, informing us of his coming this day. Between 3 and 4 Mr. Pain, Col. Kerbright [Kirkbride], and another gentleman came to our door in a waggon.

17th. At dinner Mr. Pain told us a tale of the Indians, he being at a meeting of them with others to settle some affairs in 1776. The Doctor visited Mr. Pain.

19th. Performed a trifling operation for Mr. Pain.

22d. A remark of Mr. Pain's—not to give a deciding opinion between two persons you are in friendship with, lest you lose one by it ; whilst doing that between two persons, your supposed enemies, may make one your friend.

24th. This evening pulled Mr. Pain's Boy a tooth out.

Dec. 12. With much pain drawd the Board in at Hanna's chamber window to work Mr. Pain's bridge on. I pinned 6 more arches together which makes the whole 9. I sweat at it ; Mr. Pain gives me some wine and water as I was

very dry. Past 9 o'clock Dr. Hutchinson called in on Mr. Paine.

[The December journal is mainly occupied with mention of Paine's visitors Franklin, Gouverneur Morris, Dr. Rush, Tench Francis, Robert Morris, Rittenhouse, Redman. A rubber of whist in which Paine won is mentioned.]

Sunday Jan. 1st 1786. Mr. Paine went to dine with Dr. Franklin today ; staid till after tea in the evening. They tried the burning of our candles by blowing a gentle current through them. It greatly improved the light. The draught of air is prevented by passing through a cold tube of tallow. The tin of the new lamp by internal reflections is heated and causes a constant current. This is the Doctor's conjecture. [Concerning Paine's candle see p. 87.]

Feb. 25th. Mr. Paine not returned. We sent to all the places we could suppose him to be at and no tidings of him. We became very unhappy fearing his political enemies should have shown him foul play. Went to bed at 10 o.c, and about 2 o.c. a knocking at the door proves Mr. Paine.

March 10th. Before 7 o'c a brother saint-maker came with a model of machine to drive boats against stream.[1] He had communicated his scheme to H. who had made alterations and a company had taken it and refused saint-maker partnership. He would fain have given it to Mr. Paine or me, but I a stranger refused and Mr. Paine had enough hobbys of his own. Mr. Paine pointed out a mode to simplify his apparatus greatly. He gave him 5s. to send him one of his maps.

April 15th. Mr. Paine asked me to go and see Indian Chiefs of Sennaka Nation, I gladly assented. They have an interpreter. Mr. Paine wished to see him and made himself known to him by past remembrance as Common Sense, and was introduced into the room, addressed them as "brothers" and shook hands cordially. Mr. Paine treated them with 2s. bowl of punch.

Bordentown Letter, May 28. Colonel Kirkbride is the gentleman in whose family I am. My patron [Paine] is likewise a boarder and makes his home here. I am diligently employed in Saint making, now in Iron that I had before finished in wood, with some improvements, but you may come and see what it is.

Letter, June 4. Skepticism and Credulity are as general here as elsewhere, for what I see. In this town is a Quaker meeting and one of another class—I suppose of the Baptist cast— And a person in town a Tailor by trade that goes about a-soulmending on Sundays to various places, as most necessary, or I suppose advantageous to himself ; for by one trade or the other he has built himself a very elegant frame house in this town. This man's way to Heaven is somewhat different to the other. I am informed he

---

[1] Hall calls inventions "saints." This saint-maker is John Fitch, the "H." being Henry of Lancaster. This entry is of much interest. (See p. 269.) The first steamer seems to have gone begging !

makes publick dippings &c. My Employer has *Common Sense enough* to disbelieve most of the Common Systematic Theories of Divinity but does not seem to establish any for himself. The Colonel [Kirkbride] is as Free as John Coltman.

[Under date of New York, July 31st, Hall writes an account of a journey with Paine to Morrisania, to visit Gen. Morris, and afterwards to the farm at New Rochelle, of which he gives particulars already known to my reader.]

Letter of Paine to John Hall, at Capt. Coltman's in Letitia Court, Market St, between Front and Second St. Philadelphia :

"Bordentown, Sep. 22, 1786.—Old Friend : In the first place I have settled with Mr. Gordon for the time he has been in the house—in the second I have put Mrs. Read who, you know has part of our house Col. Kirkbride's ¡but is at this time at Lancaster, in possession by putting part of her goods into it.[1] By this means we shall have room at our house (Col. Kirkbride) for carrying on our operations. As Philadelphia is so injurious to your health and as apartments at Wm. Foulke's would not be convenient to you, we can now conveniently make room for you here. Mrs. Kirkbride mentioned this to me herself and it is by the choice of both her and Col. K. that I write it to you. I wish you could come up to-morrow (Sunday) and bring the iron with you. I shall be backward and forward between here and Philadelphia pretty often until the elections are over, but we can make a beginning here and what more iron we may want we can get at the Delaware Works, and if you should want to go to Mount hope you can more conveniently go from here than from Philadelphia —thus you see I have done your business since I have been up. The enclosed letter is for Mr. Henry who is member for Lancaster County. I do not know where he lodges, but if William will be so good as to give it to the door keeper or Clerk of the Assembly it will be safe. Bring up the walnut strips with you. Your coming here will give an opportunity to Joseph to get acquainted with Col. K. who will very freely give any information in his power. Compts. in the family. Your friend and Hbl. servt."

Undated letter of Paine to John Hall, in Philadelphia :

"Fryday Noon.—Old Friend : Inclosed (as the man said by the horse) I send you the battau, as I wish to present it as neat and clean as can be done ; I commit it to your care. The sooner it is got on Board the vessel the better. I shall set off from here on Monday and expect to be in New York on Tuesday. I shall take all the tools that are here with me, and wish you would take some with you, that if we should get on a working fit we may have some to work with. Let me hear from you by the Sunday's boat and send me the name of the vessel and Captain you go with and what owners they belong to at New

York, or what merchants they go to. I wrote to you by the last boat, and Peter tells me he gave the letter to Capt. Haines, but Joe says that he enquired for letters and was told there was none—wishing you an agreeable voyage and meeting at New York, I am your friend, and humble servant. Present my compliments to Capt. and Mrs. Coltman and William. Col. and Mrs. Kirkbride's and Polly's compt."

Note of Hall, dated Oct. 3 [1786] "Dashwood Park, of Captain Roberts : On Thursday morning early Sept. 28th I took the stage wagon for Trenton. Jo had gone up by water the day before to a sale of land and a very capital iron works and nailing with a large corn mill. It was a fair sale there was a forge and rolling and slitting mill upon an extensive scale the man has failed—The works with about 60 or 70 acres of land were sold for £9000 currency. Then was put up about 400 acres of land and sold for £2700 currency and I believe a good bargain ; and bought by a friend of mine called Common Sense—Who I believe had no idea of purchasing it when he came there. He took Jo to Bordentown with him that night and they came to look at it the next day ; then Jo went into the Jerseys to find a countryman named Burges but was disappointed. Came back to Bordentown and on Saturday looked all over Mr. Paine's purchase along with him and believes it bought well worth money.

Nov. 21st. Mr. Paine told us an anecdote of a French noble's applying to Dr. Franklin, as the Americans had put away their King, and that nation having formerly chosen a King from Normandy, he offered his service and wished him to lay his letter before Congress. Mr. Paine observed that Britain is the most expensive government in the world. She gives a King a million a year and falls down and worships him. I put on Mr. Paine's hose yesterday. Last night he brought me in my room a pair of warm cloth overshoes as feel very comfortable this morning. Had a wooden pot stove stand betwixt my feet by Mr. Paine's desire and found it kept my feet warm.

November 24. As soon as breakfast was over mounted Button [Paine's horse] and set off for Philadelphia. I brought Mr. Paine $120 in gold and silver.

Bordentown 27th, Monday. Day was devoted to rivetting the bars, and punching the upper bar for the bannisters [of the bridge]. Mr. Kirkbride and Polly went to hear a David Jones preach a rhodomontade sermon about the Devil, Mary Magdalen, and against deists, etc.

December 14. This day employed in raising and putting on the abutments again and fitting them. The smith made the nuts of screws to go easier. Then set the ribs at proper distance, and after dinner I and Jackaway [?] put on some temporary pieces on the frame of wood to hold it straight, and when Mr. Pain came they then tied it on its wooden frame with strong cords. I then saw that it had bulged full on one side and hollow on the other. I told

---

[1] Mrs. Read was thus transferred to Paine's own house. Her husband died next year and Paine declined to receive any rent.

him of it, and he said it was done by me—I denied that and words rose high. I at length swore by God that it was straight when I left it, he replied as positively the contrary, and I think myself ill used in this affair.

Philadelphia. Dec. 22d. Bridge packed and tied on the sled. We arrived in town about 5 o'clock took our bags to Capt. Coltmans, and then went down to Dr. Franklin's, and helped unload the bridge. Mr. Paine called on me ; gave us an anecdote of Dr. Franklin. On Mr. Paine asking him of the value of any new European publication ; he had not been informed of any of importance. There were some religious posthumous anecdotes of Doctor Johnson, of resolves he had made and broken though he had prayed for power and strength to keep them ; which showed the Doctor said that he had not much interest there. And such things had better be suppressed as nobody had anything to do betwixt God and man.

December 26th. Went with Glentworth to see the Bridge at Dr. Franklin's. Coming from thence met Mr. Pain and Mr. Rittenhouse ; returned with them and helped move it for all three to stand upon, and then turned it to examine. Mr. Rittenhouse has no doubt of its strength and sufficiency for the Schuylkill, but wished to know what quantity of iron [it would require,] as he seemed to think it too expensive.

December 27th. Walk to the State House. The Bank bill called but postponed until to-morrow. Mr. Pain's letter read, and leave given to exhibit the Bridge at the State House to be viewed by the members. Left the House and met Mr. Pain, who told me Donnalson had been to see and [stand] upon his Bridge, and admitted its strength and powers. Then took a walk beyond Vine street, and passed by the shop where the steamboat apparatus is. Mr. Pain at our house, and talking on the Bank affair brought on a dispute between Mr. Pain and the Captain [Coltman] in which words were very high. A reflection from Captain C. on publications in favor of the Bank having lost them considerable, he [Paine] instantly took that as a reflection on himself, and swore by G—d, let who would, it was a lie. I then left the room and went up stairs. They quarrelled a considerable time, but at length parted tolerably coolly. Dinner being ready I went down ; but the Captain continued talking about politics and the Bank, and what he thought the misconduct of Mr. Pain in his being out and in with the several parties. I endeavoured to excuse Mr. Pain in some things relating thereto, by saying it was good sense in changing his ground when any party was going wrong,—and that he seemed to delight in difficulties, in Mechanics particularly, and was pleased in them. The Captain grew warm, and said he knew now he could not eat his dinner. [Here followed a sharp personal quarrel between Hall and Coltman.] In the evening Mr. Paine came in and wished me to be assisting in carrying the model to the State House. We went to Dr. Franklin's and fetched the Bridge to the Committee Room.

1787. Jan. 1st. Our Saint I have assisted in moving to the State House and there placed in their Committee room, as by a letter addressed to this Speaker they admitted. And by the desire of my patron (who is not an early riser) I attended to give any information to inquiries until he came. And then I was present when the Assembly with their Speaker inspected it and many other persons as philosophers, Mechanics Statesmen and even Tailors. I observed their sentiments and opinions of it were as different as their features. The philosopher said it would add new light to the great utility. And the tailor (for it is an absolute truth) remarked it cut a pretty figure. It is yet to be laid (or by the by stand) before the Council of State. Then the Philosophical Society and all the other Learned Bodies in this city. And then to be canonised by an Act of State which is solicited to incorporate a body of men to adopt and realise or Brobdinag this our Lilliputian handywork, that is now 13 feet long on a Scale of one to 24. And then will be added another to the world's present Wonders.

January 4th. Mr. Pain called in and left me the intended Act of Assembly for a Bridge Company, who are to subscribe $33,330$\frac{50}{90}$, and then are to be put in possession of the present Bridge and premises to answer the interest of their money until they erect a new one ; and after they have erected a new one, and the money arising from it amounts to more than pays interest, it is to become a fund to pay off the principal stockholders, and then the Bridge to become free. Mr. Pain called in ; I gave him my Bill—told him I had charged one day's work and a pair of gloves.

March 15th Mr. Paine's boy called on time to [inquire] of the money spent. Mr. Paine called this evening ; told me of his being with Dr. Franklin and about the chess player, or Automaton, and that the Dr. had no idea of the mode of communication. Mr. Paine has had several visitors, as Mr. Jowel, Rev. Dr. Logan, &c.

Sunday April 16th Prepared to attend Mr. Paine up to Bordentown. Mr. Paine's horse and chair came, mounted and drove through a barren sandy country arrived at Bordentown at half past one-o'clock for dinner. This is the pleasantest situation I have seen in this country.

TRENTON, April 20th. Sitting in the house saw a chair pass down the street with a red coat on, and going out after it believed it to be Mr. Paine, so followed him up to Collins's, where he was enquiring where I boarded. I just then called to him, and went with him to Whight's Tavern, and there he paid me the money I had laid down for him. He is now going for England by way of France in the French packet which sails the 25th instant. He asked me to take a ride, and as the stage was not come in and he going the road I gladly took the opportunity, as I could return on meeting the stage. On the journey he told me of the Committee's proceedings on Bridges and Sewers ; anecdotes of Dr. Franklin, who had sent a letter by him to the president, or some person, to communicate to the Society of Civil Architects, who superintend solely over bridges in France. The model is packed up to go with him. The Doctor, though full of employ from the Vice President being ill, and the numerous visitors on State business, and others that his fame justly procures him, could hardly be supposed to pay great attentions to trifles ; but as he consideres Mr. Paine his adopted political Son he would endeavor to write by him to his friends, though Mr. Paine did not press, for reasons above. In 2 or 3 days he sent him up to Bordentown no less than a dozen letters to his acquaintance in France.—He told me many anecdotes of the Doctor, relating to national and political concerns, and observations of many aged and sensible men of his acquaintance in that country. And the treaty that he the Doctor made with the late King of Prussia by adding an article that, should war ever break out, (though never a probability of it) Commerce should be left free. The Doctor said he showed it to the French minister, Vergennes, who said it met his idea, and was such as he would make even with England, though he knew they would not,—they were so fond of robbing and plundering. And the Doctor had gathered a hint from a Du Quesney that no nation could properly expect to gain by endeavoring to suppress his neighbor, for riches were to be gained from amongst the rich and not from poor neighbors ; and a National reciprocity was as much necessary as a domestic one, or [inter] national trade as necessary to be free as amongst the people of a country. Such and many more hints passed in riding 2 or 3 miles, until we met the stage. I then shook hands and wished him a good voyage and parted.

Letter from Flemmington, N. J., May 16, 1788, to John Coltman, Leicester, England :

"FRIEND JOHN : Tell that disbelieving sceptical Infidel thy Father that he has wounded my honor. What !' Bought the Coat at a rag shop—does he think I would palm such a falsity both upon Gray and Green heads ! did not I send you word it was General Washington's. And does he think I shall slanderously brook such a slanderous indignity—No ! I tell him the first Ink that meanders from my pen, which shall be instantly on my setting foot on Brittains Isle, shall be to call him to account. I 'll haul out his Callous Leaden soul with its brother !

"In the late revolution the provincial army lying near Princeton New Jersey one Sunday General Washington and Common Sense each in their chairs rode down there to Meeting. Common Sense put up his at a friend's one Mrs. Morgan's, and pulling off his great coat put it in the care of a servant man, and as I remember he was of the pure Irish Extraction ; he walked then to meeting and then slipped off with said great coat and some plate of Mr. Morgan. On their return they found what had been done in their absence and relating it to the General his answer was it was necessary to watch as well as pray—but told him he bad two and would lend or give him one—and that is the Coat I sent and the fact as related to me and others in public by said [Common Sense.] Nor do I believe that Rome or the whole Romish Church has a better attested miracle in her whole Catalogue than the above—though I dont wish to deem it a miracle, nor ido I believe there is any miracle upon record for these 18 hundred years so true as that being General Washington's great coat.—I, labouring hard for said Common Sense at Bordentown, the said coat was hung up to keep snow out of the room. I often told him I should expect that for my pains, but he never would say I should ; but having a chest there I took care and locked it up when I had finished my work, and sent it to you. So far are these historical facts—Maybe sometime hence I may collect dates and periods to them—But why should they be disputed ? has not the world adopted as true a-many affairs without date and of less moment than this, and even pay what is called a holy regard to them ?

"If you communicate this to your Father and he feels a compunction for the above crime and will signify the same by letter, he will find I strictly adhere to the precepts of Christianity and shall forgive.—If not——

"My best wishes to you all.
"JOHN HALL."

Letter of Paine, London, Nov. 25, 1791, to "Mr. John Hall, at Mr. John Coltman's, Shambles Lane, Leicester, England."

"MY OLD FRIEND : I am very happy to see a letter from you, and to hear that our Friends on the other side the water are well. The Bridge has been put up, but being on wood butments they yielded, and it is now taken down. The first rib as an experiment was erected between two steel furnaces which supported it firmly ; it contained not quite three tons of iron, was ninety feet span, height of the arch five feet ; it was loaded with six tons of iron, which remained upon it a twelve month. At present I am engaged on my political Bridge. I shall bring out a new work (Second part of the Rights of Man) soon after New Year. It will produce something one way or other. I see the tide is yet the wrong way, but there is a change of sentiment beginning. I have so far got the ear of John Bull that he will read what I write— which is more than ever was done before to the same extent. Rights of Man has had the greatest run of anything ever published in this country, at least of late years—almost sixteen thousand has gone off—and in Ireland above forty thousand—besides the above numbers one thousand printed cheap are now gone to Scotland by desire from some of the [friends] there. I have been applied to from Birmingham for leave to print ten thousand copies, but I intend, after the next work has had its run among those who will have handsome printed books and fine paper, to print an hundred thousand copies of each work and distribute them at sixpence a-piece ; but this I do not at present talk of, because it will alarm the wise mad folks at St. James's. I have received a letter from Mr. Jefferson who mentioned the great run it has had there. It has been attacked by John Adams, who has brought an host about his ears from all parts of the Continent. Mr. Jefferson has sent me twenty five different answers to Adams who wrote under the signature of Publicola. A letter is somewhere in the city for me from Mr. Laurens of S. Carolina. I hope to receive it in a few days. I shall be glad at all times to see, or hear from you. Write to me (under cover) to Gordon, Booksellers N : 166 Fleet Street, before you leave Leicester. How far is it from thence to Rotherham ? Yours sincerely.

" P. S. I have done you the compliment of answering your favor the inst. I rec'd. it which is more than I have done by any other—were I to ans. all the letters I receive—I should require half a dozen clerks."

Extracts from John Hall's letters from London, England :

"LONDON, January 1792. Burke's publication has produced one way or other near 50 different answers and publications. Nothing of late ever has been so read as Paine's answer. Sometime shortly he will publish a second part of the Rights of Man. His first part was scrutinized by the Privy Council held on purpose and through fear of making him *more popular* deemed too contemptible for Government notice. The sale of it for a day or two was rather retarded or not publickly disposed of until it was known by the printers that it would not be noticed by Government.

John Hall to a friend in England :

"LONDON, Nov. 6, 1792. I dined yesterday with the Revolutionary Society at the London Tavern. A very large company assembled and after dinner many truly noble and patriotic toasts were drank. The most prominent were—The Rights of Man—with 3 times &c.—The Revolution of France—The Revolution of the World —May all the armies of tyrants learn the Brunswick March—May the tree of Liberty be planted in every tyrant city, and may it be an evergreen. The utmost unanimity prevailed through the company, and several very excellent songs in favor of Liberty were sung. Every bosom felt the divine glow of patriotism and love of universal freedom. I wish you had been there. For my part I was transported at the

scene. It happened that a company of Aristocratic french and Spanish merchants were met in the very room under, and Horne Tooke got up and sarcastically requested the company not to wound the tender feelings of the gentlemen by too much festivity. This sarcasm was followed by such a burst of applause as I never before heard."

From J. Redman, London, Tuesday Dec. 18, 5 p.m. to John Hall, Leicester, England : " Mr. Paine's trial is this instant over. Erskine shone like the morning-Star. Johnson was there. The instant Erskine closed his speech the venal jury interrupted the Attorney General, who was about to make a reply, and without waiting for any answer, or any summing up by the Judge, pronounced him guilty. Such an instance of infernal corruption is scarcely upon record. I have not time to express my indignant feelings on this occasion. At this moment, while I write, the mob is drawing Erskine's carriage home, he riding in triumph—his horses led by another party. Riots at Cambridge, Manchester, Bridport Dorset &c. &c. O England, how art thou fallen ! I am just now told that press warrants are issued today. February, make haste. Mrs R's respects and mine. Yours truly."

[John Hall's London Journal (1792) records frequent meetings there with Paine. " March 5. Met Mr. Paine going to dress on an invitation to dine with the Athenians. He leaves town for a few days to see his aunt." " April 20. Mr. Paine goes out of town tomorrow to compose what I call Burke's Funeral Sermon." " Aug. 5. Mr. Paine looking well and in high spirits." " Sept. 6. Mr. Paine called in a short time. Does not seem to talk much, rather on a reserve, of the prospect of political affairs. He had a letter from G. Washington and Jefferson by the ambassador [Pinckney]." The majority of entries merely mention meeting Paine, whose name, by the way, after the prosecution was instituted, Hall prudently write " P——n." He also tells the story of Burke's pension.]

" April 19, 1803. Had a ride to Bordentown to see Mr. Paine at Mr. Kirkbride's. He was well and appeared jollyer than I had ever known him. He is full of whims and schemes and mechanical inventions, and is to build a place or shop to carry them into execution, and wants my help."

APPENDIX C

PORTRAITS OF PAINE

AT the age of thirty Paine was somewhat stout, and very athletic ; but after his arrival in America (1774) he was rather slender. His height was five feet, nine inches. He had a prominent nose, somewhat like that of Ralph Waldo Emerson. It may have impressed Bonaparte, who insisted, it is said, that a marshal must have a large nose. Paine's mouth was delicate, his chin also ; he wore no whiskers or beard until too feeble with age to shave. His forehead was lofty and unfurrowed ; his head long, the occiput feeble. His complexion was ruddy,—thoroughly English. Charles Lee, during the American revolution, described him as "the man who has genius in his eyes ;" Carlyle quotes from Foster an observation on the brilliancy of Paine's eyes, as he sat in the French Convention. His figure, as given in an early French portrait, is shapely ; its elegance was often remarked. A year or so after his return to America he is shown in a contemporary picture as somewhat stout again, if one may judge by the face. This was probably a result of insufficient exercise, on which he much depended. He was an expert horseman, and, in health, an unwearied walker. He loved music, and could join well in a chorus.

There are eleven original portraits of Thomas Paine, besides a death-mask, a bust, and a seal used on the release at Lewes, elsewhere cited (p. 14). That gives some idea of the head and face at the age of thirty-five. I have a picture said to be that of Paine in his youth, but the dress is an anachronism. The earliest portrait of Paine was painted by Charles Willson Peale, in Philadelphia, probably in some early year of the American Revolution, for Thomas Brand Hollis, of London,—the benefactor of Harvard University, one of whose halls bears his name. The same artist painted another portrait of Paine, now badly placed in Independence Hall. There must have been an early engraving from one of Peale's pictures, for John Hall writes October 31, 1786: "A print of Common Sense, if any of my friends want one, may be had by sending to the printshops in London, but they have put a wrong name to it, his being Thomas." [1] The Hollis portrait was engraved in London, 1791, underlined

[1] This is puzzling. The only engraving I have found with "Tom" was published in London in 1800. Can there be a portrait lost under some other name?

"by Peel [*sic*] of Philadelphia," and published, July 25th, by J. Ridgway, York Street, St. James's Square. Paine holds an open book bearing the words, " Rights of Man," where Peale probably had " Common Sense." On a table with inkstand and pens rests Paine's right elbow, the hand supporting his chin. The full face appears—young, handsome, gay ; the wig is frizzed, a bit of the queue visible. In all of the original portraits of Paine his dress is neat and in accordance with fashion, but in this Hollis picture it is rather fine: the loose sleeves are ornamentally corded, and large wristbands of white lace fall on the cuffs.

While Paine and Jefferson were together in Paris (1787) Paine wrote him a note, August 18th, in which he says : "The second part of your letter, concerning taking my picture, I must feel as an honor done to me, not as a favor asked of me—but in this, as in other matters, I am at the disposal of your friendship." As Jefferson does not appear to have possessed such a portrait, the request was probably made through him. I incline to identify this portrait with an extremely interesting one, now in this country, by an unknown artist. It is one of twelve symmetrical portraits of revolutionary leaders,—the others being Marat, Robespierre, Lafayette, Mirabeau, Danton, Brissot, Pétion, Camille Desmoulins, Billaud de Varennes, Gensonné, Clermont Tonnère. These pictures were reproduced in cheap woodcuts and distributed about France during the Revolution. The originals were secured by Col. Lowry, of South Carolina, and brought to Charleston during the Revolution. At the beginning of the civil war they were buried in leaden cases at Williamstown, South Carolina. At the end of the war they were conveyed to Charleston, where they remained, in the possession of a Mrs. Cole, until purchased by their present owner, Mr. Alfred Ames Howlett, of Syracuse, New York. As Mirabeau is included, the series must have been begun at an early phase of the revolutionary agitation. The face of Paine here strongly resembles that in Independence Hall. The picture is about two feet high ; the whole figure is given, and is dressed in an elegant statesmanlike fashion, with fine cravat and silk stockings from the knee. The table and room indicate official position, but it is the same room as in nine of the other portraits. It is to be hoped that further light may be obtained concerning these portraits.

Well-dressed also, but notably unlike the preceding, is the "Bonneville Paine," one of a celebrated series of two hundred engraved portraits, the publication of which in quarto volumes was begun in Paris in 1796. "F. Bonneville del. et sculpsit" is its whole history. Paine is described in it as "Ex Députe à la Convention Nationale," which would mean strictly some time between his expulsion from that assembly in December, 1793, and his recall to it a year later. It could not, however, have been then taken, on account of Paine's imprisonment and illness. It was probably made by F. Bonneville when Paine had gone to reside with Nicolas Bonneville in the spring of 1797. It is an admirable picture in every way, but especially in bringing out the large and expressive eyes. The hair is here free and flowing ; the dress identical with that of the portrait by Jarvis in this work.

The best-known picture of Paine is that painted by his friend George Romney, in 1792. I have inquired through London *Notes and Queries* after the original, which long ago disappeared, and a claimant turned up in Birmingham, England ; but in this the hand holds a book, and Sharp's engraving shows no hand. The face was probably copied from the Romney. The large engraving by W. Sharp was published April 20, 1793, and the smaller in 1794. A reproduction by Illman were a fit frontispiece for Cheetham (what satirical things names are sometimes), but ought not to have got into Gilbert Vale's popular biography of Paine. That and a reproduction by Wright in the Mendum edition of Paine's works, have spread through this country something little better than

a caricature ; and one Sweden has subjected Truelove's edition, in England, to a like misfortune. Paine's friends, Rickman, Constable, and others, were satisfied by the Romney picture, and I have seen in G. J. Holyoake's library a proof of the large engraving, with an inscription on the back by Paine, who presented it to Rickman. It is the English Paine, in all his vigor, and in the thick of his conflict with Burke, but, noble as it is, has not the gentler and more poetic expression which Bonneville found in the liberated prisoner surrounded by affectionate friends. Romney and Sharp were both well acquainted with Paine.

A picturesque Paine is one engraved for Baxter's "History of England," and published by Symonds, July 2, 1796. Dressed with great elegance, Paine stands pointing to a scroll in his left hand, inscribed "Rights of Man." Above his head, on a frame design, a pen lies on a roll marked "Equality." The face is handsome and the likeness good.

A miniature by H. Richards is known to me only as engraved by K. Mackenzie, and published March 31, 1800, by G. Gawthorne, British Library, Strand, London. It is the only portrait that has beneath it "Tom Paine." It represents Paine as rather stout, and the face broad. It is powerful, but the least pleasing of the portraits. The picture in Vale resembles this more than the Romney it professes to copy.

I have in my possession a wood engraving of Paine, which gives no trace of its source or period. It is a vigorous profile, which might have been made in London during the excitement over the "Rights of Man," for popular distribution. It has no wig, and shows the head extraordinarily long, and without much occiput. It is pre-eminently the English radical leader.

Before speaking of Jarvis' great portrait of Paine, I mention a later one by him which Mr. William Erving, of New York, has added to my collection. It would appear to have been circulated at the time of his death. The lettering beneath, following a facsimile autograph, is : "J. W. Jarvis, pinx. 1805. J. R. Ames, del.—L'HOMME DES DEUX MONDES. Born at Thetford, England, Jan. 29, (O. S.) 1737. Died at Greenwich, New York, June 8, 1809." Above the cheap wood-cut is: "A tribute to Paine." On the right, at the top, is a globe, showing the outlines of the Americas, France, England, and Africa. It is supported by the wing of a dove with large olive-branch. On the left upper corner is an open book inscribed: "RIGHTS OF MAN. COMMON SENSE. CRISIS": supported by a scroll with "DOING JUSTICE, LOVING MERCY. AGE OF REASON." From this book rays break out and illumine the globe opposite. A lower corner shows the balances, and the liberty-cap on a pole, the left being occupied by the United States flag and that of France. Beneath are the broken chain, crown, sword, and other emblems of oppression. A frame rises showing a plumb line, at the top of which the key of the Bastille is crossed by a pen, on Paine's breast. The portrait is surrounded by a "Freedom's Wreath" in which are traceable the floral emblems of all nations. The wreath is bound with a fascia, on which appear, by twos, the following names: "Washington, Monroe; Jefferson, Franklin; J. Stewart, E. Palmer; Barlow, Rush; M. Wollstonecraft, M. B. Bonneville; Clio Rickman, J. Horne Tooke; Lafayette, Brissot."

The portrait of Paine represents him with an unusually full face, as compared with earlier pictures, and a most noble and benevolent expression. The white cravat and dress are elegant. What has become of the original of this second picture by the elder Jarvis? It might easily have fallen to some person who might not recognize it as meant for Paine, though to one who has studied his countenance it conveys the impression of what he probably would have been at sixty-eight. About two years later a drawing was made of Paine by William Constable, which I saw at the house of his nephew, Dr. Clair J. Grece, Redhill, England. It reveals the ravages of age, but conveys a vivid impression of the man's power.

After Paine's death Jarvis took a cast of his face. Mr. Laurence Hutton has had for many years this death-mask which was formerly in the establishment of Fowler and Wells, the phrenologists, and probably used by George Combe in his lectures. This mask has not the large nose of the bust; but that is known to have been added afterwards. The bust is in the New York Historical Society's rooms. In an article on Paine in the *Atlantic Monthly* (1856) it was stated that this bust had to be hidden by the Historical Society to prevent its injury by haters of Paine. This has been quoted by Mr. Robertson, of London, in his "Thomas Paine, an Investigation." I am assured by Mr. Kelby, of that Society, that the statement is unfounded. The Society has not room to exhibit its entire collection, and the bust of Paine was for some time out of sight, but from no such reason as that stated, still less from any prejudice. The face is that of Paine in extreme dilapidation, and would be a dismal misrepresentation if shown in a public place.

Before me are examples of all the portraits I have mentioned (except that in Birmingham), and I have observed contemporary representations of Paine in caricatures or in apotheosis of fly-leaves. Comparative studies convince me that the truest portrait of Paine is that painted by John Wesley Jarvis in 1803, and now in possession of Mr. J. H. Johnston, of New York. The picture from which our frontispiece is taken appeared to be a replica, of somewhat later date, the colors being fresher, but an inscription on the back says "Charles W. Jarvis, pinxit, July, 1857." From this perfect duplicate Clark Mills made his portrait-bust of Paine now in the National Museum at Washington, but it has not hitherto been engraved. Alas, that no art can send out to the world what colors only can convey,—the sensibility, the candor, the spirituality, transfusing the strong features of Thomas Paine. As I have sat at my long task, now drawn to a close, the face there on the wall has seemed to be alive, now flushed with hope, now shadowed with care, the eyes greeting me daily, the firm mouth assigning some password—Truth, Justice.

APPENDIX D

BRIEF LIST OF PAINE'S WORKS

Case of the Officers of Excise. Written 1772; pub. Lond. 1793.

Penn'a Magazine. Edited by Paine, Jan. 1775 —Aug. 1776. Articles enumerated in ch. iv. of this biography.

Penn'a Journal. 1775, Jan. 4, Dialogue bet. Wolfe and Gage. March 8, paper signed "Justice and Humanity." Oct. 18, paper sig. "Humanus." 1776. Letters signed "The Forester."

Common Sense, Jan. 10, 1776. Phil. Lond.

Epistle to the People called Quakers. Phil. 1776.

Dialogue between Gen. Montgomery and an American Delegate. Phil. 1776.

The Crisis. 13 Nos. and several supernumerary. 1776–1783.

Preamble to Pa. Act of Emancipation, March 1, 1780.

Public Good. Phil. 1780.

Letter to Abbé Raynal. Phil. 1782.

Thoughts on the Peace. Phil. 1783.

Dissertation on Government, the Bank, etc. Phil. 1786.

Prospects on the Rubicon. Lond. 1787. (2d ed. corrected 1793.)

Letter to Sir G. Staunton. Iron Bridges. London. 1788.

Rights of Man. Lond. 1791. Trs. French, 1791; Swedish, 1792.

Address of the "Société Républicaine." Paris, 1791.

Letter to Le Républicain. Paris. July 1791.

Address of Friends of Peace and Liberty. Lond. Aug. 20, 1791.

Rights of Man. Part ii. Lond. 1792. French Tr., 1792.

Letter to Sheriff of Sussex, June 30, 1792.

Letter to the Abbé Sieyès, 1792. Paris and Lond.

Letters to Henry Dundas, June 6 and Sep. 15, 1792. Lond.

Letters to Lord Onslow, June 17 and 21, 1792. Lond.

Address to the Addressers. Lond. Sep. 1792.

Letter to the People of France. Paris. Sep. 25, 1792.

Letter to the Attorney General of England. Nov. 11, 1792. Lond.

Speech in French Convention on bringing Louis Capet to Trial, Nov. 20, 1792. Paris. French; printed by order of the Convention.

Reasons for preserving the life of Louis Capet. Jan. 1793.

Project of a Constitution. Reported 1793. (Pub. in works of Condorcet.)

Le Siècle de la Raison (essay suppressed by translator). Paris. 1793.

Letter to Danton, 1793. Durand's Documents. New York. 1889.

Age of Reason. Part i. Paris, New York, and London, 1794.

Letter to French Convention (from prison) Aug. 8, 1794.

Mémoire à M. Monroe. Sep. 1794. Paris.

Dissertation on the first principles of Government. Paris. 1795.

Speech in Convention on the proposed Constitution. 1795.

Age of Reason. Part ii. Paris and Lond. 1796.

Decline and Fall of the English System of Finance. (Pub. in all European languages.) 1796.

Letter to George Washington. Phil. 1796.

Agrarian Justice (A la Législature et au Directoire, ou la Justice Agraire.) 1797.

Letter to Erskine. Lond. 1797.

Letter to People and Armies of France. Paris. 1797.

Discourse to the Theophilanthropists. Paris and Lond. 1797.

Letter to Camille Jourdan, on Bells, etc. (Lettre de Thomas Payne sur les Cultes). 1797.

Maritime Compact. The Rights of Neutrals at Sea. 1801.

Letter to Samuel Adams. 1802.

Letters to the Citizens of the United States written 1802. Ed. Lond. 1817.

Letter to the People of England. 1804.

To the French Inhabitants of Louisiana. 1804.

To the Citizens of Pennsylvania (on Convention). Phil. 1805.

On the Cause of the Yellow Fever. New York. 1805.

On Constitutions, Governments, and Charters. New York, 1805.

Contributions pub. in The Prospect, N. Y. 1804–5.

Letter to Andrew A. Dean. New York, 1806.

Observations on Gunboats, etc. 1806.

On the Polit. and Military Affairs of Europe, 1806.

To the People of New York. (Fortifications.) 1807.

On Governor Lewis's Speech. 1807.

On Mr. Hale's Resolutions. 1807.

Three Letters to Morgan Lewis. 1807.

On the question, Will there be War? 1807.

Essay on Dream. Examination of the Prophecies. New York, 1807.

Reply to the Bishop of Llandaff. New York, 1810.

Origin of Freemasonry. New York. 1811.

Miscellaneous Poems. By Thomas Paine. London: R. Carlile. 1819.

Paine's principal works have been translated into French and German, and some of them into other European languages.

INDEX

A

ADAMS, Henry, 86, 300
Adams, Jno., 28, 33, 38, 110, 118, 120, 124, 130, 228, 238, 265, 268, 271, 280
Adams, J. Q., 119, 120, 136, 153
Adams, Samuel, 246, 271, 282
Age of Reason, bk., 195-8, 200, 202, 208, 210, 228-45, 257, 258, 261-3, 277, 282, 288, 305, 311, 321, 324
Agrarian Justice, bk., 259
Ainslie, Rev. R., 327
Aitkin, R., 16
Allen, Ethan, 233
Amar, 194, 198
Americans in Paris, 189, 191, 193, 199-200, 201, 206, 270
Antoinette, Marie, 50, 76, 109, 118
Asgill, Capt., 76, 78
Audibert, Achille, 143, 198, 211-12

B

Bache, B. F., 225, 332
Badeau, Albert, 313, 327
Banks, Sir J., 94, 108
Barlow, Joel, 11, 26, 99, 131, 143, 183, 195, 198, 200, 206, 250, 251, 252, 270, 272, 308, 313, 314, 339
Barrère, 146, 163, 192, 193, 208-9, 211, 215
Barruel-Beauvert, 329
Bastille, key, 110, 111, 128
Bayeaux, Mrs., 292, 298, 313
Beaumarchais, 49, 57
Bell, R., pub., 27, 73
Benoit, gaoler, 199, 209
Bentabole, 195, 216
Billaud-Varennes, 202, 211, 215, 345
Blake, William, 143
Blanc, Louis, hist., 149, 157, 159, 160, 169, 170, 171, 187, 192, 252
Blomefield, hist., 2
Blount, Ch., deist, 233
Bonaparte, 267, 268, 270, 271, 273, 274, 289, 317, 329, 334, 344
Bonnevilles, The, 127, 179, 183, 250, 268, 270, 271, 276, 290, 291-2, 296-9, 312, 315-17, 322-3, 328 seq., 346
Bordentown, N. J., 46, 81, 83, 102, 108, 239, 283, 304, 340, 344
Bosville, Col., 102, 180, 280

Bourdon de l'Oise, 195
Bradlaugh, Chas., 16, 150, 320
Brissot, 115, 127, 146, 156, 160, 170, 176, 179, 187, 194, 201, 345
Brown, Senator, Ky., 218
Burgoyne, Gen., 39 seq.
Burke, Edmund, 94, 102, 113 seq., 118, 132, 134, 139, 150, 166, 168, 169, 235, 239, 273, 344
Burr, Aaron, 270, 313
Butler, Bp.; Analogy, bk., 256, 262

C

Calais, 143
Cambacérès, 218
Capital Punishment, 125, 157, 161
Carlile, Richard, 134, 141, 251, 325
Carlyle, T., 113, 115, 142, 147, 150, 158, 232, 234
Cartwright, Maj., 53
Carver, Wm., 292, 300, 301, 304, 310, 311, 312, 315-16
Cato (Rev. Dr. Smith), 28
Chalmers, G. ("Oldys"), biog., pref. viii., xii., 2, 8, 132, 134, 137-8, 251, 252
Chapman, pub., 134, 137
Chaptal, Minister, 275, 335
Chauvelin, 169, 170
Cheetham, Jas., pref. viii., xiii., 36, 296, 309-10, 312-16, 322, 338, 339
Chenier, 217
Choppin, Wm., 131, 176, 183, 196
Christie, Thos., 125, 131, 143, 165, 183
Clinton, Geo., 292, 307, 317
Clootz, Anacharsis, 143, 179, 198, 207, 208, 217, 244
Clubs, French: Republican, 126
    Do.   Jacobin, 127, 131, 157, 176, 202, 219
    Do.   Cordeliers, 175, 200
Clymer, Geo., 17, 90, 93
Cobbett, Wm., 23, 179, 181, 226, 252, 290, 321, 325, 327, 328 seq.
Cocke Family, 1, 5
Coleridge, S. T., 165, 181
Collot d'Herbois, 211, 215
Commissioners, English, 47, 77
Common Sense, bk., 25, 35, 84, 91, 93, 113, 115, 124, 141, 233, 237, 305, 330, 336
Condorcet, 118, 127, 146, 160, 161, 170-5, 179, 220

Constable, D. and W., 183, 310–11, 347
Constitution, English, 30, 170
Constitutions, American, 61–2, 118, 120, 142, 297, 298
Constitutions, French, 118, 127, 135–6, 148, 170–3, 219, 223
Cooper, Jas., 200, 267
Cornwallis, 70, 71, 333
Courtois, 188
Couthon, 170, 173, 196, 236, 240
Crisis, bk., 34, 35, 37, 38, 41, 63, 64, 66, 75, 78, 80, 82, 305, 330
Crocker, Capt., 270

D

Danton, 94, 115, 146, 148, 154, 156, 160, 177–9, 188, 207, 345
Dawson, J., 275
Deane, Silas, 30, 37, 49 *seq.*, 56 *seq.*, 71, 85, 110, 330
De Brienne, Cardinal, 94, 116
Deforgues, 192, 203, 207
Desmoulins, C., 187, 188, 207, 345
De Ternant, 191
Dickinson, John, 85
Directory, 222, 265, 267
Doniol, hist., 49, 58
Duchâtelet, Achille, 126, 127, 179
Dumont, Etienne, 126, 128
Dumouriez, 164, 169, 170, 174, 176, 178, 179
Dundas, H., 139, 140, 144, 150, 265

E

Egle, Dr., State Lib. Pa., 64, 68
England, Terror in, 166, 168, 251
Erskine, 114, 152–3, 160, 168, 206, 261, 264, 344
Evelyn, 3
Excise, 7 *seq.*, 314

F

Fauchet, Abbé, 146, 171
Fellows, Col. Jno., 292, 296, 297, 299, 300, 301, 315, 325
Fiske, J., 34, 41
Fitch, J., 269, 340
Fitzgerald, Lord Edward, 146
Foreign Affairs Com., 37, 38
Forester, The (Paine), 29
Foster, Jno., 292, 300, 301, 315
Fox, C. J., 118, 153, 160, 169, 181, 267
Fox, George, 237
France, 47, 48, 51, 54, 70 ; revolution, 95, 106, 116–7, 125
Francis, Dr., 288, 299, 301, 320, 321, 327
Frank, editor, 310
Franklin, Dr., 15, 16, 23, 27–8, 33, 37, 47, 57, 60, 62, 68, 70, 86, 92, 118, 142, 293, 340
Freemasonry, 299, 301

G

Gage, Gen., 23, 339
Gallatin, Albert, 291, 300, 322, 337
Gardiner, A. B., 41
Garrison, W. L., 21
Gates, Gen., 41
Genêt, 155, 189, 191, 192, 194, 201, 207, 225
Gensonné, 171, 345
George III., 26, 74, 99, 105, 114, 118, 130, 140, 146, 181, 217, 266, 277, 326
Gérard, de Rayneval, 32, 47, 52–7
Girondins (or Brissotins), 157, 171, 175, 179, 184, 186, 194
Godwin, Wm., 116
Gower, Lord, 154, 163, 165, 191
Grece, Dr. C. J., pref. vii., 183, 292, 311, 347
Greene, Christopher, Col., 41
Greene, Gen. Nath'l, 34, 41, 69, 333
Grégoire, Abbé, 145, 335
Grellet, Steph., 324
Grenville, Lord, 151, 163
Grimstone, Capt., 163
Gunpowder-motor, 98

H

Hall, Jno., 81, 89, 181, 239, 339 *seq.*
Hamilton, Alex., 143, 309, 320
Henry, J. Jos., 62, 233
Henry, Patrick, 84, 257
Henry, Wm., 42, 269, 462
Hérault, Séchelles, 144, 146, 173, 180, 207, 240, 331
Hertell, Judge, 301, 315, 327
Hicks, Elias, 319, 325
Hicks, Willett, 319, 323–5
Holcroft, T., 116
Hollis, T. Brand, 116, 345
Howe, Gen., 37, 42
Howe, Lord, 33, 36–7
Humanity, Religion of, 239–40, 269

I

Independence, Am., 19, 21, 23, 24, 26, 32, 38, 69, 78, 95, 100, 110
Indians, 37, 340
Inventions, 42, 87, 89 *seq.*, 92, 98–9, 338, 340
Iron Bridge, 87, 89 *seq.*, 92–3, 99, 103–6, 112–13, 239, 272, 275, 279, 283, 338

J

Jackson, Andrew (President), 327
Jackson, Major, 200, 201
Jarvis, C. W., 347
Jarvis, J. W., 305, 314, 316, 321, 324, 337, 347
Jay, John, 54, 247
Jefferson, 29, 33, 96, 103 *seq.*, 112, 119 *seq.*, 131, 137, 191, 201, 204, 206, 252, 268, 275, 279, 280, 282, 283, 293, 295, 296, 299, 304
Johnson, phys., 143, 175, 196
Johnson, pub., 116, 121, 137

Jordan, pub., 116, 121, 135, 137, 133, 333
Jordan, C., 260, 268
Junius, 15, 20

K

Kentucky, 193, 218
Kenyon, Lord, 152, 263
King, John, 155
Kirkbride, Col., 45, 81, 169, 283, 286, 290, 340
Knowler, Rev. Wm., 6
Kyd, S., 261

L

Lafayette and wife, 52, 103, 105, 110, 112, 115, 118, 124-5, 127, 137, 216, 250, 332, 345
La Luzerne, De, 32, 57
Lamartine, 70, 149, 157, 163, 210
Lambert, Mary, 6, 144
Landor, W. S., 163, 274
Lanjuinais, 171, 172
Lansdowne, Lord, 100, 104, 107
Lanthénas, 125, 128, 142, 143, 146, 171, 179, 196, 240
Larevéllière, Lépeaux, 267, 274
Lauderdale, Lord, 182
Laurens, Henry, 42, 52, 60, 344
Laurens, Col. John, 69, 71, 317, 330
Lebon, Jos., 208
Lebrun, 192, 193, 201, 273
Lee, Arthur, 37, 49 *seq.*, 56, 60, 84
Lee, Chas., 35
Lee, R. H., 29, 32, 39, 84
Lesley, Prof. Peter, 100
Lewes, 9, 141, 301, 312
Littlepage, Lewis, 105, 164
Livingston, Robert R., 25, 33, 74, 79, 275, 280, 334
Louis XVI., 49, 70, 125, 126, 130, 146, 148-9, 155, 156 *seq.*, 172, 222
Louisiana, 281, 283, 288, 291, 294
Luxembourg Prison, 195, 201, 207 *seq.*, 222

M

Macdonald, Atty-Gen., 139, 150, 152 *seq.*, 331, 344
Madison, Jas., 84, 86, 119, 120, 143, 221, 226, 293, 304, 308
Magazine, Penn'a, 17, 19, 34, 330
Maillane, Durand, 170, 171
Malmsbury, Lord, 265
Marat, 125, 149, 158-60, 171-2, 174-6, 179, 180, 240, 345
Maritime Compact, bk., 270, 272, 275
Mason, Rev. J. M., 300, 321
Masson, F., hist., 160, 175, 193, 212
Milbank, R., 272
Miles, W. A, 153, 162
Millington, F. H., 4
Mirabeau, 124, 126, 128, 345
Miranda, Gen., 164, 179
Monroe, Jas. and Mrs., 165, 188, 202, 212-19, 246, 250, 252, 264, 332

Moore, Dr. John, 149, 182
Morris, Gouverneur, 56, 71, 79, 110, 117, 119, 122, 123, 127, 137, 147, 151, 154, 160, 161, 170, 180, 188, 191, 201-7, 225, 264, 280, 295, 305, 308
Morris, Lewis, Gen., 89, 108, 112, 177, 191, 341
Morris, Robert, 51, 64, 71, 74, 75, 79, 81, 123, 190, 317
Muhlenberg, F. A., 17, 308
Munro, G., 154, 163

N

New Rochelle, 83, 177, 292, 297, 313, 314
Nicholsons, The, 86, 101-3, 299, 322
North Carolina, 22, 23, 32

O

O'Hara, Gen., 207
Onslow, Lord, 141
Oswald, Col. John, 131, 143, 190, 195
Otto, Louis, 192, 193

P

Paine Family, 1; Eliz'th, sister of Thomas, 2; Eliz'th, wife of Thos., 11, 13-15; Frances, mother of Thos., 1, 2, 14, 90, 94, 95, 112, 331; Joseph, father of Thos., 1, 2, 5, 90, 94, 95, 237, 329, 331
Paine, Thomas, pref.; early life, 2 *seq.*; struggles, 6 *seq.*; emigration, 16 *seq.*: military career, 34 *seq.*; controversies, 28, 31, 60, 79, 88; visits France, 68, 91, 331; Europe, 93 *seq.*; Rights of Man, bk., 116 *seq.*; France, 125 *seq.*, 144; England, 99 *seq.*; prosecution, 139; Fr. Convention, 142; effigy, 151-2; and Louis XVI., 158 *seq.*; Parl't, 160; outlawry, 162; residence, 180; arrest, 195, 198; liberation, 216; Convention, 217, 221; Yorke's visit, 276; in America, 279 *seq.*; death, 322; monument, 327; portraits, 344; works, 348
Palmer, Elihu, 250, 276, 296, 300, 304, 309, 316, 319
Peale, Chas. W., 338, 345
Perry, Sampson, 131, 170
Pétion, 171
Phillips, Sir R., 166, 269
Pichon, Baron, 246, 296
Pickering, T., 225, 308
Pinckney, C. C., 143, 195, 213, 218
Pindar, Peter, 97, 264
Pintard, John, 288
Pitt, the Younger, 96, 104, 118, 135, 139, 160, 164, 167-70, 187, 218, 273
Pompadour, Madame, 182
Poole, S. L., 151, 165-6
Portraits, Paine's, 93, 142, 344
Price, Dr. Richard, 114, 132, 248
Priestley, Dr. J., 114, 131, 132, 143, 230, 248, 276
Prospect, The, 301-2
Public Good, pamph., 67, 85

Q

Quakerism, 1, 2, 4 *seq.*, 8, 13, 18, 22, 29, 31, 34, 73, 94–5, 98, 126, 134, 148, 236, 243, 253, 260, 322–4

R

Randolph, Edmund, 26, 67, 119, 121, 122, 191, 204, 206, 215, 225, 227, 308
Raynal, Abbé, 73, 76–7
Rickman, T. C., pref. vii., xii., 10, 15, 60, 131, 152, 167, 180, 182, 183, 263, 268, 274, 278, 279
Rights, Declaration of, 118, 130, 171, 221
Rights of Man, bk., pref. ix., 123, 128, 134, 140–1, 145, 166, 221, 239, 264, 267, 284, 288, 343–4
Riker, Richard, 307, 308
Rittenhouse, D., 17, 39, 340, 342
Robertson, J. M., pref. ix., 297, 347
Robespierre, 125, 131, 154, 161, 170–3, 179, 184, 187–9, 192, 196, 200–1, 207, 208–12, 236, 240, 332
Robinet, hist., 93, 124
Rocquaine, F., hist., 111, 233
Roland, 171, 333 ; Madame, 183
Romaine, Dr. N., 288, 319, 322, 337
Romney, George, 131, 346
Rotherham, Paine at, 100
Rousseau, 118, 142, 241, 259
Rumsey, Jas., 105, 269
Rush, Dr. B., 17, 20, 283, 293, 323

S

St. Denis, Faubourg, 180–4
Sampson, Counsellor, 316
Shelley, 9, 181, 326
Short, Wm., 127, 131
Sieyès, Abbé, 127, 134, 146, 148, 158, 220, 270
Skipwith, Consul, 272, 273, 290, 333
Slavery, African, 17, 21, 24, 33, 63, 111, 132, 238, 276, 291, 293–6, 318, 323
Smith, Sir R. and Lady, 186, 196, 210, 250, 252, 272, 278, 279, 280, 333
Societies, polit. inq., 92 ; constitutional, 117 ; friends of lib., 143 ; the revolution, 132 ; Repub. Greens, 287 ; Tammany, 288
South Carolina, 32
Southey, 165, 181
Sparks, hist., pref. viii. 142, 206, 217
Stanhope, Lady Hester, 139, 160
Steamboat, 42, 269, 318, 340
Stephen, Leslie, pref. viii. 234
Stillé, C. J., 49, 59, 62

T

Tabor, Judge, 314
Taine, 154, 157

Talleyrand, 154, 169, 333
Theophilanthropy, 253 *seq.*, 273, 303, 326, 328
Thetford, 2 *seq.*, 94, 112, 236
Thibaudeau, 217, 246
Thorburn, Grant, 300, 317
Thuriot, 159, 211
Tooke, J. Horne, 129, 131, 137, 141, 143, 344, 347
Trenton, 35–6, 287, 330, 341, 342
Trevelyan, Sir G., 180, 232
Truelove, E., pref. vii. 346
Trumbull, John, 100, 108, 109
Turgot, 118
Tyler, Royall, 97, 264

U

Union, American, 75, 79, 82, 91
Unitarians, English, 249

V

Vadier, 198, 200, 202
Vale, Gilbert, biog., pref. xii. 309, 323, 327, 346
Vanhuile, Jos., 208, 268, 270
Vergennes, Count, 49, 58, 70, 76, 118
Vergniaud, 146, 157, 171
Voltaire, 118, 241, 321, 339

W

Wakefield, Gilbert, 248, 257
Wakeman, T. B., 239
Ward, Elisha, 305, 307, 308, 317
Washington, George, 23, 24, 25, 34–5, 40, 64, 70, 72, 74 *seq.*, 80 *seq.*, 107, 122, 123, 143, 145, 162, 201, 204, 223 *seq.*, 259, 308, 340, 343
Watson, Richard, Bp. Llandaff, 229, 230, 249, 254–8, 261, 273, 302, 306
Welling, Dr., 23
Wentworth, Paul, 32, 56, 59
Wesley, John, 234, 241, 242
West, Benj., P.R.A., 100
Whiteside, Peter, 103, 113, 200, 213, 332
Whitman, Walt, 325
Wilkes, John, 15, 50, 181
Wilkes, Zachariah, 163–4
Williams, T., trial, 261
Wollstonecraft, Mary, 183, 347

Y

York, Pa., 39, 41, 46
Yorke, H. Redhead, 276

Z

Zoroastrian religion, 244

Errata.—"Camille Jordan" should be "Camille Jourdain"; "Dr. Romaine" should be "Dr. Romayne"; "Abbé Sieyès" sometimes written "Sièyes," and sometimes also Sièyès.